Communication and Interpersonal Relations

Text and Cases

**THE IRWIN SERIES IN MANAGEMENT AND
THE BEHAVIORAL SCIENCES**

L. L. CUMMINGS and E. KIRBY WARREN   *Consulting Editors*

Communication and Interpersonal Relations

Text and Cases

William V. Haney, Ph.D.
Wm. V. Haney Associates
Wilmette, Illinois 60091

1986 Fifth Edition

IRWIN
Homewood, Illinois 60430

© RICHARD D. IRWIN, INC., 1960, 1967, 1973, 1979, and 1986.

ISBN 0-256-02834-6

Library of Congress Catalog Card No. 85–80784

Printed in the United States of America

2 3 4 5 6 7 8 9 0 K 3 2 1 0 9 8 7 6

Every writer is a product of his experiences. In the case of this book so much is due to the author's contact with one outstanding personality that special mention must be made of it. The author is deeply grateful for eight years of study and friendship with the late

PROFESSOR IRVING J. LEE

of Northwestern University. Those who have been stimulated by his writings and inspired by his person will recognize his influence. It is to the continuation of his teachings and values that this book is respectfully dedicated.

Preface

This book is designed for communicators—for people who deal with other people in organizations such as business, government, military, hospital, and educational institutions. It was written for use in college courses, management-development seminars, supervisory training programs, adult education classes, and individual self-study.

The major changes in this edition include:

—a simpler but still valid model of the perceptual process in Chapter 3. Students (undergraduates through senior executives) have found this condensed version more usable. Of course, it still stresses the essential point that we respond *not directly to reality*—but to our *programmed perceptions of reality.*

— several new cases—Nancy Sawyer, "It Really Hit the Fan," The Sally Port Episode, "Be a Millionaire!," Reification Can Kill Us, A Slight Breakdown in Communication, Résumé Expansion, A New Witch Hunt, Leonard Who? which students have found relevant and timely.

— a tightening of some of the longer more detailed cases such as Pat's Story, Preston Lee, C P A, and Mickey Mouse in Gray Flannels, so they may make their respective contributions more economically.

— one article has been deleted and its essence has been incorporated into the chapters on perception.

— an updating of the entire book, especially Chapter 2, "Organizational Culture and Communication," and Chapter 6, "Motivation and Communication." These two areas have undergone a good deal of research and development in the last seven years.

Finally, the bibliography has been pruned and renewed. A systematic review of recent literature leads to an inescapable conclusion. The body of knowledge in the broad areas of communication and organizational behavior is markedly increasing. In terms of *quantity*—which is overwhelming—*and quality*—which is impressive if not uniform—there has probably been more solid development in these areas in the last decade alone than in the entire previous history of their study. And well there might for we are being drawn inexorably into "the race between education and destruction."

To paraphrase William F. Buckley, Jr.: "Communication may not save us but without communication we will not be saved."

This book continues to consider communication in the *organizational* setting and in terms of a broad *behavioral* base for the communicative act. The communicator, after all, is a complex being with feelings, values, attitudes, perceptions, needs, and motives. To examine communication behavior apart from the whole person and apart from interpersonal relations is not only artificial but misleading. Moreover society is becoming progressively *organized*—thus an inspection of the impact of the organization on the individual's communication is necessary.

According to its title, this book is about *communication*. The title will appear appropriate or inappropriate, I suppose, to the extent that the reader's visualization of communication coincides with the author's. Perhaps it would be helpful to indicate what this book is *not* about. It does not, for example, deal with much of the subject matter usually developed in texts of public, conversational, conference, business, and professional speaking. It does not serve the purposes of texts of composition or of business writing, reports, and letters. Nor is it a book on reading or listening. These vital aspects, phases, and media of communication are treated skillfully and thoroughly in many fine works. Some of them are listed in the bibliography at the end of this book.

This book *is* concerned with the less familiar but equally critical phases of communication common to all of the modes of human interchange. It focuses on what it is that happens *inside* a communicator *before* talking and writing and *after* listening, reading, and so forth. Some might call these processes thinking and dissociate them from the communication experience. Others, including this writer, have felt no need to make such a distinction and, indeed, question the wisdom of drawing an arbitrary line between thinking and communicating. I feel perceiving, evaluating, visualizing, and interpreting are as involved in the communication process as are phonation, articulation, spelling, and grammar.

The book is also about *interpersonal relations in organizations*. That interpersonal relations and communication are inextricably interwoven is a major thesis of the opening chapters.

Accordingly, the book is organized as follows:

Part One deals with the organizational setting in which communication occurs. Part Two discusses the behavioral basis of the communicative act with special reference to the roles that perception and motivation play in communication. A basic model of communication is detailed in Chapter 7, "The Process of Communication." The model describes communication as a serial process involving the phases of encoding, sending, medium, receiving, and decoding. Each step, like a link in a chain, is crucial. Because they are by far the least understood, this book focuses on the encoding and decoding phases.

Each chapter in Part Three deals with one or more patterns of miscommunication that arise in the encoding and/or decoding phases. These miscommunications stem largely from various fallacious assumptions unconsciously held by the communicators—be they speakers or writers, listeners, or readers. The usual chapter format in Part Three includes a definition of the miscommunication pattern(s), the range and types of their consequences, some of their probable causes, and finally, suggestion of techniques for correcting the miscommunications and for preventing their recurrence.

Part Four, Overview (Chapter 18), is a digest of each of the preceding chapters. Some readers use this chapter as a preview of the book's scope, content, and organization.

The Cases

If the book's purpose were only to provide the reader with a body of information and theory about communication, it would seem sufficient to restrict it to the textual material. I hope, however, that readers will use the book to move beyond the level of acquaintance with content to the improvement of their own communication performance. And this is the function of the cases. Some suggestions on using the cases are in Chapter 1, "Introduction."

Instructor's Manual

A manual for teachers is also available from the publisher. Its intent is to assist instructors to help students obtain more value from the textbook. It is organized chapter-by-chapter to correspond with the text. Typical chapter format of the manual is:

> *Discussion Questions*—answers to the questions appended to the chapter.
> *Objective Questions*—provides numerous agree-disagree, fill-in, or multiple-choice questions that pertain to the chapter.
> *Case Analyses*—a synopsis of each case is offered plus responses and comments relevant to the questions following the cases.
> *Additional Activities*—suggestions that individual students or, in some instances, the entire class may wish to pursue.

Acknowledgments

I want to thank the students of Northwestern and DePaul Universities and the executives, supervisors, and professionals of numerous business, academic, government, and military organizations in management development seminars here and abroad who permitted me to share theories and techniques with them.

Principal among these organizations are Aetna Life and Casualty, Abbott Laboratories, Agway, Alcoa, Allegheny Ludlum, Allis Chalmers, the American Business Communication Association, The American Group of CPA Firms, American Medical Association, Anaconda, Anderson Community Hospital, Army Corps of Engineers, Ashland Oil, Carter Oil, Caterpillar Tractor (domestic and international), Chemplex Cities Service, Copeland, The Executive Committee, Firestone, Hamilton Memorial Hospital, IBM (domestic and international), Inland Steel, Internal Revenue Service, International Nickel, Liberty Mutual Insurance, Management and Business Services, Management Services, McCann-Erickson, MacNeal Memorial Hospital, Mead Johnson, Metropolitan Life, Mobil Oil (domestic and international), Motorola, New York Life, Northwest Industrial Council, Northrop, Official Airlines Guide, Otter Tail Power, Pillsbury, Presidents' Association (American Management Association), Price-Waterhouse, Prudential Life, RCA, Sentry Insurance, Standard Oil of Indiana, Swift, Teletype, the Travellers, Union Oil (domestic and international), U.S. Departments of Air Force, Army, Health Education and Welfare, NASA, Navy, Public Health, and State, U.S. Gypsum, Weiss Memorial Hospital, Western Electric, Westfield Insurance, Zenith Radio, the Ministry of Lands, Tasmania, Australia, and the Ecole des Hautes Etudes Commerciales. In addition there were the executive development programs conducted by the American College, the American Hospital Assn., the American College of Hospital Administrators, the American Institute of Baking, the Bank Marketing Association, the Battelle Memorial Institute, the Brookings Institution, the College of Insurance, Cornell University, DePaul University, Edison Electric Institute, Emory University, Louisiana State University, Loyola University, Management and Business Services, Miami University, National Association of Mutual Savings Banks, National Management Association, Northwestern University, Northwestern's Traffic Institute, Notre Dame University, the Ohio State University, Oklahoma State University, Pepperdine University, UCLA, the University of Arkansas, the University of Chicago, the University of Illinois, the U.S. International University, the University of Richmond, the University of Tennessee, and the University of Wisconsin.

My particular thanks go to Caterpillar Tractor, IBM, Mobil Oil, the Presidents' Association, and Union Oil for sending me to Europe, Africa, South America, Asia, Australia, and New Zealand to work with management groups in other parts of the world.

I am especially indebted to Standard Alliance Industries, Inc., which, with wholehearted cooperation, has permitted me in the roles of director, researcher, and consultant to explore without inhibition organizational communication and relationships.

I am grateful to the Ford Foundation for a research fellowship that, with the assistance of the Graduate School of Industrial Administration, Carnegie-Mellon Institute of Technology, enabled me to do some of the behavioral research.

Many people have aided me with their reviewing and editing of this book. Among my benefactors for this and earlier editions were M. Kendig, co-founder and former director of the Institute of General Semantics; Robert R. Hume, National Science Foundation; and Warren G. Bennis (M.I.T.); Ann Baxter (University of North Carolina); John F. Mee (Indiana University); Joseph S. Moag (Northwestern University); Victor H. Vroom (Carnegie-Mellon Institute of Technology); Karl F. Weick (Cornell University); Ogden H. Hall (University of New Orleans); Jon M. Huegli (Eastern Michigan University); James M. Lahiff (University of Georgia); Raymond V. Lesikar (North Texas State University); James E. Wade (California State University at San Jose); James T. Watt (Corpus Christi State University); and Michael Giallourakis (Mississippi State University). I am grateful, too, to the consulting editors of the Irwin Series in Management and Behavioral Sciences, Professors L.L. Cummings (Northwestern University) and E. Kirby Warren (Columbia University) for their valuable assistance.

Much appreciation goes to my wife, Arlene, who when revision times occurred somehow managed to shield me from our five wonderful but active sons and daughters. That protection is no longer necessary. But she is still my best friend—and for that I am indeed grateful.

Finally, it should be clear that any errors and shortcomings in this book are uniquely my own and undoubtedly result from good advice unheeded.

William V. Haney

Contents

4 Perception and Communication: 2. The Frame of Reference and the Self-Image   87

Your Solitary-Confinement Cell: *The Stained-Glass Window. Forming Images of Others. The Self-Image Threatened. The ERSI.*

CASES

5 Perception and Communication: 3. The Exceptionally Realistic Self-Image   108

Advantages of the ERSI. A Game Plan. Valid Clues: *Cues from Others. Cues from Psychometric Instruments. Cues from Readings. Internal Cues.* Article: *The Meaning of Active Listening. Two Examples. What We Achieve by Listening. How to Listen. The Growth of the Individual. What to Avoid. What to Do. What we Communicate by Listening. Testing for Understanding.* Problems in Active Listening: *The Personal Risk. Hostile Expressions. Out-of-Place Expressions. Accepting Positive Feelings. Emotional Danger Signals. Listening to Ourselves.* Active Listening and Company Goals: *Individual Importance. Listening and Production. Maximum Creativeness.*

6 Motivation and Communciation   164

A Motivation Model. Frustration: *Conflict.* Motivation Theories: *Maslow. Herzberg et al. McClelland. Some Process Theories.* The Value of Motivation Theory. Epilogue.

CASES

7 The Process of Communication   199

A Communication Process Model: *Encoding. Transmission. The Medium. Reception. Decoding. Feedback.* Communication: A Serial Process. *Encoding and Decoding—The Subtle Phases.*

Part Three
Patterns of Miscommunication

11 **Differentiation Failures: 1. Indiscrimination**   345
Hardening of the Categories: *Stereotypes.* The Battle of the Categories. Contributing Factors: *Self-Serving Emotions. Language Structure.* Correctives: *Become Sensitive to Differences.* The Values of Seeing Similarities.

12 **Differentiation Failures: 2. Polarization**   367
Definition: *Contradictories. Contraries. Polarization.* Consequences:
*Deluding Ourselves. Deluding Others. Polarization in America. The
Vicious Pendulum Effect.* Contributing Factors: *Similar Grammati-
cal Form. Neglect of the Middle Ground.* Correctives: *Detect the Con-
trary. Specify the Degree—Apply the How-Much Index. Separate the
Double Contraries. Guard against the Vicious Pendulum Effect.*

13 **Differentiation Failures: 3. The Frozen Evaluation**   408
The Case of Frank. The Assumption of Nonchange: *Future Change.*
Changes in People. Changes in Business. A Durable Fallacy: *Subtle
Changes. Tolerance for Change. The Language Factor.* Correctives:
*Internalize the Premise of Change. Apply the When Index. The Ad-
ministration of Change.*

14 Intensional Orientation: 1. A General Statement   433

The Graham University Tax Case. Intension and Extension. Intensionality: Some Manifestations. A Defective Tool: *Replace the Langauge. Repair the Language.* Correctives.

15 Intensional Orientation: 2. "Pointing" and "Associating"   459

The "Pointing-Associating" Confusion: *Euphemisms and Dysphemisms.* Name-Calling: *The Double Burden. Living Up to the Lables. Living Down the Labels. Positive Lables.* "Associative" Bypassing. A Possible Misunderstanding. Correctives: *The "Pointing-Associating" Confusion. Name- Calling. "Associative" Bypassing.*

16 Intensional Orientation: 3. Blindering   488

Some Consequences: *Delayed Solutions. Undesirable Solutions.* Correctives: *Remember, Defining = Neglecting. Does My Definition Blinder Me? How to Recognize Our Blinders.*

CASES

17 Undelayed Reactions   520

Three Classes of Behavior: *1. Reflex Responses. 2. Voluntary Responses. 3. Reflexlike Responses.* The Problem of Undelayed Reactions. Correctives: *Instantaneous Action Rarely Necessary. The Habit of Delay. One Hour at a Time. Humor. Advance Preparation for Emergencies. Anticipating the Undelayed Responses of Others. A Group Technique.* Epilogue.

CASES

Part Four
Overview

18 Overview   551

Introduction. Organizational Culture and Communication. Perception and Communication: *1. The Process of Perception. 2. The Frame of Reference and the Self-Image. 3. The Exceptionally Realistic Self-Image* (ERSI). Motivation and Communication. The Process of Communication. The Inference-Observation Confusion. Bypassing. Allness. Differentiation Failures: *1. Indiscrimination. 2. Polarization.*

3. The Frozen Evaluation. Intensional Orientation: *1. A General Statement. 2. "Pointing" and "Associating". 3. Blindering.* Undelayed Reactions.

Part One

COMMUNICATION IN ORGANIZATIONS

1

Introduction

Effective communication is essential in business, in governmental and military organizations, in hospitals, communities, homes—wherever people deal with one another. Interpersonal activity inevitably depends upon communication in some form or other.

The concern for communication in organizations is growing rapidly.[1] And well it might, for we are in a new age—a postindustrial age. Smokestack industries are declining. In 1972, 676,000 people worked in U.S. auto factories. Today, there are fewer than 500,000. Steel and rubber manufacturers are shrinking, too. According to Naisbitt[2] and other futurists, heavy industry is giving way to services and the processing of information. The "fungible"—the worker considered interchangeable with and indistinguishable from any other—is vanishing. Individuals must be considered as just that—individuals.

Moreover, the efficiency of a group depends largely on how well the efforts of its individual members are coordinated. But coordination doesn't just happen. Satisfactory communication is necessary if people are to achieve understanding and cooperation; if they are to cope with the problems that come with functional change, geographic decentralization, and departmental specialization; if they are to present a desirable image of their organization to its various publics. In dealing with these and many other concerns, people in organizations have become, characteristically, *communicators*.

And the higher one is on the organizational ladder, the more time and energy he or she will likely devote to communication. Studies indicate that aside from communicating—speaking, writing, listening, reading, and

---

[1]The Council of Communication Societies publishes a directory listing 64 *associations—* not *organizations* but *associations* of *organizations*—concerned with communication!

[2]John Naisbitt, *Megatrends: Ten New Directions Transforming Our Lives* (New York: Warner Books, 1984).

3

thinking (intrapersonal communication)—an organization's top administrator does virtually nothing! The typical executive spends about 75 percent of the time communicating and about 75 percent of that time in individual, face-to-face situations. Even middle- and lower-management personnel devote the bulk of their working hours to the processes and problems of communication.

With all this increased interest, one might expect improvements in the communicative process. And, indeed, there has been fantastic advancement—in some areas. With the aid of modern electronic equipment, it is possible to send, receive, process, store, retrieve, and reproduce prodigious amounts of information with mind-numbing speed—and to reach incredible numbers of people in the process.

And the ramifications are being felt at all levels. Telecommunications innovations, for example, are not only changing the ways people get information and communicate with friends and colleagues—but how they shop, invest, work and are educated.[3] With electronic mail, letters may be sent, read, and filed in on-line storage much faster than by long-distance telephone, express delivery, or facsimile transmission. Over 150,000 subscribers (doubled from last year) can choose from 26 huge data bases in numerous categories including business news, financial services, and medical information. Computerized conferencing permits immediate access to everything on file including changes and challenges. Thus, any member of a project can review the entire transcript at a moment's notice.

The advent of microchips (computers) and optic fibers (telephonic transmission) has enormously increased the versatility and availability of these means of information processing and communication.

Just how rapidly have computers, for example, been advancing? In his BBC television series, "Making the Most of the Micro," Ian McNaught-Davis analogizes: In the early postwar years when computers were very large and ponderously slow (by today's standards), the Volkswagen Beetle began to appear on American streets. Had the Bug developed at the same rate as the computer it would currently blaze about at 600 miles an hour, get 30,000 miles per gallon, and need no service for 10,000 years. The price? About 65 cents!

Of course, the Beetle didn't make that progress—in fact, it is virtually extinct. But the computer did and continues to do so at an astonishing pace. Your digital watch contains about the same amount of logic as that huge, old clunker. The prediction: Within 10 years, *today's* awesome room-filling mainframe will be replaced by a single silicon chip!

---

[3]A quick comment on education. Experts assert that with the aid of computers, children would be reading and writing at age three. A Canadian study contends that with computer assistance, a student could be *intellectually* prepared for college in 7 rather than 12 years. Just how *emotionally* ready for college a 10- or 12-year-old might be is a question that has yet to be answered.

I am personally delighted with these technical developments. One reason, I happen to be an amateur radio operator. But even if I were not, there would still have been a catch in my throat when I read this:

Good Vibrations

What do a personal computer, a shoe, and the Morse code have in common? Combined, they enable Raymond Boduch, WA2GXI, of Buffalo, New York, to lead a fuller life. Having lost his sight and hearing at a very early age, Boduch relies on a computer to keep personal files. To use his computer, he activates a device inside his shoe. The device, developed by a New Jersey electronics expert and a student at Rensselaer Polytechnic Institute, transforms the words and numbers that appear on the PC screen into Morse code impulses that Boduch can "read" with his foot.[4]

My modern solid-state, high-frequency transceiver, by the way, is not only more versatile and powerful, but it is only about ½₀th the size of the 1950s' equipment my wife had (she was a ham, too). Moreover, all five of our children are involved more or less directly with computer technology and we're eagerly anticipating a personal computer. I hope I'll get a chance to use it! In any event, more power (no pun intended) to the technologists.

But in our awe of communication science, let us not ignore one somber but compelling thought. Quantity, speed, and coverage are not the only requirements of communication. It is also imperative that we communicate clearly and precisely. But progress toward greater *understandability* has come much more slowly than the technological improvements. It is still quite possible for persons to fail to understand one another, even though they speak the "same" language; for firms to snarl orders and lose customers' confidence; for nations to break off diplomatic relations and even declare wars because of distortions in communication.

This is partly because we live in a world of flux. However, it is not just change, but the *acceleration* of change, which has so sorely tested our ability—and our willingness—to communicate with one another.

With communications satellites, we can now be in audiovisual contact with any place on Earth.[5] Yet it frequently appears that our interpersonal communication practices, as distinguished from our communication technology, have regressed.

Have we lost sight of the fact that the ultimate senders and receivers of messages, regardless of the sophisticated intervening apparatus, are human beings? To reiterate, how far have we progressed in understanding what happens inside people as they communicate or fail to communicate?

---

[4]*QST: The Official Journal of the American Radio Relay League*, LXVIII, no. 5 (May 1984), p. 85.

[5]And off the Earth, recalling the excellent color telecasts from Saturn and Jupiter.

How far can we overcome the imperfections of language?

Only slightly.

How far can we keep the relations of our thoughts and our feelings in good order?

Very slightly.

How far can we go to create a common background of knowledge and experience for all men?

Not very far.

How much can we attain the ideal of each man perfectly understanding himself without psychosis or neurosis to any degree?

Not very much.

How many of us are willing, every time we talk to another human being, to expend the effort to really do it well?

Few of us or, if ever, few times.

How many of us are free from all neurosis and in perfect possession of the moral and the intellectual virtues?

As you answer that question you will see that I am not exaggerating when I say that a fifty percent success in the process of communication would be very good, indeed. We probably do not come near that now.[6]

Adler made that sober statement almost a quarter of a century ago. I fear we have made little progress since then. Over the last three years, I have been asking top executives to calculate the cost of miscommunication in their respective organizations. In addition to the dollars lost in waste and duplication clearly induced by miscommunication, I asked them to include such difficult-to-quantify but very real costs as:

loss of customer confidence	absenteeism
hurt feelings	turnover
grudges and retaliations	grievances
office feuds	strikes
baseless rumors	sabotage
malicious obedience	production retardation

Their estimates range from 25 to 40 percent of budget! Consider just the costs associated with poor labor-management relations. As the veteran federal mediator Douglas Brown put it: "At least 99 percent of the union-company difficulties I deal with either start with or are complicated by poor, inadequate, or omitted communication."

Just what happens when people talk together, when they write, when they read? Why are they sometimes so unsuccessful in exchanging their thoughts clearly, understandably, and effectively? When Green speaks, why does White fail to "get" him, even though White tries to understand? How is it possible for an executive, earnestly wanting to communicate

---

[6]Mortimer Adler, "Challenges of Philosophies in Communication," *Journalism Quarterly*, 40, no. 3 (Summer 1963), p. 452.

with his or her employees, to make costly errors in terms of money and morale? How is it that a military commander can issue orders that can be misinterpreted so as to lead to incalculable disasters? This is the nature of the problems that concern us in this book.

PLAN OF THE BOOK

The organization of this book is something like a funnel, beginning with the large end and leading down to the small hole at the bottom. After this introductory chapter, Chapter 2 deals with the large and complex organizational setting in which communication plays such a vital role and then focuses on that critical aspect of the organization, its culture, with which communication performance is inexorably intertwined. Chapters 3, 4, 5, and 6 set out the behavioral base in which the individual is examined as an organism whose behavior (including communication behavior) is profoundly influenced by perceptions and motivations. In Chapter 7, we investigate that special but critical behavior called *communication*. This chapter also serves as a transition between what has gone before and what is to come. Chapters 8 through 17 detail numerous patterns of miscommunication—recurrent modes of self-deception and inaccuracy that lead to misunderstanding, confusion, and conflict. Each chapter describes a pattern of miscommunication, examines its prime causes, and recommends strategies and techniques for preventing or correcting its occurrence. Chapter 18, the overview, consists of a concluding rationale for the book and a summary of its key concepts.

THE CASES

The late communication authority Irving J. Lee used to say that the road to becoming a competent practitioner of communication (and of the prevention and correction of miscommunication) was marked by five milestones. First, you acquaint yourself with the subject matter—the studies, the theories, and the methods. In other words you acquire the current knowledge of the field. Second, you develop the ability to recognize and learn from proficiencies and shortcomings in the communication of others. Third, and more difficult, you come to perceive and understand them in your own behavior. Fourth, you strengthen your own communication skills. Fifth, and by far the most formidable accomplishment you learn to prescribe for the communicative problems of others.

Lee listed these steps in their order of difficulty rather than suggesting that they be strictly adhered to chronologically. He never insisted, for example, that Step One had to be mastered before Step Two was practiced, and so forth. Nor did he discourage developing skills on two or more levels simultaneously. However, some accomplishment at Step One should facilitate development at Step Two; learning at Step Two should aid in accomplishing Step Three; and so on.

Explorations into Steps Three and Four may be within grasp for some at this point. It is recommended, however, that Step Five be approached with considerable caution and constraint. In all candor, Step Five may be something of a will-o'-the-wisp. Communication habits are often so deeply rooted that change may take place only at the volition of the individual. For one to attempt to change another may arouse the other's defenses and lead to resistance. (Defense against change is discussed more fully in Chapter 4). Change, if any, would probably be superficial and temporary at best.

Given the requisite of volition, perhaps the best that one can do is to try to provide a nonthreatening environment in which the other person can perform Step Four (see Carl Rogers and Richard E. Farson, *Active Listening*, at the end of Chapter 5 in this regard).

The textual part of this book can only contribute to your realization of Step One. The cases that follow each of the succeeding chapters,[7] however, give you the opportunity to practice at the level of Step Two and, to some extent, Steps Three and Four.

Most of the cases are reports of actual happenings in which communications somehow went awry. They are offered because there is often a decided gap between one's *intellectual acquaintance* with a subject matter and ones *internalization* of it. The cases afford the opportunity to move beyond a superficial knowledge of the patterns of miscommunication to a more profound and enduring awareness and understanding of them.

You will benefit from the cases to the extent that you bore into them. Here is a good list of questions to impose on each case:

> *What* is going on in the case? What has happened?
> *Why* did it occur? What are the *underlying assumptions* of the communicators involved?
> *What could have been done* to prevent the communication failure or at least to diminish its consequences?
> *What can be done now?* By whom? When? Where? How?
> What procedures, techniques, measures would you suggest to prevent a *recurrence* of this type of miscommunication?

The cases were allocated to the chapters because they appear to this writer and to many of his students (all of the cases have been class- and/or management seminar-tested) to exemplify in some manner the content of the chapters to which they are appended. This is not to suggest that other patterns of miscommunication (including those described elsewhere in this book or in other works) cannot or should not be perceived in the cases. On

------

[7]Except Chapter 7, the transition chapter.

the contrary, you are encouraged to probe, to examine, to analyze, and to dissect as far as your insights and skills will permit.

In sum, the purpose of this book is not unlike that of medical training. Although there is no pretense of turning out Doctors of Communication, there is the earnest hope that, after acquiring some background from a given chapter, you will proceed to develop a heightened sensitivity to the communicative processes of others and your own. I genuinely hope that you will begin to acquire or reinforce awarenesses and techniques for avoiding and coping with these patterns of miscommunication in real life.

DISCUSSION QUESTIONS

1. ". . . it is not just change, but the *acceleration* of change, which has so sorely tested our ability—and our willingness—to communicate with one another." How do you react to that statement? What do you anticipate for the future? Will the situation improve, worsen? Why? How?

2. Some people feel that Adler's assessment is unnecessarily gloomy. What do you think?

3. In view of Chapter 1, "Introduction," and the Preface, what is this book about? What is it *not* about? What value might the book have for you?

4. What do you think of Lee's five-step procedure toward becoming a more competent practitioner of communication? Why might Step Five be considered a will-o'-the-wisp?   CHANGE   8

5. ". . . there is often a decided gap between one's *intellectual acquaintance* with a subject matter and one's *internalization* of it." Do you agree? Why or why not?

6. What is the best way to get maximum value from the use of the cases in this book?

7. "The sculs of emperors and cobblers are cast in the same mold. . . . The same reason that makes us wrangle with a neighbor causes a war twixt princes."
—*Michel de Montaigne*
"We are in such great haste to construct an electric telegraph between Maine and Texas. But it may be that Maine and Texas have nothing to communicate."
—*Henry David Thoreau*
What bearing might these statements have on Chapter 1?

2

Organizational Culture and Communication

For better or worse, society is becoming progressively organized. Fewer and fewer people are self-employed. Individual enterprisers—artisans, merchants, farmers, and entrepreneurs—are disappearing. Virtually everyone is temporarily or permanently involved in organizations—schools, churches, hospitals, professional firms, government agencies, business, and military organizations, the list is almost endless.

But just what is an organization?

First, it consists of a number of people, anywhere from two on up.

Second, an organization involves interdependence. If you had 1,000 artisans, each of whom designed a product, purchased materials, manufactured, sold, and shipped the product, and so on, you would not have an organization, you would have 1,000 enterprises. Individuals are interdependent when the performance of one individual affects and is affected by the performance of others, for example, when one person designs the product, another purchases the material, a third manufactures the product, and so forth.

Interdependence calls for coordination, activities to assure that the individual functions will be carried out so that the objectives of the organization will be achieved.

And coordination requires communication. Genesis describes how the building of the Tower of Babel was disrupted by the "confounding of tongues." When people no longer had a common language, when they were unable to communicate, they could not work together.

TRENDS

Communication, then, is the prime requirement of any organization. Consider now what is happening in our organizations.

1. They are getting larger. The trend toward expansion through internal growth, merger, and acquisition is unmistakable. Three automobile

firms control an industry—at least the domestic sector of it—in which there were once scores of manufacturers. The Big Three catalog chain stores— Sears, Penney's, and Montgomery Ward—handle about a third of all general merchandising sales, almost as much as all other conventional department stores combined. Twenty grocery chains control 90 percent of the market.

2. They are becoming more complex. The simple line organization of authority and responsibility is often inadequate to cope with the growing complexities of many of today's organizations, in which an individual reports to one superior for one function, to another for another activity, and so on. Complicated? Yes, but necessary. For when the organization's objectives become more demanding, a more complex grouping of its skills and resources may be imperative.

3. A closely related trend is the increasing demand, due to international as well as domestic competition, for even greater efficiency and quality in the production of goods and the provision of services.

And that competition is accelerating—especially from extranationals. Consider a few of the markets in which the Japanese, for example, have become a factor (in some cases, a dominant factor): Cameras, watches, television and radio equipment, VCRs, personal computers, appliances, autos, motorcycles, trucks, tractors, ships, and even pianos!

American CEOs are clearly concerned. Four hundred thirty-seven of them were asked, "Is there a productivity problem in the United States?" Yes, they answered with increasing vehemence as the focus moved down through the organization:[1]

Productivity a problem at the level of:	Percentage of CEOs answering affirmatively:
Executives	58
Managers and Sales	74
Other salaried and all hourly employees	90

4. Society is beginning to impose other requirements on its organizations. For one, there has been growing concern about mental health in our country. Some feel that the structure and climate of today's organizations are in many respects inimical to the emotional health and development of its members. They call for a serious reappraisal of and, where advisable, significant changes in our organizations.

5. Moreover, the organization's members, particularly its younger members, are expecting more of their employers. They insist upon higher

[1]"Productivity Strategies," BNA Policy Guide (1981), no. 505, pp. 241–321.

compensation, yes, but they also demand greater satisfaction on the job for their psychological needs.[2]

On the basis of careful research on AT&T personnel, Howard and Wilson paint a somber picture of this qualitative change and its resultant challenge to management.

> In the last decade, as the baby boom generation entered adulthood, one fact has emerged. The postwar generation, born in the joy of victory and a surge of unprecedented affluence, represents a sharp change in the social fabric of American life. In stark contrast to the overly ambitious hopes of their parents, the baby boomers are less motivated toward success, less optimistic, and certainly less committed to the large institutions that make up this society than any previous generation of Americans.
>
> Nowhere does this sharp break with traditional values cause more consternation than in the U.S. corporate world . . . will a renewed emphasis on participative management engage the hearts and minds of these disaffected young people, or will the team approach simply hasten the demise of the work ethic?[3]

In sum, when we consider the nature of an organization and the growing trends of largeness, complexity, demand for greater efficiency, and so on, one conclusion is eminently clear: Today's organization requires communication performance at an unprecedented level of excellence. And chief among the demands made upon our organizations is the increasing necessity for an organizational culture[4] compatible with the psychic needs of the organization's members.

Harris defined culture as:

> . . . the unique lifestyle of a group of people, the coping strategies and skills developed and adapted for particular purposes. It represents a body of communicable knowledge and learned behavior that humans acquire and pass on for survival and success within an environment.[5]

Perhaps an organizational culture or climate seems like some ethereal abstract. It is not.

---

[2]A key provision in a recent contract negotiated by the UAW and the auto manufacturers was the workers' right to *refuse* overtime—even though they would be paid time-and-a-half or double time. The Howard-Wilson study, which follows, suggests that older generations would regard such a clause as utterly incomprehensible.

[3]Ann Howard and James A. Wilson, "Leadership in a Declining Work Ethic," *California Management Review,* XXIV, no. 4, (1982), p. 33.

[4]The concept of organizational culture has become a fascinating focal point for a number of behavior scientists who illuminate how organizations create complex and powerful cultures (as in any society) that affect the behavior of employees at all levels. See especially: Terrence Deal and Allan Kennedy, *Corporate Cultures* (Reading, Mass.: Addison-Wesley, 1982) and Philip R. Harris, *New World, New Ways, New Management: Meta-Industrial Organizations* (New York: Amacom Book Division, American Management Association, 1983).

[5]Harris, *New World*, p. 15.

> Communication climate is real; it does exist, and it affects the way we work with and relate to other persons. This climate is created by the way we interact with one another—the way we behave. And since it is caused by our behavior, it can be managed. We can make choices about the climate we want to create.[6]

In this we-can-call-our-own-shots mentality, we turn to a managerial philosophy that is designed to establish and maintain a constructive, positive, organizational culture.

SUPPORTIVE CULTURE

"I know I'm supposed to 'know my people,' but business is just too good. Pressure for output is tremendous, the labor market is drum-tight, and turnover is high. I simply don't have time to know my people." The complaint is pervasive in many of our fast-growing sectors.

Even supervisors who have the time insist that people are more difficult to understand, more complex, that their needs are less directly satisfiable by the boss. Moreover, employees' expectations of their employers are high and growing higher—in terms of psychic as well as material rewards.

In consequence of these changes a new, more subtle postindustrial revolution is in process, and it is leading to a serious reexamination of the role of the manager and of the organization.

I would express that emerging relationship as follows:

> The leadership and overall atmosphere (climate) of an organization must be consistent with the needs of its individual members. The organization must provide a supportive culture. The essential element is trust. Management must trust that subordinates will (or can) be capable of and indeed will contribute to the attainment of organizational objectives.
>
> Conversely, employees must trust that the organization, mostly in the form of their respective managers, will reward individuals fairly and provide for the gratification of their relevant needs as they help the organization achieve its goals.

Trust and Performance

The key, then, is *trust.* By and large, high trust tends to stimulate high performance—so say the overwhelming majority of over 9,000 supervisors I have questioned in 58 organizations of varying kinds and sizes. These supervisors feel that subordinates generally respond well to their superiors' genuine confidence in them. They try to justify their bosses' good estimate

---

[6]"Communication Climate," The Atlanta Consulting Group, 1982.

FIGURE 2-1
Constructive cycle

FIGURE 2-2
Destructive cycle

of them. And, axiomatically, high performance will reinforce high trust, for it is easy to trust and respect a person who meets or exceeds your expectations. (See Figure 2-1.)

"But how can I develop trust under today's pressures and complexities?" Too frequently the circle is vicious rather than virtuous. Unable to "know their people," supervisors are unwilling to trust them and fail to provide for a supportive relationship. More often than not subordinates respond with minimal compliance and resentment. "If that's all they think of me, I might as well give it to them. I won't get credit for doing any more." Low performance, under these circumstances, reinforces low trust, and the system is self-perpetuating. (See Figure 2-2.) A supervisor's assumptions about his or her workers can easily become a self-fulfilling prophecy.

Trust and Communication

The trust-performance cycles suggest an interesting parallel—the mutual dependence of a trusting relationship and effective communication performance. When the organizational culture can be characterized as trusting and supportive, communication practice is generally good. There are a number of reasons for this.

First of all, the members of such an organization, tend to have no ax to grind, nothing to be gained by miscommunicating deliberately or by malicious obedience. The aura of openness makes possible candid expressions of feelings and ideas. Even faulty communication does not lead immediately to retaliation, for others are not prone to presume malice on the offenders' part, but instead carry them, i.e., compensate for their errors. Moreover, a lapse in communication is viewed not as an occasion for punishment but as an opportunity to learn from mistakes. Obviously, effective communication will do much to reinforce and enhance an existing trusting climate. But if communication performance begins to falter repeatedly, the trusting relationship may be jeopardized. People begin to wonder whether the slip-ups are inadvertent or whether the other person has something in mind. When self-fulfilling prophecies of intrigue and suspicion emerge, the organization may be in for trouble.

When the culture is hostile and threatening, communication tends to suffer. Not only is there a tendency toward miscommunication with malice aforethought, but in such an atmosphere, true feelings are suppressed lest one be punished for revealing them. When an organization member slips, no one carries that person. On the contrary, the individual may serve as a useful scapegoat for others who seek temporary relief from criticism of themselves. By and large, one's communication (as well as one's behavior in general) is dominated by the need to protect oneself rather than the desire to serve the interests of the organization. Unfortunately, when the climate is unhealthy, even letter-perfect communication practice can be inadequate for if people wish to misunderstand or to be misunderstood they can do so readily, as will be demonstrated in Chapter 9, "Bypassing."

Breaking the Cycle.   There are two general ways of breaking the destructive cycle and converting it to the constructive cycle of Figure 2–1. First, if the subordinates can respond to a low-trusting superior with high performance, if they can resist performing down to the supervisor's low regard, they stand a chance of eventually winning the boss's respect. (See Figure 2–3.)

However, the ability to withstand a low-trust atmosphere for a prolonged period requires considerable strength and maturity on the subordinate's part. Consider also that the subordinate is already psychologically disadvantaged simply by being in the subordinate role. Under these conditions, persistent high performance, though possible, does not seem very probable.

FIGURE 2–3
Breaking cycle on subordinate's initiative

FIGURE 2–4
Breaking cycle on a superior's initiative

Parenthetically, if the superior's low-trusting attitude is primarily a function of external conditions, such as temporary pressure for production, rather than one's own personality, say, a tendency toward paranoia, the prognosis is more favorable.

The other approach lies in the superior's ability to respond to low performance with high trust. (See Figure 2–4.)

This presents a paradox. How, indeed, can you trust someone who has not demonstrated trustworthiness? And can you con low producers into high performance by making believe that you regard them highly? Or, will the subordinates conclude that they are being manipulated?

It was this seeming contradiction that the supportive climate was designed to confront.

A RECONCILIATION

The trend toward this mutual trust system was taking shape in the 1950s. One of the first and certainly the most eloquent of the behavioral scientists to articulate it was the late Douglas McGregor.[7]

He contrasted two general modes of thought about how a manager should manage people. Theory X was his term for the traditional and still largely current philosophy of management. Theory Y was the emerging concept that promised to integrate the goals of the organization and its members.

Theory X

The *theory* of Theory X in essence holds that the so-called average person is inherently (and therefore unalterably) immature, that he or she is in-

---

[7]Douglas McGregor, *The Human Side of Enterprise* (New York: McGraw-Hill, 1960).

nately lazy, irresponsible, gullible, resistant to change, self-centered, and thus indifferent to organizational needs. The managerial practice in dealing with such persons is to apply external controls (harshly or paternalistically or firmly but fairly). External control is clearly appropriate for dealing with truly immature individuals. We externally control infants, for example, and without such management, they would perish.

While conceding that people are quite capable of immature behavior, McGregor argued that such behavior and attitudes are not manifestations of their inborn nature but the product of their experiences. Treat people as if they were children, he said—and thus chronically underestimate them, distrust them, refrain from delegating authority—and they will respond as children.

Thus, in reacting to a myth (people are unchangeably immature) with external controls, managers have stimulated subordinates' behavior, and this in turn perpetuated the myth and seemingly justified their practice, for the more one controls, the more one *has* to control and, as goes the old Chinese expression, "He [or she] who rides a tiger can never dismount."

The Hierarchy of Needs

What, then, is the nature of the "average person"? Very much the same as any other person's, and McGregor draws on Abraham Maslow's "hierarchy of needs"[8] to support his case.

Maslow held that we are all constituted in such a way that we normally seek satisfaction (and thus are motivated) through a sequence of needs:

Physiological needs—the needs to have oxygen, eat, drink, rest, be protected from the elements, and so forth—the "tissue needs."

Security and safety needs—respectively, the needs to be free of the fear of physiological deprivation and of the fear of physical danger.

Social needs—the needs to belong, to be accepted, to be loved, and so forth.

Ego needs—the needs to be respected, to be somebody, to gain recognition, prestige, status, and so forth.

Self-fulfillment needs—the needs to realize one's fullest potential in whatever guise it may take. Among the modes of self-fulfillment are religion, altruism, education, power, and artistic expression.

Two propositions pertain: The upper level needs (social, ego, self-fulfillment) ordinarily will have little or no motivating effect on individuals until their lower level needs (physiological and safety-security) have been

---

[8]Abraham H. Maslow, *Motivation and Personality* (New York: Harper & Row, 1954).

reasonably[9] satisfied. This suggests that there is little point in running off to developing nations to preach democracy and free enterprise (or any other abstraction) to people who are literally starving, they can't hear *at that level*. George Bernard Shaw in *Major Barbara* noted: "I can't talk religion to a man with bodily hunger in his eyes."

Conversely, once the lower level ends are at least reasonably fulfilled, they become inoperative on the premise that a satisfied need is no longer a motivator of behavior. The individual is thus open to motivation from the upper level needs, or, in the words of Will Rogers, "It is easy to be a gentleman when you are well fed."

And the latter state of affairs is precisely what prevails today in the United States, asserted McGregor. For the first time in history, the masses of a nation, except depressed minority groups, pockets of depression, and so on, have had their physiological and safety-security needs at least reasonably satisfied and are now susceptible to motivation from their higher level needs.

> An implication of the high degree of needs deficiency in the self-actualization and esteem categories is that managers should focus attention on strategies to correct these deficiencies. This logic assumes that attempts to satisfy these deficiencies have a higher probability of succeeding than directing attention to the already satisfactorily fulfilled lower order needs.[10]

But American management, according to McGregor, could not thwart these upper level needs more if it tried. He felt that managers were failing to understand the change that has occurred in people. Many managers still insist on attempting to motivate in the ways that were quite effective when people were preoccupied with their physiological and safety-security needs.

The Utility of Money. Take the dollar, for example. Let it be clear, first of all, that neither McGregor nor any other behavioral scientist has claimed that money is an unimportant motivator. Consider, however, that

---

[9]The word *reasonably* is used deliberately. Note the caution of Hersey and Blanchard:

In discussing the preponderance of one category of need over another, we have been careful to speak in such terms as "if one level of needs has been somewhat gratified, then other needs emerge as dominant." This was done because we did not want to give the impression that one level of needs has to be completely satisfied before the next level emerges as the most important. In reality, most people in our society tend to be partially satisfied at each level and partially unsatisfied, with greater satisfaction tending to occur at the physiological and safety levels than at the social, esteem, and self-actualization levels.

Paul Hersey and Kenneth M. Blanchard, *Management of Organizational Behavior: Utilizing Human Resources*, 4th ed. (Englewood Cliffs, N.J.: Prentice-Hall, 1982), p. 33.

[10]James L. Gibson, John M. Ivancevich, and James H. Donnelly, Jr., *Organizations: Behavior, Structure, Processes* (Plano, Tex.: Business Publications, 1982), p. 83.

FIGURE 2–5
Utility of money for need satisfaction

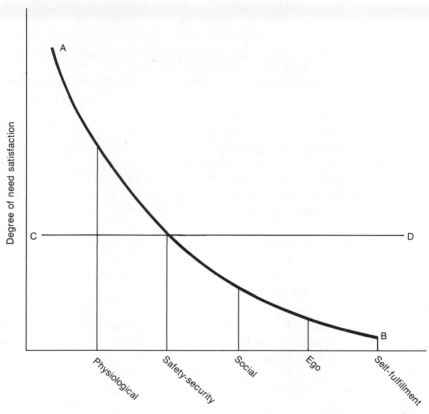

no one has a need for dollars as such, that money is a *tool*, a most versatile tool, which can be used to satisfy needs. However, the utility of a given dollar amount to satisfy diminishes as one ascends the hierarchy of needs. (See Figure 2–5.)

The A–B curve represents the degree of need satisfaction hypothetical Joe Bachelor[11] could obtain on $50 a day. Line C–D represents the minimal satisfaction level for each of his needs. If satisfaction falls below this line, Joe is hurting.

Fifty dollars is more than enough to satisfy Joe's physiological needs—to have enough food to subsist, protection from the elements, warm clothes, and so forth. Let us now imagine that some benefactor steps in and says: "Don't worry, Joe, I'll pay for your physiological needs." Joe can

---

[11]Joe Married would be a more complex example.

now spend his $50 exclusively for his security needs. If he conservatively invests his daily $50, he'll soon have a sizable nest egg, which should do a fair job of alleviating his security needs unless they are unusually extensive. Enter again Joe's munificent patron and *voilá!* he's free to spend his $50 at the third level. How well his social needs are met is largely dependent on how much Joe needs to belong and upon the dues of the group from which he desires acceptance. If Joe insists on "buying" ego satisfaction, say, through the purchase of a new Cadillac every other year, he will probably find the price exorbitant, and thus his $50 will leave him frustrated in this department. And as for self-fulfillment. . . .

Perhaps you felt that as Joe moved into the upper levels of the need hierarchy, the notion of using money to *buy* satisfaction was singularly inappropriate. How can one *buy* genuine respect, for example? Which is precisely the point. Even with unlimited funds, Joe will find it impossible to buy all of his satisfaction; the higher he goes in the need hierarchy, the more he will have to *earn* his satisfactions, and money becomes increasingly irrelevant.

Thus a management that relies largely or exclusively on monetary rewards to coax productivity from its employees is using an increasingly ineffectual means of motivation, provided that its people have their lower level needs basically satisfied.

The Ford Story.   There is a distinct irony in all of this. Consider the case of Henry Ford. Ford become eminently successful by implementing the concepts of assembly-line operation and interchangeable parts. Jobs became highly specialized portions of larger, more complex tasks. How did Ford entice a grown man to work for him, screwing in bolt 14 all day long? Simple: if the man was living marginally—and many were—just pay him $5 a day (almost twice as much as the going rate) and he would be delighted to put in his purgatory time to gain a bit of financial breathing room. But workers were not the only ones who had to play restrictive, externally controlled roles. Managers, generally, were deprived of the freedom to manage, to exercise authority, to make decisions.

Ford has been characterized as the arch-authoritarian, but no one can deny his success, two thirds of the automobile market by the early 1920s. But he was to pay a price for his one-man-showmanship. The story of the near collapse of the company is a long and involved one, but the moral is clear. People will submit to strict external control when there is no effective escape and when the controller has the power to satisfy their needs. In Ford's case, dollars proved highly successful in motivating people when their predominant needs were at the lower end of the hierarchy. But as the base of wealth broadened, as the dollars came in, these needs began to be satisfied to the extent that they were no longer the individual's exclusive preoccupation. Ironically, the very success of the methods—external controls and good wages—eventually undermined their utility as motivating agents as the needs to which they were eminently suited became fulfilled. The Ford story differs only in degree from the story of industry in general. McGregor epitomized the situation:

> Management by direction and control, whether implemented with the hard, soft, or the firm but fair approach—fails under today's conditions to provide effective motivation of human effort toward organizational objectives. It fails because direction and control are useless methods of motivating people whose physiological and safety needs are predominant.[12]

Theory Y

Thus a new management theory was necessary, one based on more valid premises about human nature and motivation. Whereas Theory X held that the average person was unalterably immature, the *theory* of Theory Y is essentially that humans are at least *potentially* mature.

> The *motivation,* the *potential* for development, the *capacity* for assuming responsibility, the *readiness* to direct behavior toward organizational goals are present in people.[13]

Managerial practice, therefore, should be geared to the subordinate's current level of maturity with the overall goal of helping him/her to develop, to require progressively less external control, and to gain more and more self-control. And why would a person want this? Because under these conditions, one achieves satisfaction on the job at the levels, primarily the ego and self-fulfillment levels, at which one is most motivatable.

Thus, Theory Y would lead to management practices that would work with rather than against the grain of human nature. The goal of management under Theory Y, then, is to "arrange organizational conditions and methods of operations so that people can achieve their own goals best by directing *their own* efforts toward organizational objectives."[14] (See Figure 2–6 below for a summary of Theory X and Theory Y.)

Flexibility. For a time, Theory Y was misconstrued by some as the soft version of Theory X, a sort of sugar-coated or manipulative system.

Theory Y permits access to the full range of management approaches from external to self-control. Where on the spectrum to peg one's approach depends on the supervisor's judgment of the subordinate's current state of development. For example, if the subordinate is new and inexperienced, rather close supervision and guidance may be necessary initially.

---

[12]Douglas McGregor, "Adventures in Thought and Action," Proceedings of the Fifth Anniversary Convocation of the School of Industrial Management, Massachusetts Institute of Technology, Cambridge, April 9, 1957, p. 28.

[13]Ibid. Italics are mine. See also, Harold Kerzner, *Project Management for Executives* (New York: Van Nostrand Reinhold, 1982), pp. 351 and 355.

[14]Ibid.

FIGURE 2–6

Theory	Resulting practice

Theory X—The "average person" is inherently (unalterably) immature.

Therefore, it is necessary to control and motivate him or her *externally*. While the manager may have a *range of modes* by which to apply controls, he or she has no choice as to *whether* external control will be imposed. The *theory* of Theory X precludes anything other than external control.

However, external controls tend to perpetuate themselves, for they keep people immature, emotionally undeveloped, unable to shoulder responsibility, etc.

Theory Y—The "average person" is *potentially* mature.

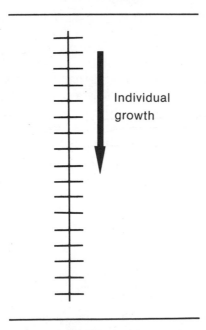

Balance of external control and self-control

Therefore, select the *appropriate balance* between external control and individual freedom commensurate with the individual's *current stage* of development. A new dimension is now open. It is no longer only a question of *how* to administer external control but of *how much* external control is desirable.

The overall objective is to build the constructive cycle (see Figure 2–1): Given skillful coaching and the opportunity to grow (less external control; more freedom to exercise his/her initiative, to make decisions, etc.), the individual will indeed be motivated to grow (because growth renders satisfactions particularly at the ego and self-fulfillment need levels).

By growing, he or she will become more capable of responsible, more self-controlled behavior which serves the best interests of his or her organization as well as his or her own best interests. In sum, the more growth—the more self-control; the more self-control—the more growth; etc.

But external control gradually decreases as the individual learns to make decisions and takes independent action. The two theories might be epitomized as follows:

Theory X: John, I want you to be able to swim. However, you cannot swim. Therefore, do not go into the water until you can swim.

The illustration is absurd but not irrelevant. The net result is that John does not learn to swim, remains undeveloped and dependent upon his superior, which is what the superior may have intended, at least unconsciously, in the first place.

Theory Y: John, I want you to be able to swim. However, you cannot swim. Therefore, I shall teach you and let you practice in three feet of water. If you show some prowess there, you may try five feet, and so on.

The key to the art of managing under Theory Y is the ability to *trust appropriately.* Chronic undertrusting leads to apathy or resentment and the conditions that generally prevail under Theory X. Overtrusting can be equally destructive. To carry the swimming analogy further, the overtrusting manager throws John into 10 feet of water. Since John is currently incapable, he begins to sink and the boss must rescue him. There tend to be two destructive consequences: (1) John's self-confidence has been destroyed or at least badly battered; (2) the boss's confidence in John may be destroyed, and thus the boss may be sorely tempted to run back to rigorous external control, "You'll never get a chance to fail me again!" with the ensuing pattern of John's nondevelopment. Ironically, the boss fails to recognize that it was faulty judgment that triggered the fiasco.

THE FREEDOM-ORDER DICHOTOMY

Prior to McGregor, some traditional management philosophers and managers seem to have been burdened with a myth—that freedom (of the individual to satisfy his or her needs) and order (coordination to achieve the organization's objectives) existed as polar opposites on a single continuum, and that freedom would be attained only at the expense of order, and vice versa. (See Figure 2-7.)

Business management had attempted to work out its role at various points along the continuum—hard, soft, firm but fair (See Figure 2-6), but

FIGURE 2-7
The freedom-order dichotomy

FREEDOM   ORDER
|||||||||||||||||||||||||||||||||||||||||||||||

has generally gravitated toward the high order-low freedom end. The rationale appears to have been essentially as follows:

1. Free enterprise has been demonstrably effective in motivating high quality and quantity performance, "No one works harder than the self-employed."
2. But economic and technological reasons require complex, interdependent, well-ordered organizations.
3. Nos. 1 and 2 appeared to be in conflict, and 2 usually prevailed, "Let people work for themselves when and in the manner they wish, and the result is usually *chaos!*"
4. Thus the institution has generally striven for coordination often at the cost of passivity and antagonism on the part of its employees.

On first analysis, we are faced with a dilemma. On one side, there is the force for logic, order, and control; on the other, the drive for individual expression and need satisfaction. The immediate necessity in industry seems to be for logical planning, executing, and controlling. Accordingly, the concepts of organizational structure, job simplification, and control systems seem mandatory. Unfortunately, they tend to develop submissive and dependent performance on the part of employees. Occasionally, such measures generate active or passive revolt. More frequently the outcome is simply overwhelming dullness and minimal compliance.

But the dilemma is more apparent than real. It has become increasingly clear that freedom and order are not necessarily extremes on a single continuum but can exist as two distinct dimensions. (See Figure 2–8.)

Real-life counterparts for the four quadrants in Figure 2–8 might be: (A) In some unfortunate Third World nations where terrorism is rampant, low order and very little freedom in the sense that citizens could not walk down the street without extreme danger. (B) The stereotypical Polynesian idyll, where life is presumably sublime but little is accomplished. (C) Stalin's Russia, Hitler's Germany, and Mao's China. And (D)? There is increasing evidence that it or something approaching it is a possibility in organizations.

Integration of Goals

D will be possible, according to Theory Y, when there is an alliance of individual and organizational goals. The prospect: the organization will encourage individuals to participate more fully in decision making, in determining the destiny of the organization—to provide them significantly more freedom to be in business for themselves—that is, to satisfy their needs but in such a way as to maintain the order necessary to achieve the goals of the organization. Thus they will simultaneously work at satisfying their

FIGURE 2-8

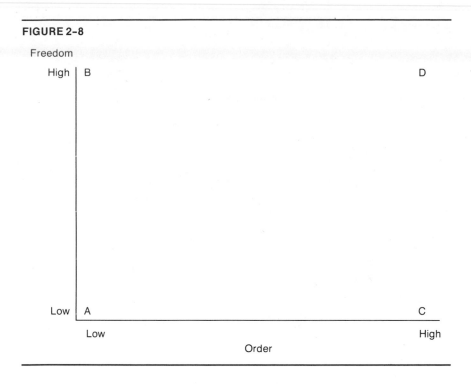

own psychic needs and at contributing maximally to their organization's objectives, in McGregor's words, a true "integration of goals."

"The concept rests on a philosophy of management that emphasizes an integration between external control (by managers) and self-control (by subordinates). It can apply to any manager or individual, no matter what his/her level or function, and to any organization, regardless of size."[15]

Vectors

We can use vectors to express the concept of goal integration. Let's simplify a business firm by dividing it into two groups, management and workers. When two or more forces are operating, they can be represented by vectors to indicate the result of the combination of their respective efforts. Examine Figure 2-9 for a hypothetical situation.

A–B represents the organization's objectives (e.g., to maintain and enhance its wealth-generating capabilities). The organization, for our pur-

---

[10]Hersey and Blanchard, *Management of Organizational Behavior*, 4th ed. (Englewood Cliffs, N.J.: Prentice-Hall, 1982), p. 182.

FIGURE 2-9

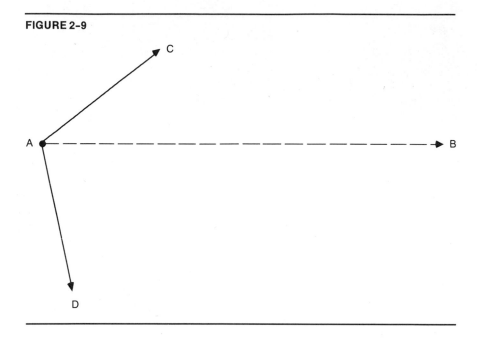

poses here, is an abstraction—neither management nor workers, nor the two groups combined. Vector A–C is management's aim, largely compatible but not totally congruent with the organization's. Managers—first-line supervisors through board chairmen, are, after all, individuals with needs and motives of their own. Vector A–D is the workers' goal, relatively self-centered and apathetic insofar as the firm's objectives are concerned.

The next step is to make a parallelogram of A–C and A–D and draw the resultant vector, A–E. See Figure 2–10.

A–E represents the combination of management's and workers' efforts. To what extent are the organization's objectives achieved? Draw a vertical line from point E up to the A–B line and place F at the point it touches the A–B line. A–F represents the degree of attainment of the firm's goals. The results are not inspiring, but payrolls are met, creditors are paid, shareholders receive dividends, and earnings may be retained for future commitments. The situation could be significantly better, or appallingly worse.

In Figure 2–11, the net organizational accomplishment, A–F is nil, in some circumstances, it could even be negative. Each group, in periods of emotionality such as a strike, is quite capable of disregarding the organization's welfare, even its *own*, in order to thwart the enemy.

The prime promise of Theory Y is that its basic premises and resultant management practices will lead to an organizational climate in which the goals of both manager and worker (A–C and A–D, respectively) will be

FIGURE 2-10

FIGURE 2-11

FIGURE 2–12

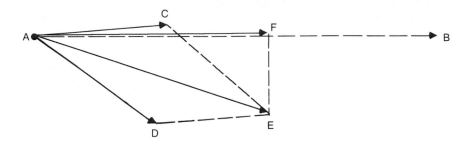

more closely aligned with those of the organization (A–B). (See Figure 2–12.) Thus A–F, the degree of attainment of the organization's objectives, will be markedly greater.

Through *participatory management* (the broader sharing of authority), workers will identify more closely with the firm for basically the same reason that top management identifies with it now. The organizational setting will offer them more opportunity for satisfying their needs, especially those at the ego and self-fulfillment levels. And this, by and large, has been the open secret of motivating anyone at any time, offering the opportunity to satisfy needs. It follows, however, that when needs change, so should the means for satisfying them.

IMPLEMENTATION PROBLEMS

To be sure, there sometimes have been problems associated with the implementation of changes growing out of the Theory Y rationale. One is the inevitable expense of transition. The installation of a participative management approach at one company exacted a toll. The initial consequences of their changes were to boost morale sky high . . . and disrupt production! It took three months to return production to its former rate. Subsequently, though, output increased 30 percent, rejects dropped to virtually nil, the job of inspector became unnecessary and was eliminated, customer complaints fell 70 percent, and the increased flexibility of the firm permitted retooling in 2 to 3 weeks, whereas in the past, it had required 8 to 10 weeks to crank up for a new model.

Another problem arises when behavioral changes are attempted in the middle and lower echelons of an organization without reinforcement from above. "How can I be a Theory Y manager when I report to a Theory X boss?" or, "How can I delegate authority when the boss doesn't delegate it to me?" These are the plaintive cries of many managers participating in management seminars at which Theory Y is suggested.

This is probably only symptomatic of a more profound obstacle to the full implementation of Theory Y. Theory Y, in essence, calls for the fullest sharing of authority possible. Consider our current system of progression. Is it not, other factors being equal, the power-oriented individual who rises in our organizations? Participative management approaches, however, are asking such individuals to relinquish the very means of need satisfaction they strove so diligently to acquire. Maslow's hierarchy of needs suggests that a solution to this seeming dilemma lies in the prospect of the executives finding even greater need fulfillment in the sharing of power and the development of their own skills and the skills of their subordinates.

McGregor was not unmindful of such obstacles.

> Only the management that has confidence in human capacities and is itself directed toward organizational objectives rather than toward the preservation of personal power can grasp the implications of this emerging theory. Such management will find and apply successfully other innovative ideas as we move slowly toward the full implementation of a theory like Y.[16]

I would add that making Theory Y work is everyone's business. Hence this chapter on organizational culture, i.e., that all-pervading atmosphere in which a working group is immersed. Odiorne speaks of excellence.

> *Excellence results from a climate in which the search for excellence goes on at all levels, at all times.*
> Keen attention must be paid to maintaining an organizational climate which respects excellence, which tries for it, which holds it up as its standard, and which impresses the desire for it upon everyone on the payroll.[17]

Developments

Hundreds of behavioral scientists and thousands of practicing executives have confirmed, updated, and extended McGregor's initial work.

---

[16]McGregor, "Adventures in Thought and Action," p. 29.
[17]George S. Odiorne, *The Effective Executive's Guide to Managerial Excellence* (Westfield, Maine: MBO, 1983), p. 3. See also; Thomas Peters and Robert Waterman, Jr., *In Search of Excellence: Lessons from America's Best-Run Companies* (New York: Harper & Row, 1982).

Rensis Likert, for example, on the basis of considerable experimental and empirical evidence on supportive climates, devised his System 4[18] style of managing organizations.

> *System 4*—Management is seen as having complete confidence and trust in subordinates. Decision making is widely dispersed throughout the organization, although well integrated. Communication flows not only up and down the hierarchy but among peers. Workers are motivated by participation and involvement in developing economic rewards, setting goals, improving methods, and appraising progress toward goals. There is extensive, friendly superior-subordinate interaction with a high degree of confidence and trust. There is widespread responsibility for the control process, with the lower units fully involved. The informal and formal organizations are often one and the same. Thus, all social forces support efforts to achieve stated organizational goals.[19]

One interpersonal concept that received a substantial boost from Theory Y is *situational leadership*[20]. Recall that "the key to the art of managing under Theory Y is the ability to *trust appropriately.*" Thus, the best way to lead depends upon the specific situation—including the characteristics of the subordinates, the task, organizational policy and climate, superiors, peers, the leader's own characteristics and traits, and the responses of the subordinates.[21]

Leadership is not a simple one-way street in which the leader influences the group. Rather it is determined by many forces outside (as well as inside) the leader. That is why Cohen et al, concluded that a "wide variety of behaviors may be effective in particular situations."[22]

Another important outgrowth of McGregor's pioneering has been the concept of *goal setting*. This is Reitz's[23] view:

> One aspect of the organizational environment which has received considerable attention in behavior-change programs is the setting of goals toward which individuals and groups can strive. Much of this interest developed from empirical studies which showed that individuals tend to perform at higher or more effective levels when they are working toward specific goals

---

[18]Systems 3, 2, and 1 were progressively more authoritarian approaches.

[19]Hersey and Blanchard, *Management of Organizational Behavior*, p. 73.

[20]Paul Hersey, *The Situational Leader* (Escondido, Calif.: The Center for Leadership, 1984).

[21]H. Joseph Reitz, *Behavior in Organizations* rev. ed. (Homewood, Ill.: Richard D. Irwin, 1981), pp. 487–93.

[22]Allan R. Cohen, Stephen L. Fink, Herman Gadon, and Robin D. Mills, *Effective Behavior in Organizations*, 3d ed. (Homewood, Ill.: Richard D. Irwin, 1984), p. 265.

[23]Reitz, *Behavior*, pp. 528–29. See E.A. Locke and G.P. Latham, *Goal Setting: A Motivational Technique That Works!* (Englewood Cliffs, N.J.: Prentice-Hall, 1984) for a current and comprehensive appraisal of the goal-setting process.

than when they are not. In this area, a goal is defined as a level of performance whose attainment is associated with "success" and nonattainment with "failure."

One variation of goal setting that has attracted a great deal of attention in organizations has been *management by objectives* (MBO). The essence of MBO is that it combines specific goal setting, participation, and feedback into a performance appraisal system.

MBO can be properly defined as: A managerial process whereby organizational purposes are diagnosed and met by joining superior and subordinates in the pursuit of mutually agreed-upon goals and objectives, which are specific, measurable, time-bounded, and joined in an action plan; progress and goal attainment are measured and monitored in appraisal sessions which center on mutually determined objective standards of performance.[24]

The key characteristics of MBO are:

1. Effective goal setting and planning by top levels of the managerial hierarchy.
2. Commitment of the organization to this approach.
3. Participation of subordinates in setting goals.
4. Frequent performance review (feedback).
5. Some freedom in developing means for achieving objectives.[25]

Under companywide MBO programs, objectives at all levels of management and employees are set with reference to the overall organizational goal. Goal setting starts at the top and works down, with each level setting goals consistent with those of the next highest level.

MBO, while difficult[26] and time-consuming to implement, has demonstrated success in changing behavior. In one production firm, productivity had been declining at an average rate of 0.4 percent per month. After MBO

---

[24]M.L. McConkie, "A Clarification of the Goal Setting and Appraisal Processes in MBO," *Academy of Management Review,* 1979, p. 37.

[25]S.J. Carroll, Jr., and H.L. Tosi, Jr., *Management by Objectives: Applications and Research* (New York: Macmillan, 1973), p. 3.

[26]Most behavioral scientists believe that such difficulties stem from misunderstanding and faulty practice of MBO's tenets rather than from an inherently invalid concept. . .many organizations have lost the elementary insight into the essential functions of a manager. Their managers go through the motions of managing by living up to set procedures, e.g., watching time clocks, granting everyday personnel requests, selecting replacements when someone quits, focusing on minor elements while not seeing the big picture.

Advice: Costly programs with attractive packages and procedures (sort of paint-by-number sets) to reinstitute the traditional managerial functions are unnecessary. Once corporate objectives are ascertained and competent managers hired, MBO becomes a natural function. (Leonard R. Sayles, "Management by Objectives: A Reappraisal," *Boardroom Reports,* 7, no. 11 (June 15, 1978), p. 7.

was instituted, productivity increased at an average rate of 0.3 percent per month. Managers involved in the program attributed the improved productivity to performance appraisal, betting planning, and better communications resulting from MBO.[27]

Still another emphasis for which McGregor's Theory Y is a logical antecedent is organization development (OD). OD's principal objective is "to uncover and remove attitudinal, behavioral, procedural, policy, and structural barriers to effective performance across the entire sociotechnical system, gaining in the process increased awareness of the system's internal and external dynamics so that future adaptations are enhanced."[28]

The chief aspects of OD include the following:

1. It involves an unfreezing-moving-refreezing process that constitutes change in human attitudes and behavior.
2. Learning is most effective when it takes place within a natural work group.
3. Change must consider the interdependencies of the environment.
4. OD is basically a continuous method of monitoring the organization's systems and processes.[29]

Japanese manufacturers have been phenomenally successful in some areas. One of their practices, especially *quality circles*, has become increasingly popular in American organizations. Theory Y, again, is its philosophic underpinning. Teams of employees meet periodically to determine ways of improving quality and productivity. The record for reducing defects and unnecessary work procedures has often been impressive.[30]

One potential hazard, though, is that management sometimes focuses on the technical developments and insufficiently appreciates the motivational implications of bringing employees together and allowing them to influence the way the work is done.

But a broader caution is in order. There is no doubt that Japanese industrial experiences have attracted a great deal of attention worldwide. Two books[31], in particular, which compare Japanese and American management practices, have been very well received and are certainly worthy of serious study. But we must guard against the temptation to assume that

---

[27]Ibid., p. 531.

[28]R.E. Miles, *Theories of Management: Implications for Organizational Behavior and Development* (New York: McGraw-Hill, 1975), p. 191.

[29]Ibid., pp. 192–93.

[30]Robert I. Patchin, *The Management and Maintenance of Quality Circles* (Homewood, Ill.: Dow Jones-Irwin, 1983).

[31]William Ouchi, *Theory Z: How American Business Can Meet the Japanese Challenge* (Reading, Mass.: Addison-Wesley, 1981) and Richard Tanner Pascale and Anthony G. Athos, *The Art of Japanese Management: Applications for American Executives* (New York: Simon & Schuster, 1981).

that which works well for the Japanese will, *ipso facto*, work equally well in American organizations.

We must remind ourselves that the two cultures differ substantially. Rehder[32] offers an insightful contrast of the two traditional organizational and management systems. And Schermerhorn's advice is warranted:

> The final answer on how well management practices such as lifetime employment, the ringi system, and even quality-control circles work in the United States and other countries remain to be determined. For now, it appears that we should use books like *Theory Z* and *The Art of Japanese Management* for provocation and dialogue . . . . Their function, like much of the writing on Japanese management, is to help develop creative and critical thinking about the way we do things and about whether or not we can and should be doing them better.[33]

Clearly Theory Y management, eupsychian management, enlightened management, or whatever one cares to call it, and its descendants (situational leadership, goal setting, MBO, OD, and quality circles), have exciting potentials. But they also place markedly greater demand upon managers' abilities to analyze and predict human behavior (their own included), to know their people, and to communicate (encode and decode messages). The strengthening of these skills is this book's principal purpose.

We have considered the organization and the culture it generates. We will now turn to the individual and examine some of the perceptual and motivational aspects of communication behavior.

DISCUSSION QUESTIONS

1. "For better or worse, society is becoming progressively organized." How do you feel about this trend? What benefits and drawbacks are associated with this tendency? What special kinds of problems are arising in this regard, and what can be done to cope with them?

2. "Some feel that the structure and climate of today's organization are in many respects inimical to the emotional health and development of its members." Do you agree or disagree? More specifically, what might be the object?

3. "A new, more subtle postindustrial revolution is in process." What was intended by that statement? What is contributing to this revolution? Is it broader than just industrial?

---

[32]Robert R. Rehder, "What American and Japanese Managers Are Learning from Each Other," *Business Horizons*, 24, March-April (1981), p. 67.

[33]John R. Schermerhorn, Jr. *Management for Productivity* (New York: John Wiley & Sons, 1984), pp. 646–48.

4. The author asserts: "The leadership and overall atmosphere . . . achieve its goals." How does this strike you as a managerial philosophy? Is it too idealistic? Will it work? Does it have sufficient regard for organizational needs? If you were employed in an organization which adhered as closely as possible to these ideals, would you be effectively motivated to produce? If you were the boss, how would this philosophy affect your people?

5. Re: the constructive and destructive cycles. Are they valid, that is, do high trust and high performance generally tend to reinforce each other? Do low trust and low performance generally tend to reinforce each other? If high performance tends to follow high trust, why don't managers simply start "high-trusting" their subordinates, even if they don't mean it?

6. What is the relationship between *trust* and *communication* in an organization?

7. "He [or she] who rides a tiger can never dismount." How does that statement relate to this chapter?

8. Maslow's *hierarchy of needs*: Does it explain and predict human behavior to your satisfaction?

9. According to McGregor, most employees in the United States have had their physiological and safety-security needs at least reasonably satisfied. Do you agree? If so, what are the implications of this to managers and others who are concerned with the motivation of people?

10. "A management which relies largely or exclusively on monetary rewards . . . is using an increasingly ineffectual means of motivation, provided that its people have their lower level needs basically satisfied." Discuss. How does the Ford story relate to the above statement?

11. In accordance with Theory Y, managerial practice should be geared to the subordinate's current level of maturity with the overall goal of helping him/her to develop, to require progressively less external control, and to gain more and more self-control." Is this realistic? Will it work? Does it have limitations?

12. Discuss the freedom-order dichotomy. Under what conditions could these qualities coexist?

13. What are some of the problems associated with the implementation of the changes called for by Theory Y?

14. What does this chapter on *organizational culture* have to do with *communication*? What special challenges confront the manager who attempts to implement Theory Y?

15. Write an essay on organizational climate discussing the relationships among the destructive and constructive cycles, Theories X and Y, external and internal control, the hierarchy of needs, the freedom-order dichotomy, and the integration of goals.

CASES

CASE 2-1

Drexel Electronics Company*

The Drexel Electronics Company, a nationally known firm, specialized in the manufacture of communications equipment. One of its larger plants was located in a nearby suburb of a large West Coast city. Some 800 people were employed in this plant, engaged in the production and minor assembly of metal parts from sheet and bar stock. Finished parts were sent to another plant for final assembly. Local sales, public relations, and general office departments were maintained on the premises in addition to the personnel, time study, engineering, and maintenance departments. Ninety percent of the employees were engaged in the 10 production and materials handling departments.

One of the production departments, small parts, was supervised by Fred Schultz, assisted by two foremen. Some 40 men and women worked in small parts on the day shift. Another 35 on the night shift were supervised by the night foreman. Workers in this department were classified into 12 grades, according to skill and seniority. The lower grades, 1 through 3, were composed mainly of younger workers who had little experience or technical skills. Their work consisted of deburring, straightening, and assembling small parts with simple hand tools. The middle grades, 4 through 6, consisted of skilled workers who did more complex work, while grades 7 through 12 were reserved for inspectors, setup men, assistant foremen, and foremen.

Although production in this department was on an individual or job-order basis, a weekly bonus determined by the total production of the department was added to the base wage for each job grade. This group bonus plan was employed wherever feasible throughout the plant.

In July, Jack Marcell, 18, a recent high school graduate, applied for employment at Drexel Electronics. The personnel manager told Jack that the prime factor in advancement was ability and that superior workers had been known to make grade 7, the lowest grade of inspector, after five years of service. Seniority, he said, played only a secondary role and was

---

*All names and organizational designations have been disguised. Northwestern University cases are reports of concrete events and behavior, prepared for class discussion. They are not intended as examples of good or bad administrative practice. Copyright, 1964, by Northwestern University. Printed by permission.

generally rewarded with pay increases rather than with advancement in rank.

Marcell was assigned to the small parts department. The day he reported for work, Schultz took him aside for a brief interview, confirmed the personnel manager's statements about advancement, and added that all women began in grade 1, while men started in grade 2. He explained that all new workers were hired on a trial, or probationary, basis.

The maximum probationary period was five months. If a worker had attained the department standards of quantity and quality of production before the end of this period, he was considered to be on a permanent basis with the firm. Otherwise, he was released. An exceptional producer could be promoted to grade 3 anytime after a minimum probationary period of five weeks. Grade 3 represented a raise in base pay and work of a more complex, less monotonous nature. Schultz said the company's probation policy was designed to give ample opportunity for the late bloomer to prove himself and yet permit the unusual worker to advance as rapidly as his ability and production warranted.

Each worker was required to turn in a "factor time summary" at the end of each working day. This sheet showed the job orders on which the employee had worked, actual hours worked on each job, the standard rate for each, the number of parts finished, and the standard hours produced. Jack soon learned that management expected the average worker on his job to produce 8 to 10 standard hours[1] per day, while a superior worker produced 10 to 12 standard hours per day.

Most of the job rates seemed hard to make to Jack, but he learned quickly and was soon producing seven to eight standard hours per day. Within several weeks, he learned from other workers that there were certain gravy jobs that came through the department quite often. These jobs carried unusually low standard rates in relation to the amount of hand finishing necessary to complete the part. Low rates were often caused by improved manufacturing procedures in one or more of the departments which processed the parts before they reached small parts, thus making certain small parts job easier, although the rates remained unchanged. On such jobs, it was possible to produce 18 or 20 standard hours per day. Furthermore, these hours could be saved up and turned in anytime during the

---

[1]A standard hour was a measure of production. For example, if the standard rate for a particular piecework job had been set at 100 pieces per hour, then a standard hour on that job would be 100 pieces. A worker who turned out 120 pieces would have produced 1.2 standard hours of work. The group bonus was computed at the end of the week. A worker who produced 50 standard hours for the week was paid his base hourly wage for the 40 hours. His standard hours over eight per day (ten in this case) were thrown into the pot along with the excess hours of the other workers. The pot hours were divided equally each week among the workers, regardless of grade. Pay for these hours varied with the bonus rate for each worker's grade (approximately 80 percent of his base rate).

week. If a worker had a gravy job on Monday, for example, he might turn out 20 standard hours of work. However, he would report only 12 hours and save the other 8 hours to spread over the remaining days of the week. Thus, it would be possible for him to report 12 hours for each of the five days of the week, even though he had produced only 10 standard hours on each of the other four days.

It became obvious to Jack that the saving technique was designed to conceal the gravy jobs from the time study department. It was clear that only the foremen and Fred Schultz were in a position to detect these jobs. The actual starting and stopping times on each job were not revealed by the time cards sent to the payroll department but only by the route sheets or individual and group productivity reports which were forwarded to the production department. But he never heard Schultz or any foreman mention the soft touches to anyone except their older workers.

Foreman   Joe [a senior employee], I got a light one coming up. Do you need it?

Joe   Well, no—I've had a few of them already this week, so I don't need it. Why don't you give it to Tom [a younger employee]? He's had some rough ones. He'll need the hours.

In order to even up for the week, it seemed to Jack that many gravy jobs were given workers who handled a series of jobs with tighter rates. However, the distribution of the easier jobs was not entirely determined by worker need. Although all workers received gravy jobs occasionally, those closest to the senior workers and foremen were assigned appreciably more than average. This group appeared to be favored over eight younger men who ate and took their breaks together, without much contact with Schultz, the foremen, and the other workers. One of the foremen expressed what he said was the general feeling toward the out group. "They're our poorest workers. They're always complaining. The only thing they're looking for on this job is the almighty buck. They have the lowest output in the department, and if you turn your back for two minutes, they're off sneaking a smoke or goofing off in some other way. They're just punks and wise guys in my book."

Not all young workers were in the out group. Jack Marcell found no difficulty in making friends with his co-workers and foremen. Before long, he was getting his share of gravy jobs, which made it possible for him to turn in 12 standard hours per day much of the time.

At the end of the fifth week of Jack's employment at Drexel Electronics, Fred Schultz called the boy aside to tell him that he was pleased with his work and that he was being promoted to grade 3. As Jack expressed his gratitude, Schultz added, "You'd better keep this under your hat. There are two other men in the department who have been with the company four months but are still in grade 2."

Jack did not mention his promotion to his co-workers, but they soon noticed that Jack was doing more advanced work. Carson and Welles, young grade 2 men with more seniority than Jack, went to see Schultz in his office and complained bitterly.

Schultz drew a breath and said acidly, "You men knew the rules when you came in here. If you don't like it, you know where the door is."

Discussion Questions

1. What were the frames of reference, respectively, of Marcell, Schultz, the in-group, and the out-group?

2. What were the major problems in this case?

3. Since Schultz seems unlikely to take any action on Carson's and Welles' complaints, assume that Carson and Welles go to a Mr. Brown, Schultz's superior, and register their complaints. As Brown, what would you do, step by step?

CASE 2-2

East-Ohio Communications System*

The East-Ohio Communications System, an independent telephone company, served a portion of eastern Ohio. The company had seven districts. Each district served five or six towns or cities. A communications manager was in charge of each district. In each town, an office manager was responsible for the switchboard office. Under the office manager were assistant office managers (AOMs), who supervised switchboard operations. The office manager, AOMs, and switchboard operators were women.

In March, between quarters, Professor Richard Cart of Northwestern University had the following conversation with Mr. Gregory Jergens, communications manager of the Garretsville, Ohio district of the East-Ohio Communications System:

Jergens We have a problem in Newton Falls which may be of interest, Professor Cart.

Cart What sort of problem?

Jergens The service ratings have been very low. Perhaps I should explain what a service rating is. In our company, we have men who go to various towns and sample switchboard operations in order to determine how efficient the service is. Such items as slow answers and wrong numbers are recorded as errors. Slow answers are the

---

chief fault in Newton Falls. An operator is supposed to answer a call within 10 seconds after the sending party picks up his receiver to place the call. If there is no response in 12 seconds, an error is charged against the office service rating.

The men who do the rating sample about 500 calls a month from various telephones within the office area. Then they give the district a rating, which is a percentage of error-free calls to total calls sampled.

A good rating is about 94. Newton Falls was just rated 84 and has been getting poor ratings periodically for more than a year now. As a result, there has been a good deal of pressure on Mrs. Swanson, the office manager at Newton Falls, and on her AOMs.

Cart They don't know what's wrong?

Jergens We've all been working on it. A few weeks ago, I sent my assistants, Steve Hieber and Ron De Kamp, to Newton Falls to interview the operators and to try to find out what the trouble is. Ron and Steve concluded that the operators are upset because AOMs plug into the boards and take calls. The operators complain of not being given a chance. They resent interference by AOMs on the switchboards.

Cart That's a tough situation for all of you.

Jergens I went to Newton Falls with Steve and Ron. We had a very unfortunate occurrence, however. While we were talking to Mrs. Swanson and some of the AOMs, Ron De Kamp noticed one AOM, Miss Johnson, taking a call at the switchboard. Without thinking, he blurted out, "See, that's what we mean. Look at Miss Johnson over there taking a call. There's the trouble."

Ron shouldn't have done this. It's not good human relations. You can't just tell a person she is wrong. You can't scold her. You have to talk to the employee and try to get her to realize her mistakes. It must come from the employee if there is going to be any kind of cooperation and desire to do good work.

Cart Did the incident have repercussions?

Jergens Yes, it did. Later, when I greeted Miss Johnson in the hall, she sort of mumbled under her breath. I asked her what was wrong. "Nothing" was the reply, and with that she walked away. Later in the afternoon, I noticed Miss Johnson sitting by herself in the conference room. I walked up to her and said I didn't want to pry, but if she would like to discuss her problem, I would be happy to listen. She said, "What good is it to try and do anything around here? You're only reprimanded for it later." Apparently, she hadn't overheard Ron's remark, but someone told her about it later. She was very upset. As a matter of fact, Miss Johnson is rough on her employees. She reprimands them and often threatens them. I listened

to her and then asked if she could see how wrong it was to reprimand someone instead of listening to their story. I explained that
nothing was accomplished by reprimands except anger and hostility. This was an excellent opportunity to get a point across. I spoke
to Ron about the incident later in the district office. He apologized
and said he realized he had made a mistake.

Cart Do you feel the operators' complaints about AOMs taking calls
get at the basic problem?

Jergens Partly, but I'm sure this isn't the whole story. The more I
think about it, the more I'm convinced it's a human relations problem. Say, how would you like to go to Newton Falls with me tomorrow?

Cart I would like that very much.

The next day, Professor Cart accompanied Mr. Jergens to Newton
Falls. After Cart had been introduced to Mrs. Swanson, the switchboard
office manager, the following conversation took place:

Jergens Professor Cart and I were discussing the possibility that employee attitudes or other human relations problems may be causing
the low rating here, Mrs. Swanson.

Swanson I'm beginning to think so.

Jergens Would you care to give us an example, Mrs. Swanson?

Swanson Well, the attitudes of some of the operators could be causing
the trouble. I've been concerned about them. It's difficult to put
your finger on any one thing.

Jergens Could you tell us an incident that would illustrate what you
have in mind?

Swanson A few days ago, I was coming up the stairs to the switchboard room with two of the AOMs and the union president. At least
five operators turned around from their work to see what was going on. We can't have this sort of thing. An operator cannot answer
calls when she's looking at something else.

Jergens Don't you feel such a reaction is the normal thing for a person,
Mrs. Swanson? Everyone is curious to see what's going on. A quick
look wouldn't disturb anything too much, would it? Do you really
feel it would prevent answering a call in 12 seconds?

Swanson They're not always quick glances, Mr. Jergens. By the time
an operator turns around to see what's going on and then turns
back to her board, she could miss 12 seconds.

Jergens It's possible. But do you really feel we can stop this? Curiosity
is pretty normal, especially when people walk into a room. Don't
you think so?

Swanson I guess so. But service can be interrupted.

Cart   Do operators turn around and stare long enough to slow answering time?

Swanson   It happens.

Jergens   We shouldn't have that. But do you really feel we can stop a quick glance, Mrs. Swanson?

Swanson   I don't know. But it's serious when four or five operators turn around at once.

Jergens   Do you want to post notices on the bulletin board? I've seen some in other offices which say, "Are you a swivel head?"

Swanson   That may have been useful a long time ago. But notices won't do any good now. And turning around isn't the only thing. There's a good deal of talking on the job.

Jergens   Of course, we are not going to try and stop a greeting or comment when an operator comes on duty, are we?

Swanson   Oh, no. I'm referring to excessive chatter which disturbs everyone.

Jergens   We can't have that. And yet we don't want to merely tell them to keep quiet, do we?

Swanson   No.

Jergens   I think we should talk to each operator. We should listen to them in order to get their suggestions for overcoming the situation. The operators should feel they are taking part in the solution. Realization of the causes of the difficulty should come from them. With this realization will come a desire to improve. When employees are allowed to participate, they are thereby motivated with a desire to do a better job. A sense of importance and a sort of team spirit emerges. When one is able to see problems more clearly, you have set the stage for self-correction.

Group discussions would also be a good idea. When a group decides for itself, a team atmosphere is created. There is a group desire or motivation to correct the situation. They pull together to get at the bottom of the difficulty, see their mistakes, and establish means of overcoming them. The group creates a good deal of acceptance for the solution, since the solution comes from its members. We might hold short discussions of a few minutes' duration as each new shift comes on duty.

I did a similar thing in another district. Every month, I would visit each switchboard office with a chart showing a summary of service rating fluctuations. A few operators would gather around the chart, and I would ask what they thought we could do to improve our answering time. I think the discussions did a lot of good. Everyone had a desire to improve the situation, and the solutions to the problems came from them. The desire to improve must come from them. Would you like to try this, Mrs. Swanson?

Swanson Yes.

Jergens You feel individual and group discussions may help?

Swanson We can try. I'll talk to my AOMs. Something happened recently which I wanted to discuss with you, Mr. Jergens. Last Monday, one of the operators, Mrs. Frankel, asked Miss Manion (an AOM) if she could take a couple of hours off on Wednesday. She works the 12:30 to 6:30 P.M. shift. Miss Manion told Mrs. Frankel she could have the time if she switched shifts with another operator. She told Mrs. Frankel her board couldn't be left unattended for a couple of hours. Mrs. Frankel said she would get someone. But she also said she had to have the time off. On Tuesday, Mrs. Frankel had not yet arranged to switch shifts. At 12:30 on Wednesday, she called the AOM and said she wouldn't be in for a couple of hours. She had not gotten a replacement. Miss Manion told her not to bother to come in at all that afternoon, as a replacement was being put in her position. Mrs. Frankel said she was taking the time whether anyone liked it or not.

Jergens How's her attendance been?

Swanson Very poor.

Jergens What did she need the time for?

Swanson To go downtown with her son to buy a camera for him.

Jergens What do you want to do?

Swanson That's what I wanted to talk with you about.

Jergens Don't you feel she has been punished enough by being replaced on Wednesday: She lost the day's pay. Don't you want to talk to her?

Swanson Yes. I don't want to let the situation go by. I know why she didn't get a replacement. She would have had to switch with an operator on the 7:30 A.M. to 12:30 P.M.. shift. Mrs. Frankel just didn't want to get up that early.

Jergens Well, do you think we might practice the listening technique here? I'm sure if you interview her and let her do the talking, she will realize she's wrong. Don't you think so, Mrs. Swanson?

Swanson I have to do something.

Jergens Would you rather reprimand her or warn her that we won't tolerate this sort of thing?

Swanson No, but I don't want to let it go by. Then they get the attitude they can do these things, because nothing happens anyway.

Jergens You're right. But we have to be understanding. If you listen to her, she will realize her mistake. And it will come from her. It must come from her if there is going to be a desire to do a better job. She may tell the other operators you talked to her. She will say you were kind and she realizes how wrong she was. Isn't this the best way, Mrs. Swanson?

Swanson Yes. But I also believe people are different, Mr. Jergens. I think we have to treat them differently.

Jergens That's right. But the desire to improve must come from them. You cannot accomplish this by telling them or by warning them, can you?

Swanson I guess not.

Jergens You will try to interview the operators and hold the discussion sessions with them, won't you, Mrs. Swanson?

Swanson Yes, but I'll speak to my AOMs about it first.

Jergens Fine, and I think everything should be discussed—supervision, talking on the job, and looking away from the board.

Swanson As far as supervision is concerned, you must realize we are all under a good deal of pressure because of our poor service ratings.

Jergens I agree with you, Mrs. Swanson. This is a difficult situation. (*Pause*) Well, if you will both excuse me, I have some important phone calls to make. Perhaps the two of you would like to discuss the problem further while I am gone.

(*Mr. Jergens left the room.*)

Cart This is quite a situation.

Swanson You know, Professor Cart, I like Mr. Jergens very much. He is a very fair and honorable man. But I can't say I agree with some of his ideas on handling employee problems.

Cart How's that?

Swanson Well, much of our trouble stems from an attitude among operators that it doesn't make much difference what one does, because no one will do anything about it anyway.

Cart They feel they can get away with things?

Swanson They feel management is sort of wishy-washy. To the operators, management is nice but nothing more. So operators do what they please. I think we should be firm.

Cart You should let them know where they stand?

Swanson Management is a combination of fairness and firmness. Employees shouldn't be allowed to get away with questionable behavior. After all, the slow answering is affecting the whole office. When operators do things that cause slow answers, they should be told about it.

Cart The entire office could suffer from the poor service record. Operators should know that their questionable actions will not be tolerated.

Swanson That is exactly how I feel. The operators know when someone is called in because of something she did. But the way things are now, someone will ask her, "What happened?" The answer is, "Nothing. They were very nice, but nothing happened." In other words, management people are a bunch of suckers.

I think this is bad. Well, take Mrs. Frankel, for instance. She will be interviewed, and I will listen to her. But I can't let her leave my office before I am sure she realizes such behavior will not be tolerated in the future. Maybe she will realize her mistake by my listening to her, and maybe she won't. In either event, I have to be firm. Then when the other operators ask her what happened, she will tell them I meant business. There should be an attitude of: "Management means what it says, and it won't tolerate any fooling around."

Cart   Employees should feel that you mean what you say.

Swanson   Exactly. Our AOMs are wishy-washy and confused. They don't know how to handle the problem child. Not one of them would tell an operator to turn around and to stop talking. AOMs know such tactics are not accepted by higher management. The AOMs talk to operators and ask how they feel about this or that. There is no firmness at all. So the operators continue to behave in the same manner.

Why, if I did something wrong and wasn't called on it, I would feel I could do the same thing again. What would there be to stop me? No one would do anything, anyway. Our operators feel this way. Firmness is not approved. I preach the golden rule to my AOMs, Professor Cart. But I think firmness is appreciated, too. An employee respects a superior who is firm. This makes a good leader. There is no confidence or respect for a confused, wishy-washy superior.

Employees know they can walk all over such a person. We shouldn't be nasty. But we can be firm and still be fair.

Listening is good in its place. An employee with a problem should be able to go to her superior for help. But people are different, and you cannot deal with them all in the same way.

Cart   Listening and group discussion won't help the present situation?

Swanson   Not when an operator knows she can get away with anything. I don't mind quick glances round, and I don't mind when operators greet one another. But I do mind when four or five operators turn around and stare at something or someone, and I do mind excessive talking about goodness knows what.

Cart   It must be frustrating.

Swanson   I'm plenty frustrated. I almost feel as if I will explode at times. I know we can do something about the situation. And yet, we are told to listen and not reprimand. So the situation continues to exist. This is nerve-racking.

(*Mr. Jergens returned to the room with his hat and coat.*)

Jergens   Sorry to rush off, but I have to get back to the office.

(*Jergens and Cart said good-bye to Mrs. Swanson and departed.*)

Discussion Questions

1. What were the perceptions, respectively, of Jergens, Swanson, the AOMs, and the operators?

2. What plan of action do you recommend?

CASE 2–3

"My Case against Paul Brown"*

Jimmy Brown and Myron Cope

In the summer of 1957, when I first arrived in the Cleveland Browns' training camp in the town of Hiram, Ohio, a burly man named Lenny Ford took me aside and gave me a few words of advice.

"Rookie," he said to me, "if you want to get along here, listen to what I'm telling you.

"First," he said, "when you're running through plays in practice, always run 20 yards downfield. Don't just run through the hole and then jog a few steps and flip the ball back. The man doesn't like that. Run hard for 20 yards, even if you feel silly."

"Second," Lenny Ford told me, "keep your mouth shut when he speaks to you. When he tells you how to run a play, run it the way he tells you. If you have an idea for improving the play, keep it to yourself. Suggestions make the man mad. If you're pretty sure you can make more ground by changing the play, change it in the *game*. Don't change it in practice. Run it your way in the game and hope it works, and if it does, don't say anything. Just make your yardage and act like it was a mistake."

Lenny was telling me to behave in a way that sounded kind of childish to me, but I wasn't about to mistake him for an idiot. He was a feared man in professional football. I kept listening.

"Also," he went on, "don't start any conversations with the man. Don't *initiate* anything. You see something wrong, let it go. He does all the talking here."

The man being described by Lenny Ford was, of course, Paul Brown, our head coach. Working for Paul Brown in the ensuing years, I became the highest-salaried player in the history of football and have continued upward. My salary this season is more than $50,000. And thanks in part to my football reputation, I've earned substantial money in business, in broadcasting and in the movies. So I suppose I should be able to say some

---

*From *Off My Chest* by James N. Brown and Myron Cope. Copyright © 1964 by James N. Brown and Myron Cope. Reprinted by permission of Doubleday & Company, Inc.

nice things about Paul, and the truth is, I can. But I'm afraid I'll never rank as one of his leading admirers.

In 1962, I told Cleveland clubowner Art Modell that if Paul Brown remained as head coach in '63 I wanted out. Trade me, I told Modell, or I'll quit. I was not the only player to make such a threat. Nor did I relish taking a stand against Paul. I don't think it can be seriously questioned that among all of America's coaches this pale, tight-lipped, little man was far and away the genius of modern postwar football. He was the Browns' first coach, and they were named for him. His teams thoroughly dominated the old All-America Conference, then won six straight divisional titles in the National Football League. An original thinker and painstaking organizer, Paul Brown made the Cleveland Browns one of the most astonishingly successful organizations in the history of commercial sports. Then, sadly, they declined. My six years under Paul were as much as I could stomach. . . .

Although I was billed as Paul's star performer, I had no relationship with him. I wanted to, but his aloofness put him beyond approach. Yet curiously, during my rookie season I thought Paul was a great guy. Far from being the grim man Lenny Ford warned me about, Paul dazzled me with compliments and solicitude. I led the league in rushing that year with 942 yards, and we won the Eastern Division title. I had every reason to expect that I would always be happy working for Paul. But I didn't realize at the time that Paul followed a pattern in his handling of men—a pattern in which, at an almost predictable moment, he would turn off his amiability as decisively as a plumber turns off the warm water with a twist of his wrench.

Given a rookie who had outstanding promise, Paul would flatter and cajole him. But after the rookie proved himself and got acclimated in his first season, he became little more than a spoke in the wheel. I became Paul's big brute, the man who would slug out yardage for him. It seemed to me that he thought of me as nothing more than a weapon. I felt he had no interest in me as an individual.

Fair enough, I did not hanker to be babied. Yet in the atmosphere that Paul created, his players inevitably became robots. You played hard, but you concerned yourself almost entirely with your own performance. "I've done *my* job," you told yourself. When a teammate scored a touchdown, you didn't go out of your way to hug him or pat him on the fanny. When the ball changed hands, you went to the bench and sat there in silence. You cared, but the action on the field moved you to no demonstration of emotion. You were as close to being a mechanical man as a football player can get.

And as the NFL developed a balance of power that made every game a tough one, it became obvious that robots no longer would do. The Browns lacked spirit. It is my honest opinion that in Paul Brown's last five years as coach—five years in which we were also-rans every season—every one of those five squads, given its fair share of breaks and a feeling of enthusiasm, could have won the championship.

Discussion Questions

1. What are Jimmy Brown's allegations against Paul Brown?
2. Accepting Jimmy's charges at face value, what do you think of Paul's philosophy of coaching?
3. The author of this case is also its chief protagonist. How do you feel about his dual role?

CASE 2–4

Atlas Publishing Co.*

All improvements and changes at Atlas Publishing Company had, for years, been initiated and directed by Mr. Arthur Dalton, the business manager. Atlas published a variety of monthly trade and general business periodicals. It was Dalton's practice to make most of the decisions personally on problems that arose during the day's work. Some of his associates said that they often suggested changes and improvements in the various magazines but, they felt, Dalton rarely listened. One of the department heads said, "Arthur believes, because of his experience in directing the business, that he knows what should be done, what shouldn't, and when."

When Dalton wanted any change made, he simply requested that it be done. He often explained in some detail how it could be done expeditiously and effectively. As a rule, his action was taken with a minimum of discussion with the people immediately affected. Some executives felt the timing of changes was unpredictable.

For the past two years, the company's net profit had been below the industry's figures. During the 59 years of its existence, Atlas Publishing Company had consistently shown a profit, but the net profit percentage of both sales and investment had gradually decreased during the past decade. Several Atlas publications had doubled their advertising volumes in the last 10 years, but competitors had "stolen" large advertising accounts from others. Junior executives believed some of these publications had not kept up to date with developments in the interests, habits, and attitudes of their readers. In their judgment, competitors had recognized these changing trends and had revised their periodicals to meet readers' needs.

The record showed that Mr. Dalton was by no means opposed to change. He had personally initiated many modifications in editorial policy. Several staff people, however, told Arthur Dalton's son, Ben, that the reasons for these changes were not always clear to others in the business.

The consolidated balance sheet and P-and-L reports of Atlas Publishing were prepared monthly by the controller and distributed to the president, the business manager, and members of the board of directors. Arthur Dalton told his management group that he knew when the expenditure of money was justified and when it was not. Since he had a substantial personal investment in the business, he felt that "frills" as he called them, should be kept to a minimum. For example, advertisements occupied a large portion of the front covers of several Atlas publications, reducing the amount of space available for the title and contents of the publication. In the opinion of many in the trade, some of these ads were unsightly and gave a negative impression to readers. Most competitors had abandoned this practice long ago in favor of attractive four-color illustrations relevant to the contents of the issue. Their covers were designed to create a favorable "publication image," a term used frequently in the trade. It was Dalton's opinion that his competitors were wasting space and money on window dressing, with loss of potential advertising revenue. Discussion and documentation by other executives had not succeeded in convincing Dalton that Atlas should give the prevalent trade practice a try.

Mr. Dalton often said that he maintained an open-door policy. His executives could come to see him on problems whenever necessary. He didn't have to agree with them, he said, but they could secure his opinion on any subject at any time.

When some of the younger, college-trained executives met at luncheon, they often discussed their feelings about Dalton's arbitrary behavior. It seemed to them that substantive changes in the magazines might be accomplished more effectively through long-range planning. When decisions were made on a day-to-day basis, many areas, they felt, received no attention, while others were treated almost as pet projects.

Arthur Dalton had often said, "When we have the money, we'll spend it on things that are necessary. When we haven't the money, even important projects will just have to wait." One of the executives, who had studied modern magazine-business methods, thought that some improvements could be considered capital items, to be depreciated over a period of years rather than charged wholly against current income. He held the opinion that, in some instances, it might be wise for the company to borrow money for improvements instead of postponing them indefinitely merely because working capital was needed for day-to-day operations.

Dalton's son, Ben, started work with Atlas Publishing upon graduation from Yale. On the eighth anniversary of his employment with the organization, Ben was named business manager, and his father became president.

Arthur Dalton told Ben that, from then on, the operating responsibilities of the publishing company were his job. Arthur Dalton planned to concern himself primarily with broad matters of policy and community affairs.

Ben realized he had moved up swiftly through the organization. He was only superficially acquainted with many of the magazines' operating problems. He decided that he needed a firmer basis than his own experience on which to start to make major decisions. He told one of his friends that he intended to make use of the know-how of other, more seasoned executives.

Ben also recalled the opinions younger executives had expressed from time to time at luncheon meetings. He decided to encourage his staff to participate in decision making. He began to consult regularly with his associates and encouraged them in turn to consult with him. To give this idea more than lip service, he appointed a Management Committee, consisting of major heads of departments, including editorial, circulation, production, advertising, and sales promotion.

After several meetings, Ben proposed that the committee develop a long-range program for improving the business. He asked each committee member to submit projects which, in his judgment, should be initiated within the coming 12 months, plus other projects which he thought were desirable but could be deferred until the following year.

Within a month, the Management Committee agreed on a consolidated list of projects which they felt were important enough to be given top priority. The estimated cost of these improvements for the next fiscal year was in excess of $1,500,000. The program included:

1. Changing magazine formats to achieve a modern appearance.
2. Hiring additional writers and upgrading salary scales.
3. Maintaining a Washington sales office and editorial correspondent.
4. Using more pictures, which would require additional and more up-to-date photographic equipment.
5. Using four-color pictures, as well as selling four-color advertising.
6. Offering more merchandising services to back up advertising sales.
7. Conducting research on readership, magazine image, and buyer motivation.
8. Creating a new magazine to meet growing needs in a related industry.

Ben was shocked by the report. He was sure that no more than $900,000 could be appropriated for the coming 12-month period and that it would be difficult to persuade his father and the board of directors to go along with even this amount. He did not believe he could or should decide personally which items should be deferred for another year or two. All the items had been marked by the Management Committee as high priority. As he studied the list, Ben himself agreed that all were important.

Ben finally decided against launching a new magazine at this time. This alone would require an outlay of $750,000 the first year. If this project were implemented now, other urgent improvements would necessarily be tabled.

Ben explained to the committee, "Perhaps we have set our sights too high." He asked them to review the list again to determine which items should be given top priority so that a final decision could be made at the next meeting, one week later.

The committee readily accepted this assignment to prune the original proposals. They agreed on a special priority list of projects totaling $600,000. The group also concluded that all of the work could not be included in the allocations for the next 12 months. However, if $300,000 were authorized for each of the next two years, most of the recommended action could be initiated. This plan met with unanimous approval. The business manager decided he was ready to discuss it with his father.

The following day, Ben presented to his father the $600,000 program of improvements for the next two years. Arthur Dalton exploded, "We simply can't afford it, Ben. Why is this necessary now? Some of these things may need attention, but we just can't tackle them with our working capital situation in the shape it is. What else have you been dreaming up, Ben?"

Ben explained that he was not alone in feeling that these improvements were necessary. He told his father about the Management Committee he had set up to work with him in planning the needs of the business. Mr. Dalton sputtered, "How long has this Management Committee been going on? Why take the valuable time of all these people? How long did it take the group to arrive at these recommendations? If you had come to me in the first place, we could have worked this out in less than an hour and at a much lower cost than $600,000."

Arthur Dalton studied the complete list more carefully. He concluded that it might be reasonable to spend $300,000 for several items that he agreed were urgently needed. He blue-penciled the remaining proposals as he said, "Some of the other directors may be more liberal, but I personally can't justify spending more than $300,000 for improvements."

Ben went back to his office. He looked out the window and pondered the future effectiveness of his Management Committee and his own future with Atlas Publishing.

Discussion Questions

1. How is business at Atlas Publishing?
2. How do you account for this state of affairs?
3. What is Arthur Dalton's philosophy of managing people?
4. What is Ben Dalton's philosophy of managing people?
5. Arthur epitomized Theory X and Ben, Theory Y. Do you agree? Why, or why not?

6. How do you appraise Ben's actions?
7. What should Ben do now?

CASE 2-5

Mayhem House

Mayhall House is an independent men's dormitory on the campus of a large Midwestern university. The grade average of the dorm was one of the lowest of any house on campus. This was mainly because almost all of our 65 residents were majoring in either engineering or business—generally acknowledged as the most difficult schools in the university. And, of course, we had our share of goof-offs—five or six fellows who had ability but had never been able to apply themselves to their studies. We chalked them up as immature and hoped they would see the light before their academic probation ran out. But as long as they didn't disturb anyone, we felt we could get along with them.

As a matter of fact, there was very little horsing around in the house. I[1] had visited a number of the other dorms and was surprised to see college men, or rather boys, running up and down the halls yelling and chasing one another and playing silly pranks. As I said, I had always considered our house remarkably calm and dignified—until this year. Now, you wouldn't know it. Everyone's calling it Mayhem House.

The situation has become so out of hand that it's difficult to know how to describe it, but I'll try to start at the beginning.

When we started school in September, two important events (at least to me) occurred. I was elected president of Mayhall House, and a new counselor moved in. His name was John Morrison, 23, a graduate student in theology. John seemed to be very pleasant but made it clear in his first meeting with the residents of the house that he had heard our grade average was low and hoped we could raise it. He gave quite a pep talk and said if we would all pull together, we might put Mayhall near the top of the list.

I agreed with this, but I didn't see how there could be much improvement, in view of the fact that most of us were in the toughest schools.

The first evidence that John meant what he said occurred when he established his closed-door policy. The fellows had the custom of leaving the doors of their rooms open and occasionally talking across the corridor to one another. If John happened to be passing by, he would simply close the doors without saying a word. I suppose he thought the fellows would take the hint, but they only got sore about the situation and started doing more

---

[1]An undergraduate student with whose permission this case is published.

transcorridor communicating. It got to be quite a joke. John would start at one end of the corridor and close 10 sets of doors as he walked to the other end. Two minutes after John was gone, all the doors would be open, and the talking would start in again—only louder and more of it. On one occasion, a student yelled, "Go to hell, John!" after John had closed his door. John opened the door again and put the student on formal warning.

Next was the stereo episode. About the middle of November, John posted a notice:

> In order to provide proper study conditions, no stereos will be turned on after 7 P.M.; effective this date.

This seemed high-handed and unnecessary to me. Stereos had never been a problem in the house before. A few students like to study with some soft music in the background. But if anyone objected, they would turn their stereos off.

The fellows seemed to accept this as a challenge. The same night the notice was posted, about seven or eight men turned on their stereos to get them warmed up but not loud enough for anyone to hear.

Then one stereo blared full blast for a second and was quickly snapped off. John came bolting down the corridor to find the culprit. When he got near the room, another stereo blared for a moment at the opposite end of the hall. John wheeled and streaked back. At this moment, two other stereos opened up, and John started twirling around in circles! It was the most ridiculous thing you ever saw, and the fellows couldn't help bursting out laughing.

John was furious. "All right, *children!* If you can't take proper care of your *toys*, someone will have to take care of them for you!"

He then started moving from one room to the next, confiscating the stereos. It took him about three hours, but he picked up every stereo—minus speakers—in the house, put them in a storeroom, and locked the door. Maybe the seven or eight pranksters deserved this, but he took *all* the stereos, mine included!

Well, that was the sign for open warfare. What happened then was one continuous nightmare. The next night, somebody brought some firecrackers into the house, and the mayhem started! Someone tied a firecracker to a burning cigarette and laid it in front of John's door. A few minutes later, the cigarette burned down and ignited the firecracker, John threw open his door, and not a soul was to be seen. He was fit to be tied. That was a night to be remembered! All night long, about every 10 minutes, a firecracker went off somewhere—outside the dorm, in the corridor, in somebody's room, or outside John's door! John didn't even come out.

The next day it snowed, and that night it was snowballs. I won't go into the gory details, but the end result was the damage of property, including five broken windows!

This, of course, brought in the dean of men. I was surprised that he hadn't come in before. I guess John never mentioned our situation to him. The rest is history. John has been transferred to another house, and we are on social probation for the rest of the semester.

Discussion Questions

1. How do you size up John Morrison? The author of this case? The dean of men?
2. How should John Morrison have handled his assignment at Mayhall?

CASE 2–6

The Man and the Desk*

F.J. Roethlisberger and William T. Dickson

The personnel of one of the departments interviewed was moved from one building to another. In the new location, because of lack of space, it was found necessary to seat four people across the aisle from the remainder of the group. It happened that there were three women in the department who were to be transferred to other work. These women were given desks across the aisle so that their going would not necessitate a rearrangement of desks. The fourth person, a man, was given a desk there simply because there was no other place for him to sit. In choosing the fourth person, the supervisor was undoubtedly influenced by the fact that he was older than the rest of the group and was well acquainted with the three women. But, beyond that, nothing was implied by the fact that he was chosen.

Now see how this employee interpreted the change in his seating position. He felt that his supervisor evaluated him in the same way in which he evaluated the women. The women were being transferred to other types of work; consequently, he felt that he too would be transferred before long. Two of the women were being returned to jobs in the shop. He felt that he himself might be transferred to the shop; and there was nothing he dreaded more. Having dwelt on speculations like these for a while, the employee recalled with alarm that his name had been omitted from the current issue of the house telephone directory. This omission had been accidental. The house telephone director, however, constituted a sort of social register. Names of shop people below the rank of assistant foreman were not printed unless they were employed in some special capacity requiring contacts with other organizations. With the exception of typists and certain clerical groups, the names of all office people were listed. The fact that his name

Management and the Worker (Cambridge, Mass.: Harvard University Press, 1939), pp. 544–45. Reprinted by permission.

had been omitted from the directory now took on new significance for the employee. It tended to reinforce his growing conviction that he was about to be transferred to a shop position. He became so preoccupied over what might happen to him that for a time he could scarcely work.

Discussion Questions

1. There is no indication that the supervisor informed the man (let's call him Joe) of the reasons for seating him with the three women on the other side of the aisle. Why might he have failed to explain his motives for the seating arrangement?

2. Apparently, Joe failed to question his boss about the seating arrangement. Why?

3. What does this case have to do with this chapter?

4. How should the supervisor have handled the situation?

5. Assume the supervisor has observed the falloff in Joe's work. What should he do now?

Part Two

THE BEHAVIORAL BASIS
OF COMMUNICATION

3

Perception and Communication: 1. The Process of Perception

"This is nothing. When I was your age the snow was so deep it came up to my chin!"
Reprinted from Redbook *with the permission of the cartoonist, Gerry Marcus*

Dad is right, of course—as he sees it. And in this seemingly innocuous self-deception lies one of the most interesting and awesome aspects of human experience: We never really come into direct contact with reality. Everything we experience is a manufacture of our nervous systems.

Although there is never a perfect match between reality and one's perception of it, the range of disparity between reality and perception is considerable. When engineers are measuring, analyzing, testing, and the like, usually with the aid of precise gauges and instruments, their perceptions may be an extremely close approximation of reality. This is basically why bridges, tunnels, and skyscrapers not only get built but generally stay built.

But when engineers, or anyone else, are relating to and communicating with other human beings—when they are operating in a world of feelings, attitudes, motives, values, aspirations, ideals, and emotions—they are playing in a very different league, and the match between reality and perceptions may be far from exact.

THE PROCESS OF PERCEPTION

The role of perception in the practice of communication is critical, so let's examine the perceptual process more closely.

To reword the basic premise: When one deals with people—for example, when you are coping with your professors, classmates, parents, relatives, friends, neighbors, spouse, children, boss, subordinates, colleagues, customers, strangers, enemies, and so forth—one never deals directly with *reality.*

Reality

I don't pretend to get any closer to whatever it is that we call "reality" but I do presume that it exists. And it does so largely independent of us. It occurs, for the most part, outside our skins.

Stimuli

Now this reality gives off certain *stimuli*—audible vibrations, visible lightwaves, smellable smells, and so on. But most stimuli never reach us. At this instant, there may be loud noises occurring—a tree falls, two cars collide, a dynamite charge is detonated. But if these events occur beyond our ken then we are oblivious of them.

Why mention. Is it possible to be oblivious to stimuli. stimuli can't be w/o a response to the given event.

Sensation

But suppose we are in the right place, at the right time, and with appropriate sensory equipment, i.e., properly functioning auditory systems, in this case. The stimuli impact upon our respective nervous systems and we sense, hear, in this instance. But *sensation,* itself, is a thoroughly meaningless experience. William James described it as a "great, blooming, buzzing mass of confusion." The infant in the crib is bombarded by all sorts of stimuli but is unable to make much meaning out of the barrage of sounds, sights, odors, and so forth.

Stimulus to make active

Perception

It is only when we are able to and, indeed, do take the next step that the experience becomes meaningful: We perceive—we create meaning out of the sensory experiences we are having. Dunham defines *perception* as "the process by which you access information from the environment, organize, and obtain meaning from it."[1]

That describes what perception does, but how does it get that way? Why do we perceive as we do? What is it that determines how you will perceive a given event,—in addition to the event itself?

> What about your mood at the moment of perception? Elated? Depressed? Relaxed? Tense? Apathetic? Angry? Wistful? Fearful? Embarrassed? Hopeful?
>
> How about your physical state? Weary? Rested? Ill? Under the influence?
>
> Does it make a difference who is present during the event—your boss, your peers, your professor, your parents?
>
> What do you have at stake? What do you stand to gain or lose by this event?
>
> And your values? What have you come to consider as more or less important?

These are some of the potential influences on how one might perceive a given event. We can put virtually all of them under one broad heading—learning.[2]

Learning

This is *learning* in the broadest conceivable sense. I am talking not only about formal, classroom learning experiences—but about any experience, which can occur anywhere and at any time, that somehow teaches one how to perceive. Moreover, this teaching or conditioning or programming can occur at any level of consciousness—including nonconsciousness. A great deal of what we have learned, then, we have not been aware of learning.

I can demonstrate this if you will play a little word game with me. I'll make a statement and deliberately omit a word. Then you quickly jot down a word that pops into your head.

---

[1]Randall B. Dunham, *Organizational Behavior* (Homewood, Ill.: Richard D. Irwin, 1984), p. 241.

[2]One may argue that a physical state is not learned. But how we react to it certainly is. The hypochondriac may regard a cold as pneumonia, a headache as brain cancer, and so on.

Here's the scene: A young mother has just entered the living room of her home and has discovered her four-year-old son with a large, black, permanent ink felt pen drawing pictures on the wall. She says: "Johnny! You've been a _____ boy!" Supply a word for the blank.

According to cultural anthropologists, play this game with English-speaking people and the large percentage of the responses will be the words "bad" or "naughty." The issue is seen as one of morality and the usual admonition is "don't be bad" or, conversely, "be good." Greek-speaking and Italian-speaking people similarly respond. However, this perception is not universal. In lieu of "Johnny, be good," the French say: "Jean, sois sage"—be wise—or, by implication, don't be stupid or foolish or imprudent. Scandanavians speak differently. A Swede would typically say: "Jan, var snel" while a Norwegian says: "Jen, ble snil." They mean the same—be kind—don't be mean. In Germany, it is still different—at least in the so-called Prussian part of Germany—the usual expression is "Hans, sei artig"—get back in line, conform.

Let these people observe the youngster decorating the wall and you can confidently predict that they will all disapprove—but they will do so for differing reasons. And they have been taught these reasons—these perceptions—subtly but effectively by their respective cultures.

Travel has tremendous potential for self-learning. When you are suddenly deposited in another culture, you can become aware of some of the lessons you have unconsciously absorbed from your own. When you recognize what other cultures are incessantly teaching their respective residents, you can become more sensitive to what has been so subtly but effectively programmed into you.

And the learning need not stop when you return home. Your heightened awareness will help you identify the unique, unchallenged, and often arbitrary nature of your own teacher. According to G. K. Chesterton, "The whole object of travel is not to set foot on foreign land; it is at least to set foot on one's own country as a foreign land."

Response (behavior)

Thus, it is one's self-made meaning—this personalized perception that can be so extraordinarily affected by one's prior programming—that one most directly responds to or, more broadly, behaves about.

PERCEPTUAL MODEL

The perceptual model looks like this:

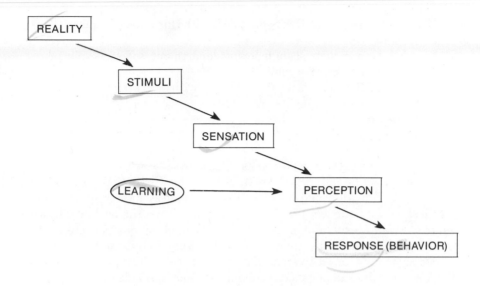

The above model is simple[3] but valid in that it depicts human response as only an *indirect* reaction to reality. That premise may be disquieting enough but there is more to come. Because there are multiple stages between reality and response, there are also multiple opportunities for us to differ from each other as we go from step to step.

Differing Responses

To illustrate the latter proposition, consider a social unit—say, an industrial organization. Just as relevantly we could have selected other units—such as your college, your sorority, or fraternity, or club, or even your family. But back to the industrial firm—just what is it? In addition to its physical and financial resources, the firm is basically a collection of individual human beings. Now let us consider how these individuals might differ among themselves as they move through the perceptual process.

Differing Stimuli.   Immediately, at the stimuli level, differences can occur. In fact, we decree them. We create elaborate organization charts with all sorts of boxes and layers and lines (solid and dotted) whereby we divide the reality. We say to various groups (and individuals):

---

[3]For a more complex model of the perceptual process, consult an earlier edition of this book: *Communication and Interpersonal Relations*, 4th ed. (Homewood, Ill.: Richard D. Irwin, Inc., 1979) pp. 56–65.

"You people are in R&D, so you'll deal with this hunk of reality (these stimuli)."

"You're in our industrial engineering department, so here's your province (another set of stimuli)."

"You're in PR, so here's what you'll cope with (still other stimuli)."

"You're responsible for cost accounting so we want you to focus on these stimuli."

And on and on and on.

And this is one of the key dilemmas of organizations—task specialization and isolation. To be fair, it isn't really feasible for General Motors to employ 100,000 individual artisans—each whom generates the requisite capital, designs a unique car, purchases or manufactures the parts for it, assembles them, tests and sells the cars, and arranges for customer financing. Parenthetically, there is some tendency to put the job back together again (or at least to enlarge it) as discussed in Chapter 2, but it is difficult to imagine an advanced economy without specialization. Unfortunately, specialization divides people, requires them to deal with particular stimuli, and the net results, too often, are sizable abysses between people who supposedly work in the same organization.

Without mentioning any names I can report that I have seen great gulfs between major functions in some companies. Here's a recent candid conversation:

Me   I don't mean to be offensive but I get the impression that you folks here in the shop producing this product don't really work in quite the same firm as those people out there in the field who are selling it and servicing it and otherwise dealing with the customer.

Them   Well, that's right. We don't really appreciate their embarrassment and tension when we fail to deliver on their promises. But at the same time, they don't really see what happens here—our pressures and frustrations and deadlines.

We already have discussed some of the ways organizations might bridge such chasms in Chapter 2, so let's leave the stimuli level for now and move on to the next phase.

Differing Sensations.   Let's be optimistic and say that the members of our mythical firm are "even", so far. That is, they have all been exposed to the same stimuli. Still they could sense them differently. There could be sensory variations among them. Suppose they all look at the cover of this book. If the group is typical, most of them will have normal color vision. Even so, will any two of them share an identical color experience? This is ultimately a subjective, inside-the-head experience and we simply do not know. Now add the more obvious sensory differences such as those that emanate from various forms of color "blindness" and from disease and injury. In my case, for example, I get different color experiences depending upon which eye I'm using. One eye was banged up in what Archie Bunker lovingly calls WW II. And from it I get—not different colors—but much greyer, dimmer hues than from my good eye.

There is a fun way to demonstrate differing sensory equipment. Sometimes I will give each member of a class or seminar a small bit of paper. Each person is to chew it up and register any taste sensations. Typically, about 20 percent of the group will start looking for water, coffee, a Coke,—anything to wash away a distinctly bitter taste. Others will be puzzled by this, because for them the paper will be sweet. Still others find the paper to be sour and a small percentage taste it as salty. And for about half the group, the paper is tasteless. So what is happening? The paper is impregnated with a chemical—phenylthiocarbamide (PTC)—which geneticists use to trace hereditary traits. Their contention: We may inherit varying sensory equipment, at least when it comes to tasting PTC.

There are indeed sensory variations among us but they probably aren't too pertinent for most of us unless, for example, one happens to be operating a restaurant, or an art gallery, or a perfumery.

Differing Perceptions.   In a sanguine mood, let us suppose that all of the members of our hypothetical organization have not only received the same stimuli—the same chunk of reality—but have similarly sensed them. However, they have one more hurdle and it is a formidable one—the very act of perceiving—of inputing meaning to experience. We have already considered some of the factors, under the comprehensive heading of learning, which can influence how one perceives. If the learning had differed, the perceiving is likely to differ as well.

For example, superiors and subordinates in organizations usually learn to perceive themselves and each other quite differently. A person looking downward in an organization may perceive very differently from a person below looking up. Rensis Likert of the Institute for Social Research (University of Michigan) reported that 85 percent of a sampling of foremen estimated that their employees felt very free to chat about important aspects concerning the job with the boss. However, only 51 percent of their men shared this view. Seventy-three percent of the foremen felt that they "always or almost always" solicited subordinates' thoughts regarding solution of job problems. Only 16 percent of their subordinates agreed with this appraisal. Ninety-five percent of the foremen said they understood their men's problems, but only 34 percent of the men felt they did.

Norman Maier, also of the University of Michigan, arrived at a similar conclusion that would be humorous, if it weren't so poignant. He studied 35 pairs of people from four large firms. A pair consisted of a manager, third echelon from the top, and an immediate subordinate. Each partner in each pair was questioned regarding the subordinate's job. On only one aspect was there substantial agreement—the content of the subordinate's duties. However, there was little agreement on the order of importance of these duties. There was only fair agreement on the job's requirements and almost complete disagreement on their priority ranking of these requirements. Finally, there was virtually no agreement on the problems and obstacles of the subordinate. These findings were discussed with all participants. Several months later, a questionnaire was sent to each participant, asking whether the superior and the respective subordinate had gotten together to discuss their differences. Only 22 pairs replied. Six of them agreed that they had gotten together; nine agreed that they had not; and seven pairs could not agree on whether they had or had not gotten together!

Unacknowledged Differences

So far we have two disturbing premises: 1) We never respond directly to reality and, consequently, 2) we can differ from each other at one or more of the steps (stimuli-sensation-perception) between reality and our response to it. This is why two or more people can respond differently to the same situation. Now, add a third element—lack of awareness and/or acceptance of these two propositions—and we have a truly explosive potential for interpersonal relations.

DEFENSIVENESS

So it is the failure to *acknowledge* these differences (differences between reality and one's perception of it . . . and differences of perceptions from person to person) that induces so much defensiveness within organizations and elsewhere. The prevailing, albeit largely unconscious, assumption is that "the world is as I see it." One who harbors this notion will find life continuously threatening, for there are many others who share this notion but not the **same world!** Such people find it perpetually necessary to protect their *worlds* and to deny or attack the other person's.

Admittedly, the premise that one deals only indirectly and often unreliably with reality can be upsetting. To those who crave a certain, definite, and dependable world (and that includes all of us in varying degrees), the admission that we respond only to what a thing appears to be rather than what it is necessarily lessens our ability to predict about the real world. Even those who intellectually accept the perception model and the roles that stimuli, sensation, learning, and so on play in determining responses may still have difficulty converting the concept into performance. A good test of the extent to which we have truly internalized such awareness occurs when we become emotionally involved with others.

For instance, suppose that you and I work in the same organization and that we observe Joe, one of our colleagues, taking home such company supplies as paper pads, paper clips, and pencils, not in large quantities, but more than he will need for official purposes. He will let the children have them, use them for his private affairs, and so on.

Now, let us say that you are the product of a rigorous, religious upbringing. You may regard Joe as dishonest. But suppose that I have none of your training and that the only part of my background that is particularly relevant is the three years I spent in the Army in World War II. There I discovered a code that was unwritten but very pervasive. It was, in effect, "You may rob the Army blind!—but you must not steal a nickel from another serviceman." I might regard Joe as honest and could readily consider his acquisitions as normal perquisites.

Let us examine the communication issue. (Permit me to disregard the moral issue without denying that there is one.) Consider the tremendous difficulty that you and I would have in discussing Joe if in our increasingly vehement statements, "Joe's dishonest!" "No, he's not!" we failed to realize that neither of us was talking about Joe. We were talking about *you* and *me*, and our respective inside-the-skin experiences. Our respective worlds were different from the outset, and there was no reason to expect them to be identical—and no rational reason to have to protect them. Why, then, did we defend them so ardently?

Let us begin with an assertion: Most reasonably mature people can tolerate fairly well differences in value judgments, opinions, attitudes, points of view—as long as they can recognize them as such. If I can realize that your *reality* is not the same as mine, then your statement about *your* reality is no threat to *mine*.

But no one can tolerate differences on matters of objectivity—matters that can be submitted to corroborative measurement and are capable of general agreement. To illustrate, suppose that you and I have a mutual superior who comes to us and says: "This may sound silly, but I'm serious. I want you two to estimate the length of that two-by-four over there (about 20 feet away) on the ground. You have to estimate because you can't use any kind of measuring device and you can't get any closer to it than you are now. Now, I want a good estimate and only one between you, so get to it!"

Now suppose that the piece of lumber is actually seven feet long but that neither of us knows this. So we start sizing up the situation, and you say, "Looks about 6-1/2 or 7 feet." And I say, "No, no—you're way short—that's a lot closer to 14 feet." Unless you have admirable constraint you would probably blurt out, "You're crazy!"

Now, why were you moved to feel that I was crazy?

Was it not partly because my statement was at least a slight threat to your sense of reality and therefore, your sanity? In other words, if I were indeed right—that is, if the board actually were 14 feet and everything were twice as big as you perceive it—would you not begin to have serious misgivings about your contact with reality? Thus, "You're crazy!" is your understandable if impulsive way of defending yourself against an attack on your sanity.

Actually, we are unlikely to have such a disparity (unless one or both of us were indeed losing touch with reality) because our perceptual lessons, when we initially learned to perceive the inch, the foot, and the yard, were likely to be very similar, regardless of where or when we learned them. And even if we were to disagree on such matters as distance, speed, and weight, we could resolve our differences by using standardized measuring devices.

But when we encounter Cézanne and Grandma Moses, Ernest Hemingway and Barbara Cartland, Mozart and John Lennon, Enrico Caruso and Michael Jackson, we are unlikely to have had identical learning experiences, and where are the standardized measuring devices? Will someone resolve a controversy with "Why, that Van Gogh is 87 percent beautiful"? Even professional critics are unable to provide universally acceptable and applicable criteria.

The point is that not only can we not tolerate differences in matters of objectivity (but what differences there may be are generally minor or resolvable by objective measurement), but we cannot accept differences on matters of subjectivity (value judgments, opinions, and so on) if we unconsciously treat them as matters of objectivity. Many important aspects of our lives, such as art, music, architecture, religion, politics, morals, fashions, food, and economic and political theory, 1) are not taught to us in standardized lessons and 2) are not, by and large, measurable by standardized scales or gauges. It is in such areas that we find it easiest to threaten one another. And when we are threatened we tend, if we do not run, to fight back—the threatener is now threatened, and the stage is set for an escalation of conflict. This progressive conflict, the "vicious pendulum," is discussed in Chapter 12.

Defensiveness appears to be so pervasive and potentially so destructive to organizational communication and interpersonal relationships that we shall examine it in the next chapter in terms of the communicator's *frame of reference* and then again in Chapter 5 in connection with increasing the validity of one's *self-image*.

SUMMARY

We have depicted human behavior as most immediately determined by the individual's programmed perception of experience. Behavior, then, is only indirectly a response to reality. One who cannot tolerate this basic uncertainty of life and who assumes that his world is the only real world may find that "world" in almost constant jeopardy. Closed and defensive, one may respond to the threats with irrational attack and/or flight.

We have conceded that many organizations are populated to some extent with more or less defensive (and thus often aggressive) people. Therefore, the challenge to anyone who aspires to be an effective leader or member of an organization (or more broadly, wishes to live an emotionally mature and deeply satisfying life) might be phrased as follows:

1.   Can one come to accept the fact that his/her and everyone else's "reality" is subjective, incomplete, unique, and to some extent, distorted? Can one, therefore, muster the courage to become open and nondefensive—to permit even contrary cues to reach one and to begin to revise, update, and make more valid one's concept of reality?

2.   Having clarified one's own perceptions, can one learn to assess accurately the worlds of others? Can the manager, for example, realize the simple but profound truth that his/her subordinates' worlds have him/her in it as a boss, whereas the manager's world does not?

In Chapter 4, we will examine how we can meet these challenges.

PERCEPTUAL ILLUSIONS

The following illusions illustrate the role of *learning* in distorting perception.

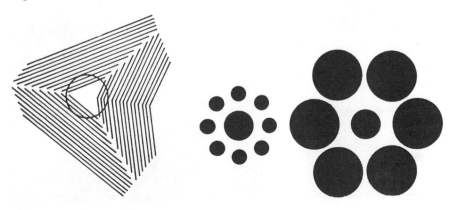

Is the circle round or lopsided?   Are the center circles the same size?

Is the vertical dimension of the hat equal to or greater than the horizontal?

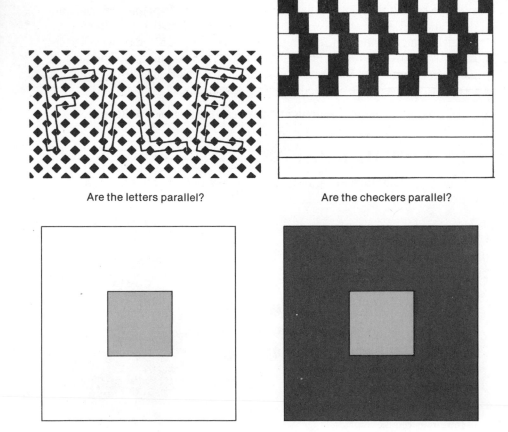

Are the letters parallel?   Are the checkers parallel?

Note how the backgrounds determine set in perceiving the center squares which are the same shade of gray.

In these illusions we perceive the *two-dimensional depictions* as *three-dimensional objects.* The impossible staircase is disturbing because we have been programmed to accept the shading of the walls as representing depth.

TRICHOTOMETRIC INDICATOR SUPPORT

0.0833 FT

10.16 CM

AMBIHELICAL HEXNUT (3.1416 REQUIRED)
MATERIAL: Ag + Au
(SILVER THREADS AMONG THE GALLED)

RECTABULAR EXCRUSION BRACKET (MIL—6—2980)

An article was recently published listing instructions for the fabrication of a Trichotometric Indicator. However, it seems that some difficulty is being experienced with the brackets which attach the indicator. As an aid toward fabricating the indicator brackets, the above illustration has been provided. It will be noted that in attaching the bracket to the indicator, a special ambihelical hexnut is used. The application of this nut is rather unique in that any attempt to remove it in the conventional manner only tightens it. Because of this design, the nut must be fully screwed on before it can be screwed off.

Sources: The illusions on pp. 67–68 and the three workmen on p. 69 are reprinted with permission from *Observation . . . Perception* published by E. I. du Pont de Nemours & Co., Wilmington, Delaware.

The "impossible staircase" is reprinted with permission from L. S. Penrose and R. Penrose, "Impossible Objects: A Special Type of Illusion." *British Journal of Psychology,* 49, 31 (1958).

The "Trichotometric Indicator Bracket" courtesy NAA "Operations & Service News." From *Approach,* May 1965.

REPERCEIVING

Here are some simple drawings. Chances are the moment you look at them, you will traverse the perceptual process in an instant: The *stimuli* in the form of light waves will bounce off the page into your eyes and you will *sense*—you will see—then, almost immediately, you will *perceive*—create a meaning for each of the drawings.

Then glance at the bottom of the page for labels for each of the drawings. If any label, not that it is any better or worse, happens to differ from your original perception note, how quickly you reorganize the pictorial data inside your own head and arrive at another perception. Keep in mind, though, that you are creating the new meaning, you are reperceiving. The stimuli and the sensing, after all, remain the same.

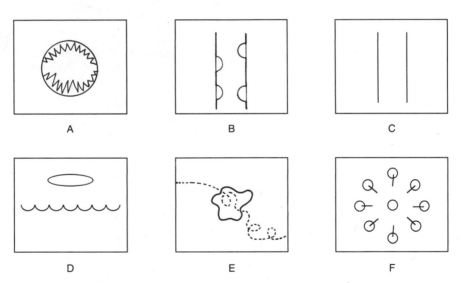

A — a vicious circle; B — large bear climbing a tree; C — small bear climbing a tree; D — a saint who thought he could walk on water; E — column of ants marching through a puddle of scotch; F — not too bright firing squad.

DISCUSSION QUESTIONS

1. What is the point of the cartoon on page 57?

2. "We never really come into direct contact with reality"? What is meant by that statement? Do you agree?

3. Perception has been described as leading to "a meaningful and coherent picture of the world." Does that suggest that meaning does not exist until perception has taken place?

4. Recalling the example of the misbehaving child being perceived by people from differing cultures, what special problems confront United Nations members, or the personnel of multinational organizations who live and work in a foreign culture, or others who communicate cross-culturally?

5. What does the *acknowledgment of differences* have to do with *defensiveness?*

6. At this writing, 25 wars are in process. Most of them, gratefully, are small, although that doesn't make their victims any less homeless, maimed, or dead. How does the perception model help explain this mutually ruinous behavior?

7. To communicate well with someone, you must agree with that person's perceptions. How do you respond to that assertion?

CASES

CASE 3–1

On a Certain Blindness in Human Beings*

William James

Some years ago, while journeying in the mountains in North Carolina, I passed by a large number of "coves," as they call them there, or heads of small valleys between the hills, which had been newly cleared and planted. The impression on my mind was one of unmitigated squalor. The settler had in every case cut down the more manageable trees, and left their charred stumps standing. The larger trees he had girdled and killed, in order that their foliage should not cast a shadow. He had then built a log cabin, plastering its chinks with clay, and had set up a tall zigzag rail fence around the scene of his havoc, to keep the pigs and cattle out. Finally, he had irregularly planted the intervals between the stumps and trees with Indian corn, which grew among the chips; and there he dwelt with his wife and babes—an axe, a gun, a few utensils, and some pigs and chickens feeding in the woods, being the sum total of his possessions.

The forest had been destroyed; and what had "improved" it out of existence was hideous, a sort of ulcer, without a single element of artificial grace to make up for the loss of Nature's beauty. Ugly, indeed, seemed the life of the squatter, scudding, as the sailors say, under bare poles, beginning again away back where our first ancestors started, and by hardly a single item the better off for all the achievements of the intervening generations.

Talk about going back to nature! I said to myself, oppressed by the dreariness, as I drove by. Talk of a country life for one's old age and for one's children! Never thus, with nothing but the bare ground and one's bare hands to fight the battle! Never, without the best spoils of culture woven in! The beauties and commodities gained by the centuries are sacred. They are our heritage and birthright. No modern person ought to be willing to live a day in such a state of rudimentariness and denudation.

Then I said to the mountaineer who was driving me, "What sort of people are they who have to make these new clearings?" "All of us," he replied. "Why, we ain't happy here, unless we are getting one of these coves under cultivation." I instantly felt that I had been losing the whole inward

---

*From *Essays in Faith and Morals,* by William James (New York: Longmans, Green, 1943). Reprinted by permission.

significance of the situation. Because to me the clearings spoke of naught but denudation, I thought that to those whose sturdy arms and obedient axes had made them they could tell no other story. But, when *they* looked on the hideous stumps, what they thought of was personal victory. The chips, the girdled trees, and the vile split rails spoke of honest sweat, persistent toil, and final reward. The cabin was a warrant of safety for self and wife and babes. In short, the clearing, which to me was a mere ugly picture on the retina, was to them a symbol redolent with moral memories and sang a very paean of duty, struggle, and success.

I had been as blind to the peculiar ideality of their conditions as they certainly would also have been to the ideality of mine, had they had a peep at my strange indoor academic ways of life at Cambridge.

Discussion Questions

1. How do you account for James' initial perception of the *improved coves?*

2. How was it possible for him to grasp the perceptions of the mountaineers?

3. Why might the Highlanders have found it difficult to appreciate or to feel comfortable in James' Cambridge surroundings?

4. How might the moral of this essay be applied elsewhere?

CASE 3-2

An Evening at the Leningrad Ballet*

Tom Burnam

Valerie didn't seem to want us to go to the ballet. She was the young, bright, and extemely attractive Intourist guide assigned to the three American couples in a party of some 40 foreign travelers at the Hotel Oktober in Leningrad. The others were mostly Finns, who had left Helsinki on the same train with us two days before.

The subject of the ballet came up at breakfast. Valerie frowned slightly. "I don't know that you would particularly enjoy the production," she said. This surprised us. Valerie, like any good guide, was not one to downgrade the attractions of her city, and Leningraders are even more proud of their ballet than they are of the magnificent baroque subway. Rivalry with Moscow has a good deal to do with it. Leningrad's subway is newer, its ballet older than Moscow's.

"What is the ballet tonight?" one of the wives asked.

"It is a modern one," Valerie said.

"Oh, that's fine," I said. "I can take ballet or leave it alone; but given a choice, I would prefer *Billy the Kid* to *Sleeping Beauty.*"

*From *The Reporter*, October 25, 1962, pp. 45–47. Reprinted with permission.

"But what's it *about?*" insisted Carl Root.

"It has to do with colored people," said Valerie. "You might find it rather dull." I am sure that she was not being sardonic; though she was not without humor, there was no malice in her. I am sure also, now, that she herself had not seen the production. At any rate, we all must have jumped to pretty much the same conclusion, although none of us said a word about it.

"I'd like to see it," said Carl. "Can you get us tickets?" "Well, yes, I suppose so," said Valerie. "How many would you like?" She was not enthusiastic.

"Six, I suppose," said Carl. We all nodded.

"Excuse me," said a woman seated at a nearby table. "I have overheard. May I, too, get a ticket?" This was Frau Schmidt, small, energetic, and German, who had elected to join our group on at least an informal basis, since like us she spoke neither Finnish nor Russian. She was a widow, traveling alone, and we learned that she was that rare phenomenon in Europe, a woman professor complete with Ph.D. Valerie turned to answer her, and I saw on our young guide's face, very briefly, that slight shadow Russians still show, as if not able to help themselves, in the presence of Germans.

"I believe I can get seven tickets," said Valerie, including Frau Schmidt indirectly.

That evening we hurried through dinner, knowing that taxicabs can be a problem in Leningrad, as they can also be in Manhattan.

[After a hectic taxi ride we were in front of the theater.] Like much of Leningrad, the theater is 18th-century baroque and does not spare the curlicues. It is a handsome place; the auditorium is spacious, acoustically superb, and quite comfortable. Our seats were good ones. There was a flimsy little program, in blue ink on white paper six by four inches. Though the language had begun to lose some of its strangeness, the letters to look less like a curious form of mirror writing, we could make nothing of the title. Anyway, I thought, it is about colored people.

It was, all right. Scarcely had the production got under way than we had seen (*a*) a Negro, evidently a student, realizing that his happy college days were over and he was back home when he was brutally pushed to the ground on a railroad-station platform; (*b*) a beefy caricature of a planter, in shorts and carrying a golf club, lording it over the field hands; (*c*) a fearful, tremulous, secret, and foredoomed affair between the blonde daughter of the brutal plantation owner and the young Negro home with his B.A.

You must remember that so far as we could know we were the only Americans in the very large audience; we were almost in the center of the sold-out house, in seats we had taken away from Russians, one might say, and we felt very conspicuous. All around us, we could notice members of the audience studying us discreetly, turning to whisper to their companions; above, in the balconies, we seemed invariably to catch someone's eye if we looked up. Certainly there was nothing overtly impolite about it, but I suppose it must have got to us a little.

Anyway, I am sure that as the first act progressed, we all stopped really *seeing* it; or we saw it through the glass of our Americanism, with a rising sense of tension. Of course the dancing and the music were superb; the Russians simply do not permit themselves anything less in their ballet. The audience, caught up in the production, frequently interrupted with bursts of applause. By the time the first-act curtain fell at last, to really thunderous handclapping and cheers, I was almost beginning to feel that the loud approval of the audience, the very smiles and bows of the prima ballerina, were somehow directed at us.

At intermission time in Russia a queer kind of promenade goes on, like the Grand March at a high school's Senior Ball. Several abreast, often with arms linked, those of the audience who do not stay in their seats move solemnly around and around the lobby, which is usually large enough and bare enough to permit this kind of entr'acte exercise. The six of us rose while Frau Schmidt stayed in her single seat a row or two away. But we did not feel like joining in the promenade, so we stood at its vortex, while the Russians wheeled around us like slow-motion hostiles circling a wagon train.

"Let's get out of here," said Carl's wife, Lois, "It's fairly obvious this thing is full of blatant anti-American propaganda. Do *you* feel comfortable in this audience?" She nodded at the solemn promenaders around us.

"You afraid they'll turn on us, or something?" Carl asked. "Russians don't act that way. At least, not unless they're told to."

"Oh, I know it," said Lois. I'm not really frightened, I guess. It's just—well, uncomfortable. Did you see that set? It was absurd. I suppose it was meant to represent the American South, but what in the world was that big billboard, or whatever it was, supposed to mean?"

"The one with the giraffe?" Carl said. "That's all they know about America. Like Coleridge putting tigers on the Susquehanna."

The set had a ramshackle tarpaper hut with Negro children gathered around it, the billboard, and a modern building in the background.

"What was that sign that said something like 'Afrikan'?" I asked.

"Must be Russian for 'Negro,' " said Lois. "That was supposed to show how the schools are segregated, I imagine."

At this point the warning bell sounded, and the promenaders broke up their march to return to their seats. Our group followed.

"You go ahead," I said to my wife. "I want to buy a souvenir program." But the elderly woman who had been selling the programs shook her head: she was sold out. As I turned away, a young Russian with the look of a student about him was at my elbow.

"Please," he said in English, "take my program."

"Permit me, then, at least to pay you what it cost," I said.

"No, no," said the Russian youth. "*Nyet.*" Russians speaking English sometimes seem to lapse into "*nyet*" when they really mean it.

"But this is not fair," I said; I knew the program had cost him 30 kopecks.

The youth smiled. "You are a guest," he said. "We do not see so many Americans in Leningrad, especially at this season." His smile seemed almost to be making amends for something. "Do take it; I insist."

I could not, without rudeness, push the issue further. I thanked him and hurried on in.

Frau Schmidt was in my seat, talking to the others. She rose at once and moved back to her own. Carl and Lois and my wife seemed somewhat subdued. I raised my eyebrows questioningly, and my wife said, "Do you know what Frau Schmidt just told us?"

"She can read Russian, just a little," Carl said.

There was a pause. "Well?" I asked.

"The damn thing has nothing at all to do with America," Carl said. "It's about Africa. Africa, and all the troubles in the Congo, and apartheid, and so on."

"I suppose we should have figured it out long ago," Lois said. "The giraffe and all. I just thought they didn't know any better than that about the South. Everything falls into place now."

And everything did, then and for the remaining two acts. The burden of secret defensiveness we had carried in the first act—indeed, since our morning talk with Valerie—fell away. Nobody was out after us; though we still could not follow the story line precisely, it was obvious that the pith-helmeted tyrants were the Belgians, the Boers, and (possibly) the British. Our reaction to the rest of the ballet, in retrospect, amuses me and saddens me a little, too. For we enjoyed what followed, I must say, enormously. Something like "Give 'em hell!" must have shown on our faces as we watched the violent plot unfold: this was just the kind of treatment apartheid deserved, by God.

When it was all over, to crashing applause and cheers, with flowers pelting onto the stage in true Russian fashion, everyone in the auditorium standing, the dancers returning again and again, we were all right up there on our feet with the rest of the audience, cheering and clapping. When at last we turned to thread our way out, we nodded and smiled to others in the crowd, who nodded and smiled back in the friendliest possible fashion.

Discussion Questions

1. Why did the American tourists believe they were the center of hostile attention in the theater?

2. Discuss this case in terms of the perception model.

3. How can we protect ourselves from distorting reality in this manner?

CASE 3-3

Is This Man Mad?*

Imagine that the individual described in the following brief case history came to you for treatment. How would you diagnose his ailment and what therapy would you recommend?

All through childhood, K. was extremely meditative, usually preferred to be alone. He often had mysterious dreams and fits, during which he sometimes fainted. In late puberty, K. experienced elaborate auditory and visual hallucinations, uttered incoherent words, and had recurrent spells of sudden coma. He was frequently found running wildly through the countryside or eating the bark of trees and was known to throw himself with abandon into fire and water. On many occasions he wounded himself with knives or other weapons. K. believed he could "talk to spirits" and "chase ghosts." He was certain of his power over all sorts of supernatural forces.

The Actual Diagnosis

Believe it or not, K. was not found insane, nor was he committed to the nearest institution for the mentally ill. Instead, in due course, he became one of the leading and most respected members of his community.

How this strange turn of events could come about may become more plausible to you if we supply an important bit of information that was purposely left out of the case history above.

K., we should have told you, was a member of a primitive tribe of fishermen and reindeer herders who inhabit the arctic wilderness of Eastern Siberia. In this far-off culture the same kind of behavior that we regard as symptomatic of mental illness is considered evidence of an individual's fitness for an important social position—that of medicine man or shaman.

The hallucinations, fits, manic episodes, and periods of almost complete withdrawal that marked his early years were considered signs that he had been chosen by some higher power for an exalted role. His behavioral eccentricities were, in fact, prerequisite to his becoming a shaman, just as balance, solidity, self-confidence and aggressiveness are prerequisite for the young person who hopes to be successful in American business.

Sociologists and anthropologists explain that shamanism serves two socially useful purposes in Siberian society. In the first place, it provides an approved outlet for the person of unstable temperament. It allows him to

---

*State of Mind, published by Ciba Pharmaceutical Products, Inc., Summit, N.J., 1, no. 1. (January 1957). Reprinted by permission.

let off steam through an emotionally satisfying dramatic performance in which he summons spirits and manipulates the supernatural. In the second place, shamanism provides entertainment for other tribesmen and welcome relief from the monotony of their bleak environment.

Discussion Questions
1. What is the main point of this case?
2. Does this case have broader implications for us?

CASE 3–4

Business Customs from Malaya to Murmansk*

H. K. Arning

The cultural differences between nations have developed on the basis of religious, political, and economical traditions. Some of them may appear unimportant to the foreigner—but ignorance about them can be dangerous to the success of business operations abroad. It is worthwhile, therefore, to look at some of the areas in which international marketers may experience difficulties that can be embarrassing or costly—and that in some cases can cost the company further business.

Personal Manners

Business outside North America follows rather conservative rules, and the personal appearance, including dressing habits, are more formal than in Canada or the United States. To arrive at a business appointment without coat and tie indicates lack of respect in any country, but particularly in Asia the question of respect is more important than in many other parts of the world. One can always take off his coat if everybody else does, but as a rule it is advisable to keep on the formal side. Physical attitudes can also be important: For example, it is considered rude in Southeast Asia, particularly in Thailand and Laos, to display the sole of the foot or to sit with the legs crossed. In the same area it may be considered offensive to place your hands on your hips; many Chinese will regard it as signifying that you are angry.

Physical contact should be avoided throughout the Middle and Far East. Handshaking is commonly accepted in most of the Asian countries, but particularly in India and Thailand the initiative in this respect should be left to the national hosts, who often regard any physical contact with strangers—even handshaking—as distasteful. In Moslem countries, avoid linking arms or putting your arm around the shoulders of your wife; it may

---

Management Review, October 1964. Reprinted by permission.

be unlawful, and would in most cases cause some embarrassment, since such physical contact is regarded as a private matter that should be confined to private quarters.

There is a sharp contrast between the attitude toward physical contact in large parts of the Middle and Far East on the one hand, and Latin America on the other. Again, it is undoubtedly helpful to let the host take the lead. Foreign visitors to Latin American countries have often attempted to avoid the repeated embracings, but such attempts are as a rule misunderstood by the local nationals, who interpret them as a sign of reserved attitude—which in turn breeds distrust. The same applies to a certain extent in respect of the distance between the faces. Asians will as a rule prefer a substantial distance compared to North American standards, while Latin Americans tend to be more comfortable with a distance of just a few inches. Thus, a businessman from North America may easily appear to be crowding in Asia, and give the impression of running away from his host in Latin America—neither of which is conducive to a relaxed business climate.

No Trespassing

The European concept of privacy may sometimes appear unreasonably exaggerated to North Americans. Europeans consider it distasteful to talk about their family in the office or the plant, and it is not usual to meet colleagues on a social basis after business hours; family, evenings, and weekends are private matters that most Europeans prefer to keep separate from business. People may live for 20 years in the same house without ever inviting their neighbors over for a cup of coffee or a drink; they are courteous and friendly to each other, but they preserve their privacy. Such attitudes may possibly explain why the American-style cocktail party has not gained very wide popularity in Europe.

First names are seldom used outside the Western hemisphere, possibly because of the differentiation of the word *you* which occurs in many languages. The polite form of *you* expresses respect, while the familiar form is more intimate and is employed only within the family or between very close friends. For business purposes the respectful form is used almost without exception, and to combine it with first names would be comparable to saying Mr. Bob or Mr. Jim in English. The resentment against use of first names is particularly evident among North Europeans, who often will feel embarrassed when business acquaintances infringe on what they consider strictly private.

Dinner at Eight

In most countries it is not customary to invite nonrelatives to dinner at home; business acquaintances are entertained in clubs or restaurants. To receive an invitation to a private home is a great honor, and it should be kept in mind that an Indian, for example, never extends such invitations for the purpose of furthering business aims; that would be a violation of sacred hospitality rules. The codes in this respect vary with geographical areas and, generally speaking, only Australasia and the Scandinavian countries come fairly close to North American practices. A detail worth remembering overseas, especially in Scandinavia and the Netherlands, is the custom that the visitor brings some flowers or a box of confectionery to the hostess when he is invited to dinner. The cost or size of the gift is not important; it is the courtesy that matters.

All over the world it is usually appreciated when foreigners follow local eating customs. Often, local food can be very worthwhile, and to experiment with chopsticks, for example, can be highly entertaining—particularly for the host. It is a practical exercise in applied goodwill, and if you give it an honest try and prove that you cannot manage, your host will not be offended if you ask for knife and fork. It may be useful to remember that Chinese dinners usually consist of eight courses, and that the guest is supposed to remain hungry throughout the seven first ones. The eighth course is usually fried rice or noodles, and at that stage it is customary for the guest to help himself to a modest quantity, thus indicating that he has had enough; otherwise the host will order still further dishes. In Chinese homes it is common practice that the guest will respectfully decline to be the first to help himself from any course, no matter how much the host insists. In Scandinavia it is proper etiquette to shake hands with the hostess thanking her for the meal when the dinner is over. It is much appreciated when foreign visitors are aware of this courtesy.

The Asian attitudes to consumption of alcohol range from partial prohibition in India to various degrees of liberal drinking in Chinese and Japanese company. Contrary to common belief, the local brews are not very potent, and although the principle of temperance is highly recommended, it may be wise to follow the hosts even into simulating a slight degree of intoxication. Complete abstinence from drinking is often regretted, but it is also respected.

In this context, it should be noted that in an Asian society where a rigid code of formality has been deeply ingrained from childhood, the relaxing effects of alcohol may perhaps be more appreciated than in Western societies; for business purposes there may be special reasons to keep that in mind.

In Mediterranean countries and in Latin America, it is rare indeed to see intoxicated people in public. The nationals of these countries are proud of their wines and they enjoy them frequently, but in modest quantities. Scandinavians are said to be heavy drinkers, but that reputation is hardly justified, at least not in business circles.

Pride and Status

In countries that recently have obtained political independence, the government and its policies are a matter of considerable pride. Most people will be delighted for an opportunity to explain political and also religious questions to foreigners, but it is advisable to avoid unfavorable comparisons with other systems or religions. There is little satisfaction and still less business to be derived from hurting the host's pride or from questioning his religious convictions.

Some North American businessmen tend to judge business acquaintances abroad on the basis of their status symbols. Many times such judgments are made subconsciously or automatically, and it may be useful to keep in mind that the yardsticks abroad are different. The top floor is not necessarily the executive suite; in Japanese department stores, the top floor is reserved for bargain counters. The location and size of the office or the carpeting of the floor may be subject to practical, legal, or climatic considerations. In fact, in a number of countries the nationals will flatly deny that they have any system of material status symbols at all. There may be many reasons for that, among which could be mentioned that differences in caste or class may make such symbols distasteful; sometimes the language or diction will express status, sometimes the name or title will indicate proud traditions or great wealth. Family, relatives, connections, and friendships are in most cases by far the most important status symbols and, actually, materialistic symbols would often be completely out of place.

Business Manners

Through the centuries, it has been a custom in most countries that the eldest son follow the line of his father in career fields such as civil service, the armed forces, and certain professions. The introduction of communism brought an abrupt end to such bourgeois traditions in Eastern Europe. Presently, however, there are indications that the former aristocracy in the communist countries quietly continue their old traditions: the medical families still raise doctors, and the offspring of the merchant clans join the state trading monopolies. This does not in any way imply a change in the communist doctrine, but it is noteworthy that some of the old and proud traditions are carried forward, notably the sense of honor and integrity that prevailed in business circles in Russia, Poland, Hungary, and Czechoslovakia before the communist upheaval. At that time, the East European countries were in many respects similar to the conservative Western Europe, and some of the old cultural attitudes are still recognizable. Due to the nature of the political system, however, the businessmen have not been exposed to the modifying influence of frequent contact with foreigners, and consequently, they often appear rigidly formal, which is evident in their dress, speech, and observance of traditional business rituals—as well as in their meticulous fulfillment of contract obligations.

Behind the Iron Curtain

Westerners sometimes find it difficult to appreciate that import and export agencies in the East European countries are part of the enormous communist civil service, and considerable time is required before a decision can be made on a Western business proposal. Plans and suggestions have to be approved by a seemingly endless number of committees, and in some cases it has happened that several years have elapsed before a final word is forthcoming.

Russian negotiators often have formal training in both bargaining and chess playing, which may explain why every move they make is so carefully planned. They never seem to get tired, and their negotiating skills may often test the Westerner's professional and human endurance. When agreement on one point apparently has been reached, they may start the next day by going through all the same motions again, pinning down every little detail. As purchasing agents they are shopping all over the world for the most advantageous deals, and they are fully aware that the centralization of the communist purchasing functions puts them in a favorable bargaining position: The orders are not numerous, but they are sizable.

Late deliveries are a nuisance in most countries, but they may be more than that for East Europeans: A delay of just a few days may upset their quota system, and thus deprive them of their bonus. Western suppliers who are unable to meet the rigid communist system of quotas and deadlines will be unlikely to receive new or additional orders.

Little White Lies

It may not be pleasant to learn that truth is a relative matter, which actually is the case in a number of countries both in the Far East and in Latin America. Form may be more important, and it is obvious that that may complicate regular business transactions. If the foreign visitor is pressing hard to obtain an agreement, he may find that his host will sign the deal just to be pleasant, and without any intention of keeping to the contract. Similarly, and particularly in the Far East, it may be considered rude to say straightforwardly that the Westerner's product or service is unsuited for the Oriental customer's purpose, and the sale may be kept hanging in the air simply because the buyer does not want to be unpleasant.

When a trader in the Middle East asks a price that is 20 times higher than what he actually expects to obtain, we have a situation where the buyer obviously will be pleased when he has managed to haggle the price down to size. Both seller and buyer have made a good deal, and both are satisfied. Pleasantries are considered important, and the time required is immaterial.

Both in Latin America and in the Orient it is customary to spend considerable time talking around the business on hand, sometimes about completely irrelevant matters. One of the reasons for this habit is a traditional distrust of foreigners, which they try to overcome by developing a first stage of friendship before they come down to business. It should be noted in this context that friendships in many parts of the world are considered obligations to a much greater extent than is customary in North America and that such obligations may imply substantial help over and beyond what may be agreed on in the contract. (This is one of the reasons why business with relatives and close family friends has priority over any other business in most parts of the world.)

From Here to Eternity

In Japan, it is not unusual to have long periods of silence in the middle of negotiations. Although it may be nerve-racking, it usually pays off handsomely if the Westerner can restrain himself enough to outwait the silence of his hosts. It may take 30 minutes, perhaps more, but in the meantime his silence is negotiating for him, usually better than he could do orally. Sometimes Oriental businessmen take advantage of the fact that time has become almost an obsession in Western countries. A Japanese once said that Westerners have a most convenient weakness: If they are kept waiting long enough they will agree to almost anything. Consequently, negotiators visiting Japan will often be asked how long they have planned to stay. Once that is known, they will be pleasantly entertained, while negotiations are kept inconclusive until a couple of hours before they are scheduled to leave, when the real business starts. Another aspect of time is the common lack of punctuality for business appointments in the East. The Westerner will learn that an hour or two is just an insignificant slice of eternity.

In fact, the question of punctuality is considered liberally in most parts of the world except in Northern Europe, where it is customary to arrive before the scheduled time. To be late for a business appointment in Northern Europe is often regarded as so disrespectful that it may hamper subsequent business relations.

Cash and Credit

The terms of payment in many countries follow rules that are different from what is commonplace in North America. In Japan, it is not unusual to regard 90-day or 6-month promissory notes as cash payment. Good customers of Chinese business houses have an almost unlimited credit. A Chinese does not want to ask a rich man for money, and consequently the renowned Chinese tailors in Hong Kong may wait for years before they issue a bill to Westerners living in the Crown Colony. On the other hand, a Chinese is highly reluctant to grant credit to strangers, even if he knows that the customer has an important position in a large business corporation and carries fully satisfactory credit credentials. There are old and deeply ingrained traditions which form the reasons for this apparently contradictory attitude.

For exporters it may be useful to remember that interest rates in Asia often range from 8 to 12 percent per year for bank loans—in Latin America, from 1 to 2 percent per month. A liberal extension of credit may therefore be a strong sales argument in both areas. In Europe, the cost of capital is comparable to North American levels.

In most of the Orient, entertainment bills should be checked before they are paid. It is not at all unusual to overcharge foreigners, and if one only starts to add up the items, the bill will frequently be taken away for correction. In a number of Asian countries, the price for smaller services should be agreed on in advance, as the negotiating right is forfeited when the service has been performed. It may be rather embarrassing, for instance, when taxi drivers in the Middle East at the end of the trip start arguing at the top of their voices and with arms raised over the head, claiming a fare that is many times higher than what you are used to or might have agreed on before you hired the taxi.

Bribes or Gifts?

Bribery is a relative matter, depending on the country and the circumstances. In Asia, the practice of giving gifts follows local rules which are too complicated to be discussed here. It should be noted, however, that in a number of countries civil servants are notoriously underpaid, and it is more or less understood that they perform certain services against a reasonable reward, provided receipts are not required. Such services may consist of such things as speeding up the handling of applications, arranging meetings with higher officials, cutting red tape, or extending the validity of visas and import licenses. It is highly advisable, however, to ask reliable advice, preferably from your consular service, before doing anything that might be construed as compromising the integrity of a civil servant abroad. What may be common practice in one country may be severely penalized in another.

Advertising Abroad

A substantial amount of literature about international advertising is available in North America, but as almost all of it is intended for West European or Latin American markets, it may be useful to mention a few points that should be taken into consideration when advertising is prepared for communist countries and for the Far East.

Marketing of Western consumer products in the Soviet Union may not be so remote any longer, and it may be worthwhile to note that since consumer articles have been in short supply for a long time in Eastern Europe, there has been no need to advertise whatever was available. However, advertising has been resorted to in order to dispose of slow-moving or substandard articles, and that has to a certain extent brought advertising into disrepute. The situation would make marketing difficult for Western businessmen who are accustomed to rely heavily on advertising, and it would appear to be advisable to put stress on quality and guarantees if an advertising campaign is to be launched.

Another difference between Western and communist advertising is in the use of female models: East Europeans regard as distasteful the use of models to attract attention for commercial purposes. An enterprising Russian garment manufacturer was recently criticized in *Pravda* because he used models in advertisements for bathing suits. The display of naked skin was, in Pravda's opinion, a sign of degeneracy.

Some elaborate advertising campaigns that have been launched in Asia have turned out to be complete failures because the marketers did not research and explore beyond the conventional data, particularly regarding the religions and superstitions of the countries concerned. Asia is composed of so many countries, religions, languages, and cultures that only wide diversification of the advertisements and a careful selection of media will render satisfactory returns.

There may even be a diversity of languages within the boundaries of the same country: the Commercial Manager of Air India, Mr. S. K. Kooka, has suggested that advertisers may use the Tamil language in South India, Hindi in North India, and Gujerati around Bombay. Also, it is almost impossible to translate directly from an alphabetic language into the characters and symbols of Chinese and Japanese, and still retain the same message.

The choice of illustrations is largely influenced by religious factors, for pictures of birds or animals or animal products may have specific religious connotations. Even pictures of people have to be selected to fit the cultural environment of the local market.

Lucky Colors

Colors have to be used with utmost care. To the Chinese, red is a lucky color; the Thai would prefer yellow for the same reason. The combination of purple and green is acceptable in several Asian countries, supposedly from the time when the leaders of the Shinto religion wore those colors. On the unfortunate side, the combination of black, white, and blue is suggestive of a funeral to the Chinese. Throughout the Far East there is a substantial amount of what Westerners usually call superstition connected with almost any color or combination of colors. For business purposes, superstition has to be respected; one cannot ignore it.

There are many pitfalls in international business that are caused by cultural differences, and to be trapped in one of them may have undesirable and sometimes costly consequences. Among foreign businessmen there is a small but increasing awareness of the existence of such differences, and over the long run the most extreme of them may be modified so that the gap is lessened. It is important, however, that visitors do not openly attempt to speed up any such development or to change the cultural habits of the local nationals. Such attempts will understandably be resented, and the repercussions on business will hardly make them worthwhile. Even when people are imitating knowingly, they like to feel that they have developed something themselves, and to tear down their illusions in that respect does not serve any useful purpose—at least not as far as the cultural differences that affect international business are concerned.

Discussion Questions

1. How does this case pertain to the topic of this chapter?

2. What aspects of differing cultures are likely to be particularly troublesome for the American transacting business overseas?

3. Many American firms have operations literally around the world. Should Americans living in a foreign country and supervising or reporting to, or otherwise dealing with, nationals in those firms anticipate any special problems relating to cultural differences?

4. "The American abroad—even when he is most successful—is likely to voice such sentiments as, 'After all, when you get to know them, they are just like the folks back home.' "—Edward T. Hall, *The Dance of Life* (New York: Doubleday, 1983), p. 96. Your reaction?

4

Perception and Communication: 2. The Frame of Reference and the Self-Image

We have examined the perceptual process in which we relate indirectly and imperfectly to reality. We now turn to the *frame of reference* concept: a singularly useful tool for helping one not only to understand and communicate with others, but also to understand and communicate with oneself.

YOUR SOLITARY-CONFINEMENT CELL

Visualize that each person lives continuously in an individual, solitary, confinement cell. This person never gets out and no one ever comes to visit. The somber point is that no one ever gets inside your head and has experiences exactly as you do. At this highly personalized level, we are all isolated from one another. The most we can do to represent what we are thinking or wishing or believing or dreading, and so on, by some form or other of communication.

The Stained-Glass Window

Let's get more optimistic. Inside your cell, there is a window—one aperture through which you have all of your contact with the rest of the world—including the people you deal with. The window is what behavioral scientists call your *frame of reference*.

Unfortunately, the window is not a pane of clear glass. If it were clear glass for everyone, I would anticipate a paradise on Earth in which we would all perceive reality realistically and deal with it appropriately. Thus there would be no wars, little if any crime or emotional disturbance, no hurt feelings or grudges or feuds or sabotage or strikes, no riots or mass burnings or pogroms, and certainly no prejudice.

Regrettably, what we have is much more like a stained-glass window filled with a variety of peculiarly tinted, distorting lenses. And the lenses are the products of the past. They represent the programmed—acquired—ways by which we distort our perceptions of reality. Having a stained-glass window is inevitable. After all, everyone has to be born in some particular place at some particular time and thus will be exposed to and programmed by some special people. The earliest ones were probably called Mom and Daddy. Later came the siblings and other relatives and neighbors and classmates and instructors and so forth. And each of these "teachers" has a unique stained-glass window.

The question, then, is not whether or not we have such windows but can we do anything about them? Are we destined to live out our lives peering through such spurious media? Emphatically, no! We can cope with these delusions essentially the same way we deal with any distortion. Stick a pencil into a glass of water. The pencil will appear to bend abruptly. But if we can understand the nature of the deception—refraction, in this case—we can learn to compensate for it. Thus, we can aim at where the pencil appears not to be and hit it.

To repeat: We can cope with distortion provided we can understand it and correct for it. This principle applies, albeit more profoundly, to the distortions in our respective frames of reference, as well.

The Self-Image.   But here we must face up to a formidable challenge. In the center of one's frame of reference is a huge lens. Actually, it's a complex of lenses. It is known as one's self-image.

The psychology of the self-image goes like this: When a human being is born (some would say before one is born) he or she begins to create an increasingly complicated, multifaceted, ambivalent, dynamic picture or concept or image of self. This image-manufacture is wholly unconscious at the onset, gradually becomes more conscious as the person matures, but probably never becomes a fully conscious activity.

Your self-image is your most precious possession. You never leave it behind. And you protect it accordingly. Some authorities contend that the most basic drive of humans is not self-preservation but self-image preservation.

Perhaps so, but let me raise another question. If your self-image is so all-fired important that you will protect it at virtually any cost, what, then, are you protecting it against? What is the most fundamental, grievous threat to your, or anyone's, self-image?

Failure? Ridicule? Rejection? These can be quite painful especially if you feel rather good about yourself. But there are people who are self-admitted losers, who don't and perhaps have never felt very positive about themselves. These are people for whom success, praise, and acceptance can be uncomfortable—even frightening.

The most severe menace to anyone's self-image is *change*—provided three conditions exist. To be truly threatening the change must be: (1) large enough and (2) quick enough and (3) uncontrolled enough (uncontrolled, that is, by the possesor of the self-image).

So any big, sudden, uncontrolled change of self-image can be unbearably terrifying, regardless of the direction of the change. Perhaps the last part of that assertion seems dubious. Can we actually be appalled by excessively positive change?

Assume that you are a young man or woman, say 22 years old, who graduated from college six months ago. At that time you took a position with a very large, prestigious organization, say IBM. And suppose that one evening you receive a phone call.

Operator I have a long distance call from Armonk, New York, for (your name).

You This is he (or she). (To yourself: Armonk? That's IBM's head shed!)

Operator Go ahead, sir.

Voice Hello, is this (your name)?

You Yes, who is this?

Voice This is John Opel with the company in Armonk.

You (Gulp! Opel is the chairman of the board! Moreover, this voice squares with the one I recall from a videotape I saw during induction training!) Why . . . er . . . uh . . . yes, sir?

J.A. I know this is rather sudden, but the President (another big name!) has just asked me to come to Washington to take over one of the Cabinet positions, and I can't refuse him. The point is, we need a replacement for me here, and the board has decided you're our man [or woman]!

You *(After five seconds of silence)* I'm your wh-a-a-a-t!!?!?!?!?!

Assuming that you're convinced that this is not a case of mistaken identity or that Mr. O has not taken leave of his senses, how much sleep will you get tonight? May I suggest why that call could be highly disturbing for you? If (and try to accept this *if*, for the moment) Mr. Opel is *right*—that is, if, despite your youth and inexperience, you are that brilliant and competent, *so* good that you can go to Armonk and direct that huge, complex, multinational corporation—do you know what that means to you? It means that your current self-image is quite unrealistic, that your contact with reality is suspect; in short, your sanity is in question.

I grant that the phone call illustration is an absurd one—but it is absurd only in degree—not in kind. Organizations have frequent examples of people passing up promotions, balking at enlarged responsibilities, and in general resisting positive feedback—because those cues, albeit favorable, constituted too great a disparity from those people's current self-images. In sum, one's self-image is threatened by big, sudden, uncontrolled change—whether the change is negative or positive. The basic threat comes across as: "You are *not* who you think you are—you do not have contact with reality!"

But how big, how sudden, and how uncontrolled must the change be in order to constitute a threat? The answer depends upon one's comfort zone.

The Comfort Zone.   Consider the operation of a thermostat. It serenely maintains its status quo—that is, it continues to break or complete an electric circuit—until its comfort zone is violated. At this point the instrument "protects" itself by reversing itself—that is, it either closes or opens the circuit—which returns the temperature of the environment to the instrument's comfort zone.

There is a kind of thermostat in each of us that throws up defenses whenever the comfort zone of our self-image is exceeded by feedback. This can be illustrated most concretely when the feedback is quantitative—as in a golf score.

Over the years my scores have fallen quite consistently in the 90 neighborhood. Visualizing myself as a 90 (plus or minus 5 strokes) shooter, I could readily accept any score from 85. to 95. 96, 97, 98? Also acceptable, but hardly elating. 99, 100, 101? I'm beginning to feel uncomfortable—am I slipping? And a 130? Unbelievable! That is the precise word for my reaction. That feedback is so discrepant from my self-image that, while I must concede the score, I would be compelled to defend against it—to deny its validity as a reflection of my ability. How? Like most duffers, I have an inexhaustible repertoire of rationalizations—bad weather (gusts up to seven mph at times), poor groundskeeping (the fairway hadn't been mowed for a good eight hours), headache (how can they expect an invalid to play this game?), evil companions, etc., etc.

My comfort zone has a limit in the positive direction, too. Suppose that, suddenly, one day I shoot a 70! Thrilling, worth six years of locker room stories, but again, incredible! And, psychologically, I would have to defend my self-image against this score as well—it just isn't me! My alibis are less developed here because I have had fewer occasions to use them, but "gigantic fluke," "my horoscope was just right," and "an enormous celestial error" come to mind.

There are no specific scores that abruptly turn me off (as happens with a thermostat). But there are regions of scores (the vicinities of 98 and 82, respectively), above or below which I cannot play without increasing uneasiness.

My self-image, then, is surrounded by a comfort zone—the margin of disparity between my self-image and feedback concerning it that I can currently tolerate without feeling compelled to be defensive. This is not to suggest that comfort zones or, for that matter, self-images do not change.

For example, if I really paid serious attention to my golf game (played every day, took lessons from a pro, and so forth), I am confident that I could signficantly lower my scores. And after gradually (perhaps over a period of six months or so) moving into the lower 80s and upper 70s and playing there consistently, suppose that I were to card a 70. Probably, I could now accept it—it might stretch my comfort zone, but it would not rupture it as it would have done before. The entire comfort zone would have shifted— but note that the change was in small, gradual, and above all, self-controlled increments—I engineered my own change.

Forming Images of Others

How about the images we form of others? How much time and energy do you spend creating, modifying, defending, discarding images of other people?—especially of the key people in your life, such as parents, siblings, teachers, fiancé, friends, spouse, offspring, bosses, subordinates, colleagues, and customers? The question is difficult to answer in specific terms. So much of our image-making is a largely unconscious affair. Moreover, it is often a substantially nonrational process. But in addition to how we fashion the images and how much time and energy we spend doing it, the question arises: *Why?* What motives do we have for forming accurate images of others? Is it to:

Determine common ground with them?
Protect our own self-image?
Communicate with them?
Determine whether or not we wish to associate with them?
Use their performance to develop standards?
Win them over to our point of view?
Determine how much to trust them?
Understand them?
Determine how they can help and/or hurt us?
Help them grow?
Be liked, accepted, approved by them?
Please them? satisfy their expectations of us?
Cooperate with them?
Determine how to compete successfully with them?
Sell to them?
Assign them to roles, duties, responsibilities?
Determine whether we should vote for them?
Know how to interact with them?
Use or manipulate them?

Encourage them?
Impress them favorably?
Evaluate them?
Satisfy our curiosity about them?
Protect ourselves from them?
Learn from them? emulate them?
Win their support?
Deceive them?
Assess their strengths and weaknesses?
Love them?
Be more comfortable with them?
Hone our image-making skills?
Know how to play "games" with them?
Protect the image that we desire them to have of us?
Categorize them in order to expedite relationships with them?

All of these motives (and a good many others) may be relevant at various times, depending upon who the other person is and his/her relationship to us. In the interest of manageability, this lengthy list can be compressed into perhaps three basic motives. You form an image of the other person because you need or want to:

1. *Predict his/her behavior*—or his/her reaction to your behavior. This, in turn, should enhance your ability to—
2. *Cope or deal with him/her* in whatever manner is required by the situation. Accordingly, you should be better able to—
3. *Satisfy your needs* in respect to the relationship. Needs are defined broadly here as including the kinds of needs you gratify when you do very selfless and altruistic things—as well as needs which are more self-centered.

To check the adequacy of that trimotive concept, consider this question: Do you recall a time when someone extremely important to you abruptly began to behave in ways that quite contradicted your image of that person? If so, do you recall how you felt at that time—what your emotions were? Fear? Disillusionment? Embarrassment? Bewilderment? Sense of betrayal? Rage? Depression? Guilt? Anxiety? Shock?

These are negative sentiments. Does it make a difference if that abrupt shift is in a positive direction—that is, suddenly the individual is behaving in the ways that are far more favorable than your image led you to expect?

Suppose that you and I have a boss who is an utter tyrant, an absolute despot. However, one day, for no apparent reason, she walks into the office, wreathed in smiles, laughing and joking. You and I and our colleagues would leap to our feet, chirping: "Goody! The boss has finally turned over a new leaf!" Right? **WRONG!** Rampant suspicion reigns: "What's she up to?" or, more contemporaneously, "What's she *on?*"

We would dearly love to believe that a permanent change is in the offing, but we are not about to accept it on such limited data. The point is: We can work for an SOB—as long as he or she is a *consistent* SOB. That doesn't make it pleasant, but it may make it possible. As long as we can predict the behavior, we have a reasonable chance of coping in such a way as to satisfy our needs concerning the SOB.

Indeed, the individual who is most capable of contributing to your bleeding ulcer, your hypertension, or your emotional breakdown is a key person (such as your parent or boss or spouse) who turns it on and off *unpredictably*. If you are dependent upon this person for the satisfaction of essential needs in your life, you have a real problem. For to satisfy those needs, you must successfully cope with the individual; but to cope you must be able to predict that person's behavior and that is where the sequence breaks down. The prime basis upon which you predict the other person is your image of him or her, and it just isn't holding up.

The Self-Image Threatened

If a sudden, dramatic change of behavior on the part of another can destroy your image, cost you your predictability, and thus your capability regarding that person, and lead to painful, frightening, and destructive consequences,. consider what could happen if you were suddenly to have your own self-image challenged.

You stand the risk of losing the ability to predict, control, and *know* yourself. It is difficult to imagine a greater internal upheaval than suddenly not to know oneself—to lose contact with oneself.

Anyone who has suffered through a deeply traumatic experience— whether related to a parent, a spouse, a child, school, religion, vocation, narcotics, alcoholism, job loss, illness, injury, lawsuit, and so forth—will probably find in retrospect that his or her self-image was being severely threatened.

The "Great Chemist."   My own experience is a case in point. As a high school freshman, I hit upon chemical research for a career. I was encouraged by an older boy I admired who also aspired to chemistry. He had built a laboratory in his basement, so of course I had to have one, too. I remember collecting hundreds of jars and bottles and other treasures that might somehow be useful in my lab. I can also recall spending hour after hour thoroughly enjoying mixing potions of every description, and some beyond description. (I recall without quite so much relish the time I brewed some chlorine and nearly gassed myself unconscious!)

I devoured the chemistry course in my junior year. I must admit to having felt rather smug during this period, for I had a ready response to the recurrent question from grown-ups: What are you going to be? Most of my friends had either a hazy answer or none at all. My self-image in this regard was forming and solidifying.

I graduated from high school during World War II and immediately entered the service. Somehow the Army gave little consideration to young men who were long on aspiration but short on experience, and consequently I had three years of singularly nonchemical activities. In fact, most of my Army career was devoted to protecting our nation from invasion—invasion from Juarez, Mexico. (Let it be recorded that not one Japanese Zero reached El Paso, Texas!)

But none of these nonadventures dissuaded me. Finally, the war ended and I was discharged. I immediately enrolled in a chemical technology program at a university reputed in this field.

Suddenly, reality began to catch up with my self-image. I had not realized that a chemist was also expected to be a pretty fair mathematician. I had done well enough in high school math courses, but the Army years were nonmathematical as well as nonchemical. At any rate, I foolishly disregarded the math refresher course (my self-image said I didn't need a crutch) and charged headlong into college algebra, where I was in competition with students fresh from high school math. While I was rusty, it would be unfair to say that I didn't understand the math; I did get it, but usually about a week *after* the exams—poor timing! The net result was the first *D* I had ever received in my life. What was the consequence, did I trade in my self-image for a new model? Hardly; my comfort zone had been violated. Rather than yield, I fought tenaciously and found a ready explanation for my plight: Aside from the Army's rusting me, the instructor had it in for me. Among other evidences, he had a Scottish name, and I was convinced that he was anti-Irish!

I was practicing what some writers call perceptual defense. Confronted with feedback that challenged my self-image, I managed to distort the incoming data. Result: The feedback, which I misperceived in self-serving ways, was no longer a contradition to my self-image. As a communication authority, David K. Berlo paraphrased the Bible: "Seek and ye shall find— whether it is there or not!"

The next quarter? I received a *C* in math. The instructor had an Irish name, but he didn't like me either! (I suspected that he was from Northern Ireland!) In the middle of the third quarter and another math *D*, my self-image had withstood all the onslaught from harsh reality that it could. And for two to three weeks (at the time it seemed like six months) I was in a state of unrelenting depression. I became very nervous and had difficulty eating, sleeping, and studying, which only intensified my problem. A large section of my self-image had been shot away. The most appalling aspect of the experience was that I realized that I didn't know myself.

I began to lose the ability to predict my behavior. Increasingly, I found myself exclaiming: "Now, why did I do *that*? That's not me!" Then came the hallucinations. I recall that on one or two occasions, I looked into a mirror and glimpsed someone else's face where mine was supposed to be! I was truly frightened, and for the first time sought counsel.

Ultimately, I took a battery of placement and aptitude tests, changed my major, and transferred to another university (closer to comforting home). Gradually, and often painfully, I constructed a revised self-image in which I could place some of that former faith and confidence.

The Great Chemist Debacle, then, is just one example of what can happen when a person undergoes a sudden (a few months versus seven years is sudden), dramatic, and uncontolled change of self-image. For seven years I had been creating, nurturing, and cherishing a dream—a self-image that pictured me in my immaculate lab coat, inventing world-saving concoctions in my shimmering, crystalline laboratory, the walls of which were adorned with Nobel Prize plaques! Quadratic equations, cosines, and differential calculus were never in that picture!

Far from being a peripheral, avocational aspect, the Great Chemist was the core of my self-image. And when it was finally destroyed, I had nothing to replace it.

Resistance to Image Change.   Anyone who has undergone a traumatic experience will understand why the individual generally resists image change—particularly sudden, dramatic, uncontrolled change. And herein lies one of the greatest obstacles to the full development of an effective communicator and, for that matter, an effective person. Psychiatrist Karen Horney contends that the neurotic process is a special form of human development that is the antithesis of healthy growth. Optimally, one's energies are directed toward realizing one's own potentialities. But under inner stress one becomes estranged from the real self and protects oneself by creating and protecting a false, idealized self, based on pride, but threatened by doubts, self-contempt, and self-hate.

Take the case of a high school friend. After graduation he, too, went into the service, but he was more fortunate (in a sense), for the Army put him through three years of an engineering curriculum. Then the war was over, and he was discharged. But he decided that he did not care for engineering and could not bring himself to take a final year of course work to earn an engineering degree. Any yet he could not bear the thought of starting all over again in another field. The net result was that, for all practical purposes, he did nothing. He took a clerical job in a nearby insurance firm and has been there ever since. Through the years, his perhaps largely unconscious philosophy of life has evidently been: "I can't stand another failure [he probably regarded not completing the engineering degree as a failure], and one sure way not to lose a race is not to enter it." In sum, here is a person who has apparently protected his invalid self-image at the cost of a stunted life.

The handicap of inaccurate self-knowledge and the unwillingness to reconstruct a more realistic self-image seem to be very widespread. In 30 years of organizational research and consulting, I have known scores, if not hundreds, of men (and some women), particularly in the middle eche-lons of their organizations, who seemed to have all the requisites for continued success—intelligence, education, experience, drive, ability, am-bition. But they had one vital failing—they did not know themselves. The image they held of themselves was pitifully out of phase with that which they were projecting to others. They seemed chronically annoyed and/or bewildered by the reactions of others to them. What was happening? Because of their unrealistic self-images they found it too threatening to entertain contrary cues from other people. By fending off the reactions of others variously as "those malicious/crazy/misinformed/ornery/perverse/stupid people," they had been successful in perpetuating and even rein-forcing their respective self-myths. Thus, they had ineffectualized them-selves; squandered their nervous energies. The masterful Robert Burns captured the poignancy of self-deception two centuries ago:

> *Oh wad some power the giftie gie us*
> *To see oursels as ithers see us!*
> *It wad frae monie a blunder free us,*
> *An' foolish notion.*

The ERSI

Why does this detailed consideration of the self-image appear in a text on communication and interpersonal relations? My principal assumption about most of the readers of this book is that they are currently working—or within a few years will be working—in organizations. I further assume that their positions will be people-related, perhaps even people-centered. Accordingly, they will probably deal with people from various socioeco-nomic strata, with differing ethnic, religious, technological, and educational backgrounds, who occupy a variety of positions within and outside of the organization—bosses and colleagues, perhaps subordinates, customers, sales personnel, union representatives, governmental regulatory officials, and so on.

To successfully discharge the responsibilities of a challenging, people-oriented position requires the possession of a more-than-ordinarily-realistic self-image—an exceptionally realistic self-image (ERSI, for short).

The various blessings associated with an ERSI and various approaches by which one can attain and maintain an ERSI are the province of the next chapter.

SUMMARY

The frame of reference concept was likened to a stained-glass window in a solitary confinement cell. Experience is severely limited; the window's size and orientation are finite; thus comparatively few stimuli can enter the cell. Moreover, experience is often distorted; the lenses in the window represent prior programmings—biases, values, preconceptions, and so on.

One can correct for distortion provided that one understands its nature. But the window's most significant lens, the individual's self-image presents a special problem: Self-perpetuation.

The peculiarity of the self-image is that it is "capable of being threatened" by *change*—sudden, dramatic, uncontrolled change (even if the change is favorable). The self-image is surrounded by a comfort zone that determines which inputs can be accepted or at least tolerated and which constitute excessive change. The latter inputs (even though they may be valid) are generally resisted and warded off by the individual's defense mechanisms.

The irony is that an unrealistic self-image can not only perpetuate itself but, deprived of corrective intelligence, can grow increasingly invalid.

We also form images of others primarily to predict them in order to cope more effectively with them so as to best satisfy our own needs with respect to them. These three basic motives apply to one's self-image as well. One needs to predict his/her own behavior, and so on. Traumatic image change, as exemplified by the Great Chemist Debacle, generally thwarts these motives and leads to stressful disorientation.

This chapter dwelt on the frame of reference and self-image constructs in order to provide a conceptual foundation by which a person preparing for or currently holding a people-oriented position could purposely strive for a progressively more realistic self-image.

DISCUSSION QUESTIONS

1. The stained-glass window is a figurative analogy designed to clarify an aspect of human behavior. In what respect do you feel that it is a valid (or invalid) depiction?

2. The most fundamental threat to one's self-image is *change*. Do you agree? Disagree? Why?

3. Change of self-image is most harrowing if the change is big and fast and uncontrolled. Agree? Disagree? Why? Are there other important characteristics of change? Are they equally critical?

4. What was the point of the illustration involving IBM's John Opel's phone call?

5. A common complaint of the weekend golfer: "Why is it that whenever I burn up the front nine, I blow up in the home stretch?" How could this behavior be explained in terms of the self-image and comfort zone concepts?

6. It was asserted that three primary motives for forming an image of others are to *predict* them in order to *cope* with them in order to *satisfy one's needs* with respect to them. Do you agree? Are there basic motives in addition to or in lieu of these three motives?

7. According to Horney, under inner stress, one becomes estraged from one's real self and spends oneself creating and protecting a false, idealized self, based on pride, but threatened by doubts, self-contempt, and self-hate. Does that strike you as a valid assertion? What might it have to do with communicating and relating to others?

CASES

CASE 4–1

Frank Corbett's Problem*

At the age of 41, Frank Corbett was the managing partner of Corbett & Wilde, a rapidly growing advertising agency serving a large metropolitan area in the eastern United States. Corbett had been instrumental in the establishment of the firm, having merged his firm with that of Gordon Wilde, 36. There were 37 persons in the employ of the partners.

Frank Corbett, clearly the dominant partner in the firm, was a dynamic man, full of ideas and drive. Wilde, an artist, was a quiet person by temperament, content to let Frank Corbett manage the firm. "Frank is a dynamo," said Wilde. "He likes that sort of thing, and I prefer to work on the creative end." Corbett felt that Gordon Wilde was a topnotch commercial artist.

Of the account executives, Carlton Phelps was regarded by Frank Corbett as the most promising partnership material. In fact, Corbett felt that he would either have to make Carl Phelps a partner soon or run the risk of losing him.

Phelps, 35, came to Corbett & Wilde from a large nationwide advertising firm where he had been an account executive. Claiming that he was given no room for independence of action, he had resigned and applied to Frank Corbett for a position. Corbett hired him on the spot. Within three years, Phelps was made a senior account executive responsible for a considerable number of clients.

Some of the accounts which Phelps supervised were those he had brought in himself. And there seemed to be no doubt that he was highly popular with his clients. Corbett was continually hearing of the wonderful service clients were getting from Phelps.

Yet, Frank Corbett had come to believe that Carl Phelps was a very difficult problem indeed. So when he was approached by Alvin Mahoney, a university case writer, he was eager to unburden himself. These are his comments:

> I hired Carl because I thought he would be just the kind of man I wanted in this organization. He has a lot of drive and originality. Furthermore, I know I can trust him and depend on his loyalty. The way I operate, I need a loyal organization who will put my interests first all the time.

---

*All names are disguised.

He is positively sensational in the way he keeps the clients happy. And he even brings in new clients—quite a number of them.

So what's the problem? I'll tell you. Carl has no feeling for the organization. He is the most unpopular man in the firm. My people feel that he pushes them around.

For example, he puts pressure on Harry Klein, the office manager, to get the people he wants, and, of course, those he wants are the topnotchers that everyone else wants, too. If Carl gets a person assigned to him that he doesn't want, he usually just sends him back to Harry. This is hard on the person, and so Harry feels that he can't assign any but our best people to Carl's accounts.

The other account executives claim that Carl doesn't train on the job. Instead he grabs off the people that they have trained. They complain that Carl doesn't pull his own weight.

Whan a client asks Carl for a special favor, you should see him operate. He is a past master at getting other people to give service to *his* clients. For example, he may get a request from a client to speed up a magazine layout—say, from next week to tomorrow night. He goes straight to the artists, photographers, copywriters, and so on, until he gets *his* work done. Of course, other people's work gets put aside.

It doesn't make any difference to Carl that he has kicked the schedule to pieces and gotten everybody mad at him. Of course, the client is enthusiastic and recommends Carl and the firm to new clients.

Everyone says they like Carl personally, but it is impossible to work with him. I suppose there is some jealousy of him, too.

I have talked with Carl many times about this. I've given him hell, pleaded with him, tried patiently to point out the results of the way he operates. For maybe a week after one of those sessions, he will be better, and I begin to think that things will work out, and then, bang, he's off again and has people mad at him.

I suppose that in many respects Carl is like me. I can appreciate what he is doing and why he is doing it. I didn't get where I am by being a pantywaist. If I wasn't managing partner, with all that that means in getting things done, I suppose I might do just about what Carl does. You see, I have a lot of sympathy for his point of view.

So, I guess you can see my problem. Should I fire Carl? That doesn't make too much sense. In fact, Carl should probably be a partner—if not immediately, then soon. Here is a man who has real talents and abilities. He is valuable. Yet he is a liability, too. Should I order him to work with the organization, or else? What would that do to his enthusiasm and the enthusiasm of the clients who are so crazy about him? And I might find myself in a position where I'd have to fire him.

But if I just let things go, isn't there real danger to my organization? My staff will think I have given Carl the green light, and maybe they will transfer their antagonism to me. I can't afford that.

Having expressed himself, Frank Corbett seemed relieved. He added, "I suppose you are going to have these remarks typed up. I suggest you show them to Harry Klein and get his views."

Mahoney did just that. Klein read through the transcript, thought for a moment, and said:

> Well, it is a difficult thing to put into words, but I feel that basically Carl Phelps is one of the most selfish men I have ever known. He is not selfish in the ordinary sense of the word, but rather in his all-consuming conviction that everything is important only to the extent that it affects him personally. In many ways he is genuinely friendly and generous. On many occasions he has been most considerate and helpful to individuals in this firm. But beneath it all, I'm convinced that each action he takes is unconsciously linked with his own personal progress. I doubt very seriously if he ever realizes it, because he had been brought up that way.
>
> Carl is generally regarded in the firm as the man most likely to be taken into the partnership. Not that this is popular with the staff, but they feel pretty helpless about it because he is Frank's fair-haired boy. It seems to me that if the partners make him a partner, they will be making a mistake. Carl is a man of inherent narrowness of purpose, and the firm will suffer.

Discussion Questions

1. What are the frames of reference of the people in this case? That is, how do they perceive what is going on?

2. Is anyone's self-image being threatened in this case?

3. What should Frank do?

CASE 4–2

The Cocktail Party*

The following conversation occurred between Fred Lyons and William Baird at a cocktail party. Both men were in their early 30s. Lyons had been practicing dentistry for six years, and Baird had just been graduated from law school. Each man had worked part time to supplement his income during his years in college. They had known each other on a casual basis for about a year.

Lyons   Well, Bill, I hear you're about to take your bar examinations. What are your plans if you get by them?

Baird   There's no *if* about it, Fred, But to answer your question, I'm lining up a practice right now.

Lyons   Do you mean to tell me you have no doubts about passing the bar?

Baird   None, really. This is the way I look at it: I attended one of the better law schools in the country, and I was one of the better people in my class. So I really don't have any qualms at all

---

*Adapted from a case prepared by Eleanor Lynch Roeser. Printed by permission.

Lyons *(Slightly sarcastically)* And I suppose you have no qualms about succeeding in law, in general?

Baird No, I'm really quite confident that I'll make a go of it.

Lyons Well, buddy, you've got a lot to learn. [He then began to recount at length some of his own difficulties and disappointments in starting in his profession.] And when you come right down to it, it's a plenty tough uphill climb to establish a reputation and a following. Frankly, Bill, you're going to have trouble attracting a clientele with this superconfidence of yours.

Baird There's where you're dead wrong. A man has to have assurance and confidence in himself, or no one else will have confidence in him. Do you think a person would want his legal problems handled by a fellow who didn't give the appearance that he was dead certain he knew what he was doing?

Lyons To be honest, I think the average person would be repelled rather than attracted by this attitude. Your client, the man in the street, wants to feel that his lawyer is his type of man. You've got to speak his language in order to convince him you understand his problem. Here, I'll give you a test. Suppose I come to you with a problem. [He then posed a legal question concerning income tax.] How would you handle it?

Baird I can't give you an opinion on that. I'd have to have a good many more facts, and I'd have to study them.

Lyons Now, do you see? Be honest with yourself, Bill. You don't have the experience, and if you parade around with that cocksure attitude of yours, you're not going to get to first base.

Baird *(Both men were somewhat angered by now.)* Now, listen, Fred. Law is a science of the mind. Dentistry is more of a mechanical science where you might expect to solve some problems immediately. And even in dentistry you can't pass judgment on an oral problem without an examination and maybe even an X ray.

Lyons Well, all I can say, Bill—if you don't learn a more humble approach; if you don't bring your speaking and attitude down to the level of the average person, you're asking for trouble.

Baird Well, if you ask me, the "average person" isn't going to have much confidence in anyone who is *too* average.

The afternoon was saved by a third person who broke into the conversation and managed to switch the subject to baseball.

Discussion Questions

1. Why did Baird respond, as he did, to Lyons' original three questions?
2. Why did Lyons disagree with these responses?
3. What might have happened had a third party not distracted the two men?
4. Assuming the absence of the third party, how might either Lyons (or Baird) have averted a "vicious pendulum"? (See Chapter 12.)

CASE 4-3

The Sally Port Episode

> One of the real questions facing working people is how much to suck up to the boss. Do you give him the treatment he deserves (utter contempt) or the treatment he expects (slavish devotion)? Most people reach a simple solution: You show devotion to his face and contempt to his back.*

That's one way of resolving it. But what do you do when your boss's expectations conflict with getting your job done correctly?

Here's what happened, according to Simon:

Scene The rear sally port (area between the outer and inner gates) at the Pontiac (Illinois) Correctional Center—a prison.

Principal Characters Michael Lane, director of the Corrections Department. Kevin Finefield, 24, a guard.

Finefield's duties include searching incoming and outgoing vehicles in the sally port. The objective is to prevent guns, drugs, liquor, and so forth from being smuggled into the prison—and, more important, to intercept any prisoners from being smuggled out of it.

On the day in question, Finefield was checking an outgoing truck. Lane approached the gate. He concedes that there was no emergency and that he was in no hurry.

Lane's version. "I came in the back way. I walked up to the gate where the guard was searching a truck in the sally port. The truck was on its way out of prison. I was not impatient. It was evident to me that the guard noticed me when I was approaching. I was with the Deputy Director of Adult Institutions. We both wore suits.

"I waited. And after a while I said: 'Officer, get the gate.' I asked to be let in. The guard didn't do it. So I identified myself. I said, 'This is Director Lane. Open the gate.'

"The guard did not have a conversation with me. I must have waited a total of six minutes. There were some inmates who were close enough to monitor what was going on. A correctional captain appeared on the scene and got the guy to open the gate. I went in."

Lane immediately complained to the warden and shortly thereafter Finefield was told that he was suspended pending discharge and was escorted out of the prison.

---

*Roger Simon, "Guard does his job, gets the gate," *Chicago Sun Times*, May 17, 1984, p. 7.

Finefield's version.   "I had a bread truck coming out and I had to check it. I was doing that when I heard this voice say, 'Open up.' I said: 'Sir, you'll have to wait.'

"Then the guy says, 'I'm Michael Lane and I'm giving you a direct order: Open up.' I said, 'Sir, I can't do that until I'm done searching the truck. A prisoner might escape.'

"I had to go underneath the truck—there's a pit—to make sure nobody was hiding under there and I had to search behind all the racks in the truck. Well, Lane didn't have to wait more than five minutes. But when he came in, he was screaming. Fifteen minutes later, I was escorted out of the prison.

"You know, I was accidentally shot by a tower officer a while ago. He fired his shot gun and it ricocheted and hit me. I didn't sue the state. I just do my job and it's a tough job.

"I have an 18-month-old daughter at home and now I'm fired. All I was doing was trying to make Lane look good. I was trying to keep prisoners from escaping."

Norma Duba's version.   Norma Duba, representing the American Federation of State, County, and Municipal Employees, spoke in Finefield's behalf:

"The Corrections Department sometimes does check to see if everybody is doing his job. Previously at Pontiac, a correctional official hid in a truck to see if the guard would find him. The guard did. For all Finefield knew, Lane was checking security.

"You can't interrupt a search, because if you do, a prisoner can slip into the area you've already searched.

"This is just an ego thing. Lane's ego was hurt and so he hands down this extreme punishment. The simple question is which is more important: Lane's ego or the security at Pontiac?"

Lane's response.   "This man was clearly insubordinate to me, his superior. My conduct does not show ego or arrogance. I waited and waited and waited. I am running a paramilitary-type organization and I cannot allow this kind of thing to happen."

Is there a moral in all of this? Simon thinks so:

Take care of the boss before you take care of your job.
And, while you're at it, it wouldn't hurt to click your heels.[1]

Sequel.   According to a source who did not wish to be identified, Finefield was discharged. In November 1984, his case was appealed. A settlement

---

[1]Ibid.

was reached. Finefield was reinstated but he was placed on suspension for 25 days. He returned to the job, served a few days, then resigned.

Discussion Questions

1. Just what is the problem here?
2. What do self-images have to do with this case? .
3. How objective was Simon?
4. How might this type of episode be prevented from recurring?

CASE 4–4

Nancy Sawyer*

Nancy Sawyer had risen rapidly in the Coleridge Corporation, a large insurance company headquartered in Hartford, Conn. She had joined the firm immediately after receiving a law degree from a prestigious midwestern university. She was 23 at the time. Previously, she had earned an MBA from the same university.

Sawyer was clearly considered fast-track material. She had moved through several of the major functions of the company: claims, underwriting, and marketing. She had also had brief stints in actuarial, investment, and EDP. Currently, she was the claims department vice president.

Today, President Richard Schramm called her into his office. Schramm tapped his fingers together as he invariably did when he was about to propose an idea.

"Nancy, I have an idea I'd like you to mull over. As you know, we've acquired the Dolton company, a smallish life company, about a month ago."

"Yes, sir. They're in Milwaukee, right?"

"Yes, but what you don't know is that we're thinking about sending you out there to turn that situation around for us."

"You mean as a trouble-shooter?"

Schramm looked out the window briefly, then swung back to Nancy.

"Well, yes, but as a permanent assignment. You'd move out there. You'd be the CEO."

Sawyer was stunned; she hoped it didn't show. Her feelings were mixed.

"Wow! Milwaukee's a long way from Hartford! . . ."

"It is indeed . . . about 850 miles, I should say."

Nancy recovered. "Of course, it's my old stomping ground, it's the area where I went to school."

---

*All names are disguised.

"That's part of the reason we thought of you. You're basically a Midwesterner. Some of our Eastern types might have a little trouble fitting in."

"Well, this is quite a development, Dick. I knew we had Dolton, of course, but it never occurred to me . . . ."

"What about John?" John Swanson was her husband; they had no children. "Think he'd go for it?"

"Well, I really don't know . . . he's a Midwesterner, too . . . we'd have to talk about it."

"Certainly."

"Of course, there are plenty of hospitals in Milwaukee. I just don't know how he'd react to a move."

"Why don't you two talk it over . . . we have some good contacts in Milwaukee who could help him line up something. What is he now, associate administrator at Mercy General?"

"That's right. Another thing, too . . . he's awfully close to finishing up on his M.H.A. here."

"Well, you'd surely want to take that into consideration. So why don't you talk it over with him . . . of course, this assumes that you're interested . . . ."

"I'm certainly interested, but this all comes from out of the blue . . . I knew of the acquisition, but I had no idea that I was being considered . . . ."

"I know. Chet (Chester Rizzo, executive vice president) and I have been keeping this under wraps. Frankly, there are people around here who think they should be tapped, and some of them have quite a few years on you. And, of course, most of them are men . . ."

"Oh, yes . . . I've been wrestling with that one for the last 10 years. I keep trying to remind myself that these are the years I'll be able to tell my granddaughters about!"

"I realize some of the crap you've had to put up with, Nancy. But I think you've handled it beautifully."

Nancy was touched. "Well, thank you, Dick, I appreciate that."

"And, frankly, that's another reason why Chet and I thought of you. We know you can handle yourself. You'd be president of the subsidiary and let's see . . . salary . . . you're what? . . . $60,000?"

"62."

"Okay, let's say you start in Milwaukee at 75 . . . oh, hell! Let's not be chintzy . . . make it 80. And, of course, there'd be increased stock options, profit sharing, pension benefits, and so on. And that's just the start of it if things pan out."

Nancy's face fell. "That's very generous, Dick . . . but do you think there'll be a problem?"

Schramm pursed his lips. "Well, not really . . . but, after all, Dolton is a bit of a bag of worms. Otherwise, we couldn't have bought it at a discount."

Schramm and Sawyer continued to discuss details. A half hour later, Schramm concluded the conference. "So Nancy, why don't you and John hash it over . . . what would be a reasonable deadline . . . two weeks?"

"Yes, Dick, I'm sure I can give you an answer within that time."

"Excellent. Keep it on the Q.T. and get back to me or Chet if you need any additional fill-in."

They rose and shook hands. Sawyer left the president's office and headed for her own. She was elated, yet troubled. The money—the challenge—they were exciting. But how would John react? Perhaps he would welcome it. He had seemed somewhat restive during the past year. He was basically happy at Mercy but with a young administrator in charge, he recognized he was in a deadend job—at least for the near term.

And how about herself? She had heard rumors about Dolton's "bag of worms." How would they take to a woman—and a young one at that? What if she took the job and flopped? She had never had so much responsibility and autonomy. Milwaukee was a long way from Hartford . . . and Dick. She was acutely aware that Dick had been her informal mentor over the years. He had known Nancy's father intimately and she always felt Dick had had a personal concern for her development and welfare. Could she stand alone?

And what if she turned down the offer? Would that derail her from Coleridge's fast track?

Nancy Sawyer felt she had a great deal of thinking to do.

Discussion Questions

1. What should Nancy Sawyer consider in reaching her decision about the Dolton Company?

2. What does Sawyer's self-image have to do with this case?

5

Perception and Communication: 3. The Exceptionally Realistic Self-Image

The previous two chapters, by developing the *perceptual* process and the *frame of reference* and *self-image* constructs, laid the foundation for this, the payoff chapter.

The central premise is that in order to communicate with or deal with others—to organize and lead them, motivate them, teach them, aid them, sell to them, collaborate with them, trust them, meet their expectations of us, satisfy their needs, delegate assignments and authority to them, hold them responsible—to do these things (and countless others) and to do them well, one must have an unusually authentic conception of self—an *exceptionally realistic self-image* (ERSI),

exceptionally realistic self-image

ADVANTAGES OF THE ERSI

Depending upon where one begins, the process of attaining and maintaining an ERSI can be an exacting project. But the goal is generally well worth the effort and fortitude required. For with an ERSI, one is more likely to:

1. *Be a liberated person.* To the extent that one's self-image is invalid, it is likely to be challenged by cues from reality—feedback whose basic message is: "In some respect or other you are not who you think you are." If this contradiction exceeds one's comfort zone, the image is threatened and the usual (although not inevitable) response is defense. And defensive behavior requires energy expenditure.

An ERSI will tend not to be attacked—at least not by the cues from reality. On the contrary, they are signaling: "You are basically who you think you are." Therefore, energy-consuming defensiveness is not provoked. Accordingly, energy that would otherwise have been preempted for self-image protection is now freed and available for more constructive pursuits, such as contributing more productively and creatively to one's organization, family, and community.

2. *Maintain and increase self-image validity.* Because the ERSI obviates defensiveness, the individual tends to be more open and receptive to feedback. Thus one is able to receive inputs that can keep this self-image updated and even increase its validity.

3. *Read others validly.* Analogically, one can only perceive others through one's own self-image—the central lens in one's frame of reference. If this lens is clouded or distorted, it follows that one's view of the world (including the people one deals with) is prone to be unrealistic. One has a head start in understanding others (forming accurate images of them) if one begins by truly understanding oneself. "An individual who is genuinely in touch with his own feelings, weaknesses, and needs is much more likely to understand the human qualities and failings of associates."[1]

4. *Screen inputs accurately.* One of the characteristics of a responsible, integral position in an organization is that the incumbent is constantly barraged with inputs—data, information, feedback, cues—from other people. Some of this influx is garbage—inaccurate, phony material. Part of the trash is deliberately contrived, as in the cases of ax-grinding, special pleading, lobbying, calculated fraud. Some of it is unintentionally misleading, as when the inputer is defending his/her own self-image.

The obvious protection against garbage is simply to close the shutters on one's window and preclude all inputs. This would ward off the fallacious—but it would prohibit the valid inputs as well. And considering the high degree of interdependence required by organizations, playing the hermit would be untenable.

The appropriate stance would be to keep the shutters open so as to receive the inputs but to develop the screening skills by which to separate the wheat from the chaff—the valid from the invalid inputs.

An ERSI is a prerequisite to acquiring such skills. An erroneous self-image can be a serious deterrent to one's learning to read inputs accurately. Suppose that a manager makes a decision which is then mildly criticized by the boss. Let us say that the manager has an inaccurate self-image which contributes to insecurity and leads the manager to interpret criticism far more personally than intended. Thus he may *over*react to the perceived threat—perhaps by irrational resistance or grovelling acquiescence.

5. *Choose realistic personal goals.* The poet Lew Sarett said: "Everyone needs basically two things: A block of granite to stand on and a star to guide him." In this chapter's terminology, he would probably say that each of us needs a currently realistic self-image partly in order to extrapolate into the future and choose realistic goals to which to aspire.

In the interests of a productive, happy, emotionally healthy life, it is important to have goals. "No wind favors him," wrote Michel de Montaigne,

---

[1] Robert M. Fulmor, *Practical Human Relations* (Homewood, Ill.: Richard D. Irwin, 1977), p. 30.

"who has no destined port." But it is also important that those goals be realistic. For if I shoot for an unrealistic star I am likely to pay a price for my inaccuracy. If my goal is extravagantly high, I am courting failure and frustration, which, if chronic, can degenerate to disillusionment and even demoralization.

If my goal is unchallengingly low, I may be settling, perhaps unwittingly, for semivegetation—a psychological stagnation that augurs well for neither health nor happiness.

One of the most important blessings of an ERSI (the block of granite) is that it enhances one's ability to choose appropriate, attainable growth goals.

The foregoing list is not exhaustive. But it does highlight several of the key values associated with the ERSI—suggesting why the ERSI is worth the price of attainment. And it does exact a price in terms of effort, time, honesty, patience, and, above all, courage to endure the temporary discomfort sometimes required by image change through reprogramming. I use the term *reprogramming* because one's self-image is a programmed product—that is, it is learned. It follows then that if the self-image is, in some respects, inaccurate, that self-image can be *re*learned. But desirable reprogramming requires that the inputs be both valid and tolerable. Valid—so that the modified self-image will indeed be more realistic. Tolerable—so that one's comfort zone will not be violated by sudden, dramatic, uncontrolled change leading to one's defenses either screening out the inputs or being crushed by overwhelming inputs.

A GAME PLAN

Accordingly, the following is a game plan designed to help one gain and maintain an ERSI through reprogramming by valid and tolerable inputs.

1. *Make a commitment.* Considering the aforementioned price of attaining an ERSI, it is evident that if you are to make significant gains in self-discovery and self-understanding, you must truly want to do so. You must adopt the scientific attitude: "Regardless of where the chips may fall, who am I really?"

2. *Identify and reduce your defenses.* The most important single reason most of us do not understand ourselves better lies in our own internal fortifications that seal us off from contrary, disturbing cues from reality. Considering that many of these bastions are rather well formed by the age of seven, the biblical age of reason, it would be astounding if anyone were aware of all his or her defenses.

So the challenge is progressively (it is a lifetime project) to recognize the existence of such defenses and to find ways of reducing them. In more rustic language—to identify the particular shutters on your window, to push them open, and to keep them open.

3. *Receive and evaluate the inputs.* With the shutters open, you are now able to receive the inputs. But not all feedback is authentic, so you must also evaluate, weigh, sift, and analyze it in order to separate the valid from the invalid.

VALID CUES

Input sources can be usefully classed into two categories: Those that originate from outside one's skin (external cues) and those generated from within (internal cues).

The remainder of this chapter will consist of a litany of sources of valid external and internal cues.

Cues from Others

For most of us, the greatest potential source of valid external cues is other people, especially those who have had the opportunity to observe us over a period of time under various circumstances.

This is not to say that everything everyone has to offer will be unfailingly authentic. Garbage is conceded. But it seems safe to assume that some of the feedback some of them could give is quite valid and potentially very helpful—if only we could communicate our receptivity to it. This seems a simple enough nostrum. Indeed, it is simplistic. For being receptive to feedback of any substance—and receiving it—on a continuing basis implies a relationship.

The Johari Grid.   An insightful model involving feedback in the context of a relationship has been devised by psychologists Joseph Luft[2] and Harrington Ingham. They called it the Johari (pronounced, uncoincidentally, Joe-Harry) Window. Johari *Grid* seems more appropriate, because their construct represents a *person*, not an opening for air and light or any other conventional usage for "window."

More specifically, the Johari Grid portrays *an individual as he or she relates to others*. To illustrate this construct in simplest terms, let us visualize a one-on-one relationship between, say Bob, a boss, and Ed, one of his subordinates.

Figure 5–1 represents *Bob* (we will see Ed's grid later) *as he relates to Ed*. Two premises apply: (1) Everything in the large rectangle is valid in-

---

[2]Joseph Luft, *Of Human Interaction* (Palo Alto, Calif.: National Press Books, 1969); and Joseph Luft, *Group Processes: An Introduction to Group Dynamics* (Palo Alto, Calif.: National Press Books, 1970).

FIGURE 5–1

	Known to self (Bob)	Unknown to self (Bob)
Known to the other (Ed)	Public area	Blind area
Unknown to the other (Ed)	Hidden area	Unconscious area

Bob
(as he relates to Ed)

formation (including feelings, facts, assumptions, beliefs, personal values, prejudices, and needs); and (2) everything in the large rectangle is pertinent to Bob's relationship with Ed. The only distinction the grid purports to make is who has knowledge of which information.

The *public area* represents that part of Bob that relates to Ed and is known to both of them. It includes such details as the fact that Bob is the administrator of the X Memorial Hospital; that Ed is one of his immediate subordinates, along with Sally, Stu, Morris, and Jane; that when Bob is absent (out-of-town meetings, vacations, etc.) he appoints Ed to serve as acting administrator; and so on. Bob's public area with respect to Ed represents common ground. Because it is mutually perceived and acknowledged, it ordinarily presents no unrecognized problem for Bob or for Ed. If difficulties do arise in Bob's public area, Bob and Ed become conscious of them, identify what they are disagreeing about, and have at least the opportunity to reconcile their differences.

The *hidden area* is that part of Bob that relates to Ed of which Bob is aware, Ed is not, and about which Bob may prefer to keep Ed in the dark. For example, despite the fact that Ed serves as administrator in Bob's absence, Bob does not consider him as his crown prince. Bob regards Ed as an excellent director of personnel but feels that he lacks the potential to become a full-time administrator. Bob has been offered the reins of a larger hospital in another city. Should he accept the new position, he plans to recommend Sally to the board as his replacement. But none of this has he confided to Ed.

Bob's hidden area with respect to Ed includes that which he has simply not yet had occasion to reveal to Ed, as well as that which he is deliberately concealing from Ed.

The *blind area* is that part of Bob that relates to Ed of which Ed is aware, Bob is not, and Ed has not as yet seen fit or felt free to bring to Bob's attention. For instance, Bob has an MBA, has attended many management seminars, and has read widely in management literature. He feels that he practices a highly participative style of leadership by trusting his subordinates implicitly and delegating freely to them. Ed knows better. He recognizes, as do his colleagues, that Bob is a soft-spoken, beneficent autocrat who merely gives lip service to liberal delegation.

Ed, thus, has knowledge that could reduce Bob's blind area. Whether it actually does reduce it depends upon two interrelated factors: Ed's willingness to share the information and Bob's willingness to receive and accept it. If Bob has consciously (or more likely, unconsciously) communicated his nonreceptivity to Ed's feedback, he is unlikely to have the information proffered to him.

The *unconscious area* is that part of Bob that relates to Ed, and of which neither man is aware. Theoretically, then, they are powerless to change this sector. Thus, if a sufficiently severe problem arises in Bob's unconscious area, psychotherapy may be required.

However, another alternative is possible. When the one-on-one relationship is a very open, trusting, receptive one, the two intimates—husband and wife, parent and child, friend and friend, even boss and subordinate—may sometimes stumble onto something in the unconscious area, thus putting it into one of the other three sectors, depending upon whether one or the other party or both parties become aware of it.

Leveling and Feedback Solicitation.   The size and shape of the grid's four sectors are determined by two basic communication processes:

Leveling is synonymous with opening up, coming clean, revealing one's thoughts and feelings, being honest and candid. It is represented by the vertical dimension in Figure 5–2.

Soliciting feedback, the lateral dimension, involves genuinely seeking and requesting feedback from another person, expressing the willingness to receive inputs, even negative ones, without becoming feisty, defensive.

FIGURE 5-2

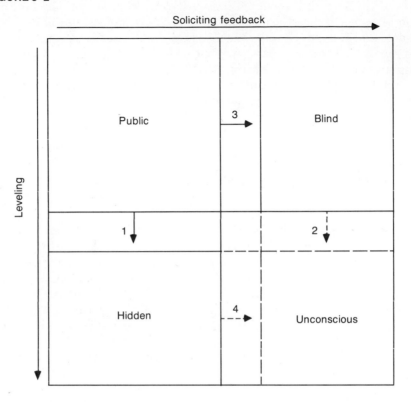

To the extent that Bob levels with Ed, he will be enlarging his public area while reducing his hidden sector (see arrow 1). It does not necessarily follow that the new floor on the public area will be extended across the grid increasing the blind while reducing the unconscious (see arrow 2). This will occur only to the extent that in leveling with Ed, Bob is actually revealing more to Ed than Bob is aware and that Ed does not share this new information with Bob.

Similarly, to the extent that Bob's solicitation of feedback from Ed is successful—that is, he actually receives the feedback—Bob's blind area will be diminished, increasing his public sector (see arrow 3). Again, the new wall will not necessarily extend downward, enlarging the hidden while reducing the unconscious (see arrow 4). This will only happen to the extent that as Ed offers feedback he is giving more information than he thinks he is. Thus Bob learns more than Ed thinks he has. If Bob keeps this bonus knowledge to himself, it is considered hidden area material.

FIGURE 5–3

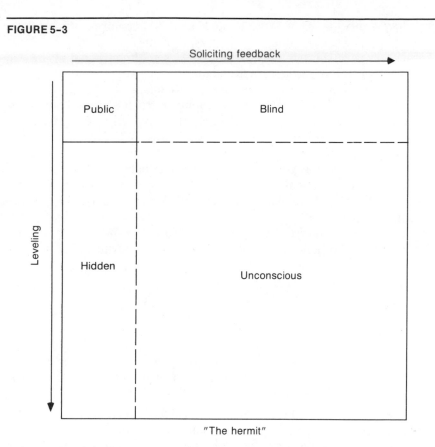

We have acknowledged that the public area's new floor and wall do not necessarily extend, respectively, across and down through the grid. Accordingly, in subsequent grids, the blind-unconscious and hidden-unconscious boundaries will be expressed by dotted lines.

Interpersonal Styles.   Note that we have not been discussing Bob in isolation—but in his relationship with a particular person at a particular time. Like most of us, Bob relates differently to different people. He also relates differently to the same person at different times.

Let us examine several interpersonal styles and consider their implications for both parties—the possessor of the grid and the person to whom he or she is relating.

Figure 5–3 shows a Johari Grid characterized by a tiny public area, sizable hidden and blind areas, and a huge unconscious area. Suppose that this grid represents Bob as he deals with Ed. It implies that Bob has been unwilling or unable to level with Ed and has also been unreceptive to feedback from Ed. This hermit style will pose problems for both Bob and Ed.

For Ed's part, there is so much that he does not know about his boss in terms of their relationship (hidden and unconscious areas) that Ed is likely to have a very limited and perhaps inaccurate image of Bob. He will have difficulty in predicing Bob's behavior, coping with him, and satisfying his own (Ed's) needs with respect to Bob. He will have only a fuzzy notion of what Bob expects of him or of how he stands with Bob. Moreover, he will be reluctant to offer candid feedback, for Bob's large blind area implies that he has not been especially receptive to feedback that could have reduced that sector. In addition, since Bob is likely to be quite reserved—maintaining his substantial hidden area would require this—Ed is likely to be cautious as well.

Clearly Ed will be frustrated should Bob assume the hermit posture. But how Ed will be affected *specifically* depends largely upon his own particular needs and motivations.

> Subordinates whose manager employs such a style . . . will often feel that his behavior is consciously aimed at frustrating them in their work. The person in need of support and encouragement will often view a [hermit] manager as aloof, cold and indifferent. Another individual in need of firm directions and plenty of order may view the same manager as indecisive and administratively impotent. Yet another person requiring freedom and opportunities to be innovative may see the [hermit] interpersonal style as hopelessly tradition-bound and as symptomatic of fear and an overriding need for security.[3]

Bob's plight, if anything, is worse than Ed's. With an enormous unconscious area coupled with a significant blind area, he is unlikely to have a very complete or valid self-image. His faulty self-perception may lead to erratic behavior on his part, which, incidentally, makes him even less predictable to Ed. Moreover, for Bob to protect his hidden area against revelation will require constant security. Indirectly, as suggested above, Bob's maintaining a large hidden area will constrain Ed from offering candid feedback.

The hermit style is particularly troublesome in an organizational context. For it is extremely difficult to report to someone who comes on as a hermit, or to supervise or attempt to collaborate with a person who manifests this style. It is singularly frustrating to be required to interact with a person who simply will not—or cannot—relate.

The most prominent feature of the Johari Grid in Figure 5–4 is its immense hidden area. This is the pumper style, for it is created when a person is successful in sucking information out of another while giving little if

---

[3]Jay Hall, "Communication Revisited," *California Management Review,* 15, no. 3 (Spring 1973), p. 60.

FIGURE 5-4

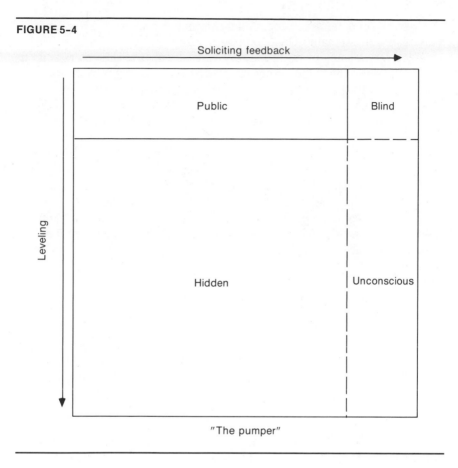

any in return. The motives for pumping could be broadly classed as defensive and offensive.

Defensively, pumpers reveal very little of themselves, thus concealing their inadequacies and vulnerabilities from those who might take advantage of them. Offensively, they gain knowledge which they may be able to use to attack, influence, or manipulate others. If knowledge is power, the pumper may be attempting to build a dynasty.

Maintaining security on one's huge hidden area can be an exhausting compulsion for the pumper. It requires considerable energy to keep secrets, to play "games," to keep people in the dark. An uncomfortable thought: Have you ever told a lie and then had to live with it? Do you recall how it drained you to keep the fiction intact? "Oh, what a tangled web we weave," wrote Sir Walter Scott, "when first we practice to deceive!"

From the pumper's standpoint, another major problem with pumping is that it is often detectable. Once "pumpees" realize that they are involved in a lopsided relationship wherein they are virtually always the givers and rarely the takers, they may grow suspicious and wary. "What's going on here?" ponders the pumpee. "He knows everything about me—my views of our boss, our mutual colleagues, our organization, even of himself—yet he never seems to commit himself. Why does he need all of this from me? What is he going to do with it? Hurt me?"

At this point, the pumpee has turned defensive and may withdraw to the hermit posture by avoiding the pumper. If he or she senses that the pumper is oblivious of the unbalanced relationship, the pumpee may confront the pumper and demand reciprocal leveling. Or the pumpee may come on as a counterpumper. But this usually eventuates in a "You tell me!"—"No, you tell me!" standoff. A more drastic defense is to feed the pumper some false information. Although this tactic may "cure" the pumper of trying to tap this particular source, it may have some destructive by-products. For if the pumper uses the fallacious material, it may harm others—perhaps himself or herself—and the pumpee may have created a vengeful enemy.

In any event, the success of the pumper style tends to be short-lived because when pumpees suspect that they are on a one-way street, they are apt to thwart the pumper's needs for accurate and intimate information.

I call the interpersonal style depicted in Figure 5-5 the blabbermouth. If Bob were playing the blabbermouth with respect to Ed, he would be doing a great deal of talking and very little listening. The net result could be a vast blind area.

Why does Bob talk so much? Among the possibilities: He's on a constant ego trip—needs applause; he's whistling in the dark—to shore up his own flagging spirits; he's venting his spleen—thus forcing the listener into the role of therapist; he's truly arrogant—genuinely assured of his own opinions and values; he has an authoritarian personality—feels that decision making should be centralized in himself; he's paternalistic, dictatorial, and so on.

Why does Bob listen so little? Perhaps he lacks respect for Ed's views; possibly he fears that Ed's views may challenge his own; his obsession with being right brooks no contrary feedback; and so on.

Ed, to the extent that he is not a captive audience, may escape some of Bob's excessive leveling by retreating to a hermit role and simply hiding from him. But this tactic may not suffice for some of the problems that Bob's blabbermouth style presents for Ed.

Bob's tiny hidden area may indicate that he is not very circumspect—"he lets it *all* hang out." Thus, Ed may be justifiably concerned about Bob's discretion regarding the confidences Ed has shared with him.

FIGURE 5–5

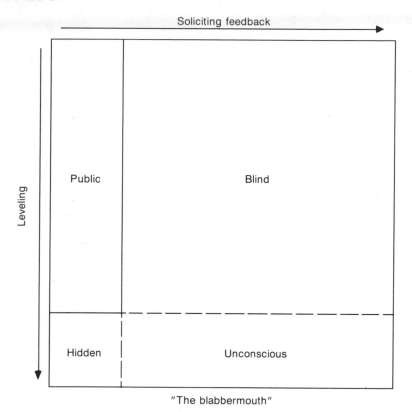

Soliciting feedback

Leveling

| Public | Blind |
| Hidden | Unconscious |

"The blabbermouth"

But it is probably Bob's nonreceptivity to Ed's feedback that pains Ed most acutely. Ed may feel disenfranchised and may perceive that Bob has little use for his contributions or little concern for his feelings. As a result, Ed may feel resentful, insecure, and bitter and may retaliate by perpetuating Bob's blind area by "withholding important information or giving only selected feedback . . . this is a reflection of the passive aggressiveness and unarticulated hostility which this style can cause."[4]

But Ed may occasionally resort to active aggression. If Bob is highly authoritarian, this can be perilous for Ed, but it can be dangerous for Bob as well. Since their relationships are dominated by blind areas, blabber-

---

[4]Ibid., p. 61.

FIGURE 5-6

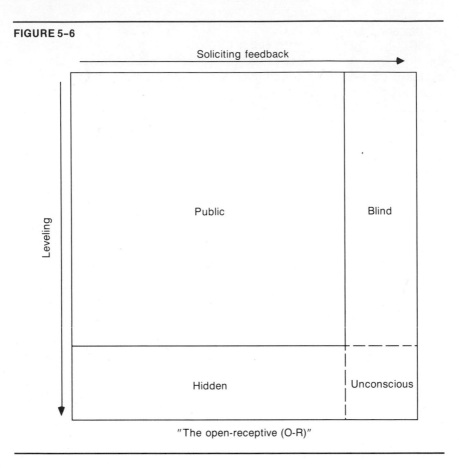

"The open-receptive (O-R)"

mouths, according to Jay Hall, "are destined for surprise whenever people get enough and decide to force feedback upon them, solicited or not."[5]

The grid in Figure 5-6 represents the open-receptive or O-R style. It occurs when there is a balanced combination of generous leveling and a genuine willingness to receive feedback. The consequence, assuming that feedback is received, is a grid dominated by the public area.

If Bob deals with Ed in the O-R fashion, a number of significant advantages over other styles can accrue. Ed will be able to form a more accurate image of Bob, due largely to Bob's uninhibited leveling—this is in stark contrast with the hermit and pumper styles, in which Bob is largely an unknown quantity for Ed. Ed will not be inhibited for fear of offending or threatening Bob, as is the case in the blabbermouth style, because Bob has made it clear that he welcomes feedback and will not punish Ed for his candor.

---

[5]Ibid.

The O-R style should enhance Bob's chances of gaining an ERSI, at least in his relationship with Ed, for Bob's receptivity to feedback promises to reduce his blind area to a minor sector. Bob's unconscious area is also likely to be diminished, subject as it is to fortuitous stumbling by intimates. Not the least of the ERSI benefits that Bob may enjoy is the freedom from having to "play games" with Ed, keeping him in the dark.

The obvious drawback to the O-R style is its vulnerability. Anyone who is this open and receptive could be hurt. Thus, the O-R style is only appropriate (and, indeed, possible) when mutual trust and trustworthiness exist between the parties to the relationship. For a White House staff member to have attempted to relate to others in the O-R manner during the Watergate period would have been naive—he or she would have been devoured.

Your OPA.   We have been comparing the advantages and limitations of several interpersonal styles. But is there an *ideal* Johari Grid? Not for all circumstances. To determine the best grid, or more specifically the best public area, for a given situation, I suggest this formula:

$$OPA = f(Y,O,C)$$

Translated, your optimal public area is a function of at least three factors: *you*, the *other* to whom you are relating, and the social or organizational *culture* within which the two of you are interacting.

The most appropriate public area for you depends to a considerable extent on the basic kind of person *you* are. Are you generally a withdrawn, recessive person? Do you find it difficult to reach out to people? to trust them? to share confidences with them? Does intimacy threaten you? If so, this doesn't mean that you can't have open, receptive relationships. But you may require more time, energy, and courage to build them than would a more outgoing person.

And how trusting is the other person? There are limits to how intimate you can become with a confirmed recluse. And what of his or her trustworthiness? It would be foolhardy to open up with a person who would abuse your trust.

Even though you and the other person may be basically trusting and trustworthy, the climate in which you are interrelating must be considered. An organizational jungle, such as the aforementioned Watergate White House, is no place to let it all hang out.

Suboptimal Public Areas.   How do members of organizations normally relate to one another? When the public areas in boss-subordinate, colleague-colleague, or staff-line relationships are less than optimal, in which direction do they usually miss the mark? Are they dangerously open or needlessly closed?

Judging from reports by most managers in my seminars and from my own observations, people in organizations tend to have unnecessarily small public areas. Their dealings with one another are excessively aloof and guarded. An ironic survival of the most defensive seems to be mainly responsible. Visualize two company employees. Considering their environment, each has an inappropriate public area. A's is vulnerably large, whereas B's is over cautiously small. The predictable outcome? A will promptly receive painful feedback clearly signaling: "You're too open and defenseless!" In short, he will be burned. He may leave the organization. If he remains, he will become more self-protective. Indeed, he may overreact—polarize[6]—and shrink his public area excessively.

B, however, will not have his trust abused—he'll never proffer it. He is unlikely to be seared by negative feedback. His defensive posture precludes it. He is even shielded from corrective intelligence which challenges: "You're too closed and insulated!"

In a hostile environment, natural selection favors the best protected. So the Bs remain; the As who stay become Bs; and everyone is obsessed with defense.

Add the collective time and energy spent "playing games," protecting inaccurate self-images, fending off disturbing feedback, bristling against criticism, playing it close to the vest, smoke-screening, passing the buck, scapegoating, and watching out for Number One, and we begin to appreciate the exorbitant price an organization pays when its people are preoccupied with personal defensiveness rather than with organizational objectives and working together to get the job done.

Enlarging the Public Area.   Such organizations would do well to encourage their members to enlarge their public areas. This ultimately occurs at the one-on-one level, so let us examine a method by which Bob and Ed can expand their respective public areas. It consists of gradually and reciprocally increasing the flow of information between the two men—that is, progressive leveling and feedback solicitation.

Suppose that Bob and Ed have maintained a hermit-hermit relationship (see Figure 5-7) for some time and that at least one of them, say Bob, wants to alter it. Bob's first step is to deliberately reveal a bit of his hidden area to Ed—to tell Ed forthrightly something he had been concealing from him: "Look, Ed, this is how I really feel about . . ." (see arrow 1). Beyond this overt information, Bob is sending a second message covertly: "See, Ed? I'm letting my guard down. I'm taking you into my confidence. Convince me that it's safe to disarm like this with you, so please don't get alarmed or feisty, and don't abuse my trust, and if you want some more candor then reciprocate, man; let *your* hair down a bit."

---

[6]See Chapter 12.

FIGURE 5-7

PROGRESSIVE LEVELING

FIGURE 5-8

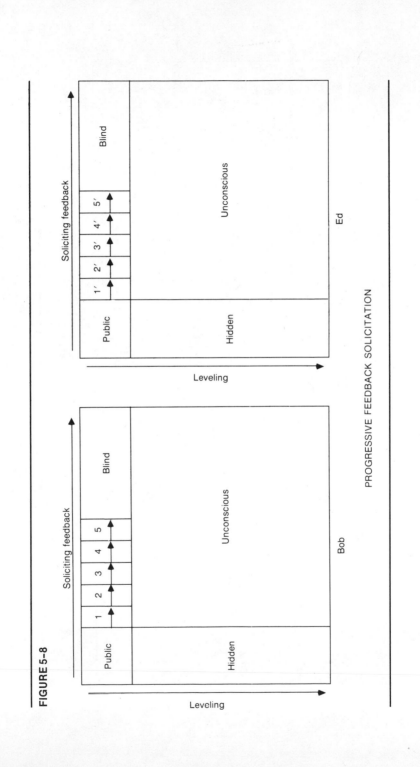

PROGRESSIVE FEEDBACK SOLICITATION

If Ed gets this second message and trusts it, then he reciprocates and shares some intimacy with Bob (arrow 1'), coupled with the same reciprocity plea. Hopefully, Bob will interpret Ed's intent and respond accordingly (arrow 2), and so forth.

Simultaneously with this progressive leveling, mutual solicitation of feedback may occur (see Figure 5–8). Let's say that Bob again initiates the process: "Ed, what is your honest opinion of . . .?" Once more, there is a second veiled message: "Lay it on me, Ed—I can take it. I promise that if you express yourself frankly, I will not make it difficult, unpleasant, or threatening for you."

If Ed takes Bob at his word, he will offer some unvarnished, valid feedback. And suppose that Bob is able to accept it without defensiveness. Thus, Bob has learned something (his blind area is reduced—arrow 1), but so has Ed. "That Bob is a pretty big man," he muses, "he can really take it. Well, maybe I can, too." Through gradual, reciprocating solicitation and reception of feedback, each man's blind area shrinks.

The net result of these two concurrent communication processes is an inverted L-shaped public area (see Figure 5–9) for each man, which is con-

FIGURE 5–9

FIGURE 5–10

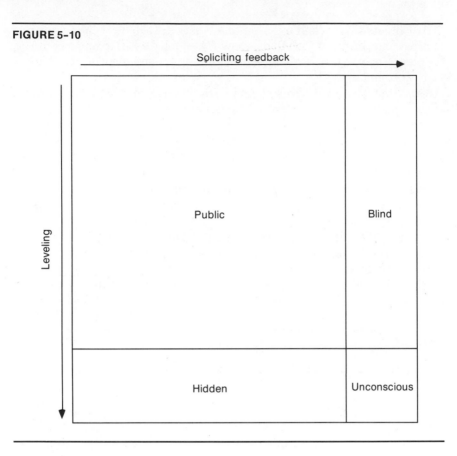

siderably larger than those of the former hermits. But there are two additional prospects for increasing the public area—or, at least, for shrinking the unconscious sector. One is the previously mentioned fortuitous stumbling of intimates. The other is the constant possibility that the sender (be he leveling or offering feedback) may be communicating more than he intends to the receiver. Thus unconscious material may be transferred variously to hidden or blind or public areas, depending upon whether one man or the other or both become aware of the newly developed information. If the transfer is primarily to the public area, Bob's and Ed's grids may approach that depicted in Figure 5–10.

The Johari Grid depicts interpersonal relationships in terms of one's willingness and ability to level with and receive feedback from others. Its relevance for self-image validity is clear. For candid feedback is a prime source (for most of us) of external cues by which one can ascertain and increase the authenticity of his or her self-image.

We will now touch upon some special concepts and approaches by which one can receive useful feedback from others: sensitivity training, group therapy, and transactional analysis.

Sensitivity Training. Uninhibited group interactions, variously termed "sensitivity training," "T-groups," "laboratory education," "group dynamics," "encounter groups," and so on, have gained increasingly enthusiastic supporters and equally energetic detractors in recent years, and the dust has yet to settle.

The format is to create a nonstructured atmosphere in which participants feel free to level with and to seek feedback from one another.

The objectives of sensitivity training have been many and varied. Some have focused on "group process phenomena, attempting to improve the ability of individuals to understand, predict, evaluate, and change the way groups work. Still others have worked on particular aspects of behavior, like the use of power and influence, leadership skills, listening ability, and giving and receiving feedback."[7]

Most relevant here, though, is that the approach has considerable potential for helping one to increase the validity of his or her self-image at least insofar as the here-and-now dynamics of the present groups are concerned.

But some precautions seem well advised; there should be, for example, professional leaders and psychologically screened participants. "Sensitivity training," warn some of its critics, "is too rough for sick people."[8]

Group Therapy. Superficially, group therapy and some forms of sensitivity training are similar. The setting is informal and seemingly unstructured. People speak and are responded to spontaneously, without an apparent agenda. But the most important distinctive characteristic of group therapy is control. The therapist, usually a highly trained professional, realizing that the participants are vulnerable, generally exercises more control on interactions than is ordinarily the case in sensitivity training.

Transactional Analysis. Conceived by the psychiatrist Eric Berne, "TA" was originally used as a tool for psychotherapy. More recently, it has also been used to aid in understanding and coping with interpersonal relations—especially those pertaining to families (spouse-spouse, parent-child, sibling-sibling, and so forth) and organizations (boss-subordinate, colleague-colleague, salesperson-customer).

---

[7]Allan R. Cohen, Stephen L. Fink, Herman Gadon, and Robin D. Willits, *Effective Behavior in Organizations*, 3d ed. (Homewood, Ill.: Richard D. Irwin, 1984), p. 366.

[8]For a balanced discussion of the pros and cons of sensitivity training, especially as relates to development in people in organizations, see: James L. Gibson, John M. Ivancevich, and James H. Donnelly, *Organizations: Behavior, Structure, Processes*, 4th ed. (Plano, Tex.: Business Publications, 1982), pp. 550–59 and 580–82.

TA's central premise is that each person consists of three ego states: Parent-Adult-Child. The objective of TA is to assure that the Adult dominates the personality and that neither an excessively critical Parent nor a primitive, self-deprecating Child is permitted to foul up transactions or relationships with others.

The individual, therefore, needs to learn to recognize which of the ego states is controlling his or her thoughts, feelings, and behavior at a given moment. With practice, one can sense who is in charge. For example, let us assume that you have never heard of TA before reading this brief description. Tune in on your current feelings. If your inner voice is saying, "Oh, this is just more drivel those behavioral scientists have cooked up!" this may be your critical, fault-finding Parent reacting. Are you temporarily withholding judgment? "This is the first I've heard of TA—sounds interesting, but I think I'd better learn more about it before passing judgment on it." This sounds like your rational, objective Adult. Or if you are immediately enthusiastic (or turned off): "Gee, this sounds like fun—figuring out who's running me—and using it to psych out others, too!" or "Transactional analysis!—that's just one more term I have to memorize for the exam," your Child seems to be controlling you.

As its name implies, TA is concerned with the transactions or communications between people—each of whom consists of a Parent-Adult-Child. The principal issue as A and B relate is: Which ego state in A is transacting with which ego state in B? Generally, when transactions are *parallel* they are considered constructive, beneficial, or at least harmless. Visualize a mother who needs to know the time. She knows that her 16-year-old son can tell her. Her Adult asks a straight-forward question directed to her

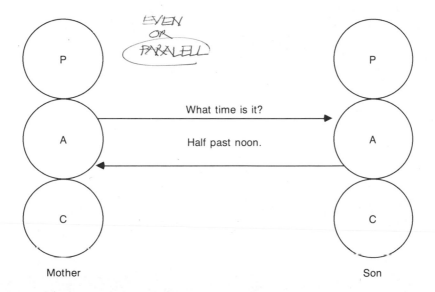

son's Adult. And the son responds out of his Adult (assuming that he is giving valid information insofar as he knows it) directed to his mother's Adult.

The key aspect of parallel (complementary) transactions is that the sender receives the expected response.

But some transactions are crossed, and the consequences may be undesirable. The sender gets an unexpected response. Imagine the same mother asking the same question with the same intention—that is, learning the correct time:

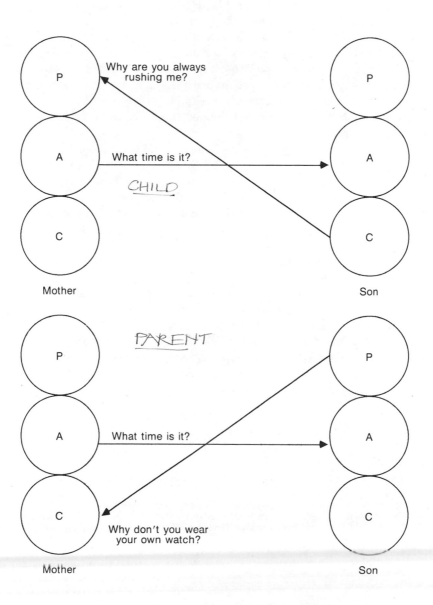

deep hatredly animosity

In neither case does the mother receive the desired information, and in both cases the stage has been set for a rancorous, unprofitable series of exchanges.

Particularly relevant to organizations is the concept of *games*—deceptions that members of the firm and others unconsciously (to some extent) perpetrate on one another. Regardless of who wins these games, the organization is a certain loser. The costs in terms of hurt feelings, retaliations, absenteeism, turnover, and grievances may be difficult to quantify on a profit-and-loss statement but that does not diminish their counterproductivity.

To illustrate games, go back to the mother-son transactions. In each case, there was the potential for a mutually destructive game known as *uproar*. In the first exchange, the mother might have understandably retaliated with, "Don't talk that way to *me*, young man!" with an appropriately fierce facial expression. The problem with that approach is that her son is now likely to be convinced that his original interpretation of her question was correct, and the wedge that divides them has been driven in more deeply.

The mother would have been well-advised to keep her cool and remain in her Adult state. Something like, "I didn't mean it that way, John, but can you tell me what time is it?" might have defused the situation.

In the second case, again, the advice is for mother to stay in her Adult and not let the other party dictate her response. The idea is not to get into her Child, for example, and to defend or alibi or quibble. Recommendation: "You're right, John, but can you tell me what time it is?"

Granted, neither of these Adult responses is likely to reconcile mother and son, especially if their alienation has been going on for some time. But at least they will not refuel their respective animosities. And, who knows, the mother might even find out what time it is!

There is *much* more to TA:[9] "ulterior transactions," "strokes," "life positions," "trading stamps," "scripts," "persecutor," "victim," "rescuer," and so forth. TA has been amply described in books by Berne, Harris, James and Jongeward, and Meininger. See the annotated references to these books later in this chapter.

Cues from Psychometric Instruments

Another approach for obtaining information by which we can increase the validity of our self-images is through standardized psychometric in-

---

[9]For implications of TA for interpersonal relations in organizations see Paul Hersey and Ken Blanchard, *Management of Organizational Behavior: Utilizing Human Resources*, 4th ed. (Englewood Cliffs, N.J.: Prentice-Hall, 1982), pp. 67–77 and 227–30; also James H. Morrison and John J. O'Hearne, *Practical TA in Management* (Reading, Mass.: Addison-Wesley, 1977).

struments. Granted that tests in general and intelligence tests in particular have been in controversy. (They have rarely been out of controversy in the past three decades!) Nevertheless, it seems reasonable to assume that some instruments, especially if these are selected, administered, and interpreted by professionals, can offer useful feedback in terms of abilities, skills, achievement, aptitudes, attitudes, interests, values, temperaments, motivations, and so on.

I use instruments in my courses and management seminars for a very specialized purpose: To offer potentially useful leads that will aid the test-taker in his or her own self-appraisal. My premise is that a human being is an enormously complex entity and that a major challenge to self-understanding is to select aspects about oneself that are specific enough to observe and study. Therefore, if a modest amount of time and money spent on an instrument or two helps one to reduce his or her area of search, then the investment seems warranted.

The instruments I use must satisfy these criteria:

1. They must have at least face-validity—that is, they must appear to a reasonable, objective observer to measure what they purport to measure.
2. They must measure behaviors or characteristics that the individual can recognize in on-the-job or in-the-home communications with others. Test results should be considered hypotheses to be tested by subsequent observations.
3. They must be capable of *self*-administration and *self*-scoring. The point here is that the results of many instruments are "fudge-able"—that is, capable of being distorted to suit the test-taker's purposes. Self-scoring tests, therefore, assure that the individual *alone* will see the scores and thus will only be doing a disservice by responding less than candidly.
4. They must measure behaviors and characteristics that the individual accepts as truly relevant in dealings with other people, for only then will one be genuinely motivated to learn about oneself in these respects.

The following are a few of the instruments[10] I have found helpful. I assert no particular claim for their validity and reliability, but they have proven useful as focus sharpeners and search-area narrowers.

---

[10]For a comprehensive annotated list of published tests, see Oscar K. Buros, ed., *The Eighth Mental Measurements Yearbook* (Highland Park, N.J.: Gryphon Press, 1978). See also: Louis Aiken, *Psychology Testing and Assessment*, 5th ed. (Newton, Mass.: Allyn & Bacon, 1984).

FIRO-B—
Consulting Psychologists Press, Inc. (Palo Alto, Calif.). Purports to indicate one's characteristic behavior toward other people in the areas of inclusion, control, and affection.

Management Style Diagnosis Test—
Organizational Test Ltd. (Fredricton, New Brunswick, Canada). Purports to indicate one's management style in terms of task orientation, relationships orientation, and effectiveness.

Orientation Inventory—
Consulting Psychologists Press (Palo Alto, Calif.). Purports to indicate one's tendency to be oriented toward *(a)* self-aggrandizement, *(b)* pleasant relationships with others, and *(c)* the group task at hand.

Personnel Relations Survey—
Teleometrics, International (Conroe, Tex.). Based upon the Johari Grid concept and purports to measure the size and shape of one's public area, that is, one's willingness to level and to solicit feedback as one relates to members of the organization at three levels: employees, colleagues, and supervisors.

Strength Deployment Inventory—
Personal Strengths Assessment Service (Pacific Palisades, Calif.). Purports to assess one's interpersonal orientation when all is going well and then again in the face of conflict and opposition.

Study of Values—
Houghton Mifflin (Boston). Purports to indicate one's value system with respect to six factors: theoretical, economic, aesthetic, social, political, and religious.

Uncritical Inference Test—
William V. Haney Associates (Wilmette, Ill.). Purports to indicate one's tendency to jump to conclusions and, conversely, one's awareness of inferring.

Cues from Readings

Can reading a book or article help a person to better understand oneself? Although readings do not offer feedback, per se, they can provide concepts, insights, tools, and techniques by which we can interpret and learn from the feedback that we do receive from interpersonal experiences. Such readings are almost too abundant. The problem is to choose sound, competent, useful works from the profusion available. The list below includes several books that I and others have found particularly germane and helpful:

Eric Berne, M.D. *Games People Play.* New York: Grove Press, 1964. A psychoanalyst's application of transactional analysis concepts to interpersonal relationships. The games are the deceptions we employ (at varying levels of consciousness) in our dealings with others in order to satisfy our needs.

Roger M. D'Aprix. *Struggle for Identity.* Homewood, Ill.: Dow Jones-Irwin, 1972. This book focuses on the discrepancy between reality and what we have been programmed to believe about the relationship between the individual and the organization. It discusses the growing resistance to being molded into organization people and the struggle of the individual to maintain a personal identity, integrity, and intellectual freedom against the increasing pressure of organizational forces.

George Bach and Herbert Goldberg. *Creative Aggression.* Garden City, N.Y.: Doubleday, 1974. Whereas Freud asserted that the repression of sexual expression was the root of most personal and interpersonal evils, these authors contend that today's counterpart culprit is the repression of aggression. Accordingly, they offer rationale by which aggression can be released in safe, constructive, and even creative ways.

George Bach and Peter Wyden. *The Intimate Enemy: How to Fight Fair in Love and Marriage.* New York: Avon Books, 1968. The operative word is *fair.* The authors offer a sound and sensible approach for resolving or at least diminishing conflict and increasing intimacy. Admittedly couched in terms for the couple, the book is nevertheless highly relevant to on-the-job relationships.

David Goleman, *Vital Lies, Simple Truths: The Psychology of Self Deception.* New York: Simon & Schuster, 1985. This book is about blind spots of the mind—certain kinds of experiences we unconsciously blank out by ignoring or forgetting. Some of these repressions protect us from overly painful experience. Others perpetuate our ignorance. Goleman's prescription is to follow "the path to sanity and survival—somewhere between the two poles of living a life of vital lies and speaking simple truths."

Amy Bjork Harris and Thomas A. Harris. M.D. *Staying OK: How to Maximize Good Feelings and Minimize Bad Ones.* New York: Harper & Row, 1985. How to identify and dispel the oppressive voices from the past that undermine us in the present. The authors prescribe specific steps to examine parental messages recorded when we were children along with the often distorted assumptions we made about them.

Thomas Harris, M.D. I'm O.K., You're O.K.: *A Practical Guide to Transactional Analysis.* New York: Avon, 1982. The bestselling translation and application of Berne's transactional analysis. The book's title stems from the most desirable of the four life positions underlying people's behavior and interpersonal relationships.

Muriel James and Dorothy Jongeward. *Born to Win: Trans-actional Analysis with Gestalt Experiments.* Reading, Mass.: Addison-Wesley, 1971. A highly regarded popularization and application of TA and Frederick Perls' interpretation of gestalt therapy. The book's objective is "discovering and fostering awareness, self-responsibility, and genuineness."

Sidney M. Jourard. *The Transparent Self.* New York: Van Nostrand Renihold, 1964). This book asserts the thesis that we can be healthier, more fully functioning, and more helpful to others if we gain the courage to be our real selves with others. Concealing feelings and thoughts prevents intimate relationships and brings on emotional sickness.

Jut Meininger. *Success through Transactional Analysis.* New York: Grosset and Dunlap, 1973. A sound treatment of TA specifically directed to on-the-job relationships. It offers insights and techniques by which one can deal with people problems in organizations and change unsuccessful personal patterns of behavior.

Carl Rogers. *Client-Centered Therapy.* Boston: Houghton Mifflin, 1951. The basic text on the theory and practice of client-centered psychotherapy, from which the ideas of acceptance and active listening were derived.

_____. *On Becoming a Person.* Boston: Houghton Mifflin, 1963. A collection of Rogers' papers concerning his thinking about therapy, education, the self, the healthy individual, and the helping relationship.

Also Worthwhile

Linda Adams. *Effectiveness Training for Women.* New York: Wyden Books, 1979.

Joe Alexander. *Dare to Change: How to Program Yourself to Success.* New York: New American Library, 1984.

Eastwood Atwater. *Psychology of Adjustment: Personal Growth in a Changing World.* Englewood Cliffs, N.J.: Prentice-Hall, 1983.

Alban N. Bacchus. *Personal Wellness and Self-Realization.* Washington, D.C.: Oryn Publications, 1985.

Eric Berne. *What Do You Say After You Say Hello?: The Psychology of Human Destiny.* New York: Grove Press, 1972.

Richard Nelson Bolles. *What Color Is Your Parachute?: A Practical Manual for Job Hunters and Career Changers.* 2nd ed. Berkeley, Calif.: Ten Speed Press, 1984.

Paul J. Brouwer. "The Power to See Ourselves," *Harvard Business Review,* 2, no. 6 (Nov.–Dec., 1964).

Leo Buscaglia, *Living, Loving and Learning.* Thorofare, N.J.: Slack, 1982.

Wayne Dyer. *The Sky's the Limit.* New York: Simon & Schuster, 1980.

_____. *Your Erroneous Zones.* New York: Avon, 1977.

Martha Friedman. *Overcoming Your Fear of Success.* New York: Sea View Press, 1980.

M. Robert Gardner. *Self-Inquiry.* Boston: Little, Brown, 1983.

Wendell Johnson, *People in Quandaries: The Semantics of Personal Adjustment.* New York: Harper & Row, 1946.

Dorothy Jongeward et al. *Everybody Wins: Transactional Analysis Applied to Organizations.* Reading, Mass.: Addison-Wesley, 1973.

_____ and Dru Scott. *Women as Winners.* Reading, Mass.: Addison-Wesley, 1976.

C.G. Jung, *The Undiscovered Self.* Especially chapter 4, "The Individual's Understanding of Himself," New York: New American Library, 1957.

Gordon MacDonald. *Ordering Your Private World.* Chicago: Moody Press, 1984.

Maxwell Maltz, M.D. *Psycho-Cybernetics.* Englewood Cliffs, N.J.: Prentice-Hall, 1960.

Norman Vincent Peale. *The Power of Positive Thinking.* Englewood Cliffs, N.J.: Prentice-Hall, 1952.

John Powell, S.J. *Why Am I Afraid to Tell You Who I Am?* Chicago: Argus Communications, 1969.

Dru Scott, *How to Put More Time in Your Life.* New York: Rowson Wade, 1980.

Hans Selye, M.D. *Stress Without Distress.* Philadelphia: J.B. Lippincott, 1974.

Carol Tribe. *Self World Understanding: Analysis and Observation Manual.* Dubuque, Iowa: Kendall Hunt Publishing, 1983.

Maurice F. Villiere. *Transactional Analysis at Work: A Guide for Business and Professional People.* Englewood Cliffs: N.J.: Prentice-Hall, 1981.

Abe Wagner. *The Transactional Manager: How to Solve People Problems with Transactional Analysis.* Englewood Cliffs, N.J.: Prentice-Hall, 1981.

Theodora Wells, *Keeping Your Cool Under Fire Communicating Non-Defensively.* New York: McGraw-Hill, 1981.

Internal Cues

Let us now examine some of the ways in which one can acquire valid internal cues—that is, in formation and insights which originate within the individual.

Cues From Psychotherapy.   Although psychotherapy is conducted in a wide variety of ways, its basic purpose is to help the patient (or client) to better understand how his/her self-image, on the one hand, and his/her self, on the other, may be out of alignment. For when the map and the territory are out of sync, the individual's ability to function—to perform adequately as a spouse, parent, student, manager, employee—and to live a creative, productive life can be impaired.

To the extent that the therapy is nondirective or client-centered, it is the individual who engineers any changes in his or her self-image and/or self. Desirably, such changes lead to increased congruity between the two, thus liberating the person from internal conflict. In sum, psychotherapy is a professional mode of reprogramming.

Cues from Active Listening.   But can lay people be helpful to friends and associates? The answer is a guarded yes, provided that the person is not seriously disturbed. But being genuinely helpful sometimes requires a good deal of sensitivity and skill.

Have you ever tried to help someone who seemed unhappy, fearful, angry, envious, guilt-ridden, or insecure, and found yourself drawn rapidly into a quarrel? If so, you have discovered how unhelpful or even downright threatening your well-intentioned aid can be perceived by the other person. Incidentally, it is quite likely that your friend was suffering at the self-image level.

The challenge, then, is to help people who really need assistance but cannot accept it directly because they too readily see the helper as a threatening change agent. Carl Rogers and Richard Farson have proposed a safe and sound approach that they call Active Listening. Their article of the same title appears in this chapter. In essence, their method consists of helping beleaguered persons to help themselves. If any change of self-image is necessary, the individual will conduct it—the changer and the changee will be one and the same.

It would be redundant to preview the article here, but these suggestions may increase its value to you:

1.   The article's title, "Active Listening," may be misleading. Active listening is not simply attentive, careful listening. Therapeutic or empathic listening would be more apt.

2.   The authors distinguish between sympathy and empathy. To keep on their wavelength, you might recall the Greek roots of those terms:

Sym (with) + *pathos* (feeling). When you sympathize with others you feel with them—you literally share their feeling. If they are grief-stricken, you are sad, too. If they are enraged, you are angry as well.

Em (in) + *pathos* (feeling). When you empathize with others you do not share their emotion, but you do understand how they feel. You imaginatively project yourself into their solitary confinement cells and accurately perceive what they are experiencing.

3.)   Probably the most important skill for the listener to develop is the ability to determine whether the speaker needs external inputs (information, data, assistance, authority, advice—something that the listener can provide directly or help the speaker find) or internal inputs (feedback of the speaker's own thoughts, feelings, values, convictions, which may help the speaker understand oneself better).

One major caveat is to avoid giving internal inputs when external inputs are needed, and vice versa. To wit, these facetious but relevant illustrations:

Scene: A business office
Needed: External input
Provided: Internal input

Sam Salesman, visiting a customer firm for the first time, stops by Oscar Obtuse's open office door: "Pardon me, can you tell me where the men's room is?"

Oscar replies, "If I sense your feelings accurately, sir—you're experiencing some internal pressures, aren't you?"

Even in this liberated age, I fear Sam's response would be unprintable!

Scene: Same
Needed: Internal input
Provided: External input

Bristling with rage, Section D's supervisor, Mary, stomps into Oscar's office and with clenched teeth and obvious restraint says: "Boss, can you tell me precisely who has the responsibility for Section D?"

Oscar rummages through his cluttered desk, pulls out a yellowing organization chart, and benignly smiles,: "Well, it looks like your name is in that box, Mary."

Aside from Archie Bunker, also fictional, it is difficult to conceive of anyone as dense as Oscar. But the distinction between internal and external input needs is not always so obvious as in Sam's and Mary's cases—especially when the individual's problems require both kinds of inputs.

Although it is demanding, active listening can be an exceedingly useful communication skill for managers, teachers, parents, spouses, and others who want to help effectively.

Cues from Videotaping.   The advent of closed-circuit television taping has opened a unique and exciting avenue for providing cues at the self-image level. Videotaping has important advantages over certain other modes of feedback.

Authenticity.   Technically, videotaping offers highly valid and immediate feedback. I blush for the many times TV's instant replay proved my calls incorrect—invariably calls I had made in favor of my team or player.

Visual Feedback.   Videotape is obviously superior to audiotape (alone) in that it adds the visual dimension.

Objectivity.   A major advantage of videotaping over the mirror is that one can monitor oneself other than in real time. Thus, one can study oneself dispassionately and repeatedly as one appeared at previous times. The motion picture has the same capability, but videotape's economy and ease of operation—no film-developing time, simple lighting needs, the operator can be trained in the rudiments in a matter of minutes—places it in a class by itself.

Permanence.   Videotapes can be stored indefinitely for replay at a subsequent date. Among other applications, this permits the assessment of skill development by comparisons of a person's performances over intervals of time.

Impact.   Videotape gets to you! I am 15 pounds lighter than I used to be. Once I saw how I filled up the screen, my self-deceptions disintegrated. While feedback from others can sometimes be challenged and dismissed as ax-grinding, there is really no defense against videotape.

I recall a public accounting firm for which I conducted a seminar. Following our first video exercise one young CPA, who sported a prominent mustache, watched a replay of himself and promptly disappeared! Twenty minutes later he returned without his bushy appendage! He explained that his wife had repeatedly complained about his adornment but that he had discounted her feedback until he saw the walrus on TV!

Safety. Although videotape makes an impact, it is nontraumatic. Recall that threatening cues are generally those that embody the prospect of big, sudden, uncontrolled change. Videotape feedback involves none of those characteristics. Granted that you may have a few mild surprises concerning your appearance and behavior. But you will be quite able to accept the feedback largely because you (rather than some external agent or event) are providing it, albeit through the aegis of an electronic instrument.

In this vein, I will never forget Big George. Along with a group of fellow bankers, he came to one of my seminars. The group as a whole was splendid, as have been the large majority of the people I have met in my 25 years of teaching courses and conducting seminars. But Big George was a rousing exception. The man was incredibly arrogant and insensitive. The other members of the group were thoroughly disgusted with him. But they were powerless to feedback to him because George's defenses rendered him impervious to insult!

I recall one exchange in particular. George had just made a typically inane remark, and one exasperated participant looked him directly in the eyes and said in a voice dripping with sarcasm: "George, some people are fatheads, aren't they?"

George smiled knowingly, obviously assuming that the comment had been directed elsewhere, and replied earnestly: "You're damned right, Harry!"

Big George had the hide of an elephant—and I was crawling the walls! My job included helping people gain some self-image validity, and nothing seemed to be working with George.

Fortunately, I had four full days with the group and the availability of videotape. I used it generously. And, to be fair, George did participate. But I could detect no change. Finally, the seminar was concluded and many of the participants queued up to say good-bye to me—and Big George was in line!

I waited in some trepidation because George outweighed me by 80 pounds! Eventually he appeared, grasped my hand with both of his (a double handshake must be significant body language!), stared directly into my eyes, and said softly: "Thanks, Bill"—and left . . .leaving me with a folded-up note in my palm.

With superhuman restraint, I pocketed the note and bade farewell to my remaining seminarians. At long last they were all gone and I retrieved the note. It was a poem evidently composed by Big George. In stubby-penciled block letters:

> *There was a man that I knew well,*
> *I knew him to a tee,*
> *His looks, manners, voice, and dress*
> *Until I saw me—on TV.*

That's no Shakespearean sonnet, and I may be guilty of wishful thinking, but that was so much more of a response than I ever expected from Big George! And if, indeed, he did receive feedback he could accept, that his marvelous defenses would not shield out, I don't believe they came from me or even from the group—but from the videotape. *He* put that feedback on the tape, and from himself he could take it!

One need not be a callous boor in order to profit from videotape. If you are interested in receiving safe, authentic, impactful feedback, I enthusiastically recommend that you grab any opportunities to get before the camera, particularly as you are interacting with others, and then view the replay.

These two suggestions may add value to your TV experiences:

Cosmetic Effect.   If you have never or rarely seen yourself on tape, you will probably have to overcome the do-I-really-look-like-that? syndrome. You are likely to be quite enthralled with your physical appearance and mannerisms. Accordingly, I like to give my people the option of viewing their replays a number of times. Once the cosmetic effect has been dissipated, they are ready for more challenging exercises in such areas as conflict resolution, problem solving, decision making, communication skills, role behavior, and conference leadership and participation.

Relevant Activity.   Some people who are unaccustomed to videotaping may be initially uneasy and overly aware of the camera. A good antidote is to be so involved with the activity that one is oblivious to the taping and free to be oneself. Thus, I try to arrange to have people doing things that are directly related to their needs and interests.

For example, I recently conducted a seminar for sales managers of wholesale grocery products from H. J. Heinz, Pillsbury, Coca-Cola, Beatrice Foods, Kellogg, General Foods, and so forth. They sell at the district levels to A&P, National, Ralph's, Safeway, Jewel, Kroger. To add reality, I hired three professional buyers. The latter were real-life customers (or their counterparts) of the salespersons.

Then came the role-playing. A salesperson would enter a buyer's "office" and proceed to make a pitch. (The salesperson had been asked to bring his/her tools—samples, ads, displays, data, and so on.) The buyers had been requested to be themselves and to respond to the salespersons as they normally would on the job. A camera recorded the interview while a small audience—two of the salesperson's colleagues, the other two buyers, and I—monitored the meeting in another room.

After the session ended, the salesperson joined us in the monitor room, received our critique (which centered on what to look for in the replay), and finally saw the replay. The next salesperson then interviewed a second buyer, and the process continued until each salesperson had interviewed each of the buyers. Postseminar evaluations indicated that the salespersons regarded the videotaping as exceptionally helpful largely because of the realism of the activity. Granted that it was role-playing—a simulated sales interview—but the players were portraying their real-life roles.

An acid test for determining whether those taped have been thoroughly involved and relatively unconscious of the camera? If they heartily resent being cut off at the end of their allotted camera time: "Get lost—we want to finish our business!" I can assume that the videotaping has been unobtrusive.

Cues from Personal Stocktaking.   Concluding this list of techniques for gaining a more valid self-image through internal inputs, I recommend two approaches to personal stocktaking. One is periodic—usually annually—and the other is current—as the occasion arises.

The Personal Inventory.   Basic requirements: A pen, a pad of paper or a notebook, an hour of solitude, and a generous measure of self-honesty.

Caption page 1 thus: (your name): Who is he (or she)?[11] (date)

Then answer the following questions as objectively as possible:

1.   What are his (or her) principal strengths? (In what one, two or three areas are you especially strong and able? This is no time for false modesty—no other people will ever see this document unless you let them. So, what do you do well? Where do you *really shine?*)

2.   What are his (or her) principal deficiencies? (No point in pulling your punches here either. Restrain your shame or guilt—in what one, two, or three significant areas do you fall short?)

3.   What are his (or her) values? (What do you really treasure? What are your priorities? What comes first with you? Second? Third? Wealth- fame- love-food-education-power-accomplishment- security-health-art-sex-work-religion-family-career-? If you had one week to live—and knew it—what would you be certain to do? Caution: List your values as they are, not as you feel they should be.)

---

[11]Suggestion: Refer to yourself as "he" (or "she") rather than "I" to help maintain your role as impartial observer.

4.   What are his (or her) principles? (What do you believe in? What maxims have you gleaned from experience that you truly accept? Again, these are the guidelines that you actually adhere to, not the ideals that you wish you could measure up to. Don't list the golden rule, for example, unless you genuinely buy it and try to abide by it.)

5.   What games does he (or she) play with his (or her):

—boss?	—spouse?	—teachers?
—subordinates?	—children?	—siblings?
—customers?	—parents?	—others?

(What repetitive deceptions do you attempt to play with other people? Do you feel compelled to keep up the game-playing, or can you risk a gameless, more intimate relationship? Suggest that you review Berne or Harris or James and Jongeward [listed earlier in this chapter] to help you answer this question.)

6.   What are his (or her) most important *"hangups"?* Specifically, what, if anything does he (or she) plan to *do about them,* and when and how does he (or she) plan to do it? (This question will be discussed in more detail in the next section.)

7.   Within the next year, what one or two attainable things could he (or she) do in order to wind up the year liking himself (or herself) more?

When you have completed the Inventory, lock it up so that no one, especially yourself, will see it. Then circle a date on your calendar a year hence to the day. When that day finally rolls around, repeat the Inventory, using the same format. Then—but not until then—get out your first edition and compare it with the one you have just written.

I make you two promises: (1) Provided that you were honest with yourself on both inventories, you will find some fascinating comparisons and changes! (2) If you prepare your Inventory twice—that is, two years in a row—you will find this annual assessment so rewarding that you will be sold on continuing it for the rest of your life!

The Personal Inventory is akin to the electrocardiogram in a sense. Cardiologists say that a single EKG has limited value. They would prefer a series of readouts spaced over a period of time to get a more accurate conception of the trends that are occurring. This enhances their ability to predict and thus to prescribe and control.

The objective of the Personal Inventory is similar. If you have a readout on yourself now and another a year from now you will have some basis for predicting rather than blindly, wishfully guessing how that readout will look in the third year. And accurate predictions enable you to control more of your personal development.

What is your philosophy of action? Do you prefer that life more or less happens to you—or do you want to call more of the shots? If you are inclined toward Socrates' sentiment that the "unexamined life is not worth living," you may find the Personal Inventory or your adaptation of it extremely worthwhile.

The Crisis Journal.   The Personal Inventory lends itself to a long-term, periodic self-assessment. But we can also capitalize on the immediate, specific, concrete learning opportunities that we call crises. I don't mean only life-and-death matters, but the times when we are frightened, infuriated, embarrassed, disillusioned, jealous, bewildered, disgusted, depressed, or, in general, roundly upset.

These distressing episodes can be acute learning experiences, provided that we treat them as such—if we can consider them in the dual senses that the Chinese do, as both dangers and opportunities. Accordingly, I recommend the *Crisis Journal* as a technique for gaining self-image knowledge during the periods when we are being tested.

Your only investment is a small notebook that you can carry with you constantly. Then the next time you find yourself in the midst of a crisis—you're uptight, offended, worried, guilt-stricken, angry—get off by yourself, cool off a bit (but not too much), and record[12] your answer to this question: What happened? Who, including myself, said or did what?—or failed to say or do what?—and why?

Important: Do not try to be rational or objective. Because at this moment your passions have taken over. Your IQ has temporarily dropped about 75 points, and you are an analytic imbecile! In transactional analysis terms, your Parent and your Child are having a raging battle and your Adult is out to lunch—powerless, ineffectual.

Do the one thing you can do now—and cannot do later: Record your data. Capture the rampant emotionality, the distorted value judgments, the defensiveness and irrationality erupting within you. Spill your guts as fully and uninhibitedly as you would to a thoroughly trusted confidant. You can expect two important benefits from this disgorging:

1. *Catharsis:* You will feel better immediately. Granted, the ventilating will not dissipate all the bad vibes, but it will alleviate some of the most acute discomfort and tension and, not incidentally, help restore some of your objectivity and judgment.
2. *Authenticity:* The primary objective of answering the what-happened question, however, is to record your current feelings accurately for future analysis. This can rarely be done as validly in retrospect. Who has not been embroiled in a heated argument only to find that later he or she was incapable of reconstructing the chain of events?

---

[12]Speaking into a tape recorder would be even better, for this would preserve your vocal cues, which could communicate an additional dimension of emotional information to you when you are able to listen dispassionately. I suggested the notebook only because of its portability, for you never know when you will need it.

This is because you are asking your Adult to report on what happened. Sorry, your Adult was probably so contaminated by your Parent or Child or both that it is unable to give an accurate account.

The next step is to cool off enough for your Adult function to return. This may require anywhere from 10 minutes to a day or longer, depending upon you and the circumstances. Then get out your *Crisis Journal*, read the recorded information, and write answers to two additional questions:

1. *Was I defensive then?* Was my self-image somehow threatened, and accordingly, was I compelled to protect it? If your honest answer is yes (which is highly likely), answer the next question.

2. *What part of my self-image was I defending?* What facet of my self-image was contradicted (threatened with change) by the external cues (usually what others said and did)? To what part of me did the cues say, "No, you're not what you think you are"? Is this aspect of my self-concept, then, so frail and insecure that I simply cannot bear to have it challenged and thus am driven to throw up my defenses?

This completes the project insofar as Crisis Number One is concerned. Just keep your journal at the ready for the next crisis.

The first step of the *Crisis Journal* technique calls for one, in the throes of a crisis, to do something constructive—specifically, to record current emotional data for subsequent processing. This is contrary to how most of us habitually respond to crises. Typically and understandably we immerse ourselves in the passions of the moment. Therefore, for the first few times that you attempt to apply the *Journal* technique, it will seem unnatural—at the time you won't feel like doing it.

Thus, you must convince yourself in advance that this is the best and, in fact, the only time that you can capture your feelings and perceptions so accurately. Resolve that you will temporarily resist the urge to indulge yourself. As the *Crisis Journal* begins to produce insights and self-understanding, you will find the technique increasingly easy to use.

When does the payoff occur? That depends—upon the type of person you are, upon the kinds and frequency of your crises, upon your skills in recording and analyzing your behavior and feelings, and so on. (Those skills, incidentally, will sharpen with practice.) A reasonable expectation is that the technique will begin to bear fruit after about a half-dozen episodes.

On a day when you are feeling particularly sturdy and willing to face reality—when your Adult is definitely in charge—read through the half-dozen accounts, looking for patterns, for threads that seem to run through most if not all of the vignettes. The chances are that you will find some. And those recurrent themes can be valuable clues for you because they may reveal some aspects of yourself about which you are *not* totally sure—some fears and shortcomings that you have not recognized or admitted to yourself. Most likely, those feelings have been repressed.

The process usually occurs like this: Everyone has his or her own inadequacies and insecurities. There is no Superman or Wonder Woman other than in fiction. Such feelings can be uncomfortable, sometimes decidedly so, especially if one erroneously assumed that he or she is uniquely afflicted. As pain-avoidance organisms we often resort to defense mechanisms such as repression to diminish the discomfort.

Repression (semideliberate forgetting) consists of progressively squeezing the uncomfortable thoughts and feelings down and down until they submerge just below the level of consciousness. Then they just seem to go away and cease to bother us—consciously. But they never do go away—they are still there, lurking in that subterranean cellar, haunting us, gnawing at us in that nebulous, ill-defined, unscratchable-itch kind of way that we experience as vague feelings of guilt, anxiety, irritability, unease, depression, and so on.

These ghosts are our unconscious hangups—the ones we have hidden from ourselves because we have never been quite able to face up to them.

The objective, using the clues gleaned from the *Crisis Journal*, is to dredge up those hangups one at a time; to appraise them in the light of *today's* competence, strength, wisdom, and resources; and to decide what to do about them. They will fall along a continuum ranging from the whippables on over to the acknowledgeables—with many gradations between them.

The whippables are the hangups that we can now overcome because, having grown, we are bigger, stronger, and smarter than we were when the bugbears were too much for us. But if we have concealed our fear of a whippable by suppressing our consciousness of it, we cannot beat it until we bring it to the surface again and comprehend what it is that we must conquer.

For one example of a whippable, I cite my own experience. You may not be afflicted with this particular malady, but I can assure you that innumerable people are. They are the legion of poor souls who have a morbid dread of getting up and giving a talk before other people. Untechnically, this is called stagefright and I was a prime victim.

In my junior year in high school, I pulled every conceivable string to get out of that required public speaking course. And I succeeded! I didn't have to take it—what a narrow escape!

But in my senior year, I made a grievous error. I somehow got elected to class office; then realized I would have to give a 30-second acceptance speech before all 600 of my classmates! On the day of that meeting, I was very uncoincidentally home and sick, sick both ways to be clinical about it! And I couldn't get better until I personally called the school to be sure that the accursed meeting was past history. The conversation (which should have won me an Academy Award) went like this:

Me I'm really under the weather today . . . I think I'm going to die . . . but the worst thing is that I guess I'm not going to able to give this terrific speech . . . I've been looking forward to giving . . . .

Voice You already missed it . . . assembly period's over!

Me Oh, wow, that's terrible (this is the great acting part). Well, I guess we have our disappointments . . .well, . . . click!

Only then could I get my stomach back to where it was supposed to be. And that monkey rode my back for six long years—three in the Army and three more in college. Finally, I pulled myself by the scruff of the neck and said, "Haney, when are you going to face up to this idiotic, juvenile fear—when are you going to start to grow up?" And the resounding answer was a feeble, "Well, . . ." and I went out and did perhaps the most courageous thing I've ever done in my life—I enrolled in a public speaking course. And it was terrifying at first. My speeches were horrible and I was quaking in my boots . . . but I was finally beginning to like it! To face up to one of your bugbears, to get a toehold, to make a little progress, that is joy, unadulterated joy.

So that's an example of a whippable. In fact, I've made my living the last 30 years getting up and giving talks before groups of people. And in all honesty I have to ask myself, would I be in this profession of meeting with groups and still getting a great deal of satisfaction from doing it, if that stagefright nightmare had not been part of my history?

At the other end of the spectrum are the hangups that the individual still cannot and perhaps never will conquer, but perhaps can acknowledge and accept. An example of an acknowledgeable is offered by Marie, a 45-year-old mother, who describes an event that occurred 16 years earlier:

We went to the park for a Sunday excursion. I was sitting in a swing with our eight-month-old, Judy. Our 2½-year-old, Sharon, was climbing on a jungle gym. Our five-year-old, Larry, was on a merry-go-round. My husband was about 15 feet away, watching Sharon as she climbed. She reached the top, stepped across to the center post, slipped, and fell headfirst, landing on rocks at the bottom. She was unconscious; she had several head lacerations; her right shoulder, elbow, and knee were terribly scratched; and we thought she might have a broken neck.

Her father picked her up; we yelled for Larry; I carried Judy, and we ran to the car and on to the hospital. . . . She regained consciousness.

X rays were taken. She was stitched up, and we were told to watch her for any signs of concussion. We all went home. Sharon's only concern was her painful but superficial elbow and knee injuries. She seemed fine.

The next day, however, the doctor called and told us that Sharon had a fine-line skull fracture. But it was in a complete circle, so she would have to be watched carefully so that the area could not be hit again—risking the fracture slipping, chipping, or causing some other type of damage. It would take about six weeks to heal.

She *was* watched carefully. There was no hard playing, no climbing of any kind allowed, including stairs—I carried her. Even poor Larry was restricted from vigorous activity.

Over the next two years I found myself looking for excuses for not going to certain places where the children would climb or be in dangerous areas. And this went on for all three children—not just Sharon. If they looked as if they were going to go up something, I managed to be there and direct them elsewhere. I didn't really realize I was doing this.

One day, while looking through the kitchen window, I saw Sharon heading for the very climbable tree in our backyard, and I headed for the back door to ward her off. Suddenly I stopped as if I had hit a brick wall and heard the words, *"Stop doing that!"* To this day I don't know if I actually said this or heard a voice. But the words were there: "Stop doing that, let those kids grow." I ran back to our bedroom, shut the door, and just sat. I don't recall even thinking at that time. After a while I took a deep breath and went back to the kitchen. I didn't look out the window. Soon Sharon came in, unhurt, very happy, but I didn't ask her if she made it up the tree. I still don't know if she did.

Since then there have been plenty of trees, mountains, and other danger areas that the three have gotten into—and out of—in their manner. *I still haven't lost my fear.* But I have learned that they have their needs to climb and grow and that I can't stop them—nor do I want to.

All that was 16 years ago, but occasionally I have reminders. Larry once called me from boot camp: "Hi, Mom, guess what I'm doing? Skydiving!"

Mom took a deep breath: "That's great, Larry—that's something I've always wanted to do!" It's *not* what I've always wanted to do, and it never will be. But he will never know how that old fear grabbed at my heart again.

Marie, by her own admission, has not conquered her fear. But she has done the next best thing. She has been able to acknowledge its existence and to realize how her overgeneralized fear was causing her to smother her kids.

Let us return to the analogy of the stained-glass window in one's solitary confinement cell. The window, one's frame of reference, is composed of a myriad of colored, distorting lenses. Its most significant lens or, more accurately, complex of lenses is one's self-image. Repressed fears and inadequacies may be the most acutely deceptive lenses of all. I can personally vouch for that assertion. I still recall how that fear of public speaking contaminated my perceptions—my contact with people, my career plans—everything tainted by that one corrupting lens. Thus, when one exposes a hangup he or she is able at long last to recognize the existence of the lens.

If the bugbear is essentially whippable, and the individual does indeed conquer it, or cut it down to size, this is tantamount to plucking the lens out of one's window. If the best that one can do is to acknowledge and accommodate the bugbear, then one can at least understand how the lens has been coloring his or her perception of reality and learn to compensate for the distortion—as in correcting for a bent pencil in a glass of water.

Whether by removing the lens or correcting for its distortion, one clarifies a frame of reference to that extent. Thus one is able to perceive reality more realistically and to deal with it more appropriately and intelligently. This is the bottom line result for which the foregoing list of external and internal cues have been proposed.

SUMMARY

This chapter began with the premise that a person in a responsible position needs to have an exceptionally realistic self-image (ERSI) in order to function well. With an ERSI, one is liberated from constantly expending energy for self-image defense; more capable of maintaining and increasing the validity of one's self-image; able to understand, predict, and cope with others more effectively; better able to distinguish valid from invalid inputs; and more likely to select realistic personal goals.

For those who wish to make a concerted effort to attain and maintain an ERSI, I offered a three-step program:

1. Make a commitment—decide that you really want to know yourself better and that you are willing to pay the price (time, effort, temporary unease) which may be required.
2. Learn to recognize and to reduce your defenses against the cues from reality.
3. Receive and evaluate those cues in order to assess how your current self-image and your authentic self may be incongruent.

The major categories of external cues (feedback from outside one's skin) included feedback from others (the mechanism of which was discussed in detail in connection with the Johari Grid concept), psychometric instruments, and readings. Internal cues can be acquired through psychotherapy, active listening, videotape playback, and personal stocktaking techniques such as the *Personal Inventory* and the *Crisis Journal*.[13]

The ultimate objective, again, was an exceptionally realistic self-image and a substantial measure of emotional maturity—high rewards. There was no promise that the venture would be without effort or discomfort. For, to augment the Bible, "The truth shall make you free . . . but for a while it may make you a bit miserable.

---

[13]For more suggestions for better understanding oneself, see Richard Hatch, *Communicating in Business* (Chicago: Science Research Associates, 1977), chapter 11, "Job Applications: The Planning Stage," and chapter 12, "Job Applications: The Communicating Stage" and Anita Taylor et al, *Communicating* (Englewood Cliffs, N.J.: Prentice-Hall, 1977), chapter 4, "How We See Ourselves: Self-Concept, the Central Attitude System." See also the books by Atwater (1983), Bacchus (1984), and Gardner (1000) listed on page 134.

DISCUSSION QUESTIONS

1. The central premise of Chapter 5 is that an ERSI is required in order to communicate with or deal with others well. What is the rationale for this assertion? Do you accept it?

2. What do you think of the five advantages associated with attaining and maintaining an ERSI? Do you agree with them? Are there other advantages that are equally or even more important? Are there disadvantages in possessing an ERSI?

3. Lew Sarett said, "Everyone needs . . . a block of granite to stand on and a star to guide him." What is so important about the star? About the block of granite?

4. "Desirable reprogramming requires that the inputs be both valid and tolerable." Why?

5. "The most important single reason most of us do not understand ourselves better lies in our own internal fortifications that seal us off from contrary, disturbing cues from reality." Do you agree? Disagree? Why?

6. Should the public area dominate the Johari Grid?

7. Is it best to reduce the hidden area of the Johari Grid to nil?

8. Is it best to reduce the blind area of the Johari Grid to nil?

9. Since one's unconscious area is known neither to the Johari Grid's owner nor to the person to whom he or she is relating, can that area be reduced only through psychotherapy?

10. What is the best way to cope with a pumper?

11. Your optimal public area depends upon *you*, the *other* person, and the *environment* in which the two of you are interrelating. Do you accept this assertion? Would you delete any of these factors? Add others?

12. What do you think of TA? Is it a valid construct? Do you feel that it might be helpful to you? If so, how?

13. What do you think of the author's use of psychometric instruments? Can they really be helpful as focus sharpeners and search-area-narrowers?

14. The author states that readings, per se, do not provide self-image feedback. How, then, can they be helpful?

15. Psychotherapy's basic purpose is to help the patient (or client) bring his or her self-image and self into greater congruity. What do you think of this view of psychotherapy?

16. Active Listening—in what ways is it like or unlike nondirective psychotherapy?

17. Why is feedback from videotape considered safe?

18. How do you feel about doing the Personal Inventory? Eager? Curious? Queasy? Indifferent?

19. Probably the most difficult step in the *Crisis Journal* technique is answering the first question: *What happened?* How can you develop skill in executing this step?

20. If one cannot overcome a fear or weakness, what is the value of merely acknowledging it?

ARTICLE

Active Listening*

Carl R. Rogers and Richard E. Farson

The Meaning of Active Listening

One basic responsibility of the supervisor or executive is the development, adjustment, and integration of individual employees. He or she tries to develop employee potential, delegate responsibility, and achieve cooperation. To do so, he must have, among other abilities, the ability to listen intelligently and carefully to those with whom he works.

There are, however, many kinds of listening skills. The lawyer, for example, when questioning a witness, listens for contradictions, irrelevancies, errors, and weaknesses. But this is not the kind of listening skill we are concerned with in this booklet. The lawyer usually is not listening in order to help the witness adjust or cooperate or produce. On the other hand, we will be concerned with listening skills which *will help* employees gain a clearer understanding of their situations, take responsibility, and cooperate with each other.

Two Examples

The kind of listening we have in mind is called "active listening." It is called "active" because the listener has a very definite responsibility. He does not passively absorb the words which are spoken, but he actively tries to grasp the facts and the feelings in what he hears, to help the speaker work out his own problems.

To get a fuller picture of what is meant by active listening, let us consider two different approaches to the same work problem.

Example No. 1

> **Foreman** Hey, Al, I don't get this production order. We can't handle this run today. What do they think we are?
>
> **Supervisor** But that's the order. So get it out as soon as you can. We're under terrific pressure this week.
>
> **Foreman** Don't they know we're behind schedule already because of that press breakdown?

---

* Reproduced by special permission of the authors and The University of Chicago's Industrial Relations Center.

Supervisor Look, Kelly, I don't decide what goes on upstairs. I just have to see that the work gets out and that's what I'm gonna do.

Foreman The guys aren't gonna like this.

Supervisor That's something you'll have to work out with them, not me.

Example No. 2

Foreman Hey, Ross, I don't get this production order. We can't handle this run today. What do they think we are?

Supervisor Sounds like you're pretty sore about it, Kelly.

Foreman I sure am. We were just about getting back to schedule after that press breakdown. Now this comes along.

Supervisor As if you didn't have enough work to do, huh?

Foreman Yeah. I don't know how I'm gonna tell the guys about this.

Supervisor Hate to face 'em with it now, is that it?

Foreman: I really do. They're under a real strain today. Seems like everything we do around here is rush, rush.

Supervisor I guess you feel like it's unfair to load anything more on them.

Foreman Well, yeah. I know there must be plenty of pressure on everybody up the line, but—well, if that's the way it is. . .guess I'd better get the word to 'em.

There are obviously many differences between these two examples. The main one, however, is that Ross, the supervisor in the second example, is using the active-listening approach. He is listening and responding in a way that makes it clear that he appreciates both the meaning and the feeling behind what Kelly is saying.

Active listening does not necessarily mean long sessions spent listening to grievances, personal or otherwise. It is simply a way of approaching those problems which arise out of the usual day-to-day events of any job.

To be effective, active listening must be firmly grounded in the basic attitudes of the user. We cannot employ it as a technique if our fundamental attitudes are in conflict with its basic concepts. If we try, our behavior will be empty and sterile and our associates will be quick to recognize this. Until we can demonstrate a spirit which genuinely respects the potential worth of the individual, which considers his rights and trusts his capacity for self-direction, we cannot begin to be effective listeners.

What We Achieve by Listening

Active listening is an important way to bring about changes in people. Despite the popular notion that listening is a passive approach, clinical and research evidence clearly shows that sensitive listening is a most effective agent for individual personality change and group development. Listening brings about changes in people's attitudes toward themselves and others, and also brings about changes in their basic values and personal philosophy. People who have been listened to in this new and special way become more emotionally mature, more open to their experiences, less defensive, more democratic, and less authoritarian.

When people are listened to sensitively, they tend to listen to themselves with more care and make clear exactly what they are feeling and thinking. Group members tend to listen more to each other, become less argumentative, more ready to incorporate other points of view. Because listening reduces the threat of having one's ideas criticized, the person is better able to see them for what they are, and is more likely to feel that his contributions are worthwhile.

Not the least important result of listening is the change that takes place within the listener himself. Besides the fact that listening provides more information than any other activity, it builds deep, positive relationships and tends to alter constructively the attitudes of the listener. Listening is a growth experience.

These, then, are some of the worthwhile results we can expect from active listening. But how do we go about this kind of listening? How do we become active listeners?

How to Listen

Active listening aims to bring about changes in people. To achieve this end, it relies upon definite techniques—things to do and things to avoid doing. Before discussing these techniques, however, we should first understand why they are effective. To do so, we must understand how the individual personality develops.

The Growth of the Individual

Through all of our lives, from early childhood on, we have learned to think of ourselves in certain, very definite ways. We have built up pictures of ourselves. Sometimes these self-pictures are pretty realistic but at other times they are not. For example, an overage, overweight lady may fancy herself a youthful, ravishing siren, or an awkward teenager regard himself as a star athlete.

All of us have experiences which fit the way we need to think about ourselves. These we accept. But it is much harder to accept experiences which don't fit. And sometimes, if it is very important for us to hang on to this self-picture, we don't accept or admit these experiences at all.

These self-pictures are not necessarily attractive. A man, for example, may regard himself as incompetent and worthless. He may feel that he is doing his job poorly in spite of favorable appraisals by the company. As long as he has these feelings about himself he must deny any experiences which would seem not to fit this self-picture, in this case any that might indicate to him that he is competent. It is so necessary for him to maintain this self-picture that he is threatened by anything which would tend to change it. Thus, when the company raises his salary, it may seem to him only additional proof that he is a fraud. He must hold onto this self-picture, because, bad or good, it's the only thing he has by which he can identify himself.

This is why direct attempts to change this individual or change his self-picture are particularly threatening. He is forced to defend himself or to completely deny the experience. This denial of experience and defense of the self-picture tend to bring on rigidity of behavior and create difficulties in personal adjustment.

The active-listening approach, on the other hand, does not present a threat to the individual's self-picture. He does not have to defend it. He is able to explore it, see it for what it is, and make his own decision as to how realistic it is. And he is then in a position to change.

If I want to help a man reduce his defensiveness and become more adaptive, I must try to remove the threat of myself as his potential changer. As long as the atmosphere is threatening, there can be no effective communication. So I must create a climate which is neither critical, evaluative, nor moralizing. It must be an atmosphere of equality and freedom, permissiveness and understanding, acceptance and warmth. It is in this climate and this climate only that the individual feels safe enough to incorporate new experiences and new values into his concept of himself. Let's see how active listening helps to create this climate.

What to Avoid

When we encounter a person with a problem, our usual response is to try to change his way of looking at things—to get him to see his situation the way we see it, or would like him to see it. We plead, reason, scold, encourage, insult, prod—anything to bring about a change in the desired direction, that is, in the direction we want him to travel. What we seldom realize, however, is that, under these circumstances, we are usually responding to *our own* needs to see the world in certain ways. It is always difficult for us to tolerate and understand actions which are different from the ways in which *we* believe *we* should act. If, however, we can free ourselves from the need to influence and direct others in our own paths, we enable ourselves to listen with understanding, and thereby employ the most potent available agent of change.

One problem the listener faces is that of responding to demands for decisions, judgments, and evaluations. He is constantly called upon to agree or disagree with someone or something. Yet, as he well knows, the question or challenge frequently is a masked expression of feelings or needs which the speaker is far more anxious to communicate than he is to have the surface question answered. Because he cannot speak these feelings openly, the speaker must disguise them to himself and to others in an acceptable form. To illustrate, let us examine some typical questions and the type of answers that might best elicit the feeling beneath it.

Employee's question	Listener's answer
Just whose responsibility is the toolroom?	Do you feel that someone is challenging your authority in there?
Don't you think younger able people should be promoted before senior but less able ones?	It seems to you they should, I take it.
What does the super expect us to do about these broken-down machines?	You're pretty disgusted with those machines, aren't you?
Don't you think I've improved over the last review period?	Sounds as if you feel like you've really picked up over those last few months.

These responses recognize the questions but leave the way open for the employee to say what is really bothering him. They allow the listener to participate in the problem or situation without shouldering all responsibility for decision making or actions. This is a process of thinking *with* people instead of *for* or *about* them.

Passing judgment, whether critical or favorable, makes free expression difficult. Similarly, advice and information are almost always seen as efforts to change a person and thus serve as barriers to his self-expression and the development of a creative relationship. Moreover, advice is seldom taken and information hardly ever utilized. The eager young trainee probably will not become patient just because he is advised that, "The road to success in business is a long, difficult one, and you must be patient." And it is no more helpful for him to learn that "only one out of a hundred trainees reach top management positions."

Interestingly, it is a difficult lesson to learn that positive *evaluations* are sometimes as blocking as negative ones. It is almost as destructive to the freedom of a relationship to tell a person that he is good or capable or right, as to tell him otherwise. To evaluate him positively "may make it difficult for him to tell of the faults that distress him" or the ways in which he believes he is not competent.

Encouragement also may be seen as an attempt to motivate the speaker in certain directions or hold him off rather than as support. "I'm sure everything will work out OK" is not a helpful response to the person who is deeply discouraged about a problem.

In other words, most of the techniques and devices common to human relationships are found to be of little use in establishing the type of relationship we are seeking here.

What to Do

Just what does active listening entail, then? Basically, it requires that we get inside the speaker, that we grasp, *from his point of view*, just what it is he is communicating to us. More than that, we must convey to the speaker that we are seeing things from his point of view. To listen actively, then, means that there are several things we must do.

Listen for Total Meaning.   Any message a person tries to get across usually has two components: the *content* of the message and the *feeling* or attitude underlying this content. Both are important, both give the message *meaning*. It is this total meaning of the message that we try to understand. For example, a machinist comes to his foreman and says, "I've finished that lathe set-up." This message has obvious content and perhaps calls upon the foreman for another work assignment. Suppose, on the other hand, that he says, "Well, I'm finally finished with that damned lathe set-up." The content is the same but the total meaning of the message has changed—and changed in an important way for both the foreman and the worker. Here sensitive listening can facilitate the relationship. Suppose the foreman were to respond by simply giving another work assignment. Would the employee feel that he had gotten his total message across? Would he feel free to talk to his foreman? Will he feel better about his job, more anxious to do good work on the next assignment?

Now, on the other hand, suppose the foreman were to respond with, "Glad to have it over with, huh?" or "Had a pretty rough time of it?" or "Guess you don't feel like doing anything like that again?" or anything else that tells the worker that he heard and understands. It doesn't necessarily mean that the next work assignment need be changed or that he must spend an hour listening to the worker complain about the set-up problems he encountered. He may do a number of things differently in the light of the new information he has from the worker—but not necessarily. It's just that extra sensitivity on the part of the foreman which can transform an average working climate into a good one.

Respond to Feelings.   In some instances, the content is far less important than the feeling which underlies it. To catch the full flavor or meaning of the message one must respond particularly to the feeling component. If, for instance, our machinist had said, "I'd like to melt this lathe down and make paper clips out of it," responding to content would be obviously absurd. But to respond to his disgust or anger in trying to work with his lathe recognizes the meaning of this message. There are various shadings of these components in the meaning of any message. Each time the listener must try to remain sensitive to the total meaning the message has to the speaker. What is he trying to tell me? What does this mean to him? How does he see this situation?

Note All Cues.   Not all communication is verbal. The speaker's words alone don't tell us everything he is communicating. And hence, truly sensitive listening requires that we become aware of several kinds of communication besides verbal. The way in which a speaker hesitates in his speech can tell us much about his feelings. So too can the inflection of his voice. He may stress certain points loudly and clearly, and may mumble others. We should also note such things as the person's facial expressions, body posture, hand movements, eye movements, and breathing. All these help to convey his total message.

What We Communicate by Listening

The first reaction of most people when they consider listening as a possible method for dealing with human beings is that listening cannot be sufficient in itself. Because it is passive, they feel, listening does not communicate anything to the speaker. Actually, nothing could be farther from the truth.

By consistently listening to a speaker, you are conveying the idea that: "I'm interested in you as a person, and I think that what you feel is important. I respect your thoughts, and even if I don't agree with them, I know that they are valid for you. I feel sure that you have a contribution to make. I'm not trying to change you or evaluate you. I just want to understand you. I think you're worth listening to, and I want you to know that I'm the kind of person you can talk to."

The subtle but most important aspect of this is that it is the *demonstration* of the message that works. While it is most difficult to convince someone that you respect him by *telling* him so, you are much more likely to get this message across by really *behaving* that way—by actually *having* and *demonstrating* respect for this person. Listening does this most effectively.

Like other behavior, listening behavior is contagious. This has implications for all communications problems, whether between two people or within a large organization. To insure good communication between associates up and down the line, one must first take the responsibility for setting a pattern of listening. Just as one learns that anger is usually met with anger, argument with argument, and deception with deception, one can learn that listening can be met with listening. Every person who feels responsibility in a situation can set the tone of the interaction, and the important lesson in this is that any behavior exhibited by one person will eventually be responded to with similar behavior in the other person.

It is far more difficult to stimulate constructive behavior in another person but far more profitable. Listening is one of these constructive behaviors, but if one's attitude is to "wait out" the speaker rather than really listen to him, it will fail. The one who consistently listens with understanding, however, is the one who eventually is most likely to be listened to. If you really want to be heard and understood by another, you can develop him as a potential listener, ready for new ideas, provided you can first develop yourself in these ways and sincerely listen with understanding and respect.

Testing for Understanding

Because understanding another person is actually far more difficult than it at first seems, it is important to test constantly your ability to see the world in the way the speaker sees it. You can do this by reflecting in your own words what the speaker seems to mean by his words and actions. His response to this will tell you whether or not he feels understood. A good rule of thumb is to assume that one never really understands until he can communicate this understanding to the other's satisfaction.

Here is an experiment to test your skill in listening. The next time you become involved in a lively or controversial discussion with another person, stop for a moment and suggest that you adopt this ground rule for continued discussion: Before either participant in the discussion can make a point or express an opinion of his own, he must first restate aloud the previous point or position of the other person. This restatement must be accurate enough to satisfy the speaker before the listener can be allowed to speak for himself.

This is something you could try in your own discussion group. Have someone express himself on some topic of emotional concern to the group. Then, before another member expresses his own feelings and thought, he must rephrase the *meaning* expressed by the previous speaker to that individual's satisfaction. Note the changes in the emotional climate and the quality of the discussion when you try this.

PROBLEMS IN ACTIVE LISTENING

Active listening is not an easy skill to acquire. It demands practice. Perhaps more important, it may require changes in our own basic attitudes. These changes come slowly and sometimes with considerable difficulty. Let us look at some of the major problems in active listening and what can be done to overcome them.

The Personal Risk

To be effective at all in active listening, one must have a sincere interest in the speaker. We all live in glass houses as far as our attitudes are concerned. They always show through. And if we are only making a pretense of interest in the speaker, he will quickly pick this up, either consciously or unconsciously. And once he does, he will no longer express himself freely.

Active listening carries a strong element of personal risk. If we manage to accomplish what we are describing here—to sense deeply the feelings of another person, to understand the meaning his experiences have for him, to see the world as he sees it—we risk being changed ourselves. For example, if we permit ourselves to listen our way into the psychological life of a labor leader or agitator—to get the meaning which life has for him—we risk coming to see the world as he sees it. It is threatening to give up, even momentarily, what we believe and start thinking in someone else's terms. It takes a great deal of inner security and courage to be able to risk one's self in understanding another.

For the supervisor, the courage to take another's point of view generally means that he must see *himself* through another's eyes—he must be able to see himself as others see him. To do this may sometimes be unpleasant, but it is far more *difficult* than unpleasant. We are so accustomed to viewing ourselves in certain ways—to seeing and hearing only what we want to see and hear—that it is extremely difficult for a person to free himself from his needs to see things these ways.

Developing an attitude of sincere interest in the speaker is thus no easy task. It can be developed only by being willing to risk seeing the world from the speaker's point of view. If we have a number of such experiences, however, they will shape an attitude which will allow us to be truly genuine in our interest in the speaker.

Hostile Expressions

The listener will often hear negative, hostile expressions directed at himself. Such expressions are always hard to listen to. No one likes to hear hostile action or words. And it is not easy to get to the point where one is strong enough to permit these attacks without finding it necessary to defend himself or retaliate.

Because we all fear that people will crumble under the attack of genuine negative feelings, we tend to perpetuate an attitude of pseudo-peace. It is as if we cannot tolerate conflict at all for fear of the damage it could do to us, to the situation, to the others involved. But of course the real damage is done to all these by the denial and suppression of negative feelings.

Out-of-Place Expressions

There is also the problem of out-of-place expressions, expressions dealing with behavior which is not usually acceptable in our society. In the extreme, forms that present themselves before psychotherapists, expressions of sexual perversity or homicidal fantasies are often found blocking to the listener because of their obvious threatening quality. At less extreme levels, we all find unnatural or inappropriate behavior difficult to handle. That is, anything from an "off color" story told in mixed company to seeing a man weep is likely to produce a problem situation.

In any face-to-face situation, we will find instances of this type which will momentarily, if not permanently, block any communication. In business and industry, any expressions of weakness or incompetency will generally be regarded as unacceptable and therefore will block good two-way communication. For example, it is difficult to listen to a supervisor tell of his feelings of failure in being able to "take charge" of a situation in his department because *all* administrators are supposed to be able to "take charge."

Accepting Positive Feelings

It is both interesting and perplexing to note that negative or hostile feelings or expressions are much easier to deal with in any face-to-face relationship than are truly and deeply positive feelings. This is especially true for the businessman because the culture expects him to be independent, bold, clever, and aggressive and manifest no feelings of warmth, gentleness, and intimacy. He therefore comes to regard these feelings as soft and inappropriate. But no matter how they are regarded, they remain a human need. The denial of these feelings in himself and his associates does not get the executive out of the problem in dealing with them. They simply become veiled and confused. If recognized, they would work for the total effort; unrecognized, they work against it.

Emotional Danger Signals

The listener's own emotions are sometimes a barrier to active listening. When emotions are at their height, when listening is most necessary, it is most difficult to set aside one's own concerns and be understanding. Our emotions are often our own worst enemies when we try to become listeners. The more involved and invested we are in a particular situation or problem, the less we are likely to be willing or able to listen to the feelings and attitudes of others. That is, the more we find it necessary to respond to our own needs, the less we are able to respond to the needs of another. Let us look at some of the main danger signals that warn us that our emotions may be interfering with our listening.

Defensiveness.   The points about which one is most vocal and dogmatic, the points which one is most anxious to impose on others—these are always the points one is trying to talk oneself into believing. So one danger signal becomes apparent when you find yourself stressing a point or trying to convince another. It is at these times that you are likely to be less secure and consequently less able to listen.

Resentment of Opposition.   It is always easier to listen to an idea which is similar to one of your own than to an opposing view. Sometimes, in order to clear the air, it is helpful to pause for a moment when you feel your ideas and position being challenged, reflect on the situation, and express your concern to the speaker.

Clash of Personalities.   Here again, our experience has consistently shown us that the genuine expression of feelings on the part of the listener will be more helpful in developing a sound relationship than the suppression of them. This is so whether the feelings be resentment, hostility, threat, or admiration. A basically honest relationship, whatever the nature of it, is the most productive of all. The other party becomes secure when he learns that the listener can express his feelings honestly and openly to him. We should keep this in mind when we begin to fear a clash of personalities in the listening relationship. Otherwise, fear of our own emotions will choke off full expression of feelings.

Listening to Ourselves

To listen to oneself is a prerequisite to listening to others. And it is often an effective means of dealing with the problems we have outlined above. When we are most aroused, excited, and demanding, we are least able to understand our own feelings and attitudes. Yet, in dealing with the problems of others, it becomes most important to be sure of one's own position, values, and needs.

The ability to recognize and understand the meaning which a particular episode has for you, with all the feelings which it stimulates in you, and the ability to express this meaning when you find it getting in the way of active listening, will clear the air and enable you once again to be free to listen. That is, if some person or situation touches off feelings within you which tend to block your attempts to listen with understanding, begin listening to yourself. It is much more helpful in developing effective relationships to avoid suppressing these feelings. Speak them out as clearly as you can, and try to enlist the other person as a listener to your feelings. A person's listening ability is limited by his ability to listen to himself.

ACTIVE LISTENING AND COMPANY GOALS

"How can listening improve production?"

"We're in business, and it's a rugged, fast, competitive affair. How are we going to find time to counsel our employees?"

"We have to concern ourselves with organizational problems first."

"We can't afford to spend all day listening when there's a job to be done."

"What's morale got to do with production?"

"Sometimes we have to sacrifice an individual for the good of the rest of the people in the company."

Those of us who are trying to advance the listening approach in industry hear these comments frequently. And because they are so honest and legitimate, they pose a real problem. Unfortunately, the answers are not so clear-cut as the questions.

Individual Importance

One answer is based on an assumption that is central to the listening approach. That assumption is: the kind of behavior which helps the individual will eventually be the best thing that could be done for the group. Or saying it another way: the things that are best for the individual are best for the company. This is a conviction of ours, based on our experience in psychology and education. The research evidence from industry is only beginning to come in. We find that putting the group first, at the expense of the individual, besides being an uncomfortable individual experience, does *not* unify the group. In fact, it tends to make the group less a group. The members become anxious and suspicious.

We are not at all sure in just what ways the group does benefit from a concern demonstrated for an individual, but we have several strong leads. One is that the group feels more secure when an individual member is being listened to and provided for with concern and sensitivity. And we assume that a secure group will ultimately be a better group. When each individual feels that he need not fear exposing himself to the group, he is likely to contribute more freely and spontaneously. When the leader of a group responds to the individual, puts the individual first, the other members of the group will follow suit, and the group comes to act as a unit in recognizing and responding to the needs of a particular member. This positive, constructive action seems to be a much more satisfying experience for a group than the experience of dispensing with a member.

Listening and Production

As to whether or not listening or any other activity designed to better human relations in an industry actually raises production—whether morale has a definite relationship to production is not known for sure. There are some who frankly hold that there is no relationship to be expected between morale and production—that production often depends upon the so-cial misfit, the eccentric, or the isolate. And there are some who simply choose to work in a climate of cooperation and harmony, in a high-morale group, quite aside from the question of increased production.

A report from the Survey Research Center at the University of Michigan on research conducted at the Prudential Life Insurance Company lists seven findings relating to production and morale.[1] First-line supervisors in high-production work groups were found to differ from those in low-production work groups in that they:

1. Are under less close supervision from their own supervisors.

2. Place less direct emphasis upon production as the goal.

3. Encourage employee participation in the making of decisions.

4. Are more employee-centered.

5. Spend more of their time in supervision and less in straight production work.

6. Have a greater feeling of confidence in their supervisory roles.

7. Feel that they know where they stand with the company.

After mentioning that other dimensions of morale, such as identification with the company, intrinsic job satisfaction, and satisfaction with job status, were not found significantly related to productivity, the report goes on to suggest the following psychological interpretation:

> People are more effectively motivated when they are given some degree of freedom in the way in which they do their work than when every action is prescribed in advance. They do better when some degree of decision-making about their jobs is possible than when all decisions are made for them. They respond more adequately when they are treated as personalities than as cogs in a machine. In short if the ego motivations of self-determination, of self-expression, of a sense of personal worth can be tapped, the individual can be more effectively energized. The use of external sanctions, or pressuring for production, may work to some degree, but not to the extent that the more internalized motives do. When the individual comes to identify himself with his job and with the work of his group, human resources are much more fully utilized in the production process.

---

[1] "Productivity, Supervision, and Employee Morale," *Human Relations*, series 1, report 1 (Ann Arbor: Survey Research Center, University of Michigan).

Maximum Creativeness

There may never be enough research evidence to satisfy everyone on this question. But speaking from a business point of view, in terms of the problem of developing resources for production, the maximum creativeness and productive effort of the human beings in the organization are the richest untapped source of power still existing. The difference between the maximum productive capacity of people and that output which industry is now realizing is immense. We simply suggest that this maximum capacity might be closer to realization if we sought to release the motivation that already exists within people rather than try to stimulate them externally.

This releasing of the individual is made possible first of all by sensitive listening, with respect and understanding. Listening is a beginning toward making the individual feel himself worthy of making contributions, and this could result in a very dynamic and productive organization. Competitive business is never too rugged or too busy to take time to procure the most efficient technological advances or to develop raw material sources. But these in comparison to the resources that are already within the people in the plant are paltry. This is industry's major procurement problem.

The decision to spend time listening to his employees is a decision each supervisor or executive has to make for himself. Executives seldom have much to do with products or processes. They have to deal with people who must in turn deal with people who will deal with products or processes. The higher one goes up the line, the more he will be concerned with human relations problems, simply because people are all he has to work with. The minute we take a man from his bench and make him a foreman he is removed from the basic production of goods and now must begin relating to individuals instead of nuts and bolts. People are different from things, and our foreman is called upon for a different line of skills completely. His new tasks call upon him to be a special kind of a person. The development of himself as a listener is an important first step.

Discussion Questions
1. What is the purpose of active listening?
2. What is *not* the purpose of active listening?
3. When is active listening appropriate?
4. Why does active listening work?
5. Can active listening help a company in which it is practiced effectively?
6. Note that passing judgment, either critical or favorable, inhibits free expression. Discuss why even positive, favorable evaluations are barriers to communication.
7. Discuss the ways the business culture encourages negative rather than posi-

tive feelings—the tendency to view the human need for warmth and intimacy as soft and inappropriate to business.

8. Discuss what the listener communicates when engaged in active listening.

9. Discuss the risk of the listener being changed.

10. Discuss how the group feels more secure when an individual member is listened to with concern and sensitivity.

6

Motivation and Communication

In Chapter 3, we briefly considered the effects of needs, physiological and psychological, upon perception and thus upon communicative behavior. Indeed, the influence of needs[1] is so pervasive and telling that they deserve at least a chapter if we are to consider adequately communication in a behavioral setting.

"Relevance to one's needs is the most important determinant of one's personal view of the world."[2] Whatever these needs and their respective intensities may be at a given moment can affect one's behavior—even at the physiological level. Market researchers, for example, conclude that one tends to buy signficantly more in a supermarket when hungry than directly after a full meal. A bachelor friend tells me that he prepares his breakfast and packs his lunch before going to work. He discovered that he had to make an adjustment because his lunch was either too abundant or too skimpy, depending upon whether he packed it before or after eating breakfast.

The potency of needs in affecting perception has been demonstrated repeatedly. The early studies in hunger, for example, reported that hungry persons will complete words such as ME_____ more frequently as food words such as MEAT or MEAL than will nonhungry persons. Moreover, hungrier subjects saw more food objects in very unstructured stimuli than did less hungry ones.

---

[1]Need is defined simply but adequately as "something within an individual that prompts that person to action" (Paul Hersey and Kenneth H. Blanchard, *Management of Organizational Behavior: Utilizing Human Resources*, 4th ed. [Englewood Cliffs, N.J.: Prentice-Hall, 1982], p. 16).

[2]H. J. Leavitt, *Managerial Psychology*, 4th ed. (Chicago: University of Chicago Press, 1978, p. 35.

A MOTIVATION MODEL

Let us consider more specifically the role of *motivation* in human behavior. Leavitt[3] provides a model which he derives from three basic premises:

1. Behavior is *caused*. The things we do don't just happen—there are always underlying reasons. This does not mean, necessarily, that these reasons will be apparent even to the individual who is doing those things.

2. Behavior is *directed*. Ultimately, there is no aimless behavior. We are always pursuing some goal or other. Again, there is no necessity to assume that we are conscious of our goals or that we are approaching them most efficiently.

3. Behavior is *motivated*. Underlying what we do are motives, drives that provide us with the energy to attain our goals, or at least to move in the direction of our goals.

Relate these three ideas, says Leavitt, and you have a system for understanding behavior (see Figure 6–1):

> With the help of these ideas, human behavior can be viewed as part of a double play from cause to motive to behavior-toward-a-goal. And it is also helpful to think of the three as generally forming a closed circuit. Arrival at a goal eliminates the cause, which eliminates the motive, which eliminates the behavior.[4]

FIGURE 6–1
A basic model of behavior

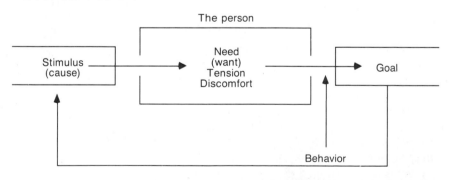

Source: H. J. Leavitt, *Managerial Psychology*, 4th ed. (Chicago: University of Chicago Press, 1978), p. 9. For a more comprehensive conception see, "An Integrated Model of the Motivational Process" J. L. Gibson, J. M. Ivancevich, and J. H. Donnelly, Jr., *Organizations: Behavior, Structure, Process*, 4th ed. (Plano, Tex.: Business Publications, 1982), p. 81.

---

[3]Leavitt, *Managerial Psychology*, pp. 7–12.
[4]Ibid., p. 8.

One's empty stomach sends neural impulses which the individual perceives as "feeling hungry"; the hunger feeling is the motive that directs energy toward food seeking; if the effort is successful, the individual is filled with food, thus eliminating the hunger feeling. If that person now ceases to seek food and thus fails to consume food for several hours, the hunger feelings will reappear and the cycle will be repeated.

This cyclical process also applies to other types of needs. Suppose that a person is psychologically "hungry" (e.g., has a need for freedom from fear of physical deprivation or a need for acceptance and/or esteem from others). This individual now has the motive for seeking satisfaction and if the resultant behavior is successful, the psychological stomach is filled and hunger ceases for the time being. And the same person is quite prone to become hungry in this sense all over again if those psychological appetites are not recurrently appeased.

The analogy breaks down to an extent here, for it is apparent that some psychological appetites, varying with the individual, are rarely if ever fully sated. But they can be momentarily and partially satisfied, and the cause-motive-behavior-toward-a-goal cycle decreases in intensity if it does not halt altogether.

This cyclical process involves the concept of *homeostasis*, which assumes a normal state, and when conditions depart from this state, homeostatic mechanisms return the body to its normal level of functioning.[5] Thus equilibrium is protected or pursued if lost.

> . . . the ultimate condition of man can be thought of as an equilibrium condition in which he need not behave. This ultimate will be unattainable as long as one fly after another goes on landing on man's rump to stir up some new need and to force him to go on swishing his tail.[6]

There appears, at this writing, to be no dearth of flies in our environment— nor any danger of their extinction.

FRUSTRATION

No discussion of human motivation would be adequate without a consideration of frustration—any interference with goal-directed behavior.[7] The sources of frustrating obstacles include the environment, other people, our personal defects or limitations, and conflict situations.

Generally speaking, when a man (or a woman) is confronted with an obstacle he or she becomes aggressive. If confident, this aggression is ordi-

---

[5]Audrey Haber and Richard P. Runyon, 3d ed. *Fundamentals of Psychology* (Reading, Mass.: Addison-Wesley Publishing, 1983), p. 192

[6]Leavitt, *Managerial Psychology*, pp. 10–11.

[7]Thomas V. Bonoma and Gerald Zaltman, *Psychology for Management* (Boston: Kent Publishing, 1981), pp. 117–23.

narily directed toward the obstacle. If a person is unsure and pessimistic about his or her ability, that person tends to direct aggression inwardly and feels blameworthy, inadequate, and so forth. The key to the direction of aggression, then, is the self-concept, as we discussed in the previous chapters.

"Many obstacle situations are depriving rather than frustrating because the obstacles do not seem insurmountable or the goals are not central to the self."[8] That same person will experience fewer frustrations, therefore, if there is a larger repertoire of alternative routes around blocks or if there is sufficient self-confidence within to obviate the need for providing self-worth each time the individual meets a problem. Intimately related to experiences of frustration are aspirations. If they are commensurate with abilities, then frustration will be less frequent. To the extent that aspirations are beyond one's capacities, the person will tend to experience frustration and perhaps ultimately—if the thwarting is chronic—demoralization. Let us remind ourselves that self-confidence is generally a product of repeated success, but that success is what we perceive it to be.

Conflict

A severe species of frustration is conflict—a seemingly escape-proof frustration.

> Conflict[9] [is] . . . a pulling in two directions at the same time. The obstacles one meets are not brick walls but drags that pull back as one goes forward . . . frying-pan-and-fire situations, or donkey-between-the-bales-of-hay situations.[10]

Conflict situations involve choosing and decision making and are generally of three types: *approach-approach*—the individual is between two equally attractive alternatives and to move toward one would pull away from the other; *avoidance-avoidance*—the individual is between two equally unattractive or repulsive alternatives, so that in escaping from one

---

[8]Leavitt, *Managerial Psychology*, p. 42.

[9]We are currently considering *intra*personal conflict, but *inter*personal conflict has received increasing attention of late. For helpful accounts of this burgeoning concept and of how to deal with conflict constructively, see: Bernard Taylor and Gordon L. Lippitt, eds., *Management Development and Training Handbook* (London: McGraw-Hill, 1975), pp. 379–80, 393–94, 507; Thomas L. Quick, *Person to Person Managing* (New York: St. Martin's Press, 1977), Chapter 7, "Dealing with Conflict"; George Bach and Herbert Goldberg, *Creative Aggression* (Garden City, N.Y.: Doubleday, 1974); A. C. Filley, *Interpersonal Conflict Resolution* (Glenview, Ill.: Scott, Foresman, 1975); the section on "Conflict and Stress in Organizations," in L. L. Cummings and Randall B. Dunham, *Introduction to Organizational Behavior: Text and Readings* (Homewood, Ill.: Richard D. Irwin, 1980), pp. 573–96; and Chapter 17, "Managing Conflict, Change, and Organization Development" in John R. Schermerrhorn, Jr., *Management for Productivity* (New York: John Wiley & Sons, 1984).

[10]Leavitt, *Managerial Psychology*, p. 43

alternative, that person moves closer to the other; *approach-avoidance*—the individual is both attracted and repelled by the same object.[11] Frustration tolerance, the ability to retain normal reactions under stress, varies greatly among individuals. Some are quite capable of maintaining problem-solving actions directed toward constructively resolving the conflict in which they find themselves. Others are more prone toward compensatory or subterfuge reactions.[11] Some of these reactions resemble homeostasis, in the form of physiological compensatory activity that strives to maintain a constant state. Their prime purpose is not to solve problems but to cushion the ego (one's feelings of self-esteem) against threats of deflation. These ego-defensive reactions include: *fantasizing* (wish-fulfilling dreams, daydreaming), *projecting* (inputing one's thoughts and desires to others), *rationalizing* (finding justifiable reasons for behavior or convincing ourselves that the goal is really undesirable—assuming a sour grapes attitude), *repressing* (attempting to ignore, deny, or forget troublesome things), *regressing* (reverting to childish ways), *identifying* (becoming ego-involved with others), *blaming others* (excusing ourselves by finding others responsible for our failures—scapegoating), *overcompensating* (trying to overcome one's deficiencies, to make up for one's failings—but in an excessive manner), and *sublimating* (getting indirect but socially acceptable satisfaction).

The list is neither inclusive nor mutually exclusive, but it does suggest some of the unconstructive responses to frustration.

How, then, can we really resolve our conflicts? A conflict is a conflict because one *perceives* it to be one. Rather than an external condition, frustration is a state of the organism. A conflict exists for you when certain needs seem mutually exclusive. Therefore, you can resolve a conflict by (1) finding a new way to satisfy both needs simultaneously, (2) reducing your valuation of one need or the other, or (3) reorganizng the situation so that it is perceptually no longer a significant conflict.

Let us now examine in more detail the human need system that is subject to so much frustration and conflict.

MOTIVATION THEORIES

What can we say with confidence about motivation? Is there any rhyme or reason to our needs? Are there any grounds for predicting people's behavior on the basis of their needs?

Let us examine three of the most important theories that purport to answer those questions: Maslow's need hierarchy, Herzberg's two-factor the-

---

[11]For a detailed treatment of intrapersonal conflict, see: K. Lewin, *A Dynamic Theory of Personality* (New York: McGraw-Hill, 1935); L. A. Festinger, *A Theory of Cognitive Dissonance* (Stanford, Calif.: Stanford University Press, 1962); David Cohen, *Psychologists on Psychology* (New York: Taplinger, 1977), pp. 126–44; and Thomas V. Bonoma and Gerald Zaltman, *Psychology for Management* (Boston: Kent Publishing, 1981), p. 123–41.

ory, and McClelland's learned needs theory. All three were devised over a generation ago, but they continue to capture management's imagination and spawn further research. They are undoubtedly not the final word but they clearly merit our close attention.

Maslow

There had been need-classifiers long before Abraham Maslow and the earlier models helped sort out the myriad human behaviors. But they did little to aid managers, or anyone else, to predict future behavior. And if managers cannot predict behavior they are powerless to control or influence it—in this case, to channel individual energies in such a way as to achieve organizational objectives. Thus, it was the promise of predictability that was a most attractive feature of Maslow's model. It is one of the more popular of the motivational concepts, so let us examine it carefully.

The model[12] (mentioned in Chapter 2) involves five types of needs: *physiological* (the need for air, water, food, elimination, temperature control, sleep); *safety and security* (the need to be free of the fear of physical danger and deprivation); *social* (the need to be accepted and approved, to belong); *ego* (the need for recognition, to be important, to be somebody, to have status, fame, reputation);[13] and self-fulfillment (the ultimate need—to realize one's fullest potential as a human being; to be creative in the broadest sense of the term).

The principal distinction of Maslow's model is that these needs exist in a prepotency pattern, a hierarchy of needs, as depicted in Figure 6–2.

FIGURE 6–2
Maslow's hierarchy of needs

---

[12]Abraham H. Maslow, *Motivation and Personality*, 2d ed. (New York: Harper & Row, 1970).

[13]Maslow distinguishes between ego needs satisfied privately (self-esteem) from those that were satisfied publicly (esteem from others).

Maslow's basic propositions are:

1. *The lowest unsatisfied needs must be sufficiently appeased before the needs above them normally become operative, that is, are able to motivate the individual.*

Ordinarily, until a person's physiological needs are reasonably satisfied, none of the higher needs will significantly influence behavior. A desperately hungry man may risk his life, to say nothing of his honor, for food. Even Jesus, who preached, "Man does not live by bread alone," was clearly aware of the importance of bread, for he fed the multitudes.

When the physiological needs are sufficiently appeased, one begins to be concerned with future deprivation as well as with present and future danger. Let us say that a hungry person, motivated to work for food, is rewarded with a meal. But now that person continues to work. Clearly working—not for another meal, for it could not be eaten now if available—but for the assurance of the next meal. To stretch the point, it might be argued that some people, particularly those scarred by earlier poverty, are working today predominantly for the assurance of meals 20 or 30 years from now.

And so it is that as the needs at one level are sufficiently satisfied, the level immediately above begins to play a role in one's behavior.

2. *To the extent that needs are satisfied, they will become inoperative, that is, they cease to motivate the individual, for a satisfied need is no longer a motivator of behavior.*

As previously stated, the hungry person who has eaten is no longer hungry. Thus subsequent work efforts are temporarily not motivatable by hunger. And, in fact, if this individual is completely improvident, as many animals are, the person will cease work altogether until hunger feelings reappear sufficiently as a motivation to attain food again. Most of us, of course, are not so casual about the future, and our security needs (e.g., to be free of the fear of hunger) continue to impel us.

Some Qualifications.   Perhaps this discussion of the Maslow model suggests that the prediction of human behavior is merely a matter of discovering where a person currently is on the need hierarchy so as to determine where the next jump will be. Unfortunately, the situation is more complex, for the sequence of need occurrence and the sequence of need satisfaction are not necessarily the same.[14] However, if we impose a few qualifications on the need hierarchy, the model gains in applicability.

---

[14]The model has been criticized as simplistic. For example, see, M. A. Wahba and L. G. Birdwell, "Maslow Reconsidered: A Review of Research on the Need Hierarchy Theory," *Organizational Behavior and Human Performance*, April 1976, pp. 212–40; Benjamin Schneider and Clayton P. Alderfer, "Three Studies of Need Satisfactions in Organizations," *Administrative Science Quarterly*, December 1973, pp. 489–505; and Edward L. Lawler, III and J. L. Suttle, "A Causal Correlation Test of the Need Hierarchy Concept," *Organizational Behavior and Human Performance*, April 1972, pp. 265–87.

Multiple Levels.   First of all, the dotted lines on Maslow's model, separating the need levels, suggest that the boundaries of the levels are permeable and that one may move up and down the ladder rapidly. Within a typical day, a person working in a factory may be motivated at one time or another by all five need levels. That person certainly becomes physically hungry at least three times a day and concerned about safety when operating a machine—and may experience anxiety about the family's financial security; this individual may do or refrain from doing many things to maintain or gain social acceptance by associates; at the same time there may be a striving for advancement and/or deriving a sense of achievement from the job at hand; there may even be some thoughts about ultimate destiny, a contribution to humanity, and so forth.

Need Conflict.   Not only is there considerable mobility up and down the hierarchy of needs during even a relatively short period of time, but it is quite possible for a person to be motivated by two or more need levels simultaneously. When one's needs are sufficiently strong and/or urgent and yet cannot be satisfied simultaneously, there may be need conflicts. Take the familiar case of the man (or woman) bucking for promotion. If the methods used do not coincide with the codes of the peer group, that person is likely to be made aware of his or her deviant behavior in no uncertain terms, with the group threatening various sanctions. Here is the classic conflict of social and ego needs. Will the individual resist the group and if necessary suffer its punishments? Or bow to group pressure and suppress his or her ambitions?[15] Maslow's hierarchy of needs suggests that this person will usually take the latter alternative, for social needs appear to be more primary than ego needs, but the situation is not quite so easily predictable, as we shall presently discuss.

Modifying Factors.   There are at least two factors that suggest why the Maslow model cannot be applied literally in every situation. They are the presence of varying appetites, which can be partially accounted for by the concept of dependency, and the role of self-discipline.

   1.   *Varying appetites.* There is no doubt that physiological needs vary from person to person. Some people simply require less sleep, food, protec-

---

[15]Of course, there are often escapes from this seeming dilemma. A person may be able to convince the group that a particular end is acceptable. For example, the need for additional income for extraordinary expenses—family medical bills, and so forth. Or the individual may modify the *means* of approaching a goal so that they will be acceptable to the group. The able student often faces a similar peer response with efforts to obtain good grades. A person may be able to justify extra effort by explaining that good grades are required to enter graduate school and by studiously avoiding unacceptable means for attaining good marks, such as apple polishing.

tion from the elements, and the like than do others. There is ample evidence to suggest that our need requirements vary at higher levels as well. Recall the individual striving for promotion? A major determinant of the response to group pressure may be just how much of a social need appetite versus an ego need appetite the person has. If he or she has learned to seek satisfactions primarily within oneself rather than through or from others, it may be fairly easy to shrug off the group and proceed.

In addition, we must ask, does the individual have alternative need-satisfaction routes? Can these social needs be satisfied through other groups—on or off the job—and, thus, for *this* situation have limited social needs?

2. *Dependency.* The concept of dependency helps to explain why the appetites, the widths of the need bands, particularly the social and ego bands, seem to vary so much among individuals. Consider that the human infant comes into the world with a fairly well-developed set of needs and an almost completely undeveloped set of means for satisfying them. In other words, he or she is necessarily dependent upon others to satisfy those needs. What seems to be critical in the personality development of the child is whether dependence is associated primarily with satisfying or with dissatisfying experiences.

If the infant's needs are usually satisfied promptly and sufficiently by others and if this becomes a generalized pattern through the formative years, the child will tend thereafter to rely upon others for need satisfaction—to develop a broad social-needs band. If, however, one's needs are normally *not* thusly satisfied and this pattern is repeatedly reinforced, one will come to rely less upon others and more upon oneself for the satisfaction of needs and thus develop a broad, demanding ego-needs band.

In actuality, the infant's needs can neither be completely frustrated (or it would not survive) nor completely satisfied (mother is only human). As a consequence, that child will develop both social and egoistic needs, but there is likely to be a dominance of one over the other. In any event, it is the internal conflict between the drive to be dependent and the simultaneous drive to be independent that fosters much of the anguish that teenagers (and their parents) experience.

3. *Self-discipline.* Another factor that complicates the use of the model is, in old-fashioned language, willpower. We can refrain from indulging our food and sleep needs to a degree. It is reasonable to assume that we can deny ourselves satisfactions at the subsequent need levels as well. Our friend seeking the promotion may decide to suffer the group's slings and

arrows in anticipation of a compensatory reward. This does not mean that this person is without social needs or that they are meager—but that he or she is suppressing them. This may help to explain people such as Albert Schweitzer, Tom Dooley, and Mohandas Gandhi—men who seemingly lived primarily at the self-fulfillment level. Among possible speculations: Were these men who possessed iron wills capable of deferring or more or less permanently denying the gratification of their more material needs? Were their lower needs relatively narrow bands to begin with? Was the wine of self-fulfillment so heady that the lower need satisfactions became pallid by comparison?

It can be argued that some people seem quite content to obtain a modicum of satisfaction at the lower two or three levels. They seem to have no ambition, no drive to get somewhere or to be somebody. It is possible that these people were behind the door when the needs were passed out? Not likely. But it is quite possible that they have *learned* not to try to satisfy some of their needs.

I recall dimly an experiment that our undergraduate biology professor described. It involved a tank of water about 12 feet long, 4 feet deep, and 4 feet wide. A glass partition was inserted, separating the tank into two six-foot segments. Then a northern pike, which had been deprived of food for some time, was placed in one compartment and a bucket of minnows was poured into the other. The pike immediately rushed for the minnows and bumped its nose, which hurt, I assume. But the pike was persistent and continued to bump its nose an average of 165 times. At this point, it stopped trying. It had apparently learned that to seek satisfaction for its needs resulted not only in a thwarting of its hunger drive but in pain as well. The experimenter could now remove the partition, and the minnows (which were evidently more stupid than the pike) swam into the other section, but the pike wasn't having any—it had learned its lesson. And in most cases, it would starve to death midst abundance!

The experiment may be apocryphal, but it does offer a provocative analogy. Substitute a child for the pike and substitute childhood experiences for the tank. Suppose that this child has a skin of a certain color, or a nose of a certain shape, or a certain last name, or a physical impairment, or lives on the wrong side of the tracks. Now suppose that this child tries to achieve some social or ego satisfaction and bumps his or her nose. This is a human being and therefore learns much more rapidly than the pike to stop trying—that way at least. Hopefully, the human learns other ways of dealing with the obstacle, such as were discussed in the sections on frustration and conflict.

But suppose instead that this person generalizes the painful, failing experiences and, by way of defense, denies these needs. In effect, the individual learns to stop trying altogether. Incidentally, since humans learn by concepts as well as by stimulus, they can learn this lesson vicariously from others (parents, older brothers and sisters, friends) who have also learned the lesson—directly or vicariously.

It is likely that when this child has become an adult, the mere opportunity for need satisfaction will often be insufficient to overcome decades of conditioning. The adult may have to undergo a thorough and prolonged process of relearning—of coming to understand that not only are there certain needs, but that there is an acceptable way of satisfying them.

Validity versus Simplicity.   The qualifications imposed upon the Maslow model of needs have two consequences: (1) they have, I hope, increased the model's validity in accounting for human behavior; (2) they have complicated the model's use as a predictive tool, suggesting that ordinarily it cannot serve as a simple template to predict the next move. The model in no way enables one who would communicate effectively to dispense with perceptive analysis. But if the trade-off has increased validity even at the cost of simplicity, the bargain would appear to be a good one.

Herzberg et al.

So much for Maslow. Let's move on to another conception of motivation. Herzberg[16] and others don't really contradict Maslow but they have developed an interestingly different way of looking at human needs. Having studied a number accountants and engineers, they conclude that people have two kinds of drives: growth needs and avoidance needs. They report that certain job factors (motivators) have potency for satisfying growth needs. These include achievement, recognition, the work itself, responsibility, and advancement. Other job factors (hygiene factors) are important largely for their capacity to dissatisfy the individual—and thus trigger avoidance needs. These include company policy and administration, supervision-technical, salary, supervision-interpersonal relations, and working conditions. The motivators are associated with job content, whereas the hygiene factors are related to the job context or environment. The major conclusion of the study was that the job factors capable of satisfying growth

---

[16]F. Herzberg, B. Mausner, and B. Snyderman, *The Motivation to Work*, 2d ed. (New York: John Wiley & Sons, 1962). See also: Frederick Herzberg, "One More Time: How Do You Motivate Employees?" *Harvard Business Review*, 46, no. 1 (January–February 1968) pp. 53–62, Frederick Herzberg, *The Managerial Choice: To Be Efficient and to Be Human* (Homewood, Ill.: Dow Jones-Irwin, 1976), and William F. Christopher, *Management for the 1980s* (New York: AMACOM, 1980), pp. 118–19.

needs are largely irrelevant to avoidance needs and that the job factors related to avoidance needs are of little or no consequence with respect to growth needs. For example, management's improvement of substandard working conditions will reduce avoidance needs but will be ineffective in motivating the worker to greater productivity and creativity.

> When these [hygiene] factors deteriorate to a level below that which the employee considers acceptable, then job dissatisfaction ensues. However, the reverse does not hold true. When the job context can be characterized as optimal, we will not get dissatisfaction, but neither will we get much in the way of positive attitudes.[17]
>
> All we can expect from satisfying the needs for hygiene is the prevention of dissatisfaction and poor job performance.[18]

The Expensive Change-Room.   Here's an example of overkill in the hygiene department. A friend took a job as an executive with a steel forge company. A day or two before I was to fly to Europe on an assignment, I drove out to visit him in his new location. He gave me a short tour of the shop.

I had seen many other factories but the environment in this one was overwhelming. The ear-splitting din, the fumes, the jarring from the huge power hammers, the excrutiating temperature from the heat-treat furnaces and the incandescent blooms and billets—what a litany of hygiene factors! There was credence in the old joke about hammersmiths never having to go to hell. They'd already lived there—eight hours a day!

We returned to Bob's office. He was eager.

Bob   Well, what do you think?
Me   What do you mean?
Bob   Any suggestions for us?
Me   Technical improvements? I'm no engineer. . . .
Bob   I know. . . but anything you saw that we could work on?
Me   Well, if you insist. . . it might be a good idea to spruce up the employees' change-room. Frankly, it's a horror now.
Bob   You're dead right! We'll do it.

Three months later, I returned from Europe. There was a note to call Bob. . . he wanted me to come out to the plant again for a big surprise. He was waiting for me when I pulled into the parking lot. "Wait till you see the new change-room!"

I was dumbfounded. The room would have been the envy of most country clubs—completely new plumbing and electrical fixtures, indirect light-

---

[17]Ibid., pp. 113–14.
[18]Ibid., p. 115.

ing, elegant lockers and benches, wall-to-wall carpeting! The bill, I discovered later, was $27,000!

And what did the company get for its handsome investment? Greater productivity? Less scrap? Fewer pieces needing reworking? Hardly. What they got was simply no complaints about a horrendous change-room. I didn't have the heart to tell Bob—at least not then—that he probably could have achieved the same effect at a fraction of the cost from a thorough paint job and the replacement of a broken commode and a few light fixtures.

Speaking of complaints, now it was management's turn. They were griping that the workers were spending too much time in their luxurious change-room!

Critics.   One of the attractions of the Herzberg model is that it is work-oriented. "There is no need to translate psychological terminology to everyday language."[19] However, his work has had its detractors. For one, its universality has been questioned.[20] His initial study group was made up solely of engineers and accountants. One might wonder if the results would apply equally to such different occupational groups as nurses, medical technologists, salespeople, computer programmers, clerks, and police officers.

Lawler[21] had another reservation. He claimed that little attention has been focused on the motivational and performance implications of the theory.

The jury is still out on the two-factor theory,[22] but the work of Herzberg and his colleagues does effectively squash the old motivational notion that more of something good is only better. Managers are cautioned not to expect too much from expensive office fixtures, Muzak, nicely decorated lounges for breaks, high-base salaries, and other hygiene factors.

> Herzberg's distinction between job context and job content reminds managers that there are two important aspects of all jobs: (1) what people do in terms of job tasks—job content and, (2) the work setting in which they do it—job context.[23]

---

[19]James L. Gibson, John M. Ivancevich, and James H. Donnelly, Jr., *Organizations: Behavior, Structure, Process*, 4th ed. (Plano, Tex.: Business Publications, 1982), p. 87.

[20]Joseph Schneider and Edwin Locke, "A Critique of Herzberg's Dual-Factor Classification System and a Suggested Revision," *Organizational Behavior and Human Performance* (July 1971), pp. 441–58.

[21]Edward E. Lawler, III, *Motivation in Work Organizations* (Monterey, Calif.: Brooks/Cole Publishing, 1973), p. 72.

[22]Steven Kerr, Anne Harlan, and Ralph Stogdill, "Preference for Motivator and Hygiene Factors in a Hypothetical Interview Situation," *Personnel Psychology*, 27 (Winter 1974), pp. 109–24.

[23]John R. Schermerhorn, Jr., *Management for Productivity* (New York: John Wiley & Sons, 1984), p. 241.

McClelland

A third conception of motivation that merits inspection is David McClelland's *learned needs theory*. We acquire our motives from our respective cultures.[24] He addresses the needs for:

—*achievement*—to set challenging yet attainable goals for oneself, to work hard to achieve those goals, and to use the skills and abilities needed to do so.

—*affiliation*—to establish, maintain, and repair social relationships . . . to have warm, friendly associations with others.

—*power*—to acquire a reputation and to have influence and impact on others. McClelland distinguishes between: *socialized* power used in the interests of the group, the department, the organization, as a whole; and *personalized* power used primarily for self-aggrandizement, often at the expense of the group. Needless to say, he recommends that executives exercise the first kind of power and avoid the second.[25]

Managers find the McClelland theory especially germane on two counts. First, along with the Maslow and Herzberg models, they feel it helps them understand people's behavior on the job. If one's needs are accurately assessed, they may help locate that person in a desirable position. See Figure 6–3.

FIGURE 6–3 Work Preferences of Persons High in Need for Achievement, Power, and Affiliation

Individual need	Work preference	Example
High need for achievement	Individual responsibility, challenging but achievable goals; feedback on performance	Field salesperson with challenging quota and opportunity to earn individual bonus
High need for affiliation	Interpersonal relationships; opportunities to communicate	Customer-service representative; member of work unit subject to group wage-bonus plan
High need for power	Control over other persons; attention; recognition	Formal position of supervisory responsibility; appointment as head of special task force or committee

Source: John R. Schermerhorn, Jr., James G. Hunt, and Richard N. Osborn, *Managing Organization Behavior* (New York: Wiley, 1982), p. 113.

---

[24]David C. McClelland, *The Achievement Motive* (New York: Appleton-Century-Crofts, 1953).

[25]David C. McClelland and D. Burnham, "Power is the Great Motivator," *Harvard Business Review* (March–April 1976), pp. 100–111.

Second, if needs indeed are acquired, then a person supposedly can learn to adopt a new profile that is required for a given role.

On a much grander scale, McClelland is convinced that entire nations, especially in the "third-world," can buck up their flagging economies by stimulating the achievement motive in their general populations.[26] Of course, McClelland has had his critics, too. Their concern is threefold:

> *Method*—McClelland uses the projective Thematic Apperception Test (TAT) to gather his data. It is difficult to validate this approach.
> *Learning Decline*—The notion that needs can be learned seems at odds with a good deal of research and observation that hold that motives are acquired in childhood and are very difficult to modify later on. McClelland cites evidence in politics and religion to assert that adult motivation can indeed be altered.
> *Durability of Change*—A third criticism centers on whether needs can be permanently acquired. So far this question is unresolved.

There is a great deal more to motivation. In fact, what we have been examining are three representatives of just one family of motivation conceptions—*content* theories. They have to do with factors within a person that energize, control, sustain, and or halt behavior. There is another family of theorems—*process* theories. They are certainly worthy of careful study. But since the emphasis is on the *process* of how one's behavior is energized, these theories are more appropriate in a book on organizational behavior than one on interpersonal communication. Accordingly, I will briefly describe a few of the more popular theories and recommend some sources where they be examined in detail.

Some Process Theories

Expectancy theory holds that motivation is a function of (a) *expectancy*—the subjective probability that after a certain behavior, a particular outcome will ensue; (b) *valence*—the value one assigns to work-related outcomes (positive-desired; negative-not desired; zero-indifferent); (c) *instrumentality*—the individual's perception that first-level outcomes will be associated with second-level outcomes.

Equity theory holds that one is motivated to obtain equity between his or her inputs/outputs and those of a comparative person. More simply, we tend to compare our efforts and rewards with those of others in similar work circumstances. We have a desire to be treated equitably, at least as we perceive equity.

---

[26]David C. McClelland, "Business Drive and National Achievement," *Harvard Business Review* (July–August 1962), pp. 99–112.

Reinforcement theory holds that behavior followed by pleasant outcomes will tend to be repeated whereas behavior followed by unpleasant outcomes will probably not be repeated. Thus, positive reinforcement can be applied to motivate behavior.

These three process theories and others are discussed much more thoroughly in:

Gibson, James L., John M. Ivancevich, and James H. Donnelly, Jr. *Organizations: Behavior, Structure, Processes.* 4th ed. Plano, Tex.: Business Publications, 1982. Chapter 4, "Motivation: Theories and Principles."

Schermerhorn, John R. *Management for Productivity.* New York: John Wiley & Sons, 1984. Chapter 12, "Leading Through Motivation."

Dunham, Randall B. *Organizational Behavior: People and Processes in Management.* Homewood, Ill.: Richard D. Irwin, 1984. Part III, "Theories in Organizational Behavior."

See also, Reitz; H. Joseph. *Behavior in Organizations.* Rev. ed. Homewood, Ill.: Richard D. Irwin, 1981. Chapter 3, "Motivation."

Cohen, Allen R.; Stephen L. Fink; Herman Gadon; and Robin D. Willits. *Effective Behavior in Organizations.* 3d ed. Homewood, Ill.: Richard D. Irwin, 1984. Chapter 7, "Basic Human Needs and Rewards."

THE VALUE OF MOTIVATION THEORY

Much of this discussion of motivation, need models, and conflicts can be broadly categorized as theoretical. So let us pause to consider the practicality, indeed, the inevitability of theory. Theory is a most practical matter. For without theory—without underlying beliefs, assumptions, premises, and so on—we would be unable to act save through our reflex and autonomic responses. Theory and practice are inescapably linked.

If we are to communicate with others, serve as a subordinate, manage others, and the like, we must have some kind of theory—valid or not, conscious or not—about human motivations and relationships. Otherwise we will be unable to function at all. If we are to control or to influence behavior—our own at any rate—we must be capable of predicting reasonably accurately the responses of others—and of ourselves. These are prime reasons for forming images of others and of ourselves, discussed in Chapter 4.

The objective of this chapter is not to sell any particular theory—content or process. Rather its objective is to urge the reader to bring his or her theory to the surface and to examine the premises of that theory consciously and critically—to do this rather than to make decisions, to take action, and to communicate on the basis of unconscious, unexamined, and, possibly, untenable theory.

EPILOGUE

My reason for placing this and the previous chapters in a book on communication is that the act of interpersonal communication never occurs in a vacuum. In its simplest format, that act is one person communicating out of his or her world of feelings, perceptions, values, and needs to another person in his or her world. To treat communication merely at the level of techniques, devices, and media is to imply an unseemly simplicity for a very complex process. To understand human communication as fully as possible, we must attempt to understand the communicator, the relationships between the individual and those with whom that person communicates, and the organizational setting in which they are communicating. Mason Haire summarized the challenge to the communicator over two decades ago. It is still timely:

> There are three outstanding basic facts that we must remember if we are going to be able to understand human behavior. The first is that the environment itself does not provide an organization. If we make a separation between the physical world outside of us, on one hand, and the psychological environment, or the world we see, on the other, we come to see that the order and organization is not in the physical stimulus but in the observer, and that one of man's greatest problems is to make sense of his environment. The second fact is that man's behavior depends, not on what is actually out there, but on what he sees; not on the way the world is actually organized, but on the way he organizes it. This is at first a deceptively simple point, but it is possible that more misunderstanding in human relations arises from this than from any other single factor. The third point is related to the other two: man has a great deal of anxiety attached to his organization of the world. Man's environment is not organized in itself; he must organize it. His organization determines his behavior. His behavior and its appropriateness to the environment determine whether he will be successful or unsuccessful—in many cases, whether he will survive or not. For this reason, he is reluctant to give up any organizations that seem to work, because of the danger that is involved in being lost in a disorganized environment.[27]

The communicator's "behavior and its appropriateness to the environment" are the central concerns of this book. In the next chapter, we will examine that critical form of behavior—the process of human communication.

DISCUSSION QUESTIONS

1. Why does this chapter which deals with needs and motivation appear in a book on communication?

---

[27]Haire, *Phychology in Management*, 2d ed. (New York: McGraw-Hill, 1964), p. 29.

2. Leavitt's behavioral model: Does it explain human motivation to your satisfaction? Can you visualize any motivated behavior that would not be accounted for by this model?

3. Give examples of need conflict involving various needs posited by Maslow, e.g., conflicts between physiological and safety-security needs, between social and ego needs, between ego and self-fulfillment needs.

4. What does the dependency concept have to do with varying appetites?

5. The Maslow hierarchy of needs—in general, does it account for human behavior? What do you think of the various qualifications imposed upon the model? Are they necessary?

6. Herzberg's major conclusion was that growth needs and avoidance needs where different needs: the need to be happy is different from the need not to be unhappy. Moreover, the two needs are related to different job factors. For example, the elimination of subpar physical working conditions cannot be expected to have a significant impact on productivity. Assuming these conclusions to be valid, what implications do they have for managers in business and industry? For educators? For the leaders of the executive and legislative branches of federal, state, and municipal governments?

7. Re: Herzberg's motivators and hygiene factors and Maslow's hierarchy of needs. Do these theories regarding needs and motivation appear to be compatible? How or how not?

8. McClelland's central contention is that certain needs are learned rather than inherited. What are the implications for management?

9. What do you think of Haire's "three outstanding basic facts that we must remember if we are going to be able to understand human behavior"?

CASES

CASE 6–1

The Accident*

E. C. St. John

The scene is the personnel office of an industrial firm. Bill, the personnel manager is questioning the second shift printing foreman about an accident that had occurred the previous night. Pete, the printing foreman, is a middle-aged man who has come up through the ranks. He is conscientious, energetic, and proud of his production record.

"Bill, I don't know what makes these guys pull these crazy stunts," Pete said as he lit his cigarette. The cuticles of the fingers holding the match were stained from years of washups and makereadies on the presses. "You front office guys are always harping on this, 'Why do accidents happen?' business too much anyway," he continued. Leaning forward in his chair eager to make his point, he waved a finger under the personnel manager's nose. "Accidents are bound to happen," he stated. "I've been trying to tell you ever since you came to this plant. You take this one you're asking about now. Ross just did a dumb thing, that's all. He knew better than to adjust the gate on the hopper while the press was running, but he just didn't think. Stupid, I guess."

"Stupid?" the personnel manager questioned.

"Oh, I don't mean stupid really," Pete continued. "He's got more education that I have, and when it comes to figuring he's tops, but last night he just didn't care."

"It must have played the devil with your production to have a man almost lose his finger. Besides the time taken getting him to first aid, you had to run the press a man short," Bill said.

"Well, no," Pete said as he tapped his cigarette out. "You see, when they came in, I cornered the whole bunch and told them we had this big beer ad run to get out and I wanted these presses running red hot. I remember telling Ross he wouldn't have time to worry about that baby that's coming soon, cause we were gonna hang up a record for the first shift to shoot at. I had to climb on him a little later for taking so long with his makeready. Then at lunch break he said he was having trouble with his register. I told him not to kid me, I'd run presses when he was reaching for his baby bottle, and I knew he could finish that order if he wasn't too lazy. He didn't get

---

*All names have been disguised. Printed by permission.

hurt until about an hour and a half after lunch. By then we had two thirds of the order run, so by holding the guys for half an hour, we finished it."

"You say he hurt his hand because . . ." Bill questioned. "Cause he's just plain careless," Pete interrupted.

"OK, Pete," the personnel manager said quietly. "I think I understand."

Discussion Questions
1. Why did the accident occur?
2. What role, if any, did the foreman play in the accident?
3. How do you account for the way he is responding to Bill's questions?
4. What does this case have to do with motivation?
5. What did Bill mean by "OK, Pete, I think I understand"?
6. What should Bill do now?

CASE 6–2

Arno Annello, Machinist*

The standards department of the Schoonway Machine Company recommended that Arno Annello, who operated a battery of automatic gearcutting machines, be discharged for failure to attain required minimum production as set by the standards department. The foreman in whose department Annello was employed objected to the recommendation. The matter was placed before the production manager for final decision.

Arno Annello came to this country from Finland. He had received the equivalent of a grade school education in his native land but had practically no knowledge of the English language. He secured a job as a floor cleaner in the Schoonway plant. He showed himself to be industrious and thorough, and the foreman of the milling and gearcutting department became interested in him. One day he suggested to one of Annello's friends that the floor sweeper should apply for a better job. When Annello heard this, he signified his desire to become an operative of the automatic sharpening machines. These machines were used to sharpen the teeth of cutters after the cutters were otherwise finished. They were automatic in operation, and with proper setup, there was very little danger of spoiling the work. The foreman or an experienced assistant personally supervised each setup. The operative inserted and removed the work, started and stopped the machines, and dressed the emery wheels when necessary. He operated from four to eight machines, depending on the character of the work.

---

*Reprinted by permission from *Introduction to Industrial Management*, by Franklin E. Folts, Copyright 1949, McGraw-Hill Book Company.

When a vacancy occurred in the department, the foreman decided to give Annello a chance, and obtained his transfer (on trial) from the cleaning department. Over a period of several months, Annello, with the assistance of the foreman, became proficient in operating the machines, and was given a permanent job. For the next two years, Annello showed steady improvement. He became known in the department as a first-class operative of automatic cutter-sharpening machines and finally developed into a skilled machine setter. While he improved as a machinist, Annello showed no aptitude in mastering the English language, and any extended or involved conversation had to be handled through an interpreter. The foreman, however, believed that Annello had the makings of a first-class machinist and was willing to put up with this inconvenience.

The company decided to install a new battery of gear-cutting machines for milling the teeth in cutters, and the foreman was confronted with the task of getting additional operatives to run these machines. The work of operating the automatic gear-cutting machines required considerably more skill than was necessary to run automatic cutter-sharpening machines. The machine attendant had to set up the indexing mechanism for the cutter blank, set the tooth-milling center at the correct distance off the center line of the blank, see that the cutter was properly sharpened, and set the machine for the correct stroke. The machine fed and indexed automatically, but considerable care was necessary on the part of the operative to keep the indexing at exactly the proper adjustment. The foreman approached Annello with the suggestion that he prepare himself to work on the new machines. Annello was highly pleased and put in all his spare time trying to familiarize himself with the work. He succeeded so well that by the time the machines were finally installed, the foreman felt that Annello was sufficiently qualified and gave him a place on the new battery. Here Annello worked along with the other workers, all of whom had been trained at one time or another by the foreman. He appeared to do average work and was well liked by the other men.

The standards department of the Schoonway Machine Company decided to institute a series of studies relative to the operations of gear-cutting machines for milling teeth in cutters. After the routine research had been made, the standards engineer announced the minimum amount of output that a worker must attain in order to be considered efficient. No bonus could be earned until this standard was exceeded.

During the period in which the studies were made, Annello was nervous. He appeared unable to keep his machine in proper adjustment. The pieces which he turned out where inferior in quality, and the total number gradually fell below the point at which the minimum standard was finally set. Engineers from the standards department, knowing that Annello was a protégé of the foreman, sought to ascertain the cause of his trouble, but he was unable to make an intelligible explanation. They warned him of the seriousness of the situation. For several days there was no change. Then, at the suggestion of the foreman, time-study men retimed Annello, in an endeavor to find the cause of his failure. His showing was worse than ever. The engineers began to question whether or not he had the native ability to do the work. The head of the standards department expressed that doubt to the foreman. The foreman insisted that Annello was a first-class worker. The standards department believed that the foreman was prejudiced because he did not object when they suggested that Joseph Smith be discharged. Smith had been employed on the new battery for about the same length of time as Annello, and his output was not as low.

With their watches concealed in their pockets so as not to arouse Annello's suspicion, the time study men clocked him for a third time. Still he showed no improvement. After that, the standards department became insistent that Annello be discharged. The foreman was obdurate, and the standards department appealed to the production manager for a final decision. The latter listened to the recommendations of the standards department and to the objections which the foreman raised, and then made a ruling that at the end of one week the standards department was to make another clocking of Annello's work. If it still was unsatisfactory, the foreman was to be given an additional week in which he could take any measures he chose in attempting to bring the machinist's work up to standard. If he failed to do this within the allotted period, Annello was to be fired for inability to attain the minimum standard.

At the end of the first week, the new timings were made. Annello showed no improvement. When the foreman received this information, he went to Annello accompanied by a friend who acted as interpreter. The foreman told the machinist that his work was coming along well and that he had no need to fear the time study men, that they would bother him no more. He said he would see to it personally that nothing happened to Annello and that as long as he tried his best, he always could have a job with the Schoonway Machine Company. Annello thanked the foreman profusely and said that he always tried to do his best. The next morning he appeared at work smiling and happy. His output for the day was just at the minimum, but the quality was excellent. The next day his output increased. At the end of the week, he was earning a good bonus. Six months later the standards department, as well as the foreman, rated him as the best worker on the automatic gear-cutting machines.

Discussion Questions
1. What was the relationship between the foreman and Arno before the advent of the standards engineers?
2. Why did Arno become nervous when the standards engineers started their studies?
3. Why did the engineers deal with Arno as they did?

4. How did their behavior affect Arno?

5. Why did the foreman reject the engineers' recommendation that Arno be replaced?

6. What do you think of the way the foreman handled the situation once the production manager declared an ultimatum on Arno?

7. Is it likely that everyone will live happily ever after?

CASE 6–3

The Crown Fastener Company*

During the summer between his junior and senior years at Dartmouth College, Edgar Hagan took a job as a student trainee with the Crown Fastener Company, a medium-sized manufacturer and distributor of nuts and bolts. The training program Hagan was placed in consisted of four weeks in the company warehouse, four weeks in the company factory, and two weeks in the company offices. There were five students in the program, all of whom had the understanding that they would receive jobs as salesmen with the company after two summers in the program.

On the first day of work, all five of the trainees met in the office of John Cusick, the superintendent of the warehouse. Cusick was a man in his middle 30s, a former decorated Navy Veteran, and a graduate of Dartmouth College. After outlining the work program for the next four weeks and assigning each of the trainees to a specific department for the first two weeks, he offered this advice to them: "Fellows, I would be very careful in my relationships with the employees here if I were you. The majority of the people here are a pretty crude bunch. Their work is pretty much physical and routine in nature, and as a result, we can afford to hire men of generally low intelligence. They're all either Italians, Poles, or Negroes from the slums, and they're tough customers. So watch out for your valuables, and don't start any trouble with them."

For the first two weeks, Hagan was assigned to the sixth-floor hexagon nut department, under the supervision of Guildo Bovanni, a man who had been with the company since its inception 22 years before. Bovanni, a short but extremely powerful man, spoke in broken English and had quite a difficult time reading any material with which he was not previously fa-

---

*Case material of the Harvard Graduate School of Business Administration is prepared as a basis for class discussion. Cases are not designed to present illustrations of either correct or incorrect handling of administrative problems.

Copyright © 1955 by the President and Fellows of Harvard College (Ea-C 265; ICH 3H14). Reprinted by permission. This case also appears in Paul R. Lawrence and John A. Seiler, *Organizational Behavior and Administration*, rev. ed. (Homewood, Ill.: Richard D. Irwin, 1965), pp. 411–14.

miliar. When Cusick introduced Hagan to Bovanni he said: "Guildo, this is Edgar Hagan, a college trainee who'll be with us for the summer. I've decided to have him work here for the first two weeks, and I'd like you to teach him all you know about nuts. Give him all the odd jobs you have so he'll get experience with as many different types of nuts as possible. Well, good luck, Hagan. We'll get together again soon."

After Cusick had left, Bovanni said to Hagan. "A college boy, eh? I'll learn ya about nuts, but I'll do it my way. I guess Cusick there thinks I can learn ya in two weeks what I've learned in 20 years. Christ! Don't pay no attention to him. We'll start ya helping the packers so ya can work with the nuts we ship most of. You'll be lucky if ya can learn them in two weeks. Then each day I'll try to learn ya a few of the nuts we don't see very often."

Hagan was amazed that each of the nine employees in the hexagon nut department quickly told him about the same thing as soon as he was alone with them. Typical of these comments was this statement by Ted Grant, an elderly Negro packer: "If I were you, I'd stay on the good side of Guildo. He's one hell of a good foreman and really knows his stuff. He can teach you more about nuts and bolts than any guy in this place. Work hard for him, and you'll get along swell here."

Hagan did his best to follow this advice and soon found that Bovanni was spending more and more time with him. He was very surprised when, on Friday, Bovanni said: "Grab your lunch, and let's go eat across the street." Bovanni regularly ate his lunch in a little bar across from the warehouse with a group of about seven other foremen. The conversation ranged from families to sports but soon settled on Cusick. Hagan was amazed at this because he, a newcomer, was there, and interpreted this to mean that Bovanni must have spoken to the men, saying that he was "OK." It was quickly obvious that Bovanni was the leader among the group, and when he summed up the conversation in the following manner, everyone seemed in complete agreement with him. "Cusick tries hard. He's tried to improve things here, but he hasn't had the experience. He must be able to handle Charley Crown,[1] though. Look at the money he's got us for new equipment. But, Christ, then he screws up and buys the wrong stuff. He just don't know what to do and won't listen when we tell him."

On Friday of Hagan's first week, Cusick issued a bulletin stating that all forms used in the routing of materials in the warehouse would be changed to a slightly more complicated type on which material locations could be designated more precisely. The bulletin was handed out to all warehouse employees with their pay envelopes at the close of work Friday. Included was a group of the new forms. The bulletin simply stated that the change was to be made and requested that each man familiarize himself with the

---

[1] The president of the Crown Fastener Company.

new forms over the weekend so that he could use them correctly on Monday. The men just took the material and stuffed it into their pockets in their haste to catch their streetcars home.

On Monday morning, everyone in the hexagon nut department quickly went to work distributing the backlog of materials that had been delivered on Saturday, making a note of each shipment's ultimate location. As was the practice in this department, all of the department personnel met at Bovanni's desk at 10:30 A.M. to give this information to Bovanni so that he could copy it onto the formal forms which went to the office for inventory control. Bovanni claimed he used this procedure so that all the forms would be uniformly filled out and not mutilated by the men carrying them around as they worked. It was quite obvious, however, that his main purpose for insisting on this procedure was that he wanted to know where every shipment on his floor was located, so that when orders came through from the office he could tell the men exactly where the material ordered was located, from memory. Hagan had been constantly amazed by Bovanni's ability to remember exactly where, within each tier and row, a certain shipment was located. This ability had been built up over a period of years, and Bovanni was obviously quite proud of it.

At the Monday morning meeting, there was a considerable difference of opinion among the various department personnel as to how the locations should be entered on the new forms. Bovanni insisted that it should be done in the same manner as before, where the aisle and tier of each shipment was recorded, while most of the other men protested that additional information as to the exact location within each aisle and tier should be noted. Bovanni argued that this would provide unnecessary detail and would only confuse things. He was quite adamant about this, and the other men quickly acceded to his point of view.

The next morning Cusick came up to the sixth floor and walked directly to Bovanni's desk. He said in quite a loud voice: "Guildo, you're filling out the forms all wrong. Didn't you read the notice? You're still doing it the old way, and that's just what we're trying to get away from. Do you think we would go to all this trouble only to have things done in the same old way? Now you've really got the office all fouled up. We need new forms on all the materials you received yesterday. You'd better get at it right away so they can make orders out on some of that material."

Guildo was sitting at his desk, looking up a catalog number, while Cusick was talking to him. He was obviously getting madder and madder as Cusick spoke. Finally he broke in: "Look, Mr. Cusick, this department never had no trouble with its locations before. We've been getting along fine. Why do you have to foul us up by making us change everything? I've been running this department for one hell of a long time, and I guess to Christ I know as much about it as you do. Why don't you handle the top brass and let me handle my department. As long as I get the work done, what do you care how I do it? When those orders come through, I'll be able to find those kegs just like I always have."

Cusick That's the trouble with you, Guildo, you only think of yourself. I've made this change in the entire warehouse. You're the only one bitching about it. From now on the office wants a complete record of exactly where everything is. Now, dammit, as long as I'm running this warehouse, we're going to do it my way!

Bovanni was getting madder all the time: "Listen, Cusick, you may run this warehouse, but I run this floor. Nobody really needs to know those locations except me, and you know it. The way we're doing things here works fine, and you know it. Why pick on me? Why don't you go climb on some of the other boys that don't get their work done? Why come nosing around here telling me how to do my job?"

Cusick moved around next to Bovanni and put his hand on Bovanni's shoulder: "Calm down, Guildo, remember who's boss here. I won't stand for your talking to me that way. Now just calm down and quit shouting."

Bovanni Wait a second. Who started the shouting? You come up here and broadcast to everyone that I don't know what I'm doing. I've run this floor for ten years, and you can't tell me how to do my job. Don't tell me to calm down, and take your Goddamn hand off me!

Cusick (*patting Bovanni's shoulder*) There's no sense in your getting all steamed up about this. You know damn well you're going to end up doing it my way.

Bovanni Get your hand off my shoulder!

Cusick Let's not argue about it. You're wrong, and you know it!

Bovanni Take your hand off my shoulder before I slug you!

Cusick (leaving his hand on Bovanni's shoulder) Listen, no one talks to me that way. I won't stand for any punk telling me what to do. You'd better learn your place around here!

Bovanni You heard me! Get your hand off me!

Cusick (*with his hand still on Bovanni's shoulder*): Hold on, Mac—.

Bovanni then whirled and hit Cusick squarely on the shoulder, knocking him back into a stack of kegs, Cusick recovered his balance and walked away, saying: "OK, buster, if that's the way you want it. . . ."

Discussion Questions

1. How do you size up Cusick? Bovanni?
2. Why did Bovanni resist the new procedure?
3. Why did Cusick confront Bovanni as he did?
4. How do you analyze the accelerating conflict between the two men?
5. What can be done now?

CASE 6-4

"He's Really Coming!"*

Charlie Thorp, with 15 years of management experience with the Darron Company, was regarded as company-minded, cooperative with associates, and a good operator. When his bookkeeper retired, Thorp hired John Pasek to replace her. It soon became apparent that Pasek's ambition was to become a salesman. John was a likable young man; so when an opening occurred, Charlie recommended to Bob Norlach, district manager, "that John, given the opportunity and the leadership, has the qualities that could be developed to make him a successful salesman in my area."

Norlach, Thorp, and Pasek met to discuss the job and its performance standards and to arrive at a mutually acceptable budget. Pasek was installed as a salesman.

Norlach asked for periodic progress reports on John, and Charlie invariably responded: "He's really coming! He is ahead of budget in both new accounts and volume of sales during the period. He's right on target."

After six months of favorable reports on young Pasek, Charlie visited Norlach and complained: "We gotta get rid of John. His production stinks. He has not performed up to standard or budget."

Norlach was astounded: "But haven't you been reporting to me how well John has been doing? Why the sudden change in your evaluation of his performance?"

Charlie answered: "I just wanted to encourage him. I figured that if I reported his real output he'd be getting a lot of pressure and he might never shape up. So I was crediting him with all my own new sales and reporting that to you."

Discussion Questions

1. Why did Charlie Thorp behave as he did?
2. What did you think of Charlie's rosy reports on Pasek? Would you appraise them differently if John *had* shaped up?
3. What should Bob Norlach do now?

CASE 6-5

Pat's Story*

Early Promotions

Considering that I had only a high school education and no business experience, I think I did pretty well at the bank, at least at the beginning.

---

*All names have been disguised

After three years, I was made a branch manager. Three years later I became assistant treasurer, but still stayed at the branch as manager.

During this time, my home life and work life were happy and it was rare when I wasn't smiling. In fact, most of the customers would comment if I wasn't kidding or laughing. They'd think I was sick.

Promoted to Treasurer

Still another three years passed—then I got a shock! On February 1st, Mr. Stockton, the president of our Mutual Savings bank, came over for his usual weekly visit. Over the years, we had become close friends. He was sometimes very unreasonable, but knowing him and his good qualities, I grew to love him. If something were to happen to him tomorrow, I would feel as badly as if it were my own dad.

He said he had a problem and could I spare a few minutes. I assumed it was the usual gab and proceeded to the lunchroom with him. There he told me that Ted Roberts, our treasurer, had given one month's notice, at which time he would go to a competitor.

I thought to myself, "God help us. We'll have to close the doors." I asked Mr. Stockton if he had tried to get Ted to stay. He said he did, but I can't imagine him trying very hard, knowing he would be too proud to admit to Ted that the bank needed him.

Mr. Stockton said frankly he didn't know what he should do. Mr. Wirtz, with all his years at the bank, couldn't qualify. Six years ago, when our senior assistant treasurer, died, and he tried it, he was out for five months with a nervous breakdown. Juan Balboa, our other assistant treasurer in the mortgage department, was new and Stockton hadn't much confidence in him yet.

The vice president, who was being groomed to take Stockton's job when he retired, had been let go in January because of lack of aggressiveness and productivity, and there was no one else but me!

"Me? I don't know, Mr. Stockton, I just don't know!" Ted was always crabbing about how he got everyone's operational problems, how stupid his help was, and how bad his ulcers were getting, and besides, I still depended on Ted for certain technical questions.

Mr. Stockton said he had approached the board of investment and really built me up, and he and they decided I could to it. Well, I don't know how these men could evaluate my capabilities. I've known me for 27 years, and I don't know what they are.

But here was a man who didn't care that I was only a 21-year-old female when he made me branch manager and at 24 made me an assistant treasurer, telling me that he needs me. I couldn't live with myself if I didn't at least try. I made up my mind in 10 minutes that I'd try to get as much knowledge from Ted as possible before he left.

Learning the Job

The next day I arrived at the main office, where Ted informed me as to his duties and tried to teach me the things I didn't know.

Well, I discovered there was a hell of a lot I didn't know. And being so content in my own little world at the branch, I never bothered to learn things that didn't pertain to branch operations.

After one day, I went home very depressed and immediately went to bed. I laid there for six or seven hours, telling myself to throw in the towel and at the same time giving myself all the reasons why I couldn't.

What would my folks think! They were so excited about the idea of me as treasurer. And my kid sisters and brothers all patting me on the back, saying, "We know you can do it, Pat." And last, but not least, I will have failed my boss. ("God, I can't throw in that towel; I'd rather die first.")

My second day was worse. While Ted is explaining, I'm not really getting it because I'm constantly thinking, "I've got to get this in a month, I've got to cram 35 years' experience into one month."

When I returned home that evening, I went to my room, closed the door, and had a damn good cry. Not only did it seem there were 3 million jobs being funneled through Ted's desk, but 3 million questions from the tellers. It seemed like they couldn't blow their own noses without checking with Ted first.

I couldn't help thinking that if these interruptions didn't stop, I'd never catch on to anything.

After one week of depression, tears, and frustration, I decided to tell Mr. Stockton to forget it. I don't want to go nuts like Mr. Wirtz, and I don't want to lay awake nights tossing and turning.

I marched into Mr. Stockton's office the next day and said, "Mr. Stockton, I . . . !" and with this he said, "Well, how's my girl doing? You certainly haven't smiled much this week, but you're a worrywart . . . take your time, be yourself, you're smart, and you'll get it."

Well, what could I say, but, "One thing good that's happened to me is I've lost 9 pounds this week, and I could stand to lose about 20 more." We both laughed, and I marched out, undetermined and unconvinced.

My morale was fairly good, at least for one day.

Three weeks of lying in bed every night, going over the day's instructions, saying, "What the hell is this amortization all about? Depreciation on the buildings and the furniture and amortizing our insurance over the life of the policy. God help me, when he leaves, I'm going to look like the world's biggest jerk! With me running the show, in two months' time we'll have to close down."

Ted didn't help very much, telling me goodies like, "Forget it, kid, when bookkeeping is out, you won't get anything done. That goof in the back room has been doing this job for 16 years, and she still doesn't know where to look when she's out."

Gee, bookkeeping was out practically every day. When do I do my work? And I don't know where to look myself. I don't know a thing about the general ledger except which column to put the amortization and accrued interest in, and that's providing I know what the hell amortization and accrued interest is by the time he leaves.

By the final week, even my folks were discouraging me, saying: "The money and the job aren't worth it!" "You look awful; you better tell Mr. Stockton you can't handle it."

At this time I owned my own house. Keeping house, and all, the whole business was getting me down. I was too tired to even wash my face before going to bed, let alone take care of the problems of a house. I decided to sell.

Well, that was a doozy of an idea! Now I had people bothering me with phone calls, plus selling furniture. Boy, I was beginning to look like death warmed over. Now, I no longer dreaded going to work, but home, too.

In the final week, Ted showed me how to reconcile the computer sheets, payroll, trustee reports, state tax computation, recording new securities, report for estimated earnings, who to collect rent from on our parking lot, and when to pay the board of investment and the board of trustees. Prior to my arrival, both Ted and Mr. Wirtz had handled it, along with our vice president, who had been fired, and Mr. Wirtz was now managing our new branch.

I was now making noontime visits to the nearest church. I don't really know if I was praying for success or just to keep from going nuts. I don't think I smiled once during the entire training. Little did I know, I wouldn't be smiling for some time to come.

Ted seemed touched when I started crying when he said goodbye. I don't think he knew I was crying for me.

The weekend prior to my being on my own was spent in bed. If I didn't know better, I would have thought I was pregnant. I was having morning sickness (which lasted for several weeks).

The First Day on My Own

The first day on my own was hell. All the young help decided that Pat was a soft slob, so let's hit her with gripes we were afraid to mention to Ted.

It was the first of the month and we were getting all our coupons and interest checks in, which had to be recorded on the bookkeeping sheet and checkbooks, plus the usual monthly reports, all of which I was supposed to do on my own.

Mr. Stockton left at 11 A.M. for his usual Monday meeting.

As soon as he was gone, Ann from the mortgage department came in.

Ann   Gee, Pat, I was wondering about our Blue Cross.

Me   Wondering about what?

Ann   How come the bank pays the family plan for the guys but not the girls?

Me   That's our policy, I guess.

Ann   When I get married in four months, my husband'll still be in school. I'll be the main support, so why won't they pay?

Me   Did you ask Ted? I really don't know very much about it. It's one thing he didn't mention.

Ann   Well, he was always so busy, I didn't want to bother him.

This kid had insulted me! What does she think I've been doing, sitting here picking my nose?

Me   Well, I can talk it over with Mr. Stockton and see about it.

Ann   It isn't a fair policy. If they can spend $72.80 a month on David, who's a jerk, why can't they spend it on me? I do more than my share.

Me   Ann, I've got 9,000 things piling up. Please let's not discuss this any further. I will find out for you.

Well now, I can get back to work!

Maria   Pat?

Me   (*Now what?*) Yes, Maria?

Maria   Do you suppose we could have a suggestion box?

Me   Sure, why not, it sounds great.

Flora then asked me if she could keep a dentist appointment that was scheduled in three more weeks. She had already gotten Ted's consent. I answered, "If I'm still alive in three weeks, you have my permission. If I don't make it, you'll have to check with the next guy."

By this time it's 11:30 A.M. and everyone seems to be puzzled as to what lunch hours they were to take. Everyone wants to eat with their friends. I was thinking, "If I went in the vault and took those guns out of joint control, these people wouldn't have to worry about eating."

As everyone bickered over the schedule, I decided that when I got home, I'd make one up and post it, but that wasn't helping me today. I decided to let them work it out themselves, provided some of them stayed to wait on the counter.

Every item I put on the bookkeeping sheet was questionable. I kept running to check with Flora. But Flora went and got last month's work to check. I thought: this is the blind leading the blind.

It was now 12:15 P.M., and my desk looked worse. Everything that these people got that seemed a little different was thrown on my desk, plus both inter-office envelopes from the branches were lying there for the contents to be distributed among the help. After sorting the stuff from the envelopes, it was now 12:30. Well, at least I've gotten two things off this desk.

Boy, when Mr. Stockton gets back at 1:00, he's going to think I was goofing off for two hours.

At 12:30 P.M. the janitor appeared.

Ernie   Pat, I've got this can of 30W oil, and the paper on the boiler calls for 20W oil. Think it would make much difference?

Me   Ernie, about the only difference in oil that I know of is real olive oil and corn oil, and that difference to me is the taste. Maybe we should taste the oil and see.

Ernie   You made a funny!

Me   Did I? That's the first one in a month.

Ernie   All kidding aside, what do you think?

Me   I think there are two people in this bank who know very little about oil, so you buy whatever oil the boiler calls for. I doubt that it will bankrupt us.

Ernie   OK. Can you give me the money? I'll bring back the receipt.

Me   Sure. Tell Charlie what you need, and he'll give it to you.

God, it's 1:00 and I've accomplished practically nothing.

Then Flora makes the grand announcement of the day: "Pat, bookkeeping is out $1.67."

A fantastic thought: Maybe I could put Flora in the boiler room and get Ernie to do the bookkeeping.

I gave Flora a consoling half smile. If I could smile, she might watch for my crow's-feet and not see my tears. "Well, let's start hunting."

I at least had Charlie to rely on. Ted seemed to have fed him a lot of info that the rest of the help didn't get.

Me   Hey, Charlie, would you mind helping us look for $1.67?

Charlie   Cripe, I've got my own crap sitting here to do, and besides, when the heck are you going to take my teller window away so I can devote my time to this important stuff?

Me   Look, Charlie, we'll consider that possibility later, but unless we can find $1.67, we'll never leave here tonight.

Charlie   Well, in that case I'll help out.

I thought "If I didn't need this bratty 24-year-old, I'd kick his a--."
It was now 1:15 and Mr. Stockton popped in.

Stockton   Having problems?

Me   I really don't know, we've just started looking.

Stockton   What have you checked?

Me   Well, I've started adding the check books, but I don't know what Charlie has checked. He's out front.

Stockton I guess you've got everything under control.
Me Yes, more or less.

As Charlie did the directing (which I might add, was his bag), we checked just about every possibility. It was now 2:15, and neither Flora nor myself had had lunch.

I decided we should leave for a few minutes just to clear our heads.

Me Charlie, keep looking. Flora and I are going to lunch. Check with the mortgage department again. Ask Juan to do it. We're running out of places to look in savings.
Charlie If he'd get off his butt instead of having those idiot kids checking for him, we might get results.

As I was thinking the very same thing myself, I kept my mouth shut and proceeded toward the door.

Teller #1 Pat, the coin machine's jammed. I can smell burning.
Me You're right, it's the motor. Is it shut off?
Teller #1 No, I didn't think it would make a difference!

God, what did I ever do to deserve such a fate?

By the time I handcranked the cylinder, it was 2:45, and I finally got out the door.

I didn't eat with Flora. Instead I went to Saint Mary's Church six blocks away. On my way back I grabbed a sandwich. At 3:15 I returned— no change. We looked and looked and finally I threw in the towel.

The help usually get out at 4:00, and it's 3:55.

I'll have to tell Mr. Stockton we can't find it.

Me Mr. Stockton, we've checked everything. I don't know where else to look.
Stockton Everybody will be fresh tomorrow; we'll look then.

Fresh? Is he kidding? The way I've been sleeping, I'll be dead tomorrow. (For a moment, I thought that might be a blessing.)

That night on my way home, I bought a bottle of rum. By 9:00 I was soused. I crawled into bed and finally got a good night's sleep.

The Next Two Days

I wasn't tired the next morning, but I sure as hell was nauseated. I arrived at work early.

As cocky as Charlie was—he was early, too.

We started from scratch, checking everything step by step. I had accomplished a bank first! Never before had the daily statement been out for two days. In fact, it had never been out for one.

Plus two days' work still sitting on my desk. Finally, on the third morning, after Flora finished blocking her mortgage cards, she announced that the cards were $1.67 out. Juan had made a wrong correction on the back of the control sheet.

I was so happy at the moment, I couldn't really be mad with Juan. Then it hit me that none of his work had been interrupted and nothing was piled on his desk, plus he left on time with everyone else!

I decided then I would take one day at a time and stop worrying.

The next day I started off in a pretty good mood. I decided this place was not going to get the best of me.

My problem this day was Mr. Stockton. He must have gotten up on the wrong side of the bed. It seemed that everything he looked at was fouled up. As he proceeded to tell me how messy everything was, I noticed the item to which he was referring had been wrong for two years.

"Look, Mr. Stockton, I don't mind being bawled out for my own mistakes, and I make plenty. That's something that has been handled wrong for two years, and I'll try to correct it, but I do not wish to be criticized for it."

This didn't set too well, as he grabbed his hat and coat and mumbled about no one having any respect for his authority and walked out.

I felt crushed. I don't believe he realized just what I was feeling. I thought I'd never catch on to all the detailed things.

Showdown with Stockton

After two months I was slowly gaining confidence, then it hit the fan!

The third week of June, Charlie gave two weeks' notice. Maria, our secretary, got a better paying job. Another teller was being sent to our branch, and another teller from our new branch quit on the spot.

In one month's time, I had five new savings tellers, three of which had less than one month's experience.

I had to train the new help in as short a time as possible. Their instruction was very poor, as I was now being interrupted every two minutes with questions.

Another two months of turmoil. Mr. Stockton was getting complaints that the help in his organization was giving out wrong information to customers, both over the counter and the telephone. I was certainly bawled out.

I finally got up enough nerve to lay the cards on the table.

"Mr. Stockton, I am not a miracle worker. Just an average person. Before I arrived, things were pretty mixed up. At that time, you had an assistant treasurer making $15,000, a treasurer making $22,000, and a vice president making $30,000. They all leave, and I replace them for $18,000. I'm not complaining about the money, but I only have one head, two hands, and a limited amount of time in the day. I have come to the conclusion that I haven't complained enough for you to recognize all of our problems. I ask nothing of you except consideration. Before screaming, look at the entire picture. I realize we're preparing to merge with another bank and that's why we're not replacing our officers, but the load is getting me down. Especially in that you think this place can run just as efficiently now as it has in the past."

He smiled and said I was right and that he was irritable lately because he was doing a lot more, too.

My little speech cleared the air and has made it a lot easier on both of us.

The Pressure Eases

In October, Juan gave two weeks' notice. He had worked for the bank we were to merge with and wasn't too crazy about going in that direction. He left for a competitive bank.

Things have been looking better the last three months. However, the commissioner refused our merger, so many changes will be needed.

I have some ideas for improvement that I hadn't tried due to the anticipation of a change anyway. Now I want to move.

There are two things which I have come to realize. Most important is the realization that these people are not goofs or idiots.

For example, in 16 years, when bookkeeping was out, it was taken away from Flora and the officers would do the search. She could never look for herself and broaden her knowledge. If it hadn't been for Flora I probably would have fallen on my face when I came to the general ledger. She has become more independent and less of a burden on me.

The moral is—let them think for themselves.

The second thing is make everyone feel his job is important. Through staff meetings, I find that the kids are volunteering a tremendous amount of their ideas and time. Morale has really picked up.

And now that I've stopped fumbling around in the dark, I want to make as many changes as possible to make our organization as smooth-running and as pleasant as possible.

I feel should any great change occur, I will face it, and should I fall, be able to pick myself up and start again.

I really love banking and am now enjoying every minute of it. I have a small ulcer, acquired five months ago, but it's all worth it.

Discussion Questions

1. What makes Pat run?
2. What do you make of Mr. Stockton?
3. What should Pat do now?
4. What do you think of Pat's management philosophy?

7

The Process of Communication

Now to focus on that critical, challenging, sometimes agonizing human process—communication. Let us begin by examining a very simple, mundane communication experience. Imagine two people, A and B, in an office. A feels warm and asks B to open a window, which B does. We can discuss these events in terms of a model of the communication process.[1]

A COMMUNICATION PROCESS MODEL

Encoding

Consider the steps in this incident. First, A had a need—she felt warm, uncomfortable. Next, she went through a remarkable (for such a simple situation) problem-solving sequence in which she decided, among other things, how best to satisfy her need without thwarting other people's needs; whether to take the action herself or to ask another to take it; and, if she decided to enlist the aid of another, how best to approach that person—when to communicate; what communication medium to use; what choice of words, tone of voice, rate and loudness of speaking; and so forth.

Let's suppose the experience is a familiar one and that B is well known to A, much of A's choice-making is routinized, carried on by conditioned responses—that is, A need not be conscious of making many of those choices.

---

[1]See Figure 7-1. For more detailed models of the communication process, see, D. K. Berlo, *The Process of Communication* (New York: Holt, Rinehart & Winston, 1960); C. Shannon and W. Weaver, *The Mathematical Theory of Communication* (Urbana: University of Illinois Press, 1962), p. 5; and W. Schramm, "How Communication Works," in *The Process and Effects of Mass Communication* (Urbana: University of Illinois Press, 1954), pp. 3–26. See also Robert S. Goyer, "Definitions of Communications," special report no. 25, Center for Communication Studies, Ohio University, September 1970; and Norman B. Sigband, *Communication for Management and Business*, 3d ed. (Glenview, Ill.: Scott, Foresman, 1982), chapter 1, "The Process and Problems of Communication; and Randall B. Dunham, *Organizational Behavior* (Homewood, Ill.: Richard D. Irwin, 1984).

FIGURE 7-1

A has been going through the process of *encoding* a message—perceiving her experiences and formulating a series of symbols with which to express her desire. The *code* part of encoding is important, for the term *code* as we are using it is a system of symbols, and a symbol is something that stands for something else.

The most that the communicator can do is to *represent* feelings, ideas, desires, values, and the like with symbols.

Experiential Isolation.   In other words, each of us is experientially isolated from all others. Thomas Wolfe, from the viewpoint of a baby in a crib, captured this insularity.

> He understood that men were forever strangers to one another, that no one ever comes really to know any one, that imprisoned in the dark womb of our mother, we come to life without having seen her face, that we are given to her arms a stranger, and that, caught in that insoluble prison of being, we escape it never, no matter what arms may clasp us, what mouth may kiss us, what heart may warm us. Never, never, never, never, never.
>
> He saw that the great figures that came and went about him, the huge leering heads that bent hideously into his crib, the great voices that rolled incoherently above him, had for one another not much greater understanding than they had for him; that even their speech, their entire fluidity and ease of movement were but meagre communicants of their thought or feeling, and served not to promote understanding, but to deepen and widen strife, bitterness, and prejudice.[2]

Complacency.   Considering our state of isolation, communication is indeed a challenge. And yet there appears to be a general denial, albeit un-

---

[2]Thomas Wolfe, *Look Homeward, Angel* (New York: Charles Scribner's Sons, 1929), p. 37. Reprinted by permission.

conscious, of this. For several years I have been asking people in organizations how they assessed their communication performance as compared to that of others. Specifically, I asked, by anonymous questionnaire: "In terms of the abilities to understand others and to be understood by others, how do you compare with (a) your superior? (b) your subordinates? (c) people at your rank? (d) your department as a whole? (e) your organization as a whole?" I have questioned over 11,000 people in universities, business firms, military units, government agencies, hospitals, and so on, and in some cases every individual in the organization was included. The main conclusion of the study was that virtually everyone felt that he or she was communicating at least as well as and, in many cases, better than almost everyone else in the organization!

Most people readily admit that their organization is fraught with faulty communication, but it is almost always *those other people* who are responsible. With such complacency about personal communication practices, it is small wonder that communication performance in organizations remains depressingly mediocre. The term *complacency* may suggest a superficial condition that can be ameliorated by just getting people to become a little more humble.

Actually, however, the problem is a function of the individual, the organizational structure, and the nature of communication itself. Many individuals find the admission of communication inadequacy tantamount to admitting inadequacy as a person. And recalling our previous discussion of the self-image, it is clear how threatening such an admission can be. Moreover, organizational processes are generally such that it is often very hard to pinpoint responsibility for a miscommunication. Indeed, it is likely that a number of people cumulatively contributed to the breakdown. Accordingly, it is extremely difficult to assess cause accurately; few, if any, are aware of their full contribution to the confusion. Thus the motivation to upgrade communication performance is generally lacking.

Still another factor inducing complacency about one's communication is the nature of the communication process itself. Consider these aspects, among others: First, communication success (or failure) is a product of the behavior of two (or more) people. Since no one person has total control over the communication process, its success cannot be measured solely in terms of how well one speaks or writes, or how well the other person listens or reads. Conversely, it is generally very difficult to isolate and thus to measure an individual's communication performance because it is so intertwined with that of another.

Second, there is often no objective or clear-cut criterion for communication success. If I try to jump a crossbar at five feet, I will receive immediate and unequivocal feedback (if I am still conscious) as to my success, or lack of it. But in communication, the feedback from my recipient, may not necessarily be either immediate or unequivocal (e.g., even if the person does not understand me that individual may also be reluctant to admit it).

Finally, consider the false assurance that wishful *intra*personal communication (the talking we do to ourselves) can generate: "It's clear, logical, acceptable to me, so she's bound to see it the same way!"

In sum, people in organizations generally seem to be unwarrantedly and dangerously complacent about their communication performance. This is partially because of factors in the individual, the organization, and the communication process that tend to shield the individual from recognizing and/or accepting how deficient his or her performance actually is. And when people are unable or unwilling to acknowledge a deficiency, they are hardly in a position to do anything constructive about it.

But even if we recognized these great barriers to communication—experiential isolation and complacency—and took pains to overcome them, we would still not be assured of an adequate communication. There are four critical steps to go.

Transmission

A's message has been or is being encoded. The next step is to make it available to B. Let's say that A chooses to speak (a memo—"Dear B: Re: Window. Please open" . . . doesn't seem quite appropriate here, unless A and B were not on speaking terms).

Some neural impulses are sent from the brain to the abdominal muscles (for air power), the larynx (for phonation), and the articulatory organs (jaw, teeth, tongue, glottis, lips, and so forth), and A is now *transmitting*. Transmitting what? Words? Thoughts? Meanings? Ideas? Feelings? The message? No, vibrations, simply compressions and rarefactions of molecules in the air.

Parenthetically, why not say that words are coming out of A's mouth? And just what is a word? Consider this: hydroherphamorphastyklebackasoriumperpendercularosis. Is that a word?

It is (or was) a word, and here is the silly but true story to support it: This happened when I was 12 years old. About 100 of us had arrived at summer Boy Scout camp in southern Michigan. The campmaster assigned us to tents, eight boys to the A tent, eight boys to the B tent, and so on, and instructed us to choose a name for our tent (patrol) that began with the letter of the tent. We were supposed to use those names at the evening retreat ceremony.

Retreat came, and each patrol leader, in turn, strode out in front of his patrol and reported in: "All members of the Armadillo Patrol present or accounted for"; "All members of the Bear Patrol. . . ."; and so forth. H tent (ours) had been unable to agree on a name for our patrol, so when his turn came, our patrol leader stepped forward and out of desperation and disgust reported: "All members of the *Herphamorpha* Patrol present or accounted for!" A nonsense word, of course, but it received something we hadn't expected, a loud, appreciative guffaw from the other patrols! (They were 12 years old, too.)

The following morning, at reveille, it was the Hydroherphamorpha Patrol—another chortle—and on it went getting a new syllable or so at each retreat and reveille. It probably would have gotten longer, but camp was only for two weeks.

The point is that that noise became a word, nonsense became sense. When that noise was made or heard, meaning was occurring—people were understanding something—*communication* was taking place. A word, after all, is a subjective matter. When one is born into a particular linguistic culture, he or she acquires (without knowing it at the time) a host of previous agreements as to what would be meant or understood when certain sounds are made or heard or when certain marks are put on a piece of paper or are seen there. (In Chapter 9 on *bypassing*, we shall discuss the sometimes grim and costly consequences of the fact that many of the agreements are hardly airtight.)

The Medium

The vibrations occur in a *medium*, usually air. Of course, there are numerous modes of transmitting—speaking, writing, gestures, raised dots on Braille cards, smoke signals, flags, and so on with media to match.

Reception

The vibrations now reach B's ears, and B receives these physical stimuli, which, in turn, are relayed to the brain via an intricate combination of processes in the form of electrochemical-neurological impulses.

Decoding

We do not fully understand what happens at the reception stage, but we understand even less what is yet to happen. Somehow B converts these impulses into symbols and the symbols into meaning. B decodes. How successful has the communication been? The prime criterion for judging the success of a deliberate communication is the extent to which *B's decoding matches A's encoding.*

Feedback

Let us assume that B has decoded A's message as intended. Technically, the communication is now complete. But A will not know there is a match, or mismatch, unless B proceeds to provide feedback, to say or do something or even fail to say or do something by which A can ascertain how B decoded and perhaps felt about A's message.

COMMUNICATION: A SERIAL PROCESS

Mismatches can occur, sometimes with extremely costly, even fatal, consequences.

The process of communication is extremely susceptible to distortion and disruption because, among other reasons, it is a *serial process*, a step-by-step process. If you are interested in interfering with or preventing a communication, you need attack it at only one phase, for as a chain, the entire process is as strong as its weakest link. Broadly speaking, you would create *noise*, a deterioration of effectiveness, at that particular link.

A's communication to B could be faulty if: A did not transmit adequately, for example, did not speak distinctly or slowly or loudly enough; or if A and B were trying to communicate in an environment where there were competing vibrations, such as in a forge shop or around a jet engine (B could scarcely distinguish A's feeble vocal vibrations from the barrage of noise assaulting his tympanic membranes); or if B had reception difficulty, for example, a hearing loss.

Transmission, medium, and reception are critical phases of the communication process, but this book will not deal with them. I am presuming that the great majority of my readers do not have horrendous problems in the physiological transmission and reception of communication stimuli.[3] I presume, too, that they do not ordinarily encounter serious barriers in the physical media they use.

Even when we have difficulties in the middle three phases of the communication process, we generally have one or two important advantages. First, we are usually *aware* that we are indeed having a problem in our communications, and furthermore we have a good idea of where it lies. Thus we usually have the opportunity to cope with the problem—to avoid it or prevent it or correct it or compensate for it.

Encoding and Decoding—the Subtle Phases

But when we have problems in our encoding and decoding, we often have neither of the advantages mentioned above. We know relatively little about what really happens *inside* a communicator as he or she sends or receives messages, and herein lies the irony I alluded to in Chapter 1.

While investing billions in communication research—and receiving commensurate returns—we have virtually ignored the equally critical end processes. Ultimately, there are *human* encoders and decoders no matter how much sophisticated instrumentation we place between them. The computer people have a phrase for it: GIGO, garbage in, garbage out.

---

[3]There are skilled practitioners in the areas of speech and audiological therapy, ophthalmology, and so on, available to deal with difficulties in these functions.

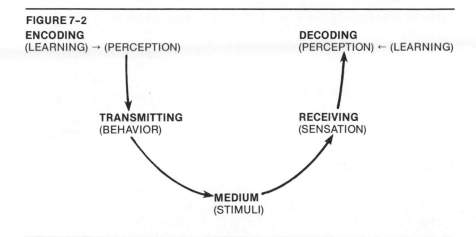

FIGURE 7-2

ENCODING
(LEARNING) → (PERCEPTION)

DECODING
(PERCEPTION) ← (LEARNING)

TRANSMITTING
(BEHAVIOR)

RECEIVING
(SENSATION)

MEDIUM
(STIMULI)

The incongruity is hardly a new one, as evidenced by the wry Josiah Stamp of England's Inland Revenue Department, 1896–1919:

> The government are very keen on amassing statistics. They collect them, add them, raise them to the nth power, take the cube root and prepare wonderful diagrams. But you must never forget that every one of these figures comes in the first instance from the village watchman, who just puts down what he damn pleases.

We have been constructing the communication chain with enormously strong, forged links in the center and paper clips at the ends.

And so, the emphasis in this book is on encoding and decoding, mainly because they are the least understood. To set the stage, examine Figure 7–2 for a superimposition of the perceptual model (page 61) on the communication process.

Let's return to the example of A trying to get B to open a window. A *encoded* her message on the basis of her *perception* of the situation—including her assessment of the problem to be solved, her anticipation of B's response to her request, and so forth.

Her subsequent transmission (speaking) was her *behavioral response* to that perception. Then the consequences of her behavior—audible vibrations (*stimuli*)—were conveyed via the medium to be received in the form of auditory *sensations* (B was hearing). But those sensations only became meaningful when B decoded—that is, *perceived* them—created meaning from them.

The roles may switch very quickly. Suppose B replies: "Sure, I'll open the window," or "Can't do it—my back's bothering me" or "No way! It's already too cold in here!" Suddenly B has become the encoder transmitting for A's consumption.

The one element we've disregarded so far is *learning.* Our prior programming, as discussed in Chapter 3, can have a direct bearing on how we perceive (and encode and decode). For example, read the phrases in these triangles:

Almost everyone reads them as "Snake in the grass," "Paris in the spring," and "Once upon a time." But look again—it's "Snake in the *the* grass," and so on. Why do we read them incorrectly? What programmings might have caused us to miss the repeated *the* and *a*?

For one, they are enormously familiar expressions. We often read what we anticipate will be there rather than what *is*.

Another factor, consider the reading ability you've developed through years of practice. You no longer read word-by-word but in clusters of words. Give the triangles to youngsters who are just learning to read—laboriously working out each letter, syllable, and word—and they'll catch the repetitions. This is no condemnation of speed reading, but it does make us easy prey to the triangle stunt.

Would the trick have worked as well if *snake* or *grass* or *Paris* had been repeated? Probably not. The articles *the* and *a* are extraordinarily frequently used words. In fact, in written English, they are respectively the first and fourth most common words.[4] But it's not only English. Use *el* and *la* or *le* and *la* and the Spaniard or Frenchman will be equally vulnerable.

Again, the separation of the repeated words, which is seemingly legitimated by triangles, probably threw us off. The same words stretched out on a straight line don't fool as many people. We could have been misled, too, by our predisposition to gloss over apparent typographical errors.

The Role of Assumptions.   Learning provides our memory content including our values, goals, attitudes, habits, and most relevantly here, our *assumptions*. Let us return to A and B to examine the role of individual assumptions.

Suppose that in expressing her desire about opening the window, A chose to say: "Let's get a breath of fresh air in here." By this, she intends to express simply that she feels warm and that she would like B to open the

---

[4]Lest your curiosity deprive you of sleep, *of* and *and* are second and third.

window. Now note some of the assumptions that may be underlying A's remark and of which she may be quite unaware. She could be assuming that because she is warm, B also feels warm and will welcome the idea of opening a window. She could be assuming that because B is closer to the window, B is the logical one to open it and that B will understand and agree with this. She could be assuming that because she means something by her words, B will understand them as A intends them.

Actually, none of these assumptions is necessarily warranted. B may be quite comfortable or even chilly with the window closed and thus be offended by A's apparent selfishness. Furthermore, he may fail to see A's logic about B's proximity to the window and instead resent A's pushing him around. B may even fail to interpret A's words as they were intended. He may, conceivably, hear A's remark as an indictment against B's failure to have opened the window previously. It is even possible that B may feel that A is not interested in opening a window at all but is sarcastically alluding to B's habits of personal hygiene! B as the receiver is, of course, just as prone to contribute to a misunderstanding influenced as he is by his own assumptions.

Consider these three propositions:

1. Everyone has assumptions—certain underlying beliefs, premises, notions, suppositions, rationales, generalizations, principles.
2. Some of these assumptions are false; they are not borne out by reality.
3. The individual is partially or, in some cases, totally unaware that he or she is laboring under fallacious notions. Many of them are primitive postulates, acquired before the age of reason. They have been semiconsciously learned at best and have never been examined critically.

The third proposition should not be difficult to accept, for does it not stand to reason that most people would not tolerate false assumptions, that they would supplant such assumptions with more valid premises? But if they are not *aware* that the assumptions are false or even that they hold such assumptions, what will prompt them to do anything about them? As the 19th-century humorist, Artemus Ward put it: "It ain't the things we don't know that hurt us. It's the things we do know that ain't so."

We are all victims, more or less, of unconsciously holding certain fallacious assumptions, which in turn materially, destructively, and insidiously affect our encoding and decoding. The frequent result is miscommunication, sometimes with grievous consequences.

Since our concern is expressly with communication, one category of fallacious assumptions, in particular, merits our attention. These are the assumptions that we develop partially or largely from our language system. For example, one of these fallacies is that words, rather than being merely labels for things, are somehow inextricably linked with that they represent.[5] This is false, of course, but we do not always behave as if it were. In fact, our reaction to a thing is sometimes distinctly colored by its label.

An incident occurred while the late Professor Irving J. Lee was giving his exceedingly popular course, Language and Thought, at Northwestern University. Dr. Lee had several graduate assistants who were occasionally given the opportunity to lecture before a class of 200 to 300 undergraduates. On one such occasion, an assistant set out to dramatize the tendency to react to labels rather than to the objects that the labels represented. He distributed bits of food that resembled dried biscuit and assured the class that the food was sanitary and nutritious and added that most of them had probably never eaten this type of food before. Each student was to taste the food and decide how much he liked or disliked it. Most of the students found it relatively tasteless and reported an indifferent reaction. A few said that they liked it slightly and even fewer expressed a mild dislike. Not *one* said that he or she liked or disliked it extemely.

The assistant tabulated the results on the blackboard and suggested that perhaps the food would be tastier with cream and sugar. He added that it was quite inexpensive and readily available. At this point, he reached behind his desk and held up a large, distinctly labeled box and said, "Just go to your grocer's and ask for _____ Dog Biscuits!" The reaction was precisely what he had hoped for—a great deal of groaning, shrieking, laughing, feigned nausea (and some not so feigned). Whereupon he triumphantly cried out: "Now just what are you reacting to—those innocuous bits of food or to the words on this box?"

Elated by his success, the assistant repeated his dramatization during the next term. But the word had spread, and the students had come to expect such things from the course "where they served dog biscuits." Undiscouraged, he changed his tactic. For the third term, he baked some special cookies, passed them out to the class, and tabulated the results. The cookies were sweet, and the reactions were unanimously favorable.

"Glad you liked them. I'll give you the recipe," he volunteered, "so you can bake some at home if you wish." The recipe: So much flour, sugar, shortening . . . and two cups of carefully cleaned grasshoppers!

He admitted later that even had he been able to restore order, he would not have dared to ask: "Now, what are you throwing up about . . .?"

The Map-Territory Analogy. For focusing attention on the subtle role that language plays in influencing human behavior we are primarily indebted to the late Alfred Korzybski.[6] Korzybski contended that the relation of our assumptions, unconscious or otherwise, to the phenomena with

---

[5]This particular fallacy is developed more fully in Chapter 15.

[6]Alfred Korzybski's *Science and Sanity: An Introduction to Non-Aristotelian Systems and General Semantics* (Lancaster, Penn.: Science Press 1933).

which they are concerned (people, things, theories, processes, relationships, and so on) is analogous to the relation of maps to the territories they represent. Geographic maps are pictures, or abstractions, of their territories. Our assumptive maps, similarly, are pictures of the territories they are used to represent. We rely on both kinds of maps as guides in our dealings with their respective territories.

But there is an essential difference between our geographic and our assumptive maps. Cartography has advanced to the point that most geographic maps can be followed with great confidence. On the other hand, our assumptive maps are often inadequate and distorted representations of their territories. And we are misled by them because we rely upon them so unquestioningly.

Korzybski felt that we are largely *unaware* of the power the structure of our language has over us. Unconscious of such influence we are in an unlikely position to take action against it. As the biologist J. H. Woodger put it, "Man makes metaphysics just as he breathes, without willing it and above all without doubting it most of the time.

Perhaps this book appears to be at least as much about thinking as it is about communicating. Actually, it is about thinking-communicating for the two processes are inseparable.

SUMMARY

The first seven chapters have attempted to prepare a foundation for the balance of the book, to delineate its scope, and to set out a rationale. In subsequent chapters, we focus on the encoding and decoding of a perceiving, need-satisfaction-seeking individual communicating in an organizational setting.

The approach to communication here is a "psychosemantic" one, the basic premises of which can be summarized as follows: Behavior, including communication behavior, is largely the product of one's perceptions which in turn are acutely affected by one's prior learning. And a most critical part of that programming stems from the individual's language system. A major contention is that one's language system spawns certain fallacious, and often unconsciously held, assumptions.[7] Such assumptions pave the way

---

[7]*General Information Bulletin*, no. 6, of the International Society for General Semantics asserts the influence of language:

Nor do we realize how grammar warps our "thinking." When we make sentences, we force symbols (words) into certain set relationships. Yet the things which these symbols represent often have quite different relationships. This happens because our grammar preserves many ancient wrong guesses about the world we live in, such as: similar things may be treated as identical; the "essences" of things never change; parts may be considered without relation to the whole; qualities are properties of "things"; an event has "a cause." Such notions once fit man's knowledge of the world. But our century has seen the birth of the relativity theory and atomic fission. Today, primitive language habits serve only to widen the frightening chasm between our lagging civilization and our leaping technology.

for miscommunication and other forms of foolish, immature, dangerous, unsane behavior. Indeed, our chief concern will be with *self-deception* for, in the words of Goethe: "We are not deceived; we deceive ourselves."

Thus, the remaining chapters explore a number of recurrent, delineable patterns of miscommunication. The patterns are not mutually exclusive. Rather they might be considered as so many handles with which to grasp and cope with some of the most prevalent and serious anomalies of a complex and vital function—communication.

DISCUSSION QUESTIONS

1. Anatole Rapaport has said: "Experience cannot be transmitted as *experience:* it must first be translated into something else. It is this something else which is transmitted. When it is received it is translated back into something that resembles experience."

   Do you agree with the above statement? What are its implications—for communicators? For the mass media? For organizational communication? Or for any form of communication which goes through a series of people?

2. Compare the model of communication with those of Berlo, Shannon and Weaver, Schramm, and Dunham (see footnote 1). What are the relative strengths and weaknesses of these models? In what ways are they different, similar? Does their adequacy and validity depend to some extent on what kind of communication experience is represented? What are the underlying premises for each model.

3. The issue of communication complacency: Do you agree that most people are unrealistically confident about their communication ability? What do you think of the various reasons offered to account for this attitude? Can you suggest others?

4. The Boy Scouts and the "Hydroherpha. . . Patrol." Can literally any nonsense syllable (or polysyllable) become a word? Under what conditions? How do words get to *be* words? Suppose that you invent a gadget and contrive a brand-new word to represent it. What potential communication problems do you foresee?

5. This book focuses on the encoding and decoding phases of the communication process. Why?

6. What "advantages" are there for having problems in the transmission, medium and reception phases as opposed to having them in the encoding and decoding phases?

Part Three

PATTERNS OF
MISCOMMUNICATION

8

The Inference-Observation Confusion

Let me begin the first of these patterns of miscommunication by inviting you to test yourself.

Instructions

Read the following little story. Assume that all the information presented in it is definitely accurate and true. Read it carefully because it has ambiguous parts designed to lead you astray. No need to memorize it, though. You can refer back to it whenever you wish.

Next read the statements about the story and check each to indicate whether you consider it true, false, or "?". "T" means that the statement is *definitely true* on the basis of the information presented in the story. "F" means that it is *definitely false*. "?" means that it may be either true or false and that you cannot be certain which on the basis of the information presented in the story. If any part of a statement is doubtful, make it "?". *Answer each statement in turn, and do not go back to change any answer later, and don't reread any statements after you have answered them. This will distort your score.*

To start with, here is a sample story with correct answers.

Sample Story

You arrive home late one evening and see that the lights are on in your living room. There is only one car parked in front of your house, and the words "Harold R. Jones, M.D." are spelled in small gold letters across one of the car's doors.

Statements about Sample Story

1. The car parked in front of your house has lettering on one of its doors.   (T)   F   ?
   (This is a "definitely true" statement because it is directly corroborated by the story.)
2. Someone in your family is sick.   T   F   (?)
   (This could be true, and then again it might not be. Perhaps Dr. Jones is

paying a social call at your home, or perhaps he has gone to the house next door or across the street.)

3. No car is parked in front of your house.   T (F) ?
   (A "definitely false" statement because the story directly contradicts it.)
4. The car parked in front of your house belongs to a man named Johnson.   T F (?)
   (May seem very likely false, but can you be sure? Perhaps the car has just been sold.)

So much for the sample. It should warn you of some of the kinds of traps to look for. Now begin the actual test. Remember, mark each statement *in order*—don't skip around or change answers later.

The Story[1]

A businessman had just turned off the lights in the store when a man appeared and demanded money. The owner opened a cash register. The contents of the cash register were scooped up, and the man sped away. A member of the police force was notified promptly.

Statements about the Story

1. A man appeared after the owner had turned off his store lights.   T F ?
2. The robber was a *man*.   T F ?
3. The man who appeared did not demand money.   T F ?
4. The man who opened the cash register was the owner.   T F ?
5. The store owner scooped up the contents of the cash register and ran away.   T F ?
6. Someone opened a cash register.   T F ?
7. After the man who demanded the money scooped up the contents of the cash register, he ran away.   T F ?
8. While the cash register contained money, the story does *not* state *how much*.   T F ?
9. The robber demanded money of the owner.   T F ?
10. A businessman had just turned off the lights when a man appeared in the store.   T F ?
11. It was broad daylight when the man appeared.   T F ?
12. The man who appeared opened the cash register.   T F ?
13. No one demanded money.   T F ?
14. The story concerns a series of events in which only three persons are referred to: the owner of the store, a man who demanded money, and a member of the police force. T F ?
15. The following events occurred: someone demanded money; a cash register was opened; its contents were scooped up; and a man dashed out of the store.   T F ?

---

[1]The story and statements are a portion of the "Uncritical Inference Test," copyrighted, 1955 and 1983 by William V. Haney. The full-length test is available for educational purposes from the International Society for General Semantics, P.O. Box 2469, San Francisco, California 94126.

If you will permit me to withhold the answers for a few pages, I would like to describe a classic study.[2] It is the oldest of its kind I could find and has been repeated in many forms since then, but always, to the best of my knowledge, the results of the Otto experiment have been corroborated.

The scene is a University of Wisconsin classroom. (See Figure 8-1.) A carefully planned incident is about to occur. Of the 75 students present, only four, A, B, C, and D (and the instructor), are in on the stunt. At a given signal the following events occur: (1) While the instructor is collecting papers from students in the front row, A suddenly hits B with his fist, and B retaliates by striking A with a book, and the two fall to quarreling very loudly; (2) at the same time, C throws two silver dollars into the air, permits them to fall to the floor, scrambles after them as they roll away from him, and picks them up; (3) the instructor now orders A, B, and C from the room; (4) as he does so, D simply gets up and walks from the room at a nor-

FIGURE 8-1

---

[2]M. C. Otto, "Testimony and Human Nature," *Journal of Criminal Law and Criminology,* 9 (1919), pp. 98-104.

mal gait; (5) as A, B, and C are preparing to leave, the instructor walks to the blackboard at the front of the room, glances at his watch, writes "9:45" on the blackboard, erases it, and writes it again; (6) A, B, and C leave the room, and the instructor turns to the class and says, in effect: "You have all seen what has happened, and you know that you may very well be called upon to give testimony.[3] Let us now take time to write out reports of what we have observed." And with the instructor's assistance the class composes a series of questions to give order to their reports. The following are some of those questions and some of the answers to which these eyewitnesses were willing to testify.

Q: Where was the instructor when the disturbance began?

Twenty-two of the students reported that he was near the front of the room; 20 that he was about in the middle; and 21 that he was in the rear. A number of students scattered all over the room said they would have testified under oath that the instructor was at his (the student's) desk collecting his paper!

Q: Where was the instructor, and what was he doing when the students left the room?

Only 5 of the 75 reported the "9:45 business" with any accuracy. The attention of the others was obviously fixed elsewhere. However, only six said they did not know. The others gave very definite testimony. Three said the instructor was holding the door open for the students to pass through. One said he was standing in the middle of the room muttering, "I'll break this up, or know the reason why." Three remembered him sitting dejectedly at his desk with his face buried in his hands. The consensus of the remaining students was that he was sitting at his desk nervously toying with, variously, the papers he had collected, class cards, his watch chain, a piece of chalk, etc. He appeared "as if not knowing what to do," and "his face wore an expression of embarrassment and uneasiness."

Q: What did C do?

You will recall that C had thrown two silver dollars into the air. They fell to the floor, and he hurried to pick them up. Some students reported that either A or B, in their fighting, had dropped some money; that these coins had rolled to the front of the room; and that C had scrambled to pick them up. Other students said that an adjustable desk arm from one of the classroom seats had been broken off (and A, incidentally, had tried to poke B with it) during the fighting; that the little ratchet ball inside had fallen out and had rolled to the front; and that it was this ball that C had rushed to pick up. The student sitting next to C, ironically enough, insisted that he had seen a little steel ball come rolling out between C's feet and that C grabbed it and put it in his pocket.

---

[3]At this time the university was on a student self-governing basis. This meant that any student disciplinary case, as this incident was to all appearances, would be submitted to a student court and testimony would be taken. In other words, it is most likely that the students saw the situation as quite real and one for which they might very well be asked to appear in court to give testimony.

Q: How did A, B and C look as they left the room?

The reports corresponded directly with the observer's attitude toward the instructor's action. If the student felt that the instructor had been fair and justified in sending the men from the room, then they tended to look "embarrassed" and "ashamed." If, however, the student thought the instructor too severe, the men looked "angry," "injured," and "abused." C's neighbor, who had perceived C do nothing more heinous than pocket a steel ball, reported that C had looked "very angry," while A and B appeared "sheepish."

Q: What did D do?

This question was quite accidental. While the class was deciding the questions to be answered for their reports, one student asked: "Are we to include the fact that D rushed from the room at the beginning of the disturbance?" The instructor replied noncommittally: "Please report what you saw as completely as you can, but report no more."

It seems highly likely that, with a vociferous struggle having just been waged in an opposite section of the room, only a few at most would have noticed D's casual departure. Yet the suggestion of the student's question plus the obvious fact that D was now absent was apparently enough to convince over 85 percent of the students that they *had* seen D leave, and most of them were quite confident about the specific manner in which he left —saying, variously, that he had "rushed," "hurried," "bolted," or "made a wild dash" from the room.

Otto, who was concerned with the bearing of this sort of behavior on the taking of legal testimony, seems amply justified in his alarm:

> The importance of these facts is obvious. If it is impossible for a witness to reproduce an occurrence as it took place in his presence, even when asked to do so directly after the occurrence; if it is his very nature to demand consistency in such items as he does get, to the point of rejecting some and creating others; if such a thing as sending three men from a room at the same time may act as a suggestion around which is built up what the witness believes himself to have observed concerning them; what are the chances of arriving at the truth under conditions[4] which often obtain where testimony is taken?[5]

It may seem incredible that people could be capable of observing, remembering, and reporting an incident so distortedly—that they could fail so utterly to distinguish between what they had observed and what they only inferred.

THE UNCALCULATED RISK

We need to dig deeper into what we call the inference-observation confusion.

---

[4]Referring to such factors as the time lapse between the observation and the giving of testimony (involving sometimes hours, days, weeks, or even years); the third-degree tactics of examining authorities; the leading, confining, and suggestive questions of cross examining attorneys; and so on.

[5]Otto, "Testimony and Human Nature," p. 104

"Taking a calculated risk" is a phrase that we ordinarily use to describe a situation in which a person has decided to take an action that may have undesirable consequences—embarrassment, loss of money, injury, and so forth. But we imply that he or she is aware of these potential effects and, furthermore, has assessed the likelihood that they will occur. Generally speaking, when we take calculated risks, we are apt to be in a better position to avoid the hazards, or at least to cope with them should they occur.

The inference-observation confusion, on the other hand, involves taking uncalculated risks. Take this actual traffic accident case, [6] for example.

FIGURE 8–2

Diagram A shows Driver White halted at a stop sign. Driver Black is approaching the intersection from the south. His right directional signal is blinking. White *assumes* that Black is going to turn right at the intersection and, acting on this inference *as if* it were fact, starts to cross the intersection. Black does *not* turn but continues northward and is unable to avoid a costly collision with White (Diagram B). The directional signal? Black had intended to turn right into a driveway—50 yards beyond the intersection. Who was liable for the personal injuries and property damage? Usually White, for failing to yield the right-of-way.

Let us go back and examine White's response more closely. We shall presume that he saw Black approaching and that he noted the blinking directional signal. At about this time he must have made his key assumption that Black was going to turn right at the intersection. Somehow in the process, however, this inference became fused with his observations. Perhaps

[6]See William V. Haney, "Are Accident-Prone Drivers Unconscious-Inference-Prone?" *General Semantics Bulletin,* nos. 20 and 21 (1957). Reprinted in *Traffic Digest and Review,* 5 (March 1957).

he forgot that he had, in fact, guessed—or perhaps he was never fully aware that he was in the realm of inference. At any rate, his crucial error occurred at the moment he treated the inference as if it were not an inference.

It was at this point that he took his uncalculated risk. White, in entering the intersection with Black approaching, was taking a very definite risk. But, since he apparently failed to perceive his inference as an inference—that is, as a situation involving a degree of uncertainty—he did not realize the risk he was taking and thus was hardly prompted to calculate its probability.[7]

In sum, the inference-observation confusion apparently occurs as follows: (1) Someone makes an inference, (2) fails to recognize or remember that he or she has done so, (3) thus does not calculate the risk involved, (4) proceeds to act upon the assumption as if it were certain, and (5) ends by taking an unrecognized and uncalculated risk that may prove costly, dangerous, or even fatal.

This is the pattern that appears to be responsible for the worst disaster in aviation history: the collision of two 747s in Santa Cruz de Tenerife, Canary Islands, on March 27, 1977. A Pan Am plane had landed but had not yet cleared the runway when a KLM plane inexplicably attempted to take off, ramming into the Pan Am plane. The complete explanation may never be known because the KLM pilot perished along with almost 600 others. But according to one safety official: "The key to the investigation is why did not the captain [KLM pilot] verify the assumption that he had takeoff clearance, especially after being questioned by another crewmember, or did he *not realize that it was an assumption.*"?[8]

So much for how the uncalculated risk occurs. But why does it happen, and what can be done to prevent it?

OBSERVATIONAL AND INFERENTIAL STATEMENTS

Why, after all, does the inference-observation confusion and thus the uncalculated risk happen? Clearly, emotions often play an important role. Consider this incident:

---

[7]Thomas Fansler, of the National Safety Council, described the phenomenon in this manner: "In checking over case histories of traffic accidents, an observer cannot help being impressed with the number of times the idea of suddenness or unexpectedness occurs. After the accident, the driver will report, 'Suddenly the man ran in front of my car,' or 'I expected the other fellow to stop but instead. . . .' The inference that may be drawn from this is that there was an *expected* pattern of circumstances in the minds of the drivers and that the change from the *expected* pattern to a 'sudden' or 'unexpected' pattern was partly responsible for the accident." Howard Pyle, National Safety Council, has attributed 90 percent of traffic accidents to driver error.

[8]*Aviation Week & Space Technology,* May 2, 1977.

Razor-in-Apple Tale Proves Hoax[9]

PHILADELPHIA (AP)—A man was released from jail and six young girls were arrested Wednesday—the result of a Halloween hoax in which the girls said they were given an apple with a razor imbedded in it.

Based on the girls' stories Jack Thomas, 52, an unemployed father of three, was jailed Saturday in lieu of $10,000 bail, charged with intent to maim and cruelty to children. He was released from jail Wednesday afternoon.

The six girls admitted Wednesday morning their stories were false after Matthew Blelochi, 44, a guard in the housing project in which they live conducted an investigation of the girls' stories.

Grace Wisotzkey, 12, one of the girls arrested, had told police Thomas had given her an apple with a razor in it.

Under Blelochi's questioning Grace admitted she had gotten an apple with a soft spot from Thomas, and her friend, Debbie Connors, prodded her into burying the blade in it, then showing it to her mother, police said.

The six girls were, Grace; her sister Carole, 14; Debbie, 13; Jean Hammond, 10; Catherine O'Leary, 10; and Joan Twilley, 11. All were charged with making a false report and conspiracy.

After Thomas was jailed, police said, infuriated neighbors threatened to burn his house.

Municipal Judge Benjamin Segal told the defendant at the time of his arraignment: "They should have whipping posts for people like you."

Here's a more tragic example. Life had not been easy for Chicago West Sider, Carey Epkins, a deaf-mute since birth. Relying upon the intricate system of sign language, even simple communications were a struggle.

Recently, however, things took a decided turn for the better. Epkins, 25, married his childhood sweetheart, Phyllis, also a deaf-mute. Naturally, the ceremony was conducted in sign language.

But on a cold night in March, Carey's short and painful life came to an end. Accosted by an 18-year-old gang member, Epkins tried to signal that he meant no harm. Instead, police said, the gang member *thought* Epkins was using signs to say he was a member of a rival gang. So the street tough drew a .38-caliber handgun and shot Epkins twice.[10]

But emotions constitute only one broad category of variables provoking uncalculated risks. I devoted a lengthy chapter in my Ph.D. dissertation to

[9] *The Atlanta Constitution*, November 6, 1969, p. 4–C. Reprinted by permission.

[10] Tom Maier and Mark Brown, "Sign Language Fails. Deaf-Mute Slain," *Chicago Sun-Times*, March 7, 1983, p. 4. Italics are author's.

merely listing and documenting some of the factors that appear to contribute to the inference-observation confusion. They include limited and impaired senses; physiological conditions, such as those associated with hunger, thirst, and fatigue and those incurred with the ingestion of alcohol and narcotics; and a host of psychological factors, including emotion and stress, habit and set, values and needs, and group and social influences. In a category by itself was a seldom suspected agent: *our language!*

A central theme running through the various patterns of miscommunication covered in Part Three of this book is that how we think and behave is influenced in no small measure by our language—the linguistic tool by which we reason and communicate.

But what does language have to do with the inference-observation confusion? Practically speaking, there are two kinds of declarative statements that I can make about what I observe (see, hear, smell, taste, and so forth). Assuming that my vision and the illumination are normal, I can look at a man wearing a tie and say: "That man is wearing a tie." This is called a statement of observation because it corresponds directly to what I have observed. On the other hand, I can look at the same man and say just as confidently: "That man bought that tie." But unless I actually observed him purchasing the tie, this statement is for me a statement of inference. I *infer* that he bought the tie because (1) he's wearing it; (2) he looks honest; (3) he appears to be the kind of person who would select his own ties; and so on. I may be right—but I may be wrong. Perhaps someone gave him the tie—or loaned it to him. Perhaps he found it. The point is that, since I did not *observe* him buying the tie, the statement for me is necessarily an inferential one.

Observational and inferential statements are often extremely difficult to distinguish. Certainly the structure of our language offers no indication of their differences. There may be no grammatical, syntactic, orthographic, punctuational, or pronunciational distinctions between them whatsoever. Moreover, the tones or inflections in which they are uttered may sound equally certain.

You and I can point to this page, and each of us can say: "William Haney wrote this material." Your statement was inferential; mine was observational. Yet the statements were the same.

In other words, nothing in the nature of our language (or any other language to my knowledge) makes it inescapable that we discriminate between inferential and observational statements. Our failure to distinguish on these verbal levels contributes appreciably to the difficulty that we have on *nonverbal* levels, namely, our propensity to confuse inference and observation. Thus, we find it enticingly easy to make inferences and to utter inferential statements with the false assurance that we are dealing with facts and the consequences of acting upon inferences as if they were observations are often less than pleasant.

"Mother, I wish I didn't look so flat-chested," said my 15-year-old daughter as she stood before the mirror in her first formal dress.

I remedied the matter by inserting puffs of cotton in strategic places. Then I hung around Mary's neck a string of seed pearls—just as my grandmother had done for my mother and my mother for me.

At midnight her escort brought her home. The moment the door closed behind him Mary burst into tears.

"I'm never going out with him again," she sobbed. "Mother, do you know what he said to me? He leaned across the table and said, 'Gee, you look sharp tonight, Mary. Are those real?'"

"I hope you told him they were," I said indignantly. "They've been in the family for three generations!"

My daughter stopped sobbing, "Oh, the pearls. Good heavens, I'd forgotten all about them."

—Mrs. J. L. H. (*Alabama*)[11]

Lest the reader feel that the inference-observation confusion pertains only to teenage girls and University of Wisconsin students of 1919, let us bring the matter somewhat closer to home. Here are the answers to the test that I trust you took at the beginning of the chapter.

1. ? Do you *know* that the "businessman" and the "owner" are one and the same?
2. ? Was there necessarily a robbery involved here? Perhaps the man was the rent collector—or the owner's son—they sometimes demand money.
3. F An easy one to keep up the test-taker's morale.
4. ? Was the owner a *man?*
5. ? May seem unlikely, but the story does not definitely preclude it.
6. T The story says that the owner opened the cash register.
7. ? We don't know who scooped up the contents of the cash register or that the man necessarily *ran* away.
8. ? The dependent clause is doubtful—the cash register may or may not have contained money.
9. ? Again, a robber?
10. ? Could the man merely have appeared *at* a door or a window without actually entering the store?
11. ? Stores generally keep lights on during the day.
12. ? Could not the man who appeared have been the owner?
13. F The story says that the man who appeared demanded money.
14. ? Are the businessman and the owner one and the same—or two different people? The same goes for the owner and the man who appeared.
15. ? "Dashed?" Could he not have "sped away" on roller skates or in a car? And do we know that he actually left the store? We don't even know that he entered it.

---

[11]From "Life in These United States," *Reader's Digest*. Reprinted by permission.

CORRECTIVES

An effective technique for avoiding the inference-observation confusion is a four-step process:

1. Detect the inference.
2. Calculate the risk.
3. Get more data—if the risk is a poor one.
4. Recalculate the risk.

1. Detect the Inference

There is an apocryphal story that goes something like this:

The Case of the Raging River

Four men—Adams, Baker, Carson, and Dawson—are camped alongside a raging river, as diagramed below:

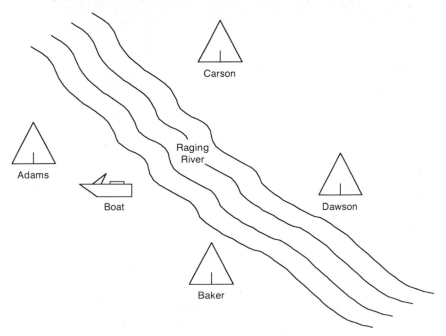

It is dangerous to cross the river in a boat and impossible to swim it. Aside from a boat, which Adams owns, there are no means of crossing within 50 miles of this point on the river.

One day a young woman, Elaine, approaches Adams and asks him to transport her across the river to Carson, her lover. Adams agrees to do so, but only on the condition that she sleep with him. Elaine refuses and asks Baker to intercede for her with Adams. Baker says that he does not want to become involved. Desperate, Elaine returns to Adams and agrees to his terms.

Afterward, Adams takes her across to Carson. Elaine immediately tells Carson what happened, and he becomes furious and throws her out. Desolate, she walks to Dawson and explains her plight, and he takes her in.

The usual challenge is to rank the five persons in the order of their morality—who behaved the most morally, the next most morally and so forth. Anyone who accepts this chore would necessarily make a host of assumptions because the case is loaded with ambiguities and information gaps. So to make the story an exercise in detecting inferences I would propose this question: What additional information would you need in order to feel more competent about ranking the five? In other words, what relevant things do you *not* know about the case?

Among other things you would probably want to know a good deal more about:

1. *Relationships.* Were any of these people related to each other in the past? If so, how? Were any of them married? If so, to anyone in the case?

2. *Motives.* Why did Elaine want to reach Carson? How would you evaluate her if she were on an errand of mercy, for example? Why did Baker refuse to become involved? Is it conceivable that Baker is on bad terms with Adams and that Baker's intercession would be the kiss of death for Elaine's chances of crossing the river on Adams' boat? What were the motives of Adams' bargain with Elaine? Why did Carson throw Elaine out? What were Dawson's motives in taking her in?

3. *Circumstances.* When and where did this case occur? Would it matter to you if the setting were puritanical Salem, Massachusetts in 1690? Or modern-day America? Or some aboriginal culture whose mores differed greatly from ours? What were the ages of these people? Eight? Eighteen? Eighty? What were the physical features of the situation? For example, how viable an option was the next crossing? Would Elaine have had to wade 50 miles up and back hip-deep in alligators and water-moccasins? Or was there a convenient highway and readily available transportation?

4. *Ambiguity.* Precisely what was meant by such phrases as "sleep with him" and "takes her in"? What actually happened between Elaine and Adams? Between Elaine and Dawson?

5. *The Criterion.* The key issue is, what is meant by morality? Ranking the five persons is tantamount to evaluating or judging them. So what is the measuring rod? How do you define morality? For example, do you prefer an orthodox conception, such as the Ten Commandments? Or do you lean toward a more humanistic view, such as doing the most good and the least harm to people? (How, then, do you define good and harm?) Clearly, how one defines morality can greatly influence how he or she ranks the five.

Each of the above questions highlights an awareness of something we don't know. Detecting the inference is easily the most critical phase of our four-step process. For if we are *unaware* that we are inferring, we are hardly likely to take any of the other three steps.

Here are three simple checkpoints for heightening and maintaining your inference-detecting ability.[12] Memorize, practice, and habituate them so that they occur to you almost automatically:

1. (Source) Did *I* make the observation?

What someone else tells you about his or her observation remains hearsay—inferential—for you if you have not personally observed it.

2. (Scope) Did my statement stay with and not exceed my observation?

Back to the aforementioned man and the tie he is wearing. I can make observational statements about the length, width, color, design, and so on, of the tie, but a statement about its *purchase* would exceed my observation and thus be inferential.

3. (Timing) Did I make the statement *during* or *after* but *not before* my observation?

Again the man with the tie: Five minutes *before* I saw him, I could have said that he was wearing the tie. The statement might very probably have been correct, but it would nevertheless have been inferential.

If you can say yes confidently to each of these questions, you are likely to have made an observational statement. If you have to say no or even maybe to any one of them, then be alert. You are probably inferring, which is why you need Step 2—and possibly Steps 3 and 4.

2. Calculate the Risk

Once I recognize that I am dealing with an inference I am ready for Step 2, the calculation of the risk, that is, the assessment of the probability that the inference is correct.

Visualize a continuum with an infinite number of gradations. Label one end "the extremely probable," and the other "the extremely improbable." We are constantly going through the process of pegging our inferences (provided that we recognize them as such and try to assess their probability) somewhere on this scale. For instance, the inference that the earth will continue to turn on its axis tomorrow seems so extremely probable that we literally bet our lives on it. Or we stake our lives on the improbability of the inference that the sun will be destroyed within a week.

To return to my inference about the man with the tie—that he bought it. I might peg this guess at the 50-50 mark. Why? It's just my judgment. Ties

---

[12]Studies indicate clearly that we can indeed increase our inference awareness. See William V. Haney, "Measurement of the Ability to Discriminate between Inferential and Descriptive Statements," unpublished Ph.D. dissertation, Northwestern University, 1953. A précis of this dissertation appeared in *General Semantics Bulletin*, nos. 16 and 17 (1955). See also my article "Police Experience and Uncritical Inference Behavior," *General Semantics Bulletin*, nos. 22 and 23 (1958).

are very popular gifts. Moreover, wives often buy them for their husbands. And who knows? Maybe the man does his shopping after the stores have closed!

I might be willing to wager a quarter that he bought the tie, but probably not a dollar and certainly not five. I consider this a poor risk in need of Steps 3 and 4.

3. Get More Data

To improve the quality of my risk, I need more data. Suppose that in answer to my question the man says in all apparent sincerity and confidence: "Yes, I clearly remember buying this tie." This still does not make it an observation for me, of course, but I may now be willing to revise the point on the probability scale.

4. Recalculate the Risk

If I know and trust the man, I may now feel that the risk is a very good one and be willing to wager a considerable sum on my inference. Let me add a fifth step, which applies when we are dealing with other people:

5. Label Your Inferences

When I am communicating with others, do I label my inferences as such and try to get them to label theirs? I was recently discussing this fifth point with a group of industrial engineers. After the seminar one of the men came up and said: "Am I glad you made that fifth point! That's the core of my problem. I have a man who is constantly giving me his inferences *as if* they were his observations. Maybe he's afraid to tell me they are only guesses, but in any event I go upstairs and report them as certainties to my superior—and sometimes they're wrong and then *I'm* in hot water. I think I know now how to deal with this fellow. I'll tell him: 'Look, management doesn't expect us to *know or see* everything, but they do expect us to know the *difference* between what we know and what we're only guessing at.'"

TWO QUESTIONS

Two particular questions sometimes arise when the inference observation confusion is discussed. They concern creativity on the one hand and decisiveness on the other.

Creativity

What bearing does inference awareness have on creativity? Wouldn't the rigor required to distinguish inference from observation tend to curtail the imagination?

I see no incompatibility between rigor and creativity. Suppose that Officer Jones observes a motorist racing through a stoplight. As the officer gives chase he will very probably be trying to infer the driver's motive in order to determine the manner by which to apprehend him. Suppose that the officer assumes the driver was simply in a hurry and felt that he could get away with it. And suppose that Jones fails to recognize this as an inference but blithely treats it as an observation. That probably ends the policeman's analysis of the situation, and we can only hope that in his interest, at least, his inference is correct.

On the other hand, if Jones is aware and remains aware that his first inference was just that —his first inference—he is more likely to try to imagine other possible motives for the motorist's action. Is the driver ill or under the influence of drugs or alcohol? Is he preoccupied and unaware that Officer Jones has seen the violation? Is the car out of control, for example, is the accelerator jammed? Is the driver taking a sick or injured person to the hospital? Is he deliberately flouting the law and egging the officer on? Has he committed a felony, and is he now attempting to escape his pursuers? And so on.

Aware that he is inferring, the officer will be continuously alert for signs that may help him calculate the probability of these various motives and perhaps suggest additional ones. Thus, he will be prepared to deal more appropriately with the situation.

The point is that had Jones confused inference for observation at the outset—had he treated his first inference as observation—he would hardly have been prompted to invent and test the additional alternatives.

Decisiveness

In urging the distinction between inference and observation, do I appear to be saying: "Don't take risks. Stay away from inferences. They are dangerous. They only get you into trouble"? Am I advocating analysis paralysis—the sort of academic impotence that George Bernard Shaw scorned when he asserted that "if all the economists in the world were laid end to end, they still wouldn't reach a conclusion"? Nothing could be farther from my purpose. In the first place, we could not avoid inferences if we tried. We assume incessantly. You and I are assuming that the chairs we are seated on (I am assuming that you are sitting on one) will not collapse beneath us. We are assuming that our next inhalation will not be noxious and kill us. When we eat, we make a host of inferences about the source, content, and preparation of the food. Whenever we post a letter, we make inferences about the speed and safety of our mail. Whenever we take advice from a doctor, attorney, or cleric, and whenever we read a newspaper, magazine, or book (this one included), we make inferences about the credibility of the statements we hear and read. We might be able to reduce the number of our inferences by resigning from life and living in bed as a vegetable. But, even so, we would have to make inferences about those who attended us.

In sum, one must deal with inferences. Visualize a woman who is the chief executive officer of her firm. How much does she know from *her* own direct observation about her employees, her products, her markets, her competition, her suppliers, her stockholders, the governmental agencies that may regulate her enterprise, her firm's financial status? And to what extent must she rely upon the observations and inferences of others, who in turn rely upon the observations and inferences of still others, ad infinitum?

Inferring and risking are inescapable parts of living in an active world. The semanticist Stuart Chase once stated: "We cheerfully trust our lives to total strangers in the persons of locomotive engineers, subway motormen, airplane pilots, elevator operators, steamship captains, taxi drivers, traffic cops, and unhesitatingly consign all our worldly goods to bankers and insurance companies."

In short, we live in a world of risk; some risks we can avoid, many we cannot or should not avoid. This chapter does not advocate inaction and indecision. The capacity to infer, after all, is essential in the arts and in the sciences. Analysis, problem solving, planning—all involve inference. Think of any creation—a skyscraper, a portrait, a computer, or a picnic—without inferences, none of these would have been possible.

Your success (or lack of it) in life will depend largely upon your ability—and upon your willingness—to risk . . . to make inferences. A decision invariably involves risking.

> The mark of an educated man [or woman] is the ability to make a reasoned guess on the basis of insufficient information.
>
> —A. Lawrence Lowell
> Late president of Harvard University

The point is this: Since we must make inferences anyway, is it not better (1) to be aware that we are making them so that (2) we will be prompted to calculate the risk involved and, if necessary, (3) get more data to upgrade the quality of the risk? This story of a dining-car waiter makes the point:

> It seems that a prosperous-looking man walked into the train's diner, sat down, and ordered a doughnut and coffee. When he finished, he was presented with a check for $1.45. He fished two one-dollar bills out of his wallet and handed them to the waiter. Shortly afterward the waiter returned with his

change on a plate—a half-dollar and a nickel. The man gave a grunt of annoy-
ance, pocketed the half-dollar, and looked up, expecting to see a resentful
waiter. Instead the waiter grinned widely: "That's all right, sir—I just gam-
bled and lost!"

Aside from miscalculating his risk, the waiter showed considerable maturity. There is a world of difference between professional and novice infer-
rers. The novice goes out to the racetrack, say, and bets his life's savings
on what he is completely convinced is a dead-sure thing. The pro may bet
the same amount (which he can just as ill afford to lose), but he knows the
odds against him. Both may lose their money, but the novice is likely to
lose a great deal more than money.

Let me add an important adjunct here. Much of our risk-taking is not of
the simple, one-chance, win-or-lose, horse-racing variety. A good deal of it
occurs in a process—a flow of events—which can be modified (or to which
our behavior can be adapted) in midstream, so to speak. Few of our decisions are intrinsically irrevocable. Take the automobile collision of White
and Black, for instance. If sometime during the process, beginning with
White's noting of Black and ending with the crash, White had become
aware that he was taking a bad risk, there were numerous actions that he
could have taken to avoid, or at least diminish, the consequences. He
might, for example, have speeded up to get through the intersection before Black reached it, sounded his horn or arm-signaled to alert Black of
the danger, braked his car sooner, veered off to his right, and so forth. In
other words, even a poor decision is not necessarily an injurious one if we
stay alert to the effect of changing circumstances upon our inferences and
risk calculations.

The objective, then, is not the *avoidance* but the *awareness* of risking,
of inferring. And to suggest the occasional absurdity of refusing to risk I
pass along a letter that was purportedly written by a corporation attorney.

It seems that the attorney's company had purchased some land in Louisiana and was now seeking a loan on it from a federal agency. Before
granting the loan, the agency asked for a record of the titles to the land.
The attorney sent in titles dating back to 1803. The agency's response:
"Who owned the land before that?" to which the lawyer replied:

Gentlemen:
    Your letter regarding titles in Case #2515619 received. I note that you
wish titles to extend farther than I have presented them.
    I was unaware that any educated person in the world failed to know that
Louisiana was purchased from France by the United States in 1803.
    The title to the land was acquired by France by right of conquest from
Spain. The land came into the possession of Spain by right of discovery in
1492 by an Italian sailor named Christopher Columbus, who had been granted
the privilege of seeking a new route to India by the then reigning monarch,
Queen Isabella.

The good queen, being a pious woman and careful about titles (almost as careful, I might say, as your agency), took the precaution of securing the blessings of the Pope of Rome upon the voyage before she sold her jewels to help Columbus. Now the Pope, as you know, is considered by some as the emissary of Jesus Christ, who is regarded by many to be the Son of God, and God, it is commonly accepted, made the world.

Therefore, I believe, it is safe to presume that God also made that part of the United States called Louisiana. And I hope to hell you're satisfied.

> *To recognize what things you know,*
> *And what things you do not know—*
> *This is wisdom.*
> *—Confucius*

DISCUSSION QUESTIONS

1. When one jumps to a conclusion, what really happens?

2. Precisely what is involved in the concept of inference-observation confusion?

3. How can one avoid the inference-observation confusion?

4. How can one help others to avoid taking the uncalculated risk? Without offending them?

5. List five occupations in which inference awareness would be especially important.

6. List five occupations in which inference awareness would be unimportant.

7. About inferences—how do you go about calculating your risk?

8. What do you think of the four-step process for avoiding the inference-observation confusion? The author feels step one—detecting the inference—is the most critical of the four steps. Do you agree? Disagree? Why?

9. Regarding the three checkpoints for heightening and maintaining your inference-awareness: Are there exceptions to these recommendations? Can you make additional recommendations?

10. Are there limits to the extent to which one should become inference-aware? Could preoccupation with inferences lead to indecision, inaction? To stultification of one's imagination? Explain.

11. Describe an incident, possibly involving yourself, in which the inference-observation confusion occurred. Analyze specifically why it occurred, what might have been done to prevent its occurrence, and what measures would prevent its recurrence.

CASES

CASE 8-1

56 Minutes before Pearl Harbor*

Hugh Russell Fraser

My task was to investigate the 56 minutes of warning we had of the Jap air attack on Pearl Harbor, December 7, 1941. What I learned amazed me. I reported every detail to the Assistant Chief Signal Officer—specifically, Maj. Gen. James A. Code.

Now, nearly 17 years later, I can tell that story. The facts, incredible as they are, became a part of my history of the U.S. Signal Corps in World War II. To most Americans who know merely that we had some radar warning of the sneak Jap attack on the "Day of Infamy," the history of those 56 minutes will come as a shock.

Radar could, and did, detect the approach of the Jap air fleet. But not, of course, as it should have been detected, and not as it would have been detected if authorized radar equipment had been installed. Actually, the island of Oahu was to have been ringed with permanent radar-warning installations. It was not. As early as November of the year before, the Corps of Engineers was directed to install six permanent radar-warning sets to be operating around the clock beginning July 1, 1941.

These sets were not installed by July 1. They were not installed by December 1, nor by December 7. Four mobile radar-warning units, mounted in trucks, were provided in their place. Regarded generally by the men assigned to them as toys to experiment with, they were in operation only from 4:00 A.M. to 7:00 A.M. Why were those hours chosen? Probably it was because those were the 3 hours out of the 24 when the enemy—any enemy—was most likely to attack. If this was the theory, then it came very close to being 100 percent right!

The Opana mobile radar set, manned by Privates Joseph Lockard and George Elliott, was the one that detected the approach of the Jap air armada. Singularly enough, it was supposed to be shut down promptly at seven o'clock on the morning of December 7, but, by one of those fortunate accidents of history, the truck coming at that time to take the two men back to base camp and to breakfast was late. So Lockard and Elliott decided to leave the set on until it arrived.

Thus, after 7:00 A.M., the Opana unit was the only radar unit on the island operating. The other mobile sets, also mounted in trucks, had shut

---

American Mercury, August 1957, pp. 80–85. Reprinted by permission.

down promptly. One was located at Punaluu on Kahana Bay, 20 miles to the southeast; another on the extreme west side of the island near Makua; and the fourth near Waipahu on the southwest coast, 11 miles west of Pearl Harbor itself.

The Opana unit, which made history, was located about 22 miles due north of Pearl Harbor and about 28 miles northwest of the city of Honolulu. In other words, it was north of the mountains on the island of Oahu, which itself is about 43 miles long and 30 miles wide.

As the seconds after seven o'clock ticked off, Lockard, who kept his eye idly on the machine, noted nothing unusual until, suddenly, at 7:02 A.M., there appeared what he later described as a "huge blip of light—bigger than anything I had ever seen before on the set—moving slowly from the extreme left side of the scope to the right. It was, you might call it, a pillar of light. It startled me, for the flight of one plane is represented by a mere dot, several planes a collection of white dots, but here was something different. The whole left side of the scope suddenly took on light!

"My natural reaction," he continued, "was to infer the radar unit was out of order. So I asked the mechanic, Elliott, to check it. He did so in a couple of minutes and reported it was working all right. By then it was 7:04 A.M. Something unusual, I knew, was before my eyes. Elliott thought so, too, although neither of us could imagine what it might be.

"Quickly we plotted it. The calculations were easily made, and it appeared to be definitely a large flight of planes approaching from due north, three points east, and about 137 miles away.

"We looked at each other, and Elliott was the first to reach for the phone. At first he couldn't get anybody at the Army Information Center at Fort Shafter. The line was dead. Then he tried another line. It was open, and soon Private Joseph McDonald at the switchboard answered. Tersely, Elliott told him what we were seeing on the scope. McDonald's answer was: 'Well, what do you expect me to do about it? There's nobody around here but me.' Elliott told him to find somebody and then hung up.

"What happened, I learned later, was that there was an officer reading a book in the next room. McDonald had supposed he had gone. He was Lt. Kermit Tyler.[1] McDonald told him what Elliott had reported. Lieutenant Tyler looked up from his book, thought awhile as if to take it all in, then said: 'It's all right, never mind.'

---

[1] A report of the Army Pearl Harbor Board which was published in the *Army and Navy Journal*, September 15, 1945, reads in part: "The Navy was supposed to have detailed officers in the Information Center to be trained as liaison officers, but had not yet gotten around to it. In the Information Center that morning was a Lieutenant Kermit A. Tyler, a pursuit officer of the Air Corps, whose tour of duty thereat was until 8 o'clock. It was Tyler's second tour of duty at the Center, and he was there for training and observation, but there were no others on duty after 7 o'clock except the enlisted telephone operator. He was the sole officer there between 7 and 8 o'clock that morning; the rest of the personnel that had made the Center operative from 4:00 to 7:00 had departed." (Reprinted by permission.)

"Joe McDonald then ca.led back, and I answered the phone. He told me what Tyler had said. I thereupon insisted on talking to the officer myself. I was a little excited and puzzled and didn't want to let the matter end with McDonald. Joe then asked the lieutenant if he would be good enough to talk to me. The officer then came on the phone and said, 'What is it?'

"I made my reply as brief as possible. 'The scope,' I said, 'indicates a large flight of planes approaching Oahu from due north, three points east, about 137 miles away at the last reckoning.'

"There was a pause for a few seconds. Then Tyler said, 'That is probably our B-17s coming in from San Francisco.' I knew there was such a flight coming in, but I knew also those planes would hardly be approaching us from due north.

"At once I made this point clear, and he replied, 'Well, there is nothing to worry about. That is all.' The last words he said with some emphasis, and I judged he didn't want to hear anything further about it, so I said: 'All right, sir,' and hung up.

"Meanwhile, somewhat startled by the whole business, although not alarmed, as now the matter was out of my hands, I continued to watch the set. The pillar of light, or 'blip,' as I call it, continued to move steadily from left to right, and the truck still had not arrived. At 7:25 A.M. we made a quick computation, and the flight of planes, whatever it consisted of, was 62 miles out. At 7:39 A.M., just as we heard the truck arriving outside, I made my last computation, and the flight was 22 miles away!

"It was at 7:39 A.M. that we closed down the radar unit and climbed into the truck for a long ride back to base. I was still turning over in my mind what we had seen on the scope as the truck bounced over the badly rutted road. I said nothing to the driver about it, nor did Elliott—not because we were alarmed but because I knew that what didn't make sense to us would hardly make sense to him.

"After we had been driving about 20 minutes, the driver called our attention to a heavy black pall of smoke that lay on the Pearl Harbor horizon to the south. 'Looks like oil smoke,' he commented. Soon we were hearing what sounded like explosions and even antiaircraft fire. It was all very puzzling, and somebody suggested it was a practice raid on Pearl Harbor.

"However, on we went over the rugged road. Actually, it was only 20 miles back to base camp, but because of the road it took almost 40 minutes. As we hove into view of the camp and the truck slowed down, we saw a lot of soldiers running toward us, shouting questions the words of which I couldn't quite at first make out. Finally, it was plain they were asking, 'What happened?' 'Did you report it?' and the like. I never saw a camp so collectively excited.

"As we started to get out of the truck, a major came elbowing his way through the group of men surrounding us and said, sharply, to us: 'Shut up! Don't say a word! I'll talk to you.'

"With that he took us off to his office and questioned us for 15 minutes. It was not until then I realized the Japs were at that very moment attacking Pearl Harbor, and that what we had seen on the screen was the Jap air fleet approaching.

"Now, as I look back, the position of the flight, the vast number of planes, made sense. I learned later the enemy aircraft carriers had sailed far to the north so that when the planes took to the air they would be coming in from an unexpected direction."

Lockard at one point told me that except for the brief questioning by the major on the island of Oahu on the morning of December 7, 1941, I was the first to interrogate him in detail as to those 56 minutes—namely from 7:04 A.M., when Elliott reported the set was not out of order, to the time the first bomb fell on Pearl Harbor.

The tracing of the history of these 56 minutes, however, led me into a further investigation of why the permanent radar sets had not been installed on the island of Oahu by July 1. Here I ran into a curious and amazing story which I tried in vain to have the Congressional Investigating Committee explore.

My investigation disclosed that the colonel in the Corps of Engineers, who was charged with the duty of having these permanent radar sets installed and operated around the clock by July 1, 1941, had spent most of his time in the summer of 1941 drinking. His entire record demonstrates incredible negligence of duty. Not only did he fall down on his job, but the toll in lives and ships that we had to pay for his failure was heartbreaking.

I tried to bring my evidence before the committee. To that end I prepared a long memorandum, setting forth the facts as I saw them. I requested that this colonel be summoned and be cross-examined under oath.

To my surprise, the Democratic members of the committee, whom I knew personally and regarded highly, handled my request—made in my capacity as a citizen—as if it were a hot potato. They not only refused to act on it in any way, or request that he be summoned, but they told me in essence "to forget it"!

Amazed that members of my own party would take this view, I turned to the Republicans. I knew only one personally. He was Representative Bud Gearhart of California. Mr. Gearhart read my memorandum carefully and promised to do his best to get the colonel summoned. Later he reported back he had failed, but he had tried his best.

"Why won't they go into this question of radar units?" I asked. "Surely, you know their importance!"

"Yes," he said, "of course. My opinion is that somebody failed and failed terribly, but I ran up against a stone wall. The chairman flatly refused me, and when I asked one of my Democratic friends what was the real reason for what I thought, and still think, was an obvious runaround, he said, 'Look, Bud, you can do what you please and maybe you can get somewhere, but don't forget I'm a Democrat and a loyal one, and I take my orders from my commander in chief, and my commander in chief happens to be president of the United States!' "

Discussion Questions

1. Analyze the series of blunders and miscalculations that rendered Oahu's defense system so ineffectual and that squandered the 56-minute warning of the Japanese air attack.
2. Why was this case placed in the inference-observation confusion chapter?

CASE 8-2

Tyler Industries, Inc.*

Len Williams, manager of the Export Parts order section of Tyler's North European division, was puzzled and troubled. Something had obviously gone sour, but what?

Len had always prided himself on the relaxed, friendly atmosphere in the section. Good-natured bantering had been the order of the day, and the men would frequently stop by his desk for an informal chat.

Suddenly, things were different. Len hadn't had a "visitor" for over a week, and everyone seemed too busy with his own affairs for intraoffice needling. With the men becoming more taciturn, Len felt himself growing progressively uneasy and unwilling to go out of his way to initiate conversations.

The change had occurred shortly after young Paul Brock had joined the section. But how could there be a connection? Paul seemed eager to learn and gave every indication of wanting to be a good "team player," but the group had clearly not accepted him.

Tyler Industries, Incorporated was a large multidivision organization headquartered in Cleveland and operating in the Americas, Europe, Africa, the Far East, and Australia. The service functions of the corporation were organized by geographic areas such as the Great Britain division, the North European division, and so on. Some of these functions were located in the regions they served. Others, such as Export Parts, were centralized in Cleveland.

The North European division's Export Parts order section consisted of Williams and seven order interpreters. Their eight desks were arranged in a straight line. Williams' desk was at the head of the line, and Brock's was second. This desk had been vacated by Lou DeWitt, who had just been promoted to chief of another section. Williams assigned the desk to Brock because Paul was new to the corporation as well as to the section and would

*All names have been disguised.

probably need considerable coaching. Moreover, Len confided to a friend, "I want to avoid that silly desk reshuffling the guys did two years ago when Jack Rosen was promoted out of the section." Coincidentally, Rosen had occupied the second desk.

Discussion Questions
1. What is your analysis of what has happened?
2. What should Williams have done?
3. What should he do now?

CASE 8-3

The Case of the Ledgers*

W. C. Lohse

Alfred Gregory, bank examiner, and his two assistants were making a routine examination of a country bank. The procedure in such bank examinations is to see that all the various bank ledgers are proved by adding machine to see that they reflect the same figures as those shown on the bank's statement for that particular day. In examination circles, it is customary to refer to the loan ledger as a liability ledger and to checking accounts as commercial ledgers; the general books, in which all entries ultimately arrive and from which the daily statement is made, are called the general ledger. One of the two assistant examiners had been on the examination force for only two or three months, and since he was a novice, he did most of the machine work.

Mr. Gregory and his two assistants, Bill, the recruit, and Mac, the experienced assistant, entered the bank promptly at 7:30 A.M. as Leonard Brace, the cashier and vice president, was opening the bank for business. The examiners' credentials were shown to Brace, and the examination proceeded as scheduled. At this point it might be pointed out that no banker is ever aware of when an examination might take place.

> **Gregory** Bill, as soon as you have counted the cash, run the liability ledger and then report to Mac.
>
> **Bill** OK! (*Bill was elated because he had been put on his own for the first time.*)

Bill succeeded in counting the cash and balancing it in a fairly short time, and proceeded to hunt up the liability ledger. This bank was considerably different from those Bill had been in before. Here, they kept all the

---

*All names have been disguised. Reprinted by permission.

ledgers in one place and they were not labeled. Bill picked up a ledger and proceeded to run it on an adding machine.

Gregory and Mac were working in the directors' room, whose open door faced the open door of Brace's office. Bill entered the directors' room and went over to Mac with the total he had on his adding machine tape.

Bill   Here you are, Mac. I ran the liability ledger, and this is the total that should be on the statement.

Mac (*looking at the statement*)   Boy, you sure goofed. This isn't even close. Run it over again.

Bill   OK!

Gregory   Say, Mac, you better have him stick with it; good experience.

Bill returned to his work, tabulated the ledger again, reported to Mac, and was again dismissed as having the wrong total. This procedure was repeated several times more before the morning was over. From where he sat in his office, Brace could see the repeated trips Bill made between Mac and the ledger. At noon, Mr. Gregory explained to Brace that the examiners would have to leave for lunch and that since Bill had been unable to strike a balance with the liability ledger, the ledger would have to be sealed until they could check it out after lunch.

After lunch the examiners came back to the bank and Bill was sent to Mr. Brace's office to pick up the liability ledger that Brace had sealed. Bill returned to the directors' room, apparently distressed.

Gregory   What's the matter, boy?

Bill   Boy, I've really messed this up.

Gregory   What do you mean?

Bill   I have been running the wrong ledger all morning. I was running the commercial ledger—no wonder I couldn't balance.

Gregory   That's all right, son, no harm done. Here, take this liability ledger back and run it now.

Bill was passing Mr. Brace's door with the ledger, when Brace called to him.

Brace   Wait a minute. I'd like to talk to Mr. Gregory and you fellows.

Bill and Brace walked back to the directors' room.

Brace (*perspiring heavily*)   Well, I guess the jig's up, Mr. Gregory.

Gregory (thinking Brace was joking, as most bankers do with examiners)   Yep.

Brace   I didn't think that some young fellow would catch me. If I had to be caught I hoped it would be an old-timer like yourself.

Gregory (*now that it is clear that Mr. Brace is serious*)   Well, now that we know of this situation, would you please aid us in ascertaining how far it has gone?

Mr. Brace readily agreed and proceeded to show the examiners where, over the past eight years, he had embezzled $28,000 and the methods used to penetrate the defalcation. Gregory asked what had given him the idea that the examiners had discovered the defalcation. Mr. Brace said that when he had seen Bill repeatedly going to the ledger, he figured that something was wrong, because in all the years that he had been under various examinations, it had never taken an examiner more than an hour to run and balance his ledger.

Brace was subsequently tried and convicted. Despite his family's reimbursement of the major portion of the embezzlement, he was fined $25,000 and sentenced to 10 years.

Gregory admitted privately that it was quite unlikely that the defalcation would have been detected by the routine examination.

Discussion Questions

1. How do you analyze Mr. Brace's behavior?
2. What is the moral of this case?

CASE 8–4

General Patton and the Sicilian Slapping Incidents*

Henry J. Taylor

Headquarters Seventh Army
APO #758, U.S. Army
29 August, 1943

My Dear General Eisenhower:

Replying to your letter of August 17, 1943, I want to commence by thanking you for this additional illustration of your fairness and generous consideration in making the communication personal.

I am at a loss to find words with which to express my chagrin and grief at having given you, a man to whom I owe everything and for whom I would gladly lay down my life, cause for displeasure with me.

I assure you that I had no intention of being either harsh or cruel in my treatment of the two soldiers in question. My sole purpose was to try and restore in them a just appreciation of their obligation as men and soldiers.

In World War I, I had a dear friend and former schoolmate who lost his nerve in an exactly analogous manner, and who, after years of mental anguish, committed suicide.

Both my friend and the medical men with whom I discussed his case assured me that had he been roundly checked at the time of his first misbehavior, he would have been restored to a normal state.

---

*From the book *Deadline Delayed* by Members of the Overseas Press Club. Copyright, 1947, by E. P. Dutton and Co., Inc., New. Reprinted by permission.

Naturally, this memory actuated me when I inaptly tried to apply the remedies suggested. After each incident I stated to officers with me that I felt I had probably saved an immortal soul. . . .

Very respectfully,

(*Signed*) G. S. Patton, Jr.

Lieut. General, U.S. Army

General D. D. Eisenhower
Headquarters, AFHQ
APO #512—U.S. Army

When General Patton gave me a copy of this letter he lay back on the bed in his field-trailer and said, "What does that sound like to you?"

"It sounds to me like only half of the story," I said.

So, first, let's see what actually happened.

Private Charles H. Kuhl (in civilian life a carpet layer from South Bend, Indiana), ASN 35536908, L Company, 26th Infantry, 1st Division, was admitted to the 3d Battalion, 26th Infantry aid station, in Sicily on August 2, 1943, at 2:10 P.M.

He had been in the Army eight months and with the 1st Division about thirty days.

A diagnosis of Exhaustion was made at the station by Lieutenant H. L. Sanger, Medical Corps, and Kuhl was evacuated to C Company, 1st Medical Battalion, well to the rear of the fighting.

There a note was made on his medical tag stating that he had been admitted to this place three times during the Sicilian campaign.

He was evacuated to the clearing company by Captain J. D. Broom, M. C., put in quarters, and given sodium amytal, one capsule night and morning, on the prescription of Captain N. S. Nedell, M.C.

On August 3d, the following remark appears on Kuhl's Emergency Medical Tag: "Psychoneurosis anxiety state—moderately severe. Soldier has been twice before in hospital within ten days. He can't take it at front evidently. He is repeatedly returned. (*signed*) Capt. T. P. Covington, Medical Corps."

By this route and in this way Private Kuhl arrived in the receiving tent of the 15th Evacuation Hospital where the blow was struck that was heard round the world.

"I came into the tent," explains General Patton, "with the commanding officer of the outfit and other medical officers.

"I spoke to the various patients, especially commending the wounded men. I just get sick inside myself when I see a fellow torn apart, and some of the wounded were in terrible ghastly shape. Then I come to this man and asked him what was the matter."

The solder replied, "I guess I can't take it."

"Looking at the others in the tent, so many of them badly beaten up, I simply flew off the handle."

Patton squared off in front of the soldier.

He called the man every kind of a loathsome coward and then slapped him across the face with his gloves.

The soldier fell back. Patton grabbed him by the scruff of the neck and kicked him out of the tent.

Kuhl was immediately picked up by corpsmen and taken to a ward.[1]

Returning to his headquarters, Patton issued the following memorandum to corps, division, and separate brigade commanders two days later:

> Headquarters Seventh Army
> APO #758 U.S. Army
> 5 August, 1943
>
> It has come to my attention that a very small number of soldiers are going to the hospital on the pretext that they are nervously incapable of combat.
>
> Such men are cowards, and bring discredit on the Army and disgrace to their comrades whom they heartlessly leave to endure the danger of a battle while they themselves use the hospital as a means of escaping.
>
> You will take measures to see that such cases are not sent to the hospital, but are dealt with in their units.
>
> Those who are not willing to fight will be tried by Court-Martial for cowardice in the face of the enemy.
>
> (*Signed*) G. S. Patton, Jr.
> *Lieut. General, U.S. Army*
> *Commanding*

Five days later General Patton, not a medical man, again took matters into his own hands.

He slapped another soldier.

Private Paul G. Bennett, ASN 70000001, C Battery, field Artillery, was admitted to the 93d Evacuation Hospital on August 10th at 2:20 P.M.

Bennett, still only 21, had served four years in the Regular Army. He had an excellent record. His unit had been attached to the II Corps since March, and he had never had any difficulties until four days earlier, when his best friend in the outfit, fighting nearby, was wounded in action.

Bennett could not sleep that night and felt nervous. The shells going over bothered him. "I keep thinking they're going to land right on me," he said. The next day he became increasingly nervous about the firing and about his buddy's recovery.

A battery aid man sent him to the rear echelon, where a medical officer gave him some medicine which made him sleep. But he was still nervous, badly disturbed.

On August 10th the medical officer ordered him to the 93d Evacuation Hospital, although Bennett begged not to be evacuated because he did not want to leave his unit.

General Patton arrived at the hospital that day.

Bennett was sitting in the receiving tent, huddled up and shivering.

---

[1]There Kuhl was found to have a temperature of 102.2° F, gave a history of chronic diarrhea, and was shown by a blood test to have malaria.

Patton spoke to all the injured men. He was solicitous, kind, and inspiring. But when he and Major Charles B. Etter, the receiving officer in charge, reached Bennett and Patton asked the soldier what his trouble was, the soldier replied, "It's my nerves," and began to sob.

Patton turned on him like a tiger, screaming at him:

"What did you say?"

"It's my nerves," sobbed Bennett. "I can't take the shelling anymore."

In this moment Patton lost control of himself completely. Without any investigation of the man's case whatever, he rushed close to Bennett and shouted: "Your nerves, hell. You are just a . . . coward, you yellow b_____."

Then he slapped the soldier hard across the face.

"Shut up that . . . crying," he yelled. "I won't have these brave men here who have been shot seeing a yellow b_____ sitting here crying."

Patton struck at the man again. He knocked his helmet liner off his head into the next tent. Then he turned to Major Etter and yelled, "Don't admit this yellow b_____, there's nothing the matter with him. I won't have the hospitals cluttered up with these SOB's who haven't got the guts to fight."

Patton himself began to sob. He wheeled around to Colonel Donald E. Currier, the 93d's commanding medical officer. "I can't help it," he said. "It makes me break down to see brave boys and to think of a yellow b_____ being babied."

But this was not all. In his blind fury, Patton turned on Bennett again. The soldier now was managing to sit at attention, although shaking all over.

"You're going back to the front lines," Patton shouted, "You may get shot and killed, but you're going to fight. If you don't, I'll stand you up against the wall and have a firing squad kill you on purpose.

"In fact," he said, reaching for his revolver, "I ought to shoot you myself, you _____ whimpering coward."

As he left the tent, Patton was still yelling back at the receiving officer to "send that yellow SOB back to the front line."

Nurses and patients, attracted by the shouting and cursing, came from the adjoining tent and witnessed this disturbance.

Patton made no initial report of these affairs to his superior, General Eisenhower, who was then in his headquarters at Tunis on the North African mainland.

"I felt ashamed of myself," General Patton told me, "and I hoped the whole thing would die out."

But an official report by Lieut. Colonel Perrin H. Long, Medical Corps consulting physician, was already on the way to Allied headquarters through Medical Corps channels.

"The deleterious effects of such incidents upon the well-being of patients, upon the professional morale of hospital staffs, and upon the relationship of patient to physician are incalculable," reported Lieut. Colonel Long. "It is imperative that immediate steps be taken to prevent a recurrence of such incidents."

General Eisenhower received this report on August 17th. His communication to General Patton was sent off that night.

In his message, which Patton showed me, the commanding general told Patton of the allegation, told him that he could not describe in official language his revulsion, informed Patton that he must make, on his own initiative, proper amends to the soldiers involved and take steps to make amends before his whole army.

"This all happened practically on the eve of a new attack in which I had been written in for a large part of the plans, already issued," Patton explained, "and General Eisenhower stated therefore that he would temporarily reserve decision regarding my relief of command until he could determine the effect of my own corrective measures.

"Then Eisenhower did four things: He sent Maj. General John Porter Lucas to Sicily to make an investigation of the charges, sent the theater's inspector general to investigate command relationships in my entire army, sent another general officer to interview the two soldiers, and made a trip to Sicily himself to determine how much resentment against me existed in the army.

"Eisenhower's problem was whether what I had done was sufficiently damaging to compel my relief on the eve of attack, thus losing what he described as my unquestioned military value, or whether less drastic measures would be appropriate.

"I went to see both Kuhl and Bennett," Patton continued, "explained my motives, and apologized for my actions.

"In each case I stated that I should like to shake hands with them; that I was sincerely sorry. In each case they accepted my offer.

"I called together all the doctors, nurses, and enlisted men who were present when the slappings occurred. I apologized and expressed my humiliation over my impulsive actions.

"Finally, I addressed all divisions of the 7th Army in a series of assemblies, the last of which was an address before the 3d Division on August 30th.

"I praised them as soldiers, expressed regret for any occasions when I harshly treated individuals, and offered my apologies as their commanding general for doing anything unfair or un-American.

"Beyond that, except to leave the Army and get out of the war, I do not know what I could have done."

Discussion Questions
1. How do you analyze General Patton's behavior?
2. What patterns of miscommunication seemed to have occurred in this case?
3. How do you appraise General Eisenhower's actions?

CASE 8–5

"It Really Hit the Fan"*

I've been in the Civil Service since my college graduation eight years ago. I've been making good progress and I've been very happy with my job. But today, it really hit the fan. It all started a week ago Monday when my boss called me.

Harry   Keith, we got instructions from the Director's office. Your unit's got to have another GS 9.

Me   Why... what does that mean?

Harry   It means promote somebody—the organization chart calls for it and it's got to be in place when we finalize our budget next week for the new fiscal year.

Me   Well... who do I pick?

Harry   That's up to you. You know your people better than I do. Pick somebody, push him up to GS 9, and make him a first-line supervisor.

Me   A supervisor of what?

Harry   That's up to you, too... maybe you need an aide, whatever.

Me   When am I supposed to make this move?

Harry   By Friday at the latest... no, sooner than that. I've to approve it and then Mary's got to approve my approval. Personnel has the final say-so on these things.

Me   So when's the deadline?

Harry   Get it to me by noon sharp, Wednesday. Clear?

Me   Well, it's clear enough ... I just wish I had a little more lead time. ...

Harry   You and me, both ... and so would my other three group managers ... I just called them ... all four of you guys are in the same boat.

Me   Well... okay, Harry... I'll do my best ... Wednesday?

Harry   That's it, buddy. Wednesday noon ... this is bigger than both of us.

Me   Well... I'll get right on it.

I really didn't need that right then. I'd been up to my eyeballs preparing for the budget proposal. At any rate it was almost quitting time so I collected a bunch of personnel records and headed home.

Fortunately, my wife is understanding ... at least I hope she is. She had to keep the kids off me all that evening while I was going over the files. By

---

*All names are disguised. Author's name is withheld at his request.

midnight, I had narrowed it down to six people. My head was aching so I called it a night.

I don't think I slept more than an hour that whole night. I was so keyed up. I had promoted people before, but I always had plenty of time to make a choice. This time the pressure was really on.

I finally gave up on trying to sleep at about 5 A.M. I got up and made some coffee and tried to get back to the files. But my head was still spinning. At seven I gave up. Betty had made some french toast, but I just couldn't eat anything. My stomach was in a knot.

Then it was out to the car and on to the office. No chance to think in the car; the traffic was lousy. I was 10 minutes early but my in-basket was already stacked, and I had two meetings that morning and another two in the afternoon.

In a way, it was good that I had so much to do because it got me away from the promotion thing. I really couldn't think about that again until I was driving home after work. Miraculously, my mind was clearer again and with a little more homework, I whittled the list down to three.

There were Susan and Laurie and Scott. They were all in their early 20s. Each had had a good education and each had been with the Department two or three years. They were all good people and I felt any one of them would have made a good supervisor. I thought I had gone as far as the records would take me, so I figured I'd chat with each one of them tomorrow and see if that wouldn't help me make up my mind.

I slept much better that night.

The next morning I got to the office a good half-hour early, but still my in-basket was loaded. They must have little gremlins who run around at night and cram the baskets. Well, anyway by the time I finally got that stuff squared away, it was almost 10 A.M. so I called all three of them in at the same time.

I told them that I had good news and bad news. The good news was that I was going to make someone a GS-9 and that each of them was being seriously considered. The bad news was that I could only pick one of them.

Well, I guess they were surprised . . . and they laughed a little, maybe it was more of a nervous laugh. I tried to get them talking, but, I don't know, they seemed so self-conscious with one another. It was getting embarrassing and I was beginning to regret I had gotten all three of them in at the same time. Well, anyway, I decided to call a halt and asked them to keep it under their hats for the time being. I told them I'd make a recommendation to Harry for his approval then he'd pass it to Mary for her okay, and then I'd get the word to them—probably Friday.

The three of them left and I felt depressed. I knew I had handled it poorly but I just didn't know what to do. Dammit! It's the Department's fault, springing this on a guy at the last minute.

Well, I had to make a decision and have it on Harry's desk by noon. I already knew who it would be. My intuition had me leaning toward Susan from the beginning. She's young and inexperienced, but hell! so are the other two. I just sensed she'd be a good bet. So she was my choice and I made Harry's deadline. Now that I had that out of the way, I could get on with my regular work.

Friday came and went; no word from Harry. But I didn't notice. I had just forgotton about the whole business.

No word on Monday either. Harry finally called me today (Tuesday). He said everything was okay and Susan was in.

So I called her to my office and closed the door and told her the good news. Frankly, I hadn't expected her reaction. She didn't actually cry, but she sure teared up. She explained what a strain the weekend had been—not hearing anything. She was sure that someone else had gotten the promotion and that she hadn't been told anything.

So I told her to dry her eyes and not tell anyone anything until I had a chance to talk to Scott and Laurie. She left the office kind of dabbing at her eyes. I noticed that several people were watching her as she headed for the restroom.

Next, I called in Scott and told him the facts of life. He took it pretty well, I think. I told him I still needed to get to Laurie so I asked him to put on a smile and pretend nothing had happened.

Well, he put on a smile, all right. He wasn't three steps out of my office when some joker yelled across the main office: "I know what that grin means, Scotty! Congratulations, old boy!" And several other people came over to clap him on the back.

Discussion Questions
1. What uncalculated risks seem to have been taken in this case?
2. What was the purpose of the promotions?
3. How should Keith have handled the promotion?

CASE 8-6

The Stardust Motel

It was 7:15 Saturday morning, and Al, Ben, Charlie, Don, Ed, and Frank were driving up to Lake Winnipaninni for a day's fishing. As they passed the Stardust Motel, they caught sight of their mutual superior, George Gilbert, vice president for public relations, First National Bank, and his secretary, Mrs. Gloria Golden, emerging from the motel. Curiously, no one said anything, but each was certain that the others had seen George and Gloria.

Subsequently, the men responsed as follows:

Al phoned George's wife and said: "Mrs. Gilbert, I know it's none of my business, but in your and the children's interests, I think you ought to know what I saw this morning. . . ."

Ben phoned George and said: "George, I think you ought to know that Al, Charlie, Don, Ed, Frank, and I saw you and Gloria this morning. Of course, I'll keep mum, but I don't know how far you can trust the others."

Charlie was called by George Saturday night. "Charlie, I understand you fellows saw Gloria and me this morning. If the wrong people hear this, my marriage could be threatened and I could be ruined at the bank. I appeal to you, Charlie, you're the leader of that group. Can't you get them to clam up?" Charlie responded: "Sorry, George, I'll keep my own mouth shut, but I just don't want to get involved."

Don caught Harold Hayes, executive vice president and Gilbert's boss, at the coffee machine Monday morning: "Mr. Hayes, I hate to do this. But in the bank's interest I think I should tell you what I saw Saturday morning . . ."

Ed made a red valentine and posted it on the bank's bulletin board.

Discussion Questions

1. Rank the people in this case according to the morality of their behavior. That is, identify the person who behaved most morally (or least immorally). Then who would be next, and so on.

2. What inferences would you have to make in order to feel more confident about your ranking?

CASE 8-7

A SLIGHT BREAKDOWN IN COMMUNICATION*

William E. Burrows

At exactly 9:20 on the night of May 8, 1978, National Airlines Flight 193, carrying 52 passengers and a crew of six from Mobile, Alabama, to Pensacola, Florida, turned into its final approach to the Pensacola Regional Airport. The plane was four miles from the edge of the airport's Runway 25 as it eased down rather quickly through the fog and haze that drifted through the darkness over Escambia Bay.

At 9:20 and 11 seconds James Stockwell, the flight engineer, who sat behind the pilot and co-pilot, scanning the final approach checklist—the list of things that had to be done before the jet could safely be landed—called out, "Landing gear and lever."

"Down three green," answered Leonard G. Sanderson Jr., the co-pilot. Sanderson was telling Stockwell and George T. Kunz, the pilot, that the three green lights on the instrument panel representing the plane's landing gear were glowing green, showing that the gear was down and locked.

At 9:20 and 15 seconds, the Ground-Proximity Warning System, a device that warns when a plane is too close to the ground or to water relative to where it's supposed to be, or is coming down too quickly relative to its altitude, went off with a loud, whooping sound and a flashing red light on the instrument panel. Then, for good measure, it said, "Pull up, pull up!" in recorded English that rang with unmistakable authority and urgency. The warnings continued for nine seconds until Stockwell, believing that he was acting on his pilot's orders, turned off the GPWS.

At 9:20 and 31 seconds Sanderson, the co-pilot, looked out his window and noticed that the Boeing 727 was skimming over Escambia Bay at an alarmingly low altitude. "We're down to 50 feet," he told the others. Two seconds later National 193 hit the water three miles short of Runway 25 and settled in 12 feet of water. Three passengers drowned before the crew of a nearby barge rescued everyone else.

A head-on picture of the 727, lying still and abandoned in water that lapped over its nose and almost up to its windshield, made Page 1 all over the country the next day and has since been used to represent the kind of foul-up that can happen to technological man and his machines despite the best laid of his plans.

The National Transportation Safety Board decided after examining a great deal of evidence that National 193 had crashed because of several errors made by its flight crew. These included the fact that the crew did not monitor the 727's altitude and rate of descent as it approached Pensacola;

*Psychology Today. November, 1982, pp. 44–45. Reprinted with permission from Psychology Today Magazine. Coyright ©1982 (APA).

the co-pilot did not call out the plane's altitude and other indications of performance to the pilot, as he was supposed to do; there was a failure to use all of the instruments available to gauge the plane's altitude; the GPWS was turned off in error; and more. The evidence made a classic case for what is loosely called "pilot error." But that evidence, as described in the NTSB's 46-page report, makes "error" a gross oversimplification.

Were it not for the tragic consequences of that accident, in fact, Flight 193's last 30 seconds could almost be said to have been a comedy of errors. Captain Kunz was descending at a rate of 2,000 feet a minute from an altitude of 500 feet. Kunz later testified that he had misread the altimeter, he wasn't wearing his glasses, and thought that it said 1,500 feet. When the alarm went off, it was so loud that it made conversation very difficult. Kunz responded to the flashing light, whooping, and "Pull up, pull up!" warning by slowing the plane's rate of descent slightly. At the same time, Flight Engineer Stockwell turned off the alarm because, in all the confusion, he thought that Kunz had ordered him to do so. Then the captain, seeing that the alarm had stopped sounding and flashing concluded that the situation was again under control. Still, he continued to descend without checking the altimeter, according to the NTSB, until National 193 went in.

The National Transportation Safety Board report went on to note that enough time remained during the four to six seconds after the alarm was turned off for Kunz to level off so that he could have another go at Runway 25.

National 193 plowed into Escambia Bay because of serious problems in crew communication, integration, operation of the plane's systems, and decision-making.

Discussion Questions

1. This case is appended to the Inference-Observation Confusion chapter. Why?

2. What part did Captain Kunz play in Flight 193's inadvertent ditching?

3. Did Flight Engineer Stockwell contribute?

4. How do you feel about Co-pilot Sanderson's failure to notify the pilot of altitude and other indicators of the plane's performance?

9

Bypassing

DEFINITION

Belden, West, and Bartell[1] was a medium-sized brokerage firm with approximately 95 employees. The accounting department had 17 employees, of whom three were middle-aged women who operated the bookkeeping machines. With an average volume of business, all three wre normally finished with their posting about one hour before the usual quitting time.

On February 21 one of the bookkeepers, Elizabeth Morley, phoned in to say she was ill and would be unable to report for duty. The other two pitched in and completed about 75 percent of the absent woman's posting before the normal quitting time. The supervisor then approached one of the bookkeepers, Jane Dover, and said: "Elizabeth just called and said she'll be absent again tomorrow, so the balance of her work [25 percent of her normal work load] will have to be completed the first thing in the morning.

Dover, a very conscientious and somewhat unassertive woman, said nothing. The following morning the supervisor found that Dover had worked until 8:30 P.M. the previous evening to complete Morley's posting. The supervisor had intended that she and the other bookkeeper continue with the remainder of Morley's work in the morning before starting on their own posting.

The foreman was passing Henry Morris, a machinist working on a bearing. Noticing some oily waste, a fire and accident hazard, the foreman remarked: "Better clean up around here."

Ten minutes later the foreman's assistant called: "Hey, boss—that bearing Morris is working on. It's due in the Engineering Department pronto, right?"

"It sure as hell is. Why?"

"Well, he said you told him to drop it and sweep up his whole area."

"Now, how in hell did he get that idea?! Get him right back on that job—Engineering is expecting it in 15 minutes!"

---

[1]All names have been disguised.

A motorist was driving on the Merritt Parkway outside New York City when his engine stalled. He quickly determined that his battery was dead and managed to stop another driver who consented to push his car to get it started.

"My car has an automatic transmission," he explained, "so you'll have to get up to 30 to 35 miles per hour to get me started."

The second motorist nodded and walked back to the car. The first motorist climbed into his own car and waited for the Good Samaritan to pull up behind him. He waited—and waited. Finally, he turned around to see what was wrong.

There was the good Samaritan—coming at his car at 30 to 35 miles per hour!

The damage to his car amounted to $2,400.

In each of the preceding instances, there was talking and there was listening. There were people sending messages and other people receiving them. But somehow the communication went awry. The speaker didn't get through—the listener didn't "get *him*." The listener presumably heard the same words that the speaker said, but the communicators seem to have *talked past* each other.

This communication phenomenon is called *bypassing*. Figure 9–1 diagrams the bypassing between Morris and his foreman.

It is evident that the foreman had one meaning for "better clean up around here" and Morris had another. Their meanings bypassed each other without meeting. Bypassing, then, is the name for the miscommunication pattern that occurs when the sender (speaker, writer, and so on) and the receiver (listener, reader, and so forth) miss each other with their meanings.

FIGURE 9-1

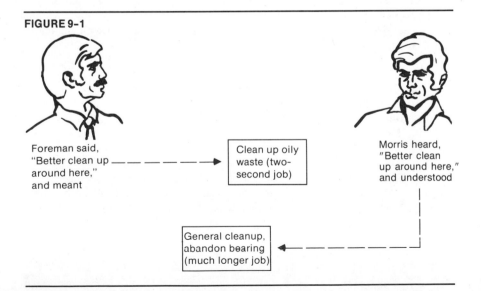

Foreman said, "Better clean up around here," and meant

Clean up oily waste (two-second job)

Morris heard, "Better clean up around here," and understood

General cleanup, abandon bearing (much longer job)

Same Word—Different Things

Before going on, it should be noted that three bypassing illustrations took the form of one person sending and the other receiving the same words but attributing different meanings to them. Jane Dover, for example, heard the same words her supervisor had said but interpreted them quite differently for what he had intended. This is a very common type of bypassing, but it has an equally prevalent counterpart.

Different Words—Same Thing

Bypassing may occur just as readily when people are using different words to represent the same thing. I once witnessed with thinly disguised amusement a heated and fruitless argument between my 12-year-old nephew and a Massachusetts soda fountain clerk, only a year or two older. Jimmy, born and reared in Illinois, was visiting the East Coast for the first time. The conversation went something like this:

Jimmy Do you have pop?
Clerk What?
Jimmy Pop.
Clerk I don't know what you're talking about.
Jimmy *(scornfully):* You never heard of pop?
Clerk No, and neither did you!
Jimmy Listen, it's that stuff that comes in a bottle—you shake it up, and it fizzes out?
Clerk Oh! You mean a soda!
Jimmy No! I dont want a soda! (*A "soda" where Jimmy lives is made with ice cream, flavoring, and soda water.*)
Clerk Well, the, what *do* you want?
Jimmy Never mind! You wouldn't have it anyway!

At this point, I partially reconciled the two antagonists by suggesting that they were both talking about the same thing. Jimmy, incidentally, finally got his "pop," "soda," "tonic," "minerals," "soft drink," or whatever it is called in your part of the country.

A particularly exasperating aspect of our language is that we have words which would appear to represent opposites but in fact we use the words interchangeably:

Verbal Paradox[2]
Inflammable and flammable
Burn with an equal flame;
Bested at chess, or worsted,
My plight is just the same;

---

[2]From "Pepper . . . and Salt," *The Wall Street Journal*, Oct. 29, 1981, p. 29. Reprinted with permission.

Sleeves raveled and unraveled
Are but a single kind;
Both boned and deboned filets
Are boneless cuts, I find.
In short, what seems antonymous
May really be synonymous.
—Richard Bardolph

Both types of bypassing (same word—different things and different words—same thing) have a common basis, of course. Both types involve people missing each other's meanings, and the consequences of both types are equally worthy of consideration.

SOME CONSEQUENCES

Bypassing may occur under such a variety of circumstances that it may be helpful to suggest something of their range.

The Range of Consequences

Bypassing is certainly one of the most prevalent and potentially costly and dangerous patterns of miscommunication in organizations or virtually anywhere else. But bypassing isn't always serious, hazardous, or even important. Much of the time its effects are inconsequential. Sometimes its results may be amusing or even hilarious. In fact, much of our humor is based on bypassing. A personal story makes the point. It happened on my first day of college teaching, years ago. Mustering as much dignity as was possible for a neophyte, I walked into the classroom and announced that I was going to seat the class alphabetically. I explained that I had difficulty in associating names with faces and that in seating them alphabetically, "I will get to know you by your seats." You may be quite sure the class bypassed me!

But I did not have the only red face that day, for 20 minutes later a young, innocent freshman woman rose to describe her initial campus impressions. She said that she was particularly fond of the serenades—when the fraternity men would come as a group to sing beneath the women's dormitory windows. "We girls love it so," she emphasized, "we wish the boys could stay all night!"

Unfortunately, not all bypassings end so delightfully (at least from the audience's point of view). Bypassings occurring every day in industry, in government, and in homes result in enormous wastes of time, money, effort, and tempers. History is full of examples of bypassings that have led to catastrophes. There is even disturbing evidence to suggest that a bypassing on a word in the Japanese response to the World War II Potsdam ultimatum may have led to the dropping of the atom bombs on Japan and to Russia's declaration of war on Japan—events that have had irrevocable effect upon world affairs.[3]

Immediate Consequences

Before we leave this cursory review of bypassing, we should note that the immediate effects of this breakdown in communication generally fall into one or the other of two broad classifications.

Apparent Agreement.   Most of the bypassing illustrations we have been considering have had apparent agreement as their immediate consequences. That is, the initial result of the bypassing was such that those involved felt that they were in harmony with each other. Henry Morris and his foreman, Jane Dover and her supervisor, and the well-intentioned driver and the stalled motorist, for example, believed that they had had a mutual understanding. The bypassing, however, concealed an actual disagreement (i.e., the people involved differed on meanings).

It is acting on the false assurance of agreement that so frequently leads us into trouble.

> Jeannie, nine, called to her mother upstairs: "Mom, may I fix the Easter eggs?" "Yes, dear," mother called back, "We'll need three dozen eggs. Be sure to cook them for at least 15 minutes."
>
> Jeannie placed the eggs in the largest kettle she could find and filled it with cold water. Then she set the kettle on the stove and turned on the gas.
>
> After 15 minutes of eager clock-watching, Jeannie removed the eggs from the water (which had not yet begun to boil) and set them on the table.
>
> While she was preparing the Easter egg dyes, her brother Tom, 14, walked into the kitchen and picked up an egg. "Are you sure you cooked these long enough?" he asked. "Sure. Exactly 15 minutes, just like Mom said." "Well, ok—say, want to see what a hard head I have?" And with that Tom cracked a very uncooked egg on his head!

Apparent Disagreement.   But bypassing that conceals actual agreement by manifesting apparent disagreement can also be disconcerting.

Major Gregory Klimov, who served for two years as an official of the Soviet Military Administration in occupied Berlin and later fled to the West, recounts the first meeting of the Allied Control Commission, Economic Directorate. After routine matters had been settled, the head of the American delegation proposed that the first item on the agenda should be: "The working out of basic policy for the economic demilitarization of Germany."

> The interpreters now translated the chairman's phrase into Russian as: "Working out the policy of economic demobilization." Another of these bor-

---

[3]William J. Coughlin, "Was It the Deadliest Error of Our Time?" *Harper's Magazine*, March 1953, pp. 31–40.

derline cases in linguistics! The English formula had used the word "policy." The interpreters translated this literally into the Russian word "politik," although the English word had a much wider meaning, and the Russian phrase for "guiding principles" would have been a more satisfactory translation.

At the word "politik" General Shabalin sprang up as though stung. "What politik? All the political questions were settled at the Potsdam Conference!"

The American chairman, General Draper, agreed: "Quite correct, they were. Our task is simply to translate the decision into action, and so we have to lay down the guiding policy . . ."

The interpreters, both American and English, again translated with one accord: ". . . politik."

General Shabalin stuck to his guns: "There must be nothing about politics. That's all settled. Please don't try to exert pressure on me."

"But it's got nothing to do with politics," the interpreters tried to reassure him. "The word is policy."

"I see no difference," the general objected. "I have no intention of revising the Potsdam Conference. We're here to work, not to hold meetings."[4]

And this futile battle over the awkward word *policy* was the beginning of the first of many long and similar arguments around the conference table.

Whether the immediate consequence of bypassing is an apparent agreement or an apparent disagreement, the subsequent effect *can* be unpleasant, unproductive, and even fatal. Let us now consider some of the factors that contribute to this often troublesome pattern of miscommunication.

THE UNDERLYING MECHANISM

To understand harmful bypassing, we must examine its underlying mechanism. Just what happens when people bypass? What kind of thought process occurs that leads to such dangerous and costly miscommunication?

Let us return to the Morris-foreman incident. They bypassed each other, that is, missed each other with their meanings. But *why?* Let us presume that neither *intended* to miscommunicate. Certainly the foreman did not use any big, foreign, or unfamiliar words. Why, then, did the communication go askew?

Suppose that we asked Morris and the foreman what they thought went wrong in their communication. Their responses might follow this pattern:

Morris I was sure I knew what the boss meant—clean up my messy work area. I never thought he was talking about just cleaning up the oily waste.

---

[4]Gregory Klimov, *The Terror Machine: The Inside Story of the Soviet Administration in Germany* (New York: Frederick A. Praeger, 1953), pp. 146–47. Reprinted by permission.

Foreman I was certain Morris would understand what I was driving at. It never occurred to me that he would put a different interpretation on my remark.

"I was sure . . . I never thought . . ."; "I was certain . . . It never occurred to me . . ." These men are revealing the key assumption underlying their behavior—the assumption that *words mean the same to the other person as they do to me.*

That is an enormously pervasive assumption. Most of us act on that assumption much of the time. And more often than not people do interpret our words as we intend—and usually we decode their words appropriately as well. But consistent success sometimes leads to overconfidence and complacency—the ideal attitudes for bypassing.

There are at least two additional reasons for the epidemic prevalence of the assumption. First, it is a highly enticing notion. We want to feel that we are understanding and being understood by the other person. Second, the assumption supports our basic egocentrism, as is evidenced by this passage from Lewis Carroll's *Through the Looking Glass:*

> Humpty-Dumpty said: "There's glory for you." "I don't know what you mean by 'glory,' " Alice said. Humpty-Dumpty smiled contemptuously. "Of course, you don't till I tell you. I meant, 'There's a nice knock-down argument for you.' " "But 'glory' doesn't mean a 'nice knock-down argument,' " Alice objected. "When I use a word," Humpty-Dumpty said in a rather scornful tone, "it means just what I choose it to mean, neither more nor less."

Few of us are frank as Humpty-Dumpty, thought we are frequently as arrogant. We would not call it arrogance (unless we were talking about the other individual) because we are largely unaware of the prevailing egocentrism which so frequently accompanies our use of words. If a man (or a woman) were to watch his own language use scrupulously during a 24-hour period, he would almost certainly catch himself talking or listening (writing or reading) dozens of times with the Humpty-Dumpty attitude. He would find himself assuming, "I *knew* what the other person understood or meant simply because that was the way I used or would have used the words."

It is understandable why so much communicating occurs under the influence of such an assumption. But the stark fact remains: the assumption is not unfailingly valid—and we have already suggested the consequences of acting unconsciously upon the assumption when it is false.

Digging more deeply, we find the assumption is supported by two pernicious fallacies. One is that words are used in only one way ("the way *I* am using them")—that words have mono-usage. The other is that words have meanings. I shall attack each of these fallacies, for they lie at the foundation of bypassing.

Fallacy That Words Have Mono-Usage

The first of the fallacies underlying bypassing is the assumption of mono-usage. The notion that words are used to convey one and only one meaning is so patently ridiculous that it hardly appears necessary to refute it. Yet so much of our communication seems to be based on this misconception that I must comment on it.

To begin, let me ask a question: How many words are used in only one way? Except for certain technological terms, virtually all of our common words (as far as I have been able to determine) are used in more than one way. That is, the words we generally use in our day-to-day communications almost invariably have multi-usage. In fact, for the 500 most commonly used words in our language there is an aggregate of over 14,000 dictionary defintions! Take the word *fast*, for instance:

> A man is *fast* when he can run rapidly.
> But he is also *fast* when he is tied down and cannot run at all.
> And colors are *fast* when they do not run.
> One is *fast* when s/he moves in suspect company.
> But this is not quite the same thing as playing *fast* and loose.
> A racetrack is *fast* when it is in good running condition.
> A friend is *fast* when s/he is loyal.
> A watch is *fast* when it is ahead of time.
> To be *fast* asleep is to be deep in sleep.
> To be *fast* by is to be near.
> To *fast* is to refrain from eating.
> A *fast* may be a period of noneating—or a ship's mooring line.
> Photographic film is *fast* when it is *sensitive* (to light).
> But bacteria are *fast* when they are *insensitive* (to antiseptics).

And note the versatility of *call* in this gripping narrative:

> Jim *called* on Joe to *call* him out for *calling* him up at midnight and *calling* him down, but their wives *called* in friends who got the fight *called* off.[5]

If one recognizes the prevalence of multi-usage in our language, one will anticipate that words can readily be understood differently by different people. *Parade Magazine* made this point graphically when it conducted an interesting demonstration. Each of three artists was given a copy of a paragraph from the *Encyclopedia Britannica*. The paragraph described

---

[5]The sentence hardly suggests the multi-usages of *call*. Webster's Unabridged lists 40 different definitions for the word. Other kaleidoscopic words: *turn* (54 defintions), *fall* (50), and *touch* (46).

(words only, no pictures) an animal that none of the artists had purportedly ever seen:

> The body is stout, with arched back; the limbs are short and stout, armed with strong, blunt claws; the ears long; and the tail thick at the base and tapering gradually. The elongated head is set on a short, thick neck, and at the extremity of the snout is a disc in which the nostrils open. The mouth is small and tubular, furnished with a long extensile tongue. A large individual measured 6 ft. 8 in. In colour it is pale, sandy or yellow, the hair being scanty and allowing the skin to show.[6]

From this purely *verbal* description, the artists were asked to draw what they conjured up from the words. The results are shown in Figure 9-2.

The animal (lower right) is an aardvark or anteater. Bizarre and diverse as these drawings appear, note a significant point: Each is a legitimate interpretation of the paragraph. Note that while a detail may be interpreted *differently*, it is, nevertheless, consistent with a common usage of the term. Who can deny, for example, that in each instance the back is "arched," that the ears are "long," or that the tail is "thick at the base and tapering gradually"?

Neologisms

The prevalence of multi-usage in a language is directly related to the extent of the *neologizing* occurring in that language. When something new appears—an invention, a novel event, a new relationship or combination, and so on—how does it become named? Basically, there are two neological tacks: (1) invent a new word (word coinage); or (2) use an old word in a different way (usage coinage).

1. Word Coinage.   The coining of words is a fascinating art. Manufacturers sometimes pay handsome rewards to those who contrive new names which most aptly and appealingly represent their products. Especially impressive are the fabricated labels for the miracle ingredients of some products. Somehow these labels suggest a mystique of power, romance, or virtue which even the Federal Trade Commission finds difficult to refute.

A special kind of word coinage is the acronym, such as:

AIDS: *A*cquired *I*mmune *D*eficiency *S*yndrome
RADAR: *RA*dio *D*etecting *A*nd *R*anging.
SCUBA: *S*elf-*C*ontained *U*nderwater *B*reathing *A*pparatus.
LASER: *L*ight *A*mplification by *S*timulated *E*mission of *R*adiation.
LEM: *L*unar *E*xcursion *M*odule.
RAM: *R*andom *A*ccess *M*emory

---

[6]From "Aardvark," *Encyclopaedia Britannica* (1957) p. 4. Reprinted by permission.

FIGURE 9-2

SNAFU: (The ubiquitous term from World War II) *Situation Normal: All Fouled Up.*[7]

YUPPIE: *Young Urban Professional.*

Sometimes words are coined by combining words or parts of words: television, gridlock, phonevision, input, motel, petrodollars, interface, op-art, econometrics,teenager, camcorder. Or they are nicknames for longer words or phrases such as *fan*, which is short for *fanatic, nincompoop*, which is a telescoped version of *non compos mentis*, and *nuke* which stands for a *nuclear power generator—*or, as a verb, *to destroy with nuclear weapons*. Often common nouns spring from the name of the person who innovated, discovered, or was otherwise associated with the referent.

Charles C. Boycott	Jules Léotard
Lord Cardigan	Ernst Mach
François-René de Chateaubriand	Colonel Martinet
Nicolas Chauvin	George Pullman
Lord Chestérfield	Vidkun Quisling
Gaston Chevrolet	Lord Raglan
Earl of Davenport	Earl of Sandwich
Rudolf Diesel	Antoine Sax
Daniel Fahrenheit	Étienne de Silhouette
Henry Ford	James Watt
Joseph I. Guillotine	Count Ferdinand von Zeppelin

And women have not been totally neglected: Amelia Bloomer, Marie Curie, Madame de Pompadour, Shirley Temple, Mae West.

And to whom are we indebted for the first flushing toilet (1770)? A Chelsea sanitary engineer, Thomas Crapper.

Flowers seem especially beholden to individuals for their names. Among their benefactors:

Michel Bégon	Alexander Garden
George Camel	Matthias de l'Obel
Anders Dahl	Joel Poinsett
William Forsythe	Caspar Wistar
Leonard Fuchs	Johann Gottfried Zinn

Our language is occasionally enriched when the proper name of a fictional character or place becomes a generic word: *babbitt—gargantuan—malapropism—mentor—quixotic—pollyanna—robot—serendipity.*

Still another way in which we add words to our language is simply to lift them from other languages. We are indebted to the Spanish for *fiesta, siesta,* and *adios;* to the French for *liaison, ambience, rendezvous, and rap-*

---

[7]*Approximate translation.*

prochement; to the Germans for *blitzkrieg, kindergarten,* and *wanderlust.*
Less obvious contributors:[8]

Algonquian	*Skunk, pecan, squaw, chipmunk*
Arabic	*Almanac, mattress, admiral, sheikh, hashish, fakir, harem*
Araucanian	*Poncho*
Australian aborigine	*Kangaroo, boomerang, koala*
Basque	*Bizarre, jai alai*
Carib	*Canoe*

2. Usage Coinage.   The kind of neologism that more is more germane to
bypassing, however, is that which occurs when a new usage is made of an
existing word. But briefly in defense, were it not for usage coinage, puns,
sad to contemplate, would be impossible. Thus, we would have been deprived of the delightful liberties taken by the suppliers of names for the
colors of the '69 Maverick: *Thanks Vermillion, Hulla Blue, Anti-Estab-
lish Mint, Last Stand Custard, Freudian Gilt,* and *Original Cinnamon.*
Maverick's marketers opted not to use *Come-and-Get-Me Copper, Gang
Green,* and *Statutory Grape.*

In connection with the frequency of usage coinage, consider these
words now being used in ways quite different from (and in addition to) the
ways in which they were defined only a decade or so ago.

aces	deep six (verb)
acid	demonstration
AIDS	dove
Apple	downer
apple	drop out
bad	dude
bag	far out
black	fat cat
blitz	flake
boomerang	flash
boned	flip
bread	freak
brother	gas
buff	gay
buns	generic
busing	grass
cat	gross
coke	Guardian Angels
crash	hackers
data base	hang-up

---

[8]From "39 Indo-European Languages which Have Contributed Words to the English
Language," a list which appears in David Wallechinsky, Irving Wallace, and Amy Wallace,
The Books of Lists (New York: William Morrow, 1977), pp. 168–69.

hardware	ram
hawk	rap
head	right on
heavy	rock
high	Ronald Reagan
hijack	rouge
hip	rug
hit	score
hog	scum
hunk	silo
into	smack
joint	soul
kill	speed
kinky	split
mace	squeeze
macro	stoked
main	stoned
man	stonewall (verb)
matrix	straight
menu	streaking
micro	terminal
militant	topless
moon	transplant
pad	trip
oreo	turkey
Panther	turn off
Peacemaker	turn on
pig	upper
pot	video
program	vigilante
punk	y'know?

This constant piling on of usages moved one anonymous bard to express his frustration in verse:

> Remember when hippie meant big in the hips,
> And a trip involved travel in car, planes, and ships?
> When pot was a vessel for cooking things in,
> And hooked was what grandmother's rugs may have been?
> When fix was a verb that meant mend or repair.
> And be-in meant merely existing somewhere?
> When neat meant well-organized, tidy, and clean,
> And grass was a ground cover, normally green?
> When groovy meant furrowed with channels and hollows,
> And birds were winged creatures, like robins and swallows?
> When fuzz was a substance, real fluffy, like lint,
> And bread came from bakeries and not from the mint?

When roll meant a bun, and rock was a stone,
And hang up was something you did with the phone?
It's groovy, man, groovy, but English it's not.
Methinks that our language is going to pot.

The accumulation of usages occurs incessantly in a living language. And if we consider some of the special kinds of usage accumulation we will be alerted to some of the areas of potential bypassing. Among them are: (*a*) etymological shifts, (*b*) regionalisms, and (*c*) technical/common usage.

(a) Etymological Shifts.   A great many of our older words have undergone etymological shifts. That is, they have acquired new usages as they have been passed down through time. Some of the usages drop out after a while, but many remain, and the result is often a formidable accumulation of defintions, all of which are operating at present. The word *mess* is a good example. A Latin term, it originally stood for "something sent." This usage is still reflected in such words as *message, messenger, mission, missle, missive, missionary, emissary, emission,* and *remission.* Later, mess came to represent food sent from the kitchen to the dining table; then a quantity of soft food (mess of porridge); than a sufficient quantity of a certain kind of food for a dish or a meal (mess of peas). Still later, mess referred to the entire dining situation, including the people sitting at the dining table (the soldiers were at mess). Finally, mess came to denote the various dinnerware, glasses, and dishes, with the unfinished food still clinging to them, which were piled together in a heap after dinner, and thus to represent any general disorganization (what a mess!). We even speak of emotionally disorganized people in this way. (Is he a mess!)

We have a great knack for using old words in new ways. The words listed on pages 260–61 are among the thousands of words that have acquired new usages in recent years. Incidentally, I have found that whether one approves of such new usages or not, it is generally wise to keep abreast of them. Recently, my office was chilly, and I walked into my young secretary's office to ask: "Are you cool in here?" "Crazy man!" she responded gleefully.

The rapidity of the etymological shifts is one reason why learning English is so difficult for foreigners. Although they may have mastered the grammar and the conventional usages (both of which remain relatively constant), they may have trouble keeping up with the ever-changing idiom. Not long ago a student from India enrolled at Northwestern University. On his first day at the university, an American student generously escorted him about the campus, helpfully pointing out the buildings in which the new student would be having classes, the cafeterias, the library, and so on. Finally, they returned to the Indian's dormitory room. When the American had seen that the new-comer was comfortably situated, he left with a cheery, "See you later!" The Indian stayed up until three o'clock in the morning, for he did not want to be so impolite as to retire when his new friend had obviously promised to return!

A Thailander enrolled at another midwestern university. He eagerly waited for an opportunity to meet the university's president, a renowned scholar. Finally, he was granted an appointment. With the utmost solemnity, he walked into the president's office, bowed humbly to the president, and said: "I am most honored to meet with you, sir. I know that you are a very wise guy."

Perhaps someone should have said something to the proprietor of a smart dress shop in Paris who felt that he would entice English-speaking patrons by advertising "Gowns for Streetwalking."

Sometimes the tables are turned. Copywriters for General Motors discovered that "Body by Fisher" became "Corpse by Fisher" in Flemish. Chevy's Nova sold poorly in South America until a name change. *No va* is *no go* in Spanish! And one U.S. airline learned after a vigorous advertising campaign that its luxurious "rendezvous lounges" were misconstrued. In Portuguese, *rendezvous* denotes a room hired for assignations. And a sales vice president of a large American firm ended a talk to the firm's Spanish-speaking representatives in Colombia with an exuberant and (he thought) supportive declaration: "We at the home office are behind you all the way!" Unfortunately, the instantaneous translation was: "We at the home office are watching your every move."

(b) Regional Variations.   Word usages vary not only from time to time but from geographic region to region. In his quest for pop, Jimmy learned this the hard way. What a "sweet roll" is in some areas is a "bun" in others and a "Danish" in still others. "Evening" in some parts of the South is the period from noon through twilight. In the rest of the country, however, it generally refers to the period from sunset or from the evening meal to bedtime.

The Pennsylvania Dutch present a special communication problem. These good people speak English all right, but often using a Germanic-type grammar. The results are sometimes quite charming:

> "Throw Papa down the stairs his hat."
> Girl to her brother chopping wood: "Chonny—come from the woodpile in. . . .
> Mom's on the table still . . . and Pop's et himself already."

But how would you respond to the pleasant chap, standing in front of you in a line at the Lancaster post office, who asks: "If a body goes quick out and comes right aways back in again, will he be where he was yet?" And no one will convince the American motorist that the English speak English.

British	American
Road Up	Road Repairs
Diversion	Detour
Corner	Turning
No Overtaking	No Passing
No Waiting	No Parking
Pavement	Sidewalk
Bonnet	Hood
Caravan	Trailer
Bump	Collision
Double Bend	S-Curve
Dual Carriageway	Divided Highway
Halt	Stop
Mews	Alley
Hackney Carriage	Taxi
Boot	Trunk
Petrol	Gas

And better carry a *torch* in case you have to change a *tyre* in the dark.

Small wonder that George Bernard Shaw described us as two great nations separated by the barrier of a common language.

It was this transatlantic rift that so effectively stymied a young friend of mine who was visiting England with his wife and infant son. The robust baby, who was bottle-fed, quickly demolished the supply of nipples that his mother had brought from the states.

Accordingly, father was dispatched to a nearby pharmacy where he asked a buxom clerk: "Do you have nipples?" The young lady stiffened and blushed profusely. Puzzled, my friend tried again: "You know, rubber nipples for a baby bottle?"

The clerk brightened: "Oh, I understand, sir—yes, I have teats."

Now it was the customer's turn to flush over what seemed a thoroughly unnecessary proclamation.

(c) Technical/Common Usage. Specialists (and almost everyone is a specialist to some degree) tend to develop their own private language. Salespeople speak of closure (the completion of a sale); plumbers, of wiping a joint (applying molten lead with a pad to join pipes); publishers, of fillers (short items to fill our columns); television directors of stretching (slowing up to consume time); and laundry personnel, of mangling the wash (smoothing it by roller pressure). Ordinarily, these specialists use such terms to good effect when communicating with fellow specialists. Many of these words and phrases, however, are also used by the general public, but in quite different ways. Let the technician forget that the outsider is not accustomed to these words in his specialized sense, and the results are more likely to be confusing at best.

I learned something of the intricacies of plain English at an early stage in my career. A woman of 35 came in one day to tell me that she wanted a baby but that she had been told that she had a certain type of heart-disease which might not interfere with a normal life but would be dangerous if she ever had a baby. From her description I thought at once of mitral stenosis. This condition is characterized by a rather distinctive rumbling murmur near the apex of the heart, and especially by a peculiar vibration felt by the examining finger on the patient's chest. The vibration is known as the "thrill" of mitral stenosis.

When this woman had been undressed and was lying on my table in her white kimono, my stethoscope quickly found the heart-sounds I had expected. Dictating to my nurse, I described them carefully. I put my stethoscope aside and felt intently for the typical vibration which may be found in a small but variable area of the left chest.

I closed my eyes for better concentration, and felt long and carefully for the tremor. I did not find it and with my hand still on the woman's bare breast, lifting it upward and out of the way, I finally turned to the nurse and said: "No thrill."

The patient's black eyes snapped open, and with venom in her voice she said, "Well, isn't that just too bad? Perhaps it's just as well you don't get one. That isn't what I came for."

My nurse almost choked, and my explanation still seems a nightmare of futile words.[9]

Miscommunication is also possible, of course, from specialty to specialty. The dentist's closure (the extent to which the upper and lower teeth fit together when the jaw is closed) differs from the salesperson's. And the parliamentarian's closure (a method for ending debate and securing an immediate vote on a measure) differs from both. Consider the machinist who ordered a tree. "What caliper size do you want?" inquired the nurseryman. "About three inches," said the machinist, whose calipers measure *diameters*. The tree man brought a sapling only one inch across, for his calipers measured *circumferences*.

Computers and Multi-Usage   Because of the multi-usage of English (and many other languages), it is unlikely that computers will replace human translators—at least in the near future. The very precisioin that the computer requires of its inputs severely limits its ability to cope with a highly ambiguous natural language.[10] For example, when asked to interpret the sentence "Time flies like an arrow," one computer gave several answers including: "Check the speed of flies as fast as you can," and "Certain flies have a fondness for an arrow."

---

[9]Frederic Loomis, M.D., *Consultation Room* (New York: Alfred A. Knopf, 1939), p. 47.

[10]In fact, artificial languages such as FORTRAN, ALGOL, COBOL, BASIC, and PASCAL, had to be devised to accommodate the computer.

And when computerized translation between natural languages is attemted, the problem is compounded. In one test, the computer received in English, "The spirit is willing, but the flesh is weak." This was translated into Russian as, "The liquor is still good, but the meat has gone bad." In an English-Japanese attempt, the output was "Invisible lunatic." The input? "Out of sight, out of mind."

The Fallacy that Words Have Meanings

The persistent delusion that words have meanings stems from what the late Irving J. Lee called the container myth:

> If you think of words as vessels, then you are likely to talk about "the meaning of a word" as if the meaning were *in* the word. Assuming this, it is easy to endow words with characteristics. Just as you may say that one vessel is costlier or more symmetrical than another, you may say that one word is intrinsically more suitable for one purpose than another, or that, in and of itself, a word will have this or that meaning rather than any other. When one takes this view, he seems to say that meaning is to a word as contents are to a container.[11]

Lee suggested that when a person acts upon the unconscious assumption that words *contain* meanings, he is insidiously led to assume that when he talks (or writes), he is handing his listener (or reader) so many containers of meanings. If this is the case, the recipient is bound to get the correct meanings.

Saint Augustine recognized this fallacy 16 centuries ago when he argued in his *Christian Instruction* that words do not possess intrinsic meaning. "Rather, they 'have' a meaning because men have agreed upon them."

Words, of course, do not contain or have meanings. Apart from the people who use them, words are merely marks on paper, vibrations in the air, raised dots on a Braille card, and so on. Words really do not mean at all—only the users of words can mean something with the words they use. This is a sensible enough statement to accept—intellectually. Unfortunately, our behavior with words very frequently does not abide by it.

But just what *do* words do—or, more precisely, what do people do with them? What happens inside people as they use words? By way of examining this internal verbal behavior, perhaps you will respond to the three questions below.

Question 1. In a redwood forest in northern California stands a huge tree—15 feet in diameter at breast-high level. Clutched to the bark at this

---

[11]Irving J. Lee, "On a Mechanism of Misunderstanding," in *Promoting Growth toward Maturity in Interpreting What Is Read*, ed. Gray, Supplementary Educational Monographs, no. 74 (Chicago: University of Chicago Press, 1951), pp. 86–90. Copyright, 1951, by the University of Chicago.

FIGURE 9-3

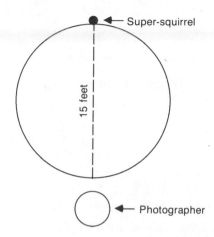

level is Super-Squirrel. (Why *Super*-Squirrel will be clear in a moment.) On the opposite side of the tree is a photographer who would like to take Super-Squirrel's picture.

However, when the photographer walks to his right, Super-Squirrel senses the photographer's movement and does the same. When the photographer moves to his left, so does Super-Squirrel. No matter how fast or quietly the man moves, Super-Squirrel is a match for him and manages to keep the tree's diameter between them. The photographer decides to back off a mile or two and sneak in from behind, but the uncanny squirrel detects this as well.

A squirrel hunter would suggest throwing a stone or stick to one side of the tree to scare the squirrel around to the other side. And that might work with an ordinary squirrel, but this is *Super*-Squirrel! And a given in this case is that Super-Squirrel keeps the tree's diameter between itself and the photographer at all times.

Another given: There is no elevation change, such as tree-climbing or mountain climbing, by either Super-Squirrel or the photographer.

The question: Can the photographer circle Super-Squirrel?

Question 2.   Would you pay $25 for a slightly used but fully functioning Zalunk?

Question 3.   Does $x + 3 = 5$?

I have no way of knowing your answers, but I can report the answers given by over 4,000 people, including college students, business and government executives, police administrators, military officers, and hospital and medical personnel, distributed among 137 groups. Their answers were confined to three choices: "Yes," "No," and "I don't know."

	Yes	No	I don't know
Question 1 (Super-Squirrel)	59%	39%	2%
Question 2 (Zalunk)	11	32	57
Question 3 (x)	5	2	93

Note two aspects of the above figures:

1. The apparent controversy generated by question 1 in particular. (You might try the Super-Squirrel problem at your next party or coffee break—if you are willing to risk group disintegration!)
2. The rapidly mounting "I don't know" answers and, conversely, the decreasing assurance of answers as we move down through the questions—that is, 98 percent positive answers (yes or no) to question 1 but only 7 percent to question 3.

And yet the three questions share a basic feature. Each contains a key variable, and the question cannot be answered yes or no until that variable is fixed, that is, defined.

The clearest example is question 3. Obviously, the answer is yes, *if* one fixes the variable x as 2—or no, if it is fixed as other than 2. And perhaps that is why there were so few yes or no answers. Since the question-asker did not fix the variable for them, people recognized the active role that they would have to play in fixing it for themselves.

But this was also true of the other two questions. However, significantly fewer people seemed aware that *they* were the variable-fixers. To say yes to the Zalunk question, one (unless answering facetiously) would presumably have had to fix (define) Zalunk as something that was worth $25 to own, or at least to satisfy one's curiosity about. To answer no would require defining Zalunk as not worth $25 to own, and so on.

The question with which responders seemed *least* conscious of their roles as variable-fixers was the first. Many steadfastly held that the photographer could circle the squirrel, and others just as tenaciously claimed that he could *not*. Put these opposing camps in the same room, and observe the decibels rise!

The yes-responders generally argued that the photographer could walk all the way around the tree. That would cause the squirrel to scamper all the way around it too, so that the photographer's path would encompass the squirrel's route. And that, according to the "Yes-ers," is circling the squirrel."

"Hardly," the no-responders retort. "Circling the squirrel requires that the photographer orbit the squirrel, with the latter as the orbit's axis—or at least pass around the back of the squirrel. Since a given in the case prohibits the photographer from being on the same side of the tree as the squirrel (to say nothing of the photographer's passing *through* the tree!), this cannot occur. Thus, the photographer cannot circle the squirrel."

FIGURE 9-4   FIGURE 9-5

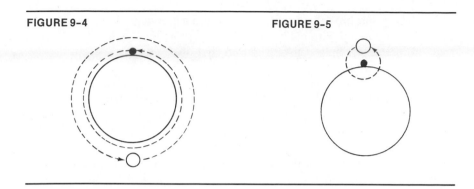

So either answer is correct, depending upon whose definition we accept.

Now, why do people quarrel over silly, petty questions like this—and even sillier and pettier ones? Partly because they *think* they are disputing *facts*—they are not. They are disagreeing about what *name* they will give to those facts. The issue is not physical but semantic.

The cardinal delusion is their belief that words have meanings—apart from the people using them. Words are just so many meaningless variables—like x and y and Zalunk—until someone fixes the variable, that is, chooses to intend or interpret the words in a particular way.

When we assume that words have meanings, we fail to realize the active role that the communicator (sender or receiver) plays as a variable-fixer. The communication problem, then, is *not* that people fix variables (i.e., define words), for we could not communicate otherwise. The problem arises only when (1) the speaker (or writer) fixes a variable one way, (2) the listener (or reader) fixes the variable differently, and (3) each assumes that the other is or should be fixing it in the *same* way.

DELIBERATE BYPASSING

Up to this point, we have been assuming that the communicators, regardless of their degree of success or failure, intended to understand each other. Clearly, this is not always a warranted assumption. The speaker (or writer) may desire to be bypassed. Or the listener (or reader) may just as earnestly contrive to miss meanings. The motives of the communicators, therefore, must be considered in an analysis of a bypassing.

The story is told of the congressman running for reelection who was speaking before a group of constituents. At the conclusion of his prepared talk, a question came from the floor: "Congressman, you didn't say anything about Social Security. Just how do you feel about Social Security?"

Realizing that his audience was evenly and irreconcilably divided on the issue, he responded with a wink and a knowing smile: "Don't worry about that subject, my friend—I'm all right on that one!"

And *everyone* applauded!

And a certain used car dealer used purposeful bypassing to his advantage with this advertisement: "Money cheerfully refunded in 24 hours if not satisfied." Some wishful-thinking buyers were convinced that they were being offered an unlimited guarantee on their purchase and that it would require only a day for the dealer to refund their money. Weeks (or days) later, when some of the secondhand autos began to break down, expectant owners approached the dealer, who reported: "The advertisement? Oh, that meant I was giving you a one-day guarantee!"

Until military conscription was abolished, the draft was a major concern for many young men. Understandably, this ad which appeared briefly in a number of newspapers attracted much attention:

How to Avoid the Draft

Legally and Honorably

Send $1

For his dollar, the customer received one word on a postcard:

Enlist

I nominate for first place among deliberate bypassers the international propagandists who make an art of misunderstanding—and of being misunderstood. Consider this example, which emanates from an international fair. It seems that the Russians were displaying their small car, the Ziss. In the U.S. display was an American subcompact. Someone thought of having an automobile engineer from a neutral nation examine each car carefully and decide which was superior.

The engineer decided in favor of the American auto. However, the Russian news agency triumphantly reported the news to the home folks in these words: "In comparative tests of Russian and foreign automobiles, the Russian Ziss placed second while the American car was next to last."

I would award honorable (perhaps it should be dishonorable) mention for intentional bypassing to the pedestrian who was arrested in Washington, D.C., for walking on the "Don't Walk" sign. His alibi in court was that he thought the sign was an advertisement for the taxi company!

Purposeful bypassing can be used constructively as well. Take the case of a certain labor-management conciliator. The union contract had only a week to run. The union had adamantly refused to discuss terms with management and was preparing to strike. When the conciliator asked union officials why they had refused to bargain, he was told: "Why, we want a substantial increase [they told him confidentially that this meant 35 to 40 cents per hour], and we're dead sure management won't go along with us, so why waste time?" Nothing the conciliator could say would persuade them to meet with management. Finally, he turned to the company, where he

"Reverend Benson says for you to call later. He just got into the bathtub."

was told in confidence that it was willing to give fifteen cents. "Would you say this would be a 'substantial increase'? he asked. "It certainly would be," he was assured. He then returned to the union officials and reported that the company was willing to talk in terms of a substantial increase. With that, he was able to coax the union's representatives to meet with the company's. With his guidance, the two parties were able to reach a compromise in time to avert a strike that neither side wanted.

Of course, the *receiver* of communication may bypass intentionallly just as readily as the *sender*. Our legal system takes this into account by insisting that a law must be obeyed not merely in accord with its letter (words) but with its spirit (intent). The law recognizes that the letter of even the most cautiously written statute may be subject to willful misinterpretation.

Gobbledygook

Before leaving the topic of intentional miscommunication we should consider gobbledygook. This is the smoke-screen kind of communication which, through the use of technical jargon, involved sentences, and polysyllabic words, seems more calculated to obscure than to inform.

In the pursuit of total organizational flexibility and integrated management mobility, one must consider such factors as systematized transitional capability and synchronized logistical programming as well as parallel reciprocal contingencies. Perhaps, however, the most significant factor of all is the basic balanced policy concept. For after all without optional digital and incremental projections the network is by and large merely a functional second- or third-generation time-phase continuum.

If that has you reeling, it has served its purpose. Erudite, sophisticated— but utterly nonsensical. I composed it from the now famous (infamous?) Systematic Buzz Phrase Projector, which purportedly originated in the Royal Canadian Air Force. For aid in constructing your own esoteric prolixities and verbose amphibolies, here are the raw materials:

Column 1	Column 2	Column 3
0. integrated	0. management	0. options
1. total	1. organizational	1. flexibility
2. systematized	2. monitored	2. capability
3. parallel	3. reciprocal	3. mobility
4. functional	4. digital	4. programming
5. responsive	5. logic	5. concept
6. optical	6. transitional	6. time-phase
7. synchronized	7. incremental	7. projection
8. compatible	8. third-generation	8. hardware
9. balanced	9. policy	9. contingency

Simply think of a three-digit number, and select the corresponding buzz words from the three columns above. For example, 230 produces "systematized reciprocal options," an expression bound to bring instant impressiveness—and confusion.

The New Yorker has the delightful policy of reprinting material that had appeared elsewhere—then adding its own comment.

APPLIED THEOLOGY 142. Sociology of Religion and Teaching.
This is a macro/micro humanistic approach to the sociology of religion and teaching containing four components: (1) Examination of historical paradigms; (2) Field studies of radical sociological change in religious states; (3) Analysis of social-cultural continuities and discontinuities, derived and underived religious posturing, dimensions of tension, crisis confluence and synthesis in cross-cultural states; (4) A correlation of sociology and teaching enabling the student to distill transcendent processes as well as to develop a more cogent language of religion in the context of educational goals. *Harvard Divinity School* catalog.

The New Yorker's response? "Those who pass go straight to heaven."
Gobbledygook leads not so much to miscommunication as to noncommunication. It is often the refuge of insecure writers (or speakers). (If you can't say it clearly and simply, to paraphrase composer Jean Sibelius, you don't understand it.) Unsure of what they mean or of how their ideas will

be received, they—like the proverbial cuttlefish—evade their enemies by disappearing in a cloud of ink.

But whether bypassing be purposeful or not, the pattern of miscommunication is essentially the same and the corrective measures are equally applicable.

CORRECTIVES

There is no panacea for harmful bypassing, but these time-tested techniques can prevent a great deal of it:

1. Be person-minded, not word-minded.
2. Query and paraphrase.
3. Be approachable.
4. Use backup methods.
5. Employ the PTA.
6. Practice the PRA.
7. Delay a day.
8. Get and provide the "telling" response.
9. Be sensitive to contexts.

Make these techniques habitual. Make them your conditioned response to a communication situation. Consider them as finely tempered muscles of the athlete. Even after these habits have been established, they must be practiced and strengthened daily.

Be Person-Minded—Not Word-Minded

Communicators who habitually look for meanings in the people using the words, rather than in the words themselves, are much less prone to bypass or to be bypassed. They realize that the important issue in communication is not what the words mean, but what the *user* means by them. When alert communicators talk or write, they are aware that their listeners or readers may *not* necessarily interpret the senders' words as they mean them. When they listen or read, they are aware that the speaker or writer may have intended the words other than as they (the receivers) are interpreting them at the moment. They recognize that communication involves variable-fixing by the sender—and by the receiver.

To keep person-minded in your communications, frequently ask yourself:

This is what it means to me, but what does it, or will it, mean to them?
What would I mean if I were in another's shoes?
Does my interpretation of their words coincide with their viewpoint (as I see it)?
Are the sender and receiver fixing the variables in the same way?

Query and Paraphrase *mirroring*

Query the Speaker or Writer. Some of the best parental advice children receive somehow becomes lost as they grow older. Almost everyone has been told: "If you don't understand your teachers, ask them what they mean." But as time goes on, something happens to us. We evidently become too inhibited or proud or embarrassed to ask others what they mean.

A common complaint among my colleagues in college teaching is that students do not ask enough questions in the classroom—the very place where questions should abound![12] It is almost as if we believed that asking a question of a speaker or writer (assuming that circumstances permit) would lead them to doubt our intelligence! Nothing could be farther from the truth. Professors and exeuctives alike indicate that they respect a thoughtful question. To them it indicates interest and a sense of responsibility rather than stupidity.

To be sure, some managers (and teachers) resent questions from subordinates. But more about that later under the heading "Be approachable."

So, ask questions when:

1. You don't understand or can't make sense of what you have heard or read.
2. You think there may be a legitimate interpretation other than the one which first occurred to you.
3. You sense something out of alignment—something that doesn't quite mesh with the rest of your knowledge of a situation.

A special suggestion for the boss: You can ask questions, too, but avoid closed-ended questions. They often begin with do or is and can be too easily answered with yes or no. Then you still don't know if your receivers have understood you or how they feel about your message. Ask the open-ended question that cannot be answered with the communication stopping monosyllable. You encourage your people to give a fuller, more honest indication of their comprehension and feelings.

Closed-ended   Did you understand me ? Is that clear?
Open-ended   How would you go about doing that?
              What's your reaction to that idea?

Paraphrase the Speaker or Writer. Putting a speaker's or writer's communication into your own words and asking if your paraphrasing is acceptable is one of the oldest, simplest, most useful, and most neglected techniques in communication.

---

[12]Business executives express much the same concern. "What do you have to do to get people to ask questions?" a vice president of a manufacturing firm asks. "If people would only make *sure* they got it straight, we'd save five hundred thousand dollars a year."

I once observed a fascinating series of business meetings in which the technique of paraphrasing was put to a special use. The meetings involved the regular executive conferences of a certain firm, but a new touch had been added. An outsider was engaged to serve as moderator. The requirements were that the moderator be reasonably intelligent, have a good memory for spoken communication, and develop the knack of paraphrasing the statement of another without making embellishments, judgments, deletions, or additions.

This is how it worked. The agenda having been set up previously, the meeting began with the moderator stating; "Ladies and gentlemen, the meeting is convened. Who would like to begin?" Some of the participants raised their hands, and the moderator recognized, say, Executive A, who then made a statement. Then, before anyone else was permitted to speak, the moderator paraphrased A's remarks. A would now either accept the moderator's rephrasing as accurate (in which case the next person would be permitted to speak) or correct it. In the latter case, the moderator would then paraphrase A's correction, which A would either accept or correct, and so on, until A accepted the moderator's paraphrasing without qualification.

After A and the moderator agreed on A's communication, any other member was permitted to query or paraphrase what had been said if they were still in doubt about A's meaning.

The procedure sounds laborious, and indeed it was for the first few meetings. But soon, this group of executives was holding conferences (which had been notorious for their miscommunications) with startling equanimity and progress. I have never experienced group discussions with so few instances of bypassing; moreover, many potential bypassings were revealed by the moderator's rewordings. An additional benefit, according to the executives involved, was that with the moderator's paraphrasings, the speaker was assured that at least one other person in the room understood fully what was said—a very satisfying and previously infrequent experience!

The meetings, it is true, were somewhat longer[13] than usual, but who can estimate the amounts of time and the money, effort, and nervous tension saved by thus preventing miscommunications?

The simple techniques of the query and the paraphrase can be potent defenses against bypassing. But discretion must be exercised. Occasionally a person may go to absurd lengths, making the techniques an end in themselves rather than a means toward clarifying communication.

---

[13]Frequently, of course, B's reaction to A's statement was delayed by the moderator's interposition. For the special value of such delays, read, "Correctives," Chapter 17.

A "Peanuts" cartoon a few years ago made the point aptly. It showed Charlie Brown greeting Linus, who was making a snowman in his backyard. The dialogue went approximately like this:

Charlie   Hi, Linus. Did you have a good Christmas?
Linus   What do you mean: "Did I have a good Christmas?"
Linus   Do you mean, did I get a lot of good presents?
Linus   Or do you mean did I have a good time with all my cousins who came to visit?
Linus   Or do you mean was it good in a spiritual sense?
Linus   Or do you mean . . .
Charlie   (*Sigh*)

Be Approachable

The Responsibilities of the Sender.   So far we have been discussing the techniques of querying and paraphrasing from the receiver's point of view; that is, how the listener or reader should use them. But communication is a two-way street, with responsibilities at both ends. Senders (speakers, writers) should do their utmost to make querying and paraphrasing possible. They should not only permit it or make themselves approachable—they should encourage it, invite it—even, on some occasions, insist on it.

But some people in positions of responsibility are threatened by feedback. They may feel so insecure or so poorly versed in their field that they regard a question as a challenge that they must ward off. Ironically, such defensiveness often leads to even more destructive consequences than those feared.

For under the best of circumstances, most subordinates are somewhat inhibited in dealing with their superiors. Conditioned by past experiences with authority figures and regarding the boss as the reward-controller, the subordinate tends to be circumspect in communicating upward. So when a manager deliberately—or unwittingly—becomes unapproachable, the boss virtually assures the strangulation of the channel upward.

To the extent that communicating upward to the boss is perceived as dangerous, painful, embarrassing, or unpleasant, the upward flow of communication will be curtailed and filtered. The boss just won't get the bad news until it becomes so bad that it can no longer be concealed—until there is, indeed, a real problem.

Supervisors who thus contribute to an "approachability gap" between themselves and their people are doing a disservice to those poeple, to their organizations, and particularly to themselves.

At the risk of appearing kindergartenish, I often urge people with responsibilities to paste a sign on their respective bathroom mirrors.

It simply asks:

ARE YOU APPROACHABLE?

I hope it will trigger a daily self-examination.

> Am I approachable?[14] Do my people[15] really feel free to query, para-phrase, and, in general, communicate with me? Have I done everything pos-sible to make their channel to me free and clear—and do I *keep* it that way? Do I make an extra effort to be approachable to more timid, reticent peo-ple?[16] Am I *genuinely* receptive to feedback, and do I continually communi-cate my receptivity to others?

Strictly speaking, the admonition should be to *attain* and *maintain* ap-proachability—two verbs. For approachability is a form of trust. And trust is a precious and fragile commodity, hard to build sometimes but easily de-stroyed. And once trust is abused, it usually becomes singularly difficult to rebuild. So we have to work to achieve approachability and keep working to maintain it.

Use Backup Methods

I am frequently asked: "Which is the best communication method?" The best method depends upon the circumstances, of course, but there is no perfect method—each method has its limitations. A face-to-face conversa-tion, for example, has many advantages. If you and I are sitting opposite one another over a coffee table, we have a good deal going for us. Beyond the language of words, we are also communicating with facial expressions, postures, gestures, and vocal inflections, to say nothing of subliminal clues that we may be sending and receiving. In addition, we have the immediate opportunity to assess one another's reception of our respective messages. If I say something and see a furrowed brow or a whimsical smile, I can ask for further feedback: "How do you feel about that?"

None of these extras would we have if I were, say, sending you a memo, letter, or a report. On the other hand, what we *don't* have is a record of our

---

[14]Lest current or aspiring managers absolve themselves too readily—"My people really feel free with me"—let them consider the frequent discrepancy between the subordinate's perception of the freedom to communicate up to the boss and the boss's perception of that freedom.

[15]By "my people" I mean the manager's immediate subordinates—those who report di-rectly to him/her. By no means am I advocating violating the chain of command.

[16]This emphasis on receptivity is not intended to retard the development and maturation of employees. The manager must use discretion to assure an open communication channel without inducing excessive dependence on the part of subordinates.

communication. And if it becomes evident a week later that, despite the advantage of our face-to-face chat, we bypassed, can you visualize the futile, irreconcilable debate that would be likely to follow: "Don't you remember? You said this!" "No, I didn't. I said that!"

Since no method is complete, the obvious strategy is to shore up the inadequacies of one method with the strengths of another. Use multiple methods. In this case, how about having one or both of us jot down the salient points of our conversation and send a copy to the other. Sure, it takes time and effort—scarce commodities in most organizations. But when we consider that top administrative officers estimate that the cost of miscommunication ranges between 25 and 40 percent of budget, can we afford not to take the time and effort?

Employ the PTA

This stands for *pretransmission audit*. It is applicable when you have the time to prepare a message in advance—such as a memo, a letter, a report, or an oral presentation. After you have composed the message but before you deliver it to your final recipient, get a third party—a friend, a secretary, your spouse—to check it for bypassing possibilities. Ideally, this auditor ought to be objective and ought to have the same relevant background as your final decoder. The point is that when we prepare messages, they frequently sound entirely intelligible and acceptable—inside our heads. Some of this feeling could be wishful thinking—we would dearly want the receiver to interpret the message that way. The bald fact is that we are generally *not* the best judge of the adequacy of our own communiqués.

Practice the PRA

This stands for *postreception audit*. It is the same idea as the PTA, except that you get your auditor to check the message after you have received it but before you take action on it. Here again, the relative outsider might spot potential bypassings that had eluded you on first reading (or hearing).

Delay a Day

If possible and especially if the situation is emotional, delay a day before sending your message or before acting on a received message. Write it up and lock it up—for a day. The value of incubation is illustrated in Chapter 17, "Undelayed Reactions." Very often the quality of encoding and decoding can be improved if one takes the time to sleep on the message.

Get and Provide the "Telling" Response

If you are sending the message, it's up to you to get a "telling" response from your recipient—a response that tell you how the other person is decoding your message. What counts is now what was in your head or even what you said or wrote. The final arbiter in communication is how the receiver interprets the message. Conversely, if you are the receiver, then provide that telling response to your sender. It takes two (at least) to communicate. Each has a mutual responsibility to make the communication succeed.

> **context** \ 'kän-,tekst \ *n* [ME, weaving together of words, fr. L *contextus* connection of words, coherence, fr. *contextus*, pp. of *contexere* to weave together, fr. *com-* + *texere* to weave—more at TECHNICAL] (1568) **1** : the parts of a discourse that surround a word or passage and can throw light on its meaning [verbal context] **2** : the interrelated conditions in which something exists or occurs [situational context] : ENVIRONMENT, SETTING

From *Webster's Ninth New Collegiate Dictionary* (Springfield, MA: Merriam-Webster, Inc., 1984). Reprinted with permission.

Be Sensitive to Contexts

In view of the incredible amount of ambiguity in our language, it is surprising that we communicate as well as we do. Our primary aid is context— the surrounding words (verbal context) and the surrounding circumstances (situational context). The context provides the prime body of clues that we use to interpret each other's messages.

This is how it works. (To get the best effect from this demonstration, cover up the remaining lines on this page and the top section of the next page and reveal one line at a time.)

A single word or short phrase is like a single piece of a jigsaw puzzle— difficult to understand until you combine it with other pieces. Suppose that I say simply: "one eighty-three." You might feel that you have no idea of what I mean. Actually, you have too many ideas. It probably will occur to you that I might mean:

a bowling (hopefully not a golf) score.
a street address.
a price—$1.83 or $183. If a Realtor® says it, you might interpret the
    number as $183,000!
a page in a book.
a highway route.
miles per hour at, say, the Indianapolis Speedway.
a temperature.
a length in inches, feet, yards, or miles. Or in millimeters, centimeters,
    meters, or kilometers.
a post office box number.

the atomic weight of a chemical element in the periodic table.
a hotel room.

But suppose that I start adding a few words. Note how quickly you create a meaningful interpretation of "one-eighty-three" as you combine the jigsaw pieces:

First, pounds of weight.
Then, woman.
Then, five feet tall.
Then, 17 years old.
Finally, sitting in her doctor's office waiting for an appointment.

Let us take a more detailed look at the role of verbal context.

Verbal Context.   Suppose that I overhear two men talking. However, they are so far away that the only word I pick up is *plufe*. What under the sun did they mean? The men are drawing closer, and now I hear: "Say, Ralph, could you plufe me a dollar? I'll pay it back tommorrow." Then later: "It was raining last night when I landed at O'Hare. So the stewardess plufed me an umbrella, to get from the plane to the terminal."

While I may wonder at that strange word, I am now reasonably confident that I understand what they are saying. But why? No one defined "plufe." No one said "This is what I mean by plufe . . ." I guessed at what the men meant by this term from the verbal context in which it occurred. Using the surrounding words as clues, I zeroed in from an almost unlimited number of possible interpretations to one—a synonym for lend.

Verbal context is not limited to the accompanying words in a sentence, but consists of the neighboring sentences, paragrpahs, and so on, as well. If you hold up an object and ask: "What's this?" the appropriate response might be "off-white," "a shirt," "$7.50," or "broadcloth," depending upon whether we had been talking about colors, classifications of garments, prices, or fabrics.

It is largely the verbal context by which we deduce what others mean (how they are fixing the variables)—and how they interpret what we mean.

Sometimes, however, we are admonished to reduce the verbal context—"boil it down," "be concise," "don't camouflage your meaning with excessive verbiage." Pliny the Elder, confessed: "I am writing you at length because I do not have time to write a short letter." The Lord's Prayer consists of 56 words and the Gettysburg Address has 266. But the Pentagon somehow needed 16 single-spaced pages of specifications for a plastic whistle used by military police and drill instructors.

Can you devise clearer and more economical expressions of the following sentiments?

Do not, however disadvantageous the circumstances, permit yourselves to be forced into a position in which you must acquiesce in the transfer of ownership of this vessel to persons owing allegiance to a country whose interests are inimical to those of ours.

I must be given maximum latitude to enjoy the benefits of our country, unfettered by degrading restrictions on my activities; if I am denied this privilege I would prefer to be permanently deprived of the exercise of my viable functions.

"Don't give up the ship" and "Give me liberty, or give me death" would do very nicely.

Obviously, discretion must be exercised by the sender, who must avoid unnecessarily long and repetitious communications, for they can be as confusing as if they were intended to deceive.

Dr. George Russell Harrison recalled this incident:

A plumber of foreign extraction wrote the National Bureau of Standards and said he found that hydrochloric acid quickly opened plugged drainage pipes and inquired if that was a good thing to use. A scientist at the Bureau replied that "the efficacy of hydrochloric acid is indisputable, but the corrosive residue is incompatible with metallic permanence."

The plumber wrote back thanking the Bureau for telling him that hydrochloric acid was all right. The scientist was disturbed about the misunderstanding and showed the correspondence to his boss—another scientist—who wrote the plumber: "We cannot assume responsibility for the production of toxic and noxious residue with hydrochloric acid and suggest you use an alternative procedure."

The plumber wrote back thanking the Bureau for telling him that hydrochloric works fine. Greatly disturbed, the scientists took their problem to the top boss. He broke with scientific jargon and wrote the plumber: "Don't use hydrochloric acid. It eats hell out of pipes."

But an equal if not greater danger lurks in *under*—communication which provides such scanty context that bypassing is virtually invited. This memorandum appeared briefly on a federal agency bulletin board:

Those department heads who do not have the services of full-time secretaries may take advantage of the stenographers in the secretarial pool.

Somehow that reminds me of Groucho Marx's reply to the airline stewardess who informed him that "You can smoke your cigar if you don't annoy the ladies." "You mean there's a choice?" eagerly asked Groucho. "Then, I'll annoy the ladies!"

Because of the necessity for conciseness, signs are particularly vulnerable targets for bypassing. Among my collection: Sign over a combination greasy-spoon diner and gasoline station:

> Eat Here And Get Gas

One wonders whether the proprietor was (1) obtuse, (2) banking on others sharing his sense of humor, or (3) issuing a fair warning.

Sign outside a church announcing a forthcoming sermon:

> Do You Know
> What Hell Is?
>
> Come hear our
> new organist.

Another church sign:

> If You're Tired
> Of Sin—Come In

Penciled beneath: "If you're not—phone 366-5619.

In the interests of sanitation and aesthetics this sign was posted in a University of Colorado cafeteria:

> Shoes Are Required To Eat In The Cafeteria

Added gratuitously was: "Socks can eat wherever they want."

This sign appeared at a dingy nightclub:

> Clean And Decent Dancing
> Every Night Except Sunday

The unsolicited addition: "You must do a big business on Sundays!"

If you visit Myrtle Beach, S.C., stop in at Dave's Bait and Tackle Shop. In addition to the usual necessities for fishing, Dave's features sandwiches, beer—and a remarkable sign:

> DAVES
> EAT
> WORMS

Evidently, gentlemen there with a certain first name have unusual dining habits. If you catch them at dinner it might make an unforgettable part of your trip.

And while we're in the category, Harry's Fly, Bait, and Tackle Shop (address mercifully withheld) was recently burned. The local newspaper announced that repairs had been completed and Harry's Fly is now open.

And finally, this sign at a power station in Ireland:

> To Touch These Overhead
> Cables Means Instant Death
> Offenders will be prosecuted.

Which seems only just for such a shocking offense.

Classified advertisements are another fertile field for inadvertent bypassing. The ad placer, keen on reducing costs, reduces his context:

> Apartment for Rent, View takes in 4 counties, 2 bedrooms.
> For Sale: 1979 Cadillac hearse. Body in good condition.
> For Sale: Large Great Dane. Registered pedigree. Will eat anything. Especially fond of children.
> Wanted: Man to handle dynamite. Must be prepared to travel unexpectedly.

Quoting out of Context.   Lifting words or even sentences, paragraphs, and chapters out of context is a well-known ploy of propagandists and others who seek to distort communication. This is hardly a new deceit. Witness this circular used by Republicans in the campaign of 1928:

> They quoted an article from the presumably unbiased *Encyclopaedia Britannica* (11th ed., Vol. XXVI, p. 392), to show the corruption of Tammany Hall, and the danger of putting a member of the Tammany Society in the presidential chair. They quite failed, however, to quote the very relevant final sentence of the *Britannica* article, namely: "The power of the organization in the state and in the nation is due to its frequent combination with the Republican organization, which controls the state almost as completely as Tammany does the city."[18]

Quoting into Context.   Wordsmiths are still using elections as opportunities to persuade the electorate to vote their way. The larger, if less glamorous, part of the Chicago area ballot in 1984 involved 35 incumbent judges

---

[18]Edwin Leavitt Clarke, *The Art of Straight Thinking: A Primer of Scientific Method for Social Inquiry* (New York: Appleton-Century-Crofts, 1929), p. 348. Reprinted by permission of Appleton-Century-Crofts, Inc.

of the Cook County Circuit Court. Voters were to decide which of them should be retained. For several days preceding the election, newspapers carried an advertisement.

VOTE **YES** ON THE
GREEN JUDICIAL BALLOT
NOV. 6, 1984
RETAIN JUDGES OF EXPERIENCE, INTEGRITY AND ABILITY

The judges were listed and each name was followed by **YES** and the candidate's ballot number. Also, three dignitaries were quoted:

> "I strongly urge all voters to retain qualified judges on the Judicial Retention Ballot." Governor James R. Thompson
>
> Mayor Harold Washington says: "It takes a YES vote of 60 percent to retain a judge on the bench. I HOPE AND URGE MY SUPPORTERS AND FRIENDS TO VOTE UNANIMOUSLY TO RETAIN THOSE GOOD JUDGES THAT ARE ON THE JUDICIAL RETENTION BALLOT."
>
> U.S. District Attorney Dan Webb says: "I personally know many of the judges that are running on this retention ballot. In my opinion, there are judges on this particular retention ballot that are among the finest jurists in our nation."

A quick impression of the overall context of the ad, highlighted by the large heading and the long and conspicuous columns of yeses, would lead the reader to believe that the governor, the mayor, and the district attorney had enthusiastically endorsed all of the candidates. But a more careful interpretation of the statements is that the endorsers had left it to the public to determine which were "qualified" and "good" and "finest."

Little wonder that Thompson et al. were cautious. The candidates had been evaluated by several interested organizations and some of them had been found wanting. Fifteen of the 35 received a "not recommended" or "not qualified" appraisal from one or more organizations. One judge was rejected by the Chicago Bar Association, the Chicago Council of Lawyers, the Cook County Bar Association, the Woman's Bar Association of Illinois, and the West Suburban Bar Association!

Now, who devised this artful ad? Perhaps it was lack of pride of authorship but you might need your magnifying glass to read Paid for by the 1984 Judicial Retention Committee at the bottom of the ad.

Did the ad work? Like chicken soup, it didn't hurt. Receiving a higher than average vote (77–84 percent) all 35 were retained!

Returning to the issue of inadvertent bypassing—an answer to the problem of insufficient verbal contexts is, of course, for the sender to provide and/or the receiver to obtain enough related information to determine the intent of the excerpt.

In conclusion, be sensitive to verbal contexts, the surrounding words and sentences that may help to determine the meaning of any word, phrase, or passage. Ask yourself: Is this word, phrase, and so on, taken out of its verbal context? Might I interpret it differently if I knew what went before or after it? Am I giving my receiver sufficient (but not too much) context to understand my communication?

Situational Context. What lies beyond the context of words and phrases?[19] How does this communication fit into the larger framework of people and happenings? Make a habit of orienting yourself toward the situational context of the message.

Suppose that we reenact the Morris-foreman case with one change— Morris now has a sensitivity about the bigger picture:

Foreman Better clean up around here.

Morris OK. (*Then moments later after the foreman has left.*) Wait a minute! The boss has me working on this bearing. It's supposed to be a rush-order job. Now he tells me to drop it and clean up my work area. Something is wrong somewhere—I'd better check.

Clearly, if Morris had checked (queried or paraphrased), the delay and embarrassment presumably would have been avoided. Sometimes, lack of awareness of the situational context is a good deal costlier.

Scram-ble!

KEMBLE, England (UPI)—Four Royal Air Force jets were speeding across England Tuesday when the rear pilot radioed: "You are on fire—eject."

Flight Lt. John Rust, 30, bailed out of one plane.

Flight Lt. Richard Duckett, 27, bailed out of another.

Rust's plane was on fire. Duckett's wasn't. Both pilots landed uninjured. Both planes, worth $960,000 each, crashed.[20]

---

[19]If the situational context is clear and mutually understood, we may need very little *verbal* communication. The epitome of this was perhaps the exchange of messages between Victor Hugo and his publishers. In 1862, after completing his monumental *Les Misérables*, Hugo went on holiday. Anxious to know how the novel was selling he wrote Hurst and Blackett. His letter consisted of simply "?" Knowing what was uppermost in the author's mind, the publishers responded with "!"

[20]*Chicago Daily News*, December 17, 1969, p. 3. Reprinted by permission.

Granted that the rear pilot should have been more specific, but will Lieutenant Duckett ever forgive himself for not having asked, "There are three of us; which one of us are you talking to?"

NONVERBAL AMBIGUITY

The focus of this chapter, as is the whole of Part Three, is on verbal communication. But nonverbal exchanges can be ambiguous, too, especially when we try to communicate interculturally. In an intriguing book, Morris[21] et al. list 20 widely used gestures. What is intended by the gesturer may vary greatly in different parts of the world. It may even be equivocal within a limited area.

For example, among other meanings, the thumb-up gesture can be perceived as: O.K.—all is well; simply one; a sexual insult; a hitch-hike request; and a direction. The authors suggest hitch-hikers avoid this gesture in northern Greece and southern Sardinia. It is likely to be interpreted as "get stuffed" and does not encourage drivers to stop, except to pick a fight. They recommend a loosely waved, flat-hand gesture as practiced by the local hitch-hikers.

SUMMARY

Bypassing occurs when communicators miss each other's meanings. It may take place when they use the same word to mean different things or when they use different words to mean the same thing. The effects of bypassing may range from the trivial and humorous to the serious and even catastrophic. In general, the immediate consequence of a bypassing may be either an apparent agreement on meanings when a disagreement actually exists, or an apparent disagreement when an agreement actually exists.

Basically a person bypasses because of the assumption, often unconscious, that words mean the same to other persons. Underlying this assumption are two insidious fallacies. The first fallacy, that words have mono-usage, thrives despite the manifest multi-usage of so many words in our language. The second fallacy is that words have meanings. This fallacy obscures the fact that words are not containers of meaning but rather are variables to be fixed (defined) by those who use words in sending and receiving messages. In this sense, bypassing occurs when (1) the sender fixes a variable one way, (2) the receiver fixes it another way, and (3) each assumes that the other is fixing the variable in the identical way. Deliberate bypassing was acknowledged. It is relatively easy to misunderstand or to be misunderstood, if one intends to do so.

---

[21]Desmond Morris, Peter Collett, Peter Marsh, and Marie O'Shaughnessy, *Gestures* (New York: Stein and Day, 1979), p. 195.

Several commonsense but uncommonly used techniques are effective in curbing bypassing. (1) Be person-minded—not word-minded; (2) query and paraphrase; (3) be approachable; (4) use backup methods; (5) employ the PTA; (6) practice the PRA; (7) dealy a day; (8) get and provide the "telling" response; (9) be sensitive to contexts (verbal and situational). To be truly effective, these techniques must become deeply embedded habits which, in a sense, are on the alert even when we are not.

DISCUSSION QUESTIONS

1. If you were looking for a church to join and were invited to a church that professed to be based on communistic beliefs, would you;
   (a) Refuse the invitation?
   (b) Report the group to the proper authorities?
   (c) Take some other action? If so, what?

2. Our Declaration of Independence states that "all men are created equal," but evidence clearly indicates that babies are born with great variations in mental and physical capacities. Discuss the apparent discrepancy.

3. During a discussion among friends, someone suggests that "more socialistic concepts should be incorporated into our federal government." Then he turns to you and says: "What do you think?" How would you respond?

4. Doing some research on differing socioeconomic classes, you spend a couple of weeks in a tiny and remote village in Appalachia. These people refer to their shoes as "holy bibles." How would you respond to this? Why?

5. Precisely what is entailed in bypassing?

6. What unconsciously held, fallacious assumptions contribute to bypassing?

7. Why might people find these assumptions attractive?

8. How can one prevent bypassing? As sender? As receiver?

9. How can you help others to avoid bypassing without insulting their intelligence?

10. "Our communication would be just as effective if the large sphere in the sky that shines at night were called 'the sun,' if children who wear dresses were called 'boys,' and if members of the Republican party were called 'communists.' " How do you respond to this assertion? Why?

11. "Words mean the same to the other person as they do to me." Why would communicators make this assumption?

12. The words *sandwich, diesel, bloomers, martinet,* and *quixotic* have what in common?

13. What did G. B. Shaw mean when he defined England and the United States as "two great nations separated by the barrier of a common language"? Can you think of analogous situations?

14. What are the principal advantage and the principal limitation of computer languages compared to such natural languages as English?

15. Give an example of deliberate bypassing. Are there walks of life in which deliberate bypassing tends to be practiced? Is deliberate bypassing ever defensible ethically?

16. Discuss the techniques for reducing bypassing. Are there limitations to their use? Can you think of other preventives?

17. Regarding the "Product-Information Program," (Case 9–2) which pictures—Steger's or Robbins'—was more correct? Explain your answer.

18. Describe an incident, possibly involving yourself, in which bypassing occurred. Analyze specifically why it occurred, what might have been done to prevent its occurrence, and what measures would prevent its recurrence.

CASES

CASE 9-1

Was There a Noise?*

In Sweet Esther, Wisconsin, Bert Johnson and Fred Carter were hauled into court on a disorderly conduct charge. They had been picked up fighting in a drugstore. When the judge asked them for their story, Johnson replied:

"Well, your honor, we're neighbors, and Carter, here, told me he was going down to the drugstore—did I want anything? I said I'd go along with him.

"Well, sir, on the way down Carter says, 'I got a puzzle I bet a dollar you can't figure out—suppose lightning strikes a tree in the middle of the forest and the tree falls down. Now, there ain't no animals or birds or insects or people or instruments anywhere near the tree. Was there a noise when it fell?'

"Well, quick as a wink I says: 'Sure, there's a noise—it don't matter if people ain't there.' Then Carter gets on one of them superior grins and says: 'I guess you ain't as bright as you think you are—there ain't no noise if nobody can hear it."

The two men glared at each other, and Johnson continued: "Well, you know how it is, your honor—I'm saying there's a noise and Carter saying there ain't, and we start talking louder and louder—one thing leads to another—I guess I gave Carter a little shove—then he shoved me—and so on and so on—only by this time we were in the drugstore, and I guess we messed the place up a bit."

Discussion Questions

1. Was there a noise when the tree fell?
2. What must you do in order to answer yes or no to that question?
3. When groups discuss the noise question, there are often disagreements. Why? What assumptions to discussants often make?
4. What does this case have to do with bypassing?

---

*The case is fictitious, but hardly unrealistic.

CASE 9-2

The Product-Information Program*

The Meridian Corporation is one of the nation's leading manufacturers of television and radio receivers as well as other electronic instruments. It had been the policy of the firm to hold an annual national convention to which its 200 district distributors were invited and attended at company expense. One of the more important events of the convention was the Product-Information Program. This program consisted of a speech coupled with whatever visual aids (video cassettes, motion pictures, sound-slide films, and so on) were appropriate. The purpose of the program was to introduce the new models and to explain their features.

Each distributor was given a duplicate set of materials (script, video or audio cassette, films, recordings, and so on) so that he or she could stage a similar Product- Information Program for the district salespersonnel.

To accomplish this, the materials were reproduced 200 times and shipped to the distributors' respective home addresses while they were still in conference. Thus, on returning home, they would be able to commence their own Product-Information Program meetings immediately. Beginning the meetings immediately was essential if the salespeople were to be able to capitalize upon the national advertising campaign conducted by the firm simultaneously with the conclusion of the convention.

Daniel Steger, merchandising manager of Meridian, was usually in charge of preparing and presenting the Product-Information Program at the national convention. He would write the script and ordinarily engaged the Raymond Company, an audio-visual aids firm in the city, to prepare his other materials. On this occasion he needed a rather lengthy sound-slide film. A month before the convention, Ted Robbins, a technician from Raymond, and Steger went over the plans for the film in detail. Robbins submitted sketches for each frame, which Steger approved.

Two weeks later, Steger phoned Robbins.

S   Say, Robbins, is it too late to add another frame to our film?
R   No, I don't think so—what do you have in mind?
S   Well, this comes between the 16th and 17th frames, so we'll call it frame number 16A. I would like a picture of a stationary core with three or four small dots circling around it—do you get what I mean?
R   Sure, I got you—any other changes?
S   No, that'll just about do it.

---

*All names have been disguised.

R OK, fine, we'll add 16A, and you'll have the finished product the day before the convention.

S Can't make it any sooner?

R 'Fraid not—we're swamped already.

S OK then—make that change, and I'll see you in two weeks.

The sound-slide film was delivered on schedule on the day before the convention. Steger previewed it, and when frame number 16A appeared, he stared in amazement. This is what he saw:

This is what he had in mind when he phoned Robbins two weeks earlier;

Steger jumped to the phone and demanded that the frame be changed. The Raymond Company assigned a double crew which worked the rest of the day, all of the night, and half of the next morning to replace the 200 sound-slide films and to deliver a copy to a badly shaken Steger, barely in time for him to make his appearance before the convention. The total cost of replacing the films was $6,250.

Discussion Questions

1. How do you analyze what happened?

2. Can you draw still another picture that would satisfy the "stationary core . . ." description?

3. Can you express Steger's picture in words that cannot be misinterpreted?

4. How could this costly error have been avoided?

5. Who should pay the $6,250?

CASE 9–3

Jack McGuire*

The company I work for is engaged in selling metals to industrial accounts. These metals are steel, aluminum, brass, copper, stainless steel, nickel, Monel and nickel alloys for foundry work, as well as for fasteners (machine screws, washers, nuts, and so on), pipe fittings, rivets, and other items, such as nails, studs, and so forth.

The policy of the company in regard to sales personnel is to hire a man and train him in the plant for about a month to familiarize him with the products sold. The next step is to have him come in the office where he learns office procedures, basic facts about metals, pricing setup, company policy in regard to returned goods and other matters. An important step in this process is listening to a veteran salesman handle customers on the phone, as well as observing how customers who come into the office are handled.

Jack McGuire, a personable young sales trainee, had recently gone through this procedure and was now handling customers by phone. Jack had joined the company immediately after his graduation from high school, where he had been an outstanding athlete.

In preface, it should be noted that during an average week, a salesman receives about one or two calls wherein the customer has contacted the wrong company or the customer has a misconception about the products handled by the company.

One day McGuire received a call from the purchasing agent of one of our large industrial accounts.

> **Buyer** *(without announcing his company's name)* Do you have any track spikes in stock?
>
> **McGuire** *(with a little chuckle)* No, I am afraid you called the wrong place. You will have to try a sporting goods house like Dooner's.
>
> **Buyer** *(angrily)* Thank you for the information (bangs down the receiver).

One week later, our regular salesman, Frank Clifford, called on the account and was confronted by the buyer in an angry manner, "What are you hiring now, wise guys? I called up for track spikes to be used in our scrap metal yard, and your salesman told me to go to Dooner's."

Clifford explained that the man was new and that it probably was an honest error. Later, Clifford explained to McGuire that what the buyer had wanted were railroad track spikes which are used like steel nails where heavy timber is involved.

---

*All names have been disguised. Printed by permission of the author, whose name has been withheld by request.

Discussion Questions
1. What is your analysis of this case?
2. How could Jack have avoided this unpleasantness?

CASE 9–4

Room 406*

It was 4:56 P.M. on Tuesday on the surgical floor of John Randolph Memorial Hospital. Nurse Rhoda Fleming, an efficient woman with 15 years' service in the hospital, was in charge of the floor that afternoon. She was making her final check of the rooms prior to the arrival of her relief, who came on at 5:00 P.M. In Room 406, she found that Mr. Henry Youstra, who had undergone surgery the week before, and who had not responded well, had finally died. Mentally, she began to review the procedure on expirations—call a doctor to pronounce death; notify various administrative departments, including Admissions and Reception; wrap body; and so forth. Suddenly recalling that she had a 5:15 P.M. dental appointment, she decided to ask her relief, who generally arrived early, to handle the procedure.

While depressed with the death, she couldn't suppress a feeling of relief, for bed space was a critical problem at the hospital. She would tell her relief to prepare the room immediately for a new patient. She returned to the floor desk, which was located near the elevators. The night nurse, Ann Simmons, had already arrived and was waiting at the desk.

"Anythig new, Rho?" she asked.

"406 just died, so that room's all set to go again. I hate to see them go that way, but we can certainly use the space. I'm pressed—will you take over?"

"Sure. How about 411, did you give her her shot yet?"

"No, and you'd better do that soon. Old Doc Anders might be up, and he'd have a conniption of she hadn't had it yet."

"Does the office know that 406 is ready?"

"No, you can tell them after you get things cleaned up."

Nurse Fleming then left, and Nurse Simmons gave 411 her shot and went about her other routine duties. At about 6:30 P.M. Nurse Simmons called the office and told them that room 406 was ready for occupancy, though she had not checked that room herself. She was told that a Mr. Leopold would be down from emergency surgery later on and would be given that bed. She then carried on her other activities.

---

*All names are disguised. Printed by permission of the author, whose name has been withheld by request.

Visitors' hours began at 7:00 P.M. at Randolph Hospital, and as was her custom Mrs. Henry Youstra left home at 6:00 P.M. so as to arrive just at 7:00. Over the weeks of visiting her husband, she had acquired the habit of asking for her visitor's card by the room number, as the cards were issued by room number. The woman at the front desk gave her the card prepared for visitors of Mr. Leopold, and she took the elevator to the fourth floor. Nurse Simmons was at the fourth-floor desk when Mrs. Youstra arrived there. Nurse Simmons recognized Mrs. Youstra as a nightly visitor and smiled professionally at her, not recalling which patient she visited, nor looking at the name on the card. Nurse Simmons placed the card in the desk file, and Mrs. Youstra went down the hall.

At 8:00 P.M., the end of visiting hours, Nurse Simmons checked each room to see that all visitors had left. In Room 406 she found Mrs. Youstra dead on the floor beside the bed containing her husband's body.

Discussion Questions

1. Analyze in detail the critical exchange between Nurses Fleming and Simmons.

2. In summary, how do you perceive what has happened?

3. What patterns of miscommunication seem to have occurred here?

4. What measures will help to prevent a recurrence of this sort?

CASE 9–5

The Sturdy Corporate Homesteader*

deliberate
bypass !!!

In a happier time, so a U.S. Chamber of Commerce speaker tells us, the government used the public domain to "give every man a chance to earn land for himself through his own skill and hard work." This is the sturdy homemaker sob with which the air will presently resound when this gentleman's associates get to work on Congress. He may have been thinking of the California redwood forest. It was so attractive a part of the public domain that in this generation we have had to raise millions of dollars from rich men and schoolchildren to buy back a few acres of it here and there for the public.

Under a measure called the Timber and Stone Act, a homemaker who had his first citizenship papers could buy 160 acres of redwood forest from the government for $2.50 an acre, less than a panel for your living-room costs. Agents of a lumber company would go to a sailors' boardinghouse on the San Francisco waterfront. They would press a gang of homemakers and lead them to a courthouse to take out first papers. Then they went to a land office and each filed claim to 160 acres of redwood: a quarter-section

---

*From Bernard De Voto's "The Easy Chair," *Harper's Magazine* (May 1953), pp. 57–58. Reprinted by permission.

whose number the lumber company had supplied. At a lawyer's office, they transferred to the lumber company the homesteads they had earned by skill and hard work, received $50 for services rendered, and could go back to the boardinghouse. "Fifty dollars was the usual fee," a historian says, "although the amount soon fell to $10 or $5 and eventually to the price of a glass of beer."

Under this act, four million acres of publicly owned timber passed into corporate ownership at a small fraction of its value, and 95 percent of it by fraud. Under other acts supposed to "give every man a chance to earn land for himself," enormously greater acreages came to the same end with the sturdy homemaker's help.

The laws stipulated that the homemaker must be in good faith. Erecting a "habitable dwelling" on his claim would prove that he was. Or if it was irrigable land, he had to "bring water" to it, for a homemaker would need water. Under a couple of dozen aliases apiece, employees of land companies or cattle companies would file claim to as many quarter-sections or half-sections of the public domain and after six months would commute them, get title to them at $1.25 per acre.

The sworn testimony of witnesses would prove that they had brought water to the claim; there was no reason for the witnesses to add they had brought it in a can. Or the witnesses swore that they had "seen water" on the homestead, and so they had, having helped to throw it there cupful by cupful. Or to erect a "12 by 14" cabin on a claim would prove good faith. Homemaker and witnesses neglected to mention that this "habitable dwelling" was 12 by 14 inches, not feet. Alternatively, a "shingled residence" established that the homemaker intended to live on his claim; or could be created by fastening a couple of shingles to each side of a tent below the ridgepole. Sometimes a scrupulous corporation would build a genuine log cabin 12 by 14 feet, mount it on wagon wheels, and have the boys drive it from claim to claim, getting the homemaker a lot of public domain in a few hours. In a celebrated instance in Utah the efficiency of this device was increased by always pushing the truck over the corner where four quarter-sections met.

In six months the homemakers, who meanwhile had been punching cows or clerking in town, commuted their two dozen parcels of the public domain. They transferred them to their employers and moved on to earn two dozen more quarter-sections apiece by their skill and hard work. Many millions of acres of publicly owned farmland and grazing land thus passed economically into the possession of corporate homemakers. If the corporation was a land company it might get half a million acres convenient to a railroad right-of-way or within a proposed irrigation district. Or a cattle company could thus acquire a hundred thousand acres that monopolized the water supply for miles and so graze a million acres of the public domain entirely free of charge.

Lumber companies could operate even more cheaply. Their employees need not pay $1.25 per acre or wait to commute their claims. They could pay a location fee, say $16 per 320 acres, and the company could forthwith clear-cut the timber and let the claims lapse. At 20 cents an acre virgin stands of white or ponderosa pine, Douglas fir, or Norway or Colorado spruce were almost as good as some of the damsites which, our propagandist hopes, will presently be offered to the power companies.

These are typical, routine, second-magnitude land frauds in the history of the public domain out West—to describe the bigger ones would require too much space. Enough that in the golden age of landgrabs, the total area of the public domain proved up and lived on by actual homesteaders amounted to only a trivial fraction of the area fraudulently acquired by land companies, cattle companies, and lumber companies. Among the compelling reasons why the present public-land reserves had to be set aside was the headlong monopolization of the public domain that was threatening the West with peonage.

Those reserves were also made to halt the waste of natural resources which the United States had dissipated more prodigally than any other nation. They had to be made so that a useful part of our national wealth could be preserved, developed, wisely managed, and intelligently used in future times. They had to be made so that the watersheds which control the destiny of the West could be safeguarded. But no one should forget for a moment that they were, besides, necessary to prevent Eastern and foreign corporations from taking over the whole West by fraud, bribery, and engineered bankruptcy.

Discussion Questions

1 What is the relevance of this article to communication?

2. Could this egregious bypassing have been prevented?

CASE 9-6

Garnishment Policy*

The loose credit policies of many retail stores have created a serious problem for many employers. These policies have permitted their employees to extend their credit far beyond their budgeting capabilities. Thus, they become delinquent with their payment contracts. Creditors, to effect repayment of their contracts, resort to legal means of collection. They file wage assignments or garnishments with the individual's employer and by so doing make the employer a collector of indebtedness.

---

*The author's name has been withheld by request. All names have been disguised.

In the Glennon Company, the policy regarding garnishments had been to withhold the required amount from the employee's weekly paycheck and send a separate check for this amount to the creditor. With delinquencies mounting, the Payroll Department became increasingly burdened by the policy.

Finally, Glennon's board of directors adopted a new policy that complied with the law yet promisied to ease the work load of the Payroll Department. Accordingly, the president sent a memo to the department:

> Effective immediately. Honor assignments of wages but do not remit. Hold for full amount and make creditor prove claim.

Austin Horlick, a machine operator with an excellent work record, was a victim of the easy credit stores, and when he found it impossible to pay all of his obligations as contracted, he skipped payments and became a delinquent on the books of his creditors. It was just a question of time before one or more of them, failing to have their accounts brought to date by credit letters and phone calls, filed wage assignments with his employer.

The Quick Money Loan Company was one of these creditors. Tom Lederer, the Quick Money's manager, called Alan Curland, Glennon's paymaster, to inquire about the status of his assignment. The men were acquainted through many similar contacts.

Tom Al? Tom, at Quick Money. What is the status of my assignment against Austin Horlick?

Al Hello, Tom. Just a moment until I check his file. (*Pause*) You're first, Tom.

Tom Thanks, Al. Paydays are still Friday, aren't they?

Al Yes, Tom, but there has been a change in the company policy. I will not be able to send you a payment each week. The new policy is to hold for the entire balance.

Tom That will be OK, Al. I'll mark my records up for a month and check with you at that time as to the amount you have on hand.

Al OK, Tom, the plant is working a lot of overtime, so you will probably have about $30 a week held up.

Tom Thanks, Al. The balance of the account is $171.23. At that rate it will take about six or seven weeks to wipe out the debt. Maybe Horlick will make other arrangements and get a release before then. Thanks again, Al, I'll be talking to you. Good-bye.

Al Goodbye, Tom.

The following day, George Smith, a co-maker for Austin Horlick, called at the Quick Money Loan Company and made a payment of $100 in exchange for his release from the contract. This payment was made the day after Lederer had talked to Curland. Smith's payment reduced the debt so that the balance could possibly be liquidated by the wage assignment withholdings in three weeks. Lederer marked the record to call Curland again in two weeks to advise him of the correct payoff figure. When the time had elapsed, he called Curland.

Tom   Al, Tom Lederer.

Al   Hello, Tom. What's on your mind today?

Tom   The Austin Horlick case. I received payment on the account from the co-maker and I wanted to give you the payoff figure.

Al   Fine. How much do you need?

Tom $80.46 will take care of it.

Al   Hold on a minute while I get the file. (*Pause*) Say, Tom, I can't send you the money yet: we haven't withheld enough.

Tom   How much do you have?

Al $92.

Tom   That's more than is necessary. I only need $80.46.

Al   The assignment is for $171.23 plus the accruing interest, and that is what I will have to hold for.

Tom   Why? I just told you that I had received a payment from the co-maker and I will only need $80.46.

Al   I'm sorry, Tom, but the policy now is to hold for the entire balance.

Tom   But, Al, the amount has been changed and you will be holding more than will be required.

Al   Can't help it, Tom. I have my orders, and I have to comply.

Tom   There is something wrong with that kind of thinking. Hadn't you better call your home office for clarification?

Al   No. They told me what to do, and that is what I'm going to do.

Tom   I thought that the company was trying to avoid trouble? This stand is going to cause you to be deluged with lawsuits.

Al   I know it, but it is out of my hands, and from what they have said to me in the past, I'm not going to cross them again. I told them that we would be spending more time in court than before, but they don't seem to care. Guess they want to give the legal staff something to do.

Tom   OK, Al, I'll check with you later to see if you can't work something out. I hate to send this to our attorney as it will increase the debt that Horlick has with me. I don't see any reason for him to be penalized because of this foolish misunderstanding.

Discussion Questions

1. Why was the garnishment policy issued?

2. How do you evaluate the policy and the manner in which it was issued?

3. How does this case resemble or differ from "The Product Information Program" and "The Sturdy Corporate Homesteader"?

CASE 9-7

The Expensive Expense Accounts*

John Holland, controller of Lawton Pharmaceuticals, Inc., contacted Harry Triemstra, partner of Froehling, Winthrop, and Triemstra, public accountants. Holland wanted an audit of one of Lawton's divisions, and hopefully, because of a current profit squeeze, at the lowest possible fee. Triemstra assured Holland that the job would be done competently and inexpensively as possible.

Triemstra assigned Nils Swenson, a capable and experienced senior, to the account, emphasizing Holland's concern about the fee.

"Let's make a good impression, Nils," Triemstra said, "Lawton could be a big account for us."

Jeff Watkins, a bright but inexperienced young junior, was also assigned to the job, under Swenson's supervision. Swenson and Watkins began their examination on Monday, and despite the fact that this was Watkins' first audit, the work went smoothly. Swenson was eager to complete the assignment quickly, not only to please the client but to be free to attend a technical seminar in Chicago the following week. Late Friday afternoon he reviewed the work and determined that the examination had been completed except for analyzing a few small expense accounts.

"Jeff, it looks to me as if we've just about wrapped this one up except for vouching the expense accounts. So why don't you do those, and I'll be back from the seminar a week from Monday to review the work papers. And, incidentally, Jeff—you've done a very good job, considering this has been your first audit."

Jeff was obviously pleased with the compliment, "Thanks, Nils, it was a pleasure working with you. I'll have those accounts ready when you get back."

The following Friday, Harry Triemstra received another call from John Holland.

Holland Say, Triemstra, I thought we were in agreement that the costs on this job would be minimal.

Triemstra Exactly. What's wrong?

Holland Then why has this greenhorn accountant of yours been spending a solid week vouching all our expense accounts? I can tell you there's no way we're going to pay for those 40 hours of vouching work!"

---

*All names have been disguised.

Triemstra He's been vouching expense accounts all week? Frankly, this baffles me. I'll check with our senior, Nils Swenson, and find out why he decided to extend their tests. I'll get back to you.

As soon as he finished his conversation with Holland, Triemstra buzzed his secretary: "Diane, get hold of Swenson immediately. He's in Chicago at that [expletive deleted] seminar!"

Discussion Questions

1. How did this miscommunication occur?

2. Who was responsible and to what extent?

3. What were the consequences of this miscommunication?

4. How could it have been prevented?

CASE 9–8

"But I Thought You Said . . . ."*

David P. Mayer†

The daily pressures of the supervisor's job sometimes prevent him from communicating with his subordinates as well as he should. And he may also neglect the important job of training his subordinates to give him the information he should have. In the ensuing dialogue between a boss and his secretary, the reader will find some glaring cases of noncommunication on both sides. Probably nobody is this bad, but it's just possible that the reader may get some clues to where he could improve the effectiveness of his own communication and that of his subordinates.

Boss Barbara, please type this cost report and let me have it by five o'clock.

Secretary Right, Mr. Lohr, five o'clock.

Boss And you better check my figures.

Secretary OK. Will you want any extra copies?

Boss Well, ah . . . oh, prepare the usual number.
(*Time passes—it is now five o'clock.*)

Secretary Here's the report, Mr. Lohr. I was afraid I wouldn't make it.

Boss Do my figures check out?

Secretary They add up.

Boss Good. I didn't know if the last column checked out with the Accounting Department.

---

*Reprinted with permission. *ETC.: A Review of General Semantics*, 33, no. 2 (June 1976), pp. 185–88.

†Former Chief of Personnel Program Management, U.S. Veterans Administration.

Secretary Oh! . . . I didn't check with them.

Boss I told you to.

Secretary I'm sorry. You said to check your figures, so I just verified your totals.

Boss I ran those totals on a tape myself.

Secretary There was no tape attached to your worksheets.

Boss Well, check those last line entries with Mr. Adams in Accounting.

Secretary Mr. Adams just left; it's after five.

Boss What? After five! I wanted this report to go out this evening.

Secretary You said you wanted it ready by five o'clock. You usually take this report home and review it.

Boss I know, but it's due out this evening.

Secretary It's not due till the 15th. We still have three days.

Boss No, no. The due date was changed.

Secretary It was?

Boss Yes, you knew that.

Secretary No, I didn't know it.

Boss Didn't you check your reports-control card?

Secretary I did, and it still shows the 15th due date.

Boss Your card is wrong. The date was changed.

Secretary This is the first I've heard of it.

Boss It was changed in a recent letter from the home office.

Secretary I don't see those instructional letters any more.

Boss You don't?

Secretary No. You told Betty to handle them so she could learn the office control system.

Boss But you're still handling the reports-control cards. Didn't you ask her to keep you informed of any changes?

Secretary No, I thought you did.

Boss You should have done it yourself.

Secretary I'm not her supervisior, and her boss is a little touchy about . . . !

Boss Now I wonder how many more control records are inaccurate.

Secretary I don't know.

Boss Well, that's another problem to look into tommorrow. . . . Will you check out those cards in the morning?

Secretary Yes, but will you let her supervisor know that I'm following your orders?

Boss Remind me in the morning.

Secretary OK—now, what about mailing this report?

Boss Call and see if Mr. Johansen is still here so we can get it signed.

Secretary What about those figures . . . ?

Boss We'll just have to take a calculated risk.

Secretary . . . and by the way, Mr. Johansen left at two o'clock.

Boss What?

Secretary His secretary told me he was going to leave at two o'clock and anything needing his signature should be sent up to him before then.

Boss Why didn't you tell me?

Secretary You were out, so I left a note on your desk.

Boss Your note said that Mr. Johansen wanted the outgoing mail before two.

Secretary Well . . . ?

Boss Well, what? We're supposed to get all outgoing mail to him by two o'clock every day. I thought this was just a reminder that we've been slipping on this a little. Now I'll have to stop off at his house and . . . .

Secretary He's not at home. He left to attend a meeting in Columbus.

Boss Why doesn't someone *tell* me these things?

Secretary He announced it at his staff meeting yesterday.

Boss I wasn't here yesterday.

Secretary It's in the minutes.

Boss I haven't seen any minutes.

Secretary There's a copy in your mail basket.

Boss I haven't had time to check my incoming mail.

Secretary You know, Mr. Lohr, I think you'd have more time if you let Mr. Covington do this report.

Boss He doesn't know how; he's too new.

Secretary We should train him—he's waiting for assignments.

Boss I don't have the time to train him.

Secretary You do too much yourself, Mr. Lohr.

Boss I have to if I want things done right. Well, Mr. Johansen's assistant lives next door to me—I'll get him to sign the report.

Secretary I'll call and tell him you're coming over.

Boss Good, and don't forget to send the Accounting Department a copy of the report in the morning.

Secretary Ah, I didn't make an extra copy.

Boss And why not?

Secretary You said the "usual number."

Boss What I meant by the "usual number" was enough copies to distribute to all concerned.

Secretary Well, I didn't know Accounting wanted a copy. We've never sent them one before.

Boss For some reason or other they asked for one this time.

Secretary You mean they sent us a request?

Boss Last week. I thought you knew. Well, have Rachel make a copy for them in the morning.

Secretary Rachel won't be in tommorrow.

Boss She didn't mention anything to me about taking off.

Secretary Sure she did.

Boss When?

Secretary The day before yesterday. She asked you right after your long-distance telephone conversation with . . .

Boss Oh, yes, now I remember. I was so preoccupied about that call, Rachel's request just didn't register.

Secretary You know, there doesn't seem to be too much communicating around here.

Boss People just don't listen . . . that's the trouble.

Secretary I agree.

Boss Agree with what?

Secretary That people just don't listen.

Boss You're right. Tommorrow we're going to start a campaign to improve communication in the office.

Secretary That's a wonderful idea.

Boss And now I'd better get this over to Mr. Johansen's assistant.

Secretary Don't forget you have a dental appointment at 10:30 tomorrow.

Boss I canceled it.

Secretary Oh, no! And I canceled your two office appointments for tomorrow morning.

Boss But that's why I canceled the dental appointment—to keep those interviews. They're important.

Secretary You didn't tell me.

Boss Well, tomorrow we start that campaign.

Secretary Right, good night—see you tomorrow.

Boss Oh, that reminds me, I won't be in until ten tomorrow—have to take my wife to the doctor.

Discussion Questions

1. The author concedes he has telescoped a litany of miscommunications. However, as an exercise in communication analysis dissect this case speech by speech. What patterns of miscommunication are occurring here?

2. How might these patterns of miscommunication be prevented in the future?

3. Do the author and/or Lohr exhibit sexism?

10

Allness

An employee You can't get anywhere around here. What's the use of coming up with any new ideas? They won't listen to you anyway!

His supervisor My people are automatons—no drive, no ambition, no initiative. They won't move unless I push them!

Motorist Never try to reason with a cop. They're obsessed with their authority!

Police officer I get fed up taking abuse from the typical idiot behind the wheel!

A father I can't let my son use my tools; he'd ruin them in two seconds!

His son I just *look* at those "precious" tools and Dad blows his cool!

Have you noticed the tone of finality and absoluteness in which people sometimes talk? When they speak in this way, it is almost as if they were declaring: "What I am saying is all there is to say about the subject—there is nothing more." It is hardly a rare characteristic. Stop in at your barbershop or beauty salon or unisex hair stylist and listen to the ease and dispatch with which the intricate problems of national and international affairs are neatly and conclusively solved. Listen to the talk of quarrelers, and you will find a similar note of arrogance, of unseemly assurance and know-it-allness—or *allness*, for short.

Underlying much of this dogmatic, unqualified, categorical, close-minded thinking and communication are two assumptions—both are fallacious, and both are usually held unconsciously by the communicator.

TWO FALSE ASSUMPTIONS

(1)It is possible to know and say everything about something. (2) What I am saying (or writing or thinking) includes all that is important about the subject. These assumptions are so patently ridiculous that it seems point-

less to refute them. And yet a considerable proportion of communication is apparently based upon them. Perhaps, as the late J. Samuel Bois said, we need to crack through the hard shell of the obvious.

We can go about it this way. Pick up a simple object, say, a piece of schoolroom chalk. Examine it; study it. What could you say about it? You might mention that it is white, small, lightweight, cylindrical, nonedible, inexpensive, a writing instrument, tasteless, hard, smooth, soluble in water, about four inches long, about a third of an inch in diameter, a piece of matter, and related to our national economy. You might add that it is a mineral, usually calcium carbonate, capable of squeaking on a blackboard, brittle, a manufactured product, a schoolroom necessity, used in children's games, a domestic product, powdery when crumbled, likely to soil dark clothing, usually shipped in sawdust or in a protective box, inorganic, and so on.

While you might be quite willing to stop talking about the subject, you would not contend that you had said everything about it. But just how long would it take to say everything about it? A half hour? An hour? Two hours? A day? When we consider the origin of the material, its countless evolutions, and its dynamic atomic structure, it is evident that to say or know *all* about even the simplest object is impossible. This story about Agassiz, the great naturalist and teacher of scientists, is pertinent:

> A scientist, he thought, was a man who sees things which other people miss. . . . One of his students has left an account of how he trained them:
>
> "I had assigned to me a small pine table with a rusty tin pan upon it. . . .Agassiz brought me a small fish, placing it before me with the rather stern requirement that I should study it, but should on no account talk to anyone concerning it, nor read anything relating to fishes, until I had his permission so to do. To my inquiry 'What shall I do?' he said in effect: "Find out what you can without damaging the specimen; when I think that you have done the work I will question you." In the course of an hour I thought I had compassed the fish; it was rather an unsavory object, giving forth the stench of old alcohol. . . . Many of the scales were loosened so that they fell off. It appeared to me to be a case of a summary report, which I was anxious to make and get on to the next stage of the business. But Agassiz, though always within call, concerned himself no further with me that day, nor the next, nor for a week.
>
> "At first, this neglect was distressing; but I saw that it was a game, for he was . . . covertly watching me. So I set my wits to work upon the thing, and in the course of a hundred hours or so I thought I had done much—a hundred times as much as seemed possible at the start. I got interested in finding out how the scales went in their series, their shape, the form and placement of the teeth, etc. Finally, I felt full of the subject and probably expressed it in my bearing; as for words about it then, there were none from my master except his cheery 'Good morning.' At length, on the seventh day, came the question 'Well?' and my disgorge of learning to him as he sat on the edge of my table puffing his cigar. At the end of the hour's telling he swung off and away, saying 'That is not right.'

"It was clear that he was playing a game with me to find if I were capable of doing hard, continuous work without the support of a teacher, and this stimulated me to labor. I went at the task anew, discarded my first notes, and in another week of ten hours a day labor I had results which astonished myself and satisfied him."

After this arduous assignment was over, Agassiz did not praise his pupil . . . but gave him a more difficult task of observation and comparison. This was all the praise the pupil could expect, for it meant: "You are becoming a more competent scientist."[1]

Obviously, we can never know or say all about anything. But we need to discuss how these fallacious assumptions arise and how we can cope with them.

THE PROCESS OF ABSTRACTING

The structure of our language contributes to the problem of allness. Just what do we do when we use language—when we talk, write, listen, read, think, and so forth? We abstract. Let me demonstrate this by first of all listing a few details about a certain person I know. Among many, many other things this person is a(n):

male	redhead
gardener	salesperson
husband	father
veteran	human being
citizen	car owner
tax exemption	taxpayer
golfer	10 lb.-overweight person
Scout leader	possessor of civil rights
moderate drinker	avid detective-story reader
registered voter	teller of droll jokes
churchgoer	lover of music, rose growing, and
baseball fan	swimming
Rotary member	student of current political cam-
hater of soap operas, bridge, and	paign issues
tardy people	newspaper reader
consumer	son

Now, what happens when I say something about this person? Suppose I say: "He is a good voter." What I am doing, in effect, is calling your attention and mine to some details about this person; perhaps to such details as a citizen, a registered voter, a student of political campaign issues and candidates, and so on. But, at the same time, I am neglecting and inducing you to neglect that he is redheaded, a husband, a father, a veteran, a car owner,

---

[1]From Gilbert Highet, *The Art of Teaching* (New York: Alfred A. Knopf, 1950), pp. 242–43. Reprinted by permission

a golfer, a churchgoer, and literally thousands of other details that we might have attended to.

This characteristic of language use—this process of focusing-on-some-details-while-neglecting-the-rest—is called *abstracting*. When we talk, write, listen, read, and so on, we are necessarily abstracting. However, this is often difficult to remember. And when we are unaware that we are attending to some details about a situation, a person, and so forth, while simultaneously overlooking a host of others, it becomes extremely easy to assume that what we know or what we say is all that we really need to know or say. John G. Saxe has depicted the obfuscating property of abstracting on a physical rather than a verbal level in his charming verse about the six blind scholars and the elephant.

> *It was six men of Indostan*
> *To learning much inclined,*
> *Who went to see the elephant*
> *Though all of them were blind*
> *That each by observation*
> *Might satisfy his mind.*
>
> *The first approached the elephant*
> *And, happening to fall*
> *Against the broad and sturdy side,*
> *At once began to bawl:*
> *"Why, bless me! But the elephant*
> *Is very much like a wall!"*
>
> *The second, feeling of the tusk,*
> *Cried: Ho! what have we here*
> *So very round and smooth and sharp?*
> *To me, 'tis very clear,*
> *This wonder of an elephant*
> *Is very like a spear!"*
>
> *The third approached the animal,*
> *And, happening to take*
> *The squirming trunk within his hands*
> *Thus boldly up he spake:*
> *"I see," quoth he, "The elephant*
> *Is very like a snake!"*
>
> *The fourth reached out his eager hand*
> *And felt about the knee:*
> *"What most this wondrous beast is like*
> *Is very plain," quoth he:*
> *"'Tis clear enough the elephant*
> *Is very like a tree!"*

> The fifth who chanced to touch the ear
>   Said: "E'en the blindest man
> Can tell what this resembles most—
>   Deny the fact who can:
> This marvel of an elephant
>   Is very like a fan!"
>
> The sixth no sooner had begun
>   About the beast to grope
> Than, seizing on the swinging tail
>   That fell within his scope,
> "I see," quoth he, "the elephant
>   Is very like a rope!"
>
> And so these men of Indostan
>   Disputed loud and long,
> Each in his own opinion
>   Exceeding stiff and strong;
> Though each was partly in the right,
>   And all were in the wrong.[2]

Of course, this kind of difficulty is not uncommon even among those of us with 20/20 vision!

ALLNESS DEFINED

Allness, then, is the attitude of those who are unaware that they are abstracting and thus assume that what they say or know is absolute, definitive, complete, certain, all-inclusive, positive, final—and all there is (or at least all there is that is important or relevant) to say or know about the subject. Allness, as one wag paraphrased the above definition, is what people have who think they know everything about everything—which is quite annoying to those of us who do!

THE CRAVING FOR CERTAINTY

> Just when the speaker convinces me
> Of what he has brilliantly planned,
> Just when I bow to his wisdom he says,
> "On the other hand—"[3]

This bit of doggerel reminds us of the comfortable feeling of knowing, of being sure. We may tolerate ambiguity and discontinuity to a certain extent, but conversely, in varying degrees, we crave certainty.

---

[2]By John G. Saxe and printed in Lowrey and Johnson, *Interpretative Reading* (New York: D. Appleton-Century, 1942), pp. 44–45.

[3]Arnold J. Zarett, "Ambidextrous," *The Wall Street Journal*, May 20, 1971, p. 12.

"The demand for certainty," wrote Bertrand Russell, "is one that is natural to man, but is nevertheless an intellectual vice."[4] On a doubtful day, propose an outing to your children and note how they insist that you declare whether the day will be fair or foul—and their disappointment when you cannot give a firm answer. The same sort of dogmatism, Russell contended, is demanded, in later life:

> So long as men are not trained to *withhold judgment in the absence of evidence*, they will be led astray by cocksure prophets, and it is likely that their leaders will either be ignorant fanatics or dishonest charlatans. To endure uncertainty is difficult, but so are most of the other virtues. For the learning of every virtue there is an appropriate discipline, and for the learning of *suspended judgment* the best discipline is philosophy.[5]

But he warned against philosophy teaching no more than skepticism, for while the dogmatist may be dangerous, the skeptic is ineffectual.

> Dogmatism and skepticism are both, in a sense, absolute philosophies; one is certain of knowing, the other of not knowing. What philosophy should dissipate is certainty, whether of knowledge or of ignorance.[6]

Bacon expressed it more succinctly: "Learning teaches how to carry things in suspense without prejudice till you resolve."

The craving for certainty leads easily to oversimplification. Senator Patrick Moynihan said: "One of our greatest weaknesses as Americans is the habit of reducing the most complex issues to the most simplistic moralisms." As one historian put it, "The essence of tyranny is the denial of complexity."

Recognizing the increasing interrelatedness of business with its environment, James McSwiney, former President of the Mead Corporation, cited the urgent need for "complexifiers."

> Yesterday—so to speak—the man who could cut through the web of detail and get at the heart of the matter was the hero. He often moved to the top of the organizational ladder. He never seemed to be in doubt!
>
> . . . But *today* we worry more about the person who is *too ready* to fire off an instant decision that solves one problem and creates *twenty* more.
>
> No one welcomes indecision in management. . . . The need is not to *agonize*, but to really *analyze*—and to take *intelligent action*. . . .
>
> The point is *intelligent action* today must include an understanding that a business decision can have political, social, cultural, technological, even religious, as well as economic ramifications. The complex problems of our society which once might have been considered peripheral to business are now *central* to making *intelligent* decisions.

---

[4]Bertrand Russell, *Unpopular Essays* (London: George Allen and Unwin, 1951), p. 26.
[5]Ibid., p. 27.
[6]Ibid.

For some the craving for certainty seems essentially motivated by internal insecurities. Others, in fairness, have omniscience thrust upon them by the roles they play in society. We dearly want the doctors diagnosing our illnesses, the attorneys handling our cases, and the police officers protecting our lives and property to be *right*.

Is it any wonder that when constantly pressured to fulfill the roles of authority, people can sometimes be seduced by it? Internally generated or externally imposed, the need for certainty and simplicity often leads to elaborate defense mechanisms which assure that certainty and simplicity. The allness attitude, buttressed by its two enticing but false assumptions is such a mechanism.

MODES OF ALLNESS

More specifically, what sorts of problems does allness contribute to? The following suggest a few of the various manifestations of the allness attitude.

Allness Will Tend to Occur:

1. *When we talk or write (or abstract in any manner)* unaware *that we are abstracting, and thus assume that we have covered it all.*

This attitude, which is exemplified by the paired statements at the beginning of this chapter, is epitomized by the expression "often in error—but never in doubt." This is not to suggest that close-minded people never change their minds but that with them it seems to be a process of moving from one state of certainty to another.

Now let us consider what may happen when such abstractors get together.

2. *When two or more people abstract different details from a given situation, are unaware that they are abstracting, and thus both assume that what they know is all.*

The six students of the elephant were a case in point, and the almost inevitable consequence of this state of affairs is the rigid drawing of lines and unintelligent, destructive conflict. "Behind every argument," said Justice Louis Brandeis, "is someone's ignorance."

Letters-to-the-Editors columns of newspapers and magazines provide abundant examples of this mode of allness. Each letter is, of course, an abstraction—it represents a selection of some details and the omission of others. But so frequently letter writers seem unaware that they have abstracted—that they have not covered it all. Consider this series of reactions[7] to a *Life* article:

[7]*Life*, June 20, 1969, p. 22A.

Sexy Movies

Sirs:

The name of the photographer who captured that phalanx of Chadron, Neb. "mothers" ("Sexy Movies? Chadron, Neb. Tries Gentle Persuasion," May 30) might well have been Grant Wood, for this is surely American Gothic 1969! I look at these frozen, rigid, closed faces and suddenly for the first time I understand what the youth rebellion is all about.

Sirs:

You have published your all-time champion picture! Those seven women of Chadron! Good old-fashioned Americans mad as hell! More people like these ladies and we would soon be back to normal.

Sirs:

How vile, disgusting, vulgar and completely filled with sin! I refer to the small minds of certain people, a few of whom seem to reside in Chadron, Neb. as well as New York, London, Hong Kong. When will they learn that sex, in all of its many forms, is wholesome and normal in every respect?

Sirs:

What our area expected and what it got from *Life* were two different things. Once again the city slickers east of the Hudson have succeeded in labeling the ranchers and rubes of Nebraska as Rip Van Winkles to whom the 20th century may yet become obvious.

It's nice to see our area get national publicity, and maybe the ladies' approach to the sex movie problem could be copied elsewhere. I just wish that one time someone, somewhere would let the eastern seaboard know that out here on the Great Plains we do hold full membership in the human race. Otherwise, some future Barry Goldwater may do more than just threaten to saw off the Thirteen Colonies.

I had begun to fear that these readers would never reconcile their differences when a fifth writer seemed to settle the whole matter.

Sirs:

Thank God for those saviors of morality and decency in Chadron, Nebr. It should be quite clear by now that there is a nationwide Communist-supported plot to encourage the moral decay of our youth through sex education in oohoolo and lowd motion pic tures featuring perversion and nudity. Besides, if the good Lord wanted us to be photographed running around without any clothes on, we would have been born that way.

How's that for unassailable logic!

When one assumes that only one viewpoint or abstraction is correct, it follows inexorably that all other perceptions become quite intolerable. Which recalls a cartoon of a few years ago showing a driver and a companion. In front of their car—*six inches* in front of their car—is another car. And the driver is saying disgustedly: "Look at how close that maniac is driving ahead of us!" As Jonathan Swift said 300 years ago: "It is impossible to reason a man out of something he has not been reasoned into."

It is difficult under the best of conditions to concede points of view that are different from our own. Davis has an interesting diagram[8] showing how a production expert's perception of a problem tends to differ from that of a sales expert. We see our own bailiwick as the central problem area and others as only related problems.

When conducting management seminars, I sometimes ask the executives present to "please raise your hand if you do *not* work in *the key func-*

FIGURE 10-1

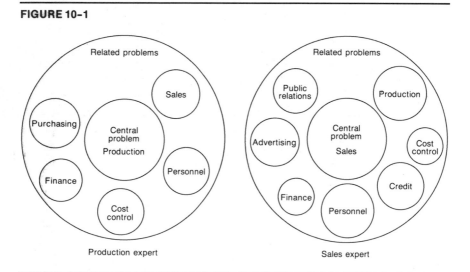

Production expert   Sales expert

---

[8]By permission from *Human Behavior at Work*, 6th ed., by Keith Davis. Copyright, 1981, McGraw-Hill Book Company.

tion of your organization." I have seen very few hands over the years.[9] During a recent winter, Washington, D.C. suffered a heavy snowfall, and an emergency announcement was made on TV and radio that night: "Only essential personnel need report for work tomorrow morning." The next day the agencies reported one of the highest attendance records in history!

3. *When we evaluate a group on the unconscious assumption that our experience with one or a few members holds for all.*

This is still another form of reacting to the abstraction as if to the totality. Consider this letter to a newspaper's advice column.

Dear Mrs. Landers:

You are wrong when you tell the girls that there is a man shortage. I am 29, have a successful law office and a car. For several years I have tried·every conceivable place, including church, to find a girl friend but have had no luck. Many girls marry when they are about 20. They marry men with whom they grew up. Most of the other girls are going steady. I can't even meet young women who are not married or going steady!

I am not quite average looking, so women have snubbed me for about 14 years. I now hate all American women and especially USO and Red Cross girls. USO girls snub any man who isn't handsome or doesn't meet their specifications. When Red Cross girls are not on duty they will have nothing to do with enlisted men and date only officers.

My hatred for women now is such that if I saw a woman dying I would not walk a step out of the way to help her. If I handle an eviction suit, a woman tenant gets no break from me. When it is a collection case, if a woman doesn't pay immediately, I have her wages garnisheed even though I know she will lose her job. Why shouldn't I? It looks as though I will have to go to Europe to get a wife.

HOMELY

Admittedly, Homely's letter does sound extreme—but then some people do talk, and think, this extremely on occasion. Supposedly here is a man who has had some unfortunate experiences with some members of the opposite gender. But these women can represent only an infinitesimal fraction of the group. However, Homely has apparently forged an all-embracing, unyielding generalization about females that may well constitute a self-fulfilling prophecy. Thus, his subsequent relationships with women are likely to continue to be unsatisfactory.

---

[9]My purpose here is not to discourage pride in or commitment to one's job or department. My concern is with destructive provincialism: preoccupation with one's own function to the exclusion of and possible detriment to others. A salesperson, for example, might hype sales with extravagant promises about the qualities and delivery of the product. The resultant customer complaints could wreak havoc in engineering, production, and service.

Sidney Harris write this article over 30 years ago. Unfortunately, it still seems valid:

> Some weeks ago, I presided as toastmaster at a large luncheon sponsored by the National Conference of Christians and Jews. A few hours later, I flew to New York to visit some friends living in Greenwich Village.
>
> As I taxied into New York from the airport, the relationship between these two events suddenly struck me. To the average mind, the phrase "Greenwich Village" conjures up a definite set of images, most of them bad, and most of them false.
>
> To the reader of sensational journals or to the casual tourist, Greenwich Village is a weird neighborhood in lower Manhattan, composed largely of ranting poets, crazy artists, ridiculous perverts and "Bohemians" of the lowest order of depravity.
>
> Actually, this is only a part of the truth and not the larger part. Anyone who has stayed in the Village for more than a few weeks learns that the painters, the poets and the perverts are only the most obvious tenants of the neighborhood.
>
> The great bulk of the population in the Village is made up of substantial citizens living in well-kept homes, with well-tended children, dogs, and back gardens. The houses along 10th St. are charming and almost austerely Early American. Washington Square is bursting with roller skates, softballs and all the springtime signs of bourgeois maternity.
>
> Now, what the ignorant majority thinks of "Greenwich Village" is exactly what it thinks of other races and creeds. It is always the obvious undesirables that, in the public mind, characterize a group or a neighborhood. It is the deplorable habit of human nature to identify any object with its worst attribute.
>
> If a man drinks, we describe him as a "drinker," never adding that he is kind, humorous, brave and truthful. The part we dislike becomes the whole—until we get to know the whole. And, until "brotherhood" among people becomes a reality, we will be as unfair toward other races and creeds as we are in our ignorant and partial judgment of Greenwich Village.[10]

The second to last paragraph smacks a bit of the all-inclusiveness that the author himself is condemning. However, the expression, "the part we dislike becomes the whole—until we get to know the whole," is poignant. If I don't like the part, am I likely to get to know the whole? Will I not tend to avoid it, to perpetuate my ignorance about it and thus my prejudice against it? Is it a case of knowing what we like—or of *liking what we know and disliking what we don't know?* After all, isn't prejudice, as the psychoanalyst Judd Marmor expressed it, "being down on something you're not up on"?

---

[10]"The Village Is Sadly Misjudged," *Chicago Daily News*, April 14, 1954. Reprinted by permission.

4. *When we become closed to the new or different.*

"I can't get *through* to him." "He simply won't listen." "His mind is made up, he refuses to be disturbed by facts." Familiar expressions? They are usually directed at a person who appears to have *alled* himself in. His tolerance for the new or different is nil. He seems to have lost—or suppressed—one—of the most distinctive characteristics of human beings—our viability—our apparently unlimited capacity to learn, to grow psychologically.

Watch babies, and observe how natural it is for them to learn. They are constantly reaching, probing, grasping, fingering, testing, looking, tasting, listening. Later their insatiable curiosity, when they become agile enough to exploit it, may drive their mothers up the walls. But it is graphic evidence of our deeply ingrained drive to know, to discover, to grow.

And yet often by the time we reach college, or well before, we have lost much of this viability. Why this transformation occurs is too complex a problem to explore in detail here. But let me suggest one way of thinking about the progressive psychological arthritis that seems to afflict many of us.

As we grow older, more and more of what we learn is actually *re*learning. To learn something new or especially something different may require that we relinquish something we already hold—that we discard certain accepted assumptions and cherished beliefs. This can be an unpleasant, uncomfortable experience. But some people find it a distinctly threatening state of affairs. And when we are threatened we often resort to some defense mechanism or other. Allness can be a particularly effective bastion at such times.

To the extent that I come to believe genuinely that I know all there is to know—or at least all I need to know—I really need not expose myself to novel, contrary, or disturbing experiences and ideas.

Unfortunately, I must pay a price for my insularity, comforting though it may be: I do not learn—I cease to grow. "It is impossible for anyone to begin to learn what he thinks he already knows." Epictetus' 1,900-year-old admonition is still valid. If we think we know—whether we do or not—we simply do not have the motive to expend the energy to do the growing—and it does take energy to grow psychologically.

And we must *will* to learn—for one cannot *be* taught. Gibran, the Lebanese poet-philosopher, understood that learning was largely an act of the student's volition when he described the province of the teacher:

> *If he is indeed wise he does not bid you*
> *enter the house of his wisdom,*
> *But rather leads you to the threshold*
> *of your own mind.*[11]

[11]Kahlil Gibran, *The Prophet* (New York: Alfred A. Knopf, 1963, originally copyrighted by Gibran, 1923), p. 55.

FIGURE 10-2

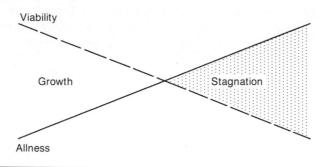

All of which suggests that there is an inverse relationship between allness and viability (Figure 10–2).

When your viability is high, your allness is correspondingly low. The
gap between them represents the potential for psychological growth.
Note, however, that as the allness increases, the viability decreases and
the growth potential diminishes until the allness exceeds the viability, and
now the potential for nongrowth, for psychological stagnation, increases.

This is not to imply that you will live out your life at a fixed balance between a certain level of viability and a corresponding level of allness. Indeed, if you plot an average day on the above chart, you might find considerable variation. The key questions: How much gray area does one generate?
And does it occur at critical times? The following might be a typical day in
the life of a hopefully atypical student:

FIGURE 10-3

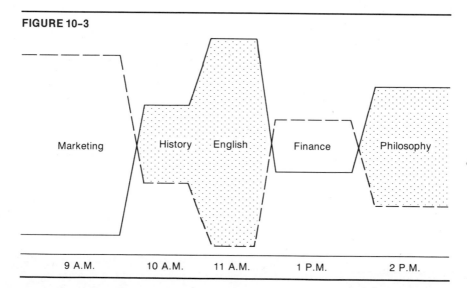

If he were to verbalize his fluctuating attitude, it might sound something like this:

> *"Marketing*—Now there's a field for you! I'm really fascinated by the ways they find out what the public wants to buy and what merchandising techniques are effective and so on. I'm going to be able to *use* this course.
>
> *"History*—Frankly, this bores me. What good is it to know what happened so long ago? Times have changed. Life is different now, so why dig up the dead?
>
> *"English*—I positively can't stand this! I've had this stuff drilled into me for 12 years. When will they let up? When I go into business, I'll have a secretary writing my letters.
>
> *"Finance*—This is all right, but it's plenty stiff. Some of it is practical, but a lot of it I'll never use.
>
> "Philosophy—Man, is this stuff up in the clouds! I just hope I can bull through the exams."

A college student with this much shaded area isn't getting his (or his father's) money's worth out of his education.[12] But there is a more subtle danger here. Aside from the possibility of flunking out, the student is cultivating a pernicious habit. Getting by and stagnating can become a way of life. His innermost feeling may be: "If I can just get through this horrible course—or curriculum—and get my diploma—then I'll be free—then I'll start to grow![13]

I wish him well, but I am not too optimistic about his prospects. Not infrequently, the young person who begins to vegetate habitually during college days—or earlier—continues to die psychologically more or less the rest of his life. "Anyone who is too old to learn," said Harry Hoskins, "has probably *always* been too old to learn." Our habit patterns can be insidious tyrants. God may forgive us our sins—but our nervous systems won't!

DELIBERATE DECEPTION

Abstracting, to recapitulate, involves simultaneously singling out some details while ignoring the remainder. When people are unaware that they are abstracting, they are in danger of unwitting, undesirable allness reactions such as those we have just examined.

However, the deliberate and judicious selection and suppression of detail can be a most cunning device for deception. The *Slovar Inostrannykh Slov* is the *Russian Dictionary of Foreign Words*. Here is its definition for:

> Boy Scout: A member of a bourgeois children's organization having a military-political character in capitalist countries.

---

[12]Employees with this much shaded area aren't giving their employers their money's worth.

[13]Lest these remarks be construed as pertaining only to college students, let us recognize that we are students all of our lives—or should be. An academic *commencement*, after all, is intended to designate a *beginning*, not an ending.

A gross slander? Perhaps. But why is it difficult to refute? Let us dissect it.

> "bourgeois"?—Admittedly most Scouts *are* middle-class kids—but that is because most of the population of "capitalistic countries" is middle-class. The definition gains additional leverage because *bourgeois* is an inflammatory word in Ivan's lexicon.
>
> "military"?—Granted, if being organized into "patrols" and "troops," and having rank, the close-order drill and saluting, and so forth, are "military."
>
> "political"?—Conceded, if pledging allegiance to their nation's flag and helping to get out the vote (without respect to party or candidate) on election day are "political."

Moreover, the "military-political character" suggests Hitler's youth movement of the 30s, the Jugendbund, or Mao's teenage Red Guard of 1966–67.

The shrewdness of this fallacy lies not in what is said but in what is not said. Where does the definition include the essence of scouting—the character building, the good deed a day, the fitness of body, mind, and spirit, and so forth? These aspects are artfully omitted, for apparently they do not fit the predetermined purpose of the definer.

This is skillful abstracting. If an out-and-out lie is told about us, we can combat it with the truth. But when a partial truth is insinuated as the whole. . . . How does one respond to "Is it true that you're not using coke now?" without leaving a residue of doubt?

SUMMING UP

Now for a review. The rationale of this chapter can be stated as follows:

1. We can never say or know everything about anything.

    > One of the most tantalizing truths we know is that there is so much we may never know. . . . We simply cannot overtake the coy horizons of the sea of unawareness that surround our modest island of perception. On this fact rests securely the conviction that humility is a vital part of wisdom.[14]

2. Thus, when we talk, listen, write, read, think, observe, and so on, we necessarily abstract—that is, select some details while omitting the remainder.

    > Talking, for example, is an enormously selective process. No culture has created a way of talking that does not emphasize some things at the expense of others.

3. However, the very process of abstracting can conceal its own nature—that it is a selection-omission act.

---

[14]Wendell Johnson, *Your Most Enchanted Listener* (Harper & Row, 1956), p. 73.

Consider the tone of the paired statements at the beginning of this chapter. Does it not suggest the extent to which the speakers were unaware that they were abstracting?

4.   Thus the speaker, listener, and so on, has no warning that he or the other person is leaving out details, and oftentimes the more one leaves out, the harder it is to recognize that one has left out anything.

Bertrand Russell said: "One's certainty varies inversely with one's knowledge." And four centuries earlier Michel de Montaigne in *Of Divine Ordinances* had written: "Nothing is so firmly believed as what we least know."

5.   To be unaware that one has abstracted, that one has left out details, that one has not covered everything, is the ideal condition for allness.

The greatest of all faults is to be conscious of none.

—Thomas Carlyle.

CORRECTIVES

What, then, can we do about our abstracting to correct allness—or better, prevent it from occurring? Stop abstracting—or at least reduce the amount of abstracting we do? The first alternative is impossible—aside from breathing, digesting, and carrying on other autonomic nervous system processes, virtually everything we do involves abstracting in some fashion or other. The second alternative is possible, but it could be undesirable. Students, for example, do very little except abstract. They listen to lectures, participate in discussions, take notes, write research papers, give oral reports, read books and articles, take exams, choose a major, plan a career, interview employers. These activities and hundreds of others inside and outside the classroom require the ability to abstract. In fact, much of students' training is calculated to develop and refine their abstracting skills.

And consider people working in organizations. The chances are that their principal value to their employer is the special kinds of abstracting they do. For example, what do accountants do? They take myriads of individual, unorganized data and glean from them meaningful abstractions, such as a profit and loss statement, which they and others can use to make important decisions. Imagine carting 30 bushels of raw data into a board of directors' meeting and announcing: "OK, folks, here's the information you wanted!"

Generally, the higher people rise in an organization, the more critical their abstracting skills become. Indeed, often an extremely important factor leading to one's rise is that he or she had or was developing the abstracting skills required by the more responsible position.

How could a business firm, a government, or any kind of organization function if there were not people who could conceptualize, theorize, ex trapolate, plan, organize, coordinate, categorize, catalog, codify, generalize, evaluate, analyze, synthesize, and carry on other abstracting processes?

No. The antidote for allness is not the *avoidance* but the *awareness* of abstracting.

Some suggestions:

1. *Develop and maintain a genuine humility[15]—a deep conviction that you can never say or know everything about anything.*

Such as the humility displayed by a witness in court while being sworn in:

> **Bailiff** Do you swear to tell the truth, the whole truth, and nothing but the truth, so help you God?
>
> **Witness** Look, if I knew the truth, the whole truth, and nothing but the truth—I would *be* God!

Disraeli said: "To be conscious that you are ignorant is a great first step toward knowledge." Lawrence A. Appley, of the American Management Association, holds a similar view with reference to management development:

> Before the executive can communicate effectively or, in fact, handle any of the other tasks of management, he must first know that he doesn't know. When a man develops the humility to admit that perhaps he doesn't know all the answers after all, then he is ready to begin to learn. It's at this point that management training becomes a wise investment.

And doubting (of this sort) does not come easily, wrote Anatole France. It is . . . "rare among men. A few choice spirits carry the germ of it in them, but these do not develop without training." Nor without effort, we might add.

2. *Recognize that you inescapably abstract (i.e., select and omit details) when you talk, listen, write, read, think, and observe—for when you* **consciously** *abstract:*

. . . you are inclined to evaluate the quality of your abstractions more judiciously—and, if necessary, to upgrade their quality.

Leo Rosten regards as shallow and shoddy the abstractions—not of young people in general—but of those who presume to speak for them:

> I have read a slew of articles by the young—about their (and our) problems. The writers are bright, articulate, unfailingly earnest. Their grievances, as distinguished from either their knowledge or their reasoning, are often legitimate and moving. . . .

---

[15]Humility not in the sense of meekness and self-abasement but in the older usage of the word—*openness to truth.* As such, humility is an antonym for arrogance, close-mindedness.

There *is* plenty wrong in this muddled, unjust, horrid world. But our problems are outrageously oversimplified by the glib (old *or* young), and by airy assumptions that money can solve everything, can solve it painlessly, can solve it swiftly. . . .

What idealists ignore are the objective *consequences* of their reforms. (Southern farm labor thronged North, into already explosive metropolitan slums, when relief payments were raised there; minimum-wage laws *created* unemployment among those unskilled, dropouts, minorities they tried to help.)[16]

The oversimplifiers notwithstanding, it has taken humanity thousands of years to acknowledge that no one has all the answers—that the best we can expect from many of our social problems with their subterranean complexities is to reach a shaky compromise which nobody really likes but with which the various interest groups can live.

This is a worn but serviceable kernel of knowledge that one generation should be able to pass along to the next. But so frequently the new generation (my own included, when it was new) seems to become infatuated with its own oversimplifications. And by the time its idealism and its realism finally become congruent, it has dissipated much of the irreplaceable zeal and energy of youth.

. . .you tend to be more empathic—to sense that the other person may not be abstracting as you are.

"Tell me," said the blind man, "what is white like?"
"It's like newly fallen snow," replied his sighted friend.
"Lightweight and damp?"
"No, it is more like paper."
"It rustles then?"
"No, no . . . well . . . it is like an albino rabbit."
"I understand—soft and furry."

. . .you are more prone to be exploratory and innovative; you are less tyrannized by habit, precedent, and tradition.

Chapter 16, "Blindering," develops this aspect of conscious abstracting.

3. *Make a habit of adding or at least silently acknowledging the etcetera when you abstract.*

Adding the etcetera is an extensional device urged by general semanticists[17] to help keep ourselves aware that we never cover it all. "The word 'and,' " said William James, "trails along after every sentence. Something always escapes."

---

[16]If you wish to evaluate the quality of Rosten's abstractions, see Leo Rosten, "Who Speaks for the Young?" *Look*, May 15, 1970, pp. 16 and 18.

[17]So highly regarded is "etcetera" that it is the title of the professional journal published by the International Society for General Semantics.

Alfred Korzybski went a step farther. He arbitrarily defined the period (punctuation mark) as etcetera. He said in effect, "When you see a period in my writing or hear one in my talking, please translate it as etcetera. It will remind both of us that I have not covered everything." Editor Leo Lerner expressed it thusly:

> The important thing about etcetera is that we should think it even when we don't say it. When we make a statement and think of the "and so forth" at the end of it, we show we realize that we have not said all that is possible to say about the subject, that we have uttered an approximation, a fragment, a partiality. The use of etcetera is an exhibition of the consciousness of ignorance, a humility, a sincere modesty.

The point is not to make a fetish of conspicuously "etcetering" every statement. This may suggest (sometimes correctly) that one is bankrupt for ideas or further examples.

"Buy my used car. First of all, its depreciation will be nil. Second, personal property taxes on it will be very low if not nonexistent. Third, if you buy this used car instead of a new car you won't agonize about getting that first dent. *Etcetera, etcetera, etcetera.*" The three etceteras translated: "I really can't think of a single additional claim for the rusty old hulk, but admitting this to you isn't likely to close the deal."

"Etcetering" can also be used as a ploy to conceal the audacity of the speaker's views. The king of *The King and I* was wont to make the most imperious assertions and then to attempt to disclaim any arrogance by vehemently ending the statement with "etcetera, etcetera, etcetera!"

4. *Frequently ask yourself: Do I have an "all-wall"?*

Do I find myself fending off the new or different? After all, I do have the power to protect myself in large measure from such "disturbing changes."

> *Who is so deafe or so blinde as hee*
> *That willfully will neither heare nor see.*
> *—John Heywood (1546)*

CHALLENGING A MYTH

The crux, once again, is the *awareness* of abstracting, not the *avoidance* of it. While extolling the virtues of viability, open-mindedness, and flexibility, in no way do I advocate a posture of indecision, diffidence, or vacillation.

Yet there exists a subtle but pervasive myth in our society—that the ability to decide and take action is fundamentally incompatible with the ability to learn, grow, and change. It is as if decisiveness and viability were polar opposites on a single continuum:

DECISIVENESS ←————————————→ VIABILITY

Thus, according to this myth, one could become decisive only at the expense of an open mind. Conversely, one could become open and viable only at the cost of the capacity to act. This is the oversimplification which H. L. Mencken helps to perpetuate:

> *It is the dull man*
> *who is always sure.*
> *It is the sure man*
> *who is always dull.*

The epigram is cute, pithy, and quotable. But it is a fiction.

Why the myth came to be I shall leave to the historians and the anthropologists. Perhaps it has something to do with the action orientation of Western thought—as distinguished from the passive and contemplative Eastern mentality. Is it mere coincidence that so many of our folk heroes have been "men of action," "quick on the draw," "faster than a speeding bullet"?

Be that as it may, the single continuum is simplistic. I submit that decisiveness and viability are independent variables, that a more valid diagram would consist of two continua.

At A we see the vegetable, at B the ineffectual intellectual, at C the impulsive menace. The myth suggests that D is impossible—and that is why it is a myth. The D type orientation is not only possible but mandatory for leaders in our complex organizations.

An old Arabic apothegm is roughly analogous to the chart above.

> He who knows not and knows that he knows not,
>   he is simple—teach him.
> He who knows but knows not that he knows,
>   he is asleep—wake him.
> He who knows not but knows not that he knows not,
>   he is a fool—shun him.
> He who knows and knows that he knows,
>   he is wise—follow him.

Action and Viability

The objective, then, is to be able and willing to resolve problems and take action while remaining open to experience. The goal is an attainable but difficult one. "It is hard to be strong and not rash," goes a Japanese proverb.

A leader, wrote Eisenhower, must constantly make distinctions. "One of his problems is to keep his mind open, to avoid confusing necessary firmness with stubborn preconception or unreasoning prejudice."[18] G. K. Chesterton expressed the thought more trenchantly: "I am firmly convinced that the purpose of opening the mind as in the opening of the mouth is to close it on something solid."

George Counts confronted the paradox deftly.

> There is the fallacy that the great object of education is to produce . . . the individual who adopts an agnostic attitude towards every important social issue, who can balance the pros against the cons with the skill of a juggler, who sees all sides of every question and never commits himself to any, who delays action until all the facts are in, who knows that all the facts will never come in, who consequently holds his judgment in a state of indefinite suspension, and who before the approach of middle age sees his powers of action atrophy and his social sympathies decay. With Peer Gynt he can exclaim:
> > Ay, think of it—wish it done—will it to boot,—
> > But do it—No, that's past my understanding.
> This type of mind also talks about waiting until the solutions of social problems are found, when as a matter of fact there are no solutions in any definite and final sense. For any complex social problem worthy of the name there are probably tens and even scores, if not hundreds, of "solutions," depending upon the premises from which one works. The meeting of a social situation

---

[18]Dwight D. Eisenhower, *Crusade in Europe* (New York: Doubleday, 1948), p. 256.

involves the making of decisions and the working out of adjustments. If we wait for a solution to appear like the bursting of the sun through the clouds or the resolving of the elements in an algebraic equation, we shall wait in vain. . . . society requires great numbers of persons who, while capable of gathering and digesting facts, are at the same time able to think in terms of life, make decisions, and act. From such persons will come our real social leaders.[19]

Profile of Viable Men[20]

Viable—capable of living or developing, as viable seeds, physically and psychologically fit to live and grow.

I know some viable men.

They keep pushing beyond the horizons of what they already know.

They refuse to be stuck in yesterday. They won't even remain rooted in today.

They are teachable.

They keep learning. They continue to see and listen. All their horizons are temporary.

They don't deny today's wisdom—rather, they add dimensions to it.

They have strong beliefs, faith, aspirations, but they know the difference between belief and bigotry—between knowledge and dogmatism.

They are acutely aware of the limits of what they know.

They are more likely to wonder and inquire than to dismiss and deny.

They know a great deal, but they also know that they do not know it all.

I also know some stunted, deadened men.

Their outlooks have been blighted—their interest diminished—their enthusiasm restricted—their sensitivity limited.

They are the old fogies, though they may be young in years.

They strive only to stay where they are.

They see only the dimensions of what has already been explored.

They search with their eyes only for what is old and familiar. They have frozen their views in molds.

They have narrowed the wave lengths.

They are imprisoned in the little community—the little dusty dungeons of their own minds.

They are the conflict carriers.

*****

> Not ignorance
> But ignorance of ignorance
> Is the death of knowledge.
> —*Alfred North Whitehead*

---

[19]George S. Counts, *Dare the School Build a New Social Order?* (New York: John Day Pamphlets, 1942), no. 11, pp. 20–22.

[20]This was written by Dr. Irving J. Lee, a truly viable man, shortly before his death in 1955. From Irving J. and Laura L. Lee, *Handling Barriers in Communication* (New York: Harper & Row, 1950), pp. 148–49. Reprinted by permission.

DISCUSSION QUESTIONS

1. "The essence of tyranny is the denial of complexity." What is meant by this?

2. "Dogmatism and skepticism are both, in a sense, absolute philosophies; one is certain of knowing, the other of not knowing. What philosophy should dissipate is *certainty*, whether of knowledge or of ignorance."—Bertrand Russell. Do you agree, disagree? Why?

3. "Prejudice is being down on something you're not up on."—Judd Marmor. Agree? Disagree? Why?

4. Why is it sometimes so difficult to accept or even tolerate viewpoints or abstractions that differ from our own?

5. How could you best teach nonallness to others? How might a supervisor help reduce the allness of a subordinate? Vice versa?

6. Precisely what is allness? Is it the same as abstraction? Explain.

7. What is the relationship, if any, between allness and viability? Between allness and decisiveness?

8. Are there any occupations in which allness is particularly difficult to avoid? Why?

9. Some people seem to equate nonallness and weakness. Discuss.

10. Some apparently single-minded leaders, such as Napoleon, Hitler, Stalin, and Mao, have been outstandingly effective for varying lengths of time. Discuss them in relation to the allness concept.

11. Describe an incident, possibly involving yourself, in which allness behavior occurred. Analyze specifically why it occurred, what might have been done to prevent its occurrence, and what measures would prevent its recurrence.

CASES

CASE 10-1

The Kiss and the Slap*

In a railroad compartment, an American grandmother with her young and attractive granddaughter, a Romanian officer, and a Nazi officer were the only occupants. The train was passing through a dark tunnel, and all that was heard was a loud kiss and a vigorous slap. After the train emerged from the tunnel, nobody spoke, but the grandmother was saying to herself, "What a fine girl I have raised. She will take care of herself. I am proud of her." The granddaughter was saying to herself, "Well, grandmother is old enough not to mind a little kiss. Besides, the fellows are nice. I am surprised what a hard wallop grandmother has." The Nazi officer was meditating, "How clever those Romanians are! They steal a kiss and have the other fellow slapped." The Romanian officer was chuckling to himself, "How smart I am! I kissed my own hand and slapped the Nazi."

Discussion Questions
1. What does this story have to do with allness?
2. Why did the grandmother, granddaughter, and the Nazi officer perceive the situation so differently?
3. Could this case be analyzed in terms of other patterns of miscommunication?

CASE 10-2

Aldermanic Election†

Allenshire, population 50,000, a suburb of a large city in New England, is largely Republican and predominantly Protestant. Many of its citizens are well-to-do executives and professional people. The per capita income of the suburb is well above the national average.

In an aldermanic election Martin J. Stewart, the incumbent alderman of the 3d Ward, was opposed by Ronald Green. Stewart's supporters distributed the following leaflet:

---

*Alfred Korzybski, "The Role of Language in the Perceptual Processes," *Perception: An Approach to Personality*, eds. Robert R. Blake and Glenn V. Ramsey. Copyright, 1951, The Ronald Press Co. Reprinted by permission.

†All names have been disguised.

Alderman Martin J. Stewart	*Ronald Green*

Residence

212 Grey. Homeowner. Allenshire resident 24 years.	609 Wilson. Homeowner. Allenshire resident 8 years.

Family Status

Married. 2 children, 4 grandchildren.	Married. 2 children.

Occupation

Businessman. President, National Office Supplies Co.	Lawyer. Partner, law firm of Green, Weisman, and Epstein. Former EPA lawyer.

Political Activities

Assistant secretary, Allenshire Republican Club.	Vice president, Allenshire Democratic Club. Active in last November's campaign for Levine, Democratic nominee for sheriff.

Local Government Experience

Alderman the past two years. 12 years on Park District Board without salary. Now president.	None

Civic Activities

Deacon, First Methodist Church. Charter member, Northwest Allenshire Community Club. Air raid warden during the war. Civilian Defense Chairman for Allenshire during the war.	Member, Temple Beth Israel. "Active participant in community and charitable activities."

Endorsements

Allenshire Young Republican Club. Allenshire Women's Republican Club. 3d Ward Young Republican Club. 3d Ward Women's Republican Club. Service as alderman rated very highly in poll of fellow aldermen and city department heads. 3d Ward Residents for Stewart.	Allenshire Democratic Club. 3d Ward Independent Citizens for Green. Committee of 100 Nonpartisan 3d Ward Neighbors.

3d Ward Young Republican Club.

Ronald Green's supporters distributed the following leaflet:

Biographical Sketch

of

RONALD GREEN

Candidate for
ALDERMAN—3D WARD
Allenshire   Election: April 7

Born: [Nearby city], 1944

Married: One son, seven years old; one daughter, six months old.

Residence: 609 Wilson Avenue, Allenshire (own home). Allenshire resident 8 years.

Education: [Local university], 1966, School of Law, 1968 (Scholarship student—top man in class).

Community and charitable activities:
Participated in community activities such as factory zoning problem in south end of ward, Northwest Allenshire transportation problem, and represented community (without fee) in litigation concerning the Jackson School corner—gasoline station zoning problem. Member of several Allenshire civic, social, and religious organizations; lecturer on municipal, governmental, and legal problems; member, participant, and attorney for charitable organizations.

Experienced educator:
Member of faculty [local university, School of Law] since 1977. Presently serving as a member of that faculty.

Governmental experience:
Formerly Assistant Regional Attorney, U.S. Government Agencies (four New England states).

Professional experience:
Practicing attorney since 1968. Admitted to practice before state and federal courts, U.S. Court of Appeals, and U.S. Supreme Court.

Professional associations:
Member, Allenshire Bar Association; State Bar Association; Federal bar Association; [list of national and honorary legal fraternities].

Discussion Questions

1. What is the 3d Ward Young Republican Club trying to accomplish—and how?

2. What are Green's supporters trying to accomplish—and how?

3. What does this have to do with allness?

4. Are there other patterns of miscommunication involved here?

CASE 10–3

Interview with Miss Winkler*

Schuyler Dean Hoslett

This conversation takes place in the office of Mr. Zurch, director of personnel for an organization employing about 3,500 persons. Miss Winkler has been reported by her supervisors as doing unsatisfactory work; they ask that she be transferred on the basis of a list of charges outlined in a memorandum. Mr. Zurch has sent for Miss Winkler, who enters his office while he is talking to an assistant about another matter. Also present in the office at the time of the interview, but presumably not able to hear the conversation and doing other work, were Mr. Zurch's secretary, his assistant, and the recorder of the interview. Inasmuch as Miss Winkler spoke in a low tone, all of her comments were not audible to the recorder, especially as she became more emotional and finally tearful, but the conversation was substantially as follows:

W Did you send for me, Mr. Zurch?

Z Yes, I did; I'll be with you in just a minute. *(Mr. Zurch continues to talk to his assistant for seven minutes. During this time there is considerable confusion in the office, with the telephone ringing often, and with Mr. Zurch becoming more and more concerned over some matter about which he talks loudly, interspersing his rather definite comments with considerable swearing. This, it may be noted, is his usual manner under stress. Mr. Zurch continues:)* Now, look, Miss Winkler *(takes several minutes to look over her file and to talk to his assistant about another matter)*, you remember we talked together in March and at that time B Division was not satisfied, and since you have been with Mr. Newton, and he was not altogether satisfied.

---

*Reprinted from "Listening to the Troubled or Dissatisfied Employee," *Personnel*, July 1945, pp. 54–56, by permission of the American Management Association.

W   He didn't tell me anything like that. *(Speaks in a low, courteous voice.)* He told me after I left that he wanted me back. . . .

Z   Now you have been in C Division and there is a report on your work there. Now Miss Winkler, we take each employee and try to fit her in where she can do the best job. We realize that people sometimes can't get along because of the supervisor, or fellow employees, and we try to make adjustments. *(This comment is given in Mr. Zurch's usual direct and belligerent manner.)* Now you have been in a number of positions. How many have you occupied?

W   *(After thinking a moment)* Four or five.

Z   Do you agree with the comments made in this report? *(Quotes from report before him on the desk.)* "Shows little interest in work and says she doesn't care for filing."

W   *(Miss Winkler's voice is growing husky now, and her response is almost inaudible, but she explains that she doesn't like filing and that she wasn't hired to do that kind of work. She was to be a stenographer.)*

Z   We don't have the work always to everyone's satisfaction.

W   But I wasn't told that was what the job would be.

Z   But we can't give everyone a job he wants. . . . *(Interview has turned into something of an argument at this point; Mr. Zurch presents next charge.)* "Deliberately slows down on the job."

W   No, I do not. *(Miss Winkler seems quite incensed at this charge.)*

Z   "Uses business hours to write letters."

W   I did that once.

Z   "Doesn't keep up to date with her work."

W   They put in a new system up there, and the supervisor asked me to help with it, and I said I would. But I couldn't keep up to date on my own work and do that too. The supervisor asked me to do this at the same time that I had more than enough work of my own to do. *(Though deeply disturbed at these charges, Miss Winkler's responses are direct; by this time, however, she is on the verge of tears.)*

Z   "Leaves 15 minutes before 12 and returns 20 to 25 minutes late."

W   If I went before 12, I returned earlier.

Z   "Uses rest room facilities on second floor instead of third as required by the rules."

W   They were dirty on the third floor.

Z   We can't be in those rooms every minute of the day. When I went in there *(apparently at an earlier complaint)*, it wasn't dirty—only a few papers thrown around. It wasn't like any bathroom at home, but it wasn't dirty.

W   I have seen it at times when you couldn't use it.

Z Why didn't you report it?

W I did—But that's a petty thing (*i.e., the complaint*).

Z Yes, but it means five to ten minutes more away from your desk. Listen, Miss Winkler, I think the supervisor doesn't have an ax to grind; maybe all of these things aren't true, but a certain amount is.

W I did the work I was told to do, but some had to be left over. They expected me to get the mail out, and certain work had to be left.

Z That's right, but there are those times when you were away from your work. (*Mr. Zurch explains the limitations on the number of persons the organization may hire; that each girl must do her work, or the organization will get behind.*)

W I still think the charges aren't fair.

Z Well, tell me, are there any differences between you and Jones (*her immediate supervisor*)?

W I'd rather not say.

Z Don't you get along?

W Oh, sometimes.

Z Please tell me the story. . . . (*When it is apparent that there will be no response*) Did you go over this with Miss Counce (*the counselor*)?

W (*Miss Winkler replies that she did, but by this time she is crying softly, and the exact words were not heard.*)

Z We have a reputation of being fair. We try to analyze every factor in a report of this kind. . . . You have been here two years, long enough to know the whole story. . . . Do you think you aren't in the right job?

W I want to leave the job.

Z (*In a milder tone*) Now that's not the right attitude. We won't get anywhere that way. Has Mr. Achen (*a higher supervisor*) ever talked to you?

W Not once.

Z Has the principal clerk of the department talked to you about it?

W Yes, once. (*Two sentences not heard.*)

Z Do you think your work too heavy?

W I can keep it cleaned up at times, but not all the time. There are days when with dictation, etc., I can't.

Z Well, why don't we have the job analyzed on a week's basis and see if there is too much for one person.

W A week wouldn't be right; once I was behind for three weeks.

Z Honestly, haven't you taken extra time off?

W No, absolutely not. I've noticed other girls going out when they weren't supposed to, though.

Z Are you getting along with other employees?

W Yes.

Co. has reached definition of a unsatisfactory employee
(1.) ①us. how bus. letter
② bathroom 3rd flr
③ leaves early come back / etc.

Z Well, I'll tell you, you go back upstairs after you get set *(i.e., after she has made repairs on her face because of the crying)* Do you have any other comment to make?

W I feel he *(supervisor)* has been very unfair about my slowing down on my work.

Z All right, OK, now you stay down until, let's see, it's 3:30 now, until 3:45. I'll call them to expect you at 3:45.

Mr. Zurch's comment after the interview: "This girl comes from a good family and environment and apparently feels that she has a better head than the other workers. Our problem is to get her adjusted. I disagree with this report that she purposely slowed down on the job. The fact that she didn't like filing is nothing against her; we have that trouble all the time. But there is no question that she takes time off. I think 50–60 percent of the charges are correct and the rest is put on for a good story. We'll find that the supervisor hasn't talked to her correctly. She would be a better employee under a girl who could handle her or a smart-looking man. You noted that she was especially indignant at charges of slowing down, but not so indignant on spending extra time out."

Mr. Zurch calls the immediate supervisor and the next higher supervisor into his office to discuss the situation.

Z What is it all about, this Winkler case?

Mr. Achen Her attitude is wrong. She wants to be a stenographer, and she was hired as a clerk-typist, and there isn't a 100 percent steno job up there. We give her some dictation, but can't give her full time. She doesn't want to do filing.

Jones She gets behind. *(Telephone call interrupts.)*

Mr. Achen She said to someone, "I'll let this filing pile up and just see what happens." I think for the good of the department she should be transferred. *(Another telephone call interrupts.)*

Z But we can't transfer her all the time.

Mr. Achen We spoke to her about the rest rooms, but she disregards the rules. We have given her a fair chance.

Z OK, thanks a lot. *(Apparently the decision is to transfer Miss Winkler to another department. Mr. Zurch goes off to a meeting.)*

Discussion Questions

1. Why did Zurch call in Miss Winkler?
2. What do you think of his approach?
3. Why did he level the charges one after the other without developing Miss Winkler's replies—possibly without listening to her?
4. What did Zurch learn from this interview?
5. What did you think of the manner in which the problem was resolved?

CASE 10–4

The Hayden Company*

The Hayden Company, headquartered in Dayton, Ohio, had numerous divisions in unrelated industries throughout the United States. These divisions for the most part were autonomous in their operations.

Guy Horton was attached to the personnel department in the headquarters office of the Hayden Company. He reported to the personnel director. He served in an advisory capacity and gave assistance in problems of office and laboratory personnel to the office managers in the various divisions of the firm.

These divisions did not have personnel officers as such, and all recruiting, selecting, and training were carried on through their respective office managers.

An acute problem had arisen in the Memphis division. Because of separations and expanded operations, several additional researchers would be needed within five to six weeks. The research these people would do would be in the field of farm chemistry and the application of farm products to industry.

Mr. Horton's search to find personnel to fill this need took him to several midwestern universities where he was permitted to look through alumni records and also to talk to graduating seniors who qualified. One of the schools he visited was the Rogers Institute of Technology, an institution with a high scholastic rating.

Horton sent the following report to his superior, relating his experiences at Rogers:

"I visited RIT yesterday morning and was permitted to interview several seniors and also to look at alumni records for candidates for the Memphis Laboratory. The students I talked to gave me a very unfavorable impression; their dress and speech could have been much better. After speaking to a number of them, I did not think it worthwhile to interview others. My next step was to seek out the alumni records, and believe me I did not get a great deal of cooperation on this. Some clerk showed me an enormous card file, and without further word he left. I leafed through this card file for a while but gave it up as a waste of time. I judged this school as being no more than a trade school, and it would be a waste of time to visit it in the future."

Discussion Questions
1. What do you make of the circumstances surrounding Guy Horton's visit to the Rogers Institute of Technology?

---

*All names are disguised.

2. Is allness involved in Horton's judgment of Rogers? Any other patterns of mis-communication?

3. What advice would you offer Mr. Horton?

CASE 10-5

Slovar Inostrannykh Slov

The following definitions appear in the *Russian Dictionary of Foreign Words (Slovar Inostrannykh Slov)*.

Detective literature: A kind of contemporary bourgeois adventure literature—romances, stories, tales devoted to description of "the exploits of detectives defending bourgeois property and the legal order."

Individualism: A bourgeois ideology that puts the egotistical interests of separate personalities in opposition to the interests of society.

Internationalism: International class unity and solidarity with the proletarians and the workers of all countries in the struggle for the overthrow of bourgeois dominance, the destruction of imperialism, and the building of communism in the entire world. . . . An example of real internationalism and a model of the cooperation of peoples in the U.S.S.R.

Lend-lease: A law passed in 1941 by the U.S.A. Congress for the mutual transfer or lease of equipment, raw materials, food and other goods to allied countries during the Second World War. Lend-lease deliveries brought colossal profits to the large American monopolists.

Lobby: In the U.S.A., the agents of the large bankers and monopolists having a strong influence in parliamentary circles, lobbying with Congressmen in the interests of monopoly capital as regards the making of laws.

Police: In capitalist countries, these are special administrative organs made up of armed detachments protecting the bourgeois society and its order; bourgeois states, being based on police and gendarmerie, exercise their reactionary power by anti-democratic methods of unbridled arbitrary rule directed against the people.

Wall Street: A street in New York on which are located the largest banks, financial markets, etc. Wall Street is a synonym for the plundering imperialistic interests of the American financial oligarchy.

Discussion Questions

1. How do you react to these definitions and why?
2. How would you define these terms?
3. How would your counterpart in Moscow react to your definitions? Why?
4. What does this calse have to do with allness?

CASE 10-6

Mickey Mouse in Gray Flannels

Gerry Friedman*

I am using disguised names, including my own, to prevent embarrassment to some of XYZ's employees. As the case opens, I was a sales engineer for XYZ, Inc.—specifically, the New York City district sales office.

Morale under our sales manager, Mr. Utley, was high. Apparently top management regarded him highly too, and promoted him to Product and Sales Service Manager and assigned him to the Chicago Divisional H.Q. His successor was not announced.

The following incidents concern the new NYC sales manager. They will be presented in two parts: (1) the description of the incident and (2) my interpretation of it. At the end of the case is an organization chart of the XYZ Corporation.

Christmas Party

Last December, the Eastern Division had a Christmas party. Utley's promotion had been announced, but he was not to depart until his successor had been selected and oriented.

In an unguarded moment, NYC salesman Gant remarked to the Regional Sales Manager, Heinze, "I hope you're not planning on promoting Kenton, because if you do, over half of the NYC salesmen will leave!" Heinze angrily replied, "Who the hell do you think you are to tell me who I can or can't promote!"

In early January, Heinze announced the promotion of Kenton to NYC District Sales Manager in spite of his Washington office performing under 75 percent of quota two years in a row.

---

*Gerry Friedman, 32, is a sales engineer in a midwestern city. He prepared this case for a course in organizational behavior that he took in conjunction with an evening MBA program. All names, including the author's, are disguised.

Interpretation. (Opinions stated in these interpretations are my inferences and are not presented as fact.)

Kenton was disliked by most of the NYC salesmen. Certain characteristics of his business activities were unpalatable to most of us. He appeared more interested in selling his bosses than in selling his customers and salesmen.

Gant's Christmas party prediction was not a guess. His opinion was firmly based on discussions we salesmen had among ourselves about potential new managers to take Utley's place.

Toll Receipts

Shortly after Kenton assumed his new responsibilities, he inaugurated the policy of including toll receipts with our expense reports. Tolls varied from 25 cents to 75 cents each. The date and time of day were stamped on most of these receipts.

Interpretation. This policy was not consistent with Kenton's advice that we make effective use of our time. The toll areas had automatic and manned toll booths. Only the manned booths gave receipts. It was common for us to wait from 15 seconds to over a minute for a manned booth, when we could have driven through an automatic booth in a few seconds. There are many toll areas in the NYC area (including New Jersey and Connecticut). At the end of a week it was common for me to accumulate 20 or more toll receipts. These receipts had to be stapled in chronological order. The total reimbursement on 20 toll receipts may be $5 to $8. I would think that the time required to handle these receipts was worth more than $10.

The only logical reason I see for his change of policy is that the dates and time of the day stamped on the receipts were a handy check so that Kenton could verify that his men were actually in the field. This makes me believe that he was equating his past field performance with our present performance.

Restaurant Receipts

It had always been the custom to obtain receipts for lunch and other entertainment when accompanied by a customer. If the receipts were included with the expense report, the salesmen would be reimbursed for the expense. (Each salesman's entertainment expenses were budgeted.) One of our secretaries informed some of us that she overheard Kenton calling restaurants to verify that the signatures on the receipts were actually those of restaurant employees and that the receipts were not forged.

Interpretation.   Our secretaries were also quite displeased with Kenton, consequently, they would relay information when they thought it would be useful to us. This information concerning Kenton checking our receipts backfired.

So far he had given us two main messages—he didn't trust us, and it would be more beneficial for us to impress him and other XYZ personnel than to impress customers. So we started writing neater reports; we became more exact and effective at writing letters of which Kenton received a copy; we would not turn in toll receipts if the stamped times were not in our best interests. Because he didn't trust us, we began to act in the image he created for us. It was not uncommon for two salesmen to meet for a long lunch and to turn in a receipt claiming that a customer had been along. It was never discovered, to my knowledge, whether he called customers to verify if they had been to lunch as claimed on receipts.

Utley and Kenton had been salesmen together in the NYC office several years ago. On a visit to New York, Utley pointed out that Kenton was considered a goof-off and apple-polisher at that time. Utley warned us that Kenton could not be trusted and that he would "poison his mother if it paid enough." Corporation management never seemed to interrogate employees regarding their opinion of their boss or fellow workers, so Kenton's unsavory characteristics were apparently unknown to influential corporation management.

Salesman-Stimulation Program

We had a sales meeting each Monday evening. They usually began about 5:00 P.M. and ended anywhere from 7:00 to 12:00 P.M., depending on the material to be covered. The corporation had a salesman-stimulation program which consisted of literature and cassette tapes sent to each salesman's house. We each received an average of one tape a month at home. Kenton played these tapes at the sales meetings.

Interpretation.   We resented being treated like children. We got the tapes at home and could hear them there. Kenton gave us the idea that he felt we didn't play them.

Cards and Beer

When Utley was manager, we would play cards and have a few beers at the office after the sales meetings. This practice stopped immediately after Kenton became manager. He would not allow card playing or drinking on company premises.

Interpretation.   Kenton had always been considered a good drinker and gambler in the past, so his reason was not that he disapproved of these activities. I feel he feared reaction from his superiors if they learned of the activities.

He was so preoccupied by his impression on his bosses that he could not envision his impression on his salesmen.

These Monday night card games were replaced with a bull session by the salesmen at a local pub. The conversation inevitably led to the poor working conditions under Kenton. Morale was very low. We exchanged new job leads.

Utley respected our right to enjoy a card game and a few beers in the office. This increased our morale. His attitude was "let's work hard, but take time out for play, too." I interpreted Kenton's attitude as, "Let's work hard, and don't take time out for play."

The Heinzes' Cocktail Party

Mrs. Heinze sent invitations to each salesman's wife to attend a cocktail party at the Heinzes' house. The salesmen were surprised and pleased. This would be an opportunity to become acquainted with Kenton and Heinze and their wives on a social basis. This party proved very disappointing to most of salesmen. When Kenton talked individually and privately with our wives, he was trying to find weaknesses in selling habits, such as amount of work done in the evening at home, arising time in the morning, and time spent at home during normal customer contact hours. His conversation was also designed to encourage each wife to be a company wife; that is, he apparently attempted to brainwash each wife to interact with her husband in the best interests of the company.

Interpretation.   I believe that Kenton read a book once that stressed the importance of the cooperation and commitment of wives to company goals, but he apparently didn't learn how to apply the rules.

Shortly after this party, we salesmen and our wives had another gathering and compared notes. It was apparent that Kenton's brainwashing attempt had backfired. It became obvious to many wives during their private discussion with Kenton that he was fishing for information that would point out weak work habits.

Meet the Veep

Several members of our top management were traveling to NYC for a trade show. Late Friday afternoon preceding the show, Kenton, who was out of town, phoned our office, leaving a message with one of the secretaries. Each salesman was to meet one or more of the executives at the airport, escort them to their hotels, and have dinner or refreshments with them if they so desired.

I was to meet our vice president of research and development on Sunday at 11:00 P.M. at the Kennedy Airport. This was the first and only information I had received on these plans. I explained to the secretary that I would be unable to comply.

At 2:00 P.M. on the Sunday afternoon preceding the show, we had a meeting at the Coliseum to learn the corporation plans for the coming week at the show. After the meeting was over, at 8:00 P.M., I explained personally to Kenton why I would be unable to meet the vice president.

He exclaimed that this was the first he had heard of it. Our secretary had not given him my message, nor had he asked her for any return messages. He expected his orders (even through our secretary) to be obeyed.

He had been in Washington, D.C. on business and said that I should have contacted him there. I explained that the cost for a phone call to Washington would be more than a cab ride from the airport, and that my judgment indicated that no action was necessary.

He criticized my poor business political discretion and said he would say more about this at a more convenient time for him. My reason for being unable to meet the VP that Sunday evening (even without alternate plans, I would have refused under the circumstances) was a meeting at our church in Hackensack, N.J. Even this was no justification to Kenton.

He coerced Wallace into meeting the VP. This, by the way, caused hard feelings toward me by Wallace, as he blamed me for his plight.

Interpretation.   Kenton apparently felt that we had no alternative but to follow his orders. His method of handling people typically had an adverse effect on those people. He felt that all of us were on duty 24 hours a day, and that we should drop all personal plans to work for him.

Kenton thought this was a good way for him to impress the home office. He expected top management to react something like this, "Wow, personalized taxi and guide service by one of Kenton's salesmen. Kenton must be a real good manager. He is very promotable. He will be the youngest vice president in XYZ history."

When I find that my boss expects me to devote five extra hours on a Sunday night so that he may gain a small favor in a VP's eyes, I'll refuse every time, regardless of any prearranged plans.

Kenton Writes His Own Fan Letter

Kenton prepared a typed letter and addressed it to Mr. Stein, our vice president of marketing, and gave it to salesman Stone and told him to sign it.

This letter to Stein complimented Kenton on a recent business transaction at one of Stone's accounts. Kenton's intent was to have Stein believe that Stone had written the letter himself. Stone did not agree with the contents of the letter; therefore, he did not sign it. Consequently, the letter was not sent as Kenton had intended.

Interpretation. When Stone told me this, I could hardly believe him until he showed me the letter. It was at this time that I felt Kenton must be psychologically unsound. We felt he was definitely going overboard in trying to sell himself.

Gant's Territory Offered

Kenton took me to dinner one evening. I was shocked when I learned the reason for this dinner. He explained that Gant was doing an ineffective job and that he would have to let him go. Kenton was assigning me to Gant's territory. This would be a promotion for me since Gant's territory included the most important customer in our district. Gant was unaware that he was going to be fired. Kenton was unaware that both Gant and I were actively seeking employment elsewhere. Among the salesmen in our office, Gant was my closest friend.

Interpretation. Gant had been with XYZ for over five years and had an excellent sales record working for Utley in the NYC office and previously in the Albany office.

During my sales training three years earlier, I spent one week in the Albany office and made several sales calls with Gant. My personal opinion then and now is that he is an above-average salesman.

Gant's remark at the Christmas party had doomed him to early dismissal from XYZ. True, Gant was not as effective working for Kenton as for Utley, but neither was I nor, I believe, were any of the other NYC salesmen.

Kenton had finally been able to work up a case against Gant so that he could be fired from a logical standpoint, but most of the rest of us could have been fired from the same logical standpoint if Kenton had wanted to build a case against us.

I felt very uncomfortable when I knew about Gant's dismissal before he did.

No More Playboys

At our dinner, Kenton said, "The NYC office has always been a bunch of playboys. I'm going to tighten the reins on these guys."

Interpretation. This comment was a duplicate of Heinze's attitude. It appeared that Kenton was able to alter his behavioral pattern to match that of his boss. But an alternate theory is that his behavioral pattern was developed prior to working for Heinze. The question here is, What came first—his behavioral pattern or his boss?

This playboy characterization is an overgeneralization. Heinze observed occasions when the NYC salesmen played hard. Apparently he was not aware of our work hard attitude during business hours.

Heinze did not completely approve of Utley as he was not molded in Heinze's image. It is my opinion that Heinze wanted Utley promoted out of his region.[1]

The Youngest VP

Kenton also said: "I'm going to be the youngest vice president in the history of XYZ."

Interpretation. Kenton was quite a thin man with a pretty face and wavy hair. He had about three years of college, but had not graduated. At 33, he had 12 years' experience with XYZ. Part of his success was due to the rapid growth of XYZ and part to political maneuvering. I can't see where contribution to XYZ profits had much to do with his success.

The above points suggest why he had so much drive to succeed. He wanted to impress his brother, possibly by passing him on the organizational ladder. Perhaps, during his childhood, he was not successful in sports or in winning friends, and was known as a sissy. This early consideration by others may explain his almost totally dictatorial attitude and almost complete disregard for others' feelings. He did not intend to let anything stand in his way.

Exodus

Within one year of Kenton's promotion, Fox and Stone quit and joined competitive companies. Gant and Smith were fired. (Smith was a new man hired to handle my territory in New Jersey.) Gant joined a competitor. I don't know what happened to Smith. Raymond and I both quit and moved to an unrelated industry.

Rath stayed because he felt he had a good chance to receive a promotion to district manager of a small office soon. Bolling looked for other work.

Fox became District Manager for a competitor. He offered Wallace a good job, and Wallace accepted. When Wallace resigned (he had 12 years' experience with XYZ and was considered an excellent salesman by top management), Stein, the F Division VP for marketing, finally intervened and persuaded Wallace to retract his resignation.

Gant's Christmas party prediction came true. Out of the eight original salesmen in the office, five had left, and the remaining three were unhappy with their jobs. In addition, the first man Kenton had hired was asked to leave within six months.

---

[1]Utley's promotion did not bring him up to Heinze's status on the organization chart.

EXHIBIT 1

Organization chart for the XYZ Corporation

The ages of several individuals are indicated.

Interpretation.   As each of us left, we hoped someone from the home office would investigate why we had left, but nothing was done until Wallace resigned. I don't know what was disclosed during his discussion with Stein, but my latest knowledge of the situation was that Kenton is still NYC Manager and Heinze is still Eastern Regional Manager.

Summing Up

I believe Kenton's contribution to XYZ profit, since he became NYC District Manager, was insufficient, even negative.

Three men were trained by XYZ in this field, and this training expense is now benefiting competition. Every man who was hired to replace us was given extensive and expensive training.

The most important account in the NYC area had four different men calling on it within one six-month period. This certainly resulted in some lost business (and lost image).

My three years at XYZ convinced me that it is not how one does his job, but how his superiors believe he is doing his job, that most benefits him in raises and promotions.

Discussion Questions

1. Why did Gerry write this case?
2. What is fact—and what is tint in this case?
3. What is the relevance of the self-image concept to this case?
4. Draw Johari Grids for some of the relationships in this case.
5. Suppose that Heinze acquires a copy of this case and confronts Kenton with it, how would Kenton respond?
6. What does this case have to do with allness?

11

Differentiation Failures:
1. Indiscrimination

The two accounts that follow may seem quite diverse, but they are alike in at least one important respect.

> Grand Falls, N.B., Jan. 9 (AP)—The foamy white waste products of a starch factory looked like snow to Frederick Boucher, seven, so he jumped into an eight-foot ditch filled with it. Two classmates on their way home from school with Frederick called for help, but by the time rescuers arrived the boy was dead.

> The interview was going smoothly for George Ramsey,[1] a young black man who was soon to be graduated from a well-regarded midwestern university. Judy Novak, the assistant personnel manager, was highly impressed with him on every count—academic record (upper tenth of his class), extracurricular activities, employment experience, references, and so on. Her telephone rang. It was Fred Carleton, founder and president of the firm. He had seem Ramsey apparently being interviewed for a job and insisted that Novak "ease him out of here as soon as possible." Why? In Carleton's words, Ramsey was "clearly a radical—those people with the Afros are all alike!" Judy felt that she had no alternative but to terminate the interview, explaining lamely that Ramsey's qualifications were not appropriate for the currently available positions that the company had.

In each of the above cases, a person failed to discriminate—to separate like things from one another. Whether it was piles of white material or blacks, someone overlooked important differences and saw only similarities. The president, for example, seems to have had difficulty in differentiating among young black men with Afros. To him they evidently appeared as indistinguishable as the proverbial peas in a pod.

We shall use the term *indiscrimination* to represent the behavior that occurs when one fails to recognize variations, nuances, differences; when one is unable or unwilling to distinguish, to differentiate, to separate ap-

---

[1] All names have been disguised.

parently like things from one another. *Indiscrimination* may be defined, then, as *neglecting differences* while *overemphasizing similarities*. It is one of three forms of differentiation failure that we shall examine in this book. Two others, polarization and the frozen evaluation, are discussed in the next two chapters.

HARDENING OF THE CATEGORIES

One of the most troublesome consequences of indiscrimination is an evaluational disease that we might appropriately label "hardening of the categories." Most of us have a penchant for categorizing—for classifying. Show someone something that person has never seen before—an unusual butterfly, a peculiar tree leaf, a strange rodent—and one of the first questions is likely to be: "What kind is it?" We meet a new person, and we are uneasy until we can find a pigeonhole. What *is* she?—how is she classified? Is she a salesperson, plumber, farmer, teacher, painter? Is she Protestant, Catholic, Jew, atheist? Democrat, Republican, independent? Lower, middle, upper class?

Categorizing, per se, is not undesirable. Under some circumstances, as we shall examine later, it is essential. But we are concerned here with categorization when the categories become hardened, unyielding, when they tend to deter further analysis and investigation that would be desirable. Joe White,[2] for example, as an office manager for a meat-packing firm, has developed a category for women workers over 50 years old. "They're insecure, inefficient, ineffectual, and temperamental," he will tell you. Thus, when Mary Grey, 52, a widow, applied for a clerical position, Joe did not even bother to interview her. He knew "her kind." Fortunately, another manager of the company did interview her and hired her on the spot. She has since proved to be a stable, energetic, and intelligent worker.

Stereotypes

The word *stereotype* is a useful one for our purposes. Originally a printing term, it stood for a plate that printed the same picture, drawing, and so forth, over and over again. Thus a sociological or psychological stereotype is a fixed, conventional image or picture. One who stereotypes applies the image of the group to all individuals assigned to that group. The stereotyper disregards, consciously or otherwise, any differences or distinctions that the individual may have that are different from those of the stereotyped group.

The journalist Tom Stacey depicted one group thus: "Politicians are like a bunch of bananas—they stick together, they're yellow, and there's not a

---

[2]The names are fictitious, but the incident actually occurred.

straight one among 'em." That's clever and cute and—unjust. Admittedly, politicians are easy targets for satirists and some of them richly deserve the darts. But in fairness, can we lump in with such politicians the high-minded, courageous men and women of integrity and ability who have literally given their lives in the political service of their nation?

Consider also the prevailing stereotype of poet in America. Such adjectives as thin, effeminate, meek, sensitive, delicate, and eccentric may come quickly to mind. The stereotype can exist only so long as the exceptions are suppressed. But the generalized image dissipates when one considers some of our late contemporary poets—for example, warm, wiry Carl Sandburg; barrel-chested former backwoodsman Lew Sarett; and rugged Robert Frost.

Of course, stereotypes can be expedient devices at times. Many television, pulp, and movie writers cherish them because they serve as shortcuts to characterizations. In the past, screenwriters merely depicted a lean, lanky, sad-faced black shuffling through a scene. They had tapped a familiar mold. The personality and behavior were completely predictable because the writers permitted no deviations from the established pattern.

This story is told of Metropolitan Opera Company prima donna Dorothy Kirsten's debut in motion pictures. Having always worn her hair down, Miss Kirsten was surprised when the studio requested her to change to an upswept coiffure. Reason: "They wanted me to look like a prima donna!" And the Hollywood actor John Wayne was given his first opportunity when the director Raoul Walsh decided that he measured up to the requirements: "To be a cowboy star you gotta be six feet three or over; you gotta have no hips and a face that looks right under a sombrero."

And so stereotypes can save time and effort. They obviate any additional analysis or investigation. There is no need to look for differences—a stereotype precludes them. Stereotyping permits us to set up neat, well-ordered, and oversimplified categories into which we can slip our evaluations of people, situations, and happenings.

THE BATTLE OF THE CATEGORIES

Few of us go very far in life without having to fight the battle of the categories. Try to change your line of work, to transfer from one subject major to another in college, to compete for a dramatic role in the school play when you have been classified as an athlete or a campus politician, and you invariably find people resisting your attempt to break through their categories.

A few years ago, a very capable actor committed suicide—why? Apparently out of despondency over being unable to find work. Film executives evidently felt that the public would not accept George Reeves as anyone other than Superman, a role he had played in television movies for years.

In a penetrating book about the Rockefellers, the great-grandchildren of John D. uniformly complain how they have been victimized by stereotyping. For example, Hope, daughter of John D., III, laments

> In growing up a Rockefeller, I lived with a tag, just like a Jew or a black. I'm not by any means suggesting I suffered in the same way, but it is true that when people heard the name Rockefeller, there was no way they could see the person named Hope.[3]

As one hardens categories, and accepts stereotypes, one is progressively less able to search out the differences. The characteristic response to a new person, situation, thing, or idea is to find the proper category, to slip the new object into a pigeonhole. Some persons are terribly uneasy until they can tack on a label. Does this person belong to a union? Is he a Jew? A Democrat? A Sigma Sigma? An ex-convict? These people can only relax when they find the "right" tag.

A key danger with hardened categories is that the categorizer is prone to evaluate with faulty analogies. Situation (or person) A is new, but seems similar to situation (or person) B. Anxious to complete the pigeonholing, the categorizer sweeps A into B's category with the dangerous assumption that the way to behave with respect to A is the way with respect to B.

> When his outfit was deactivated, Sergeant Vincent Bonura[4] was reassigned to another camp. He reported to his new company commander, Captain Carl Barnes, and the men exchanged salutes.
>
> "At ease, Sergeant, smoke if you like."
>
> "Thank you, sir."
>
> "Well, Sergeant, I want to get the best from every one of my men, so I'll want to check you on all your past experience so I can see best where I can use you. Let's see . . . Bonura. That's Italian, isn't it?"
>
> "No, sir, I'm Sicilian."
>
> "Ooooh, a Sicilian. . . . Well, Sergeant, I've had Sicilians in my outfits before, and I want to get one thing straight. I don't like any troublemakers in my company."
>
> "Sir, I'm not a troublemaker!"
>
> "Don't interrupt me, Bonura!"
>
> "Sorry, sir."
>
> "In Nam, I had this man . . . Mazzaro . . . Marzano . . . something like that, and from the time he came to me until I got rid of him he gave me nothing but trouble. Now I don't know why you got shipped out of your old outfit. . . ."
>
> "Sir!"
>
> "Sergeant! I don't know why you got shipped out, but if you're the hotheaded type, I'll make it plenty rough for you around here—and give you plenty of time for cooling off!"

---

[3]Peter Collier and David Horowitz, *The Rockefellers* (New York: New American Library, 1979), p. 526.

[4]The names have been disguised.

CONTRIBUTING FACTORS

Why do people behave in these irrational, rigid ways? They do so because they neglect differences and overemphasize similarities. Why do they do so? Two of the major contributing factors are (1) self-serving emotions and (2) the structure of our language.

Self-Serving Emotions

I know a bright young man who also happens to be a college instructor. He's still paying off debts he accumulated in graduate school and, in the interests of economy, he purchased a motorcycle for transportation. But he hadn't foreseen the reactions of others. Here's his account:

> I never understood much about the nature of prejudice until last year, when I bought a motorcycle. In short order, I learned what it was like to be a member of a minority group.
>
> For the first time in my life, I knew I was being judged not for myself, but for what I stood for in the minds of some. I was no longer a separate and distinct individual, but a type. Or rather, a stereotype called a motorcyclist.
>
> Even though only a small fraction of the people who ride motorcycles are hoodlums or even roughnecks, perceptions of the whole class are influenced by the conduct of the worst element. Statistically, that perception is a very crude caricature of the average motorcyclist. We are all regarded with the same suspicion and uneasiness, if not downright hostility, as if we were all charter members of the Hell's Angels. Everywhere I rode, I felt the hot breath of prejudice on the back of my neck.

My friend evidently experienced what psychiatrists call paranoid projection—the tendency to displace one's fear or anger or aggressiveness on some group easily identifiable by race, religion, political persuasion, or lifestyle that deviates from society's norms. British psychiatrist Dr. Anthony Storr said, "There can be very few of us who do not unthinkingly entertain beliefs or prejudices about groups other than our own which will not stand the light of critical examination . . . for it is prejudices of this kind which serve to bolster our self-esteem."

By projecting from some small percentage of motorcyclists to the whole group, we legitimatize our irrational fears and transfer our own latent aggressive feelings to an alien group. In England, Storr points out, the Scottish, Irish, and Welsh were the victims of the same suspicion and defamation that blacks, Jews, Latinos, and other minorities have experienced in the United States.[5]

---

[5]William B. Helmreich, *The Things They Say Behind Your Back* (New York: Doubleday, 1982) is an insightful book on stereotyping.

FIGURE 11-1

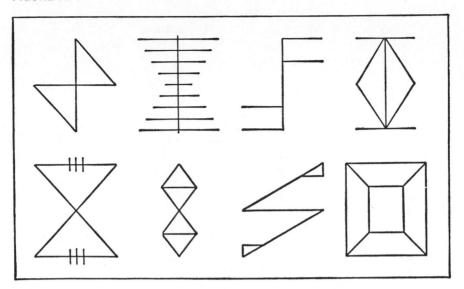

Language Structure

There is another contributor to indiscrimination worthy of attention, not merely because it is important, but because it offers a remedial approach to the problem. It constitutes a factor that can be altered and thus can effect an important change in the outcome. I am speaking of language. We can demonstrate the point if you will study Figure 11-1. Now, before you read any further, make a statement (write it down, speak it aloud, or simply say it to yourself) about what you see there.

If you responded without too much consideration, the chances are that your statement described how the items in the figure were alike. "Geometric figures," "straight-line drawings," "patterns," "forms," and so on, are common responses. Our little game illustrates what linguistic specialists have recognized for years, the English-speaking persons find it relatively easy to perceive and to speak in terms of similarities. In other words, we are often more prone to generalize than to differentiate.

Our propensity to see similarities may be explained partly by the abundance of generic nouns and verbs in our language.[6] We may use the word *wood*, for example, to stand for a myriad of objects ranging from a sliver to

---

[6]We have no monopoly on general words (or on the ability to generalize). But our language is outstanding in this respect when compared with certain other languages, particularly those of some of the more primitive cultures.

a giant Sequoia. Consider the enormous variety of fabrics that *cloth* may be used to represent. Think for a moment of the almost infinite variations in form, size, shape, color, and so forth, that such words as *African, furniture, Catholic, student,* and *animal* may represent.

Here is a curious and revealing comparison. In English, we can use the word *snow* to refer to a snowflake, a snowball, a flurry, a blizzard, an avalanche, lightly or heavily falling snow, snow that is dry, wet, caked, loose, compact, shifting, still, and so on. But the Eskimo, astonishingly, have no one word for all of these! To be sure, they have a large vocabulary of words for many specific forms of snow. For example, they have 20 specific expressions for textures of ice and snow. But they have no one general word, such as our *snow,* for all of them. This is fortunate, in a way, for the Eskimo. With their abundance of specific nouns and a dearth of general nouns, they are led to focus upon the differences in their environment. Take the case of snow, for example. The Eskimo have to be constantly on the alert for the differences in drift patterns, textures, crust strengths, and so on. If they do not attend to these, they may not provide a full dinner table for their families—they may not even get home to their families at all. And so their language, which encourages them to perceive differences, may be a definite boon in this respect.

Our preponderance of mass verbs is another case in point. We have a large number of verbs that represent, to many foreigners at least, a perplexing variety of actions. *Get, make, do, carry,* and *use* are just a few of these. *Go* is a particularly interesting example. We use this word for going on foot and also for being transported, as by vehicle. But the German has no comparable verb. When he or she goes on foot, *gehen* is appropriate. But traveling by vehicle requires an entirely different verb, *fahren.*

The language of the Navaho Indian goes much farther. When traveling by horse, the Navaho have no way to express the general notion of going by horseback. Their language requires that they specify the gait of the animal, whether it be, for example, at a walk, a trot, or a gallop. Moreover, the language insists upon another division of the generic process of going. The Navaho must distinguish among starting to go, going along, arriving at a point, returning from a point, and so forth. Such distinctions can, of course, be made in English, but they are not made consistently.[7]

> The general nature of the difference between Navaho thought and English thought—both as manifested in the language and also as forced by the very nature of the linguistic forms into such patterns—is that Navaho thought is prevailingly so much more specific, so much more concrete.[8] The

---

[7]Clyde Kluckhohn and Dorothea Leighton, *The Navaho* (Cambridge, Mass.: Harvard University Press, 1948), p. 201.

[8]Ibid., p. 199.

nature of their language forces The People to notice and to report many other distinctions in physical events which the nature of the English language allows speakers to neglect in most cases, even though their senses are just as able as those of the Navaho to register the smaller details of what goes on in the eternal world.[9]

Conversely, it appears that the plethora of general verbs[10] (and nouns) in our language both reflects and encourages our inclination to see the relationships and similarities among phenomena.

The crux of this chapter is that the process of noting similarities generally involves the neglecting of differences. Recall your reaction to the drawings in Figure 11-1. When one says or visualizes: "They are all geometric designs, figures, drawings, and so on," attention is called to the ways in which the units are alike and suppressing recognition of their differences. One neglects, for the moment at least, that the second drawing, top row, is similar to a row of telephone poles reflected in water; that the fourth drawing, bottom row, is the only rectangle, and so forth.

A language that prompts us to note similarities, then, may tend to discourage us from observing differences. And the failure to see differences, as we have discussed, may lead to the destructive and dangerous patterns of indiscrimination. Let us now examine some of the possible preventives and remedies that we may use in coping with indiscrimination.

CORRECTIVES

A difficult aspect in the treatment of hardened categories is that categorizers are usually unaware that stereotypes are affecting their behavior. They become so oblivious of their overemphasis on similarities and neglect of differences that they take the rigidly categorized world of their own making for granted.

Of course, we all carry our sets of categories around with us. You are a rare person if some sort of stereotyped image does not occur to you at the mention of at least some of these terms:

---

[9]Ibid., p. 201.

[10]English certainly has no dearth of specific nouns and verbs, especially with respect to those aspects of our culture on which we place a great deal of emphasis. Sports is an example in point. These synonyms for the verb *defeat* were gleaned from just one week's scanning of newspaper sports pages:

bash	edge	overtake	slash	stifle	trounce
batter	mangle	scalp	slaughter	top	vanquish
best	massacre	scuttle	slip by	topple	wallop
blast	maul	shade	smash	trample	whip
crush	nick	sink	smother	trim	whitewash
down	nip	skin	squeeze by	trip	zap

preppies	wife-abusers
doctors	alcoholics
Southerners	white-collar workers
addicts	damn Yankees
union officials	management
blacks	flower children
feminists	evangelists
professors	artists
extremists	teenagers
bankers	wetbacks
muggers	punk rockers

But the mere occurrence of conventionalized images to you does not necessarily make you a chronic stereotyper. Joe may be quite aware that his generalized image is just that, and often with little or no basis in fact. He says to himself, in effect: "Sure, you mention 'professor,' and I think immediately of the pedantic, absentminded fuddy-duddy, carrying a rolled-up umbrella and wearing spats. But that's just the stereotype. Actually, very few of the professors I have known even approach this caricature."

The problem of indiscrimination arises when a person is unaware of or unwilling to recognize stereotypes as such—when, in other words, the categories become hardened. Thus an approach to the dissolution of stereotypes—to the softening of categories—is to work toward the awareness of them. What can we do to alert ourselves to the influences of stereotypes upon our evaluations and communications?

Become Sensitive to Differences

Recall that this chapter holds that the overemphasis on similarities and the corresponding neglect of differences frequently lead to stereotyping. In fact, stereotypes cannot exist without the neglect of differences. The moment we begin to take differences into account, our stereotypes begin to disintegrate. As we make a deeply ingrained habit of looking for differences, we approach a self-awareness which makes possible mature, intelligently discriminating behavior in dealing with people, situations, happenings, relationships, and so forth. "The more we discriminate among," Irving J. Lee said, "the less we will discriminate against.

Internalize the Premise of Uniqueness. Perhaps the first step toward developing a heightened awareness of differences is to disavow the erroneous notion of identicalness. No two things have ever been found to be exactly identical in all respects—or even in one respect. Those two peas in the pod are actually quite dissimilar, even to the naked eye, if one observes closely. "Nature," wrote Ralph Waldo Emerson, "never rhymes her children nor makes two alike." No two snowflakes, no two blades of grass, no two grains of sand—no two of anything—have ever been shown to be completely identical. An important technique of identification is based on the presumption that no two fingerprints are exactly the same. Consider that there are nearly 5 billion persons on earth with approximately 10 fingers each and add all the people who have gone before us and are yet to come—it is an astonishing presumption. Yet it has never been disproved.

Nor have we contrived two of anything that are completely identical. A machinist friend tells me that possibly the most precise manufactured objects are Johansson blocks. Jo blocks are used to check the accuracy of micrometers (extremely exact instruments in themselves). I have seen Jo blocks so precise that placing two of them together created a partial vacuum, so that a person found it impossible to pull them directly apart! You had to twist and slide them to separate them. Are Jo blocks identical, then? They are incredibly alike—machined within a tolerance of plus or minus two millionths of an inch! But note, these are tolerances—that is, even Jo block machinists must admit that they can only approach identicalness, never attain it.

Because no two of anything have been found to be absolutely the same, we have a useful premise: There is always uniqueness, never identicalness. If we are deeply convinced that there are always differences, we may not be so prone to overlook them. We will be less likely to "disregard the individuality of nature, and substitute a generality which belongs to language."[11]

Index Your Evaluations.   One simple device which has proved successful in developing the awareness of differences is the index. Indexing is hardly a new process. Cooks index their recipes; executives their correspondence; librarians their papers and books. Each is separating items according to the essential differences among them. The habit of indexing people, things, situations, and so on, is equally, if not more, useful. The salesperson who habitually indexes will react to purchasing agent$_1$ as if he or she were different from purchasing agent$_2$—they are different.

Make a habit of indexing. The next time you hear someone (or yourself) making statements such as these below, ask yourself Which?

"Union officials are corrupt!"	*Which* officials of *which* unions!
"Women shouldn't be allowed to drive automobiles!"	*Which* women drivers?—and might there be some men drivers you would ban from driving?

---

[11]A. B. Johnson, *A Discourse on Language* (Utica, N.Y.: William Williams, 1832), p. 10.

"Doctors are mercenary!"   *Which* doctors? Would you include your hometown physician? Those who contribute half their time to charity cases? Those who work in laboratories at a fraction of the income they could command?

Doctor$_1$ is different from doctor$_2$, of course, and doctor$_2$ is different from doctor$_3$, and so on. Use the little subscript as a mental exercise, as a habitual memory jogger to call your attention to the differences.

As the next two chapters will describe two other types of indexing, let's index the indexes. To distinguish them, this chapter advocates the use of the Which Index.

THE VALUES OF SEEING SIMILARITIES

To digress for a moment, I trust that I have not given the impression that one should focus on differences at the expense of similarities. The ability to note similarities is essential in generalizing, categorizing, codifying, organizing, classifying, arranging, cataloging, and so forth. These activities, in turn, are indispensable in learning, analyzing, problem solving, innovating, decision making, and so on. For example, children learn about fractions when their teacher shows how the parts of a pie, when put together, make a whole pie. From this they can generalize to (i.e., see the similarities with) fractions of a plot of land or fractions of a container of milk. They eventually generalize to the visualization of fractions as an abstract idea.

Take another case. Suppose that you plan to build a motel and want to find the optimal location for it. Your basic approach is to analogize—that is, you will look for similarities with respect to location among successful existing motels. You may find that these motels are usually located on major highways within easy access of motorists. Moreover, they tend to be situated on the outskirts of cities, far enough out to avoid high real estate taxes and competition from hotels, yet close enough in to utilize the inexpensive urban power and water, and so forth. Thus you may be able to make a wiser decision because you have been able to abstract key similarities out of a myriad of differences among the motels.

Categorizing, cataloging, and classifying (all based on seeing the similarities) are imperative in modern business. Imagine the chaos in the offices of the comptroller, the purchasing agent, the production control manager, and so forth, if they were somehow prevented from classifying and organizing the multitudinous data and details with which they deal.

Scientific advance (or progress on any frontier) is intimately related to the perception of similarities. We learn about the unknown largely on the basis of the known. Someone must have been able to generalize from perhaps a rolling log to the notion of a wheel, from a boiling kettle to a steam engine, and from a flying kite, bird, and so on, to the visualization of an airplane.

This chapter hardly proposes to minimize the value of seeing similarities. Our goal is to achieve better-balanced perceptions—to see differences as well as similarities. To accomplish this, most of us need training in looking for differences. Thanks to our formal education, language structure, and so forth, we are already fairly adept at noting similarities.

SUMMARY

In life, there are differences as well as similarities. Our language structure, however, which subtly influences our evaluating and communicating patterns, encourages us to overemphasize similarities and to neglect differences. The frequent result is that we may behave in terms of stereotypes (neglect of differences) and react to essentially different and unique people, situations, and things as if they were identical with our self-manufactured stereotypes. We can develop a greater sensitivity to differences by internalizing the premise of uniqueness and by applying the Which Index in our evaluations of people, situations, and so forth. The deeply ingrained habit of asking "Which?" will diminish the tendencies to overgeneralize that so frequently lead to stupid, unsafe, and unsane behavior.

Remember, these are differences that make a difference—take them into account.

DISCUSSION QUESTIONS

1. In primitive societies, such as those of the Eskimo, there tend to be fewer generic words and more specific words, especially for important aspects of life. The Trobriand Islanders, for example, have no single word for *yam* but many specific words to denote the yam at its various stages of growth. What are the implications of this? Is it good or bad that a language has many or few mass words—many or few specific words? Why?

2. "The more we discriminate among, the less we will discriminate against."—Irving J. Lee. Do you agree? If people lived by this motto, would it be an effective attack on bigotry, on racial, ethnic, and sexual inequities? What are the obstacles to promulgating this concept more widely?

3. A century and a half ago A. B. Johnson warned against the tendency to "disregard the individuality of nature, and substitute a generality which belongs to language". What did he mean? Specifically, what should we do to heed his warning?

4. This chapter seems to be mainly concerned with the tendency to overlook differences. But what about similarities? Is there not value in being able to abstract them from a situation?

5. What connection is there between the ability to perceive similarities and education? Business decisions? Scientific advance? Government?

6. Prepare a report on an incident, perhaps involving yourself, in which indiscrimination occurred. Analyze why it happened, what could have been done to prevent or correct this incident, what measures are likely to prevent its recurrence.

CASES

The Dixon Company*

The Dixon Company, a national restaurant chain, recently found itself short of the cash funds necessary to establish several new restaurants. Albert Bullock, the president, instructed Walter Green, the company's 60-year-old treasurer, to enter into negotiations with a local bank for a $1.6-million loan. The bank indicated that the loan would be granted provided that the company submit a satisfactory audit report by an independent public accounting firm.

Mr. Green requested the public accounting firm of Wilscher and Wunderlich to perform the audit. Edward Thorndike, a partner in W & W, assigned Tom Scott to supervise the audit. Scott, 26, had been with W & W for five years and had proven to be a highly capable certified public accountant, although inclined to be somewhat overconfident in his manner.

Within the first few days of the audit, Scott uncovered several company accounting policies that were not in agreement with generally accepted accounting principles. After lengthy discussions with Mr. Green, Scott was able to have these exceptions corrected.

During the final week of the audit, Scott took another apparent accounting principle variance to Green.

Scott I've got another book adjustment for your approval, Mr. Green.
Green All right, Tom, what is it?
Scott As you know, accounting depreciation principles are based on the theory that certain assets purchased and used in the business produce income. If such an asset is usable over a period of more than one year, its cost should be systematically and consistently prorated over its estimated useful life. Thus, each year's income is charged with a proportional part of the cost of the equipment used to produce such income. I've discovered that while you follow this principle in regard to most assets, you do not consistently and systematically depreciate class 10 equipment (dishes, glassware, etc.). In the last three years, you charged off 5 percent, 8 percent, and 3 percent, respectively. If you had followed a correct policy, the percentages would all be the same.

---

*All names have been disguised.

Green *(Smiling)* Well, Tom, I've gone along with all your other adjustments, but you're off base on this one. I guess you still have a little to learn about the restaurant business.

Scott *(Suddenly flushing with anger)* Why any elementary accounting textbook will tell you you can't vary your depreciation rate policy.

Green You go out and find yourself a modern, up-to-date book on depreciation methods, young man. Then, you will realize you are wrong.

The conversation grew more heated and finally Scott walked angrily from Green's office, saying: "Well, I'm sorry if I can't make you understand this, but I'm going to report this to my supervisor, and I'm sure we'll have to note this exception in our report to the bank."

Scott phoned Thorndike and reported his disagreement with Green. Mr. Thorndike replied: "Tom, a dish does not *wear* out; its life ends suddenly with a crash. The normal depreciation principle often cannot be applied to a restaurant's class 10 equipment. Variable depreciation rates based on such factors as actual glassware inventory counts or current glassware purchases are acceptable. These factors give some indication of the rate of loss as the result of breakage."

When he had concluded the phone conversation with Scott, Thorndike made this notation in his assignment files: "*If* we get the Dixon job next year we will have to find someone else to handle the fieldwork. Scott seems to have clashed with the company's treasurer."

Discussion Questions
1. How does this case relate to *indiscrimination*?
2. Why did Scott insist that he was correct in challenging the company's depreciation policy?
3. Scott flushed with anger. Why?
4. How should Tom Scott have behaved differently?

CASE 11-2
Full Circle*

Henry J. Taylor

I travel the whole world, and whenever I come home, countless friends ask: "Why do Europeans dislike us Americans so much? Because of our aid? Because America is rich? Why?"

I think we should relax, and worry less about our alleged "failure to be loved." For I maintain that *Europeans do not dislike us any more than they dislike each other.* Prove it yourself:

Take a circular trip, country by country. Did you ever find a Scotsman who is on fire with friendliness for the English or the Irish, or vice versa? Cross the Channel. Most British have little more than contempt for the French, and—again—vice versa. The French do not like the Spaniards and, as for liking Italians, many Frenchmen get livid at mere mention of the name. The dislike of Italians, in turn, for Frenchmen, Yugoslavs, Albanians and Greeks is historic; and they have been fighting Austrians for hundreds of years. Austrians, in turn, detest the Czechs and Poles. The Poles detest the Austrians and Czechs.

Go north in the circle. The Norwegians do not like the Swedes. ("You stayed neutral in the war while we fought," say Norwegians. "You would have stayed neutral too if you had not been attacked," reply the outraged Swedes.) The Dutch will tell you there is no excuse for Belgium. ("Northern Belgium should be Dutch. Southern Belgium should be French. Why a Belgium?") The Belgians like neither the Dutch, Danes, nor the French. And as for liking the Germans, from one end of Europe to the other people love the Germans like a bulldog loves a tramp.

I hope we Americans make more friends in Europe, but we are wrong in thinking of ourselves as the special target for European displeasure; wrong in our mystification, wrong in our hurt feelings, and wrong in excessive and futile measures to make ourselves loved by spending money. The fact is, we can easily be too preoccupied with the attitudes toward us of peoples abroad.

Discussion Questions

1. Are Europeans guilty of indiscrimination?
2. Is Henry Taylor guilty of indiscrimination?
3. What advice do you offer?

CASE 11-3

What's Wrong with the Men?

Italian film star Gianna Maria Canale, interviewed by the press, was asked what was wrong with the men in various cultures:

Americans "They have too many muscles, always thinking of sports and not enough about their women. Besides, they drink too much."

Italians "They are exactly the opposite of Americans. They think only of women, but not in a nice way. They have a one-track mind."

South Americans   "They resemble Italians."

Englishmen   "Really too cold to be good."

Germans   "They would want to order me around as though they were the commanding officers."

French   "They lose themselves in too many compliments. Frenchmen talk too much. They're boring."

Discussion Questions

1. What does this article have to do with indiscrimination?
2. Why do news services print such articles?
3. What's wrong with Italian film actresses?

CASE 11-4

Wright Cleaners and Dyers, Ltd.*

Wright Cleaners and Dyers operated a number of retail branches throughout a large metropolitan area. Many of the older branches were located in neighborhoods that had become economically depressed. A few, such as the store established in Whitesdale six months earlier, were in upper middle-class communities.

Richard Clark, 35, an executive in a rapidly expanding firm, lived in Whitesdale with his wife and two young sons. As Clark left for a short business trip on Monday, he asked his wife to take several of his shirts to Wright's. Mrs. Jackson, sole clerk at the Whitesdale branch, promised Mrs. Clark that the shirts would be ready by Wednesday.

Mrs. Jackson, 61, a widow, had been forced by the death of her husband to obtain employment. She had been working for Wright's for six months— her first job since her marriage in her early 20s. Except for a brief indoctrination period at Wright headquarters, she had spent all of this time at the Whitesdale store.

Clark arrived home late Wednesday night and wasn't expected in the office until Thursday noon. The next morning he drove with his sons to Wright's. He walked into the store with his boys at 8:30 A.M.

Clark   Are my shirts ready yet?

Mrs. Jackson   Do you have your ticket?

Clark   Ticket? No, I didn't know you had to have one.

Mrs. Jackson   Oh, yes—I can't find your laundry without a ticket number.

Clark   Well, OK—I guess my wife has it at home.

*All names have been disguised.

Clark loaded his boys into the car, drove the mile back to his home, picked up the ticket, and returned with his children to Wright's.

Mrs. Jackson   *(after glancing at the ticket number)* Oh, that's not in yet.

Clark   But my wife said they were promised for yesterday.

Mrs. Jackson   Well, they may have come in this morning, but they would be in large boxes in the back, and it would take an hour to unpack them. You come back in an hour, and I'm sure I'll have them ready for you.

Clark   Why don't you let me help you go through the boxes? This running back and forth is getting ridiculous.

Mrs. Jackson   I can't do that—no one is allowed back of the partition.

At this, Mrs. Jackson walked behind the partition, leaving an exasperated Clark, who decided he could do no more with the situation at this point.

In an hour Clark returned.

Mrs. Jackson   Here are the shirts—I got them out for you. I'm sorry about the delay.

Clark   If you're sorry, may I assume that you wouldn't like to have this sort of thing happen again?

Mrs. Jackson   Why, yes, of course.

Clark   Well, whose rule is it that no one is allowed to help you sort out the laundry in an emergency?

Mrs. Jackson   The supervisor's—that's a store rule.

Clark   Then I would suggest that you advise your supervisor, since you are closer to the situation, that this store is in Whitesdale—not in some blighted type of neighborhood. I think you can assume that people are honest here.

Mrs. Jackson   Oh, it isn't a question of honesty. I had a woman in here a couple of weeks ago who went through the cleaning bags hanging on the racks—tearing them open—to find her cleaning.

Clark   I don't see the similarity—I had the ticket number—nothing would have had to be torn open.

Mrs. Jackson   Well, no one is allowed behind the partition. That's a store rule.

Clark   I know, and most of the time it's probably a good rule—but don't you suppose there might be an exception—an instance when a rule might be broken?

Mrs. Jackson   No, that's what rules are for. *(Mrs. Jackson quickly walked behind the partition.)*

Later in the day, Clark telephoned Wright's main office and spoke to Anthony Conti, supervisor of stores.

Clark   Mr. Conti, I didn't feel like doing you people a favor this morning, but I'm a little more mellow now. I'd like to tell you about a practice which may lose you customers. *(Clark recounted the incident with Mrs. Jackson.)*

Conti   Well, I'll tell you, Mr. Clark—I'll tell you why that happened. You see, we train our girls all alike because we may have to transfer them from one store to another, and so on. Now we tell them *never* and under *no* conditions to let anyone go back of the partition. And there are two reasons why we tell them this. Now we find that nine times out of ten whenever we get a customer back there fooling around with the cleaning, there's going to be confusion. And the second reason is the safety of the girls. You know what I mean—we can't let a man back there with the girls.

Clark   I know what you mean, but I don't think Mrs. Jackson should have been concerned. She's seen me several times in the store. And I don't exactly dress or look like an escaped convict—besides I had my two little boys with me.

Conti   Well, you have to have a rule, though—you never know, and those things can happen.

Clark   Yes, but the probability of their happening in Whitesdale is pretty remote, don't you think?

Conti   Well, maybe—but rules are rules, and we make the girls live up to them.

Discussion Questions

1. How do you size up Mrs. Jackson? Why did she respond to Clark as she did?

2. How do you size up Mr. Clark? And why did he deal with Mrs. Jackson as he did? What motivated him to call Conti?

3. How do you size up Mr. Conti? Why did he favor standardized practices? He refers several times to "the girls." Does this suggest anything about Conti?

4. What does this case have to do with indiscrimination?

CASE 11–5

The Wayland Company*

The Wayland Company, a large ore producer with its headquarters offices in New York City, maintained numerous lead, zinc, and feldspar operations. One of its larger feldspar centers was located at Bixby, Utah. Early in the spring, Robert Harris, plant manager at Bixby, flew to New York for an annual meeting with Cal Douglas, production manager of the feldspar

---

*All names have been disguised.

operations, and Fred Squires, chief cost accountant for Wayland's. Douglas and Squires were located in the New York offices.

The purpose of the meeting was to establish the standard costs[1] of the Bixby plant for the coming fiscal year. Predictions were to be made about the extent of such expenses as supplies, repair material, repair labor, fuel, and direct and indirect labor. Direct labor[2] costs were by far the largest expenditure in the plant. Direct labor is generally considered a variable cost[3] in that it varies directly with the quantity of production. Past experience at Bixby had shown, for example, that the direct labor required for producing one ton of feldspar was approximately one-half hour; for producing two tons, one hour, and so on. A measure of the efficiency of the operation could be determined by the extent to which the actual direct labor cost ran above or below this norm. It was the company policy, therefore, to hold the plant manager responsible for maintaining his variable costs, direct labor included, at the lowest feasible level. He was not held responsible, however, for fixed costs, which were beyond his control.

Cal Douglas called the meeting to order, and the three men began to go over the standard costs. As the conference reached the topic of direct labor, Fred Squires remarked: "According to our figures, the direct labor cost incurred at Bixby should be 98 cents per ton and it should be 100 percent variable cost."

Douglas I don't think you're taking into consideration the fact that our Bixby plant has recently been organized. A clause in our contract with the union states that five men have to be paid for five hours a day regardless of production. In other words, if Bixby had 100 percent downtime, these particular men would have to be paid for five hours for every day of the downtime period, whether it is for one day or for six months! It's my thinking, therefore, that all costs incurred when the plant is not operating should be classified as fixed and not be charged to the plant manager.

Harris Mr. Douglas is correct about our plant being organized and I've got to pay those five men no matter what the production situation is. If their time is classified as variable cost, then I would be held responsible for an expenditure over which I have no control. And I certainly agree with Mr. Douglas when he says these should be fixed costs.

---

[1]"A standard cost is a carefully predetermined method of what a cost should be under stated conditions." From J. D. Edwards, R. H. Hermanson, R. F. Salmonson, and P. R. Kenecki, *How Accounting Works* (Homewood, Ill.: Dow Jones-Irwin, 1983), p. 222.

[2]Direct labor is that directly related to the product.

[3]The obverse of variable cost, in accounting terminology, is fixed cost, i.e., cost incurred independently of the quantity of production, e.g., rent, property tax, depreciation, insurance, and so forth.

Squires Mr. Harris, you don't seem to realize that what you're asking us to do is contrary to all established cost accounting principles. If we classify any of your plant's direct labor as fixed costs we would incur some serious problems with respect to accounting terminology. Based on my 25 years as a cost accountant, this idea would certainly be a radical innovation, and in my opinion it just cannot be done.

Cal Douglas, sensing that the meeting had reached an impasse, suggested that they break for lunch. After lunch the conference reconvened and the controversy grew more heated. Finally, Douglas commented: "Gentlemen, it's evident that we have reached a stalemate here. Frankly, we haven't the time to work it out. I think I can see both points of view, and I realize that we're asking Fred to act against some established accounting principles, but frankly I think we must make an exception in this case. We simply must adjust our cost accounting procedure to accommodate our labor problem."

Mr. Squires replied with repressed anger: "Do you realize what repercussions this would lead to? It would change accounting terminology and procedures we've been abiding by for years. Cost accounting, by its nature, has to be consistent from period to period. If we inaugurate this procedure we'll be harming the accuracy of our total plant costing."

Discussion Questions

1. What was the position of Douglas and Harris?
2. What was Squires' position?
3. What patterns of miscommunication do you see operating in this case?
4. What do you recommend to reconcile their differences?

CASE 11–6

On a Bus*

Ruth Lebow Cogan

I was doing industrial nursing at the time of this story, and if you have ever done industrial work you know you start to work at 8:00 A.M., not five minutes after, and you finish at 4:30 P.M., not five minutes earlier.

On this particular evening I had to go to school after work, so instead of going home my usual way I caught a Jackson Boulevard bus going east. It must have been about 20 minutes to five before I caught the bus since I had to walk a block to catch the bus and had to wait a few minutes before it ar-

---

*Printed by permission of the author.

rived. The bus reached State Street about five o'clock, and it was at this time that I transferred, or tried to, to a northbound bus.

I was carrying an armload of books and no other packages when I boarded the bus. I handed the driver the transfer and started to move to the back of the bus when the driver called me back. He said, in what appeared to me to be a very accusing voice, that my transfer was an hour overdue, that it was stamped for four o'clock. I told him the other driver must have made a mistake since I had not finished work till 4:30. At this point he accused me of lying and said I was shopping for an hour and tried to get by with an old transfer. By this time he was shouting and all the people in the bus were intently watching and listening for the outcome. He asked for another fare, and seeing there was no future in arguing with him, I opened my purse and found that I had no change—only a $10 bill. I told the driver I only had $10 and asked if he could change it. His face was getting redder and redder, and he finally burst out with, "I'll change it and give you all your change in silver." By this time I was furious and told him I did not care how he changed it as long as he gave me my change.

At this point he really lost control and blared out that he knew people like me—always trying to cheat the bus lines out of a fare and that I didn't pull the wool over his eyes and that he could see through my act. He said he changed his mind, that he would not cash my ten dollars and that I would just have to get off the bus. Under fire of accusations I had no alternative but to get off, since technically he was within his rights to refuse to change a $10 bill.

Discussion Questions

1. Who is at fault?
2. What patterns of miscommunication seem to be involved in this case?

12

Differentiation Failures:
2. Polarization

Polarization may be considered as a special form of indiscrimination, but because of its relevance to what has been happening in our nation and, indeed, in many parts of the world, it warrants a separate chapter.

> A college professor may be either a top-notch researcher or an excellent teacher; he may not be either, but he certainly won't be both.

> Kids these days don't appreciate what they have. Either you sweat for what you get, or you'll take it for granted.

> The cops in this precinct are either honest and walking on their uppers, or they're grafting and living high.

Perhaps those statements seem a bit jarring. Are such statements less offensive if they are made by people of renown?

> Life is either a daring adventure or nothing.
> —*Helen Keller*

> There are but two objects in marriage, love or money. If you marry for love, you will have some very happy days, and probably many very uneasy ones; if for money, you will have no happy days and probably no uneasy ones.
> —*Lord Chesterfield*

> The world is divided into people who do things and people who get the credit.
> —Harry Golden[1]

The latter statements may be more memorable, but they are still oversimplistic. Whether expressed by celebrities or not, each of the above quotations perpetrates a *polarization*.

---

[1]Publisher and author Golden also felt that there were two kinds of people in the world: Those who insist on dividing the world into two kinds of people and those who don't (!)

DEFINITION

To define *polarization*, we must distinguish betweeen two kinds of situations that apparently present two, and only two, alternatives. One of these is a genuine dichotomy; the other is a false dichotomy.

Contradictories

At any given time and place, you will either marry or you will not marry; you will either be arrested for speeding or you will not; you will either receive a pay raise or you will not; you will either make the varsity basketball team or you will not; and so forth. These are authentic dichotomies or contradictories. Note their characteristics: (1) one alternative must occur, but (2) both cannot.[2] Take this statement: "People are either over six feet tall, or they are not." Everyone, at any given time and place, (1) must be in one camp or the other, for there is not middle ground, and (2) cannot be in both camps.

It is quite safe, sound, and sane to make either-or statements about contradictories. But there is another type of situation about which either-or statements and evaluations can be quite misleading and dangerous.

Contraries

Examine this statement: People are either tall or short. It has the either-or form, but it does not involve contradictories, for there is middle ground—countless people are neither tall nor short. And this is the key distinction between contradictories and contraries. Contradictories involve no middle ground, no other alternatives; contraries do. Moreover, the middle ground may consist of gradations, shadings, degrees—an unlimited number of them in many cases. The temperature of the air around us is a good example—it isn't simply hot or cold. The temperature varies by smooth, continuous changes that we express conveniently in arbitrary steps called degrees. Actually, there are an infinite number of gradations between 0 and 100 degrees Fahrenheit, or Celsius.

Indeed, it is as if nature abhorred contradictories. Contradictories appear to be largely human-made. Consider the computer. It operates on the contradictories of open and closed. A given circuit is either open or it is closed. to accommodate this limitation the binary numeral system was adopted. It consists of only two numerals—*0* and *1*—to represent opened or closed circuits. For those who may not be familiar with it the binary system looks like this:

---

[2]Aristotle expressed these requirements as two of his laws of thought: (1) something must be either A or non-A, and (2) nothing can be both A and non-A at the same time and place.

Decimal	Binary	Decimal	Binary	Decimal	Binary
0	0	4	100	8	1000
1	1	5	101	9	1001
2	10	6	110	10	1010
3	11	7	111	11	1011

The decimal 2, then, is not read as ten, but as one circuit closed, another circuit open.

A simpler example of such contradictories are the go no-go gauges used in industry to determine whether or not an object meets given specifications.

On the other hand, consider some of the contraries masquerading as contradictories.

Life or death. Precisely when does life begin and when does it end? With legalized abortion and organ transplants, these are no longer only philosophical questions. They have become vital physiological, legal, and moral issues. For example, when may a heart be transplanted from one person to another? When the donor dies is the over-simplified, black-and-white answer. But, *when* does he or she die? When no pulse or breath can be detected? When no reflex action can be elicited? When the heart and lungs cease to function? When an irreversible coma is recorded on an encephalograph? In a recent meeting of the American Academy of Neurology one conclusion was clear: There was *no* generally accepted conclusion as to when death comes.

Male or female. As disconcerting as it may be to male chauvinists or women's libbers, there apparently is no 100 percent male or no 100 percent female. Evidently there is maleness and femaleness in varying degrees in each of us. Again the issue is not merely academic. In a recent Olympics, 11 women athletes were disqualified because analyses revealed that they were insufficiently female to compete with other women. And recall the furor when, after a sex-change operation, Renee Richards née Richard Raskind sought to compete as a woman in tennis tournaments.

One young Englishman has successfully affected an androgynous pose. Boy George's appearances, replete with heavy cosmetics, pierced ears, and bizarre clothes have reaped a tidy income. Presumably enough for BG to fall back on when the public finally relinquishes its rigid sexual dichotomy.

Animal or vegetable. As if the foregoing were not disturbing enough, here is yet another old, comfortable oversimplification under attack: the supposed contradictories of animal or vegetable. Where do you put the *euglena* which digests food like an animal and photosynthesizes like a plant? Or where does the *ascidian* fit? It is classified as an animal, yet it produces cellulose, which has been considered a function unique to plants.

It seems fair to conclude that most of the important aspects of living involve *contraries.* Health-illness, wealth-poverty, war-peace, loyalty-treason, hero-villain, sanity-insanity, beauty-ugliness, conservative-liberal, intelligence-stupidity, bravery-cowardice, line-staff, investment-speculation, competence-incompetence, mind-body, good-bad, heredity-environment, true-false, honesty-dishonesty, guilt-innocence, and so on, are not simple, either-or matters. But people sometimes deal with these and other contraries in an irrational way. This behavior is called polarization.

Polarization

Polarization occurs when one, failing to differentiate, treats contraries as if they were contradictories; when one deals with a situation involving gradations and middle ground in strict, either-or contradictory terms. I recall quite vividly the intense conflict in a certain midwestern town over the issue of fluorine in drinking water. Impressive scientific evidence had been presented to the effect that fluorine in proper proportion to the water markedly reduced dental decay, especially in children. But nothing could persuade the majority of the town's citizens that the fluorine would not be poisonous, and the health measure was voted down.

The fluorine issue involved contraries; it was a matter of gradations. But the majority of the citizens treated it as if they were dealing with contradictories. "Fluorine," they polarized, "is either poisonous or it's safe. We know it's poisonous, so we're not going to have anything to do with it!"

Fluorine is, of course, a deadly poison—*in sufficient quantities*. But medical and dental research had demonstrated that in minute amounts (as with other "poisons" such as iodine, chlorine, and arsenic) it was highly beneficial. It was the failure of some people to see the graded uses and effects of fluorine that cost the town a valuable health aid.

Another issue involves cyclamates, a type of sugar substitute. The federal Food and Drug Administration has banned them because studies indicated that ingesting certain quantities of cyclamates caused cancer in rats. However, the estimate is that one would have to consume daily 120 cases of soft drinks to have a comparable exposure. Saccharin, a sweetener which has aided diabetics and dieters for 90 years, and aspartame, the newest synthetic sweetener, are similarly in jeopardy. The question of just how much of these chemicals are dangerous to humans has never been answered.

CONSEQUENCES

Let us examine some of the manifestations and effects of polarization.

Deluding Ourselves

Not the least of the negative effects of polarization is that we may deceive ourselves. One psychiatrist described the obsessive (either-or) disability of one of his patients:

. . .he revealed a classification of all women into contrasting classes—the thin and virtuous, the fat and vicious. He felt that he should marry, and the idea of marriage to any but a thin and virtuous woman was inconceivable. Nevertheless, he was attracted only by fat women, and his few would-be virtuous approaches to thin women had been signally successful.

As bizarre as this unfortunate man's perceptions may have been, are they really much different from the polarizations so many of us practice? I knew an aggressive young man who vowed while in college that his annual income at the age of 30 would be $75,000. Today he is 40—bitter and disillusioned, for he is making "only" $50,000. In his eyes he is a dismal failure.

> For several years the comptroller of a big firm, looking forward to his own retirement, had been grooming a man we'll call Smith as his successor. Smith was aware of this plan and worked so successfully toward the goal that he was also being considered as a candidate to step eventually from the comptrollership to the presidency. Then one day he went completely to pieces.
>
> The comptroller asked him sympathetically what was the matter.
>
> "I've just found out," Smith said after some coaxing, "that I've got diabetes."
>
> Examination by a specialist showed that he had only a mild case and that with insulin shots and reasonable care in his diet he would have no trouble. This enabled him to get to work with much of his old efficiency, but he insisted that he be dropped from consideration as the comptroller's successor.
>
> "Up to now," he explained, "I've hardly been sick a day in my life. Now I'll never again be able to think of myself as healthy."
>
> Smith destroyed his career because he saw health as an absolute. That is, he saw himself as formerly absolutely healthy and now absolutely unhealthy. He had completely obliterated from his mind the possibility of a middle ground.[3]

Deluding Others

Polarization may, of course, be used to mislead others. In their famous debates on slavery, Stephen A. Douglas attempted to use polarization to his advantage when he threw apparent contradictories at Abraham Lincoln. Lincoln neatly sidestepped the horns of the false dilemma by exclaiming, "I protest against the counterfeit logic which concludes that because I do not want a black woman for a slave, I must necessarily want her for a wife. I need not have her for either. I can just leave her alone."

Polarization is also a favored ploy for getting out from under, as per Captain Queeg's (*The Caine Mutiny*) stock reply to those who criticized his unreasonably harsh treatment of subordinates: "Well, what do you want me to do—give him a commendation?"

---

[3]Robert Froman, "How to Say What You Mean," *Nation's Business*, May, 1957. Reprinted by permission.

And parents often use polarization on children for "their own good." A friend of ours thought she had mastered the technique when she would ask her four-year-old: "Which would you rather do first, Johnny, take your bath or brush your teeth?" Johnny, of course, didn't want to do either, but how can you say no to a question like that?

But Johnny learned to retaliate in kind. One day while shopping with his mother, he pulled her over to the toy department and demanded: "What are you going to buy me, Mom, a bicycle or an electric train?"

Among the most effective polarizers in modern history were Adolf Hitler and his Nazi henchmen. "Everyone in Germany," declared Hitler, " is a National Socialist—the few outside the party are either lunatics or idiots."[4] The thesis they so successfully inculated was that an enemy of the National Socialist party was necessarily an enemy of Germany."

Unfortunately, such polarizations persist. Ever since the 1983 election, the Chicago City Council has been sharply divided racially: Mayor Harold Washington and 21 aldermen (all black) vs. Aldermen Edward Vrydolyak and Edward Burke and 29 other aldermen (all white). The resulting Council Wars are often ludicrous. The "city that works" still manages to do so—largely despite rather than because of the council. Recently, a Chicago radio station decided to survey its listeners. If you felt Mayor Washington forces were responsible for the strife, you could register your opinion by calling a certain telephone number. If you felt the Vrydolyak-Burke people were at fault, you could call another number. A large number of listeners criticized the station for exacerbating an already polarized situation. The least the station could have done, complained listeners, would have been to provide a third number where listeners could indicate that they felt both camps were contributing to the impasse.

Polarization in America

Of course, you needn't be a Chicagoan to experience political divisiveness. Consider the polarization that racked our nation in the 1960s. According to Henry Grunwald, we were in the grip of two views of reality.

> In one view of reality, America is under attack from junior barbarians devoid of all respect and patriotism, spoiled by permissive parents and spineless college administrators, misguided by essentially subversive professors and other intellectuals; under attack also from blacks ungrateful for the favors done them and unwilling to work hard enough when crime is so much easier and more tempting. In the other view, America is ruled by a hypocritical Establishment that prates of virtues it does not practice, instead putting profit above all else, fighting an immoral war for material gain and in pursuit of some insane imperialism, and racist to the very marrow of its white bones.

---

[4]*New York Times*, April 5, 1938.

On the one side, law-and-order, honor, country, decency pitted against treason, anarchy, filth, immorality. On the other, freedom, justice, "the people" against entrenched power, blind chauvinism, blood lust and repression. Two visions: two ghastly caricatures: accepted as truths by more and more Americans.

But still far from totally accepted. There are countless gradations between the two visions, and a genuine, tortured desire not to surrender to the extremes.[5]

Some historians contend that we had not been so polarized since the Civil War. Today, the American scene is less explosive but far from serene. We still have our schisms. Viet Nam is over but the loss of Marines in Lebanon is still a vivid memory. Debate continues to rage over ecological issues; poverty; racial, ethnic, and sexual inequities; wife- and child-abuse; terrorism. More recently, we were acutely divided about an urban vigilante in a New York subway who allegedly shot four young men who had "requested" $5.

How do such polarizations come to be? The answer would be encyclopedic but I will suggest just one contributor to these ruptures. It has to do with how some people use language—how they talk and write and think about the issues that divide them.

I submit that people tend to become polarized partially because they talk in polarized terms. Consider the ubiquitous bumper slogan "America—Love It or Leave It." That had a ring to it, and when uttered with sufficient fervor, it may have tingled the spine. But unfortunately, regardless of the composer's intention, it could have been an expression of a mindless retaliation against some of the equally mindless criticisms heaped upon our nation. When it was intended or interpreted thus, it became a rank polarization which seemed to offer two alternatives: (1) blind faith in and unquestioning acceptance of the status quo, or (2) give up—and get out.

This was essentially the sentiment expressed in Stephen Decatur's famous toast (Norfolk, Virginia—1816):

Our country! In her intercourse with foreign nations may she always be in the right; but our country, right or wrong.

I prefer Carl Schurz's expression:

Our country, right or wrong.
When right, to be kept right;
When wrong, to be put right.
—From an address in Congress, 1872.

So if we must sloganize, perhaps we could adorn our bumpers with a third alternative: "America—Stay and Improve It." That may not stimu-

[5]Henry Grunwald, "Thoughts on a Troubled Eldorado," *Time*, June 2, 1970, p. 18. Reprinted by permission from *Time, The Weekly Newsmagazine*, © Time Inc.

late the adrenals as much, but it seems to me that it makes eminently better sense.

The Plight of the Moderate. But the more divided a society becomes, the more difficult it is to remain temperate. One remains silent, passive, and ineffectual, or one speaks out and risks being driven to either of the poles. The distinguished critic Joseph Wood Krutch once said: "From experience I have learned that you can't criticize anything without having it supposed that you favor the opposite extreme." Horace warned against this tendency 2,000 years earlier: "When I caution you against becoming a miser, I do not therefore advise you to become a prodigal or a spendthrift."

The plight of the moderate was depicted adroitly a few years ago in a cartoon showing two men talking. The gist of their conversation:

First man Well, what's your choice—anarchy or repression?
Second man What do I get if I choose anarchy?
First man You get crime in the streets, riots, chaos.
Second man What do I get if I choose repression?
First man You get law and order, internment camps, censorship, and police brutality.
Second man And what do I get if I choose peace, brotherhood among men, and an end to poverty?
First man You get ignored. . . . So what's your choice—anarchy or repression?

America's Viability. Our nation's vitality historically has been its viability—its ability and willingness to self-examine, to adjust, to evolve. But we must protect that viability and the system that preserves it from destruction by the polarities of anarchy and suppression. Dwight D. Eisenhower wrote: "We must never confuse honest dissent with disloyal subversion."

The danger is that ideas, *per se*, will be suspect. Fear is ruinous. It compels the fearful to turn to authority, however oppresssive, for security. And for the oppressors fear is the fundamental means of control.

Ramsey Clark, a former attorney general, once told the National Students Association that "people who fear dissent will not know the truth." It is, after all, the truth, not fear, which will set us free.

Clearly, our vitality is our viability. Our Constitution is a remarkable document, but even it has been amended 26 times!

The Vicious Pendulum Effect

The most destructive consequence of polarization is the escalating conflict, or the vicious[6] pendulum effect.

---

[6]Vicious in the dual senses of savage and self-energizing (akin to the vicious circle).

The pattern is a familiar one. Two persons—or two groups or two na-tions—with perhaps only moderately differing views on a given issue begin to discuss that issue. Emotions rise, and the discussants start to swing far-ther and farther apart. Soon their positions become polarized and rigid. No middle ground appears possible, and they are engaged in a heated and seemingly irreconcilable dispute. When superpowers arrive at this "You're nuts!"—"No, you are!" stage, fingers reach nervously for nuclear missle buttons.

Assumptions.   At the root of this dangerous escalation are two erroneous and unconsciously held assumptions. One is the aforementioned polariza-tion—the oversimple either-or thinking that leads us to treat contraries as if they were contradictories. The second assumption has also been exam-ined earlier—it is the fallacious but attractive notion that "the world is as I see it" or, in short, the "I-know-reality" assumption (IKR).

Chapter 3, "Perception and Communication: The Process of Percep-tion," argued that our contact with reality is only indirect—that which we experience is not reality but our perceptions of it. And our perceptions are likely to be influenced, indeed distorted, by our past perceptual experi-ences—by our psychoprogramming.

Visualize a person who assumes, albeit unconsciously, that he or she knows reality—has direct and valid contact with it—the perceptions, therefore, are undistorted by prior programming. This person is almost certain to be a threat to and to be threatened by others who make similar assumptions about themselves but do not share this particular program-ming.

Underlying this threat is fear. Anger, profanity, physical threats, and violence notwithstanding, the primary emotion is fear of loss of contact with reality. This dread can sometimes be warranted, as those who have endured certain mental illnesses can readily attest. But the IKR fallacy evokes the fear needlessly. Indeed, it virtually guarantees it. It does so by setting up within a person a thoroughly unrealistic and unreasonable ex-pectation that is bound to be thwarted.

One's usual response to fear, real or unfounded, is defense—often an overraction. Overreaction, according to Jeb Magruder, was our former president's fatal flaw. Nixon had "an inability to tolerate criticism, an in-stinct to *overreact* in political combat. I don't know which came first, the li-berals' loathing of Nixon or Nixon's loathing of the liberals, but the pas-sions fed on one another, grew more and more bitter, until once he achieved the presidency, Nixon could not resist the urge to use his awe-some powers to get his enemies."[7]

---

7 Job Magruder, *An American Life: One Man's Road to Watergate* (New York: Atheneum, 1974). Italics are author's.

Basically, then, it is a perceived threat to one's contact with reality leading to a defensive overreaction that energizes the pendulum to swing in escalating arcs.

The Pendulum Effect.   Consider how the polarization and IKR fallacies
combine to contribute to the pendulum effect. Let a pendulum (Figure 12-1)
represent an individual's perception—especially a point of view, value
judgment, opinion, or any other expression of how this person values or
feels about something ("Your tie is nauseating!") rather than a factual description of that something ("Your tie has orange and purple stripes with
pink and yellow polka dots"). And let X represent reality or sanity or intelligence or justice or honor or rationality or morality . . . or any other virtue that seems relevant to the situation. And let Y stand for the antonyms
of these respective perceptions—unreality, insanity, stupidity, injustice,
and so on.

Let's use *reality* and *unreality* to illustrate. Note than when the pendulum is at dead center (see 1 at X in Figure 12-1) it most closely approaches
reality. Thus this viewpoint, opinion, and so on, is considered quite realistic (or sane or intelligent, and so forth). To the extent that the pendulum is
off center—either left or right of X (see 2 and 3 in Figure 12-1)—it is away
from reality and toward unreality, and thus is regarded as *less* realistic, *less*
sane.

There can be and there frequently is a discrepancy between where
one's pendulum is objectively and where one perceives it to be. But is
seems fair to assert that many people (especially when they are in conflict
with others) perceive their respective pendulums as permanently an-
chored at X. This, of course, is consistent with the IKR fallacy, and smug-
ness is perhaps the hardest of all qualities for anyone to detect in oneself.

Suppose that Jones and Smith are about to discuss a topic on which
their views are actually quite similar and, assuming objective standards,
quite close to reality. Jones's view, which is slightly liberal, is at A', and
Smith's slightly conservative view is at A—the two views are a scant two
units apart, and each view is only one unit removed from X. (See Figure
12-2.)

Smith speaks first and, operating under his IKR assumption, states his
A position as though it were at X—for he truly believes it to be there. Now
since Smith and Jones are two units apart, and Smith is seemingly at X, it
follows that to maintain the two-unit discrepancy, Jone's pendulum is dis-
placed to B'—two units from *reality!* (See Figure 12-3.) This poses a perceived threat to Jone's IKR. His feelings at the moment, if he could understand and verbalize them, might well be: "This man says he knows reality.
What he says differs from what I know. Therefore, if he is right, I am
wrong. If his position is realistic, mine is not. He is challenging my contact
with reality—my sanity!"

FIGURE 12–1

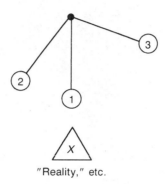

"Reality," etc.

Jones feels compelled to defend—more likely to overdefend—his sanity by attacking Smith's. Jones may overreact with a somewhat more vehemently liberal view, say at C'—two units from his original position, A', and three units from Smith's. Consistent with his IKR, Jones will express his view as if it were at X. This has the effect of bumping Smith from X to C (see Figure 12–4).

Now it is Smith's turn to be threatened. He is likely to retaliate—probably to *over*-overreact—counterattacking Jones's contact with reality (see Figure 12–5).

At this pace, it won't be long before the men, alternating between bumper and bumpee roles, progressively ram each other into unreasoning, polarized positions ignoring the middle ground (see Figures 12–6 and 12–7)—positions that neither would have supported had they not been psychologically frightened into them.

CONTRIBUTING FACTORS

Polarization, ranging from innocuous either-or fallacies to the dangerous and destructive pendulum effect, is basically the confusing of contrar-

FIGURE 12–2

FIGURE 12–3

FIGURE 12-4

"Unreality"

"Reality"

FIGURE 12-5

"Unreality"

"Reality"

FIGURE 12–6

FIGURE 12–7

ies for contradictories. We shall now examine some of the reasons for this misevaluation.

Similar Grammatical Form

Contraries and contradictories are often stated in a similar grammatical form:

> You either had coffee this morning or you didn't. (Contradictories)
> You are either a coffee fiend or a complete abstainer. (Contraries)

That both contradictories and contraries are frequently expressed in the either . . . or pattern probably accounts for some of the confusion between them.

Neglect of the Middle Ground

A more complex and important reason for polarization is the disregard or avoidance of the shadings and gradations between the extremes. The tendency to neglect the middle ground may be attributed to a number of factors. Most of the important ones fall under the headings of conditioning and expediency.

Conditioning. All through life we are conditioned to polarize. It is altogether possible that our training in this respect begins even prenatally. Note the role of simple motor activities in our conditioning. We have extensor and flexor reflexes. We can contract a muscle and relax it. We can inhale and exhale.

Consider, too, our linguistic conditioning. Let me illustrate the point by inviting you to take a little test. First of all, give the opposites of the following words:

$$
\begin{array}{r}
\text{white} - \underline{\hspace{4cm}} \\
\text{good} - \underline{\hspace{4cm}} \\
\text{polite} - \underline{\hspace{4cm}} \\
\text{honest} - \underline{\hspace{4cm}} \\
\text{success} - \underline{\hspace{4cm}}
\end{array}
$$

Simple, wasn't it? Opposites come very readily to mind. But now try the second part of the test: fill in the gradational terms between the extremes:

white — _____ — _____ — gray — _____ — _____ — black
good — _____ — _____ — _____ — _____ — _____ — bad
polite — _____ — _____ — _____ — _____ — _____ — impolite
honest — _____ — _____ — _____ — _____ — _____ — dishonest
success — _____ — _____ — _____ — _____ — _____ — failure

You probably found this part much more difficult. Actually, the cards were stacked against you. There are comparatively few intermediate terms in our language. Of course, we have the imprecise, quantifying adjectives and adverbs such as *slightly, fairly, medium, average, very, extremely*, and so on, but using them requires extra thought and effort, and we frequently neglect them.

The paucity of middle terms tends to encourage polarization. If we cannot say that a person is entirely honest, it is easier to classify that person at the opposite pole as dishonest. We disregard the infinite gradations of honest between the poles partially because we lack the quantifying substantive words to express them. A young high school graduate was reported to have hanged himself because he had failed by a slim margin to be elected to the National Honor Society. It seemed to make little difference to him that he had been president of his class, that his parents had given him a new automobile as a graduation gift, that he had been awarded a college scholarship, and that he had been accepted by one of the foremost universities in the nation. In his stage of depression, it was impossible to conceive of anything short of complete success as other than total failure.

There are many other factors in the environment that condition us to polarize with ease and alacrity. Here are a a few of them.

a.   The Two-Sided Question.   It seems as if someone is always attempting to temper a heated argument by admonishing: "Now remember, there are two sides to every question!" Our well-meaning friend may actually be more misleading than helpful, for few questions of any importance have only two sides—most such questions are multisided. Are the problems of public school integration, nuclear weapons control, street crime, or poverty simple pro and con affairs? Or, for that matter, can the problem of choosing a vocation or a mate, of raising children, or of earning a living be solved by a categorical yes or no? The reporter-columnist Nicholas Von Hoffman stated: "The illusion of objectivity is dead. The old criteria for objectivity are that there are two sides to an argument and both must be reported. This defies the realities of today, where there are 30 or 40 sides to a story."

And yet the two-sided question myth is a prevailing one. "Did you hear about the Smiths' breakup? It was all his fault." "No, she was to blame." Could not both of them have contributed to the strife, and could there not have been factors beyond the control of both—inability to have children, financial difficulties, in-law interference?

To be sure, there are legitimate two-sided questions—in law and in debate, for example. But the charges or resolutions are scrupulously phrased and defined in order to permit positions of guilty and not guilty (note the avoidance of the contraries guilty and innocent), affirmative and negative.

b.   Popular Songs.   One would not have to search long through the lyrics of popular songs to find exhortations to polarize—an influence, unfortunately, that most of us tend to underestimate. Note the utter disregard for gradations in such titles as "All or Nothing at All," "It Must Be Right; It Can't Be Wrong," and so forth.

c. Cheap Fiction.   Whether it occurs in the form of paperback novels, slick magazines, television, or the movies, cheap fiction is replete with polarization. The beauty is breathtaking, while the beast is grotesque; the rich are fabulously so, and the poor are penniless; the paragon of honesty invariably clashes with the despicably deceitful.

If there is anything adult about the current rash of adult movies, television dramas and stage plays, and novels, it is the avoidance of depicting the good guy as insufferably virtuous and the bad buy as unrelievedly evil.

d. Restrictive Laws.   Laws are sometimes written in either-or, blanket terms. Several years ago, the Food and Drug Administration was required to forbid the use of coal-tar dyes in lipsticks. Under an archaic law, an ingested product (women consume minute amounts of their lipstick) containing any amount of any toxic material had to be banned. Cosmetics industry representatives claimed that a woman would have to eat 100 lipsticks a day for 90 days to suffer any ill effects. Even the FDA admitted that the amount of dye seemed completely harmless, but its hands were tied until the law was changed.

Police officers are often faced with the necessity of modifying the letter of the law. With limited resources they must use discretion in determining the level of enforcement that is desirable and feasible.

Expediency.   It is much easier to think of a person as either intelligent or stupid rather than rating that individual more precisely along a continuum of mental ability. It might be considerably simpler for a teacher to pass or fail students. But rating them along the range of A–B–C–D–F, percentages, and so on, requires a good deal more consideration and judgment.

And, too, we are often pressured for decisions. We feel that we haven't had the time to investigate and analyze. And we are uncomfortable with the uncategorized, the unresolved—so "if it ain't this, it's gotta be that."

CORRECTIVES

To prevent polarization, habituate these techniques:

1. Detect the contrary.   *contradict*
2. Specify the degree—apply the How-Much Index.
3. Separate the double contraries.
4. Guard against the vicious pendulum effect.

Detect the Contrary

The first step in combating polarization is to detect the contrary. But how can one quickly, yet dependably, distinguish it from the contradictory? Aristotle's laws of thought are 23 centuries old, but so far as they apply, they are still valid and practical.

1. Something must be either A or non-A.
2. Nothing can be both A and non-A at the same time and place.

Use these laws to test an either-or situation.

> An employer: "The biggest problem with secretaries is initiative. Some, when they see a job to be done, will always go right ahead and do it without having to be told. But the others—you literally have to lead them by the hand—especially if it involves anything outside of their regular routine."

Which are involved—contraries or contradictories? To qualify as a contradictory, the situation must measure up to both of Aristotle's requirements. Must a secretary either always go right ahead and do it or be led by the hand? Hardly; there is abundant middle ground. The situation fails on the first criterion of the contradictory, and it is therefore a contrary.

Specify the Degree—Apply the How-Much Index

Having determined that one is dealing with a contrary, the next step is to specify the degree between the extremes. In other words, it is no longer a question of either-or but of how much.

If a person steals a 22-cent stamp from the office postage supply, we might describe the action as dishonest—or at least as not honest. If a person steals $100,000, we could say the same thing. But would we not have had an obligation to quantify—to distinguish the degree of dishonesty involved? Do other circumstances influence the degree of honesty? Is there a difference between stealing a given amount from a rich person and stealing from a poor one? Does stealing with the intent of repaying make a difference? What about stealing for a worthy cause?

To a great extent, the method of applying the How-Much Index depends upon the nature of the contrary and upon the availability of terms to denote the degrees.

Use a Quantitative Index When Possible. Some objective contraries (e.g., tall-short, light-heavy, hot-cold, large-small) lend themselves to a quantifying index. *Time* magazine writers, for example, often use a telling detail in parentheses to specify: "The boy was tall (5 feet 11 inches) for his age (13) . . ."; ". . . has the largest undergraduate enrollment (28,000) in the state.

Use Substantive Middle Terms When Available. Many contraries, of course, cannot be quantified. One cannot describe a person as 89–percent patriotic, 2.3 times more friendly than a neighbor, or ¼ ill. but some contraries do have a supply of substantive middle terms that may be helpful in specifying approximate degrees between the poles. The following adjectives, by no means as precise and as nonoverlapping as inches, pounds, or miles per hour, still may suggest some of the gradations and nuances along the beautiful-ugly continuum:

agreeable	frightful	ordinary
attractive	ghastly	passable
beauteous	glamorous	piquant
becoming	good-looking	plain
beguiling	gorgeous	pleasing
bonny	graceless	presentable
captivating	grisly	pretty
charming	grotesque	radiant
coarse	gruesome	ravishing
comely	handsome	repugnant
cute	heavenly	repulsive
dazzling	hideous	resplendent
devastating	homely	revolting
divine	horrible	stunning
drab	horrid	uncomely
dreadful	ill-favored	unprepossessing
elegant	loathsome	unseemly
exquisite	lovely	unsightly
fair	monstrous	well-favored
fetching	nondescript	winsome

Use Quantifying Terms.   Certainly, such words as *very, slightly, moderately, extremely, generally, seldom, average, fairly, often, medium,* and so forth, do not approach the specificity of the numerical indexes, but they are obviously superior to the absence of quantification. Remove the quantifying terms *most* and *generally,* from the statement below, and note how much more harsh, unyielding, and "either-or-ish" it becomes:

> Most American educators agree that the elective system in our colleges and high schools leads generally to an aimless nibbling at knowledge, or to excessive specialization.

Separate the Double Contraries

The compound polarization merits special consideration. Actually, it involves mistaking double (or multiple) contraries for single contradictories. This bit of doggerel epitomizes a common compound polarization:

> *Girls at college*
> *Are of two strata:*
> *Those with dates*
> *And those with data.*[8]

---

[8]Richard Armour, *Reader's Digest,* January 1952, p. 20. Reprinted by permission.

FIGURE 12–8

The old beautiful-but-dumb cliché. The counterpart for males: All brawn and no brain. Not only are both notions fallacious, but some evidence indicates that if there is a correlation between physical and intellectual superiorities, it is a positive rather than a negative one.

But let us return to the double contraries—how can we deal with them? The first step is to cut them down to size—to separate the contraries and work on them individually. Suppose we take the brawn-brain fable. Expanded, it would appear: People are either brainy (and puny) or brawny (and stupid). It is immediately clear that there are two continua involved—intelligence and strength. We can now proceed to specify degrees on each of them with the How-Much Index as before. Graphically, our double values might be expressed as shown in Figure 12–8.

Lest the foregoing treatment appear a bit frivolous, consider this compound polarization:

> There are two kinds of doctors; Those who are dedicated; those who are dollar-conscious.[9]

Is it not more likely that most doctors are some degree of both?

---

[9]Attributed to a high-ranking officer of a national service and fraternal organization.

Combining Contraries. Compound contraries, then, are misleading when (1) they are treated as contradictories and (2) they are falsely correlated. But sometimes contraries are related—and useful information can be expressed by combining them, provided that they are dealt with as contraries rather than as contradictories.

The Weather Bureau's temperature-humidity index (THI) does this. What is important to most of us is not how cold or hot or how humid or dry the weather will be, but how comfortable we will be. A temperature of 85 degrees Fahrenheit sounds warm, but the THI tells us that at a 25-percent relative humidity, the day will be reasonably comfortable. The THI also tells us that a more moderate 75 degrees will be rather unpleasant if it is accompanied by a humidity of over 60 percent.

The bureau has also combined the contraries of temperature and wind velocity to give us the wind-chill index. Ten degrees above zero coupled with a brisk breeze can be decidedly more uncomfortable and dangerous than 10 degrees below zero on a calm day.

Guard against the Vicious Pendulum Effect

We can minimize the pendulum effect if we are mindful of two key factors: (1) controversial issues are usually complex, (2) our perceptions of such issues are programmed by prior experiences.

Complex Issues. Controversial issues are generally highly complex. Because they are multifaceted, it is highly unlikely that any one viewpoint will be 100 percent valid. Be wary, therefore, of blanket statements. One can prevent or ameliorate the pendulum effect by analyzing the issues, carefully selecting aspects to be conceded and specifying the nuances and gradations between the polarities.

Programmed Perceptions. We have observed how polarizers progressively frighten each other, with a succession of overreactions, toward the extremities. Such people would not be so inclined to overdefend if they were not so frightened, and they would be less threatened if they were relieved of the burden of the IKR fallacy.

The IKR fallacy is their undoing. It is this fallacy that provides the psychological fuel that propels disputants' pendulums in ever-widening arcs. When a person expresses an opinion or a value judgment, regardless of how vehemently, that person is not, contrary to belief and desire, talking about reality but describing inner feelings. And that description need not frighten another person whose personal view happens to be different.

The chief antidote for the IKR fallacy, then, is to eradicate it by conscious, humble acknowledgment that no one knows reality—that no one has direct and valid contact with reality—that what we experience is not reality but our perception of it, which in turn is inevitably biased by our past experiences.

To the extent that you genuinely accept and internalize these premises, you will be impervious to threat by another person's disagreeing with your views on politics, religion, culture, art, morals, music, or any other value-judgment area. Your armor consists of these insights:

> You recognize that the other person is only talking about the programmed feelings inside his or her head.
>
> You recognize that you are only talking about the programmed feelings inside your head.
>
> You recognize that neither of you stands to lose contact with reality because you concede that neither of you had direct and valid contact to begin with.

Unthreatened, you are unlikely to counterattack and threaten the other person. Thus neither the other person's pendulum nor yours receives the initial impetus that sets it swinging.

Some specific suggestions for countering the *IKR* fallacy:

1. Determine whether you and the other party are disagreeing on facts or on your respective feelings about those facts. If the former, get out the yardstick, measuring cup, bathroom scale, speedometer, odometer, thermometer, micrometer, or whatever other standardized measuring device is appropriate and available. If the latter, try to discover and understand the underlying assumptions, needs, motives, and programmings that led to those feelings, value judgments, and attitudes.

2. Try role reversal. If the discussion seems to be degenerating into a futile and heated dispute—the pendulums start to swing—strike a bargain with each other. Promise that for the next 15 minutes you will express the other person's point of view as persuasively as you can—provided that the same is done with yours. Prediction: For the first few minutes both of you will feel awkward and artificial. But gradually, as each of you exercises discipline, and speaks convincingly from the other person's frame of reference, you will begin to realize that, astonishingly enough, there is some value, some intelligence, even some sanity in the other person's position. Role reversal will not guarantee a total resolution of conflict, but it does tend to keep the discussion on the real points in contention and to restrain the pendulum's momentum.

3. Don't get personal. Escalating pendulum effects are usually those that grow not only progressively vehement but progressively personal as well. Try to stay on the issue and off the individual.

> Say: "I can't really agree with that idea."
> Not: "That's a ridiculous idea!"
> Worse: "You're an idiot!"

4. Keep your cool. It really does take two to tango—and also to fight. When attacked, resist the temptation to overreact—to counterattack.

Unthreatened, the other person will find it unnecessary to be defensive. You can disagree without being disagreeable.

5.   Without making a fetish of it, try to label your opinions, feelings, and value judgments as such—not as objective, unassailable facts. Helpful phrases: "I believe . . ."; "I think . . ."; "It's my feeling that . . ."; "In my opinion . . ."; "According to my value system . . ."; "As I see it. . . ."

6.   Acquire the *to-me-ness* and *to-the-other-ness* habits. Preface your value-judgment statements with "to me."

> Not: "The Church is no longer relevant."
> But: "To me, the Church is no longer relevant."

Substitute "appears to me to be" for "is" when linking a noun with an adjective with the verb to be.

> Not: "Pornography is harmful to children. . . ."
> But: "Pornography appears to me to be harmful. . . ."

Similarly, when listening to the other person's opinion, add (silently) "to that person" or "appears to that person to be" to his or her declarations.

> Someone says: "Draft evaders are cowards and deserve no amnesty in any form."
> You interpret: "(To that person,) draft evaders . . ." or "Draft evaders (appear to that person to be) cowards. . . ."

These word additions and substitutions not only render value-judgment statements more temperate but more accurate as well—for they denote more explicitly that the speaker is not speaking about the facts out there but about the feelings inside.

7.   Resist absolutes; they are a telltale sign of the desperate disputant.

> "You *never* listen to me . . .!"
> "You're *always* late in submitting your reports. . . ."
> "*All* the kids have one, Mom. . . ."

Absolutes fail on at least three counts: They tend to provoke retaliatory antonyms by the other party, thus accelerating the swings of the pendulum.

> "You *never* consult me anymore!"
> "What do you mean? I *always* ask for your advice first!"

They make a graceful retreat difficult. Having committed oneself to an absurdity—"*No one ever* appreciates *anything* I do in this department!"— how does one back down without losing face?

Third, they weaken your case. They render your position vulnerable and easily challenged.

"You say you *never* receive information from headquarters. I believe you did receive the May 15 general directive and the June sales forecast. And did you not receive the revised list of corporate objectives last Thursday?"

The indiscriminate use of all-inclusive terms, such as *all, everywhere, always,* and *everyone,* often reveals one's failure to be selective. Confronted with a controversial issue, I may fail to distinguish among its components—to differentiate those aspects that I consider genuinely valid and important from those that are dubious and trivial. Rather I imprison myself with all-embracing defenses of my position and blanket indictments of my opponent's. My unconscious assumption appears to be that to concede anything weakens my case. Lord Acton's advice seems more to the point—accede in everything you can, for this strengthens the part that remains.

SUMMARY

Polarization tends to occur when contraries (situations involving graded variations, middle ground) are treated as if they were contradictories (strictly either-or affairs).

Moreover, we may be misled not only by our own polarizations but by the purposeful or unintentional polarizations of others.

One of the most destructive forms of polarization is the vicious pendulum effect—the escalation of conflict. It thrives on overreactions. Regrettably, the easiest, the most dramatic, and the most infantile response to opposition is absolute counteropposition. Such polarization has become a commonplace in America, but it is nonetheless a clear and present threat. Whether suppression or anarchy or sanity will prevail is yet to be seen. However, one cannot but agree with William Buckley's admonition: "Reason may not save us; but the absence of reason will not save us."

The factors contributing to polarization include the similar grammatical form of contradictories and contraries and, more important, our propensity to neglect the middle ground. Conditioning and expediency are among the influences accounting for the latter.

Polarization tends to be reduced when one develops habits, first, of distinguishing contraries from contradictories and, second, of specifying the degree (applying the How-Much Index). In the case of compound polarizations, the initial step is to separate the contraries. Then the gradations on each continuum can be specified.

The vicious pendulum effect can be dampened if we can recognize different perceptions as products of different conditionings and if we can acknowledge that in complex issues literally no one (including ourselves) has the one complete and unassailable viewpoint.

DISCUSSION QUESTIONS

1. "Faced with significant decreases in applicants, should colleges lower admissions requirements or contract facilities?" How do you feel about this?

2. What cases in this chapter as well as in other chapters seem to involve the vicious pendulum effect?

3. Give five examples of true contradictories and five involving contraries.

4. "Modern logic has abandoned one of Aristotle's most basic principles: the law of the excluded middle, meaning that a statement must either be true or false. In the new system a statement may have three values: true, false, or indeterminate. A close analogy to this system in the legal field is the Scottish trial law, which allows three verdicts—guilty, not guilty, or not proven."—John Pfeiffer (*Scientific American*).

   How do you react to the above?

5. Precisely what is polarization? What contributes to it? How can it be prevented?

6. What is the vicious pendulum? What are its mechanics—that is, how does it occur? Remedies?

7. Was polarization involved in the case "General Patton and the Sicilian Slapping Incidents" (Chapter 8)?

8. Does the "Craving for Certainty" discussed in Chapter 10 have any bearing on polarization?

9. "Be contented, and you'll live longer."
   "Don't be contented—or you'll stagnate."

   "War is coming—because there have always been wars."
   "War isn't coming—because neither side can win it, and both sides know it."

   "Think big—for you have to spend money to make money."
   "Watch your pennies—and the dollars will take care of themselves."

   "An objective test doesn't let you express yourself."
   "An essay test is so vague you don't know what's expected."

   Your reaction?

10. "What we tragically fail to recognize is that extremism is always a symptom of failure in the feedback process of an institution, and not a cause of anything in itself."

    —*Sydney J. Harris*

    How do you feel about the above statement? Why?

11. "I divide all readers into two classes: those who read to remember, and those who read to forget."

    —*William Lyon Phelps*

    How do you react to this statement? Why?

12. What vicious pendulum effects do you see occurring today in your community? In our nation? In the world?

13. "In nature and in the id, there are no opposites which exclude each other."

    —*Eric Berne*

    Do you agree?

14. List and discuss contraries masquerading as contradictories. For example: mind or body, heredity or environment.

15. What is the plight of the moderate? Can one be a centrist and still be effective?

16. Dr. Martin Luther King, Jr., wrote: "To retaliate in kind would do nothing but intensify the existence of hate in the universe. Along the way of life, someone must have sense enough and morality enough to cut off the chain of hate."— *Stride toward Freedom*. Bayard Rustin, a leading civil rights leader, stated: "As you get black backlash in response to white backlash, the intensity of the white backlash increases. We're in trouble because one backlash reinforces the other."
Your reaction to these statements?

17. In addition to the THI and the wind-chill index, what other combinations of contraries are useful?

18. Describe an incident, possibly involving yourself, in which polarization occurred. Analyze specifically why it occurred, what might have been done to prevent its occurrence, and what measures would prevent its recurrence.

To underscore the urgency for coping with the vicious pendulum effect, I cite a recent confrontation.

> To stem a tide of shoplifting, a college bookstore in the Northwest began to require that students check their bags and outer coats. In retaliation a group of students, male and female, entered the store and checked *everything*!

The bare facts speak for themselves.

CASES

Deadly Force*

The use of deadly force in effecting the arrest of an alleged felon is a serious problem to the police officer who is in the position of judge and jury. In a split second, the officer must at times decide the guilt or innocence of a person, which ordinarily could take a court months of contemplation to decide.

Ralph Rogers, a police officer for less than a month, was patrolling on foot. Suddenly he saw a man sprinting from a store with a woman chasing after him, screaming, "Stop that robber!" The man was running toward an idling automobile. Another man was at the wheel, evidently waiting for the runner. The officer realized that he could not possibly overtake the fleet runner and considered for a moment his terrible dilemma. He decided against shooting, and the man scrambled into the car, which was already starting to move—a screech of tires, and the car turned a corner and was out of sight.

The lady, breathless, ran up to the officer. She was furious. "Why didn't you stop him!" she snarled. "You could have shot him easily! He stole $700 from me!"

The officer's face grew crimson. "Look, lady," he choked, "what could I do? If I had shot and killed him I could have been tried for murder or manslaughter."

"But he robbed me of $700! Don't you have the right to shoot a robber?"

"Yes—but I didn't *know* he was a robber when I was chasing him. Maybe you don't know this, but if he had stolen less than $15, that would be petty larceny, and he would not be classified as a felon. That means that if I had killed the guy I could be tried for murder or manslaughter.

"So, do you see the position I'm in? If I shoot and possibly kill a man I am liable for a serious offense. If I let him get away I'm the goat. Don't worry, lady, you won't be the only one I get hell from. The chief is going to have plenty to say, and so are the newspapers! What a law we have when you're damned if you do—and damned if you don't!"

Discussion Questions
1. What do you think of Officer Rogers' dilemma? Were there alternatives?
2. What could Officer Rogers do to deal with similar situations more effectively?

---

*All names have been disguised. Printed by permission. The author's name has been withheld by request.

CASE 12–2

Evans and Borne*

Evans and Borne were a partnership with branches in four cities—New York, Chicago, Boston, and Los Angeles. Each branch was supervised by a vice president. The firm was an investment banking firm that participated in securities underwritings and also acted as a dealer and agent in the sale or purchase of securities. The company had been rapidly increasing its business volume during the last five years and currently employed 400 persons.

Due to this expansion, the accounting department had been responsible for an ever-increasing amount of record-keeping. (The department also maintained an interoffice account, necessary because each branch office kept its own accounting records.) Management decided that a consulting firm ought to look into the possibility of a basic change in procedure. Such a firm was engaged, and after a study of several weeks it submitted the following recommendation:

> Evans and Borne has arrived at a point in its operation where a decision must be made as to whether to continue operations under the present system or to install an electronic accounting system. We recommend the latter.

The consulting firm was discharged and the president, James L. Borne, called in his executive committee (the four vice presidents) to discuss the recommendation. After about an hour's discussion of the pros and cons of the two alternatives, Mr. Borne, well known for his decisiveness, rose and spoke enthusiastically:

> Judging from our talking here, we are just about unanimously agreed that the electronic system is for us. I feel the same way. The growth of our business alone convinces me that a year from now we will have no choice. The size and complexity of our operation will force us into electronic accounting. And so I firmly feel that not only should we go into the new system but that we should do so immediately. As you know, these new machines are a tremendous investment, and I want them to start paying off just as soon as possible. So, what do you say? Shall we get into electronics as soon as possible?

The system was installed within three months. It was quite evident within the first month that the company was in over its head. There had not been time to train personnel adequately, and tempers flared continuously.

The turmoil in the accounting department was such that management was seriously considering discarding the system. But by this time the com-

---

*All names are disguised. Reprinted by permission.

pany had been irrevocably committed to it; there would be no turning back. It was almost a year before the department was restored to order.

Discussion Questions

1. What does this case have to do with polarization?
2. Were there any other patterns of misevaluation operating here?
3. How should Evans and Borne have gone about the system changeover?

CASE 12-3

Preston Lee, CPA*

The day was a cold one even for February, but the sky was cloudless and sunlight streamed through the window of Professor Robert Dillon's study. Dillon was entertaining two old friends, Wallace Borden and Frank Compton.

"When you finish with a situation like we went through with Preston Lee and look back on it, you are never sure you did the right thing," said Wallace Borden. "It just makes you sick when a promising young man, who might have developed into a partner, leaves you for a routine job as a payroll auditor in an insurance company."

Wallace T. Borden was the partner in charge of the Oklahoma City office of J.D. Rodman & Co., CPAs, the headquarters office of which was located in Fort Worth, Texas. There was also an office in Austin, Texas. The firm enjoyed an excellent reputation and was particularly well-known in the oil industry, which provided a majority of its clients. The Oklahoma City office was opened in 1969, with Borden in charge, and since that time had grown slowly but steadily. In 1976, Frank Compton, an outstanding member of the professional staff, became the second resident partner in Oklahoma City. In 1985 there were four men and one woman on the professional staff in that office.

Preston Lee was 22 when he joined the firm in August 1981 at a salary of $18,500. He had graduated from the University of Oklahoma three months earlier and had then served a short tour of duty in the Air Force as required by the agreement under which he had been helped through college. A good-looking young man over six feet tall and weighing over 200 pounds, Lee had earned a B+ average on his major, accounting, and a B− average overall.

He had taken the CPA examination in May 1981, while still in college, and secured a condition. In November he took the examination again and passed it. When he resigned in December 1984, his salary was $25,500 and he was due for a raise.

---

*All names have been disguised.

Wallace Borden Tells His Story

Professor Dillon gazed vacantly out of the window of his study. Then he turned to Borden:

Dillon   How did all of this happen?

Borden   Before I tell you about Preston Lee, I should mention some related matters. In my opinion, salaries paid by the Oklahoma City office are comparable to those paid by other CPA firms in Oklahoma City. We are pretty much in the middle bracket. The University tells us that most of their graduates are going out at higher than our starting salary. But most of these men and women are going out of Oklahoma—many of them to the East—so it is hard to compare.

It is our policy to hire right out of college and develop them, so of course it is rare for them to have taken the CPA exam when hired. Press Lee was an exception. Of course, we put some pressure on our people to get their certificates. In 1981, when Lee passed the exam, he was the only person on the staff who actually had the CPA, but today they all have it. I am talking about staff, of course, not partners.

Preston Lee: The First Year

Lee had been with us only a few months when I had to throw him a curve. The accounting department of one of our clients broke down, and our other people were tied up, so Lee went in under my supervision. A key person had left the client's employ, and the records were messed up. Press moved right in, and every time I checked, which was frequently at first, I found he was on top of it, so I began to relax my supervision. He brought the job out in good shape, and naturally we developed confidence in him and began pushing him along.

We don't usually give a man that much responsibility so fast, but we had just had two seniors leave us. One of them had been unable to pass the CPA exam. The other was a CPA, but didn't quite measure up to our standards.

Shortly after the job I just mentioned, we were called in by one of our clients. The comptroller is a CPA, and he has strong ideas about being audited by a non-CPA. In spite of the fact that Press Lee was just out of college, he and this comptroller got along fine, and he was the only one who was permitted to do the audit. Naturally, this puffed him up.

A Difference of Opinion

I think it was in his second year with us that Press began to feel that our firm was lacking in aggressiveness; that we were self-satisfied and didn't have the hustle to expand the practice. He told us that he thought the firm should get much more active in social affairs, particularly at country clubs—giving parties to drum up more business—and that he thought he should have an expense account to cover the cost of lunches and drinks for clients' personnel and others. He pointed to the fact that some of the Oklahoma City offices of the big national firms were doing just that and that one had started a new office and in six years it had grown to a professional staff of about 50.

Dillon Was that so?

Borden Well, yes, we see the partners of that firm in the clubs and hotels talking to our clients. They are getting themselves well known and putting ideas in people's heads about the wonderful job they are doing, giving them brochures such as the one on the federal income tax—tips for oil companies. They have been passing these out around town in fairly substantial quantities.

We discussed the question of professional ethics with Press, and his feeling seemed to be that they were doing it, and no one was telling them they couldn't, and if we didn't do it too, we would lose out—in fact, we had already lost out, according to him.

Along toward the end of 1983 we were at a client's Christmas party and Press had had quite a few drinks, but he was not out of control, and he was talking to a business associate of the client. This fellow hit it off real well with Press. They both got pretty high and started talking about auditing, and Press said to him, "Why the hell don't you bring your audit over to our firm and let us take care of you?" and the man said, "Well, I am just going to do that."

As a matter of fact, this man's auditor is a good CPA and a friend of ours, and that sort of thing is apt to be interpreted in several ways, none of which we would like, particularly as far as the profession is concerned. So we discouraged Lee from talking to the guy anymore, and he was pretty unhappy, I'll tell you. Here he had some business all lined up, and we threw cold water on it. He was really upset.

So we weren't about to give him an expense account. We didn't think it was the proper thing to do with such a young man. We had serious reservations about whether we could control it adequately, or his behavior either. And then there was the effect on the other staff men. From Press's standpoint we were just old fogies.

By the end of 1983, we rated Lee as probably having more potential than either Condon or Burke, who were many years his senior. Our problem was to get his attitude straightened out. Press was much more concerned with selling himself to the client, and in many cases his success at this was outstanding; he made friends easily.

After Press had passed the CPA, we suggested that he take on some community work, and he joined some Jaycee committees. He always did everything with a lot of enthusiasm—or with none; when he went flat, he went really flat. So he got in the middle of their Christmas program for orphans and was active in an election campaign. What with one thing and another, I think he might have been president if he had kept pushing, but he didn't. His interest cooled off, and he dropped it. Press is like that; hot one minute, cold the next.

Just before New Year's, 1984, Press married an attractive young lady named Charlotte.

The Summer of 1984

Because we knew the staff thought that we had been giving Press more than his share of favors, we were really surprised at what happened in our counseling interview in July 1984. We review our staff people twice each year, try to assess their progress, and look at their salaries.

So in July 1984, we talked with Press and told him that from our point of view, he was making progress, that we had no particular comments to make at that time about strengths or weaknesses, and that we were raising his salary $100 a month. He sort of leaned back in his chair and said: "Same old raise, huh? There is no progress."

Dillon   How do you account for his reaction?

Borden   Frank here thinks it was outside influence. Press knew a union official who apparently believed that employers took advantage of their employees and withheld most of the fruits of their labor. I understand that he said that staff people should receive substantially all of the net fees which they generated and that partners should get their compensation from the fees that their work produced. He favored more holidays, longer vacations, and more fringe benefits. I think Lee was influenced by this fellow.

We were very surprised. We had just raised him to $25,500, against Condon and Burke at $26,000. He was raised $7,000 in three years. At the same time that we had given him a raise, we had given them none, but he didn't know that, at least not then. After the interview, he walked out into the staff office and, in typical Press Lee fashion, said to Condon and Burke: "Well, I got a $100 raise. How much did you guys get?"

As they hadn't been raised, this caused some difficulty.

I suppose he thought his rate should go up to the same level as Condon and Burke, in spite of the big difference in age and experience. He said he thought he was better than they were. His attitude was what bothered me, not his competence. He was handling responsible jobs well, but we felt his relations with the clients were a bit immature. He was always kidding with them; he seemed to us to be a bit shy on professional attitude. But we thought he needed to mature a bit.

In the conference, he said that he didn't feel that he should be asked to work under Condon and Burke any more; that he was doing as good work as they, and carrying as much responsibility, and that he was a CPA and they weren't.

I recalled that when we had put him on a job with Burke in charge he hadn't cooperated very well. It was obvious that he didn't intend to take direction from Burke. We had never had this particular difficulty with him until 1984. During the first two years that he was with us, he took supervision well.

Not long after the interview, he went out and interviewed the local office of a national CPA firm. I have a good friend who interviewed him. Apparently Press felt he had a lot of specialized tax knowledge about the oil industry that he wanted to sell to them. He made some remarks about J.D. Rodman being a nonaggressive, dead-end firm and was rather taken aback when my friend told him that they had the highest respect for us. They said they had no opening in Oklahoma City, but might be able to get him a job in Kansas City, but he didn't want to move to Kansas City, so that was that.

New Office in Stillwater

We had been wanting for some time to open an office in Stillwater, as we had a number of clients there, including a couple of good ones who kept pressing us to set up service locally. Finally, one of them went so far as to build a new building with space in it planned for us, so we had a partners' meeting and agreed to do it, with Robert Golden, a younger partner from the home office in Fort Worth, in charge.

The idea was that Golden would move to Stillwater. At the firm picnic, in August, Bob Golden's wife, Gloria, got to talking to the other wives and said that she had no desire to move to Stillwater. Gordon Campbell, our managing partner in Fort Worth, got wind of this. Here he had an office, and nobody to put in it. For various reasons, none of the other partners in Fort Worth could move and there was no staff man that seemed appropriate.

Campbell phoned me and asked whether Condon or Burke would be interested in going to Stillwater. I said they had the capacity all right but they didn't have their CPAs, and so that was dropped. So I said that it seemed to me that Preston Lee was a possibility, that he had the personality and drive to make a new office go, and would do a good job if someone stood behind him to keep him from going off the deep end. I pointed out that he felt himself at a dead end in Oklahoma City and he might welcome the opportunity. We kicked the idea around a bit, and Gordon said: "Why don't you check with Lee and see if he's interested?"

I said I didn't want to mention it to him unless it was pretty sure that he would get the opportunity if he wanted it, and Gordon said that of course he understood that.

Dillon   So then you talked with Lee?

Borden   Yes, we took him to lunch. We told him that the firm definitely was going to open an office in Stillwater and that Bob Golden was the logical man to go, but apparently he didn't want to. Would he be interested? We said we didn't know for sure that it would develop for him but that he was a strong candidate among others.

Press asked about compensation and we told him that this hadn't been discussed but that we were sure consideration would be given to the expenses involved in moving, that he would have an opportunity to grow and that his compensation would grow accordingly. We told him that he wouldn't be a partner and that we wouldn't guarantee that he would ever be a partner, but that the opportunity was definitely there.

So he talked to his wife, and they decided it would be great. She had gone to school in Stillwater and hadn't finished, so she would go back to school and finish up, and they made plans bang, bang, bang. I called Gordon, and he said, "Fine. Send him down to Fort Worth to talk and send his wife with him."

But the next morning Gordon called, and he was really upset. He had gone down to the office early, and Bob Golden came in and said he was looking forward to going to Stillwater and his wife was very enthusiastic about it, too. So of course the only thing he could do was call me and say he was sorry and that there was no point in Press coming to Fort Worth.

So Frank and I got Press in and explained to him about Golden: that he was the logical man to go and that after further consideration he had decided to go. We expressed to Press the thought that his having been so strongly considered was a great compliment, as most of the other men were older than he was, with more experience. We told him that another opportunity would come along and that we thought he had a great future with the firm.

Gordon Campbell was in town a few weeks later to see a client, and he and I took Lee to lunch, and Gordon told him he was sorry about the way things had worked out, but that he had had to make the decision on the basis of the welfare of the firm as a whole, that Lee had received very careful consideration and had been a strong candidate, and that in a few years, with a bit more experience, he would be an even stronger candidate. Gordon told Press he had a big future with the firm and that there would be another opportunity coming along.

The Last Three Months

Dillon   What happened then?

Borden   Three weeks later Press came into my office and told me he had considered the situation every way he knew how and he had arrived at the conclusion that there was no future for him in the firm and that there was no alternative for him but to resign.

So we asked him: "Well, what do you have in mind?"

And he said, "Nothing. I'm going out and get a job."

Frank and I spent a good deal of time, jointly and separately, with Press. We both told him quite bluntly that he was just plain wrong and making a mistake. There was opportunity, there was a future for the firm, and he was a part of that future. We told him that we were not proposing to hand him a big job or a partnership on a silver platter, but he could earn one through his own efforts. We weren't going to divide up the present situation and just hand him a slice, but he could build a share for himself, in time. You don't become a partner because you are a nice guy; you become a partner because you earned it.

I think that he had hoped to pressure us into a substantial raise or a junior partnership or something. Communication broke down, and I was guessing, but I think when he said he was quitting that he didn't intend to leave, but was applying pressure.

I think he wanted a rating equal or superior to Condon and Burke and he wanted equal money. I think he didn't want them telling him what to do. If we had given this to him, I really don't know whether we would have had problems with Condon and Burke or not. But I don't care to give in to that kind of pressure, and anyway it is against the policy of the firm.

The upshot was that we didn't offer him anything at all, except advice that he was being premature. Then he talked around that he could get a better job somewhere, where there was more opportunity. He made a trip to Billings, with his wife, and they didn't welcome him with open arms the way he expected. The man's wife was in the hospital, and he kept the Lees waiting around and in the end didn't offer him the comptrollership that Press thought he would get, and that was a blow. Another company offered him $12,000 for six months as an internal auditor, but that was temporary, and it wasn't a vice presidency, and Press was insulted.

In the meantime he had done a great deal of talking about the wonderful job he was going to have and then, when he had more trouble than he expected, he talked to everyone about his troubles. I guess he was getting rather desperate.

So finally, the California Insurance Company offered him $26,100 as a payroll auditor in San Francisco, and they told him that, with his CPA and all, it was a wonderful opportunity for him to move into an executive spot, and he took it and moved out of town. Up to the time that he actually gave notice, Frank and I kept trying to convince him to stay.

Comments by Frank Compton

Compton The two senior men, Graham and Corcoran, who left our staff in May 1982 may have had something to do with Press Lee's later behavior. During his first six months on the job, Lee worked closely with them and under their supervision. Both men seemed to have a lot of personal problems. Both were rather negative toward their work and apparently believed that the firm owed them opportunities which it failed to provide. Both had a strong dislike for Condon. I would say that Lee was never able to reconcile their adverse opinion of the firm and what they regarded as their inability to progress in such a firm, with our enthusiasm for its potential.

I had several talks with Lee about his negative attitude, which seemed to be focusing on Condon. Just before he told us he was leaving the firm, he said that he could not work with Condon and therefore could not be in the same organization.

I talked with him about attitude and the need to be able to work with most anybody—whether a fellow employee, or client, or client's employee—and about teamwork and what it meant to be part of an organization. I suggested that some problems take time and patience to work out in fairness to everyone. He agreed to reconsider, but later, he decided that it was unnecessary.

We thought Press had a big future ahead of him, with us. But, obviously, he didn't think so.

Incidentally, after he resigned but before he left town, he often came into the office and had coffee with us, or just talked. Early in January, after Condon gave notice, Press was having coffee with me and he mentioned the news about Condon leaving and said: "Maybe I shouldn't have quit."

Borden So that's the story, Bob. One always thinks, maybe if we had done it differently . . . .

Two days later Dillon received a note from Borden:

> Dear Bob,
> Just to round out the Press Lee affair, here's the gist of a phone call I had with California last month. Frank and I would be quite interested in your views on this situation after you've had a chance to mull it over.
> Sincerely,
> Wallace

Memorandum, January 21, 1985

Mr. Davis, personnel manager of the California Mutual Insurance Company, called to ask about Preston Lee. They are considering hiring him as an internal auditor.

I told Mr. Davis that:

> Lee's reputation for honesty and integrity is excellent. Clients have com-
> plimented us on his ability to work with their employees. There is some re-
> sistance to supervision by the immediate supervisor. His judgment needs
> maturing but overall is good. He is dependable; has no bad work habits ap-
> parently handles his finances and family affairs well. He has an excellent rec-
> ord on committee work in the Junior Chamber of Commerce and seems to
> have leadership qualities.

Mr. Davis asked if we would hire him back. I said no, that our experience is
that a man who quits for a supposed advancement does not possess qualities necessary to become a partner and usually is not a satisfactory employee.

W. T. Borden

Discussion Questions

1. What is the principal problem of this case?

2. What was Preston Lee's frame of reference?

3. What was Wallace Borden's frame of reference?

4. Regarding Borden's comment: "Maybe, if we had done it differently," what
   should have been done differently, in your opinion?

5. What does this case have to do with polarization?

CASE 12–4

Two Factions*

A problem of undeniable importance lies within the confines of the police
department for which I work. I think that I can safely say that it has directly involved a large percentage of the members of this department and,
moreover, its effect has been felt by every citizen of our city.

The problem originated years ago, but instead of diminishing with time,
it has grown to be a complex and difficult situation. This problem is now
evidenced by open dissension and strife within the ranks of those employed around me.

Approximately 10 years ago, the city's police administration tolerated
gambling and the illegal sale of liquor (bootlegging) to a considerable extent. In all probability, this tolerance was the result of some political pressures plus the desires of a few corrupt people who were interested, not in
better government, but in building large bank accounts.

This state of affairs continued unchallenged for several years, until a
group within the department began to develop. About 25 or 30 officers,

* Printed by permission. The author's name has been withheld by request.

headed by four or five recognized leaders of no great rank, held a few informal meetings. They decided that all illicit forms of entertainment in the city would be closed. It was clear that some of the officers were motivated largely by public-spirit while others joined the group because they had been excluded from the group receiving graft money and privileges.

Thereupon, this group (with the exception of a few who agreed in theory but would not shoulder direct responsibility) began to act. In groups and simultaneously, they entered establishments, effected some arrests, and closed the doors to further operation. These officers, for the most part, made these raids and arrests while on off-duty time.

Immediately, attempts were made to conciliate the two factions, but they failed. The consequences were not long in coming. The leaders of the Vigilante group were fired upon the provisions that they had been acting without authority, due to the fact that they were not actually on duty, nor did they have their supervisor's consent to act.

Within the police department, the remaining Vigilantes were met with both hatred and sympathy and a wide crack soon appeared within the organization.

Almost at once, the dismissed members began suit to regain their positions, and after a year's legal debate, full reinstatement plus salary reimbursement were ordered. All men resumed their positions with the department.

Perhaps this solved their respective problems, but it certainly was of no value with respect to the enmities created in the rank and file. In fact, the flames were fanned to the point where everyone was placed in an impossible situation—one must either associate with one group or the other or be disliked by both.

These two factions, the "Vigilantes" and the "Anti-Vigilantes," have been at great odds since that date. They refuse to speak to one another, and open condemnations are the rule. Politics play a larger and larger part in the organizational structure of the department. The Public Safety Commissioner (an elective position), if favorable to one faction, will immediately upon taking office assign favored positions to his group and thus relegate the out-group members who had been holding these positions to more or less menial stations. It should be quite evident how this constant displacement of key personnel depreciates the value of our organization and also should show quite clearly that the breach in the ranks grows deeper with each change.

Many new men have been added to our department since the trouble originated, and a large percentage of them have been drawn into the struggle. I cite my own experiences as an example: One of my best friends in the city happens to have been an active leader of the Vigilante group. Our friendship is based almost entirely on mutual interests outside our field of work, namely fishing and hunting, but because of my association with him, many say I am a sympathizer of the Vigilante faction. I have lost several friends who say that because I enjoy this man's company, I am a believer in his theories and a backer of his principles.

Upon the completion of my probationary period, I was told that it would be impossible for me to be a fence-sitter, in other words, that I would be forced to declare my sympathies for one group or the other. I laughed then because I could not see why my choice of friends should be based on such damned foolishness. But I am no longer laughing, for it has affected my working conditions and even threatens any future chance for advancement or promotion. This much has happened to me, and of a certainty it is happening and has happened to many others.

Discussion Questions
1. How do you analyze what had happened in this police department?
2. What should the author do?
3. What should the Public Safety Commissioner do?

CASE 12-5

For Men Only*

Randall Beckman

Tom DiRicco and I are managing partners of a small legal firm in a Pittsburgh suburb. We have been expanding slowly but satisfactorily, and about six months ago we decided that I should go to our local university law school to recruit one or two additions to our professional staff.

With scheduling assistance from Dean Coleman, I interviewed a dozen or so candidates and was especially impressed with two of them. Checking with the dean I learned that both had received several job offers and were probably on the verge of making a decision. Ordinarily I would have consulted with Tom, but he was out of the city, and "unreachable." I felt that I had to act fast, so I made a firm offer to both students. They promised to consider it and let me know by the end of the week. The next day, Wednesday, Tom returned to the office.

Tom   Any luck at the university?

Randy   Two hot prospects—both graduating in June—I think we have a good chance with both of them because they indicated that they would like to stay in this area.

Tom   What are their names?

Randy   Charles Timmons and Mary Klein. They're both—

Tom   Mary?

Randy   Yes, do you know her?

Tom   No—but where did you get the idea that we want a woman in here?

---

*All names have been disguised.

Randy Why not? She's sharp as a tack—upper 10 percent of her class. She already has a CPA, so she would strengthen us in tax accounting. Plans to take the bar exam in September, and I'm betting she'll pass with flying colors.

Tom Well, let her fly her colors somewhere else.

Randy What kind of attitude is that?

Tom It's sanity—that's what kind of attitude it is. Have you ever worked with a female attorney before?

Randy No, have you? (*I'll admit I was getting a bit miffed at this point.*)

Tom That's beside the point. Let me tell you what to expect of Miss Stein—

Randy Klein!

Tom What?

Randy Klein—her name is Klein!

Tom OK, take it easy. Miss Klein will require a minimum of two years before she can pull her weight here.

Randy You can say the same thing about a man.

Tom Yes, but in two years Miss Klein will be *Mrs.* somebody, and then what happens?

Randy You tell me.

Tom She will either be "with child" or moving elsewhere when her husband has his job transferred.

Randy Aren't you making some gigantic assumptions?

Tom You made a gigantic assumption offering this broad a job.

Randy She's no "broad"!

Tom Let's say none of the other things happen. How do we know what will happen when she starts working with our men? Suppose she *is* pretty good—is she going to be promoted over some of the men? We don't need a battle of the sexes here.

Randy Why shouldn't she be promoted if she's good enough?

Tom And another thing, how will our clients react if we assign her to them? Won't they feel they're getting second-class service?

Randy Why, you male chauvinist pig! Maybe Gloria Steinem has a point!

Tom She's got a point all right—her pointed head! And so do you for committing us to this girl!

Randy I *had* to—if you'd let the office know where to reach you on your junkets, I could have talked it over with you before making a decision.

Tom What do you mean "junket"? Since when is driving to Harrisburg for a trust seminar a "junket"?

Randy Forget it. What are we going to do about Miss Klein?

Tom   We aren't going to anything about Miss Klein! *You* will withdraw the offer.

Randy   I'll do nothing of the kind. If you'll cut out the bigotry crap and listen to reason—!

Tom   Will you listen to the idiot who's talking about reason?!

Our so-called conversation was interrupted at this point by a call from, as luck would have it, Mary Klein. She was regretful because she felt sure that she would have been happy working for us, but another job offer was just too good to turn down.

DiRicco and Beckman were off the hook, but it's fully six months later and the relations between Tom and me are still strained.

Discussion Questions

1. What miscommunications do you see occurring in this case?

2. How could the communications have been improved?

13

Differentiation Failures:
3. The Frozen Evaluation

This chapter deals with a third form of failure to differentiate. The previous two chapters were concerned with the necessity for indexing on a horizontal basis—that is, with the need for differentiating among people, circumstances, attitudes, objects, and so forth, at a given time. The present chapter calls for a vertical sort of indexing, to take into account the way a person, a situation, a thing, and so on, changes with time.

THE CASE OF FRANK

I want to tell you about a personable man you would probably like and respect. Frank, to give him a name, began life with two strikes against him. To make a long, sordid story short, an alcoholic, violent-tempered father, the frequent absence of a mother who was forced to work away from home, and the influence of a gang of young toughs which Frank joined at 13 were sufficient to turn him into a brash, cynical, externally callous adolescent. After numerous scrapes he finally got into serious trouble in 1941. Caught stealing a car at 18, he was sentenced to two years in prison. Actually, the sentence was a fortunate development for Frank. The grimness of prison life quickly dissolved his brashness. Under the skillful guidance of the prison chaplain and a social therapist, Frank was beginning to gain insights about himself at the time of his release. With 11 months off for good behavior, Frank felt that he had paid his debt to society—but there were those who did not agree. On his return home, his drunken father cursed him and forbade him at first to enter the house, ironically for bringing shame to the family's name. Some of the neighbors openly mocked him as he walked down the street; others pointedly ignored him. He tried to find work, but, even with an abundance of wartime jobs, no one would hire anyone with his record. Frank was understandably relieved when he was drafted two months later.

He sank gratefully into anonymity, but even in the Army there were incidents, as, for example the time an officer's footlocker was burglarized.

Frank, though innocent, was the first to be called in for questioning. But, on the whole, Frank's three years in the Army were helpful. They gave him time to think. He could now see how his environment had driven him into crime. He began to go to church, where he found solace and encouragement and firmly resolved to salvage the rest of his life.

When the war ended, Frank received an honorable discharge and returned home. His father had died during the war. His brother and three sisters had all married, and the sisters had moved away. The brother lived in the family house with his wife and two children, and Frank's mother lived with them.

It was now over five years since Frank had stolen the car, but many had still not forgotten. There was no more open taunting, but many of the neighbors seemed cool and distant. Finding a job was difficult too. It became painfully clear that his record still followed him. Once he lied about his prison sentence and was hired—only to be fired under embarrassing circumstances a week later when he was found out. Police drove up to his home twice during his first month at home to take him into headquarters for questioning about auto thefts.

Finally, Frank moved to another section of the city, and life began to improve. A kindly man hired him as a mechanic's apprentice in his garage. Three years later with steady pay increases he married. Today, he is the likable manager of the garage. He has a lovely wife, and their two children are in college. He still visits his mother from time to time, but, he much prefers to have her come to his home. The old neighborhood hasn't forgotten the old Frank.

Frank has been the victim of a special form of failure to differentiate: the *frozen evaluation*. Some people made evaluations about the Frank of 1941. The Frank of 1986 is virtually another person, but the evaluations have remained unchanged—frozen.

Not all frozen evaluations, of course, are as poignant and enduring as those concerning Frank. I was recently the delighted[1] target of one. Hurrying for an appointment, I was fortunate enough to find the one remaining curb parking space in the area. The space was the one nearest to the corner. When I returned 30 minutes later, the car in the space behind mine had left and a woman was trying energetically but ineptly to park between my car and the one in the third space from the corner. As I unlocked my door, the woman leaned out and proceeded to upbraid me most indecorously for failing to park in the second space, thus depriving her of the corner space, a much easier space in which to park! In her frustration she had unconsciously frozen her evaluation of the parking situation. She had assumed that the now-vacant second space was also empty at the time that I had parked!

[1] Delighted only because I felt that the incident would be an apt illustration for this chapter.

The parking incident was an example of an evaluation made in the present and frozen to apply inappropriately to the past—a sort of retroactive frozen evaluation. The obverse—evaluations that are indiscriminately spread over the future without respect for change, as in the case of Frank—can also have undesirable consequences. Universities, hospitals, and other institutions that receive stipulated bequests and gifts are sometimes hamstrung by this kind of frozen evaluation. Several decades ago, an Eastern college was willed $200,000—a very considerable gift, especially in those days. The donor, an ardent railroader, decided that the industry would always flourish, as indeed it did at the time he wrote his will. Thus he stipulated that his gift was to be invested in 10 particular railroad stocks in prescribed amounts. The investment was to remain undisturbed. Only the dividends were to be used by the college. A foolproof plan, reasoned the benefactor: the college would have a continually increasing endowment with commensurate dividends. Unfortunately, his prediction was faulty. As the years passed, most of the railroads on the list met with difficult times, and several failed. The college, unable to react to changing economic conditions, could only sit by helplessly and watch the investment shrink to a fraction of its original value.

But, in fairness, some wills have been admirably apt. Shah Muhammed I (1740–97), regarded as one of history's cruelest tyrants, instructed that his remains be interred in the city sewer!

When I unconsciously (or perhaps deliberately) spread an evaluation over the future and/or over the past, disregarding changes in whatever I am judging (a person, group, situation, and so on), I have frozen my evaluation. Some of our most destructive frozen evaluations are those we make about ourselves. Take this case of self-imposed torment, for example, as reported by a psychotherapist.

His client was an attractive young woman, aged 17. She had been brought to him by her parents, who were concerned with the extreme shyness she exhibited in the presence of young men or boys. With girls her own age she seemed arrogant, and with older women she appeared self-confident. But she could not even discuss young males without stammering and blushing profusely.

Investigation ruled out medical and home environmental factors. The therapist began meeting with the girl, gradually gaining her confidence. She was finally able to recount this event:

Three years earlier she had attended a children's party where a number of boys were also invited. A door accidentally closed on her fingers. The pain was excruciating, and the girl became ill and vomited. The incident was quickly forgotten by all except the girl, to whom it remained an overwhelming mortification. Although she tried not to think of it, the bitter memory was always reinstated by the presence of boys.

THE ASSUMPTION OF NONCHANGE

The frozen evaluation seems to occur most frequently when one somehow assumes nonchange. Suppose that John Brown, as a freshman, failed one of my courses, mainly through negligence and irresponsibility. And suppose that someone comes to me four years later and asks my appraisal of Brown, whom I have neither seen nor heard of since. I can very confidently say, "Oh, Brown is a poor student," if I assume that John has not changed. But how reliable is this assumption? I think you will agree that I might be doing Brown a great disservice with my obsolete evaluation.

I have frequently been impressed by late bloomers—students who started their academic careers quite unprepossessingly but then found themselves and graduated with honors that one might not have dreamed possible from their work years earlier.

Consider, for delayed maturers, this lackluster trio:

> A as a tyke roamed San Francisco streets, sometimes visiting saloons with his father. The father died (can San Francisco saloons be lethal?), and the boy's family moved back East. Here the young man enrolled at Dartmouth, soon quit, and took a job in a mill. Then he entered Harvard, and again quit. But now things began to look up. He married and taught English (extraordinarily well) at a high school, then at a normal school. But despite having embarked on a successful career, our friend suddenly chucked it all, packed up his family, and headed for England. Is there no hope for this nomad?

> B candidly states in his autobiography: "[I was] considered by all my masters and by my father as a very ordinary boy, rather below the common standard in intellect. To my deep mortification my father once said to me, 'You care for nothing but shooting, dogs, and ratcatching.' . . . As I was doing no good at school, my father wisely took me away at a rather earlier age than usual, and sent me to Edinburgh University. . . . During the three years I spent at Cambridge my time was wasted, as far as the academical studies were considered." Another inauspicious beginning.

> C's early scholastic career was described by Liam Hudson: "At sixteen he failed the entrance examination to the Zurich Polytechnic. He . . . eventually took a good degree, although not good enough to gain him a post in research. One of his professors really did describe him as a lazy dog, and his professor of physics did recommend him to try biology or medicine instead." Another loser, no doubt.

Fortunately, none of these people heeded their early press notices. They refused to freeze their self-evaluations, and they went on to great creative accomplishments. Their names? Robert Frost, Charles Darwin, and Albert Einstein. Incidentally, as children, Einstein along with Thomas Edison and Winston Churchill, would have been termed *learning disabled* had that classification been available then.

Laws, rules, and regulations are another area rife with the premise of permanence. Structures that may be justified *when* they are initially imposed tend to remain on the books long after the conditions that give gave rise to them have changed.

> In Tacoma, Washington, the law says that drivers must stop outside the city and inform the chief of police that they wish to enter Tacoma.

> In Tennessee it is illegal to drive along a highway without having a herald precede you.

> Dress up proper in Hamilton, Ontario. The law decrees that anyone appearing on the streets after midnight without a full-dress suit can be arrested.

> In Idaho it's quite all right to buy a chicken after dark—*provided* that you have a permit from the sheriff!

Ordinarily these relics do no more harm than to clutter up statute books, but occasionally archaic regulations can be troublesome. Early in World War II, Britain had to use every available weapon, even 15-centimeter guns that dated back to the Boer War. A time-and-motion expert found that the manual called for Gunner No. 6 to stand smartly at attention during the entire operation of the gun. "Why is this man doing nothing?" No one knew. Finally, the expert located a veteran of the Boer War who explained: "G-6 is holding the horses."

This leads to a much broader question: How valid is the general premise of nonchange—the assumption that appears to underlie so many of our frozen evaluations? Actually, the notion that there is rest, pause, cessation, and so on, is a pernicious fallacy.

On every level we can observe, or at least presume, process. Everywhere about us we can see evidence of incessant change—of aging, wearing out, growing, eroding, regenerating, decaying, and so forth. Even the solid earth undergoes perpetual change. Considering the dramatic changes, such as earthquakes and volcanic eruptions; the slower ravages of wind, rain, glacial movements; and the even slower migrations of continental plates, the surface of the earth is in continuous motion.

The land surfaces of the world are no more in a state of absolute quiet than are its water surfaces. Minute waves called microseisms are continuously moving through the rocks over the entire surface of the earth, as can be seen by examining a sensitive seismograph record obtained in any part of the world.

And while it may not be too apparent, "the Atlantic widens, the Pacific narrows, the Alps grow higher, Los Angeles slides northward, and Africa splits apart."[2]

And modern-day physicists postulate that on submicroscopic levels there is never-ceasing change. This inert book you are reading is pre-

---

[2]"This Changing Earth," *National Geographic*, 143, no. 1, (1973), p. 1.

sumed to be composed of infinitesimal particles whirling about at the speed of light—the "mad dance of electrons," as Korzybski called it.

On the macroscopic level, consider the exponential rate of technological changes that we have experienced. Consider the last 50,000 years—roughly 800 current lifespans. Thus 800 people living end to end could represent the entire period. Of these 800, 650 lived in caves or less. Only the last 70 had any effective means of communication. Only the last six saw a printed word or could measure heat and cold. Only the last four could measure time with any accuracy. Virtually everything in our material world was invented during the lifetime of the very last person. And more technological progress will probably be made during the first half of the 801st person's life span than during the lifetimes of the previous 800! It has been estimated that knowledge has multiplied eight times since 1850 and that 80 percent of what we know today was discovered in the last 15 years! Hence, the oft-told story of the alumnus who visited his old physics professor. After glancing at a current exam, the former student remarked: "Why, these are the same questions I answered ten years ago!" "Yes," explained the professor, "but the answers are all different now."

Future Change

These have been past changes. How about the future? Can we expect a slowdown, a tapering off? Hardly, the pace will quicken, says the 30,000-member World Future Society. Here are a few of the predictions they made in December 1984:

> By 2000, 100,000 people in the United States will be above the age of 100 and the 85-and-older group will grow faster that any other population segment.
>
> By 1990, due to the destruction of tropical forests, animal, and plant species will become extinct at the rate of one per hour!
>
> By 2020, soil erosion will be rampant. Most of the soil of southern Iowa, for example, will be gone and each acre will require 38 percent more fertilizer and 38 percent more fuel for tilling.
>
> Blue-collar workers will constitute only 10 percent of the U.S. work force by 2000.
>
> By 2050, unless there is a drastic downturn in population growth, more people will be born in *one year* than in the 1,500 years following Christ.
>
> By 1993, at the current rate of increase, health-care costs in the United States will approach 20 percent of our GNP—$1 trillion.
>
> On the brighter side, we may have only 10 percent of the current auto accidents. Sweden is experimenting with microcomputing technology controlling sensors buried in the highway to guide traffic.

Finally, robots are multiplying like rabbits, about 30 percent a year. There should be 35,000 of them installed in the United States by 1990. To replace those missing blue-collar workers?

Currently 200,000 new chemicals are developed every year, and that number will be doubled by the 21st century.

In the face of such manifest transformation—past, present, and future—it seems incredible that some people remain impervious to the realization of change. When the first atom bomb exploded, Albert Einstein said: "Everything has changed—except the thinking in men's minds."

CHANGES IN PEOPLE

And people, despite the perceptions of some, change too—often very slowly, sometimes markedly. Infants become children, adolescents, young adults, middle-aged, and finally elderly people, experiencing gradual and sometimes abrupt changes beyond enumeration.

Humorist Erma Bombeck underscores her own transformations as she records her three daughters discussing Mom:

"This is weird," said the oldest child. "Are we talking about the same Mom? The thin, bright-eyed, dark-haired girl who used to read me stories, bake cookies, paste my baby pictures in the album and giggle a lot?"

The middle child said, "The somber-looking blonde who used to put me to bed at 6:30 and bought me a dog to save on napkins?"

The baby said, "The grayish lady who falls asleep during the six-o'clock news and is going to show me my baby pictures when we finish shooting the roll at my graduation?"

I knew I should have raised 'em in separate parts of the house.[3]

The periods in which people live change too. Consider the attitude shifts of the public. In 1922, for example, *Good Health* published an article that typified current public opinion about smoking:

Tobacco benumbs all the finer sensibilities. That's why men smoke. A man who loves his wife and children is lonely when away and misses the home folks. He smokes, and at once his loneliness is gone. Tobacco fills the place of home and family. It kills the fine sentiment that made him long for the home fires and the familiar faces.

The smoker's business is not prospering. He is worried. He ought to find out the cause and remove it. He smokes instead. He is no longer worried. All is well. But the business fault is not corrected. More business enterprises have run aground in a fog bank of tobacco smoke than have been wrecked by hard times or business panics. Tobacco is an enemy of business as well as of morals. . . .

---

[3]Erma Bombeck, "They Remember Mama . . . in Three Different Versions," *Albany Times-Union*, February 8, 1978, p. 12. Reprinted by permission.

The college "Smoker" is a devil's den, a snare which has lured many thousands of promising young men to mental and moral ruin. The smoking room is sister to the saloon and must be eliminated along with its iniquitous relative, if civilization is to be saved from the demoralization which threatens it.[4]

Contrast that with the public's attitude 40 years later. In 1962, with 8 out of 10 men and 1 out of 3 women smoking, the nonsmoker was almost an oddity! Now the public's sentiments are changing again. In "Heart Facts: 1985," the American Heart Association reports that the mixture of chemicals in cigarette smoke kills 350,000 Americans yearly through heart disease, cancer, and emphysema.

Increasingly, the smoker is being considered not as a moral leper but a witless self-destructionist—even a threat to those who inhale secondhand smoke. "In a conflict between smokers and nonsmokers, whose rights should prevail?" Of 10,000 recent visitors to the Epcot Center, 53 percent sided with the nonsmokers and only 4 percent with the smokers. The remaining 37 percent felt both should receive equal consideration.

For some time, being thin has been fashionable. Cases of anorexia nervosa and bulimia are increasing. Overweight is a dirty word. But this has not always been so. Note this admonition from *The Lady's Realm* of February 1906:

> Angularity of form is invariably ugly, and is best remedied by very careful dieting. Fattening foods of all kinds should be eaten. Farinaceous foods, rice and tapioca, taken in the form of milk puddings, are excellent. Potatoes, butter and beans should be eaten freely. Sweets and pastry are useful in encouraging the development of adipose tissue. Cream also forms a delicious food with fattening properties.

Our attitudes about dress are equally transient. This mandate on beach apparel was rigorously enforced in 1925 by the Wilmette (Illinois) Park District:

> For women blouse and bloomer suits may be worn, with or without skirts, with or without stockings, providing the blouse has one-quarter arm sleeve, or close-fitting arm-holes, and providing the bloomers are full and not shorter than four inches above the knee.
>
> Men's suits must have skirt effect or shirt worn outside of trunks, except when flannel knee pants with belt are worn. The trunks must not be shorter than four inches above the knee, and the shirt must not be shorter than two inches above the bottom of the trunk.

Try posting *that* on today's nude beaches!

But attitude changes concerning smoking, anatomy, and dress seem almost tortoiselike compared to our fickleness regarding what is—or is not— *IN.*

---

[4]"The Immorality of Smoking," *Good Health,* December 1922.

According to Long and Reim's *The American Forecaster 1985:*

In	*Out*
Minivans	Granola bars
Scotch	*Penthouse* and *Playboy*
Wine coolers	*USA Today*
Pornographic movies	Cabbage Patch dolls
Gourmet mustard	Vinyl-covered car roofs
The game of squash	Suntans
Ponytails	Romance novels
Gourmet pizza	Low-alcohol beers
Colorful men's underwear	Beef
White Socks	Happy hours

Of course, by the time you read this, the ins will be outs and the outs will be ancient history. So if you want to keep up to date the authors have this advice: "When the weatherman on TV does it, it is on its way to becoming passé."

CHANGES IN BUSINESS

One of the more dynamic aspects of American life is business. Fluctuation is the rule. Booms and busts, sellers' markets and buyers' markets, inflations and deflations—nothing stands still for very long. The television market is a dramatic example. Thirty-five years ago, seven- and ten-inch black and white sets were being snapped up at high prices. Twenty years ago, dealers in TV-saturated areas were driven to considerable lengths to move their merchandise. One offered a 21-inch set for $100, no down payment. He did a brisk business, but only because of his special enticement: a no-interest $500 loan went with each set! His advertisement: "Pay off your doctor and grocer bills; buy shoes for the kids; make payments on your house, car, and appliances—and have TV too!" Fifteen years ago, *color* TV manufacturers found it impossible to keep up with the demand. Today the industry is swamped with foreign imports—principally Japanese. And tomorrow?

Change is virtually synonymous with our economy. The value of money is a case in point. A dollar is a dollar, right? Wrong! Not with inflation ravaging it. A recent article in the *Wall Street Journal* projected the value of the dollar, assuming that the current rate of inflation, 6 percent, remains constant. This is quite an assumption, incidentally, considering our recent bout with double-digit inflation. Other factors being equal, your salary would double in 12 years, triple in seven more years, and quadruple in another five years. That's the good news. The bad news is that prices would escalate as well.

Few aspects of organizational experience have changed as dramatically as the manner of supervising employees. The following were office rules insisted upon by Zachary U. Geiger, a California carriage and wagon maker, a century ago:

Office employes will sweep the floors, dust the furniture, shelves and showcases. Each clerk will bring in a bucket of water and a scuttle of coal for the day's business. Make your pens carefully. You may whittle nibs to your individual taste.

This office will open at 7 A.M. and close at 8 P.M. except on the Sabbath, when it will remain closed. Every employee should lay aside from each pay a goodly sum of his earnings for his benefit during his declining years, so that he will not become a burden on the charity of his betters.

Any employee who smokes Spanish cigars, uses liquor in any form, gets shaved at a barbershop or frequents pool or public halls will give me good reason to suspect his worth, intentions, integrity and honesty. The employee who has performed his labors faithfully and without fault for a period of five years in my service, who has been thrifty and attentive to his religious duties, and is looked upon by his fellow man as a substantial and law-abiding citizen will be given an increase of five cents per day in his pay, provided a just return in profit from the business permits it.

In summary, "The only thing constant in life," as La Rochefoucauld wrote, "is change."

A DURABLE FALLACY

Subtle Changes

It seems odd that such a palpable fallacy as the notion of nonchange should persist. Among the reasons for the fallacy's durability is that some changes occur so gradually that we are insensitive to them. We often fail to keep abreast of the changes in the people closest to us (friends, spouse, children, subordinates). Because we are with them so constantly, their incremental alterations may be imperceptible to us.

Tolerance for Change

Another factor that protects the fallacy of nonchange is that change is generally less comfortable than nonchange. Indeed change can be downright terrifying, especially if it involves the unknown, the unpredictable, the unexplained, and thus, the not understood. Alvin Toffler's title for his best-seller, *Future Shock*, was most apt. The accelerated changes that he and John Naisbitt *(Megatrends)* anticipate can be thoroughly disturbing.

Thomas Holmes[5] has been studying the cumulative effect of change upon people. His overall conclusion is that we seem to have a certain tolerance for the changes we experience in a given period. If we exceed that tolerance, we increase our chances of becoming ill. "If it takes too much effort

---

[5]See Thomas E. Holmes and Ella M. David, *Life Change Events Research, 1966–1978* (New York: Praeger, 1984).

to cope with the environment we have less to spare for preventing disease," says Holmes.

Accordingly, he has assigned numerical values to various kinds of changes. Here are the top ten on his Social Readjustment Rating Scale:

Life event	Value
1. Death of a spouse	100
2. Divorce	73
3. Marital separation	65
4. Detention in jail or other institution	63
5. Death of a close family friend	63
6. Major personal injury or illness	53
7. Marriage	50
8. Fired at work	47
9. Marital reconciliation	45
10. Retirement	45

Here's how it works—suppose in a 12-month period, a person has a marital separation (65); then a reconciliation (45); then a divorce (73); and then gets fired (47). That racks up 230 points. Holmes contends that that person has better than a 50 percent chance of becoming ill in the near future.

Some of us might become ill with far fewer points and that is part of my uneasiness with the numbers and the change categories. I believe different people value a given change quite differently. A divorce for one person might be devastating, for another, it would be relatively unimportant.

However, there are several aspects that strike me as valid and helpful:

1.   The notions of changes *piling up* on us seem authentic. What may be a minor irritation on one day may become a major stress on another day when one is oversaturated with change.

2.   Notice that good as well as bad changes can be stressful. Marriage and marital reconciliation and, later in Holmes' list, outstanding personal achievement, vacation, and Christmas may be positive, but they are still changes.

3.   Holmes is constructive suggesting that if we can anticipate life changes and plan for them, we can reduce their stressful impact.

The Language Factor

Language is another important perpetuation of the insidious assumption of nonchange.

When we trace back to the roots of our language, and we discover many clues as to why we talk and behave as we do. The basic form and structure of the English language were laid down in ancient Greece. Now consider what life must have been like then—comparatively slow, static, and unchanging. Not much written history to give a sense of process. To us the average Athenian's life would seem extraordinarily placid—one day very much like any other.

Consider, then, that our language was spawned by this relatively constant society. Is it any wonder that the Greeks created a language that reflected their static existence? The result is that, although we live in an enormously more dynamic environment, we still use a languge that strongly implies nonchange, rest, and permanence—and thus are seduced to overlook change.

Note how incredibly easy it is in our language to speak or write (or listen or read) without taking time into account. Read each of the paragraphs below, and decide the date line of each. After you have dated all three, read the answers which follow.

(A)

Prompted by widespread fears that new weapons of mass destruction might wipe out Western civilization, the Pope today issued a bill forbidding their use by any Christian state against another, whatever the provocation.

Date _____

(B)

We need law and order. Yes, without law and order our nation cannot survive. Elect us, and we shall restore law and order.

Date _____

(C)

The earth is degenerating these days. There are signs civilization is coming to an end. Bribery and corruption abound. Violence is everywhere. Children no longer respect and obey their parents.

Date _____

(A) could have been a plea by Pope John Paul II but it was actually Pope Innocent in 1139 and the weapons had nothing to do with nuclear or biological warfare.

(B) could have been contemporary campaign rhetoric but it was Adolph Hitler in Hamburg in 1932.

(C) was from an Assyrian tablet, circa 3000 B.C.

And therein lies an important inadequacy of our language system—the prevailing failure to specify time.

CORRECTIVES

The two preceding chapters described the need for discriminating among people, qualities, traits, and so forth, without regard for time differences. The current chapter calls for time differentiation. Let me say this a little differently.

The frozen evaluation was defined as a judgment set in concrete—an evaluation that remained constant and inflexible despite changes in its object. It seduces us to see now as forever. The basic problem, therefore, is to keep our evaluations in pace with past and future changes in the person or situation—whatever it is that we are evaluating. When the object changes, then the evaluation ought to change correspondingly. How can we accomplish this? How can we keep from freezing our evaluations, and how can we thaw those already frozen?

Internalize the Premise of Change

Substitute the conscious premise of change for the unconscious notion of nonchange. Believe firmly in the process nature of people, of situations, of things, and so forth, and you will be more likely to keep your evaluations up to date.

Apply the When Index

A very simple, yet effective, device for implementing the awareness of change is the When Index. Using the When Index is simply assigning a date. For example, the following Associated Press release appeared in 1950:

Williams Signs with Red Sox for Record Baseball Pay of $125,000
    Boston, Feb. 7 (AP)—Ted Williams, the Red Sox slugger, today signed the highest salaried contract in baseball history—for an estimated $125,000.
    Babe Ruth's $80,000 salary in 1930 and '31 was tops in the old days.[6]

At first glance, Mr. Williams seems to have fared considerably better financially than did Mr. Ruth. But the Foundation for Economic Education, Inc., made a revealing analysis by When-Indexing (i.e., dating) the purchasing power of the take-home dollar. See Figure 13.1.

To update this illustration: In 1985, Pitcher Rick Sutcliffe graciously accepted $1,950,000 from the Chicago Cubs for his services. You'll be re-

---

[6]Appeared in *The New York Times*, February 8, 1950. Reprinted by permission of the Associated Press.

FIGURE 13–1

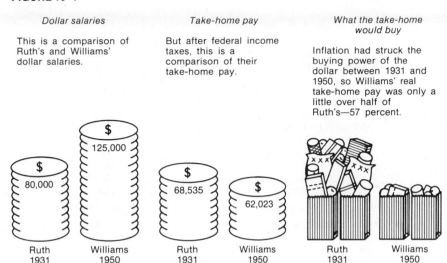

Dollar salaries	*Take-home pay*	*What the take-home would buy*
This is a comparison of Ruth's and Williams' dollar salaries.	But after federal income taxes, this is a comparison of their take-home pay.	Inflation had struck the buying power of the dollar between 1931 and 1950, so Williams' real take-home pay was only a little over half of Ruth's—57 percent.

| | $ 80,000 | $ 125,000 | $ 68,535 | $ 62,023 | | |
| Ruth 1931 | Williams 1950 | Ruth 1931 | Williams 1950 | Ruth 1931 | Williams 1950 |

If Ted Williams were to have as much buying power in 1950 as Babe Ruth had in 1931, he would have had to be paid $327,451.

lieved to know that despite inflation, taxation, and the cost of living index, Sutcliffe's purchasing power matched Ruth's—but just barely!

The advent of cryogenics has spawned a poignant story concerning the relevance of When-Indexing. It seems that a rich man with a terminal illness was nearing death. He decided that he would have his body frozen in the hope that if sometime in the future a cure would be found he could be thawed and restored to health. Sure enough, 20 years later his dream was fulfilled and he recovered. His first act was to get to a pay phone and call his brokerage house. "How's my IBM stock?" he asked. "$35,000 a share," was the response. "That's marvelous!" he exclaimed. Just then the operator interrupted, "Your time is up. Please deposit $500 for another three minutes."

That story no longer seems quite so funny—not with serious economists such as John McCarthy extrapolating that if prices change in the next 40 years as they have in the last 40, then the average family's income will be $124,000, a college president's salary will be $600,000, homes will sell for $300,000 to $500,000, and bread for $7 a loaf!

The When Index (which may be expressed as a mental or even an explicit superscript—e.g.: the United States[1986] is not the United States[1979] is a reminder of the constant flux that characterizes the world in which we live. These three brief cases suggest its usefulness:

The Case of Richard Roe[7]

Richard Roe embezzled $10,000 in 1978 and was soon apprehended, convicted, and sentenced. Roe in 1986 has served his term. Roe[1986] is not Roe[1978]. There are bound to have been changes. But this does not mean that a prospective employer does not have the right to investigate Roe thoroughly before hiring him. Indeed, it would be imprudent to fail to do so. But no employer, it seems to me, has the moral justification to refuse to hire without an investigation. To dismiss Roe summarily as an undated ex-convict may not only deprive the employer of an able worker, but more important, it may contribute to Roe's destruction as a useful citizen.

The Case of Earl Wood[8]

Earl Wood, 40, fell 25 feet to his death from a second-story fire escape door in the Ellington Company.

Police believed that Wood, an assembler, was unaware when he stepped from the door that the fire escape had been removed for repairs. Employees said that Wood frequently spent his rest break on the fire escape.

Even a structure as seemingly unchangeable as a fire escape is not always the same. Fire escape yesterday is not fire escape today. Had Wood engrained the habit of When-Indexing, he would have been prompted to look before stepping out onto a fire escape that was not there.

The Case of David

Six-year-old-David had had his experiences with inoculations, so his mother was not too surprised that he protested vigorously when she told him that he was to receive a polio shot the following afternoon.

"David," she countered, "I know how you feel, and I am willing to make a bargain with you. Now, the shot is not going to hurt you today or tomorrow morning, is it?" "No," he admitted. "And it isn't going to hurt when we leave the house and while we are driving to the doctor's office?" "No." "And it isn't going to hurt when we are sitting in the waiting room, reading the comic books?" "No." "Or when the doctor rubs your arm with alcohol and gets the hypodermic ready?" "No." "Then there would be no sense in crying or yelling at any of these times, would there?" "No, I guess not." "But it *will* hurt when he sticks the hypodermic into your arm, right?" "Yes!" "Well, young man, at that *time* you may yell your head off!"

David agreed, and when the inoculation actually occurred, a relaxed David considered the prick hardly worth yelling about, and his When-Indexing had spared him needless anxiety.

Try this sort of When-Indexing on yourself the next time you make a dental appointment or anticipate some other unpleasant experience. As Seneca wrote, "There is nothing more miserable and foolish than anticipation." A wise old professor of mine realized this as he viewed the self-

---

[7]Fictitious.

[8]The names are disguised. Otherwise the account is accurate.

imposed anxiety associated with tardiness: "I'm never late until I get there."

The Administration of Change

So much for the individual's coping with change. What about organizations? So often organizations must adapt to changes if they are to compete successfully, or even survive. Here are a few suggestions[9] for the manager who is required to administer changes:

1. *Involve your people in planning for changes.* It will help them understand rather than fear the change. Planning will allay possible concern that management is "trying to pull a fast one". The involvement may generate useful ideas from people closest to the affected activity.

2. *Use feedback so people can express their resistance.* Letting people get it off their chests usually reduces resistance. At least it will give you a more accurate conception of why they are resisting.

3. *Consider group aspects.* Will the change break up congenial work groups? Disrupt commuting schedules and carpools? Affect vacation plans? Assign people to a group with incompatible standards of conduct?

4. *Build a trusting work climate.* Mistrust and distrust occur when people have incomplete or incorrect information. They often feel helpless and impotent, sensing they cannot influence the situation.

> To build a trusting climate, tell the truth. It's been proven time and again that people would rather have bad news than no news. Given the facts, they feel they can do something about a problem.

5. *Be certain that your people know the real goals or reasons for the change.* Be sure people do not create erroneous assumptions and circulate false rumors regarding the change.

6. *Use problem-solving techniques.* (See Chapter 17, "Blindering") Identify the *real* problem. You may think: "If only I could only get Sam to retire, the morale of the group would improve greatly." It's unlikely, however, that deep-seated attitudes are caused by a single individual in a group.

7. *Be sensitive to timing.* It's generally better to get people favorably disposed toward the advent of, say, automated data processing before rather than after the installation is made.

SUMMARY

A frozen evaluation is one that is spread unconsciously (or perhaps deliberately) over the future and/or over the past, without regard for change. The frozen evaluation may take on a great variety of forms, not the least

---

[9]Gordon L. Lippitt, Jack Mossop, and Petter Langseth, *Implementing Organization Change* (San Francisco: Jossey-Bass, 1985).

serious of which are those that have to do with our evaluations of ourselves. Underlying most frozen evaluations is the assumption of nonchange—a fallacious and often unconsciously held notion that there is rest, permanence, constancy. The When Index reminds us to take change into account in our evaluations—to distinguish among time^1, time^2, time^3, and so on.

DISCUSSION QUESTIONS

1. What do indiscrimination, polarization, and frozen evaluation have in common? How are they distinguished?

2. The Case of Frank is about a man who found it difficult to live down his past. Do you know other people who have resigned themselves to others' frozen evaluations of them? Under what conditions is this most likely to happen?

3. "But always we begin by speaking as we think, and end by thinking as we speak. . . ."—Lester Sinclair. What are the implications of this statement? If we were to improve our language system, would this improve our thinking? What are the practical limitations on improving or changing a language system?

4. "No man dies in the world into which he was born."—Margaret Mead. What did she mean? Do you agree? How does this statement bear on this chapter?

5. Why is it possible in English and in many other languages to talk and write datelessly—that is, to make declarative statements, for example, without specifying the time to which those statements apply?

6. The "Case of David" suggests a way of using the When Index to minimize anxiety over future events. What do you think of this notion? Is there positive value in worry—especially if such concern helps us to prevent or avoid or cope with a problem?

7. Report upon an incident, perhaps involving yourself, in which frozen evaluations played a role. Why did the incident occur? What could have been done to prevent or correct the situation? What measures could prevent a recurrence of such frozen evaluations?

CASES

CASE 13–1

Apex Forgings*

Stan Liska

This is going to be a little hard to believe, but I swear it's true. I'm an industrial relations manager for our plant, Apex Forgings. Under Section 7, Article 17, of our basic agreement with the union, employees may bid on permanent job vacancies. These vacancies are posted on the company bulletin board. Such jobs are awarded solely on a seniority basis—the man with the longest service gets the job, regardless of his background. I don't agree with it—but that's the contract.

So, naturally, the man who gets the job often has to be trained for it. Sometimes the training is done by the lame duck who is on the job but will be released from it as soon as the new man can take over.

Last summer a job vacancy occurred in Department 23, the Axle Machining Department. Accordingly, an End Face Operator vacancy was posted. George Morales, 27, a Puerto Rican, was awarded the job, and since he had no prior experience on that job or in that department, he was to be trained by the incumbent, Fred Meister, 32. Morales' English was none too good but I wasn't concerned. He had done a good job in Department 14, and I felt he would learn quickly.

At the end of the first day Morales filled out his production record card exactly as Meister had completed his. I'm still not clear as to whether Fred knew what George was doing. Anyway, the next day Fritz Heinsohn, 55, the foreman of Department 23, really chewed out Morales.

> **Heinsohn**   What the hell do you think you're doing? The way you filled out your card there would be twice as many axles turned out as possible. We don't need any wise guys around here. You don't put nothin' on this card, is that understood?

Morales had received no previous instruction on filling out the time card, but he sensed that Heinsohn was in no mood for discussion, so he just said he understood. Morales thought Heinsohn had uttered some racial slur under his breath as he walked away, but George couldn't be sure, so he let it go.

---

*All names have been disguised.

Two weeks later Morales was considered trained, so Meister left for greener pastures and Morales was left alone. On the morning of the next day, Heinsohn appeared again and laced into George.

Heinsohn What do you mean by not putting anything on your damned card? How the hell are we supposed to know how many axles you're turning out? Do you think we're mind readers around here?

Morales started to explain, but Heinsohn interrupted.

Heinsohn Hell, you spics are all alike—if they're not punks, they're dummies. Now, you keep a record of how many axles you run and put it on the card. And don't let me hear no more crap from you.

At that, Heinsohn turned and walked away. To make a sad story short, Morales fell off a little in his production that first week and Heinsohn kept jumping on him. George finished out the week—and just never came back. My honest opinion is that we lost a good man.

You might wonder how Heinsohn is regarded by Al Mayer, our superintendent. The answer is highly. Heinsohn gets the most product out the back door. Mayer simply ignores Fritz's turnover, low department morale, scrappage, and giving a bad example to the other foremen.

Discussion Questions

1. What patterns of miscommunication seem to be involved in this case?
2. How could these patterns of miscommunication have been prevented?

CASE 13–2

"We're Better than Orange"*

Blue versus Orange!!!

Orange is the number-one team in the country according to a poll of those who know. They do not rate Blue within the top 20. Conclusion: Blue cannot possibly beat Orange next Monday night at Orange.

We must concede that the odds are against Blue. Orange is undefeated this year, and is invincible at home, having won 130 games or so in a row on its home court. Looks bad, doesn't it?

Before I go any farther, let's look at some of the records. Tuesday evening, we played Green here. The score was 88 to 55 at the end of the game, Blue on the long end of the scoring.

Earlier this year, Green played Red at Red. It lost to Red by only four points. The amazing bit in this comparison is that Red held the aforemen-

---

*The colors stand for various colleges and universities. Otherwise the above article is a reprint from Blue U's student newspaper.

tioned Orange squad to a four-point spread on a neutral court. Figuring a home floor edge of ten points, Red is only four points worse than Orange, but is worse than Green by six points. Therefore Orange is two points worse than Green. Seeing that we beat Green by 33 points at home, I subtract 10 points, which shows me that we are 23 points better than Green. Since Green is two points better than Orange, I have come to the conclusion that Blue is 25 points better than Orange on a neutral court and 13 points better than Orange at Orange.

This all makes for an interesting twist in the records, which will show you that nothing is impossible in this game called basketball. So there you are.

So, c'mon Blue, we know you can do it! We're with you!

[According to this reasoning, Blue will defeat Orange by 13 points. Blue actually lost by 21.]

Discussion Questions

1. What does this case have to do with frozen evaluations?
2. What was the author's motive for writing this piece?

CASE 13-3

Ice Cream and Advertising*

James Clifford, an account executive with a Detroit advertising firm, had learned through a friend that a certain Michigan manufacturer of ice cream had developed a revolutionary process for packaging ice cream. He reasoned that the president of the ice-cream firm might be a good prospect for an advertising program designed to capitalize on the packaging innovation. He asked his friend, who was also an acquaintance of the president, to arrange an interview for him. He had hoped to meet with the president, Mr. Shepherd, before the innovation became common knowledge among the agencies. Clifford's friend made the appointment with Shepherd's secretary.

Meanwhile, Clifford set about preparing a brochure containing a detailed plan of demonstrations in Michigan and the Midwest and several illustrations of displays for stores.

Unfortunately, Shepherd's secretary had forgotton to notify her employer of the appointment. When Clifford arrived, she suddenly recalled her error and with great embarrassment admitted her mistake to Mr. Shepherd. The president, a kindly man in his 70s, remarked; "Oh, I don't

---

*All names have been disguised.

think any harm's been done. Since the error has been on our end, he shouldn't suffer. I'm not too busy now anyway, so you can have him come in. But I think it would be best to explain the slipup to him so he will know that he'll have to start from scratch with me since I know nothing about him or the purpose of his visit."

The secretary explained her error to Clifford and showed him to Mr. Shepherd's office.

Shepherd   I'm terribly sorry this happened, Mr. Clifford, but I'm sure it won't hamper our meeting.

Clifford   That's perfectly all right, sir. Your secretary explained the situation to me, and we all slip up once in a while. *(Smiling)* After all, they're still putting erasers on pencils.

Shepherd   *(Smiling)* Well, it's nice of you to be so gracious. Now, what did you have in mind?

Clifford began to discuss the company's new packaging process and the desirability of setting up an advertising campaign. He was taking the brochure from his briefcase when Shepherd interrupted:

Shepherd   *(Sadly)* Young man, I'm afraid my secretary's error was more costly than I had thought.

Clifford   How is that, sir?

Shepherd   Why, you've made your trip for nothing.

Clifford   I don't understand.

Shepherd   Why, if I had known you were going to talk about advertising I could have saved you a trip.

Clifford   You mean you've already signed with another agency?

Shepherd   Not at all. I simply don't advertise—never have and never will.

Clifford   You've never advertised?!

Shepherd   Never. My grand-dad founded this company 80 years ago on the theory that a good product will sell itself—and he was right. My dad followed his practice, and so do I. So you see, I'm not about to waste any money now on advertising. I just don't believe in it.

Clifford made a few vain attempts to dissuade the old man, but it was obvious that Shepherd was unalterably opposed to advertising his product. In resignation Clifford returned to Detroit, where he reported to his supervisor:

Clifford   I simply don't understand the man. He's the kind of guy who wakes up in the morning to his GE electric clock; brushes his teeth with Crest; puts on his Arrow shirt, Kuppenheimer suit, and Florsheim shoes, eats his Kellogg's corn flakes, drives his Cadillac to work, and then says, "I don't believe in advertising"!

Discussion Questions

1. Are there any frozen evaluations going on in this case?
2. Is Mr. Shepherd a lost cause insofar as progress is concerned?
3. How could this evaluation be corrected?

CASE 13–4

The Frozen Andy*

William Lyon

Phil entered my office as my stomach ascended to my throat. His crimson face warned me that I was in for another unpleasant encounter. A fleeting thought reminded me that I should have better control of my inner response by now—this was not the first time.

"Why did you put Andy on the Green job?" screamed Phil with uncontrollable anger. I motioned for him to close the door. The slam echoed down the corridor.

"Why?" was my inept response.

"Why? You know damn well he's immature as hell. He doesn't know when to be serious. He'll run Tom up a tree. Just like last fall on that packing job."

I looked out the window to compose myself. The coloring of the leaves was impressive.

"But Phil, that was a year ago. Andy has advanced significantly and has had favorable reports in the last six months. I felt he could handle the job and in fact feel we have to give him something more challenging so he can grow."

"He's not going to grow on my accounts!" Phil was again at the screaming level. "I was against hiring him in the first place. He just doesn't have it—and never will!"

"But what about his favorable reports?" I queried.

"I don't give a damn what others say or feel about him. I don't want him on my jobs. It's just too big a risk. Don't you see?" he pleaded with authority. "Get him off!" The door opened, and a red neck disappeared through it.

Evidently Phil had been in personnel and had seen the long-run schedules that I had been working on. I proceeded to review the matter with Simon, the managing partner. After several minutes of discussion, he suggested that he should talk with Phil to correct the situation. I left his office somewhat relieved, feeling that Si would stand behind Andy (and me).

That afternoon my phone rang. It was Si. He said that he had had a long discussion, somewhat heated, with Phil. He told me that it didn't appear

---

*All names have been disguised.

that Phil was going to change his mind and that I should make the necessary changes in the schedule.

Discussion Questions
1. What patterns of miscommunication do you see in this case?
2. How could they be prevented in the future?

CASE 13–5

Money Troubles*

The money market can be treated in the same way as any commodity market. In general, when the supply of money is plentiful, its price (which is the rate of interest) will be lower than when its supply is short. This, however, is only part of the story, since it is widely known that federal controls on the money supply are in force. The incident arose out of the changing price of money.

As a farm loan appraiser for an insurance company's mortgage loan department, I am charged with several duties. Perhaps the most important of these are the recommendations of new loan business.

Not long ago, the money supply was diminishing significantly and mortgage money was becoming scarce. Those of us in the field were aware of the tighter money market, but no policy change in regard to the interest rate was issued from the home office. In my own case, I had two farm loan applications on my desk, to be submitted at the then prevailing interest rate. These were to be sent to the home office for approval as soon as the appraisal report was completed and as soon as proper credit checks were made. The following day, I mailed these cases to the home office and assured the applicants that their cases would be approved.

In that same day's mail, I received a memorandum stating that "all farm loan applications must be submitted at a ½ percent higher interest rate, effective as of the date of this memorandum."

The two loan applications that were submitted at the old rate were committed and mailed to the applicants at the new rate. Both applicants were very unhappy about the change in their applications. They felt that they had been double-crossed. There is no question that the company and I lost considerable goodwill not only with these people but with many of their friends to whom they complained about our treatment of them.

Discussion Questions
1. Who is responsible for the loss of goodwill described by the author?
2. What does this case have to do with the frozen evaluation?
3. What measures could have prevented or ameliorated this incident?

---

*Printed by permission of the author, whose name has been withheld by request.

CASE 13-6

John Lundy*

John Lundy, 40, had been a press operator with the Romaine Company for over 15 years. For the past four years, he had operated mechanical forming presses. His most frequent job was making top and bottom caps for water heater jackets. His raw material was a sheet of 18–20 gauge cold-rolled steel. The sheet was eight feet long and two feet wide, and it weighed about ten pounds. The procedure was to grasp the sheet with a suction cup and to slide it on rollers to a stop at which the first two feet of the strip were properly positioned under the press. He would then press two buttons simultaneously, which caused the machine to press down with a force of 100 tons, forming the cap.[1] The press would rise automatically, whereupon John reached under with both hands and lifted and removed the cap and placed it on his stack of finished pieces. He then moved the next two feet of sheet under the press and repeated the process. Thus, he made four caps from each strip.

One day the press suddenly malfunctioned. John had pressed the buttons, the press descended and rose, and he started to reach for the cap. Without warning, the press descended a second time and Lundy narrowly escaped serious injury. Cautiously he tried the machine again, and it double-hit again. He called Frank Torgeson, his foreman, and complained about the press. Torgeson immediately ordered the machine shut down and called maintenance. In the meantime, he assigned Lundy to a similar press nearby.

Three hours later two maintenance men arrived, briefly discussed the machine with the foreman and set to work. They suspected that a faulty connection in the machine's electrical system permitted a second cycle. Accordingly, they climbed to the top of the press, about 18 feet above the floor, and called to John: "Hey, Lundy, do you want to come over here and go through an operation so we can see what's happening from up here?"

"OK," John replied, and he walked to the press. He cupped the sheet, slid it into place, and pressed the buttons. The press descended, and John reached under for the cap—the press recycled, and his right hand was severed at the wrist.

Discussion Questions

1. How do you account for this tragedy?
2. What patterns of miscommunication appear to be involved in this case?
3. How could this accident have been prevented?

---

*All names have been disguised.

[1]The buttons were positioned at eye level and spread apart in such a way as to require the use of both hands to operate them, thus protecting the operator's hands from injury as the press descended.

CASE 13-7

Be a Millionaire!

In 1978, the U.S. Congress created the National Commission of Social Security. The Commission's objective was to study options in the financing of retirement. Chaired by Milton Gwirtzman, an attorney, the Commission reported its recommendations to the Congress in 1981. The report included the suggestion that virtually all individuals be allowed to invest in Individual Retirement Accounts (IRAs) and that the maximum annual amount of contribution be sizable. The proposal became law and the modified IRAs became available in 1982.

Anyone could now invest up to $2,000 of earnings or the entire amount of earnings, whichever was less, in an IRA. A married couple could invest up to $2,250. If both spouses were working, each could contribute up to $2,000 for a total of $4,000. Investors could deduct the amount of their contributions from reportable income on their federal income-tax returns. Thus all investments and any appreciation of funds in the IRAs would be tax-deferred until withdrawal, normally retirement, at which time one's taxable income would presumably be lower.

Banks, savings and loans, and other thrift institutions, and many other financial organizations began to compete aggressively for customers to open IRA accounts.

This advertisement of a certain savings and loan association was fairly typical:

BE A MILLIONAIRE!

Open an IRA with us.

Your money is insured up to $100,000 by the Federal Savings and Loan Insurance Corporation.

Your investment will be compounded DAILY at 12 percent.

Invest $2,000 a year for 30 years and you will retire with $652,000!

A couple investing $4,000 a year will have more than a MILLION DOLLARS!

Mr. Girtzman objected strongly to such advertising in a letter to Paul Volcker, chairman of the Federal Reserve Board.

Discussion Questions
1. What was Mr. Gwirtzman complaining about? What is wrong with the ad?
2. What does this case have to do with the frozen evaluation?

14

Intensional Orientation: 1. A General Statement

This chapter will not deal with a specific pattern of communication difficulty. The purpose here is to describe and discuss a general orientation toward the relationship between words and what we use them to stand for—between the map and the territory.[1] In the two following chapters, we shall examine a number of forms of misevaluation and miscommunication to which this orientation can lead.

One way to define the *intensional* (the *s* is intentional) *orientation* is to show it in action.

THE GRAHAM UNIVERSITY TAX CASE[2]

Graham is a large private university located in Allyn, a pleasant suburban community. For years, town–gown relations had been quite amicable except for one point of friction—taxation.

Graham held two types of exemption from real estate taxation. Exemption$_1$ concerned its educational property, that is, property used directly for educational purposes, such as classrooms, libraries, administration buildings, dormitories, and athletic fields. No one quarreled over this exemption, however, for it was granted to all schools and colleges.

Exemption$_2$, on the other hand, covered Graham's investment properties. These were real estate holdings that were not directly used for educational purposes, although the income from them was. It was around this exemption that the friction revolved. Interest in the issue waxed and waned, but there was always an underlying current of resentment among many of the townspeople. It was generally believed that the university's exemption had removed a sizable portion of the suburb's real estate from the tax rolls, thus increasing the taxation on the individual's property.

---

[1]See the map-territory analogy on pp. 208–9.
[2]The names have been disguised; otherwise the details are factual.

The debate became especially heated during election years. One aldermanic candidate, for example, published a statement in the *Allyn Times* to the effect that Graham's exemption$_2$ was depriving Allyn of tax revenue from 6 percent of its area and 10 percent of its assessed value. Other published statements, letters to the editor, and so on contended that the exemption covered as much as 50 percent of Allyn's real estate.

And there were citizens who supported the exemption. "So what if we have to pay more taxes," they argued, "isn't it worth it? Graham has put Allyn on the map, made us a cultural center. Moreover, Graham's thousands of students contribute to the economic health of the community with their purchases in Allyn."

And so the discussing and the contending and the arguing continued until the *Times* decided to do something about it. It hired competent real estate taxation specialists to determine the status of tax exemptions in Allyn. After a comprehensive survey, the specialists submitted their report: 16 percent of the total of Allyn's real estate was tax exempt. This included not only Graham's property, educational and investment, but that of the other colleges, the private and public schools, the churches, the municipal buildings, the libraries, the hospitals, the parks, and so forth. The subject of debate—Graham's investment property—constituted only one half of 1 percent of Allyn's real estate!

The friction disappeared almost immediately. Even the most ardent disputants admitted: "If that's all it amounts to—it's hardly enough to fuss about."

INTENSION AND EXTENSION

The Graham case involved a problem that was approached in two vitally different ways. For years people had been verbalizing, theorizing, speculating about Graham's exemption$_2$. They talked, they discussed, they disputed. The more they talked about the problem, the farther they seemed to move away from it. They became so absorbed in their personal maps of the territory that it became increasingly difficult for them to examine the territory itself. They were intensionally oriented—more concerned, that is, with the feelings, thoughts, suppositions, beliefs, theories, and so on, inside their skins than with the life facts outside.

Finally, the *Allyn Times* took a radically different tack. "Look," said the publisher, "all this talking about the problem has only succeeded in aggravating the situation. Let's quit talking for once and go out and do some looking—let's go out and see just what this exemption amounts to." The publisher's stop talking and start looking approach is characteristic of the extensional orientation.

We are oriented intensionally when we are predisposed to become absorbed with the map and to neglect the territory. This tendency is epitomized in this charming fable.

A Man Lived by the Side of the Road . . .
. . . and sold hot dogs.
He . . . had no radio.
He had trouble with his eyes, so he had no newspaper.
But he sold good hot dogs.
He put up a sign on the highway, telling how good they were.
He stood by the side of the road and cried: "Buy a hot dog, mister." And peo-
ple bought.
He increased his meat and bun orders, and he bought a bigger store to take
care of his trade.
He got his son home from college to help him. But then something happened.
His son said: "Father, haven't you been listening to the radio? There's a big
depression on. The international situation is terrible, and the domestic sit-
uation is even worse."
Whereupon his father thought: "Well, my son has been to college. He listens
to the radio and reads the papers, so he ought to know."
So, the father cut down his bun order, took down his advertising sign, and no
longer bothered to stand on the highway to sell hot dogs.
His hot-dog sales fell almost overnight.
"You were right, son," the father said to the boy. "We are certainly in the
middle of a great depression."[3]

Extensional orientation, on the other hand, is the predisposition to inspect the territory first—and then to create verbal maps to correspond
with it. One of the greatest extensionalists in history was Galileo. Time
and again he refused to be governed by the revered maps—the theories
and postulates—of his time and went instead to observe the territory for
himself. The Aristotelian law of falling bodies was one of these unquestioned maps. Postulated more than 19 centuries earlier, it held that the velocity of falling bodies was directly proportional to their weight—a notion
consistent with the prevailing theory of gravitation. But Galileo had to see
for himself and proceeded to the Leaning Tower of Pisa, where he exploded the law and started the world thinking about a new theory of grav-
ity.

Sherlock Holmes owed his success largely to his extensionality:

Dr. Watson   What do you imagine it means?

Holmes   I have no data yet. It is a capital mistake to theorize before
one has data. Insensibly, one begins to twist facts to suit theories
instead of theories to suit facts.

—"Scandal in Bohemia" (Arthur Conan Doyle)

INTENSIONALITY: SOME MANIFESTATIONS

Basically, we behave intensionally when we respond to our maps (our
feelings, imaginings, visualizations, formulations, attitudes, theories, pre-

---

[3]From a Quaker State Metals Co. advertisement.

conceptions, evaluations, inferences) as if we were responding to the territory (objects, people, happenings, relationships, things, and so on). Trouble tends to come when the map is an inadequate representation of the territory. Take the case of a young soldier in World War II. Seriously wounded and unconscious, he desperately needed a transfusion, but blood of his unusual type was unavailable, and there was scant hope of acquiring some in time. Fortunately, a black soldier in a neighboring battalion heard about the boy's condition and volunteered for a transfusion. His blood type was suitable; the transfusion was made, and the soldier's life was saved. On the road to recovery several days later, the young man was told of the man who had given his blood. The boy became almost uncontrollable with fear and rage. He was overwhelmed by a lifelong delusion that having the black man's blood in his veins would change the color of his skin and even alter the shape and size of his lips and nose, the texture of his hair, and so forth.

Instead of reacting to the territory, a situation in which he was generously given lifesaving blood, the young soldier responded in terms of his fallacious map.

Consider another kind of map. What is your image of a prison? According to studies, most people, including most prisoners, visualize stone walls, iron bars, and armed guards. So imposing is this perception, conclude some authorities, that the vast majority of inmates never even try to break out. Therefore, reasoned prison officials in Northern Ireland, in these taut economic times, could we not reduce to cost of incarceration without reducing the effect? The walls and bars are already here so let's reduce the guards. Reverend Ian Paisley reports that dummies were manning the observation posts when 38 men broke out of Maze Prison recently!

To a greater extent than most of us are aware we are conditioned to react intensionally by our environment. Society's customs, traditions, norms, mores, and so on, are maps—sometimes spurious ones—which become so ingrained in us that we often treat them as territories.

I can still recall the hubbub that occurred a few years ago when a college professor married a woman who had attended one of his courses a year before. The professor, an exceptional scholar and teacher, was 40, and his lovely and intelligent bride was 32. Though entering matrimony relatively late in life, the two were obviously well suited to each other, and their marriage has since proved eminently successful.

This was the territory, but some people paid more attention to their specious maps. One newspaper headlined the wedding story with a ridiculous, cradle-snatching implication: "Teacher Marries Pupil." Many readers, largely ignorant of the facts of the situation, raised their eyebrows and clucked their tongues, and some readers even wrote letters of protest to the college president. They had become so distraught at the imagined violation of a social taboo that they were hardly able or willing to examine the territory behind their fallacious maps.

Sometimes we behave intensionally because we want to. It is a relief, occasionally, to escape to our inner self-made worlds. There is value in daydreams, movies, television, novels, and so forth, when these serve as temporary safety valves. There is danger, however, when the world of make-believe becomes accepted as real. Children are perhaps the most susceptible. A mother caught her seven-year-old son pouring ground glass into the family stew. He wanted to find out whether it would really work, as it had with the characters in a television play he had seen. Another youngster accidentally hung himself while attempting to free himself from a trick knot from which a comic book hero had escaped. And still another boy caused a $100,000 warehouse fire by using a clever incendiary made of a burning cigarette inserted in a book of matches. He had learned the trick from a movie.

But some adults are almost as prone to delude themselves—to react to faulty or fictional maps as if they were the actual territories. Milton Caniff, originator of the comic strip "Terry and the Pirates," tells of the time that one of the characters, Hot Shot Charlie, was sent to the United States for a period. Always a precisionist, Caniff depicted him as quartered at an actual apartment in Boston. One day the strip showed Hot Shot receiving a cable with the apartment's address clearly visible on the wire. The next panels showed him packing and leaving for overseas.

A day or so later Caniff received an urgent request from the apartment-house owner. "Please print a block in your comic strip," the owner pleaded, "and explain that there is no vacancy at _____ Street!" The poor man had been deluged with eager inquiries about Hot Shot's vacant apartment!

And Bing Crosby gave an amusing illustration of the undeniable effect of another kind of map, the motion picture:

> I'd heard of the public identifying actors and actresses with roles, but this was the first time I'd got the full treatment myself. Not long after *Going My Way* was released, I attended a dinner party at the home of my friend Jack Morse. Before dinner, cocktail canapés and hors d'oeuvres were served, among them toasted frankfurters on toothpicks. They were served by a gray-haired, motherly-looking maid from the Ould Sod. It happened to be Friday, and when I absent-mindedly took one of the frankfurters, I thought she'd have a stroke. "Holy Mother! Father Crosby!" she burst out, "you're not going to eat one of those!" Obviously she was subconsciously thinking of me as the priest I'd played, and the fact that "Father O'Malley" would eat a meat canapé on Friday upset her.
>
> The other guests collapsed with laughter, and she retreated in confusion to the kitchen. I was a little confused myself.[4]

Unfortunately, the impact of popular entertainment is not always so delightful. There is increasing concern that violence, so pervasive in movies

---

[4]Bing Crosby as told to Pete Martin, *Call Me Lucky* (New York: Simon & Schuster, 1953), pp. 186-87. Reprinted by permission.

and television, has a most dangerous influence on children. Saturated with media mayhem, some children seem to consider it with insouciance—as normal. One young man freely admitted slaying an elderly woman. His defense, albeit unsuccessful, was simply that he had watched too much violence on TV!

But the most pathetic victims of the celluloid chimera are perhaps some of the stars themselves. Living in the fanciful world created by press agents and celebrity worshipers, their maps become tragically out of phase with life facts. The too frequent results are emotional breakdowns, broken marriages, and suicides.

Generally speaking, intensionality is most likely to lead to undesirable consequences (1) when one's map inadequately represents the territory and (2) when one is unaware of responding to a map rather than to the territory.

Every medical student knows that the length of the small intestine is 22 feet or thereabouts, for the textbook said so. But Dr. Betty Underhill has revealed this map to be a dangerous fallacy. In 100 autopsies, she found that men's intestines ranged in length from 16 feet to 25 feet, 9 inches; women's, from 11 feet to 23 feet, 6 inches. Differences such as these, she asserted, can be life-and-death matters in surgery.

Not a few women are incensed with a particular map known as male chauvinism. They are visibly angry and exasperated with the dependent roles to which they have been traditionally confined. They firmly denounce, for example, the rank inequity of receiving less pay for comparable work than their male counterparts. I do not presume to explore the origin of this particular map. But I can make an observation on just one way in which it has been reinforced and perpetuated.

In Chicago, Chuck Schaden, an old-time radio buff, conducts a nightly radio program. From 7 to 11 P.M., he plays transcriptions of Golden Oldies, soap operas and serials: "Suspense," "Inner Sanctum," "The Shadow," "The Whistler," "The Green Hornet," and "Gang Busters," "Jack Benny," "Fred Allen," "Bing Crosby," "Amos and Andy," "Easy Aces," "Myrt and Marge," "Vic 'n' Sade," "One Man's Family," "I Love A Mystery," and so forth.

Especially fascinating are the kid shows: "Jack Armstrong," "Captain Midnight," "Terry and the Pirates," "Dick Tracy," "Tom Mix," and so on. Almost invariably in these radio serials, the female role is a subservient one. While Jack Armstrong, Billy Fairfield, and Uncle Jim are fighting evil in far-off lands, Betty (Billy's sister) is generally tucked out of harm's way. Captain Midnight and his teenage side-kick, Chuck Ramsey, take considerable risks. But Patsy Donovan is consistently treated as a fragile incompetent— "You stay here, Patsy, it might be dangerous."

Admittedly, there was one exception—"Little Orphan Annie." But even she had to rely frequently on male stalwarts such as the Asp, Punjab, and the incredibly rich and powerful Daddy Warbucks.

Now visualize the 1930s and 1940s and the millions of little boys and girls transfixed by their families' radios night after night after night. The message—sometimes subtle, often blatant—was constant: Girls are inferior to boys.

And the kids soaked up that message without question, challenge, or reservation. That was one way myriad mental maps were formed and solidified.

A DEFECTIVE TOOL

Language, broadly speaking, is a map . . . and a map is a tool, of sorts. Now if a tool were damaged, you might repair or replace it. I obviously regard English as a defective tool—the last six chapters and the next two focus on specific deficiencies. So why not simply replace or repair the language? Unfortunately, changing a language is usually anything but simple. Let's examine a few aspects of the problem.

Replace the Language

In theory, a truly international language sounds like a good idea. It probably wouldn't cure all of the world's ills, but it would be a step in the right direction. Certainly there have been efforts to create such a language—over 100 in the last century and a half. And some of these artificial languages are considered superior to English as a communication instrument. Yet not one of them, including the relatively popular Esperanto, has really succeeded. Why?

People tend to be very touchy about their language . . . something they begin to learn long before they aware they are learning anything. Perhaps they feel, consciously or otherwise, that language is a repository of their culture. In a sense, it is. But in any event, people generally resist language replacement with remarkable tenacity. Consider a few examples:

Note the animosity that exists between some English-speaking Canadians and some French-speaking Canadians. The former insist on an all-English-speaking Canada. The latter periodically threaten to secede.

A much older rift exists in Belgium between the Flemish (similar to Dutch)-speaking Flemings and the French-speaking Walloons.

The national language of the Republic of Ireland is English. Yet there are those who persist in the teaching and perpetuation of Gaelic, even though it is an archaic language elsewhere.

We still hear of riots and loss of life in certain provinces of India because of attempts to install a national language.

France is desperately trying to preserve the purity of French. A fast-food restaurant chain was recently fined $300 for advertising "hamburger" instead of "steak haché." Other Franglais words to avoid

when you are in Paris: "Le drugstore," "le walkie-talkie," "le jumbo jet," "le hot stuff," and "le 5 o'clock shadow."
And lest we feel too smug, let us remind ourselves that a serious debate is rapidly heating up over the issue of bilingualism in the United States.

The irony is that in spite of all the rancor and even bloodshed, we will probably eventually have an international language anyway. Which one? English . . . with all its warts! And why? Simply because its speakers have spread it throughout the world by trade, colonization, conquest, and achievements in science and the arts.

Evidence? Half the world's scientific literature is published in English. It is the official language of international aviation. Major international meetings are conducted in English, or have provision for simultaneous translation into English of speeches in any other language.

English is the standard language in some countries in every continent. School children in Germany, France, Japan, and many other nations learn English as their second tongue.

So we are moving inexorably toward English as a common language. But which English? What they speak in London or Edinburgh or Swansea or Sydney? The best bet is American English largely because of the globe-circling influence of, among other things, American movies and television.

Caution: If this discussion has led you to consider dropping the foreign language you're studying don't. Given our vaunted resistance to change, neither American English nor any other tongue will become a universally used language in the 20th century, nor in the 21st, according to some authorities. So let's examine a less drastic approach for improving the tool.

Repair the Language

Repairing the language is obviously less extreme than replacing it. But we haven't fared too well in the mending department, either.

Here's a simple example: "Ain't" used to be an acceptable contraction of *am not*. Unfortunately, it began to be used by some in lieu of *isn't* or *aren't*. "He ain't going to the ball game" or "they ain't as clever as they think they are." Accordingly, the word fell into ill repute and is no longer used in *"polite"* society. So what do we say instead? *Aren't* as in "I'm going to have to lose some weight, aren't I?" We prefer to overlook the fact that the contraction uncontracted is "are not I." So join my crusade for restoring *ain't* to its former and needed usage. But let's not hold our breaths until it's re-accepted.

A far more serious illustration of resistance to linguistic change concerns phonetic spelling, spelling a word the way it sounds. English orthography is ridiculously inconsistent. Why doesn't *tomb* rhyme with *comb?*

Why do neither of them rhyme with *bomb?* Or why does *tomb* rhyme with *room,* *comb* with *home,* and *bomb* with *mom?* Why can *ough* be pronounced so differently as in *dough, through, ought, hiccough, trough, tough,* and *bough?*

How do you pronounce *whales?* Well, it could be the name of the great sea mammals. But this word could also be utterly silent, provided we take the *w* from wreck, the *h* from honesty, the *a* from loafer, one *l* from will, the *e* from hypocrite, and one *s* from dress.

If we converted to phonetic spelling, we would have to make some provision for a few homonyms (*bore* and *boar, bell* and *belle*) but think of the advantages. It has been estimated that elementary education could be reduced by two full years! What a savings in time and energy and dollars and drudgery! It would spare kids from the labor of having to learn our ludicrous spelling irregularities by rote. Perhaps then education, which is supposed to be exciting, would have a chance to be just that.

Has phonetic spelling been tried for English? Many times in many places with uniformly lackluster results. The Chicago Tribune tried going modestly phonetic many years ago. They started using *tho* for though and *thru* for through and *nite* for night, and a few others and they lost subscribers! People feel very strongly about their language and don't care for change even if the objective is eminently sensible.

Here's another example of needed but resisted change. Our language is loaded with sexist words, references, and images.

> Frequently this language ignores or even excludes women. *Manslaughter*— could killing a woman be a less serious matter? *Man overboard* might refer to a woman. *Workman's compensation*—obviously women don't qualify. Politicians concern themselves with the *man on the street* and the *common man*—never mind that women vote, too. *All men are created equal,* but not women? We write *Dear Sir* to women. We carefully note a *woman* doctor or a *female* lawyer performed professional work lest others automatically think the professional was a man.[5]

A more subtle example is that we simply don't have a generic pronoun to refer to both sexes simultaneously. Traditionally, we say *he* and *him* and *his* when we refer to a male and female together, "When the human being is attacked, *he* tends to run or fight."

Some contend that when you use these pronouns in a general sense, everyone will interpret them as referring to males and females equally. But research doesn't support this.

Janet Hyde studied groups of first graders, third graders, fifth graders, and college students. Subjects were presented with a pronoun in a sen-

---

[5] *Cleaning Up Sexist Language* (Chicago: 8th Day Center for Justice, 1980), p. 4. See also: Dale Spender, *Man Made Language* (London: Routoledge and Kegan Paul, Ltd. 1980).

tence and asked to create a story about it. When cued with *his*, only 12 percent of the stories were about females. When cued with *his* or *her*, 42 percent of the stories concerned females. Another finding: Elementary school children were far more likely to interpret the generic *his* as masculine than college students.

We often say or write man when we mean men and women—"Man does not live by bread alone," and "The nuclear bomb threatens the survival of mankind." Such has not always been the case.

> At one time, English had separate and unambiguous words to distinguish a person by sex; *wif* for a female, *wer* and *carl* for a male. *Mann* (a human being) dropped the second *n* in combined forms like *waepman* and *carlman*, both of which meant adult male person, and *wifman*, an adult female person. *Wifman* eventually became *woman* (the plural, *women*, retains the original vowel sound in the first syllable), while *wif* was narrowed in meaning to become *wife*. But *wer* and *waepman*, *carl* and *carlman* simply became obsolete—no longer needed once *man* was used to signify a male specifically and male and female generally.[6]

So how can we begin to balance the scales—to strive for a sexually inclusive language? A few changes have been made. More frequently we hear salesperson, spokesperson, and chairperson. But we still have no accepted generic pronoun. *He/she, he and/or she,* and *s/he* still look and sound ungainly and artificial.

In the meantime, we can resort to *one*—but with restraint: "When one eats one eventually becomes sated; at which point one usually ceases to eat." (One more *one* and one might regurgitate.)

Another possibility is the use of plurals—*they, them, their.* The grammarian in me cringes when we use them with singular antecedents—"everyone to rest themselves"; "it's enough to drive anyone out of their senses"; "nobody likes a mind quicker than their own." But at least we'd be in good company—those statements are from Shakespeare, Shaw, and F. Scott Fitzgerald, respectively.

If we can't do much to replace or repair our language, at least we can be aware of its flaws and misdirections and treat them accordingly. That is the purpose of this chapter. In fact, it is the basic thrust of the whole of Part Three—Patterns of Miscommunication.

CORRECTIVES

As the problem of intensional orientation has been stated only generally, at this point we can offer only general advice for dealing with it. We shall reserve for the next two chapters the task of defining intensionality in its more specific forms and of offering techniques for preventing or diminishing its consequences.

---

[6]Casey Miller and Kate Swift, *Words and Women: New Language in New Times.* (New York: Anchor Books, 1977), p. 81.

The basic advice is to get extensional. Develop the show me or let me see attitude. Develop a healthy distrust of preconstructed maps. Go to the territory, look, observe, explore, probe, examine—then make your maps. This is the tenor of the homey advice World Court Justice John Bassett Moore once gave the late radio-television commentator Edward R. Murrow: "When you meet men of great reputation, your judgment of them will be greatly improved if you view them as though they were in their underwear."

Extensionality is the *sine qua non* of scientists. They make hypotheses (tentative maps), yes, but usually on the basis of previous observation of the territories, and then they check those maps against the territories again—and again—and again. If a map matches the territory, well and good; but if it does not, one alters the map or discards it and builds another, and another, until one has a map that adequately represents the territory.

This is the scientific attitude, the territory-first-then-map approach; but surely there is great need for that approach beyond the confines of the laboratory.

SUMMARY

Intensional orientation is a general term for the tendency to be guided primarily, if not exclusively, by one's maps rather than by the territory. Trouble, confusion, and danger are most likely to occur (1) when the map inadequately represents the territory and (2) when the individual is unaware that he or she is dealing with a map rather than with the territory.

The basic technique for preventing or minimizing the injurious effects of intensional orientation, simply stated, is to develop an extensional orientation—a readiness to seek out the territory rather than a willingness to be mesmerized by one's often fallacious maps. Extensionality, in short, is the propensity to look first—then talk.

DISCUSSION QUESTIONS

1. Intensional orientation can sometimes lead to harmful, unintelligent, even self-destructive behavior. However, are there not circumstances when such an orientation would be harmless—even desirable?

2. What are the conditions in which intensional orientation would be considered undesirable?

3. If people resist linguistic change, why does slang seem to change so rapidly?

4. What does this chapter have to do with communication?

5. Report on an incident, perhaps involving yourself, in which intensional orientation played a role. Why did the incident occur? What could have been done to prevent or correct the situation? What measures could prevent a recurrence of similar incidents?

CASES

CASE 14–1

The Continental Electric Company*

The following statement is by Howard Teal, manager of the Mandota plant of the Continental Electric Company, regarding a problem he had had with an assembly line. The line consisted of 35 people working on precision electrical parts.

Two years ago, during the summer, five workers at about the middle of the assembly line began to complain of severe itching and of welts on their arms and legs. The welts resembled mosquito bites, but the employees insisted these were not mosquito bites. They said that bugs were crawling from the assembly table and biting them. They sat at the assembly table with their backs to heavily screened windows. No mosquitoes could possibly have come in from the outside.

Well, we finally called in an exterminator, who spread all sorts of insecticides around the room. Things were fine for a few days, but then the workers began complaining again. The exterminator came back every three weeks, but that didn't seem to help. By the end of the summer, 11 people had registered complaints. The unrest subsided in the fall.

With the coming of hot weather last year, the complaints began once more. This time, 15 employees insisted they were being bitten. Finally, in July, they threatened to walk off the job. I immediately called in a dermatologist, who examined the employees. He told them that they were not being bitten and that the whole thing was in their imaginations.

The workers became angry, and the complaints became more pronounced. So back came the exterminators. After a few days, the complaints began anew.

The employees claimed they had seen little green bugs crawling around their work areas. There were a few insects, small enough to get in through the screen—the things one finds on trees during the summer. I know they don't bite, but I wasn't going to argue. Instead, I had the exterminators back a few more times until the fall season started.

Then, as before, the complaints ceased.

This year, the hot weather set in about May 15, and so did the unrest in the assembly room. Some 20 to 25 employees were now convinced that they were being bitten by insects around the assembly table. Even my supervisor began to itch.

---

*All names have been disguised. Printed by permission. The author's name has been withheld by request.

I then visited Dr. Jay, an entomologist at the university. He suggested that I have the employees collect insects from the assembly room, put them in jars, and send them to him for analysis. Many employees in the assembly room collected insects with zeal. I might add that assembly line efficiency dropped somewhat. When the collection had been completed, I delivered our specimens to Dr. Jay. After a careful analysis, he concluded that none of the insects brought to him for analysis would bite human beings. But the complaints continued.

Dr. Jay decided to visit the plant. Upon arriving, he took off his shirt, rolled up his trousers, and sat at the assembly table for a long time. He was not bitten once. He then interviewed several complaining employees. He suggested that they might themselves be bringing in insects from the outside. The workers insisted that they were being bitten at work because the symptoms occurred only in the plant.

Dr. Jay then submitted a highly technical report with the scientific terms for each type of insect he had analyzed. The report suggested that these insects did not normally bite and listed various physiological causes of itching. He suggested that the welts could have been caused by intense scratching due to itching sensations brought about by perspiration or by psychological causes. I posted his report on the bulletin board for all the employees to read.

At Dr. Jay's suggestion, I painted two ordinary 150-watt bulbs purple and secured them to the floor at each end of the assembly line. The lights gave the appearance of ultraviolet ray. As far as the employees were concerned, that was exactly what they were. They were and are still unaware of what I did.

Throughout June, July, August, and September, after installation of the lights, we had only two minor complaints of employees being bitten while on the assembly line.

Discussion Questions
1. Why did the workers suffer from itching and welts?
2. What does this have to do with intensional orientation?
3. Why were the employees angered by the dermatologist's conclusions?
4. Why did the purple lights seem to work?
5. What do you think of the purple lights ploy?

CASE 14–2

The Water-American*

At my first admission into this printing-house I took to working at press, imagining I felt a want of the bodily exercise I had been us'd to in America,

*From *The Autobiography of Benjamin Franklin* (Lexington, Mass.: D.C. Heath, 1908). Reprinted by permission.

where presswork is mix'd with composing. I drank only water; the other workmen, near fifty in number, were great guzzlers of beer. On occasion, I carried up and down stairs a large form of types in each hand, when others carried but one in both hands. They wondered to see, from this and several instances, that the *Water-American,* as they called, me, was *stronger* than themselves, who drank *strong* beer! We had an alehouse boy who attended always in the house to supply the workmen. My companion at the press drank every day a pint before breakfast, a pint at breakfast with his bread and cheese, a pint between breakfast and dinner, a pint at dinner, a pint in the afternoon about six o'clock, and another when he had done his day's work. I thought it a detestable custom; but it was necessary, he suppos'd, to drink *strong* beer, that he might be *strong* to labor. I endeavored to convince him that the bodily strength afforded by beer could only be in proportion to the grain or flour of the barley dissolved in the water of which it was made; that there was more flour in a pennyworth of bread, and therefore, if he would eat that with a pint of water, it would give him more strength than a quart of beer. He drank on, however, and had four or five shillings to pay out of his wages every Saturday night for that muddling liquor; an expense I was free from. And thus these poor devils keep themselves always under.

Discussion Questions

1. In what way do the workers display intensional orientation?

2. How would you classify Franklin's orientation?

CASE 14–3

"Get Off Route 25, Young Man"*

Charles F. Kettering

My home is in Dayton, Ohio, and I was a friend of the Wright family and learned to fly on the very early Wright airplanes. Their first flight was on the 17th of December, 46 years ago. Everyone was perfectly sure that it was a crazy thing to try. The undertakers moved into Kitty Hawk with a number of caskets because they thought the Wrights would kill themselves.

When they made those first three flights on December 17, 1903, they wired their sister that they had succeeded, that they were very happy, and that they should be home for Christmas.

She thought it was a world-shaking event, so she very excitedly called a Dayton newspaper on the telephone. She rang and rang and rang. The newspaper boys were playing pinochle, but finally one of them answered.

---

*Collier's, December 3, 1949, pp. 13–14. Reprinted by permission.

He said, "Yes?"

She said, "This is Katherine Wright speaking," and very excitedly read the telegram.

He said, "Good. Glad to hear the boys are going to get home for Christmas," and hung up the telephone.

The newspaperman said to the others: "Nobody's going to catch me on that, because it has proved mathematically that a heavier-than-air machine can't fly."

***

I had a friend who was the research and development man for one of the British railroads. he came to this country to deliver a commencement address at a technical university. After the address he came to Detroit to see our laboratories.

"Ket," he said, "when you were over in London last year you told me some things you fellows were doing with Diesel locomotives and you lied to me."

I said, "Not intentionally."

"But," he said, "you told me you were running these locomotives about a hundred miles an hour."

I said, "We are."

"And that you were taking power on the front wheels; that is, the wheels that are ahead."

I said, "We are."

He said, "I have the formulas in my portfolio that say you can't do that."

I said, "For Heaven's sake, don't let the locomotive know about it."

I said to him, "I won't argue with you at all." I took the telephone, called Chicago and got him transportation from Chicago to Denver, and flew him to Chicago to make the connection. He made the trip to Denver, where I had him ride partway on the Diesel engines.

He stopped in to see me on his way back. He was returning to England. I said, "I didn't expect to see you again. Did you ride that locomotive?"

"Yes," he said.

"Did it go a hundred miles an hour?"

"It did."

"Well," I said, "that's the reason I didn't expect to see you back. Maybe you forgot to take the portfolio with the equations in it."

He said, "The thing that amazes me is why we could be so 100 percent wrong."

I said, "You weren't wrong. You didn't start in right."

The two of us got out his formulas. He wasn't talking about our locomotive at all. Our locomotive uses an ordinary truck like a streetcar's. He was talking about a locomotive with a rigid frame which would normally have a small-wheel lead truck in front of it.

I said, "What's the use of using mathematics on one kind of thing and then applying it to another which is in no way related? It isn't even a second cousin to it."

***

When we first put self-starters on automobiles, I attended a meeting of the American Institute of Electrical Engineers. They asked me if I would make a little talk on the self-starter, and I did.

One fellow got up and said, "No wonder you made your self-starter work; you profaned every law of electrical engineering."

I didn't profane any fundamental laws of electrical engineering. All I did was make the starter work. Those laws had nothing whatever to do with self-starters; they were written for something entirely different.

***

As I said before, my home is in Dayton, and we have had our laboratories for years in Detroit, which is several hundred miles away. I keep my home in Ohio and drive back and forth weekends.

Some of the people who work with me also drive between Dayton and Detroit. One said, "I understand you drive from here to Dayton in 4½ hours."

I said, "I can do that once in a while, depending on traffic."

He said, "I don't believe it."

I said, "But I do it."

He said, "I'm a much better driver than you are, and I can't do it."

I said, "I'm going down Friday. Why don't you ride along with me?"

So we rode into Dayton in about 4½ hours, or a little more, and he said, "Hell, no wonder you can do it. You didn't stay on Route 25!"

Now, Route 25 is the red line that is marked on all the maps between Detroit and Dayton. If you are a stranger, that's the road you should take. It never occurred to my colleague that you could take any other road on either side of Route 25. There's a lot of country on either side of it; in fact, half the earth is on each side of it.

Discussion Questions

1. What do the four incidents have in common?
2. How do the incidents differ?
3. What patterns of miscommunication seem to be involved here?
4. What preventive measures do you recommend for these patterns of miscommunication?

CASE 14–4

The Trials of Galileo

Galileo is perhaps most widely known and remembered for his astronomical studies. Early in life he became a convert to the Copernican ideas, ideas that conflicted with the medieval conception of the universe as established by Ptolemy. Ptolemy declared that the earth was an immovable sphere, fixed in the center of the universe, with the sun and the stars revolving about it. For many centuries the Ptolemaic system was almost undisputedly accepted. Not only did it seem to agree with the perception of the senses but it was also in harmony with the homocentric doctrine of theology, which recognized man as the principal object of divine concern. The entire universe was conceived as having been created to serve man's needs. Hence it was but natural to regard the earth, the abode of man, as the center of the universe. . . .[1]

It was not until he made a number of discoveries by means of the telescope that he boldly championed Copernicanism. Apprised that a contrivance had been invented in the Dutch Netherlands by which distant objects could be made to appear much nearer and larger, he set to work and soon constructed a telescope, becoming the first scientist to apply it to astronomical observation. With the new instrument Galileo made a number of important discoveries. He found that the moon, instead of being self-luminous, owed its light to reflection; also he proved its surface was deeply furrowed by valleys and mountains. The latter discovery shattered the Aristotelian idea that the moon was a perfect sphere, absolutely smooth. Especially noteworthy was Galileo's discovery of the four satellites of Jupiter, whose revolutions confirmed by analogy the Copernican explanation of the solar system. Galileo also perceived movable spots on the disc of the sun, inferring from them the sun's axial rotation and by analogy the rotation of the earth on its axis.

After making his discoveries with the telescope, Galileo could not restrain his enthusiasm for the Copernican system. So persistent were his activities in behalf of it and so unsparing was his ridicule of its opponents that the Church, which still adhered to the Ptolemaic theory, became alarmed. In 1615 he was ordered by the Inquisition to desist from further advocacy of the doctrine "that the earth moves around the sun and that the sun stands in the center of the world without moving from east to west." Galileo submitted, and for the next 16 years remained silent. Meanwhile, however, he was writing the great work of his life, which he published in 1632 under the title *Dialogue concerning the Two Chief Systems of the World*. The main reason for his choice of a dialogue between three persons as the medium for his thought was probably a desire to avoid committing himself openly. The work presented overwhelming proof of the Copernican theory. When it was examined by the ecclesiastical authorities, Galileo was immediately summoned to appear before the Inquisition at Rome. Near 70 and broken in spirit, he was forced in the presence of the full Congregation to abjure on his knees the doctrines defined as contrary to the

---

[1]Robert Ergang, *Europe from the Renaissance to Waterloo* (Lexington, Mass.: D.C. Heath, 1954). Reprinted by permission.

Holy Scriptures. The oath of recantation read in part, "I Galileo Galilei . . . swear that with honest heart and in good faith I curse and execrate the said heresies and errors as to the movement of the earth around the sun and all other heresies and ideas opposed to the Holy Church; and I swear that I will never assert or say anything either orally or in writing, that could put me under such suspicion." A story has it that after he recited the abjuration Galileo muttered under his breath, "*Eppur si muove* (But it [the earth] does move)." Though the legend is unsupported by historical evidence, it indicates the value of the renunciation which was obtained under duress and expresses the general belief as to what went on in Galileo's mind.

The last years of his life Galileo devoted to the study of dynamics, publishing in 1636 his famous *Dialogues on Motion,* a consolidation of his earlier work on the subject. This book not only laid the foundation for the study of mechanics but specifically served as the preliminary work for Newton's laws of motion. Soon after publishing it, Galileo became blind and also partially deaf. Yet he continued to work until his death on January 8, 1642, at the age of 78. Many historians of science regard Galileo as the founder of experimental science. His investigations of nature discredited dependence upon accepted authority, particularly upon Aristotle. Galileo's fight for the Copernican system did much to promote its acceptance and win supporters for it.[2]

Discussion Questions

1. Why did the Church find it necessary to silence Galileo?
2. Why do inventors sometimes have great difficulty in having their innovations accepted by others?
3. What is the relationship between intensional orientation and experimental science?

CASE 14–5

"They Don't Do It Our Way"*

Dr. Ina Telberg

"What the Distinguished Lady Representative has just suggested proves that women can be more than decorative—they can also be useful."

With this jovial remark, a United States Delegate looked at his Soviet Colleague in the Population Commission of the United Nations and awaited a smile of response. None came. The Russian sat stiff and unsmiling. In Russia there are no jokes about women drivers or women delegates, so be-

---

[2]Ibid. reprinted by permission.

*Reprinted by permission from *UNESCO Courier,* May 1950.

loved by the Americans. The Russian conception of courtesy, therefore, forbade the Soviet Delegate to do anything but freeze into a silent disapproval. The well-meaning American attempt to find common ground by means of a joke thus increased, rather than decreased, the psychological distance between the two delegations. . . .

One Man's Meal . . .

One of the most deeply rooted, and largely unconscious, features of any culture is what the psychologists call the *time perspective*. Within the United Nations, at least three different time perspectives operate.

"Gentlemen, it is time for lunch, we must adjourn," announces the Anglo-Saxon chairman, in the unabashed belief that having three meals a day at regular hours is the proper way for mankind to exist.

"But why? We haven't finished what we were doing," replies—in a puzzled manner that grows rapidly more impatient—an Eastern European Delegate, in whose country people eat when the inclincation moves them and every family follows its own individual timetable.

"Why, indeed?" placidly inquires the Far Eastern representative, hailing from a country where life and time are conceived as a continuous stream, with no man being indispensable, with no life process needing to be interrupted for any human being, and where members of electoral bodies walk in and out of the room quietly, getting a bite to eat when necessary, talking to a friend when pleasant; but where meetings, theater performances, and other arranged affairs last without interruption for hours on end, while individuals come and go, are replaced by others, meditate or participate as the occasion requires, without undue strain, stress, or nervous tension.

As one or the other group persists in its own conception of the time perspective, as the Anglo-Saxons demand that the duration of meetings and conferences be fixed in advance and that meals be taken regularly at fixed hours, and as the Russians sit irritated and the Latins puzzled and the Secretariat frantic—as this condition continues, mutual friction grows, murmurs of "unreasonableness" are heard around the room; and, when the issue under discussion is an important one, overt accusations are hurled across the room of "insincerity," "lack of a serious approach to the problem," and even "sabotage."

Irony or Poetry

Another frequent source of irritation, rooted deeply in the cultural differences among nations, is the *length and the style of oration*.

The Latins are usually accused of unnecessary length and of equally unnecesary flights of poetic fancy. The Russians are disliked both for the length of their speeches and for the irony and sarcasm of the speeches' content. The utilization of irony in political speeches is a long-standing tradition of *public oratory in Russia*. It has nothing to do with the Soviet Government. Mr. Vishinsky, for example, most noted for this type of oration, was born, trained, and had had considerable success as trial lawyer and political orator, long before the establishment of the Soviet Government.

It was in November 1946 that I was flown to Lake Success from the Nuremberg Trials. I was tired, sleepy, and a stranger to the United Nations. On November 15th, Vishinsky was delivering his now-famous veto speech in the Political Committee at Lake Success. A regular interpreter failed, and I was rushed to the microphone in the middle of the speech. I remember how my voice trembled when I first began to speak. I knew that I was on the air, and that many of my friends in America and England were listening. In a few minutes, however, I lost every trace of self-consciousness as Mr. Vishinsky's Russian carried me away by its sheer beauty, force, and richness of expression. Latin quotations, Russian proverbs, even Shakespearean poetry, were utilized for the purposes of his attack on the British and the American positions.

Next day I was startled by the press reactions. I myself even received some fan mail: a couple of letters that denounced me as a Communist for having interpreted the speech with such fervor, and another one that praised me for same. I realized then how unnecessarily vitriolic, aggressive, and offensive the address was when translated: in fact, how ill-adapted was the Russian oratorical style to delivery in a foreign tongue. It was not the language itself, however, that was the obstacle. It was the tradition behind the language; what I have since learned to call *speech etiquette.*

Settling a Grave Issue

The Latins, on the other hand, far from employing sarcasm, prefer to sprinkle their speeches with a liberal amount of poetic imagery, metaphysical expressions, and literary allusions.

During the General Assembly meetings in Paris, a Latin-American delegate pleaded for the inclusion of the phrase "from the cradle to the grave" in the Article of the Declaration of Human Rights dealing with social security. He wanted to ensure that a worker, or rather, a citizen, should be covered by measures of social protection in just that manner: from the cradle to the grave. He meant precisely, literally, what he said.

"Such phrases have no place in a serious document," pronounced a Western European Delegate.

"But the Declaration should be beautifully worded," argued another Latin Delegate.

"It's a legal document—not a poem," muttered a Benelux member.

A member of the United States Delegation whispered darkly into a neighbor's ear:

"Why not 'from womb to tomb'? At least it rhymes!"

Before the final text of the Article was settled upon, several other poetical versions were suggested. Some others, quite unprintable, shortly made the rounds of the corridors outside the conference rooms. . . .

The Origin of Life

Life itself is prized differently in different cultures. To die of peaceful old age is the ideal life pattern in some parts of the world. Death for a country or an ideal is the desirable social behavior in others. Nowhere have these differences been made so manifest as in the drafting of the Declaration of Human Rights.

"*Man is of divine origin, endowed by nature with reason and conscience,*" argued several Latin-American delegates.

"*All life is of divine origin, not only human life,*" a representative of a Buddhist state murmured gently. "*Is it not vanity to attribute divine origin to human life alone?*"

"*Man is not divine. He is rooted in the very land he tills, in the soil that bred him,*" once state an Eastern European Delegate from a preponderantly agricultural area. The Soviets suggested tactfully that science had reservations on the whole subject. The Anglo-Saxon bloc, evidently not quite definite on the subject of human divinity, kept still.

Confusion over China

Humor relief is not infrequently provided by the very cultural differences that are usually so productive of misunderstandings.

On one occasion, a misunderstanding was particularly startling:

"*Gentlemen, gentlemen, let us not act in this matter like an elephant in a china shop!*"

As this remark was being rendered from the Russian into English, a language in which the Chinese Delegate was following proceedings, he promptly raised his hand.

"*Mr. Chairman, I should like the Soviet Delegate to explain just what China has to do with his objections,*"

"*Mr. Chairman, I said nothing whatever about China. The Chinese Delegate must have misunderstood.*"

"*Mr. Chairman, I distinctly heard my country mentioned. I request an explanation.*" . . .

Discussion Questions

1. In terms of the *intensional orientation* concept what do Dr. Telberg's illustrations have in common?

2. In addition to language differences, what else contributes to miscommunication within the UN?

3. The United Nations has been criticized from some quarters as an ineffectual body for solving the world's problems. How do you feel about the objectives and accomplishments of the UN?

4. Two other cases are concerned with intercultural relations, "An Evening at the Leningrad Ballet" and "Business Customs from Malaya to Murmansk." Compare them with "They Don't Do It Our Way."

CASE 14–6

The Flag, the Anthem, and the Four-Letter Word

The Flag[1]

Eugene B. Colin, 46, a Skokie advertising executive, used an American flag to teach his night school class something about semantics, but learned something himself in the process.

Colin was served Tuesday night with a warrant charging him with desecrating a flag in the presence of his 15 adult pupils at Niles North Township High School September 30. He said he was only trying to illustrate the flag's semantic properties.

Colin said he held a small flag in his hand for about 30 minutes while he explained to his students that its real value lay in what it meant to them. Otherwise, he told them, it was cloth made up into stripes and stars of various colors.

Then, he said, he placed it on the floor in front of him. And that was the trouble.

"If anything, it certainly was a case of poor judgment," Colin said later. "I don't think I'm second to anyone in my reverence for everything this country stands for," he continued. "I just wanted to illustrate that the value of a thing is what we impute to it."

What the students imputed to the placing of the flag on the floor was something else. A report of the incident was given to the Skokie police, who obtained the warrant from Judge Harold W. Sullivan of the Circuit Court's Skokie Branch.

Colin, who lives at 9331 N. Forest View in the suburb and who receives no salary for his teaching, said he didn't know he had done anything wrong in placing the flag on the floor.

School officials, he said, had told him that most of the class wanted him to continue teaching, but he wasn't sure how many of them would support him when his case comes up in the court October 29.

---

[1]"Teacher Learns More about Flag," *Chicago Sun-Times*, October 16, 1968, p. 2. Reprinted by permission.

The Anthem[2]

On a Saturday evening in December 1941, shortly after Pearl Harbor, I had a dinner date with another graduate student. We went to a restaurant that had a small dance floor at the end of the room farthest from the entrance and that employed a small orchestra on weekends. We sat at the table next to the dance floor.

During an intermission three young men in Navy uniforms, who occupied a table near us and who had each downed several drinks from the bar since our arrival, went out on the dance floor and began an impromptu floor show. Their horseplay included several apparently unintentional sprawls on the floor, and the "emcee's" speech came out as "Laszh'n'szhen-'lemen" etc. Suddenly one of them seized a trumpet from the deserted orchestra stall and began playing a wavering but recognizable version of "The Star-Spangled Banner." With his two companions following, he began a stumbling parade up and down the dance floor. By the time the trumpeter had reached the second or third bar of the anthem, everybody in the restaurant had risen to his feet—except my escort. When I realized that he had remained seated, I sank back down into my own chair. One of the men in uniform stopped, looked at us, and called "Shtan' up! Shtan' up!" but we remained silent and seated. After they had returned to their table, my escort said, "I will not take part in dishonoring a symbol of my country." Shortly afterward, we rose to leave. As we made our way the length of the room to the door, it seemed to me that all talk ceased and that the eyes that followed us were filled with hostility and suspicion.

The Four-Letter Word[3]

In a suburban courtroom just north of Detroit last week, a high school teacher named Nancy Timbrook clutched a shredded Kleenex as she defended her actions before a judge. She admitted that she had, as charged, written a four-letter variant of the word *to copulate* on her classroom blackboard.

Prosecutor   Didn't you know that it was an unfit word to use in front of children?

Mrs. Timbrook   That's what I was trying to teach—that it was indecent and immoral. It's always made me sick every time I've seen it. I've seen it every day in the [school] john. I wanted to stop it.

Prosecutor   Did you know that writing that word was a crime?

Mrs. Timbrook   I didn't know I was doing anything that would send me to jail.

---

[2]By Alma Johnson Sarett. Reprinted by permission.

[3]"English Lesson," *Time*, March 28, 1969, pp. 69 and 72. Reprinted by permission.

Judge Ignorance is no excuse.

Mrs. Timbrook Perhaps I should have studied law instead of literature.

While the four-letter word under discussion has become common-place
in the works of many modern novelists, its use is far from accepted in high
school English classes. Any teacher who makes it the theme of a classroom
exercise can expect a strong reaction—if not from the students themselves, at least from their parents. Which is what happened to Mrs. Timbrook, 36, a truck driver's wife and the mother of nine children, who teaches
at Lamphere High School in Madison Heights, Michigan.

Led by God. The incident took place last month after Patrick Eady, 32, a
social studies teacher at Lamphere, invited two college-age youths who
are members of a local left-wing group called the White Panthers to address his students. Their talk was freely sprinkled with the provocative
verb (or noun, or adjective, depending on how it is used). News of the highly
unusual lesson spread quickly through the school. Annoyed by the students' snickering, Mrs. Timbrook decided to discuss the word in class the
very next day. She printed the word on the blackboard for each of her four
English classes and asked each what it meant. "I was led to do that by
God," Mrs. Timbrook, a deeply religious woman, later recalled. "I didn't
know what I was going to do until I walked into the classroom.

For the most part, the students merely giggled and answered that the
word meant sexual intercourse. But many of the 42,000 residents of the
town questioned Mrs. Timbrook's divine inspiration. She insisted that her
lecture's purpose was to prove that the word was "devoid of life and love."
Nevertheless, parents besieged the superintendent of schools with irate
phone calls and, at hastily convened meetings, vilified Mrs. Timbrook as a
"whore" and a "disgrace to womankind."

Eady was fired from his job. When Mrs. Timbrook was given nonteach-
ing duties in the superintendent's office, other teachers boycotted the
school for a full day. Then one father, Police Lieutenant William Sloan,
brought criminal charges against Mrs. Timbrook and Eady. Both were arrested on a state charge—"depraving the morals of children." Mrs. Timbrook was also charged with violating a local ordinance that forbids the
writing of "indecent and immoral language."

In court, Judge Edward Lawrence conceded that her motive had been a
moral one. But he was not inclined to minimize her offense. "People may
commit murder in the heat of passion," he said, "but that doesn't excuse
murder. People may write obscenity for various reasons, but that doesn't
excuse obscenity." While the state charge against her was dropped, Mrs.
Timbrook pleaded guilty to violating a local ordinance. She faces penalties
of up to 90 days in prison and $500 fine at her sentencing next month. Eady,
who comes to trial next month, is not likely to get much more sympathy.

Discussion Questions

1. What do these incidents have in common?
2. What do these incidents have to do with *intensional orientation?*
3. How do you analyze the incident of the flag?
4. How do you analyze the incident of the anthem?
5. How do you analyze the incident of the four-letter word?

CASE 14-7

Reification Can Kill Us*

Sydney J. Harris

You may never have heard of the word *reification*, or know what it means. But it may kill you, and me, and millions more around the globe, as it has many times in the past.

To *reify* means to treat an abstraction as though it were real and personal and existent. *Russia* is such an abstraction. *America* is another. If we go to war, these two reified abstractions will be seen as fighting one another.

Of course, no such things exist. Russia is made up of millions of individuals, and so is America. The people in Russia have nothing against the people in America, and the same is true the other way around.

If you were to walk the streets of Russia—as more than 100 Americans recently did on a Fellowship of Reconciliation tour—you would find not only no personal animosity among the ordinary citizens, but also a passionate craving for peace and a dread fear of atomic warfare.

They, just like us, want a tranquil and secure future for their children; like us also, the average citizen has little to say about his government's stance in world affairs; and, of course, they are even worse off than us, for they cannot vote out of office a regime they dislike or oppose.

The true tragedy of the current confrontation between our two countries is that it has so little to do with the ordinary citizen, and so much to do with power politics at the highest level. But it is not the generals and politicians who will be slaughtered if we go to war; it will be the rest of us, like it or not, want it or not.

The danger in reification is that it forces us to think—and to feel—in terms of these abstractions rather than in terms of flesh-and-blood human beings; that it depersonalizes the conflict and transforms it into a battle of slogans and flags and symbols that have only a tenuous relationship to the reality beneath them—the suffering, the dying, the desolation beyond belief that nuclear war will leave in its wake.

---

*Formerly, "The Process of *Reification* Makes Doom a Reality," *Chicago Sun-Times*, December 20, 1982, p. 35. From Strictly PERSONAL by Sydney J. Harris (c) by and permission of News America Syndicate.

This is not to equate the Soviet system with ours; for ours, with all its imperfections, is vastly more desirable than theirs. But it is not *systems* that are going to kill and be killed, it is people—and people far more like us than unlike us, as we would see if we had the opportunity to get to know them better.

A *country*, like a *government*, is an abstraction. There is no such thing, except on paper, or in the mind.

It is governments that start wars, or renew them, for reasons that may not have anything to do with the basic welfare of their own populace. Now it has reached the point where *no* nuclear conflict can protect or advance the welfare of any civilian population. Everything has changed except the minds of those who lead us, in nearly every part of the world.

Confucius told us long ago that all reform must begin with the reform of language. And the first thing that must go is the *reification* of words like *Russian* and *American* when we mean men and women and children of God.

Discussion Questions

1. What do you think of the title of this case?

2. Do governments start wars?

3. What do you think of the Confucian advice?

4. What does this case have to do with intensional orientation?

15

Intensional Orientation: 2. "Pointing" and "Associating"

A department store manager once received a shipment of high-quality handkerchiefs and, in an adventuresome mood, placed half of them in a pile at one end of a sales counter with a sign: "Fine Irish Linen—$1.00 Each." He stacked the other half at the opposite end of the counter with a sign: "Nose Rags—3 for 50¢." The Irish linens outsold the nose rags five to one!

A delicatessen operator performed somewhat the same sort of experiment with some first-rate cheese. She cut two large wedges from the same wheel and placed them in her showcase. She labeled one wedge, "Imported English Cheddar," and the other, "Smelly Cheese." The former, at twice the price, far outsold the latter.

And Haldeman-Julius, publishers of the little five-cent Blue Books, discovered years ago that changing titles could have a salutary effect on sales:

Title	No. of copies sold*
Markheim	100
Markheim's Murder	7,000
The Mystery of the Iron Mask	100
The Mystery of the Man in the Iron Mask	11,000
The Art of Controversy	100
How to Argue Logically	30,000
Fleece of Gold	600
Quest for a Blond Mistress	50,000

*During equal periods of time.

It is obvious that the way we react to the *words* by which things are called can affect very considerably the way we react to the *things* themselves. You will recall from Chapter 7 that the students in Dr. Lee's classes responded quite differently to the foods they were eating after they were told that the foods were dog biscuits and grasshopper cookies.

One way of understanding how our response to words can affect our evaluations of things is to recognize the versatility of language use. Among other uses, we employ and react to words as *pointers* which call attention to something. We also use and react to words as *evokers* of associations.

Suppose that you and I are riding through the country and I see a small pool of water and say, "Look at that swimming hole over there." My words may serve the purpose of a pointing finger and call your attention to a pool that you might otherwise have missed.

But if you happen to associate certain memories, experiences, and feelings, pleasant or otherwise, with the term *swimming hole*, then it is entirely possible that my words would stir you up a bit. Moreover, they might suggest to you a great deal beyond the physical pool to which I was referring.

For convenience, we will use the terms *pointing* and *associating*, respectively, to represent these two functions of language. However, we must guard against the view that words are used *either* as pointers or as associators. They are ordinarily used and reacted to as both. The situation is a case of double contraries.

Take the term *sulfuric acid*. (See Figure 15–1.) For A, who has never studied chemistry and is not especially familiar with the term in any other

FIGURE 15–1

context, the words may have little pointer or associator value; for B, whose hand was once badly burned when someone threw sulfuric acid at him, the words might usually have great associator value but perhaps comparatively little pointer value; C, a chemist, may ordinarily use and react to the term with largely pointer value and practically no associator value; and so forth.

Theoretically, depending upon the individual, the time, the place, the verbal context, and other circumstances, one may use or react to a given word or phrase with values anywhere along the infinitely graded double continua.

Even though our terms *pointers* and *associators* imply a fallacious polarization, they provide a useful distinction for describing and coping with serious patterns of miscommunication. I shall henceforth use the words in quotes to remind the reader of the multivalued and interrelated sense in which I am intending them. Let the quotation marks remind us also that people (not words) do the "pointing" and "associating" with words.[1]

It is clear that when people send and receive them, words may have many functions; "pointing" and "associating" are prominent among them. The crux of this chapter, then, is that confusion, misunderstanding, and other kinds of trouble may readily occur when communicators forget or are unaware that both "pointing" and "associating" are usually involved in communication.

The failure to recognize the "pointing-associating" duality of language may lead to several patterns of miscommunication. Three prevalent and troublesome forms are the "pointing-associating" confusion, name-calling, and "associative" bypassing.

THE "POINTING-ASSOCIATING" CONFUSION

The commonest experience of deluding ourselves with words occurs when we confuse the "associating" and "pointing" functions. We often react to the associations evoked in us by the label as if we were reacting to what the label was "pointing" to—the object itself. Most Americans shudder at the prospect of eating rattlesnake meat or French fried grasshoppers. Is it because they dislike the taste? Hardly, for most of them have never eaten these foods, which, incidentally, are regarded as delicacies in some parts of the world. It is obvious that they are reacting not to the foods themselves but to their names and to the associations that they have for the names. Consider whether you would not be somewhat more favorably disposed toward a sirloin steak than toward a slice of dead cow, even though both labels point to the same piece of meat.

---

[1] The reader has probably assumed that I am deliberately refraining from using the words *denotations* and *connotations*. These terms have come to suggest so strongly a polarized view of language use that it seemed advisable to avoid them.

Juliet understood the "pointing-associating" confusion when she pleaded with Romeo in one of literature's most quoted expressions:

> 'Tis but thy name that is my enemy. . . .
> What's in a name? that which we call a rose
> By any other name would smell as sweet.
> —*Romeo and Juliet*, Act 2, Scene 2

Euphemisms and Dysphemisms

To euphemize is to substitute an inoffensive, mild, or pleasant "associator" for one that may produce an opposite reaction. To euphemize is to put a good face on something. Calling a liquor store a "package store" or "party store" does not change the store, its contents, or its function, but it may soften the impression for many. I have coined the word *dysphemism* as the antonym of *euphemism*. It puts a "bad face" on the thing. Calling the same establishment a "booze store" still doesn't change the store, but it may change the way some people feel about it.

There are many occasions on which euphemisms or dysphemisms, used judiciously, may serve good purposes—or at least expedient ones. When consoling a friend who has just lost someone near, you would almost certainly use "passed away" rather than "croaked" or "kicked the bucket." And surely it is kinder to refer to a thin person as "on the slender side" than as "skinny" or "spindly." More appealing titles for people's jobs may also have their value:

Yesterday	Today	Tomorrow
Handyman	Repairman	Customer Engineer
Typewriter	Stenographer	Visual transcriptionist
Bookkeeper	Comptroller	Tax avoidance researcher
Garbageman	Sanitary engineer	Excess materials manager
Telephone girl	Switchboard operator	Audio connection supervisor
Head clerk	Office manager	Coffee break coordinator

On the other hand, a person running for election might not be reluctant to use dysphemisms in describing a liberal intellectual opponent as "that stubborn, radical egghead." Your children and mine may be equally energetic, but if I don't happen to like you, I may prefer to describe yours as "wild" and my own as "active." Your wife may be a "gabby gossip," but mine is an "enthusiastic conversationalist." And while my home may have that "lived-in look," yours is just "shabby."

Paradise Island, in the Bahamas, which relies heavily on the tourist trade, underwent a needed name change. One wonders how many vacationers would book an idyllic two weeks on Hog Island—its former name.

Sensitive to public criticism, the U.S. Congress no longer takes "recesses." These are now called "district work periods" by the House and "nonlegislative periods" by the Senate.

Nor is the executive branch insensitive to "how it will play in Peoria." "Reagan changed the name of the MX dense pack to the 'the Peace-keeper,' " cracked Johnny Carson, "because he figured 'the World-ender' wouldn't go over so well." Rear Admiral Eugene J. Carroll (ret.) added: "Calling the MX a peacekeeper is like calling the guillotine a headache remedy."

The White House provided another linguistic masterstroke when U.S. Marines were removed from Lebanon in late summer, 1984. After 19 months of attempting to keep peace (when there was really no peace to keep), they were recalled. The cost had been 264 killed, 137 wounded, and $59.7 million spent. But the Marines weren't withdrawn or even evacuated, according to the White House, they were "redeployed." Political satirist Mark Russell was unsympathetic. "If a Republican wants to pull out of Lebanon, it's called redeployment. If a Democrat wants to pull out of Lebanon, it's called treason."

An educational group named the U.S. State Department the winner of its 1984 Doublespeak Award. The reason: The State Department had announced that it would no longer use the verb "killing" in official reports on the status of human rights in countries around the world. Hereafter, it would be the "unlawful or arbitrary deprivation of life."

The Pentagon had provided several runners-up for the award:

Term	Pentagonese
peace	permanent prehostility
combat	violence processing
invasion of Grenada	predawn vertical insertion

One of the most acute dangers of euphemisms-dysphemisms and, in general, of reacting to "associators" as if they were "pointers" is that we tend to lose sight of the things being represented. We become so mesmerized by the name that the thing becomes obscured. On some campuses the name of one's sorority or fraternity apparently looms very large in extra-curricular matters. Fraternity men have told me that the dating of sorority women of other than the "better" houses is frowned upon by their brothers. Ironically, the "Eta Byta Pi" label on a young woman sometimes seems a more important criterion for date selection than the unique characteristics and qualities of the woman herself. But is this behavior less rational than voting a straight party ballot without any apparent concern for the qualifications of the individual candidates? Speaking of politics, have you heard of the Democratic nomination for treasurer in a Michigan county a few years ago? The Democrats discovered that they had nominated a T. Edward Aho, 52, an inmate of a state mental hospital! Aho, an unemployed worker, was not prominent, but his Finnish name had vote appeal in the Finnish-dominated county. Similarly, a certain city ward, predominantly Scandinavian, voted a Mr. Jensen into a minor office. It was only after the election that most of the voters realized that Mr. Jensen was a black man.

One-time Vice President Fritz Mondale was embarrassed a couple of years ago when an excerpt of his book, *The Accountability of Power*, appeared in *Genesis*, a magazine for sophisticated men. The issue in which Mondale's byline appeared also featured such articles as Erotic Diary of a Nympho Cheerleader. How had it happened? Mondale's publisher gave the reprint permission because "judging from its plain little letterhead and its title, the magazine sounded kind of religious."

Mr. Mondale, of course, was to suffer a much greater blow—a decisive loss in his bid for the presidency in 1984. Many of his supporters may have deserted him . . . but his sense of humor didn't. His post-election appraisal: "I wanted to run for the presidency in the worst possible way—and I did!"

There are many who readily capitalize upon our tendency to react to "associators" as if they were "pointers." Some of the most skillful of these people write advertising copy. With deft pens poised, these word-magicians sift through hundreds of words to find the term or phrase that is most likely to elicit quickly the desired response to their products. They overlook few possibilities for word appeal. In the automobile industry, for example, even the car's colors are verbally glamorized. It is no longer possible to buy a black or a red or a green or a blue auto. But you can get one in Morning Mist, Carnival Red, Fern Mist Green, Ginger Glow, Calypso Coral, or Burgundy Fire. My personal prize goes to the inventor of the name for a certain yellow color that one manufacturer used a few years ago. To me, at least, the color was a bilious gray-yellow, reminiscent of dusty mustard. Its name—the stroke of a master—was Sunglo!

Classified advertisers are generally not as adept as their distant cousins in the agencies, but they too contrive studiously to find the "right word." The favorite terms for describing a house for sale, according to a survey of 8,000 ads in eight major U.S. daily newspapers, were "cute," "a cutie," "adorable," "exquisite," "elegant," "a dandy," "magnificent," "glamorous," "spic and span," "clean as a pin," "a rare find," and a "real bargain." A farm was seldom a "farm" but a "rural hideaway," a "rustic retreat," or a "secluded estate." There were few "jobs" in the Help Wanted columns, but "openings" and "positions" were plentiful. A lost dog was frequently the "pet of an invalid grandmother" or belonged to a "heartbroken little girl." Dogs for sale were advertised variously as "love that money can't buy," "darlings," "cuddlies," and "swell pets." Possibly the most refined touch of all was the term for a bitch with a litter of pups—she was listed as a "matron."

Even the farmer who was busily building an unusual structure on his east forty had a flair for "associators." "What's it going to be?" asked a neighbor. "It all depends," was the reply. "If I rent it, it's a pastoral lodge—

if I don't, it's a cowshed." And if you happen to write restaurant menus, you had better watch your "associators," for they determine to some extent how much you can charge for the food.

Hamburger	$ 0.85
Salisbury Steak	$ 2.00
Chopped Tenderloin Steak	$ 3.00
Charcoal-Broiled Chopped Tenderloin Steak	$ 5.00
Prime Tenderloin Steak, Charcoal Grilled (Chopped)	$ 7.00
Du Boeuf Haché Grillé au Charbon de Bois	$12.50

And make certain your dining establishment has *ambience*—if it's only *atmosphere*, you'll have to reduce your menu prices.

Parents have naming responsibilities, too. They name their children. So if that obligation is in the near future for you, you may want to consider a study conducted by Deborah Linville. She asked seniors and graduate students at the Rensselaer Polytechnic Institute to rate 250 female names on a scale of 1 (nonsexy) to 7 (sexy).

According to her group, among the sexiest names were Alicia, Adrienne, Candace, Cheryl, Christine (highest rated), Dawn, Gail, Heather, Holly, Jacqueline, Jennifer, Julia, Kathy, Maria, Marilyn, Melanie, Michelle, Renae, Susan, Tamara, and Tina. Among the lowest rated: Alma, Cornelia, Doris, Edna, Elvira, Ethel (lowest), Esther, Florence, Magdalene, Myrtle, Rosalind, Silvana, and Zelda.

But there's more. Linville mixed a few of the top-rated names with a few of the lowest rated. Then she asked a second group of students to rate the names as job applicants. The nonsexy names were chosen by male raters (far more than by female raters) for employment and promotion over the sexy counterparts.

All of which seems to leave parents in a fix. They may opt for a name in the middle of the list hoping to find a reasonably attractive one which at the same time would not be a burden in their daughter's climb to the firm's (or nation's) presidency. In the middle list: Anne, Audrey, Barbara, Betsy, Betty, Carolyn, Catherine, Charlotte, Elaine, Ellen, Faith, Hope, Jean, Jill, Joanne, Joyce, Laura, Linda, Marcia, Marian, Mary, Patricia, Priscilla, Ruth, Shirley, Virginia, Wendy, and Yolanda.

Humorist Art Buchwald, on reviewing the Linville study, suggested that it might be invaluable evidence in a job discrimination suit. "If an Ethel gets promoted over a Christine, although Christine had been in the organization far longer, Christine has got one heck of a case."

Lest it appear that euphemizing and dysphemizing are merely playing with words, I submit that a key issue in a continuing controversy is whether an abortion should be regarded as "killing a human being" or "terminating a pregnancy."

NAME-CALLING

There is a species of the "pointing-associating" confusion that merits special attention. It concerns the associating labels that people apply to one another and to themselves. The names we call others or by which we are called can profoundly influence our evaluations and behavior.

The Double Burden

The child's retaliation, "Sticks and stones may break my bones, but names can never hurt me," is unfortunately only half correct. Names can hurt us, even more grievously, on occasion, than sticks and stones.

Consider the youngster who survives polio with a withered leg. The physical pain of walking and the psychic pain of watching other children run may be as nothing compared with the burden of a thoughtlessly imposed nickname such as Limpy or Gimpy. Or consider the youngster scarred by acne. A disfigured face is a sufficient trial, but a label such as Scarface may well double the burden.

Adults are not exempt from carrying a double burden. A psychologist who serves as an employee counselor with a manufacturing firm recently described the case of a young, intelligent, and attractive stenographer who came to him for help. Until recently she had been considered by her supervisor to be a superior employee, but during the last few months she had grown nervous and irritable. Her work began to deteriorate, and her supervisor finally recommended that she speak with the counselor. He learned that the young woman has been divorced three years previously but seemed to have made a satisfactory adjustment. In recent months, however, her social life was more than she could bear. Breaking down, she sobbed: "I've dated four men in the last year, and in each case things were going fine until my boyfriend found out I had been married. Two of them dropped me like a hot potato, and the other two began taking such liberties that I had to drop them. Why don't men give divorcées a chance to start over? Look, I'm decent and I intend to stay that way, but they make it pretty rough."

Living Up to the Labels

This young woman was resisting her name, but this is not always the case. People, often unconsciously, tend to live up to their labels. I shall never forget an experience in a group dynamics course in college. There were about 20 in the class, and we met twice weekly in two-hour discussion sessions. Our basic purpose was to study group dynamics by observing the dynamics of our own group. Along about the sixth week, one member of the group made a statement to this effect: "It has occurred to me that certain people in this group tend to play certain roles. I have noticed that whenever someone is being picked on, Kathy will step in to defend him—she's sort of a protector of the underdog. And when we begin to argue and the tension begins to build, have you noticed that it's often Bill who tries to relax us with a comical remark? And Don usually backs anyone who wants a change—he's 'Mr. Progressive'!" He continued to categorize three or four other members. The group responded with some chaffing of the "underdog protector," "the jokester," and so on, and the subject was forgotten—apparently. But as the weeks went on, it became obvious that some of those labeled were portraying their "roles" in and out of season! Kathy was defending underdogs more vehemently than ever; Bill was joking more than ever—even when there were no tensions to be broken; and so forth.[2]

Unhappily, living up to one's labels can have far graver consequences. Consider this statement from a social worker's file:

> I got a reputation as the town's bad girl. Sure, I did some of the things they said I did. But not until I had been blamed for a lot of things not my fault. After that I didn't care.

The double burden has become so oppressive for adolescents in trouble that authorities have been moved to speak out against such incriminating labels as "juvenile delinquent." Joseph Lohman, a sociologist and for four years sheriff of Cook County, Illinois, has said: "The name juvenile delinquent . . . sets the young person apart and may motivate further misbehavior." Mrs. Newton P. Leonard, president of the National Congress of Parents and Teachers (PTA) a few years ago, exhorted her nearly 9 million members to discard the label. "Juvenile delinquents, so-called, are children in trouble, children in conflict—with the law, with society, with themselves," she said. "The last thing they need is to be branded with a dehumanizing label and a matching set of attitudes from members of the community."

Living Down the Labels

Living up to one's labels may result in irrational and tragic behavior, but the consequences of living them down can be equally foolish and dangerous. For instance, a Claremont, California youth became so embarrassed when he failed his driver's license test that, to prove himself to his ridiculing friends, he stole a car and drove it—to Philadelphia! But for a more poignant example, consider the case of a 17-year-old who stabbed a 14-year-old boy to death. A typical attack-by-bully incident? If you were to look behind the glaring headlines, you would find a very different kind of explanation. You would discover the story of a life in torment—the story of

---

[2]In fact, their role-playing was so rigid that this was virtually the only kind of behavior they were able or willing to portray.

a boy pathetically small for his age, frail since infancy, a boy prevented by malnutrition from entering school until he was 8, a boy now 17 who weighed only 90 pounds and stood 4 feet 11 in his shoes. You could see the image of a lad taunted by his playmates with the stinging labels of Half-Pint, Short-Stuff, and Peanut.

On the fateful day, Adrian encountered two boys—each three years younger but 50 pounds heavier than he. The boys began the usual "runt" diatribe, and the conflict escalated. "Mickey started for me," testified Adrian, "and Tommy went to the side. They were bigger than me, and I thought they were gonna beat me up. I hadda use something to protect myself. He [Mickey] kept coming, and I stabbed him." The weapon was a knife that Adrian used to open boxes in the grocery store where he worked. Adrian's face clouded as he recalled that his tormentors had also called him an imp, a weasel, and Wimpy.

Positive Labels

These sobering illustrations of the possible consequences of living up to or of living down one's labels should not suggest that such behavior is necessarily negative and destructive in its effect. On the contrary, labels may sometimes have definite positive influence. I am firmly convinced that a fair share of the good in people is derived from the good that was expected of them as children. Many children, I am confident, became honest, responsible, generous adults partly, if not largely, because others, notably their parents, teachers, and playmates, expected such qualities of them and communicated their anticipations to them. By making clear to children that you know they are truthful and that you genuinely trust them, you are implicitly, if not explicitly, labeling them as "truth-teller," and the chances are that they will live up to the label. It is the genuine high expectation (which implies trust, confidence, respect) of the other which, after all, is the cornerstone of Theory Y (see Chapter 2).

But even positive labels may be dangerous. Unrealistic positive labels may entice one to overreach one's capabilities and thus lead to frustration, disillusionment—even tragedy. Consider the case of the young man described in the polarization chapter, who, on the eve of his high school graduation, was found hanged in his attic. An outstanding personality, the boy had been president of his class, active in school affairs. He had just been accepted for enrollment by one of the nation's leading universities and had been given a new convertible by his proud parents. What could conceivably have driven him to suicide? Authorities uncovered a probable reason: He had missed being elected to the National Honor Society by a fraction of a point. His self-image (his self-labels, if you will) and this overwhelming failure were evidently irreconcilably polarized in his tortured mind.

"ASSOCIATIVE" BYPASSING

This fallacious "pointing-associating" duality of language offers still another possibility for communication difficulty. An earlier chapter described bypassing as the miscommunication pattern whereby people miss each other with their meanings. We were concerned with words that were being used and reacted to primarily as "pointers." Let us now examine the tendency of people to miss each other's "associative" meanings.

"Associative" Bypassing Becomes Possible:

1.   When the sender (speaker, writer, and so on) assumes that, because his or her words are intended to be merely "pointers," they will necessarily have little or no "associative" value for the receiver (listener, reader, and so forth):

> In the earlier years of commercial aviation a cabin attendant would warn passengers: "We're flying through a *storm*. You had better fasten your *safety* belts; it will be less *dangerous*." He or she might have intended nothing more than merely "pointing" with those words, but you may be sure the novice passengers "associated" a great deal more. Today, flight personnel are trained to elicit pleasant and secure associations with: "We're flying through some turbulence now; please fasten your *seat* belts—you will be more comfortable."[3] Even so, perfection is still illusive—not long ago a vivacious young flight stewardess strayed from the script to announce gaily that we were to land soon: "Folks, please fasten your seat belts; we'll be hitting the ground in just a few minutes."

2.   When the receiver interprets words as largely or solely "pointers," whereas the sender intended them to be "associative."

> If you have ever complained: "Oh! You take things so literally," you have probably been involved in this sort of *"associative"* bypassing. It is the pathetic miscommunication which occurs when the young lady vainly tries to encourage her shy date with "Johnny, I'm cold." Whereupon her gallant escort whips off his jacket and slips it around her shoulders. She had wanted the jacket, all right, but with Johnny's arms still in the sleeves!
>
> This is the pattern, too, of sarcasm which fails. A sales manager was busily preparing for a trip which was to take him away from the office for the day. He called his filing clerk, pointed to a small pile of correspondence, and instructed: "Please file these letters." And, hoping to jar him from his usual lethargy, the manager added wryly: "Be sure to take all day with the job!" He did.

---

[3]When you fly you may be told that there is open seating. That sounds delightful—sit anywhere you wish—like owning your own airliner. You do indeed have your option, provided that someone is not already seated there! So if you don't get reasonably close to the head of the line of onboarding passengers you may find yourself seated opposite the lavatory wedged between two corpulent riders.

3.   When the communicator (sender or receiver or both) assumes that words have the same "associative" value for the other person as they have for oneself.

> Illustrative is the case of the hospital patient who was awaiting major surgery the next day. He was toying with breakfast as he worried about the operation. Suddenly a nurse appeared at his door, noticed the barely touched food, and blithely said: "Better eat—*while you can!*" The poor man immediately assumed the worst. But the nurse had only meant to imply that the food service attendant would soon pick up the breakfast tray!

A POSSIBLE MISUNDERSTANDING

If in discussing these particular pitfalls of language I have given the impression that "associators" are bad or that they are to be avoided or abolished, I have not intended to. In the first place, "associating" is not a thing that can be destroyed. It is a function of words, and it has no existence apart from people using and reacting to words. As long as people have imaginations, as long as they have the agility to leap beyond the immediate objects of their senses, there will be "associating." And let us be everlastingly grateful for it. The world would be unbearably prosaic without humor (an enormous portion of which is based upon association) and without poetry, drama—literature in general—which is designed to elicit rich associations from us. "I love you" (among the most highly "associative" phrases in our culture) would be just so many flat, commonplace words if the sender and the receiver were not able to transport themselves beyond mere "pointers."

Are we not sometimes the poorer for having cast out "associators"? Consider that in Victorian times only horses *sweated*, men *perspired*, and women—why they merely *glowed!*

No, this chapter has not been calculated to annihilate "associators" (even if that were possible). And certainly there has been no intention of debasing or minimizing their value and usefulness. On the other hand, it is clear that there are occasions when it is important, even imperative, to be *aware* of when "associators" are being used and to know how to cope with them. It is for these purposes that the following corrective measures are offered.

CORRECTIVES

It is the major thesis of this chapter that words can be used and reacted to both as "pointers" and as "associators." When communicators forget, ignore, deny, or, for any reason, are unaware of this duality, patterns of miscommunication become possible which may lead to confusion and trouble. Among these patterns are the "pointing-associating" confusion, name-calling, and "associative" bypassing. The suggestions which follow should be helpful in recognizing and dealing with these patterns.

The "Pointing-Associating" Confusion

Make a Habit of Distinguishing between Labels and Things.   Living and communicating with labels as we do, we are frequently enticed to accept them as the things they represent. Communicators must be wary of reacting to labels as if they were more than representations (and often misleading representations at that). In this vein, give Mrs. Haney credit for a sensible adjustment to what had been a distinctly distasteful task for her. As a child, she was occasionally required to fish out of the sink the potato peelings, carrot scrapings, and assorted remains from the dinner dishes. This was referred to in the family as "cleaning out the garbage," a chore (and phrase) which distressed her to the point of nausea. At Girl Scout camp a year or so later, she gained an insight. There the girls were instructed to scrape the "leftover food" off their plates. On returning home, she discovered that she could remove the "garbage" from the sink with scarcely a qualm as long as she reminded herself that it was "leftover food" she was touching.

Remember, the map is *not* the territory; words are *not* that which they are being used to represent. Ask yourself: "Am I responding to the *object* or to the *association* I have for its *name*?"

Don't Permit the Label to Obscure the "Product."   Develop the extensional habit of looking behind labels to see the product more clearly. Manufacturers who assume that consumers usually look beyond the labels have sometimes paid for their overconfidence. Several years ago a new chocolate dessert topping came on the market. The product was tasty and inexpensive, but many customers adamantly refused to try it, apparently because they were unable or unwilling to look beyond its rather colorful name—Goop!

Some companies, however, learn the lesson less painfully. "Mrs. Japp's Potato Chips" had been distributed throughout greater Chicago for sometime before World War II. But shortly after Pearl Harbor sales began to sag. It didn't take Mrs. Japp (a Danish name) long to find the answer and change the name to "Jay's Potato Chips." The product has prospered ever since. Similarly, "Mikado" wooden pencils became "Mirado."

It came as no great surprise to the sports world that the National League Cincinnati Baseball Club changed its name from "Reds" to "Redlegs" in the era of congressional investigations of Communists. This, incidentally, was the same wordwise organization which felt that "bleachers" was a somewhat unattractive name for its uncovered stands. Since then the stands have been known as the Sun-Deck, and its patrons are permitted to wear beach costumes. For night games—miracle of miracles—it becomes the Moon-Deck!

Another convincing illustration of the role that a label plays in the acceptance of labelled products occurred in Shawnee Mission, Kansas. The Home Economics course offered to 7th-grade boys was suffering considerable absenteeism. Those who did attend were assaulted with "sissy," "panty waist," and "wimp." The course's name was changed to Cooking—no change in attendance. The name was changed again to Bachelor Survival. The school can't satisfy the demand for enrollment!

Remember that, despite your intentions, your words can affect other people. Buddha recognized this 25 centuries ago when he admonished: "Whatever words we utter should be chosen with care, for people will hear them and be influenced by them for good or ill."[4]

Name-Calling

The basic advice is to recognize names for what they are—merely tags, often inaccurate, and always incomplete representations of the flesh-and-blood persons to whom they are appended. Remember that the labels in themselves are utterly powerless and meaningless. It is our reactions to the labels of others (and to our own) that can have profound effects on our evaluations and behavior. It is tempting for those who do the labeling and for those who are labeled to assume that the labels are valid and complete.

More specifically, if the labels assigned to you are negative and unfavorable, refuse to live up to them, to resign yourself to them. Resist them, contradict them with your behavior (actions are usually more convincing than words). But, on the other hand, avoid overreacting to them and assuming a manner or characteristic which is as bad as or worse than the trait originally labeled. If your labels are positive, recognize that they may serve as a beneficial stimulant, but be wary of overreaching your capacities.

If you are doing the labeling, if label you must, be careful in your selection of tags. Negative labels are seldom useful and often dangerous, whereas positive labels are often, but not invariably, beneficial. If you want someone to be honest, let the person know that you genuinely trust him or her.

"Associative" Bypassing

"Associative" bypassing occurs when communicators miss each other with their "associative" meanings. Such bypassing is similar to bypassing

---

[4]*The Teaching of Buddha*, 4th ed. (Tokyo: Bukko Dendo Kyokai, 1977), p. 246.

(the missing of "pointer" meanings), and the reader is encouraged to review the correctives section in Chapter 9, "Bypassing."

But, in addition, remember:

1. Words to which you "associate" little or nothing may be highly "associative" for the other person.

   Labor contract negotiators have learned to be alert to some of the red-flag words which upset the other party. In meeting with company representatives, union negotiators, for example, refrain from mentioning the union "demand" and substitute union "proposal" when softer associations seem in order. They find, too, that discussions with management in terms of what "your employees want" rather than what "the union (or 'we') wants" are often carried on with more equanimity and objectivity.

2. Words "associating" a great deal to you may "associate" little or nothing to the other person—they may merely "point" for others.

   Before making his final decision on a proposal to move to new offices, the head of a large company called his top executives together for a last discussion of the idea. All were enthusiastic except the company treasurer, who insisted that he had not had time to calculate all the costs with accuracy sufficient to satisfy himself that the move was advantageous. Annoyed by his persistence, the chief finally burst out:

   "All right, Jim, all right! Figure it out to the last cent. A penny saved is a penny earned, right?"

   The intention was ironic. He meant not what the words denoted but the opposite—forget this and stop being petty. For him this was what his words connoted.

   For the treasurer "penny saved, penny earned" meant exactly what it said. He put several members of his staff to work on the problem and, to test the firmness of the price, had one of them interview the agent renting the proposed new quarters without explaining whom he represented. This indication of additional interest in the premises led the agent to raise the rent. Not until the lease was signed did the agency chief discover that one of his own employees had, in effect, bid up its price.[5]

3. Your receiver (or sender) may not be "associating" as you are.

   Employed by a tool and die works, a young engineer was assigned to study the plant's production procedures in general and to devise improvements. Tool and die people are the aristocracy of factory workers, and their foremen are of correspondingly high standing. The engineer was aware of this and took great care to show respect.

   When he found one department where he thought he could make considerable improvement, he first set about making friends with the workmen and their foreman. Once he had gained their acceptance he got the foreman

---

[5]From Robert Froman, "Make Words Fit the Job," *Nation's Business*, July 1959, p. 78. Reprinted by permission.

to call the men together so that he could outline his plans to the whole group. Because he thought that several of the men might resist change, he sought to allay their fears by saying:

"Of course, at this stage what I'm proposing is only an experiment." . . .

The men not only dragged their heels but actively sabotaged his attempted innovations. Finally, the foreman went to the production manager. The gist of his complaint was that the engineer was trying to use him and his men as "guinea pigs."

You may be tempted to dismiss this as an unthinking reaction on the part of the men. But it was the engineer who sought to communicate something to them, not they to him. He wanted to make them feel that he was proposing only tentative changes which would not become permanent unless they proved successful.[6]

DISCUSSION QUESTIONS

1. Euphemisms and dysphemisms are sometimes used to deceive others. What can be done to combat such forms of misrepresentation since they are usually not direct contradictions of truth?

2. On the other hand, what should be the rights of advertisers, public relations people, editorialists, lawyers, salespersons, writers, and others who rely largely upon words to accomplish their purposes?

3. Do you agree that only half of the sticks-and-stones expression is true? Why?

4. Recalling the illustration of students living up to their labels in the group dynamics course: What can be gained or lost by such labeling?

5. What are the pros and cons of positive labeling?

6. What are the pros and cons of "associators"?

7. Report upon an incident, perhaps involving yourself, in which "pointing-associating" confusion (or name-calling or "associative" bypassing) was involved. Why did the incident occur? What could have been done to prevent or correct it? What measures would tend to prevent its recurrence?

---

[6]Ibid., pp. 76–77.

CASES

CASE 15–1

Galvanized Sheets*

Some years ago the manufacturers of galvanized sheeting were experimenting with new methods of galvanization. The object was to develop a process that would be quick and inexpensive, and yet would coat sheeting in such a manner that it could be bent sharply without the galvanizing peeling off. One firm, the Ewell Company, finally developed a process that met these qualifications.

Their method was to manufacture sheeting in a continuous roll so that it could be galvanized as it rolled through the galvanizing pit. The sheeting was then cut to specifications.

The company felt that it had a superior product but decided upon a marketing test as a precautionary measure. A few salesmen in certain pilot territories were instructed to begin selling the new products to their customers, that is, sheet metal shops, ventilating firms, and so forth. Since no trade name had as yet been selected, the salesmen were told to refer to the new product as "continous roll galvanized sheets."

Customer reaction ranged from apathy to resistance. The salesmen returned to the plant and complained that the average customer had a firm conviction that the rolling process[1] would flatten out the galvanizing to such an extent that it would be too thin to withstand severe bends without peeling.

The salesmen tried in vain to explain that the "continous roll" of their new galvanizing process didn't really involve rolling in the thinning sense at all. The reports were disturbing, but Ewell, convinced of the superiority of its product, decided to gamble. The continuous roll process was adopted throughout the plant. The product was trademarked Flex-tite in the hope that this would offset prejudices. Production began in full swing while management crossed its fingers and waited.

Within two years it was obvious that the gamble had paid off. The company, now producing Flex-tite exclusively, had doubled its total sales of galvanized sheeting.

Discussion Questions
1. Why was the original label for the new product objectionable?

---

*All names have been disguised.

[1]Rolling in the metals industries generally referred to the process of thinning strips of metal as they passed between sets of rollers. The rollers exerted great pressure on the strips and literally squeezed them down into thinner gauges.

2. Give other examples of production-oriented labels which other organizations use in connection with their products or services. Is *your* organization (educational institution, business firm, government agency, and so forth) guilty of this?

3. What relevance does this case have for this chapter?

CASE 15-2

Sticks and Stones . . .*

> Despite the child's defiant jingle, names hurt more than sticks or stones: a man can more easily bear an attack on his body than an offense to his feelings, and will remember an insult long after he has forgotten an injury.
>
> —*Sidney Harris*

Live Wire. In Christchurch, New Zealand, hauled into court on a charge of using foul language to a telephone operator, an angry subscriber countercharged that the girl just laughed and laughed after he obliged her by spelling his name: Montmorency de Villiers.

Any Other Name. In Calgary, Alberta, George and Rosie Big Belly asked the provincial secretary what could be done for them under the provisions of The Change of Name Act.

Typo. In Philadelphia, when *Inquirer* columnist Frank Brookhouser reported that Hubert B. Wolfeschlegelsteinhasenbergerdorff had registered to vote in the November elections, Hubert wrote in indignantly to say that a *u* had been left out: his name was Wolfeschlegelsteinhausenbergerdorff.

In New Haven, Connecticut, Yale graduate student Edmund D. Looney petitioned the superior court for permission to change his name, claiming that it might interfere with the practice of his future profession—psychiatry.

Tired of Living in Snake Den. Johnston, Rhode Island, residents of Snake Den Road complained to the City Council of the frightful name of their street. The council ordered the name changed to Belfield Drive.

Southern Hospitality. In Birmingham, Alabama, when the judge asked him what the initials stood for, juryman W. J. Weaver recalled: "My mother and daddy had 11 daughters in a row. They decided to call me Welcome John."

Maiden Name. All through school, Mary Hooker had been embarrassed. Her mother's solace: "Don't worry, dear. One day, you'll marry a fine young man and that will be the end of the name problem." Unfortunately, Mary fell in love with and married Elmer Tramp.

---

*All items except the Harris quote and "*Maiden Name*" are from *Time* and are reprinted with permission.

CASE 15-3

The Manatee

The manatee is excellent eating—and that is its trouble. It has been in danger of being hunted out of existence in Florida. Kirk Monroe, a state senator, sought to protect the animal with a $500 fine for killing one. He introduced a bill in the state legislature in which he omitted the mammal's common name but used only its scientific name, *trichecus latirostris*.

The bill seemed tabled for posterity until on the last day of the legislative session one senator rose and opined: "If there is a beast with any name as that in the state of Florida it ought to be protected." The bill passed unanimously.

Discussion Question

1. Why did the bill pass?

CASE 15-4

"The Four Goals of Labor"

Fortune once conducted an interesting test. A cartoon entitled "The Four Goals of Labor" was clipped from a union newspaper and duplicated. *Fortune* deleted the union apellation and indicated that the cartoon had come from an NAM Newsletter. Twenty union members (who were unaware of the reattribution) were asked whether they thought the cartoon was a fair representation of labor's goals. Four reluctantly conceded that it was. Two were undecided. The other 14 roundly condemned the cartoon, describing it as patronizing, loaded, or paternalistic. One said, "Makes me want to spit."

Discussion Questions

1. What does this experiment prove?
2. How would a group of managers respond to something that had been falsely attributed to the AFL-CIO?

CASE 15-5

Prestige Foods*

Prestige Foods—attractively packaged fruits, fowl, meats, and so forth—have found widespread favor as business gifts. The foods are generally of

---

*All names have either been disguised or omitted.

high quality and even more highly priced. The gift is invariably accompanied by a piece of sales literature. The following were sent with a smoked pheasant and a box of apples, respectively.

Smoke Dreams Come True

Rembrandt stewed over his canvas—a regular fussbudget about deep, rich browns. Stradivari swooned over a violin, working for a tone of pure gold. But they weren't in it with the way we toil, turning out our smoked bird masterpieces.

Wild life is pampered on our rolling wooded acres. Birds are urged to gorge on the fat of the land. To the plumpest we award the great adventure of the smokehouse and the great wide world, where they make mouths water and gladden hearts.

This succulent creature is ready to eat. It's been slowly smoked over fragrant hickory embers. Lazy little plumes of smoke sealed in the sweet juices, turned the outside crackly brown. We firmly believe you can't get such happy flavor anywhere else.

This bird will keep approximately two or three weeks in the refrigerator. (Hsst! Or a year in a freezer with the wrapper left on. But who's that Spartan?)

Hints for Serving

How to Slice. With any smoked bird it's gourmet-wise (not stingy) to slice it wafer thin. That lets your lucky palate savor every delicious smoky morsel. A good sharp knife will do the trick.

Getting Het Up, Whole. If—instead of eating your bird cold, just as it comes—you have a yen to try it hot, here's how. Put it in a roaster with some good strong chicken broth or consommé. Use a moderate oven and baste conscientiously.

Wonderful Canapés. Here's where a smoked bird really preens itself. Try slivers of the tender smoked meat on little squares of fresh buttered toast—goldly brown and fragrant. Top with a dab of horseradish, or better yet, our very own Dippin' Gravy.

Or mince some of the smoked meat and add to softened, well-seasoned cream cheese. Spread on crisp crackers.

Or serve thin slices of smoked meat with snowy rings of Bermuda onion on rounds of buttered rye.

Or carry out your own inspirations. This bird can't *help* being delicious!

Fancied Up

Smoked Bird á la King. And we really mean regal. Use your favorite Chicken á la King recipe, substituting whatever smoked bird you're blessed with. Just before serving, add a good stiff dose of Sherry or Madeira.

Smoked Bird Rarebit. Nestle slices of smoked bird between pieces of hot buttered toast. Cover with strips of brisk sharp cheese and slide under the broiler till the cheese starts to burble and run. Serve at once.

Smoked Bird and Scrambled Eggs. Mince the meat and add to slightly beaten eggs. Cook in double broiler, stirring thoughtfully.

Smoked Bird Salad. Toss some savory bird shreds in with your favorite mixed salad—crisp greens, dewy tomatoes, shivery cucumbers. Let it glisten with good French dressing and rejoice in a mite of Roquefort.

Glorious Leftovers

Never, *never* throw out that precious carcass till it's worked magic! Would you toss out platinum? Would you discard diamonds?

'Tis wonderful—that carcass—in soup, beautiful soup. And that goes for the glittering white bones of the most greedily denuded. Try simmering that exposed frame in a kettle of Split Pea Soup. Serve in man-size soup plates, spiked with Sherry. O tempora! O mores! And the same for Black Bean or Lentil.

Greetings From Sparkling Brook, California

Dear Epicure:—

These Golden Globe Apples were sent to you at the request of the person whose name appears on the address label.

They are grown solely by me, in a little hidden valley in the Sierra Nevada Mountains of California. Your donor is able to send them to you through having acquired a Preferred Share in the fruits of my orchard.

When I first found this valley, over 20 years ago, it was an abandoned homestead—so forlorn that folks poked fun at me, and said: "What are you going to raise, Joe—sagebrush or rabbit weed?"

But here I had found one old apple tree, with a heavy crop on it. And a native of these parts told me that every fall, for 25 years, he had helped himself to apples from it. "Hmm," I thought, "a natural apple spot if there ever was one."

So here I planted a dozen different kinds of apples—including a new one, recently discovered growing wild on a mountainside. And this new one turned out to be just the apple this little valley was waiting for.

Here our golden California sun gives its flesh and skin a golden tinge. Here our cold mountain nights develop its fruit sugars, and make it so crisp that every bite crackles. Here the volcanic ash in the soil gives it a tang no other apple has. And here the pure mountain springs from which its growth is watered fill it with a ciderlike juice which is nature's true champagne.

Because this "Golden Globe" Apple is a luxury fruit which can be gotten nowhere else, apple lovers all over America now send to me for it. If, after eating these, you would like information on my various packs, and Preferred Rights to them, I will be glad to send it.

Sincerely yours,
Joe Wilson

CASE 15–6

Flight from Scorn—A Tale of Two Boys

These two accounts, with only the names disguised to prevent further embarrassment, are factual.

Thirteen-year-old Danny detested his schoolmates calling him Fatty. Five months ago, he weighed 105 pounds—seemingly not excessive for his height, 5 feet 5 inches. But by Danny's own perception he was a bit too chubby. So be began to diet—with a vengeance. His parents were not alarmed at first but when his weight dropped to 62 pounds they took him to a hospital. Doctors ruled out glandular problems and ordered tube feeding. He gained ten pounds in five days. Finally, he divulged his secret— he'd been worried about the teasing. Now at 74 pounds he's been discharged for another crack at Mom's good home cooking.

Eleven-year-old Larry was a different target for ridicule: he has one brown eye and one blue eye. Classmates began calling him "old brown and blue eyes." Larry decided he could stand it no longer and ran away from home. But two nights of sleeping under porches proved even worse so he turned himself in to police who in turn returned him home.

Discussion Questions
1. Why did Danny and Larry behave as they did?
2. Can you give examples of older people who overreacted to name calling?
3. How can we protect ourselves against the double burden of name calling?

CASE 15–7

McCall College*

McCall College is a small Eastern liberal arts college. For many years its theater department had enjoyed an excellent and well-deserved reputation among the student body and faculty and among the community in which the college was located. The theater department presented eight or nine plays yearly, the season beginning in October and ending in May. Each play was presented for six performances—one each night from Wednesday through Sunday and a matinee on Saturday. The average attendance over the years had been gratifyingly high, 85 percent of capacity, ranging from 60 to 65 percent to frequent standing-room-only audiences.

Last year the theater's director, Doug Lawson, decided that for one of the midseason productions he would present a collection of excerpts from several plays rather than one single play. The theme was to portray the changes in theatrical production from classic Greece up to the 20th century. He titled the production, accurately enough, *Theater Styles Review*, and chose excerpts from Euripides' *Hippolytus*, representing the classic Greek theater; *Everyman* (medieval morality play); Shakespeare's *Midsummer Night's Dream* (16th century); Molière's *The Would-Be Gentle-*

---

*All names have been disguised.

man (17th century); Sheridan's *School for Scandal* (18th century); Stowe's *Uncle Tom's Cabin* (19th-century melodrama); Ibsen's *Ghosts* (19th-century realism); and Wilde's *The Importance of Being Earnest* (19th-century comedy of manners).

Lawson designed the sets and carefully rehearsed the cast. After several weeks of hard work, everyone from Lawson to the student curtain-puller eagerly anticipated the audience reaction.

Finally, on opening night Lawson peeked through the act curtain to count the house. The auditorium was virtually empty! It seemed incredible. The weather was typically unpleasant for February, but audiences had turned out on much more inclement nights. No one could think of a competing attraction in town that night, and yet there they were—or weren't!—an audience of only 20 percent capacity!

But the show must go on—and so it did, admirably. The sparse audience thoroughly enjoyed the presentation, and Lawson, despite his disappointment with the size of the audience, was justifiably proud of his company. He had rarely seen an opening night at McCall so brilliantly and flawlessly executed.

After the performance the director, cast, and crew sat down together to ponder. The only possible answer, everyone agreed, must lie in freakish chance. It just happened, someone offered, that everyone decided, for one reason or another, that he would attend on some night other than the first. But just wait, some promised bravely, we'll have overflow crowds the rest of the week!

But there were no overflow crowds. To be specific, the audiences ranged between 20 and 35 percent of capacity. Lawson was stunned. Didn't people like the excerpt format? He had had good audience reactions to it on several previous occasions. Were the performances poor? Certainly his own judgment and the demonstrably appreciative audiences precluded this as a reason. What then? Lawson called his company together and began:

> As you all know we have just had the greatest attendance flop in the 15 years I have been here. Now why? Don't tell me the audiences, what there were of them, didn't love it. And you people did marvelously. Now the purpose of this meeting is to decide what went wrong, correct it, and run the show again in May. I gambled with it once and lost, but I'm just stubborn enough, and confident enough of my product, to gamble again. Now, what went wrong?

Several suggestions for minor changes in dialogue, business, and sets were made. Someone suggested that the title might be changed. Lawson invited the troup to think of a better name. Some suggestions: *Lagniappe, Grease Paint Review, Sex through the Ages, Euripides Goes Wilde, 2600 Years of Grease Paint*. Finally, *Athens to Broadway* was selected, and the production was repeated during a week in May.

The attendance soared to the old standard. The audiences ranged from 70 to 85 percent of capacity during the six performances.

Discussion Questions

1. How do you account for Lawson's "greatest attendance flop"?
2. How could this miscommunication have been prevented?

CASE 15-8

The Bright Young Man

Bob Elgin, a district manager, had long considered the company's management training program inadequate and felt that he had a responsibility to supplement company-sponsored trainees by developing people with management potential from the ranks. Such was the case when he hired Bruce Gorman, recently discharged from the Army, for an office position in one of his plants.

Bruce immediately asserted himself and was not hesitant about offering suggestions for improvement and criticism of areas that he felt were not up to par. Bob took an immediate liking to Bruce and proposed him for acceptance into the company-sponsored management training program. Bob's request was denied, primarily because Bruce lacked a college education and because of the personnel interviewer's evaluation of Bruce as having a cocksure attitude.

Exercising his prerogative, Bob decided to put Bruce through the training program at the district's own expense.

Bob and Bruce developed considerable rapport, and with the management trainer's guidance Bruce progressed rapidly. When the opening arose, Bob was able to sell Bruce to higher management as a plant manager.

Bruce was so elated that he told Bob that in his new assignment he would break all existing records—and proceeded to do so. One of the boasts Bruce made to Bob was that he would reach a credit currency of 70 percent his first month. The plant under the previous manager had never exceeded a credit currency of 55 percent. Bruce's credit currency for his first month was 68.9 percent.

Bob was delighted. He immediately dispatched a congratulatory memo to Bruce, inserting a good-natured needle about his missing his prediction by a hair:

> To: B. N. Gorman
> From: R. L. Elgin
> Subject: Credit Currency Report
>   68.9 percent is not 70 percent, but what else can I expect from a green manager? Here's hoping you do better this month.

A week later Bob visited Bruce's plant for the first time since the credit currency report. He entered Bruce's office to find him hard at work at papers strewn about his desk.

Bob said jocularly: "That's a mighty fine impersonation of a hard worker!"

Startled, Bruce looked up and retorted sharply: "I thought I'd have more than one month to prove my worth!"

Discussion Questions

1. What were Bob Elgin's perceptions regarding himself and Bruce up to the moment Bruce gave his sharp retort?
2. What were Bruce Gorman's perceptions regarding himself, his job, and Bob Elgin up to and including Bob's remark: "That's a mighty fine impersonation . . .?"
3. What does this case have to do with "pointing" and "associating"?
4. What should Bob do now?

CASE 15–9

Leonard Who?

Would Fred Astaire and Ginger Rogers have been as light on their feet had they remained Frederick Austerlitz and Virginia Katherine McMath? Would Jack Benny and Eddie Cantor have been as hilarious if they hadn't changed from Benny Kubelsky and Edward Israel Itzkowitz? Would Boris Karloff have been as menacing as William Henry Pratt? And would Natasha Gurdin, Doris Kappelhoff, Frances Gumm, Raquel Tejada, Alexandra Zuck, and Norma Jeane Baker been as glamorous as Natalie Wood, Doris Day, Judy Garland, Raquel Welch, Sandra Dee, and Marilyn Monroe? We may never know the answers to these crucial questions but Nicholas Aloysius Adamshock, Reginald Truscott-Jones, Alexander Archibald Leach, Leonard Slye, and Spangler Arlington Brough were likely better off being known as Nick Adams, Ray Milland, Cary Grant, Roy Rogers, and Robert Taylor.

Many newer stars have eschewed pseudonyms. Anka, Baez, Cosby, DeNiro, Fonda, Gere, Hawn, Jagger, Lauper, Manilow, McCartney, Minnelli, Nugent, Pacino, Richie, Ronstadt, Sedaka, Spacek, Springsteen, Streep, Streisand, Travolta—those names don't seem particularly lyrical. But they are originals and they don't seem to have hampered their owners' careers.

And finally the old joke:

> I wonder if anyone ever needled Big John Wayne about his name originally being Marion Morrison.
> I know of one fellow who did.
> Really? I'd sure like to meet him!
> So would I but I don't think they'll dig him up just for that.

Discussion Questions

1. Why does this case appear in this chapter?
2. Most of the pseudonyms seem euphemistic compared to the originals. Roy Rogers sounds more attractive than Leonard Slye. But what about Boris Karloff?
3. What do you think of the apparent trend of performers to retain their original names?

CASE 15–10

A New Witch Hunt

We used to call them cold sores. Now they have a new name and thereby hangs a tragic tale.

Doctors now refer to the common childhood ailment as *herpes—herpes simplex* I, to be more exact. But that's close enough to *herpes simplex* II, the dreaded genital herpes that has contributed to a great deal of anguish and downright unsane behavior.

As of this writing, the most notorious victim—or villain, depending upon your point of view—is three-year-old Johnny Bigley of Anne Arundel County, Maryland.

Johnny contracted the virus at birth and cold sores periodically break out on his hands and back. That condition plus its ominous label have terrorized the Pasadena Elementary School since Johnny enrolled.

His teacher immediately asked for and received a transfer to another school. The parents of Johnny's classmates have steadfastly refused to permit their children to attend classes when Johnny is present. Lawyers representing the school and the teachers sought an injunction to keep Johnny out of school except on days on which there are no sores whatsoever anywhere on his body.

The judge decided that Johnny would submit to a daily examination by a doctor and that he would be kept home on days when there were sores on his hands. Johnny could come to school if he had sores on his back, provided he wore a one-piece jump suit—and if the school took precautions originally calculated as a protection against hepatitis.

None of these rulings have dissuaded parents or teachers who demand more stringent restrictions. The 10-day injunction has now expired and Susan Russell, attorney for the parents and teachers argues: "You have to weigh one child's right to an education against the risks to all the other children—and there is a slim risk of infection."

The rancor continues despite the fact that the risked infection is simply to cold sores to which, according to doctors, up to 70 percent of the children get anyway.

Dr. Ward Cates of the National Center for Disease Control states: "The likelihood of these children getting the virus from him (Johnny) is much smaller than of their getting it from kids without any symptoms at all." And Dr. Andre Nahmias of Emory University's medical school stresses that the herpes simplex I virus is "so ubiquitous (more than 70 percent of the adult population now carry it) that it is virtually impossible to avoid exposure."[1]

Such authoritative comments ought to be calming but they are not. Some parents can't back down even if they want to. According to attorney Russell, one parent was warned that if her child attended class with Johnny, he would not be allowed into his after-school day center.

The upshot is that young Johnny continues to arrive at an empty school, carrying all the grown-up sexual stigma associated with "herpes."

> The sobering lesson is an old one: that words are amazingly powerful. We jeer at the idea that people might once have believed in spells, or proved their innocence by reciting complicated oaths without a slip.

> But confronted by a word that conjures up a reality we can't control—a disease we can't cure or don't understand—we shy away as if Johnny Bigley had the black plague. Grown-ups can, and should, behave better.[2]

Discussion Questions

1. Why do the parents refuse to let their children attend class with Johnny Bigley?

2. What do you think of the judge's ruling?

3. What else can be done to ameliorate the matter?

4. Assuming the affair can be resolved, what is the possible long-range effect upon Johnny?

CASE 15–11

Résumé Expansion

A highlight of *The Official M.B.A. Handbook* or *How to Succeed in Business without a Harvard M.B.A.* is résumé expansion. That seems a very modest expression for the highly creative reconstructive surgery the authors propose.

The basic idea is to "transform the insipid into the inspired, the mundane into the magnificent, the illegal into the entrepreneurial." While they don't advocate outright lying, they do advise that you "repackage your achievements in terms that give them dignity and importance."

---

[1]"Herpes Hysteria in the Classroom," *Newsweek*, January 22, 1985, p. 38.

[2]Morton Kondracke, "Doublespeak and the Witch Hunt," *Chicago SunTimes*, February 2, 1985, p. 13.

Education
High School: Scarsdale High, Scarsdale New York
College: North Western U., September 1977–
June 1981
  • Made Dean's List
  • So did 82% of the class
  • Babysat a couple of times for my
    Philosophy prof. when he and spouse
    went to Chicago
  • Dealt a little marijuana to friends to
    work my way through school after
    the Old man cut me off.

Graduate Work: Harvard Business School, Septem-
ber 1981– M.B.A. expected in June
1983 (God willing!)
  • Grind in library six days a week
  • Organized Saturday Night parties
    to meet local college women with
    chicks appeal.

Work Experience
Cook: Kentucky Fried Chicken, summer 1981
  • Biggest one in Westchester
  • Cooked on swing shift
  • Took home extra chicken if I cooked
    too much
  • Taught high school kids how to
    cook chicken, and told them to hustle.

Caddy: Greenview Country Club, summer 1980
  • Found golfer's balls
  • Replaced divots
  • Told members off when they
    undertipped
  • Tended the pin
  • Arranged member's betting pools
  • Stepped on opponents balls in the
    rough

Other Experience: Won $50,000 in McDonald's
  "Build a Big Mac" contest summer
  1981
  • Spent $18,000 of winnings on new
    Corvette
  • Totalled car into front window of
    local Teamsters union hall while
    coming home blotto from party
  • Sold car to pay repair bills and
    settle with Teamsters
  • Used remaining $21,000 to pay for
    business school

They offer this illustration[3]:

> *Prentiss Robert Jackson* was a business student who used this technique. Born of humble stock in Scarsdale, New York, he had an academically successful but otherwise nondescript four years at a well-known midwestern college. On the fact of it, he was afraid that his lack of serious work experience would doom him to a decade of penal servitude in somebody's personnel department. Instead, by careful application of résumé expansion, P.R. was able to turn his meager summer experience into a corporate recruiter's dream. Follow along as we trace the evolution of Jackson's résumé from scribbled work sheet to finished product.

Discussion Questions

1. What are the differences between the pre- and post-expansion versions of Jackson's résumé?

2. What patterns of miscommunication did the expanded résumé attempt to exploit?

3. Do you advocate the Fisk-Barron résumé-expansion approach?

---

[3]Jim Fisk and Robert Barron, *The Official M.B.A. Handbook*, pp. 107–9. Copyright © 1982 by 82 Corporation. Reprinted by permission of Wallaby Books, a division of Simon & Schuster, Inc.

Career Objective: a position offering
challenge, personal growth,
and serious *dinero*

**Résumé of
PRENTISS ROBERT JACKSON**

Home address:
12 Spruce Lane
Scarsdale, N.Y.

School address:
27 Gallatin Hall
The Business School
Boston, Mass.

Education

1981–1983   **HARVARD GRADUATE SCHOOL OF BUSINESS
ADMINISTRATION**
Worked my way through school by winning $50,000
special construction contract from national restaurant
chain. (Was forced to dispose of major asset, however,
after run-in with local Teamsters organization.)
Founding member, Aflu-American Association.

1977–1981   **NORTHWESTERN UNIVERSITY**
B.A. received June 1981. Dean's List. Established
primary day-care service for faculty children. Paid for
tuition and expenses last three years by founding a
small business that marketed a complete line of
leisure products to students, achieving return on
investment of 2,048 percent. Summa cum laude thesis:
David Bowie: The Last Existential Man.

**Work
Experience**

Summer
1982

GOLF COORDINATOR, GREENVIEW COUNTRY CLUB
Responsible for revitalization of golf course to achieve
improved playing characteristics. Tripled player
through-put by utilizing batch processing. Provided
professional assistance and financial consulting
services to members. Helped ensure members'
strategic success by respositioning them vis à vis their
competitors.

Summer
1981

**SPECIAL ASSISTANT TO FRANCHISER, KENTUCKY
FRIED CHICKEN, HARRISON, NEW YORK**
Senior production officer during high-volume evening
shift. Audited inventory stocking levels and instituted
control systems to prevent exceeding storage
capacity. Conducted initial employee orientation and
instituted employee motivational seminars.

16

Intensional Orientation:
3. Blindering

FIGURE 16–1

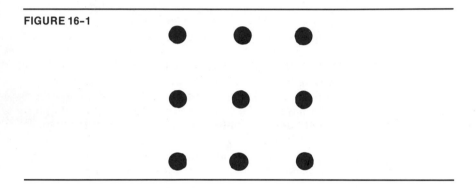

FIGURE 16–1

A good way to get the essence of this chapter under your skin is to make an earnest effort to solve the following problem.

Objective: To draw through all nine of the spots with these restrictions:

1. Start with your pencil on any one of the nine spots. (Figure 16–1).
2. Draw four straight lines without removing your pencil from the page.
3. You may cross over lines, but you may not repeat them, that is, trace back on them.
4. Some readers may already know the solution. Congratulations! Their reward is a further challenge: Do the problem in three lines! (That will teach them to be so clever!)

Most people have difficulty with the problem because they unconsciously add a fourth restriction—one that renders the problem insoluble.

Did you perceive the nine spots as a *square*? (Figure 16–2, p. 490.)

Most people in our culture would see it as such.[1] But did you then proceed to restrict your drawings of lines to the boundaries of your square: Did you assume that you could not draw beyond?

If you did (and most of us would), you were, of course, severely hampering your progress toward a solution. Once you remove the *self-imposed restriction*, the solution comes easily (Figure 16–2 on page 490).

The nine-spot puzzle illustrates one of the key difficulties in problem solving—the tendency to *restrict* one's view of the problem. Clearly, one of the most important reasons why the problem solver has a limited perception of a problem grows out of the *definition* of the problem. (Most people define or think of the problem above as the nine-spot *square*.)

A pertinent example of a restrictive problem definition occurred in a certain family I know. The wife complained that "the powder room was cold" during the winter. The husband unquestioningly accepted his wife's articulation of the problem, and together they began to work on it. Their first attempt was to cover the window and its frame with a large piece of plastic. This approach was not only unsightly but ineffective—the powder room seemed as cold as ever. The next action was to install a storm window. Since the window's dimensions were atypical, a tailor-made one had to be made—cost: $48.50. That helped but not much. Now the couple began to contemplate construction overhauls. She favored having the furnace people install another radiator in the room. He argued for tearing into the outside wall and inserting more or better insulation. Either plan would have run into hundreds of dollars.

Before taking either step, the couple, fortunately, began to reconsider the *definition* of the problem. "Let's face it," they jointly concluded, "our problem is not a cold powder room. It's a cold (and uncomfortable) *toilet seat*!" A fuzzy cover ($4.95) now adorns the seat, and the problem has been solved.[2]

In sum, the *words* we use to define a problem or situation can act as *blinders* (not unlike a horse's blinders or blinkers that prevent distractions from the side and limit its field of vision) and thus restrict us in our approach to the problem or situation.

Incidentally, the key to solving the nine-spot problem with *three* lines is to note that the challenge was simply to "draw through all nine of the spots." There was no requirement that the lines pass through the *centers* of the spots. Given the leeway of slicing through the peripheries of some of the spots, the problem can be readily solved (Figure 16–3).

---

[1]People in some cultures, such as the Trobriand Islanders, fail to perceive such connecting lines and would see, in this case, simply an aggregate of isolated spots.

[2]Ordinarily, to establish the authenticity of this illustration, I would cite the name of the family involved—but my wife would kill me!

FIGURE 16–2

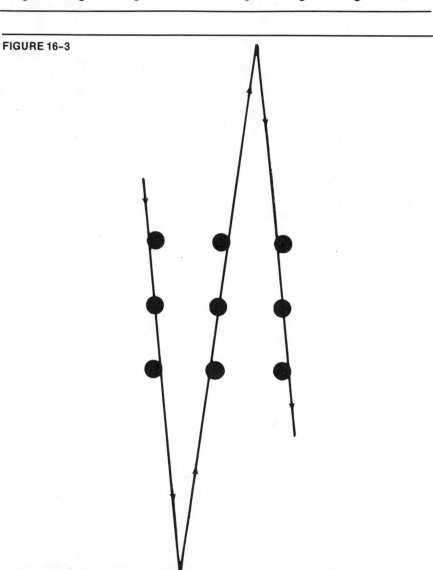

FIGURE 16–3

SOME CONSEQUENCES

Roughly speaking, blinders may lead to two broad kinds of consequences. Blindering may (1) delay or impede desirable solutions and (2) lead to undesirable solutions.

Delayed Solutions

If you are still in the mood for puzzles, try this one. Two cyclists are separated by 30 miles of straight, flat road. They begin pedaling toward each other simultaneously. At the same time, a fly takes off from the handlebars of one of the cyclists, flies to the second, turns instantaneously, flies back to the first, and so on. The fly continues to make these alternating flights as the cyclists continuously decrease the distance between themselves. Finally, the fly is smashed between the cyclists as they collide. Both cyclists were traveling at 15 miles per hour, and the fly at 40—all at constant rates of speed. The problem: What is the total distance of the fly's flight, that is, how far did the fly fly? (Don't read farther until you have tried to work out the problem for yourself.)

If you arrived at an incorrect answer, or at no answer at all, or at the correct answer in more than 15 seconds, something must have impeded your progress. Examine the assumptions you made about the problem. Did your reactions resemble one or more of these?

1. "The problem is difficult. It requires computation—paper and pencil work."
2. "The problem is incomplete. I don't have all of the necessary data."
3. "The problem is silly. I won't waste my time and energy."
4. The technicality finder: "A fly couldn't fly that fast." "How could the fly turn instantaneously—it would lose some speed."

Probably underlying each of these expressions (though only the first admits it) is the assumption that the problem is complex. Once we define a problem as complex, we are more likely to search (if we search at all) for an answer by using complex techniques, for example, by computing the sum of the decreasing distances of the fly's individual flights.

The problem, however, is quite simple—if one defines it as such. The cyclists are 30 miles apart and pedaling at 15 miles per hour. They will thus collide in one hour. The fly that travels at 40 miles per hour will thus have flown 40 miles.

I admit that I may have helped blinder you by asking "How *far* did the fly fly?" thus focusing attention on distance and away from time. Had the question been "How long did the fly fly, and therefore how far?" the correct answer would probably have come much more rapidly and easily.

The phenomenon of blindering as a factor in impeding progress is suggested by M. W. Ball:

> Oil men, through some queer quirk of herd psychology, have been great respecters of political boundaries. When oil is found in a state they are likely to search that state with enthusiasm and thoroughness, ignoring areas of equal promise just over the state line. Perhaps this explains why no oil was produced in New York until five years after its discovery in Northern Pennsylvania. . . .[3]
>
> Down in Texas, close to the southeast corner of New Mexico, the year that saw Maljamar discovered saw the discovery of the Hendricks field, one of the great fields of the West Texas Permian basin. The field was scarcely more than a stone's throw south of the New Mexico border, on a structural feature that obviously extended into New Mexico, yet for nearly three years the state line stopped the oil men cold.[4]

The Electra Story. It would be difficult to find a more poignant example of blindering contributing to a tragic delay in problem solving than that of the ill-fated Electra.

On September 29, 1959, a Lockheed Electra flying over Buffalo, Texas, crashed, killing all 34 aboard. Why it crashed was a mystery. The weather had been clear and calm. No planes or rockets were reported in the region. The pilot had reported no difficulties a few minutes previous to the crash.

The tragedy touched off one of the greatest aviation accident investigations in history. Before it was over, the investigation had involved hundreds of engineers, pilots, and government investigators.

The investigation was intensive, extensive, expensive—and for six months almost completely futile. The Lockheed and Civil Aeronautics Board investigators had made the blindering assumption "that the Electra was a sound mechanism and had presumed that the Buffalo crash was caused by some inexplicable distortion of a basically solid plane."[5]

> The engineers who designed the Electra's advanced, low-drag, high-speed wing had every reason to congratulate themselves at the time the plane was certificated on August 22, 1958. Their thin, stubby airfoil was not only enormously efficient but enormously strong. It satisfied every standard laid down by the government during a severe test program.[6]

A terrible price had to be paid for this blindering—for this delay in solving the problem. On March 17, 1960, another Electra with 63 aboard plummeted into soft earth near Tell City, Indiana.

---

[3]From *This Fascinating Oil Business*, by Max W. Ball, copyright, 1940, used by special permission of the publishers, The Bobbs-Merrill Co., Inc., p. 342.

[4]Ibid., pp. 358–59.

[5]"Brilliant Detection in Jet-Age Mystery," *Life*, July 25, 1960, p. 81. Reprinted by permission.

[6]Ibid., p. 78.

The CAB investigating team excavated 10 feet of dirt before they discovered what had happened to the plane: the 104-foot fuselage and all its contents—including 10,000 pounds of human flesh—had compressed into a cylinder of broken metal only 35 feet high as it came to rest underground. The masked investigators in glistening plastic gloves and aprons who removed this awful debris from the hole were seized with an overwhelming sense of horror, pity and physical revulsion as they worked. Those who had been concerned with the earlier Electa crash found themselves saying, "Maybe if I had been a little smarter. . . ."[7]

The circumstances of the crash suddenly made it impossible to continue to assume that the Electra was a basically sound plane.

Now, the investigators concentrated on the design of the plane itself. And finally an answer came.

As long as the Electra's outboard nacelles retained the stiffness for which they had been designed, the plane was safe and sound. But *if* the struts and braces inside the nacelle structure cracked or otherwise loosened, and *if* the wind was jolted hard by air turbulence or by a sudden pull-up, and *if* the plane was moving at high speed at the time, a curious chain reaction effect could be induced. Both the Electra's big, square-bladed propeller and its turbine engine turn at high speeds—the prop makes 1,280 revolutions and the turbine 13,820 revolutions a minute. Thus, when running, they comprise a huge gyroscope with all the same odd reactions to disturbance that children discover in toy gyroscopes at Christmas. When the sudden jolt caused the wing to flex and agitated a nacelle, this whole package of spinning metal, which projects far out in front of the leading edge of the wing, would begin wobbling in its mount, like a pointed forefinger with its tip describing a small circle.

The odds against this motion doing anything more than dampening or soothing the initial movement of the wing itself were enormous. But in the Electra the oscillating wing and the swirling power plant suddenly began "exchanging energy." Each deformation of the flexing wing forced the turbine to wobble more wildly. Every increase in the engine's wobble, in turn, fed new violence back into the fluctuation of the wing. As the wing's leading edge was twisted alternately upward and downward by this process, airflow added still more impetus to its movement. In a very few seconds with all these tremendous forces working on it in lethal rhythm like a fat man jumping harder and harder on a springboard, the wing would snap off as though it were made of glass. The mystery—in the opinion of Lockheed, of the FAA, and of the airlines involved—was finally solved.[8]

Yes, finally solved apparently, but what a horrendous price for a blindered delay.

---

[7]Ibid., p. 82.

[8]Ibid., p. 88.

We can also hope that the dread Legionnaires' Disease (which killed 36 people and hospitalized 151 at an American Legion convention in Philadelphia in 1976) has been finally, if tardily, explained. The cause, according to Dr. Joseph McDade, a microbiologist with the U.S. Public Health Service Center for Disease Control, is apparently a new bacterium.[9]

The breakthrough occurred only when McDade, having ruled out other bacteria, decided upon a new approach—to look for a strange organism rather than a familiar one. The irony is that the deadly bacterium had been known to science as early as 1947, but only as a curiosity. No one knew it then as *pneumophilia* (grisly translation, lung-loving). It surfaced again in 1959. And then in 1965 an outbreak of a pneumonia-like disease killed 16 at St. Elizabeth's Hospital in Washington, D.C. The surmise now is the lethal culprit was again pneumophilia—but it was not recognized as such.

Had blindering prevented the discovery of the cause then? Could the 187 Philadelphia casualties have been averted?

Blinder Names.   One cannot help wondering how long progress has been retarded by the assigning of inappropriate names. How much time was lost and how many lives were squandered by the term *malaria?* Contracted from the Italian words *mala aria* (bad air), the term perpetuated the erroneous notion that the disease was caused by the bad air of the swamps. And how long were the properties of *oxygen* concealed by its misleading name? Oxygen stems from the Greek terms for acid-producer—but, unfortunately oxygen does not produce acid! And how many bright and willing scientists were inhibited from even dreaming of the possibility that the *atom* (from the Greek for *indivisible*) could be split largely because its *name* said that it could *not* be divided?

Perhaps the most dramatic blinder-busting in athletics occurred on May 6, 1954. That was the day Roger Bannister ran the mile in under four minutes. Until then, it seemed to have been carved in granite that the magical four-minute mile was simply beyond mere mortals.

The record is now 3:46.31 minutes and the sub-four mile is the standard for world-class runners. In fact, between them John Walker and Steve Scott have achieved it over 200 times.

Gloria Steinem in *Advertising Age* alerts us that "working women" is a blinder term. It excludes homemakers. Instead, she says, we should talk about work outside the home or work inside the home and put an end to semantic slavery of homemakers being classified as women who don't work.

The common cold continues to elude medical science, but at least a significant semantic breakthrough may have occurred. Dr. Martin Colburn of the University of Illinois has concluded from his studies that the common

[9]Peter Gorner, "Legionella—the Rare Killer that Almost Got Away," *Chicago Tribune*, Section 2, May 31, 1982, pp. 1–2.

cold and cold weather have only the word *cold* in common. He has ascertained that cold weather *alone* does not cause colds. His explanation for the higher incidence of respiratory illnesses during cold weather is that we spend more time indoors in closer and more frequent proximity with people who bear the cold virus.

Undesirable Solutions

Blindering may not only retard or prevent the finding of appropriate, constructive solutions, but it may steer us toward improper, unintelligent, even dangerous solutions. As a young man, the renowned anthropologist Benjamin Lee Whorf, served for some time as an analyst for an insurance company. He was solely concerned at first with the physical factors in fires and explosions, for example, defective wiring and the presence or lack of air spaces between metal flues and woodwork. But he soon began to notice certain human factors as well. He found that the way people defined or labeled a situation greatly influenced their behavior toward it. For example, he found that people tended to be extremely cautious around what they called "gasoline drums." Great care was taken to prevent smoking or striking matches in their vicinity. But when the drums were emptied and were thus now labeled "empty gasoline drums," caution was thrown to the winds. Cigarettes were smoked with abandon because the situation was now defined as safe. Ironically, the "empty" drums were *full* of gasoline vapors, and one spark could be sufficient to explode them—an enormously more dangerous circumstance than when they contained the liquid gasoline.[10]

Among other similar incidents, Whorf cited the case of the tannery drying room:

> A drying room for hides was arranged with a blower at one end to make a current of air along the room and thence outdoors through a vent at the other end. Fire started at a hot bearing on the blower, which blew the flames directly into the hides and fanned them along the room, destroying the entire stock. This hazardous setup followed naturally from the term "blower" with its linguistic equivalence to "that which blows," implying that its function necessarily is to "blow." Also its function is verbalized as "blowing air for drying," overlooking that it can blow other things, e.g., flames and sparks. In reality a blower simply makes a current of air and can exhaust as well as blow. It should have been installed at the vent end to draw the air over the hides, then through the hazard (its own casing and bearings) and thence outdoors.[11]

[10]From "The Name of the Situation as Affecting Behavior," by B. L. Whorf. Published in "The Relation of Habitual Thought and Behavior to Language," in *Language, Culture, and Personality: Essays in Memory of Edward Sapir*, ed. Leslie Spier et. al. (Menasha, Wis.: Sapir Memorial Fund, 1941). This article, with the exception of the following incident involving the "blower" is reproduced in Case 16-3.

[11]Ibid.

CORRECTIVES

It is obvious that blindering can be a serious hindrance in business, education, government, science, and even in our personal lives. How, then, can we cope with it? How can we eliminate it or at least minimize its destructive influence? The following suggestions are offered.

Remember, Defining = Neglecting

Blindering is the process of narrowing one's perception, of channeling one's vision of a situation, problem, phenomenon. These restrictions are frequently introduced by the verbal (and nonverbal) definitions that one assigns to the situation, and so on. To define is "to mark the limits or boundaries of." Thus, when I define the chair I am sitting on as a piece of office furniture, I am setting up certain restrictions. I am calling attention to those attributes that my chair has in common with other office furniture, such as that it is usually found indoors, in offices (rather than in homes or on lawns), that it is largely utilitarian (as opposed to decorative), and so forth. At the same time, however, my definition is neglecting a host of other aspects which my chair does not share with office furniture in general. My definition distracts attention from a myriad of details unique to my chair—among them, its specific colors, its weight, the textures of its plastic and steel surfaces, the tensile strengths of its various materials, its style, its molecular structure, its cost, its resale value, and the origins of its materials. In short, the process of defining inevitably involves the excluding of some (actually, most) details.

The crux is that, although definitions unavoidably neglect some aspects, it is nevertheless essential that we do define, delimit, categorize, classify, organize our data and experience. The practical implication, therefore, is that it is dangerous to *forget* that defining is necessarily a process of restricting and neglecting. Remember, in other words, that you are abstracting.

Does My Definition Blinder Me?

Consider this experiment conducted with college students. One group was confronted with the problem of removing a ping-pong ball from the bottom of an upright rusty pipe. The students were not to change the position of the pipe in any way. In the room were a hammer, pliers, rulers, soda straws, pins, and a bucket of dirty water. After several futile attempts to fish the ball out with the various "tools," the group struck upon the idea of pouring the dirty water into the pipe and floating the ball up.

A second group of students was given the same problem, but with one change. Instead of the bucket of dirty water, a large pitcher of clean ice water, surrounded by crystal goblets, and set on a clean tablecloth, was placed in the room. These students never solved the problem. In this case they defined the water as *drinking water*—and their definition blindered them from other possible uses.

The same phenomenon is illustrated by the popular scissors and strings experiment. The experimenter hangs two strings from the ceiling, as in Figure 16–4. The objective is to tie the two ends together, as in Figure 16–5. The strings are so far apart, however, that the subject cannot quite reach string B while holding string A, or reach A while holding B (Figure 16–6). The subject is now given one instrument with which to solve the problem— a pair of scissors. Some individuals promptly snip off a length from one string and tie it to the other. The addition permits them to move closer to where the end was, but, alas! they find that the shorter string is now too high for them (Figure 16–7).

Their definition of scissors as a "cutter" inhibits their thinking of it as anything else. A pair of scissors, after all, is also a length, and tying it to the end of one of the strings might have given the additional length necessary to reach the second string. A pair of scissors is also a weight, and tying it to a string which could then be set in motion as a pendulum would be an effective solution to the problem (Figure 16–8).

It may be exceedingly helpful on occasion to ask oneself: "Am I blindering myself, restricting my approach to the problem by my definition, my sizing-up of the problem?"

FIGURE 16–4

FIGURE 16–5

FIGURE 16–6

FIGURE 16–7

FIGURE 16–8

How to Recognize Our Blinders

This is the crux, of course. How can we cope with our blinders if we do not recognize that we are being blindered? We scoff at the old wives' tales of yesteryear, but is it not possible that unwittingly we still accept a good many chimeras as valid?

Are there any practical, day-to-day techniques which will help us to uncover and eliminate our blinders? Here are a few that are often useful:

1. Talk with an Outsider.   There are times when we have difficulty seeing the forest for the trees. We become so immersed in a problem that we become quite unable to see it from other vantage points. One of the chief values of outside consultants to a business institution is the freshness of outlook they bring. As dispassionate observers, unencumbered with the minutiae of problems, they are often able to suggest views and insights that have eluded those closer to the situation. Bell Telephone Laboratories deliberately assigns a new person to a research team from time to time in order to get the benefit of his or her naiveté. The newcomer is often able to stir up the thinking of the scientists who have been at the problems longer, and thus to prompt them to arrive at new and better approaches.

But the outsider need not always be a professional or even well versed in a particular problem area. Often a spouse, a friend, a parent, even a child, can help one see a problem in a new light. And not infrequently, as in nondirective counseling, the very process of explaining the problem to another, of making the effort to get someone else to see one's problem, helps one to break through self-created encasements.

Emotional problems are particularly vulnerable to blindering. Often individuals are too close to such problems to perceive them objectively. Here is a letter to an advice columnist from a clearly distraught wife—and the columnist, as the outsider, provides, happily, the obvious solution:

> My husband is a minister, He does everything on a scheduled basis. And I mean *everything*.
> Sunday is our night for lovemaking. I am not complaining, because I enjoy it as much as he does. But he is very big and strong and very physical. He's not rough or abusive, but he's very affectionate and puts a lot of enthusiasm into everything. To get to the point, on Monday morning I'm exhausted, and that's the morning I do my wash.
> Any suggestions?
>
> Tired on Monday
>
> Dear Tired: Yes. Wash on Tuesday.

2. Kill "Killer" Phrases.   This apt coinage is by Charles H. Clark of Autonetics, Inc., who has compiled a list of phrases that squelch a new idea before it has a chance to be examined. "Let's be practical," "We've never done anything like that," "We've always done it this way," "It'll cost too much," "The boss won't like it," "It can't be done," "We're doing the best we can," and "The customers won't stand for it" are examples. Granted, some suggestions prove to be worthless or worse. But some, ridiculous or impractical at first hearing, may have a gold nugget in them—something which, if combined with other ideas, might prove exceedingly useful. The point is that the killer phrase will decapitate the infant idea before anyone has had the opportunity to dig for its gold, to give it a fair appraisal.

3. Brainstorm with a Group.   Brainstorming, an idea-generating technique that swept the nation some years ago, has definite blinder-finding potential. The rules of the game are quite simple. A group of people meet to make suggestions relevant to a given problem area. The goal is quantity, not quality—the more ideas, the better. At first, no one evaluates the worth of the ideas. Only afterward are the ideas sifted through for possible pearls. The key antiblindering feature of brainstorming is the interpersonal excitement and stimulation generated among the group. A may say something that sets off B and C, who in turn mention something that triggers ideas from D, E, and F, and so on. Participants are urged to build upon or modify one another's ideas. The upshot is that ideas may appear that might never have occurred to the same people if they had been working as solitary thinkers.

However, brainstorming is not without its own blindering dangers. Without skilled leadership, the flow of ideas may get started down one relatively narrow channel—one idea merely pressing another deeper into this specialized rut. Good leadership can guide the ideas through a more comprehensive and useful area.

The next two suggestions also involve groups but with lessening degrees of interaction.

4. Use the Nominal Group Technique.   The group in this approach exists largely in name only—thus, nominal group. True, the members are physically present and they are addressing the same problem. But, unlike brainstorming, there is relatively little interaction.

First, a problem is articulated and individuals independently list as many solutions as they can conceive. Next, in round-robin fashion, each person expresses a solution. Someone adds the idea to a master list. The process continues until all of the generated solutions have been recorded. The next phase is to clarify and evaluate (cite pros and cons) each solution, but not to arrive at a decision. Next, each member privately rank-orders the solutions. These individual priorities are tabulated and the aggregate evaluation of the solutions is revealed to the group.

Among its strengths, this method balances participation and influence of members. It produces a large number of creative ideas and a good deal of member satisfaction without exposing individuals to personal confrontation. Its prime limitation is that it can handle effectively only one problem at a time. Furthermore, the problem to be addressed should be quite specific and well-defined.

5. Use the Delphi Technique. This approach is useful when people cannot or for any reason do not meet face-to-face. The first phase is for the chairperson to send a statement of the problem to each participant. Each records potential solutions and returns them. The chairperson now summarizes them and sends a copy to each participant for appraisal and additional suggestions. These are again summarized and the process continues until a clear consensus appears, or a vote is taken.

This technique allows for the participation of a large number from a wide geographical area. Although not eliminated, social pressures are certainly reduced. The prime disadvantage is time; it generally takes a good deal of time to gather data from a widespread group. Perhaps with inter-computer capability, the intervals can be shortened. Any values of social interaction, however, are probably irretrievable.

Since the chairperson interprets and summarizes the individual inputs, that role is critical.

6. Start Anywhere—But Start. How many times have you tackled a creative project and had difficulty in beginning? Perhaps it was a term paper, an essay, or a report, and the main heading or the lead sentence simply did not come, regardless of your efforts to grind it out. I have wasted hours, I am embarrassed to say, because I could not begin a chapter or an article or even a paragraph in a way that satisfied me. I finally discovered what others have known for years—that it is rarely necessary to begin at the beginning. The important thing is to start—start anywhere, but start. Often when I start where I can make a start, I come back to the beginning, and the chapter title or the lead line, or whatever it was that had me blocked, falls into place.

7. Try the Reversal Technique. If your initial and seemingly normal reaction to a problem does not work, you might try just the reverse. Dr. Edward de Bono, director of the Cognitive Research Trust at Cambridge University, offers this illustration:

> An ambulance speeding along a narrow country road is suddenly confronted with a flock of sheep completely blocking the road. The "normal" response would be to try to drive through the sheep. Because the sheep would tend to walk away from you, that approach would be difficult and slow, as well as dangerous for the sheep. So, suggests de Bono, do just the reverse. Stop the vehicle, get out, and drive the sheep past your stationary vehicle.

The reversal technique can be an excellent blinder-buster because it frees one from the old and possibly fixated ways of looking at the problem.

That in itself can be helpful—even if the reversal doesn't make immediate sense. But frequently an apparently ridiculous solution works brilliantly.

> A conscientious young couple I know found their lives alarmingly changed after the birth of their first child. The baby, it seemed, needed very little sleep. Long past the age at which most infants settle into an acceptable nighttime routine, she continued to call for attention—at midnight, 2 A.M., 4 A.M., and so on. Her parents took turns walking the floor with her. ("We can't stand to hear her cry.") When, at 15 months, she still didn't sleep for more than two hours at a stretch, the pediatrician suggested a sedative. Both parents disliked the idea of drugging a baby. I proposed reversal—that the parents take the sedative—and they laughed . . . but they tried it. The very first night they slept soundly from 10 P.M. to 6 A.M. "If the baby cried, it couldn't have been for long," her mother said sheepishly. "I certainly didn't hear her." After three nights they gave up sedatives and discovered that their baby slept like an angel.
>
> My favorite example of reversal comes from a used-car salesman who loathed his job because it sometimes involved unloading questionable cars on ignorant buyers. He longed to quit, but the only thing he knew was cars. In a moment of pure inspiration he jumped the fence: He set up a used-car locating-and-inspecting service to guide the innocent. For a modest fee he helps prospective buyers locate possible cars, lists the cars' present and potential problems with repair estimates and negotiates with the owner on price. As part of his service he guarantees that if certain components fail he will replace them, and if the car proves a total loss, he offers to buy it back. Not surprisingly, he makes more now than he did as a salesman—and is a lot happier.[12]

8. Redefine the Problem. Defining the problem too narrowly can lead to limited solutions—or poor solutions—to wit, the celebrated toilet seat case previously described. Dr. de Bono cites this example: The apartments in a certain high-rise building are being changed to offices. A key problem arises—the elevators are inadequate for the greater number of people using them. Visitors and employees are complaining of long waits. De Bono suggests that if you define the problem as "How can we reduce the waiting time?" the tenable solutions are few. Installing new elevators would be quite expensive. Speeding the elevators up might be dangerous. Staggering working hours could be very complex and might create more problems than it solves. However, if you state the problem as "How can we diminish visitor and employee impatience?" many more alternatives arise. For example, provide comfortable chairs and couches near the elevators; install snack food vending machines nearby; put up a bulletin board with interesting information (suggestion box questions and answers, news about em-

---

[12]Fredelle Maynard, "How to Solve Problems like an Expert," *Woman's Day*, April 1976, p. 171. Excerpt reprinted by permission of *Woman's Day Magazine*. Copyright © 1976 by CBS Publications, Inc.

ployees and organizational tenants, social notices); provide mirrors—a sure focus of interest. The broader definition of the problem permits moving freely beyond the problem's initially apparent boundaries.

"Most people," states one management consultant, "formulate the wrong questions. It's the difference between asking, 'How can I build a better mousetrap?' and 'How can I get rid of mice?' The first question limits you; the second frees you to explore new, offbeat solutions."

9. Use Results-Oriented Planning. The Center for Constructive Change (Durham, New Hampshire) devised this technique. Its essence is to resist focusing on personalities and methods, but to define clear goals and then work backward.

> Dr. Thomas Marshall, CCC vice president, illustrates the center's approach with an explosive situation recently faced by a Pittsburgh labor relations manager. A foreman—a steady, honest, hardworking employee of 30 years—wanted to fire a young black whose performance and absentee record were unsatisfactory. The union steward charged racial prejudice and a meeting was set up. Ordinarily, Dr. Marshall suggests, the procedure would have been "Let's get the facts," followed by a shouting match of accusation and counter-accusation. Whatever the eventual decision, it would seem arbitrary and unfair to the loser.
>
> The labor manager, a CCC graduate, avoided this trap. He began by addressing the young black: "The purpose of this meeting is to help you become a productive worker for our company. That's what you'd like, isn't it?" Well, yes. Then, to the foreman, he said: "It's your job to help him become an efficient worker, right?" Sure. "All right," the manager continued. "Now if everything in your department were going the way you'd like it, what would be happening?" The foreman was happy to elaborate: This young fellow would get to work every day on time; he would produce a certain number of spark plugs, a certain maximum of scrap (unusable parts). Once the goal was defined, the manager moved backward. Are the workers informed of their production record daily? No? Well, wouldn't it help if they had this information?
>
> Then it was the worker's turn. How often had he been absent in the past month? Could he improve that record? How about making a plan for the next few weeks—a quota of so many spark plugs per day the first week, a maximum of one absence per month. The end result was a plan workable because it has built-in controls and checks, has been accepted by both parties—and doesn't depend for its success on changing individuals. (The foreman doesn't have to get over his prejudice against blacks, if indeed he has one.) . . . .
>
> . . . The CCC approach would be to set aside the immediate disagreement—or, rather, to see the "problem" as an opportunity for creative planning. "Don't focus on people, problems or on the present environment," Dr. Marshall says, "but on *where you want to be.* Instead of blaming the other person, concentrate on setting up objectives together, then work out strategies to promote those objectives."[13]

---

[13]Ibid., p. 173.

10. Break a Set. A set, in the psychological sense, is the readiness of the organism to respond in a particular way. Breaking a set, then, frees one of habitual ways of perceiving and coping. It liberates one from culture-bound and unchallenged assumptions. This vignette usually discloses one such assumption:

> The scene is an office, one of the secretaries is dying. Her water carafe has been poisoned. Three executives—Archer, Baxter, and Cummings—are looking on helplessly. The police arrive. Just before she expires, the young woman, without looking at or pointing at any of the executives, gasps: "He did it!" Why was Baxter arrested?[14]
>
> Breaking this kind of cultural set opens up new avenues for problem-solving. My housecleaner, the most efficient I've ever had, is a vigorous 25-year-old male. Laid off from a sandblasting job that he hated, he was without work a long time. But then he noticed the number of want ads for domestic help and wondered why domestic help was considered female. Men should be especially good at washing floors, putting up storm windows, cleaning garages and basements, he thought. This enterprising fellow now has a truck, two male assistants and a business that occupies him seven days a week.[15]

11. List and Analyze the Components. This technique was originally developed to promote the invention and improvement of products. It consists of examining the individual parts of a situation or an object with a view to determining how each part could be improved. A screwdriver, for example, traditionally consists of a wooden handle, a round steel shank, and a wedge-shaped end that is inserted into a screw slot. To produce a better screwdriver, we could consider how to improve each component. Could the wooden handle be replaced by plastic or rubber? It would be less likely to split, perhaps cheaper to produce, and so on. Would a square or hexagonal shank allow for the application of greater torque with a wrench or a pliers? And so forth.

12. Capitalize upon Apparent Disadvantages. The key to this technique is to focus not on "How can I minimize the liability?" but on "How can I make the most of it?" I know a high school teacher whose classes were demoralized by drugs. Her students were much more enthralled with marijuana supply sources and prices than with homework. More often than not, they came to class stoned. Instead of ignoring the drug problem, the teacher made it the focal point of the year's work. She had the students do research on the history of marijuana laws and on the effects of amphetamines and LSD; conduct interviews at a halfway house; and write

---

[14]Because Archer and Cummings are women. If this answer doesn't immediately occur to the problem-solver, could the culprit be our culture, which has conditioned us (up till now, at least) to think of executives as men?

[15]Maynard, "How to Solve Problems," p. 174.

pro and con letters concerning drug laws to the news media and lawmakers. The teacher feels that she never had a better class.

A young woman who had just graduated with a major in advertising also used a disadvantage to her advantage. She wanted to join a top New York firm. Her friends tried to discourage her. Better join a small company first and get some experience, they said—no major would hire a neophyte. Undaunted, she applied to the firm of her choice. As predicted, one of the first questions put to her was: "What experience do you have?" Her forthright answer: "Absolutely none. I want to learn this profession from a top-notch company. Hire me, and train me *your* way. I won't have to unlearn a lot of things I learned with other organizations." She got the job.

13. Break the Tension Cycle.   Sometimes you find yourself working on a problem, making reasonable headway, when suddenly there's a brick wall. You are blocked, stymied. Most people back off a few feet and run headlong at the wall to butt it down. It doesn't give, so they try it again—and again—and again. Ironically, the more frustrated they become in attacking problems, the tenser they become. The more tense, the more fixated, the less insight—the less likelihood of noticing that there may be other ways of dealing with a brick wall, perhaps going over, under, or around it. And thus the *tension cycle*, one of the most effective deterrents to problem solving, takes over.

There are several ways to break the tension cycle—among them, leaving the area of frustration, learning to relax physically the individual members of the body, participating in an unrelated activity, and so on. The last is my favorite. If I find myself stymied in my work and beginning to grow tense, I shift to another area of the same work. If this is not effective, I pull out of my desk a list of previously planned short-term and reasonably agreeable tasks. Then I spend 20 minutes, say, taking a book to the library—or out of the library, or answering a letter, or reorganizing my bookshelves, or just taking a walk around the block. When I return to my original work I am invariably more relaxed, and quite often I can now see a solution to the problem that I had not noticed before. Regardless of what you call it—intuition, the subconscious, what-have-you—there does appear to be something working inside us even if we are not fully aware of it, and often it works more efficiently when we are not consciously holding the reins.

14. Distinguish among Your Deadlines.   One of the greatest sources of personal tension in our modern world is the well-known deadline. But the relationship between deadline tension and blindering is not always clear. How is it that some people seem to work well under deadline pressure while others go to pieces? Part of the confusion may lie in the ambiguity of the term *deadline*. There are at least three types of deadlines.

1. *Those that are externally imposed and unavoidable.* Some people, especially those involved in news, work with heavy deadlines hanging over them constantly. Evidently they accommodate themselves to the pressure of time, and work with great efficiency and surprising ease. For most of us, however, unavoidable deadlines are rare occurrences. Most of our deadlines are of the following two kinds.

2. *Those that are self-imposed.* Among individuals who tend toward perfectionism there is the inclination to set up arbitrary deadlines for themselves. Before long, the deadlines seem to become quite demanding, and the tension cycle is likely to set in. Self-imposed deadlines may be helpful stimulators and guides, so long as we recognize them as such; but if we let them take on the guise of externally imposed unavoidable deadlines we are inviting tension and blindering.

3. *Those that are created through procrastination.* There are probably some students who do not procrastinate, but by and large they have avoided my classes. These deadlines actually exist, of course, but better planning could have made them less formidable. But advice of this sort is usually futile, for procrastinators usually rationalize that they work better under pressure anyway—and perhaps they do. They certainly have had a great deal of experience under these conditions!

Perhaps the best overall antidote for blindering is expressed by the motto of the Air University, *Proficimus more irrenti,* usually translated as "Progress unhindered by tradition." Major General M. K. Deichelmann phrased it more pragmatically as "Stay loose, boy—stay loose."

DISCUSSION QUESTIONS

1. Precisely what is blindering? How does it occur? Why? What are its potential dangers? What measures help to prevent or correct it?

2. How many blinder names or phrases can you think of?

3. The tension cycle was described as a cyclical process of frustration leading to direct attack on the blockage, which in turn increases frustration, which in turn leads to more fixated attacks, and so on. How can we know when we are withdrawing gracefully or giving up too easily?

4. Does blindering seem to be related to other concepts in the book?

5. Report upon an incident, perhaps involving yourself, in which blindering occurred. How and why did it occur? What could have prevented it or ameliorated its consequences? What measures could prevent its recurrence?

CASES

CASE 16–1

Puzzles to Ponder

Here are some conundrums to contemplate. Caution: You may encounter a trick in each of them. But the trick is likely to be a *self-imposed* limitation—a *blinder.* You may unconsciously assume that you *must* (or must *not*) solve the problem in a certain way. So give yourself a pat on the back if you not only solve the problem but spot the key *blinder*—the false assumption which hampers solving the problem. (If your time is short or your morale is low or your will is weak, you will find the answers following Case 16–7.)

1. George Carson and his son, Mike, were speeding along Route 30 one rainy evening when suddenly their car skidded off the road. George was killed instantly, but Mike, though seriously injured, was still alive when the police arrived. He was rushed to the hospital and immediately wheeled into the emergency room. The old surgeon looked at the patient and gasped: "My God! I can't operate—he's my own son!"

   How could the surgeon be correct about Mike's identity? (NB: Mike has two parents and no stepparents.)

   Answer: _____

   Blinder: _____

2. Move one of these coins once so that there are five coins in each row.

Answer: _____

Blinder: _____

3. The numbers below are in this order for a reason. What is it?
8—5—4—9—1—7—6—10—3—2—0

Answer: _____

Blinder: _____

4. O—T—T—F—F—S—S—E—N—T— — — — —
What are the next three letters?

Answer: _____

Blinder: _____

5. Three men checked in and paid $30 for a hotel room. Later the clerk discovered that he had overcharged them $5. He gave Jake, the bellman, five one-dollar bills to return to them. Jake, resentful that the men had failed to tip him for carrying their luggage, pocketed $2 and gave a dollar to each of the men. Thus, the men had paid $27 for the room. However, $27 plus the $2 Jake kept equals $29.

What happened to the extra $1?

Answer: _____

_____

Blinder: _____

_____

6. Ten gumball machines, each with a glass globe loaded with gumballs, are mounted on a heavy table. You have it on good authority that nine of the machines dispense balls weighing one ounce each. The remaining machine dispenses half-ounce balls. The appearance (size, shape, color) of the balls from all the machines is identical.

Using a spring scale (not a set of balances) such as is found in the grocery store, how can you determine which machine is giving the half-ounce gumballs?

Restrictions:
1. You *must* use the scale to *solve* the problem, not merely to *verify* a solution.
2. Only *one* use of the scale—that is, one registration of the dial—is permitted. Each time you add or subtract a gumball is considered a separate weighing.

Answer: _____

_____

Blinder: _____

7. What did Attila the Hun and Felix the Cat have in common?

Answer: _____

Blinder: _____

CASE 16–2

The Rawley Company*

The Rawley Company, manufacturers of custom-made metal-forming machinery, had been in business for over half a century. It was located in a large midwestern city and employed approximately 100 persons. Executives of Rawley had become aware that their company's sales had fallen considerably short of its production capacity. Stimulated by the company's president, James Howe, a dynamic man with an inquiring mind, the firm decided to approach the problem through the cooperative efforts of a group of persons to be known as the Sales Council.

The Sales Council was to be composed of representatives of various departments of the firm, some of which were not conventionally concerned with sales. The representatives and their departments included:

James Howe, *president* (designer, engineer, sales)
Donald Brewster, *vice president* (assistant general manager, manager of sales)
Raymond Prescott, *treasurer*
Clifford Carlin, *assistant vice president* (production manager)
Ralph Goodwin, *assistant vice president* (warehouse manager)
Arthur Howard, *assistant sales manager*
Chester Green, *Eastern sales*
Fred Lemec, *in charge of machinery orders*
Russell Thurston, *engineer and salesman*

The Sales Council was to operate on the assumption that ultimately every employee was directly or indirectly related to the sale of the company's products. Consequently, the combined thinking of representatives of these various sections might produce helpful suggestions for their common objective, increased sales.

---

*All names have been disguised. Printed by permission of the author, whose name has been withheld by request.

In order to expedite the meetings of the Sales Council, a professor of interpersonal communication from a local university was called in to act as moderator. It was felt that he should act as a disinterested chairman whose primary responsibility was simply to help the members of the group to understand one another as clearly and as accurately as possible. Specifically, he was to repeat and/or paraphrase the statement of each speaker immediately after the speaker had finished making it. This was to give the speaker the feeling that at least one person understood what he had tried to communicate. Furthermore, all other members of the Sales Council were to have the opportunity to agree or to disagree with the accuracy of the moderator's restatement of the speaker's statement until, theoretically, each person present was satisfied that he and the moderator had understood the speaker.

Shortly before the first Sales Council meetings were to be held, some of Rawley's executives and the professor met for an orientation session in a conference room in a nearby restaurant. The meeting was to explain to the professor what the Sales Council was, what its objectives were, and what the professor's role as moderator was to be.

After each executive present had expressed his view of these points, the professor, David Wilson, asked to have the floor.

Wilson Gentlemen, I'd like to try to sum up what I think you have been saying about the Sales Council so that you can tell me if you think I understand you. As I get the picture, you are proposing an experiment in group problem solving. Casting this approach in my own frame of reference, this going to be essentially a group—something like the conventional classroom situation—in which the lines of communication are directly between teacher and students and only indirectly from student to student. . . .

Howe *(acting as chairman, breaks in)* I see heads shaking in disagreement, Dave. Ralph?

Goodwin Dave, I don't like your analogy. This is not going to be a classroom situation at all. The moderator isn't supposed to act as an autocrat. He's trying to achieve the cooperation and communication of the group at a high level. . . .

Wilson I think you're right about the analogy being a poor one, but I only used it to describe the direction of the communication lines as I see them in the Sales Council. . . .

Carlin No offense meant, Dave, but you can't presume to act the role of a teacher, the subject-matter expert. You don't have the company background for it.

Ten minutes later:

Wilson Now, getting specifically to the role of the moderator. . . . The way I get it, he is to listen to Speaker A, filter through his personality and background what he thinks A has said, and express it to the group. . . .

Goodwin   You don't filter anything. Your job is to repeat what A has said.

Carlin   Well, he's to *paraphrase* what A has said so that A will know that at least one person has understood him.

Wilson   I get that, but how can I possibly relay a man's statement, other than through the sheer repetition of his exact same words, unless I interpret, size up what he has said? In other words, isn't it inevitable that I filter what comes to me through my own nervous system, my personality, my background?

Goodwin   Filtering is changing the substance you are conveying—that isn't your job.

Carlin   You don't *filter*—you *reflect* what has been said.

Wilson   Perhaps "filter" has been a bad figure of speech, but even in reflecting the other fellow's statement, must I not determine his meaning for myself—and how can I size up the meaning unless I relate his words to my own unique frame of experience?

At this point, dinner was announced and the subject was dropped.

Discussion Questions

1. What do you think of the conference communication technique proposed by the Sales Council?

2. Speech by speech, how do you analyze the communication occurring in this case?

3. Who is responsible for this wheel-spinning?

4. What does this case have to do with *blindering?*

CASE 16–3

The Name of the Situation as Affecting Behavior*

B. L. Whorf

There will probably be general assent to the proposition that an accepted pattern of using words is often prior to certain lines of thinking and forms of behavior, but he who assents often sees in such a statement nothing more than a platitudinous recognition of the hypnotic power of philosophical and learned terminology on the one hand or of catchwords, slogans, and rallying-cries on the other. To see only thus far is to miss the point of one of the important interconnections which Sapir saw between language, culture, and psychology. . . . It is not so much in these special uses of language

---

*From "The Relation of Habitual Thought and Behavior to Language," in *Language, Culture, and Personality: Essays in Memory of Edward Sapir,* ed. Leslie Spier et al. (Menasha, Wis.: Sapir Memorial Fund, 1941), pp. 75–77. Reprinted by permission.

as in its constant ways of arranging data and its most ordinary everyday analysis of phenomena that we need to recognize the influence it has on other activities, cultural and personal.

I came in touch with an aspect of this problem before I had studied under Dr. Sapir, and in a field usually considered remote from linguistics. It was in the course of my professional work for a fire insurance company, in which I undertook the task of analyzing many hundreds of reports of circumstances surrounding the start of fires, and in some cases, of explosions. My analysis was directed toward purely physical conditions, such as defective wiring, presence or lack of air spaces between metal flues and woodwork, etc., and the results were presented in these terms. Indeed it was undertaken with no thought that any other significances would or could be revealed. But in due course it became evident that not only a physical situation *qua* physics, but the meaning of that situation to people, was sometimes a factor, through the behavior of the people, in the start of the fire. And this factor of meaning was clearest when it was a *linguistic meaning*, residing in the name or the linguistic description commonly applied to the situation. Thus around a storage of what are called "gasoline drums," behavior will tend to a certain type, that is, great care will be exercised; while around a storage of what are called "empty gasoline drums" it will tend to be different—careless, with little repression of smoking or tossing cigarette stubs about. Yet the "empty" drums are perhaps the more dangerous, since they contain explosive vapor. Physically the situation is hazardous, but the linguistic analysis according to regular analogy must employ the word *empty*, which inevitably suggests lack of hazard. The word *empty* is used in two linguistic patterns: (1) as a virtual synonym for "null and void, negative, inert," (2) applied in analysis of physical situations without regard to, e.g., vapor, liquid vestiges, or stray rubbish, in the container. The situation is named in one pattern (2) and the name is then "acted out" or "lived up to" in another (1); this being a general formula for the linguistic conditioning of behavior into hazardous forms.

In a wood distillation plant, the metal stills were insulated with a composition prepared from limestone and called at the plant "spun limestone." No attempt was made to protect this covering from excessive heat or the contact of flame. After a period of use the fire below one of the stills spread to the "limestone," which to everyone's great surprise burned vigorously. Exposure to acetic acid fumes from the stills had converted part of the limestone (calcium carbonate) to calcium acetate. This, when heated in a fire, decomposes, forming inflammable acetone. Behavior that tolerated fire close to the covering was induced by use of the name "limestone," which because it ends in "stone" implies noncombustibility.

A huge iron kettle of boiling varnish was observed to be overheated, nearing the temperature at which it would ignite. The operator moved it off the fire and ran it on its wheels to a distance, but did not cover it. In a minute or so the varnish ignited. Here the linguistic influence is more complex; it is due to the metaphorical objectifying (of which more later) of "cause" as contact or the spatial juxtaposition of "things"—to analyzing the situation as "on" versus "off" the fire. In reality the stage when the external fire was the main factor had passed; the overheating was now an internal process of convection in the varnish from the intensely heated kettle, and still continued when off the fire.

An electric glow heater on the wall was little used, and for one workman had the meaning of a convenient coat-hanger. At night a watchman entered and snapped a switch, which action he verbalized as "turning on the light." No light appeared, and this result he verbalized as "light is burned out." He could not see the glow of the heater because of the old coat hung on it. Soon the heater ignited the coat, which set fire to the building.

A tannery discharged waste water containing animal matter into an outdoor settling basin partly roofed with wood and partly open. This situation is one that ordinarily would be verbalized as "pool of water." A workman had occasion to light a blowtorch nearby, and threw his match into the water. But the decomposing waste matter was evolving gas under the wood cover, so that the setup was the reverse of "watery." An instant flare of flame ignited the woodwork, and the fire quickly spread into the adjoining building. . . .

Beside a coal-fired melting pot for lead reclaiming was dumped, a pile of "scrap lead"—a misleading verbalization, for it consisted of the lead sheets of old radio condensers, which still had paraffin paper between them. Soon the paraffin blazed up and fired the roof, half of which was burned off.

Such examples, which could be greatly multiplied, will suffice to show how the cue to a certain line of behavior is often given by the analogies of the linguistic formula in which the situation is spoken of, and by which to some degree it is analyzed, classified, and allotted its place in that world which is "to a large extent unconsciously built up on the language habits of the group." And we always assume that the linguistic analysis made by our group reflects reality better than it does.

Discussion Questions

1. What was the central point of this article?

2. What does it have to do with *blindering?*

CASE 16–4

The Roberts Machine Company*

The Roberts Machine Company was a medium-sized firm which produced various types of shop machines—lathes, punch presses, drill presses, mill-

---

*All names and organizational designations have been disguised. Published by Northwestern University. Reprinted by permission.

ing machines, and so forth. The sales department held a dinner meeting every other month. After dinner, in a hotel private dining room, Gordon Swift, sales manager, conducted a business meeting. The October meeting was attended by Swift, Al Rockland, assistant sales manager, and 11 salesmen, 6 of whom had more than 15 years of service with Roberts. Also present was James Jacobs, sales manager of Electro-Products, Inc., manufacturers of electrical components for home appliances. Jacobs was a personal friend of Swift and known to most of the men. He had been invited to observe the meeting. Swift had previously sat in on one of Jacobs' sales conferences.

The purpose of the meeting was to review a proposed new method for communicating product information to Roberts' dealers, using an audio cassette tape to accompany the firm's catalog. The dealer, in his own shop or home, could play the tape as he leafed through the Roberts catalog. Swift felt that the pictures and copy of the catalog alone did not communicate adequately the sales appeal of their product line. The tape, in his words, "added another dimension to product communication."

Swift opened the meeting by explaining the purpose of the catalog-tape technique and asked each salesman to play the role of a dealer as he listened to the record. The salesmen leafed through the catalog as the tape called attention to the advantages of each item.

When the tape ended, Swift asked for comments. Most of the men contributed to the informal discussion which followed. Mr. Jacobs did not participate.

Pros and cons of the technique were discussed; most seemed to agree that the catalog-tape idea was basically sound—a way of communicating to the dealer in two media, visually and aurally. A few wondered whether it might be too difficult for a man to listen, look at pictures, and read text at the same time.

There was some disagreement about whose voice should be used on the cassette. Several felt that a professional announcer should do the job; the majority preferred Mr. Swift as narrator. One of the salesmen suggested that the sales manager's voice would add a note of warmth and make the process seem more personal than the colder media of catalogs, pamphlets, and newsletters.

Some thought that the tape increased the accuracy of the communication—the emphasis and inflection of the narrator's voice would help convey information more precisely than the written word alone. One man wondered whether the average dealer would have facilities for playing the cassette. Others felt that almost every home had a tape player these days.

After the discussion had continued for some 30 minutes, one of the younger salesmen, Ed Knoll, commented: "As long as we're talking about dealer communication, I think we could capitalize on the visual angle, too. I wonder if we couldn't take some film clips of several of our machines in action."

There was an audible groan from several other salesmen—one brought up another topic, and the subject of film clips was not resumed. Jacobs was puzzled about the apparent indifference and negative reactions to the film clip idea.

Although it was not strictly relevant to the catalog-tape proposal, Jacobs thought that the idea might have potential value for Roberts' overall sales program. The Roberts machines were intricate. Motion shots of machines in action could show what words and still pictures could not possibly convey. Moreover, Jacobs had always considered Knoll a bright, hard-working young man, who had shown drive and imagination during his three years with the firm. But Jacobs remained silent as the meeting continued for another hour.

At nine o'clock, Swift said:

> Well, gentlemen, I think we've kicked this around long enough, and I appreciate your comments. Al and I will get our heads together next week, and we'll let you know whether or not we decide to go ahead with the catalog-tape idea.
>
> But right now, I'd like to hear what our friend, Jim Jacobs, has to say about the performance we put on for him. He's been sitting here soaking it all in. Any reactions, Jim?

Jacobs You're right, Gordon, I have been soaking it all in, which is a bit unusual for me. I'm usually running the show rather than watching it—and I certainly appreciate your invitation. I'd like to do this more often.

> Now, if you don't mind, Gordon, I wonder if I could impose upon you and your men for about three minutes.

Swift Go right ahead, Jim. Got something cooked up?

Jacobs Well, in a way. You men all know how enthusiastic Gordon is about the subject of communication. And most of you know that I feel pretty much the same way. Gordon and I have spent hours at a stretch talking about the problems of communication in business. Heaven only knows, we've got them in our plant—and in my own department, too. Now, there was one point in this meeting that particularly interested me. You all recall that remark of Ed Knoll's about film clips? Well, I wonder if you'd oblige me by writing a short sentence or two about your reaction to Ed's comment. Don't bother to sign your name.

Each salesman wrote a brief note and passed it to Jacobs, who said: "Thank you very much, gentlemen. You might be interested in what I'm up to. Frankly, it's just a little experiment I thought of while I was sitting with my ears open for a change—instead of my mouth. I really don't know what to expect from it.

"But Gordon is giving me a lift home, so I imagine you'll be getting a feedback through him."

"Fine, Jim," Swift replied, "this might be interesting at that. And now, unless anyone has anything else to add, let's adjourn the meeting."

Swift began talking with several salesmen at the door while others were collecting their papers and getting their coats. Jacobs walked over to Knoll and said: "Ed, I wonder if you would tell me just what you had in mind with that film clip idea?"

Knoll Well, Mr. Jacobs, I thought we could shoot a short film on our own—probably wouldn't run more than 30 dollars. I have a Super 8-mm camera, and if the company would buy the film and let me rig up a few lights—

Jacobs Were you suggesting that the film would be coordinated with the tape?

Knoll Oh, no—it would be entirely apart from the catalog and tape. It would be just another way of communicating with our dealers and their customers, too. Our machines are too big, too expensive, and there are too many models for our dealers to stock the complete line. The film would be a way of showing our machines in actual operation.

Jacobs thanked Knoll and joined Swift, who was waiting to drive him home. As they rode, Jacobs read the statements aloud. There were 11 of them:

Cost!!![1]
Oh, no! Not the movie boys again!
That isn't the kind of thing we can afford to do now.
Coupled with the tape and review of the catalog, the film would be a sharp idea.
Necessity of having a projector and screen besides a tape player—too much apparatus.
Completely irrelevant in terms of a critique of the tape idea.
The idea is for catalogs and tapes to be sent out and heard. If they are going to show movies, you don't need catalogs.
Vision with the tape sounded like a good idea.
A sound film would be better than a film with a separate tape.
Book, voice, and pictures—too much to absorb.
That's all we need—another unusable film!

Discussion Questions

1. Is there any significance in the fact that the film clip suggestion came from Knoll?

2. Assuming the idea had merit, what do you think of how Knoll expressed it?

3. How do you analyze the various reactions to Knoll's suggestion?

---

[1]Swift told Jacobs that the Roberts Company had had an unpleasant, costly experience with a product film prepared by a film production firm. The film had cost $22,000 and for various reasons had never been used.

4. What connection, if any, does *blindering* have with this case?

5. Are other patterns of miscommunication involved here?

6. Jacobs seemed to be on Knoll's wavelength from the outset. Why?

CASE 16-5

Flies, Typhoid, and Publicity*

It was while I was working at the Memorial Institute that an opportunity came for me to bring my scientific training to bear on a problem at Hull House. (My efforts in the baby clinic could not be called scientific.) This was in the fall of 1902, when I came back from Mackinac to find Chicago in the grip of one of her worst epidemics of typhoid fever. At that time the water, drawn from the lake, was not chlorinated; the only precaution taken against dangerous pollution was to make daily cultures of samples from the different pumping stations and the next day, when the cultures had had time to develop, publish the results and tell the public whether or not to boil water. It was assumed that housewives would look up these instructions every day, and act accordingly, but the actual result was that typhoid was endemic in Chicago and periodically it reached epidemic proportions. On this particular occasion Hull House was the center of the hardest-struck region of the city—why, nobody knew. Miss Addams said she thought a bacteriologist ought to be able to discover the reason.

It was certainly not a simple problem. The pumping station which sent water to the 19th Ward sent it to a wide section of the West Side; the milk supply was the same as that for neighboring wards. There must be some local condition to account for the excessive number of cases. As I prowled about the streets and the ramshackle wooden tenement houses I saw the outdoor privies (forbidden by law but flourishing nevertheless), some of them in backyards below the level of the street and overflowing in heavy rains; the wretched water closets indoors, one for four or more families, filthy and with the plumbing out of order because nobody was responsible for cleaning or repairs; and swarms of flies everywhere. Here, I thought, was the solution to the problem. The flies were feeding on typhoid-infected excreta and then lighting on food and milk. During the Spanish-American War, when we lost more men from typhoid fever than from Spanish bullets, Vaughan, Shakespeare, and Reed had made a study of conditions in camps—open latrines, unscreened food—which led them to attribute an important role in the spread of typhoid fever to the house fly. That was what started the "Swat the fly" campaign.

---

*From *Exploring the Dangerous Trades* by Alice Hamilton, M D (Boston: Little, Brown, 1943). Reprinted by permission.

Naturally, my theory had to be put to the test, so, with two of the residents to help me, Maude Gernon and Gertrude Howe, I went forth to collect flies—from privies and kitchens and filthy water closets. We would drop the flies into tubes of broth and I would take them to the laboratory, incubate the tubes, and plate them out at varying intervals. It was a triumph to find the typhoid bacillus and I hastened to write up the discovery and its background for presentation before the Chicago Medical Society. This was just the sort of thing to catch public attention: It was simple and easily understood; it fitted in with the revelations made during the Spanish War of the deadly activities of house flies, and it explained why the slums had so much more typhoid than the well-screened and decently drained homes of the well-to-do.

I am sure I gained more kudos from my paper on flies and typhoid than from any other piece of work I ever did. Even today I sometimes hear an echo of it. In Chicago the effect was most gratifying; a public inquiry resulted in a complete reorganization of the Health Department under a chief loaned by the Public Health Service, and an expert was put in charge of tenement-house inspection. But unfortunately my gratification over my part in all this did not last long. After the tumult had died down I discovered a fact that never gained much publicity but was well-authenticated. My flies had had little or nothing to do with the cases of typhoid in the 19th Ward. The cause was simpler but so much more discreditable that the Board of Health had not dared reveal it. It seems that in our local pumping station, on West Harrison Street, near Halsted, a break had occurred which resulted in an escape of sewage into the water pipes and for three days our neighborhood drank that water before the leak was discovered and stopped. This was after the epidemic had started. The truth was more shocking than my ingenious theory, and it never came to light, as far as the public was concerned. For years, although I did my best to lay to rest the ghosts of those flies, they haunted me and mortified me, compelling me again and again to explain to deeply impressed audiences that the dramatic story their chairman had just rehearsed had little foundation in fact.

Discussion Questions

1. Supposedly, blindering is involved in this case. How?

2. How does this case compare with "The Electra Story"?

CASE 16-6

The Windy City

Chicago's nickname is "The Windy City."

Many people, especially visitors, think of Chicago as being a very windy

The U.S. Weather Bureau's National Climate Center lists Chicago as 16th in windiness among America's cities. Chicago's average wind speed is 10.4 mph. The top five on the center's list:

		Mph
1.	Great Falls, Montana	13.1
2.	Oklahoma City, Oklahoma	13.0
3.	Boston, Massachusetts	12.9
4.	Cheyenne, Wyoming	12.8
5.	Wichita, Kansas	12.7

What does the above combination of statements have to do with this chapter?

CASE 16–7

A Very Clean Job*

When the time came for the annual audit of the Bronson Company, Mort Smith was pleased to receive the assignment again. Smith, senior auditor for McKinley, Karten, and Steiner, public accountants, had handled the Bronson audit for nine years and was very familiar with the company's system. As he explained to his superior, "It's a joy to do the Bronson job. Their controller, Barry Revsine, is a CPA himself, and you can always count on his giving you a very clean job."

When Smith and Scott Petersen, a new junior on his first job, arrived at the Bronson Company, Revsine handed them a 30-page trial balance. During the course of the audit, approximately 20 adjusting journal entries were made. When the audit work was completed, Smith instructed Petersen to extend the trial balance, foot it, and finalize it.

Sometime later Petersen hesitantly approached Smith and said: "It doesn't balance." Smith replied curtly: "Check the footings and extensions and so forth."

Two hours later an anxious Petersen reported: "I'm sorry, but it still doesn't balance." "Listen, Scott," snapped Smith, "this is no practice set you're working on. Check your entries. See if they are posted correctly. See if they balance individually. Make a net income summary. You've done *something* wrong!"

Four hours later, a thoroughly frustrated Petersen tried a new approach. He checked the client's beginning balance and found it to be in error. Scott pondered how he would inform Smith that the client had made the mistake.

---

*All names have been disguised.

Discussion Questions

1. What kind of miscommunication was involved here?
2. How could this situation have been prevented?
3. How should Petersen deal with the situation?

ANSWERS TO CASE 16–1: PUZZLES TO PONDER

1. *Answer:* The old surgeon is Mike's *mother.*
   Blinder: Assuming that all old surgeons are males.
2. *Answer:* Place the far-right coin on *top* of the corner coin.
   Blinder: Assuming that the problem must be solved in only two dimensions.
3. *Answer:* The numbers are arranged alphabetically: Eight—five—four—nine—and so forth.
   Blinder: Assuming some sort of mathematical series rather than considering the *spelling* of the numbers' names.
4. *Answer:* E—T—T for Eleven—Twelve—Thirteen. The letters are the initials of the spelled numbers: One—Two—Three—and so forth.
   Blinder: Assuming that the letters represent a mathematical series of the ordinal positions of the letters in the alphabet (e.g., O = 15th; T = 20th) rather than simply representing initials for the names of the numbers.
5. *Answer:* $27 *minus* the $2 Jake kept equals $25. And $30 minus the $25 room charge equals the $5 the clerk *tried* to return to the men.
   Blinder: The question posing the problem is misleading.
6. *Answer:* Arbitrarily label the machines: Machine #1, Machine #2, Machine #3, and so on. Take one ball from Machine #1, two balls from Machine #2, on up to 10 balls from Machine #10. You now have 55 balls. If all the machines dispensed one-ounce balls, the 55 balls would weigh 55 ounces. Place all of the balls on the scale. Fifty-five ounces minus the balls' combined weight in *half* ounces will give you the *number* of the culprit machine. For example, if the balls weigh 51½ ounces, $55 - 51½ = 3½$ ounces = 7 *half* ounces. Thus, machine #7 is the villain.
   Blinder: Assuming that you can take only one ball from each machine.
7. *Answer:* The same middle name, "the."
   Blinder: Assuming (and perhaps wishing) that your author has higher standards for humor than he has.

17

Undelayed Reactions

Game for another little test? OK. You will have exactly four minutes to complete it. All set? Just follow the instructions.

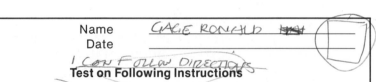

Name _GAGE RONALD_ ~~RON~~

Date _____

I CAN FOLLOW DIRECTIONS

Test on Following Instructions

(Read all of the following directions before doing ~~anything~~.)

1. Print your name, last first, on the top line following the word "Name."

2. Underline the word "print" in direction number 1.

3. In direction number 2, draw a circle around the word "underline," and in the above statement which appears in parentheses, cross out the word "anything."

4. Now, draw a circle around the title of this paper.

5. Circle the numbers of sentences 1, 2, 3, 4, and 5, and put an X over number 6.

6. Draw a circle around the word "all" in the above statement which appears in parentheses.

7. In sentence number 5, circle the even numbers and underline the odd numbers.

8. Put a circle around the number 2 in the third sentence.

9. Write "I can follow directions" above the title of this test. Start directly above the word "Test."

10. Underline the sentence you have just written.

11. Draw a square about one-half inch in size in the upper left-hand corner of this paper. Draw a circle around the square.

12. Cross out the numbers 8 through 12. Now circle the same numbers.

13. Put an X in the square inside the circle in the upper left-hand corner.

14. In the space under the last direction on this paper, copy neatly, in writing, the above statement which appears in parentheses.

15. Now that you have read all of the directions as stated in parentheses above, follow direction number 1 only. Do not follow any of the other directions; omit them entirely.

16. If you failed to follow the instructions, you are entitled to some serious suspicions about the legitimacy of your author's ancestry.

Read all the following directions before doing anything

That was diabolical, and if you fell for it, and most of us do, I hope you will forgive me. But what was the prime culprit? Was it not our reaction to time pressure? And we Americans seem especially susceptible. In some cultures where I have conducted seminars, such as in parts of Africa, Asia, and South America, people appear to be less vulnerable and the Instruction Test often flops—that is, fewer are caught by it. We have been programmed from childhood on to respect those who are quick on the draw, decisive, and "men of action." It is as if we had been taught to shoot first and ask questions later. I was an offender of the first order. When I had something new to assemble—such as a wagon for the kids—I would read the instructions as a last resort—after all of my actions have failed!

And, to be sure, there are circumstances when the snap decision is to be desired over the delayed response or no action at all. On the other hand, the consequences of some undelayed, unreasoned reactions have ranged from mild embarrassment to some of the greatest catastrophes in history. Consider the tragic phenomenon of panic. Take the famous Iroquois Theatre fire (Chicago, 1903), for example. It is generally conceded that a considerable portion of the terrible death toll (almost 600) could be attributed to the crush of fear-crazed persons who jammed the exits.

Doors, windows, hallways, fire escapes—all were jammed in a moment with struggling humanity, fighting for life. Some of the doors were jammed almost instantly so that no human power could make egress possible. Behind those in front pushed the frenzied mass of humanity. Chicago's elect, the wives and children of its most prosperous business men and the flower of local society, fighting like demons incarnate. Purses, wraps, costly furs were cast aside in that mad rush. Mothers were torn from their children, husbands from their wives. No hold, however strong, could last against that awful, indescribable crush. Strong men who sought to the last to sustain their feminine companions were swept away like straws, thrown to the floor and trampled into unconsciousness in the twinkling of an eye. Women to whom the safety of their children was more than their own lives had their little ones torn from them and buried under the mighty sweep of humanity, moving onward by intuition rather than through exercise of thought to the various exits. They in turn were swept on before their wails died on their lips—some to safety, others to an unspeakably horrible death.[1]

The veteran writer Ben H. Atwell, an eyewitness, testified to the senseless loss of lives:

Piled in windows in the angle of the stairway where the second balcony refugees were brought face to face in a death struggle with the occupants of the first balcony, the dead covered a space 15 or 20 feet square and nearly 7 feet in depth. *All were absolutely safe from the fire itself when they met death,* having emerged from the theatre proper into the separate building containing the foyer. In this great court there was absolutely nothing to burn and the doors were only a few feet away. There the ghastly pile lay, *a mute monument to the powers of terror. . . .*

To that pile of dead is attributed the great loss of life within. The bodies choked up the entrance, barring the egress of those behind. Neither age nor youth, sex, quality or condition were sacred in the awful battle in the doorway. The gray and aged, rich, poor, young and those obviously invalids in life lay in a tangled mass all on an awful footing of equality in silent annihilation.[2]

If that calamity seems remote, consider the Cocoanut Grove nightclub fire:

To a week already overcrowded with gruesome news pictures from the war, Boston added a terrible climax of civilian tragedy on Saturday night (Nov. 28) when more than 400 people[3] lost their lives in a fire at a midtown night club. It was the worst U.S. disaster of its kind since the 1903 Iroquois Theatre fire in Chicago.

A thousand merrymakers were packed in the Cocoanut Grove celebrating football victories and "getting away from the war" at 10:15 P.M. when the

---

[1] *Chicago's Awful Theatre Horror* by the Survivors and Rescuers (Chicago: Memorial Publishing, 1904), p. 36.

[2] Ibid., pp. 41–42. Italics are author's.

[3] A subsequent article ("After Cocoanut Grove," *Atlantic Monthly,* March 1943, pp. 55–57) totaled the fatalities at just under 500, the hospitalized at 250.

floor show was scheduled to start. A bus boy struck a match to see how to screw a light bulb back into its socket. A tinsel palm tree nearby caught fire and havoc took the stage. The guests' mad headlong rush for the two inadequate exits ended by completely clogging all escape. *More than the flames and stifling smoke, it was the hysteria and panic of the screaming, clawing crowds which piled up the dead like a dam.* One chorus boy kept his head in the pandemonium, directing entertainers to the safety of an adjacent roof through a second story window.[4]

Are we finally beginning to learn a lesson? Perhaps so. On May 29, 1977, the Beverly Hills Supper Club, Southgate, Kentucky, caught fire and 165 died and 70 were injured. That's tragic. But, according to authorities, with 2,400–2,800 persons present, the toll could have been much higher. A postfire appraisal concluded:

> Despite the rush to escape, there was apparently an absence of panic, at least in the aggressive, destructive sense of the word. On the contrary, patrons appeared to have confidence in the staff and the staff appeared to have confidence on the Club's management in dealing with the fire. Many waiters, waitresses, and other staff members were especially concerned about the safety of their patrons and helped them escape.[5]

Similarly, in the MGM Grand Hotel fire (Las Vegas, November 21, 1980) there were considerably fewer casualties (84 dead, over 700 injured) than might have been the case.

> The reported behavior of the guests appeared to consist primarily of cooperative and altruistic behavior during the evacuation or refuge processes.[6]

Those are certainly encouraging signs and I would like to feel more sanguine. But with three recent newspaper clippings in front of me, I can only be cautiously optimistic.

One pictures a rice riot at a Buddhist charity event in Bangkok with 19 dead and 45 seriously injured. In a mad rush for sacks of rice being given away, 3,000 stormed the hall crushing men, women, and children.

A second clipping describes a stampede at a rock concert in Cincinnati. Only a limited number of nonreserved, general admission seats were available. The waiting mob broke down a gate, surged through, and trampled 11 young fans to death; 22 others were seriously injured.

Still a third clipping concerns a riot just before the "super bowl" of European soccer at Brussels. The gruesome score: 38 dead, more than 400 injured.

---

[4]"Boston Holocaust," *Life*, December 7, 1942, © Time Inc., p. 44. Reprinted by permission.

[5]"Tragedy in Kentucky," *Fire Journal*, November 1982, p. 65.

[6]John L. Bryan, "Human Behavior in the MGM Grand Hotel Fire," *Fire Journal*, March, 1982, p. 46.

Panic, of course, is not exclusively a group phenomenon. The individual may experience solo panic that can lead to destructive consequences. I am looking at a newspaper clipping that tells of a businessman who was dozing as his commuter train sped home. The train stopped at the station just before his own and started up again, awakening the man. Startled and thinking that he was missing his station, the man dashed out of the forward door of the coach. He stumbled and fell under the train, and its wheels cut off his feet at the ankles.

Riots, lynchings, and many other forms of mob or individual violence or inaction (frozen panic)—unsanity, in any case—are almost invariable earmarked by irrational, impulsive behavior.

THREE CLASSES OF BEHAVIOR

The question is: How is it possible that normally civilized, law-abiding, peaceful, sane, and adult persons sometimes act like fear-crazed or enraged animals? How can humans, collectively or individually, lose their heads, or fly off the handle and, as a consequence, effectively contribute to the harm and destruction of themselves and others? Compare three broad classifications of human behavior:

1. Reflex Responses

Shine a light into someone's eyes, and watch the pupils contract. Draw a pointed instrument across the sole of a foot, and note the reaction of the toes. Tap the knee just below the patella, and watch the lower leg jerk. These simple reactions are called *reflex responses*. Involving no thinking, they are uncontrolled (and largely uncontrollable), direct, and immediate responses of the organism to stimuli.

2. Voluntary Responses

Now ask the same person to spell New York backward, to multiply 43 by 9, and then to estimate your weight. Assuming that this person had had no special preparation for these tasks, the responses will have characteristics opposite to those of reflexes. They will involve some thinking; they will be delayed, controllable (and controlled) responses.

3. Reflexlike Responses

Compare these two forms of behavior with a third:

> We enlisted men were playing baseball with our officers. I had walked and had visions of stealing second. Unfortunately, their pitcher caught me leaning and threw to first base. Now I was in a rundown between the lieutenant

playing first and the bird colonel playing second. I was a sure out, but just as the lieutenant threw to the colonel, I snapped to attention and saluted. The colonel promptly returned the salute and muffed the catch, and I scampered on to second!

The colonel's reaction appears to be a cross between a reflex response and a voluntary response. Like a reflex, his reaction was undelayed, uncontrolled, and apparently involved little or no thought. On the other hand, it resembled a voluntary response, in that his action was controllable (albeit largely uncontrolled in this instance). In short, his response could have been delayed, controlled, and premeditated—in other words, it could have been a voluntary response, but years of conditioning and habit militated against this. A reflexlike response, then, may be considered a potential voluntary reaction which, through habit, panic, conditioning, surprise, and so on, resembles a reflex.

Useful Reflexlike Responses.   Reflexlike responses often begin as conscious, voluntary actions. One learns to drive a car, play a musical instrument, type, throw a baseball, and so forth, quite consciously and perhaps laboriously at first. But with repetition, these actions become so habituated that they may be carried on with virtually no conscious control. Our capacity for learning these responses is invaluable to us. Consider driving an automobile. If you had to maintain conscious control of your steering, braking, accelerating, and so on, you might have considerable difficulty in coping with, say, the added complexity of having the car in front stop quickly. You simply do not have the time, under these conditions, to decide with due premeditation that you must slow up or stop your car, that you must take your foot off the accelerator, that you must put it on the brake, that you must press the brake pedal hard enough to stop in time but not hard enough to skid your car into oncoming traffic, that you must be looking for possibilities of steering around the stopped car, that you must take into account the actions of the drivers behind and beside you, and so forth. If you are an experienced driver, you have so thoroughly habituated many of these actions that you will perform them without prethought and therefore will have time and concentration for coping with the less familiar aspects of the situation. Good typists, for example, are unaware of the specific movements of their fingers. In fact, if they began to *will* that certain fingers strike certain keys, the rate would fall off markedly and the errors would probably increase. If a punch press operator had to make conscious decisions before stamping each piece, you can imagine the decreased productivity.

There is perhaps no more relevant application of appropriate reflexlike responses than in sports. Thinking is often a handicap here. The athlete who has to think about throwing a punch, fielding a ground ball, or returning a serve, is likely to flub it. Instead the athlete reacts with a lightning-fast conditioned reflex.[7]

In short, there is a great deal to be said for properly trained reflexlike responses.

Dangerous Reflexlike Responses.   There are occasions, however, when reflexlike responses can lead to trouble. Take the rookie police officer who was assigned to night duty in a downtown shopping district. He was making his rounds, checking the rear doors of the shops, when he found the door of a furniture store unlocked. He swung the door open and noticed with a start that the figure of a man loomed in the darkness inside. The officer quickly went for his gun and was dismayed to see the "other man" go for his. The policeman immediately pulled his revolver and fired—and the "man" disappeared amid the sound of shattering glass. Upon investigating, the young officer discovered that he had destroyed a $200 mirror!

Most of us might argue that we would have done the same thing as the embarrassed rookie—and so we might, for we would have been rookies, too. But veteran police officers tell us that the situation could have been handled more skillfully. They say that they have learned from experience to suspect immediately the possibility of a mirrored image. They say that there are ways of weaving, ducking, and dodging—while reaching for one's gun—which (1) make one a difficult target if the "man" should actually turn out to be there and (2) permit a check on the suspected mirror. Of course, if the other "man" doesn't weave, duck, or dodge as you do, you may have a problem on your hands! But, the veterans insist, you are usually in a better position to cope with it.

Happily, not all inappropriate reflexlike responses end negatively. Once when Lauritz Melchior was in the finale of *Die Walküre*, a fire broke out in the stage light trough. Fortunately, a fireman was present, as required by law. Unfortunately, he had fallen asleep in the warm wings. Awakened by the clamor, he dashed on stage and threw a bucket of water on Melchior! Realizing his error, he promptly retreated and returned with a second bucket and doused the flames. The tenor took eight curtain calls; the fireman took ten!

However, unthinking responses can sometimes have far graver consequences than minor property damage and embarrassment. The ironic label for the following similar tragedies could be "The Quick and the Dead":

> In Albany, Texas, two sisters were walking on a railroad trestle when a freight train bore down on them. Margie Dell Macon, 12, panicked and started

---

[7]Perhaps it is primarily because there is so much time to think that golf can be so difficult. For what could be easier than to hit a *stationary, teed-up* ball? Almost anything, answers the exasperated duffer.

to run. She stumbled, and the train killed her. Barbara, 14, remained where she was, crouched on the edge of the trestle. The train didn't touch her.

In Arlington Heights, Illinois, two brothers were walking on the shoulder of a busy road. They suddenly spotted a snake. Romeo Ramos, 6, ran onto the road into the path of an oncoming car. Roel, 11, stayed on the shoulder, unharmed. The reptile? An innocuous garter snake.

Destructive undelayed reactions are not confined to such specific situations. Consider Nystrom's analysis of extremist thinking and behavior. "Fanaticism," she wrote in a striking statement, "is a triumph of reflex over reflection."[8] She went on to explain: "It [fanaticism] differs from the more primitive reflexes in that it is conditioned . . . but it is reflex nonetheless: an absolute, fixed, undifferentiated, *immediate* response of the organism to a set of self-selected signals."[9]

THE PROBLEM OF UNDELAYED REACTIONS

The problem of undelayed reactions does not, of course, involve true reflexes, which for the most part consist of harmless and often self-protective behavior. Nor does it concern properly trained and habituated reflexlike actions which increase one's efficiency in repetitive tasks and facilitate the handling of unusual situations, as in driving an automobile.

The undelayed reactions that are of concern here are those that can and ought to be delayed, controlled, and premeditated. The correctives which follow, then, apply to the reflexlike responses which, in the interest of saving tempers, time, energy, money, and lives, could and should be delayed, conscious, voluntary responses.

CORRECTIVES

Instantaneous Action Rarely Necessary

First of all, let us recognize that very few emergencies require an immediate action. This chapter has cited numerous examples of critical circumstances ranging from a policeman's reflection in a mirror to the unforgettable Iroquois Theatre fire. In no case was immediate, unthinking response necessary. In fact, in every case, had those involved delayed their reactions for even a moment to size up the situation, the consequences might have been a good deal happier.

---

[8]Christine Nystrom, "Immediate Man: The Symbolic Environment of Fanaticism,"*ETC.*, March 1977, p. 19.
[9]Ibid.

The Habit of Delay

On the aftermath of the Iroquois Theatre catastrophe, Bishop Samuel Fallows wrote:

> Let every safeguard that human ingenuity can devise be furnished and yet there always remains the personal element to be taken into account. Habitual practice of self-control in daily life will help give coolness and calmness in times of peril. Keeping one's head in the ordinary things prevents its losing when the extraordinary occurs.[10]

The "habitual practice of self-control in daily life" is precisely what is advocated here. Frequently practice the technique of delaying your response, if only for an instant. It is especially helpful to discipline oneself under semiemergency circumstances. If, for example, someone makes a remark that seems offensive, resist the impulse to respond—instead, let your initial reaction be *delay*. Give yourself time to size up the situation: Did she really mean that? Will it be wise to retaliate in kind? What are his reasons for saying it? Could she only be joking? Hadn't I better give him a chance to clarify this? The chances are with you that your delayed reactions will be appreciably more intelligent, mature, and, in the long run, effective than your impulsive response would have been. The point is not simply to count to ten but *to size up* the situation—to analyze, detect the inferences, get more data, remember the etcetera, look for other alternatives, which-index, how-much-index, and when-index,—while doing so.

Since many of our harmful, overquick responses are vocal, a friend has developed the habit of clenching a pen or pencil crosswise between his teeth when the urge to "shoot from the lip" comes on. While the wear and tear on the writing instrument may be considerable, this little technique is a good reminder of the wisdom of delaying and rather effectively inhibits the verbal outburst.

One Hour at a Time

For repetitive undelayed reactions, one might copy the one-step-at-a-time principle that has worked wonders for Alcoholics Anonymous. This technique could be used, for example, by harried executives with the habit of losing their tempers at the slightest provocation. By resolving repeatedly not to shout for the next hour, they can probably short-circuit the anger pattern and build some confidence in their ability to retain composure. Capitalizing on behavioral modification findings, it would also help if one's secretary or colleague would occasionally commend successful restraint.

---

[10]*Chicago's Awful Theatre Horror*, p. xv.

Humor

Your sense of humor can be a marvelous tension-breaker for yourself as well as others—and a deterrent to self-defeating impulsive behavior. In the India-Burma theater during World War II, the forces of British Field Marshal Viscount William J. Slim had just suffered a resounding defeat. Searching for a way to relax his desperate staff, he remarked, "Things could be worse." "How?" came a disbelieving voice from the rear. "Well," replied Slim, "it could be raining."

Advance Preparation for Emergencies

The best general provision for emergencies is the deeply ingrained habit of delay-while-sizing-up, but more specific preparation is often possible. Generally speaking, an emergency is an emergency because it involves circumstances that are unexpected and unfamiliar and that we feel unprepared or unable to cope with. To the extent that the circumstances are anticipated and made familiar and to the extent that we are equipped to cope with them, they are no longer overwhelming crises. Training for combat is an excellent example of this. The recruit spends weeks going through many of the activities of warfare, firing his rifle, throwing grenades, taking forced hikes with full field pack, participating in bayonet drill, crawling through the infiltration course,[11] and so on. The object is to acquaint the soldier with as many of the aspects of combat as possible so that the actual experience will not seem overpoweringly complex and terrifying.

Speech training is another good example of advance preparation for emergencies. The beginning speaker is advised to become familiar in advance, insofar as possible, with the components of the speaking situation. One is urged, for example, to master the speech (in many cases this will require committing the ideas and their connectives, though not the exact wording, to memory); to learn in advance what one can about the audience (size, age, sex, interests, prejudices, and so on); to know the purpose of the occasion; the topics of any previous and subsequent speakers; and the role one's own talk will play; and to acquaint oneself with the physical aspects (acoustics, arrangement of the audience, position of the speaker's stand, lighting, and so forth). In short, one becomes able to cope with difficult and critical situations to the extent they have been predicted, prepared for, and controlled in advance.

---

[11]The infiltration course is a simulated battlefield. The trainee crawls 50 yards or so under barbed wire, with a brace of machine guns firing real bullets a few inches overhead. As an added fillip, charges explode sporadically throughout the field, throwing showers of grit or mud everywhere.

This has perhaps never been demonstrated more eloquently than when our astronauts dealt with the various dangers that confronted them. Recall that when the automatic aids to bring in his craft failed, Gordon Cooper calmly took over the manual controls and achieved a highly accurate reentry. Having practiced repeatedly for every conceivable emergency maneuver, Cooper could justifiably say: "I was not overly concerned. We had checked, checked, and double-checked. I felt right at home in the bird." He had done his homework well.

Hostage-taking, no doubt stimulated by the takeover of the American Embassy in Teheran, has become an increasingly prevalent phenomenon. Accordingly, a number of U.S. police departments are taking special preparatory training. Typically, personnel are informed that a simulation is about to occur—blanks will be used instead of real bullets. Otherwise, they have no idea of what they will be up against.

The situation might involve a crazed gunman who has commandeered a business office and taken several hostages. If the officers perform well as a team, they may resolve the situation without injury or loss of life or even property damage. If they don't, they will be given explicit feedback so they can improve their performance the next time around—even if it turns out to be for real.

Anticipating the Undelayed Responses of Others

So far, we have been concerned with measures to take that encourage our delayed reactions. Let us now consider how to deal with the harmful undelayed responses of others. First of all, it should be recognized that the tendency to react quickly varies from individual to individual, and within a given individual, from time to time. In other words, *which-index* and *when-index* the other person's propensity to fly off the handle. While Sam seemed to stand up under pressure last week, there is no guarantee that he will be as serene now.

Second, if you anticipate a potential flare-up, use the most snap reaction-proof medium of communication possible. For example, it is extremely easy for a person who becomes angry on the telephone to cut you off in an instant and proceed to act foolishly and destructively. Under some circumstances, a memo or letter, with no chance of immediate feedback from the other person and no possibility for control on your part, may be even worse. But a face-to-face communication gives you a chance to see the storm clouds forming and to forestall them. And even if the other person does "blow his top," you are there to help him regain his composure.

Third, and most important, don't match the other person's undelayed response with one of your own. Sorely tempting as they may be at times, mutual overquick reactions may make reconciliation considerably more difficult. And, after all, if you are right, you can afford to keep your temper; if you are wrong, you can't afford to lose it.

CASES

CASE 17-1

The Fateful Knob*

Any doctor, old or new, would have been glad to be called to this house, one of the most beautiful old homes in the city. I felt that my standing in the community was at stake and that it was an important moment.

At the conclusion of the examination I wanted to talk privately with the stiffly starched and immaculate nurse who was in attendance, who, too, was apparently making every effort to be perfect in her professional attitude. I wanted to give some instructions to the nurse and asked the family to excuse us for a moment while I talked to her privately. The nearest and most obvious place was the old-fashioned bathroom adjoining, and I asked her to go in. I closed the door.

"Sit down," I said, pointing to the bathroom stool, and then, as she took it, I noticed that the only place left for me was the indispensable one in any bathroom, which was covered by a gold and white lid.

I seated myself and talked for several minutes while the family waited anxiously outside for the verdict. Finally she rose and as I, too, rose, my hand automatically grasped the ornate pear-shaped knob at the end of the chain hanging beside me—and I pulled.

Why I pulled the cursed thing I'll never know. Instantly the place resounded with the familiar screeches and hisses of flushing water.

"Oh, doctor!" she gasped, "what will they think?—And the door shut!—What can I do?"

"Hell, woman," I said, my dignity ruined, "Don't ask me what you can do. I don't even know what I can do!"

I was never asked to return.

Discussion Questions

1. What is the principal pattern of miscommunication in this case?

2. Could this misevaluation have been prevented?

---

*Frederic Loomis, M.D., *Consultation Room* (New York: Alfred A. Knopf, 1939), pp. 29–31. Reprinted by permission.

CASE 17–2

You Can't Outrun a Grenade

William A. Daniels

I recently finished basic training in the infantry, and I have to report that our platoon of recruits fell for the oldest trick in the Army.

It was the first day of live hand grenade practice. Our sergeant, an apparent live grenade in his hand, was instructing us. He emphasized several times: "When you are on the receiving end of a grenade, fall to the ground immediately and present as small a target as possible. *You can't outrun a grenade.*" These admonitions were greeted with the usual smirks and *sotto voce* wisecracks.

Then, suddenly, while attempting to show how to move a live grenade safely from hand to hand with the pin pulled, the grenade slipped from the sergeant's grasp and fell sputtering to the ground. Sixty men rose as one, and scrambled, and fought, and ran to escape the grenade which would explode in five seconds.

Five seconds passed, and no explosion occurred. The men sheepishly realized that the grenade was a dummy and that the sergeant had used this as an example of the damage and injuries that could result if panic were allowed to take control.

Discussion Questions

1. Why did the sergeant drop the grenade?
2. Why is this case appended to this chapter?

CASE 17–3

The Logan Company*

The Logan Company, a manufacturer of television and radio receiver sets, employed some 2,000 persons. The firm, which had been privately owned for over 30 years, had been sold to a large electronics holding corporation four years earlier, but retained substantially the same management after the sale. Following three unsatisfactory years, the president of Logan retired. The holding corporation installed Eric Stone as general manager; he was from outside the firm but within the holding company. Stone was given

---

*All names have been disguised. Printed by permission of the author, whose name has been withheld by request.

the rank of vice president, although he carried out the functions of the president, an office now vacant. He made many changes in the upper and middle management levels, including the product-line managers. The current situation, then, may be said to be one of flux and readjustment.

Among the responsibilities of the industrial engineering department was the supervision of the installation of production lines as new products or changes in products were introduced. One of these was a new conveyor assembly line for television tuners. Formerly the tuners had been assembled by conventional bench assembly methods, with workers compensated on an individual incentive basis. Many employees had expressed dissatisfaction with the new methods, complaining that their take-home pay had been markedly reduced.

Ray Edwards, 35, six years with Logan, was the industrial engineer in charge of installing the tuner conveyor line. He found on Tuesday that it was necessary to adjust the pace of the conveyor in order to train assemblers. He realized that the product-line manager, Fred Peterson, who had joined the firm two months earlier, was under considerable pressure to increase tuner production. So he phoned Peterson at 11 A.M. to discuss the intended adjustment but was unable to reach him. As he waited for Peterson to return his call, Edwards reviewed four alternatives for timing the change:

1. Have Logan's maintenance men make the adjustment after work hours that day. To Edwards this did not appear to be a happy choice, since it would require overtime pay at time and a half for the maintenance workers. This pay would be charged against the industrial engineering department. The department's budget for such expenses was already strained for the fiscal period.
2. Wait until Saturday (a nonworking day) and have maintenance people make the installation. Their overtime pay would then be charged to the miscellaneous budget. While this would entail no loss of production time or employee pay and would relieve the industrial engineering department of overtime charges, the delay in installing the change would interfere with operator training.
3. Have the salesmen of the adjustment equipment make the change during work hours. Since he would be paid by his own firm the expense would not be charged to the industrial engineering budget. However, tuner production would be shut down, and workers would not be paid during the shutdown period.
4. Have the salesman start to make the change during the lunch period. Edwards favored this plan because it would not only remove the burden of overtime pay from his department's budget, but would require a minimum of shutdown time and loss of worker pay. How-

ever, Edwards wanted to inform Peterson that the change might take longer than the lunch period.

Peterson had spent the morning in conference in the office of the vice president in charge of manufacturing, Roy Sheldon. Also present was Tom Flynn, manager of the industrial engineering department, to whom Edwards reported. Flynn, 38, had 13 years of service with the company. At 12:45 P.M., as Peterson left Sheldon's office, he was stopped by Miss Larson, Sheldon's secretary, who gave him Edwards' message, which had been relayed to her by Peterson's secretary.

Peterson immediately picked up the phone on Miss Larson's desk and called Edwards.

Peterson   Ray, I understand you called—just got the note.

Edwards   (*The fourth alternative was now no longer possible, because the assemblers' lunch period had ended.*) Yes, Fred—we're going to have to regulate the tuner line. As you know, it has been going too fast for the workers.

Peterson   Yeah? (*Suspiciously.*)

Edwards   Well, we've purchased some new gearing that should do the trick of slowing down the line. Now, as to whom to make the change, I have a few ideas to sound out with you.

Peterson   Shoot.

Edwards   First, we could have the maintenance men do the job tonight. Frankly, I'm opposed to this, and so is Flynn. Their time would be charged to us, and we're up to the hilt right now in overtime charges. I don't think Tom would stand for it. So I thought. . . .

(*Click!*) Peterson had hung up. He charged angrily back into Mr. Sheldon's office and, in Sheldon's presence, proceeded to upbraid Tom Flynn for trying to shut down his production line in order to avoid overtime costs.

Discussion Questions

1. How would you describe the organization climate at Logan?
2. What was Edwards' frame of reference before the telephone conversation with Peterson?
3. What was Peterson's frame of reference before the telephone conversation with Edwards?
4. How do you analyze the phone conversation?
5. How should Edwards have handled the situation?
6. How should Peterson have handled the phone call?
7. Sheldon has now had the situation drop into his lap. What should he do?

CASE 17-4

The Mid-Western Telephone Company*

The general staff of the Mid-Western Telephone Company decided upon a revision in the company's billing procedure. Formerly, billing machine symbols had appeared on four portions of the bill. The change consisted in using these symbols on only one section of the bill. Thus, it was necessary to have three sets of symbols removed from each of the firm's billing machines.

Later Friday afternoon Charles Liska of the general staff notified the United Office Machine Company, which serviced the machines, to send out a repairman at the beginning of the week to remove the unneeded symbols. Liska then instructed Ted Jennings of the division staff to notify the district heads and the supervising accountants of each district of the change. Each of the supervising accountants was to have relayed the information to the supervisor under him.

These lines of communication are charted in Exhibit 17-1.

EXHIBIT 17-1

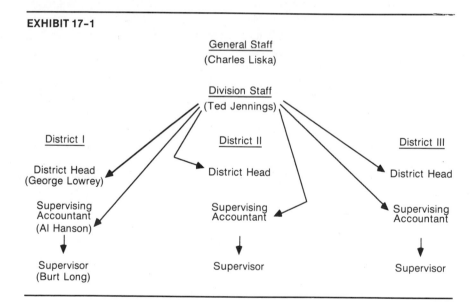

*All names have been disguised. Printed by permission of the author, whose name has been withheld by request.

Jennings tried to contact George Lowrey, the district head in District I, and was unable to reach him. Jennings then called Al Hanson, the supervising accountant in District I, and gave the message to him and requested that he notify Burt Long, the supervisor whose unit was involved.

At the time he was called, Hanson was wrestling with a production problem and was several hours behind schedule. He did not take any notes and forgot to contact Long.

Monday morning the repairman walked into Long's unit and told him that he was there to remove something, but he was hazy on whether he was to remove all of the symbols or only some of them from the machines. Long, who had not been contacted about the matter, tried to call Hanson, but Hanson was not at his desk. Long then called Lowrey to ask him what to do. Hanson happened to be in Lowrey's office when Long's call came in. Lowrey, knowing nothing of the situation, told Hanson that Long was asking what to do about symbols on the billing machines. He asked whether Hanson could handle the situation.

Hanson flushed with embarrassment as he suddenly recalled his failure to convey Jennings' message to Long. He vaguely remembered something about the removal of symbols, but because he felt that Lowrey was already holding him responsible for his current production problem he dreaded admitting his error in the presence of his superior. He clutched the phone and told Long that all of the symbols were to be removed. He silently resolved to stop the repairman and check with Jennings as soon as he left Lowrey's office. Unfortunately, the district head began a prolonged discussion of Hanson's production difficulty. Hanson became so preoccupied with Lowrey's remarks that the symbols matter slipped his mind. Meanwhile Long relayed Hanson's instruction to the repairman, who proceeded to remove all of the symbols.

Sometime later in the morning, Jennings, following up to see whether the work had been done, discovered what had happened. Upon checking with the United Office Machine Company, he was told that the correct symbols could be replaced at $55 per machine and that the machines would have to be brought into the shop for the replacement.

The end result was that the ten machines of the unit were taken out of production for several days and that a cost of $550 was necessary to replace the symbols.

Discussion Questions

1. Who contributed to this cacophony of errors and how?

2. How could this costly error have been prevented?

3. What patterns of miscommunication seem to be involved in this case?

CASE 17–5

Your Eyes Can Deceive You*

Arthur Bartlett

George Smith got home from a date with his girl about midnight. His mother was not at home. Probably she was out playing cards with friends, George thought. That had been her favorite recreation ever since her divorce, when George was six. Working all day in the candy factory, she liked to relax in the evenings. Now that George was 20, and working, and had a girl to occupy his attention, she often stayed out fairly late. So George went up to his own front room, undressed, got into bed and lay there reading the newspaper.

A bus stopped across the street, and George pulled aside the window shade and looked out. Under the street light, he could see his mother descending from the bus. A tall, heavy-set man got out behind her. The bus moved on. George was about to drop back on his pillow when his startled eyes stopped him. The man was reaching for his mother, trying to put his arms around her. George saw her push at him and try to step back off the curb; saw him grab her again and start pulling her toward him.

George leaped out of bed, pulled on his trousers and rushed down the stairs to the front door. Across the street, the man was still attempting to embrace his mother and she was struggling against him. George dashed to the rescue. Clenching his fist as he ran, he leaped at the man and punched with all his strength, hitting him squarely on the jaw. The man toppled backward and uttered a groan as his head hit the sidewalk. Then he lay there, still.

What happened next filled George with utter confusion. Dropping to her knees beside the unconscious man, his mother looked up at him with anguish in her eyes, "George," she cried, "what have you done? This is Howard Browser. . . . Howard, the candymaker at the factory . . . the man who asked me to marry him." . . .

The boy stared at his mother across the crumpled figure on the pavement. "He wasn't attacking you?" he demanded, dully.

"Of course not," she told him. "We'd been out together all evening. He brought me home. He wanted a good-night kiss, that's all. I was just teasing him."

An ambulance took Howard Browser to the hospital, but he never regained consciousness. He died the next day. George Smith spent that night in a jail cell.

---

*Reprinted by permission from the *American Weekly,* Hearst Publishing Company, Inc.

The authorities finally decided not to prosecute. George, the investigation proved, didn't know Browser; had never seen him before. He had honestly thought that what he saw was a man attacking his mother.

Take the case of Matthew J. Flaherty, a Boston policeman, some years ago. Shortly after being appointed to the force, Matt Flaherty took a bride and they moved into their own home on Newcastle Road. Eleanor Flaherty loved the house, but she was nervous about being alone in it at night, waiting for Matt to come home from his late tour of duty. Every little noise make her think that there was someone in the house or trying to get in. When Matt got home she was usually so upset that he would search the whole house, from cellar to attic, though smiling at her fears.

"No burglars," he would assure her, "except in your pretty little head."

Still, he couldn't help feeling anxious. If anyone really were prowling around his house while he was away nights. . . .

One night—they had been living in the house about two months then—he made the usual fruitless search and went to bed. But he had hardly dropped off to sleep, it seemed, when he woke with a start. What had awakened him? Naturally, his first thought was of a prowler. Listening tensely, he heard a sound—the creaking of a floor board—on the other side of the closed bedroom door. Quietly, he reached for his gun and eased himself up in bed.

Sure enough, the door began to push open. Somebody was coming right into the room.

"Who's there?" Matt Flaherty yelled taking careful aim. There was no answer but a startled gasp, and he started shooting. It was too dark to see the figure beyond the half-opened door, but whoever it was fell with a thump to the floor.

Then Matt turned on the light. That was when he realized, for the first time, that Eleanor was not there in the bed beside him. She was lying just outside the door, dead.

Discussion Questions

1. How does the title of this article strike you?

2. Is there any similarity between the two incidents?

3. How could these tragedies have been prevented?

CASE 17–6

Torment in a Neighborhood*

Walter B. Smith

What made James Lee, the Chinese laundryman, go berserk?

Why did he shoot three men, two of them police, then try to fight off 150 more cops before falling with a bullet wound through the skull?

Lying Saturday in County Hospital, his head throbbing and his left ankle shackled to the bed frame, Jimmy Lee gave his explanation of why he did it.

"I was scared," he said.

He was scared, he said, because he thought the three men had come to beat him up and perhaps take his money because he had slapped a boy.

And he slapped the boy, Lee said, because he finally had become fed up with the way neighborhood kids in general tormented him with squirt guns, name-calling, door-banging, and other mischief.

The furious gun battle took place just a week ago in Lee's laundry at 2705 Diversey.

The city was shocked—the more so because such violence is so rare among Chicago's law-abiding Chinese.

Today two of Lee's victims are dead—detectives Jeremiah Lucey and Roman C. Steinke.

The third victim, truck driver Steven Malenk, 40, father of the slapped boy, has recently been discharged from a hospital.

Lee has a sewed-up hole in his head where a bullet went right through. Doctors expect him to recover, but he may be paralyzed for life.

Lee started the shooting when the two policemen went to the laundry with Malenk to arrest Lee on a warrant charging assault.

The warrant stemmed from an incident three nights earlier when Lee had slapped Malenk's son Steve Jr., 11.

For months, Lee said, neighborhood kids had badgered him. Sometimes they spit on the floor, sometimes they threw things, sometimes they called him obscene names.

On the evening of February 3, Lee said, the Malenk boy and a companion were heckling him. (The boys say they were just looking in the window.)

Lee chased them and caught Steve, slapping him.

Soon afterward Steve came back to the laundry with his father. Lee said

---

*Chicago Daily News. Reprinted by permission

the truck driver threatened him and they struggled. The laundryman admits he batted Malenk with a flatiron, breaking his wrist.

Malenk went to the Shakespeare police court next day and got the warrant charging Lee with assault.

Lee said he did not know about that when the officers came to get him last Saturday. Why didn't he go along peacefully to the police station?

"I was scared," Lee said. "All I knew was that these three men were coming to get me and wanted me to pay them $125. I thought they were going to beat me up."

He said he did not know that the men with Malenk were police. They wore civilian clothes.

"All I could think of was to shoot first."

The mention of $125 apparently was a misunderstanding of the policemen's statement that Lee would have to post $125 bail at the police station.

Lee said he kept the pistol and shotgun with which he fought the police as protection against burglars.

He lived alone at the laundry. He has no relatives in Chicago.

Lee told his story twice. First it was in halting English to a *Daily News* reporter. Then it was in Chinese to the Rev. Philip Lee, no relation, who was pastor of the Chinese Christian Union Church at 23d Street and Wentworth.

The wounded man's chief worry was about his laundry. The Rev. Mr. Lee assured him that arrangements would be made with a Chinese friend to see that the customers got back their shirts.

The clergyman said Chinese welfare organizations were making plans to give Lee the help he needs.

Lee said he was brought to America in 1934, at the age of two. After three years in New Jersey he was brought to Chicago, where he has lived ever since.

He said he had had his laundry at the Diversey address for six years, but that the trouble with the youngsters did not start until last September.

An inquest into the death of Detective Lucey has been continued to March 9.

* * * * *

James Lee died 2½ months later from his wounds. A newspaper account included the following:

> Lee said he went berserk because he was afraid the officers were going to beat him up. However, a fingerprint check showed Lee was sought as an Army deserter, and police said that might have been the reason he feared arrest.

Discussion Questions

1. How is this case similar to the two incidents described in "Your Eyes Can Deceive You," Case 17–5?

2. Does this case differ from those incidents?

CASE 17–7

Dyer Public Relations, Inc.*

Ralph Stewart, staff writer for a business magazine with a large national circulation, was talking with Robert Dyer for the second time in early March. He had already recorded Mr. Dyer's account of the formation and development of Dyer Public Relations, Inc., as well as Mr. Dyer's personal history. Now, to round out his prospective article, he needed further information about others in the firm.

Mr. Dyer was cooperative and said, "If you uncover anything constructive about how our communications and human relations are functioning, we'd be grateful—especially me. If it doesn't come up naturally, I suggest you probe and hear what we now call the 'Office Boy Incident.' Our people know you're here, and I've requested them to be frank in their interviews with you."

Dyer Public Relations, Inc., had been founded 14 years earlier in a large West Coast city by Mr. Dyer—a driving, ambitious, dynamic young man with seemingly inexhaustible energy. The company became a nationally recognized firm, grossing over $2 million annually. Dyer, Inc., employed approximately 40 persons. A partial organization chart appears in Exhibit 1.

In addition to Mr. Dyer, the following persons were involved in the "Office Boy Incident":

> *Mark Taylor*—47, treasurer, joined Dyer 13 years earlier. Mr. Taylor also maintained a private accounting practice. He had a working agreement with Mr. Dyer that he would spend approximately half his time on the Dyer accounts and the other half on his own practice. These percentages were never adhered to rigidly. Some months, Mr. Taylor spent more than 50 percent of his time on Dyer affairs; some months, less. This had been an established arrangement between the two men, and both seemed satisfied with its operation.
>
> *William Frey*—27, held a Ph.D. in industrial psychology. He was in charge of personnel services, including testing and placement for clients and the Dyer staff. Frey had been with the Dyer firm for two years. His predecessor, Kenneth Elson, had served as director of personnel services and as office man-

---

*All names and organizational designations have been disguised. Copyright, 1964, by Northwestern University. Printed by permission.

ager. When Dr. Frey assumed the personnel responsibilities, Mrs. Lane became office manager.

Miriam Lane—26, was office manager of the firm and personal secretary to Mr. Clawson. She had six years' service with Dyer and had been office manager for the past two years. The firm's general clerical work flowed across her desk. She assigned it to secretaries who were not already busy with duties for their immediate supervisors. She had direct responsibility for the work of Russell Harmon, office boy.

Russell Harmon—21, office boy, a university student majoring in business management, had been working approximately 30 hours per week with Dyer for the past year.

THE OFFICE BOY INCIDENT

Over the past several months, because of tax deadlines and other financial problems, Mark Taylor had been devoting considerably more than 50 percent of his time to the Dyer firm. He was attempting to clear up a few personal affairs before leaving on a business trip for Dyer. He handed a typed letter about his professional fraternity to the bookkeeper, Arlene Roney, telling her to have 25 copies made. Miss Roney had been with the firm some two weeks and knew little of the firm's procedures. She knew that reproduction work was done by the office boy, Russell Harmon. She also knew that the firm owned a photocopying machine but was unaware that the company also had an offset duplicator.[1] She assumed that the letter was to be photocopied, called to Harmon as he was passing her desk, and handed the letter to him. She said, "Mr. Taylor would like 25 copies of this."

Harmon had just been told by Frey to deliver several packages to an office building across town. He glanced at the letter, realized that in its present form (without mat) he could only photocopy it, a job requiring 15 to 20 minutes, and said, "I can't do that now. I've got to run an errand. If I get back in time, I could do it before closing time, but I doubt if I can make it that soon. Guess it'll have to wait until tomorrow."

Miss Roney felt that she could do no more about the situation and placed the letter on her desk. A few minutes later, Mr. Taylor approached her. "Did Russell run off those copies of the letter yet?"

Miss Roney answered, "No, he said he didn't have time now and probably couldn't do it until tomorrow."

Taylor, visibly angered, immediately stalked to Mr. Dyer's office. "Say, Bob, I know this is my personal work, but I would think I could get a little cooperation from the personnel around here—especially when you consider the amount of time I've been putting in for you."

---

[1]The two machines served different purposes. The photocopy machine could reproduce a few copies quickly without the material having to be retyped on a stencil or a mat. However, the offset duplicator was faster and less expensive when a larger quantity of copies was required.

EXHIBIT 17-2

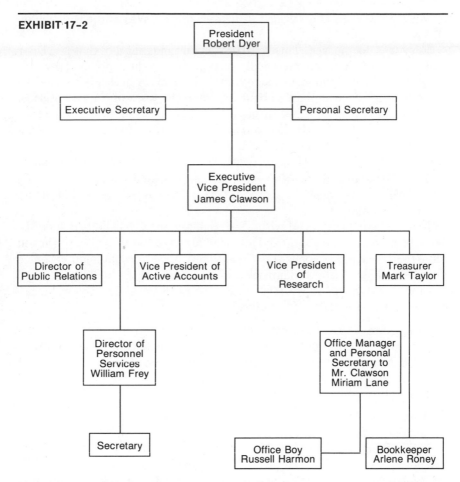

Note: The chart does not fully express the working relationships within the firm. Mr. Dyer frequently communicated directly with Mr. Taylor, the two vice presidents, and Mrs. Lane. Each of these also communicated directly with Dyer. Dyer also worked directly with Dr. Frey and the public relations director. These two men, however, rarely initiated direct relations with Mr. Dyer.

Dyer   What do you mean? What kind of cooperation?

Taylor   Why, Harmon just refused to run off 25 copies of a personal letter for me.

Dyer *(Considerably disturbed)*   Where is he? We'll just see what the hell's going on here!

Dyer walked to Mrs. Lane's desk in the main office and demanded loudly, "Where is Harmon?"

Mrs. Lane   Why, I don't know. I imagine he's out on an errand for Dr. Frey *(pointing toward Frey's office)*. He's been sending Russell to the Weber Building, on the other side of the city.

Mr. Dyer turned and strode into Frey's office. "Why can't Harmon do this work for Mark?"

Frey was nonplussed. This was the second time that day that Mr. Dyer had appeared to hold him personally responsible for the conduct of persons over whom, in his opinion, he had no authority. Earlier in the day, Dyer had come to him with complaints about errors in the work of the secretaries. Moreover, Frey had noticed through the glass partition of his office that Mrs. Lane had apparently directed Mr. Dyer to him. He was suddenly angered with Dyer's accusations and Mrs. Lane's "buck-passing" and snapped, "I don't know! Harmon doesn't work for me! He works for Lane!"

Mr. Dyer stamped out of Frey's office and headed for his own. As he passed Mrs. Lane's desk, he shouted, "When Harmon comes back, tell him I want to see him!"

Mrs. Lane was incensed with Frey. She assumed that he had sent Mr. Dyer back to her. She got up and followed Mr. Dyer into his office. "Do you have to make a scene about this?" she asked. Mr. Dyer slammed his office door behind Mrs. Lane and himself and said, "Who in the hell does Russell Harmon think he is? If Harmon refuses to work for Mark Taylor, he can just get his rear end out of this office!"

Mrs. Lane   What's this all about?

Mr. Dyer   Mark brought something to Harmon to reproduce, and Harmon refused to do it. I want to see this kid now!

Mrs. Lane   I'll find out from Russell about this.

Dyer   I'll ask him!

Mrs. Lane returned to her desk. Shortly afterward, Mr. Dyer, who had an outside appointment, left the office for the day. Harmon returned just before quitting time. When told of the incident, Harmon was bewildered. He felt betrayed by Dr. Frey, who had not, in his words "stuck up" for him by telling Mr. Dyer that he was on an errand. He remarked about Miss Roney to a friend, "I was never even introduced to the girl, and it looks like she's trying to cut me down. Why, I don't even know her!"

Mrs. Lane questioned Harmon about the affair and said she would explain everything to Mr. Dyer in the morning.

By coincidence, Dr. Frey, Mrs. Lane, and Russell Harmon were scheduled to work overtime that evening. Harmon was still disturbed. Dr. Frey saw him talking to Mrs. Lane at the water cooler and went out to join them.

Harmon   What I can't understand is why Mr. Taylor didn't come to me. I could have explained everything, and the whole thing could have been prevented. But, boy! I guess I'm in the soup now. I want to see Mr. Dyer. It doesn't seem fair that he should only hear one side of the story.

Frey Speaking about "sides of the story," maybe you would be interested in mine. (*Frey proceeded to recount how Mr. Dyer had charged into his office and upbraided him for Harmon's conduct.*)

Mrs. Lane If you ask me, I'm the gal with the responsibility. I've got to see Mr. Dyer first thing tomorrow morning.

The three continued to compare their versions of the "Office Boy Incident." Dr. Frey and Mrs. Lane were able to allay their suspicions of each other, although neither offered a formal apology to the other. Harmon, however, still felt upset. He told the others that nothing could clear up the situation until he had had a chance to explain the matter directly to Mr. Dyer, which he planned to do the first thing the following day.

Early the next morning, Mrs. Lane explained the confusion to Mr. Dyer. At first, he became angry with Mr. Taylor for not giving him the complete account of the affair and said, "That's poor communication. If Mark is having trouble with his girl, I'll give him a pamphlet on how to communicate!"

Later he grew aggravated with himself, and finally he became contrite: "I'm sorry—that's one of my failings. I should be able to control myself." Stewart was told that Mr. Dyer frequently made this sort of statement after a flare-up.

When Russell Harmon reported to work, he walked to Mrs. Lane's desk.

Harmon Is Mr. Dyer in yet?

Mrs. Lane Well, yes, but the situation is all cleared up.

Harmon Would it be all right if I saw him? I'd like to explain the thing to him.

Mrs. Lane Russell, I don't think you should do that. He knows that you weren't to blame, and I really think you should let the thing blow over.

After assurances from Mrs. Lane that he was "in the clear," Harmon decided to let the matter drop.

Several employees told Stewart that Mr. Clawson was out of town at the time of the incident. One of them added, "It probably wouldn't have made any difference if he had been here."

Discussion Questions

1. What do you make of Mr. Dyer's candor in opening his firm to Stewart?
2. Step by step, how do you analyze the series of miscommunications which occurred in this case?
3. What do you think of the organizational structure of Dyer Public Relations, Inc.?

Part Four

OVERVIEW

18

Overview

We have been examining human communications (the encoding and decoding phases, in particular) as they are influenced by assumptions held by the communicators involved. Some of these assumptions are destructive and troublesome because (1) they are false and imply an inadequate, distorted view of the world, and (2) communicators are usually unaware that their evaluations and communications are being influenced by these assumptions. Under these conditions, patterns of misevaluation and miscommunication are prone to occur and recur. Before summarizing the patterns we have considered, let us review Chapters 1 through 7, which laid the foundation for our examination of communication.

INTRODUCTION

Chapter 1 emphasized that human communication is a vital but complex and challenging process. Despite prodigious progress in the technical aspects of message transmission, information processing, storage, and reception, we still have much to learn about what happens *inside people* as they engage in communication.

The book's focus is on these latter aspects—the subtle, subjective, internal phenomena of human communication.

The organization of the book is also described in the first chapter, and the cases appended to the chapters are recommended as a means of internalizing the contents of the chapters.

ORGANIZATIONAL CULTURE AND COMMUNICATION

Chapter 2 delineated a basic setting for communication behavior—the organization. An organization consists of a number of interdependent people who require coordination if their individual efforts are to serve the organization's objectives most effectively. Moreover, organizations are growing larger and more complex. They are challenged to respond to ever greater demands from society and especially from their own members. In consequence, the organization requires greater communication competence on the part of its managers and key personnel than ever before in history.

This chapter then examines the overall culture of the organization, suggesting that a high-trust—high-performance cycle is desirable in the interests of both the individual and the organization. Conversely, a low-trust—low-performance cycle is to be prevented or, if already in effect, broken. McGregor's Theory Y, (including some of the more recent developments such as situational leadership, goal setting, MBO, OD, Theory Z) with a policy of appropriate trust coupled with personal development, seems a tenable approach. The integration of individual and organizational goals appear to be a sound objective.

PERCEPTION AND COMMUNICATION

The three chapters under the heading above focus on the individual.

1. The Process of Perception

The central premise of this chapter is that what we experience is not reality but our perception of reality. Our unwillingness or inability to internalize this truism can readily lead us into defensive and self-destructive behavior. Thus we are challenged to recognize that our "reality" is subjective, partial, unique, and subject to bias—and to ascertain accurately the perceptions of others.

2. The Frame of Reference and the Self-Image

The frame of reference concept is offered to meet the above challenges. The frame of reference was likened to a stained-glass window in one's solitary confinement cell. The major lens of this window is one's self-image. A valid self-concept is essential if one is to deal effectively with others.

3. The Exceptionally Realistic Self-Image (ERSI)

Among the advantages that a person with an ERSI enjoys are the liberation of energy that would otherwise be required for self-image protection, the ease of maintaining an ERSI, the prerequisites for developing skills for reading others and screening inputs, and the selection of realistic personal goals.

This game plan for attaining an ERSI was recommended:

1. Make an earnest commitment to discover yourself.
2. Recognize and reduce your defenses against valid feedback.
3. Receive and evaluate the external and internal cues.

External feedback includes the cues that we may receive from others (for example, the Johari Window and the transactional analysis concepts) and from psychometric instruments and also the insights that we may derive from readings. Internal feedback can be acquired from, among other modes, psychotherapy, empathic listening, videotape playback, and personal stocktaking methods, such as the Personal Inventory and the Crisis Journal.

MOTIVATION AND COMMUNICATION

Chapter 6 is also concerned with the individual, but this time as a need-satisfying organism whose needs influence perceptions and thus, behavior. I agree with Demosthenes: "The easiest thing of all is to deceive oneself; for what a man wishes he generally believes to be true." The chapter explores several motivation theories in order to determine a basis for understanding and predicting the behavior of others—mandatory skills for effective communicators.

THE PROCESS OF COMMUNICATION

Chapter 7 focuses on an individual's communication behavior and presented a model of the communication process—encoding, transmitting, medium, receiving, decoding. Encoding and decoding are the most subtle, least understood, and most neglected phases of the process. The insidious role of fallacious, unconsciously held assumptions is underscored. Such assumptions contribute to recurrent patterns of miscommunication—a consideration of some of the most troublesome of these patterns constitutes the remainder of the book.

THE INFERENCE-OBSERVATION CONFUSION

The inference-observation confusion occurs when one somehow acts upon inference as if it were observation. In essence we risk without being aware that we are doing so and are off guard, therefore, against the possibility that the inferences are erroneous. The situation is not unlike that of walking downstairs in the dark—of striding off the last step, certain that you had reached the floor level!

One of the key reasons that we often find it easy to substitute inference for observation is that our *statements* of inference can be readily confused with *statements* of observation. That is, there is nothing in the nature of our language (grammar, spelling, pronunciation, syntax, and so on) that inescapably distinguishes between the two types of statements. Thus the habit of differentiating statements of inference from statements of observation should go far in training one's acuity in distinguishing between inferences and observations on nonverbal levels.

Accordingly, a four-step procedure for coping with the inference-observation confusion was suggested:

1. Detect the inference.
2. Calculate the probability that the inference is correct.
3. Get more data—if the risk is a poor one.
4. Recalculate the risk.

Finally, it was argued that creativity and decisiveness are not incompatible with inference awareness. Creativity can be facilitated when one is conscious of inferring. And the quality of decisions can be enhanced by inference awareness. The issue is not the avoidance of inferring (risk-taking) but the awareness of it.

BYPASSING

Bypassing occurs when communicators miss each other with their meanings—either by using the same word while meaning different things or by using different words while meaning the same thing. Resulting in false disagreements (or agreements), bypassings can sometimes be innocuous, even humerous. But on other occasions, they can be significantly more costly and destructive.

Immediately underlying bypassing is the supposition that words mean the same to the other person as they do to me. This belief, in turn, is supported by two insidious fallacies: that words have *mono-usage;* that words *have meanings*.

To guard against unintentional bypassing (deliberate bypassing was acknowledged), the communicator can supplant these assumptions with two others that represent much more adequately the relation between words and meanings: (1) most words, with the exception of some technical terms, are used in more than one way; (2) meanings exist not in words but only in the people who speak, hear, write, and read them, the people, who fix the variables—that is, assign meanings to words.

Querying, paraphrasing, being approachable, using backup methods, practicing pretransmission and postreception audits, delaying, and remaining alert to contexts, verbal and situational, are some of the ways of implementing these premises.

ALLNESS

Allness is a sort of evaluational disease. It occurs when one unconsciously assumes that it is possible to know and to say everything about something; that what one is saying (or writing or thinking) covers *all* there is (or all that is important) about the subject. The assumption is manifestly fallacious, and yet it is an extremely difficult one to dislodge if we do not recognize that we are inevitably and continuously abstracting.

To abstract is to select some details of a situation while neglecting others. We abstract when we observe (see, hear, smell, and so on), talk, listen, write, read, think, and so forth.

When we fail to realize that we are abstracting, that is, leaving out details, we are in distinct danger of believing that we have left out nothing—nothing of consequence, at any rate. Arrogance, intolerance of other viewpoints, and closemindedness are frequent consequences of such false assurance.

Allness is encouraged by the craving for certainty—the intolerance of uncertainty, if you will—which afflicts all of us to some degree.

To intensify our awareness of abstracting and thus avoid allness, we should:

1. Cultivate the humility to concede that we can never say or know everything about anything.
2. Recognize that abstracting is inevitable when we talk, listen, and so on, for then we would be more likely . . .
   —to assess and perhaps improve the quality of our abstractions.
   —to be empathic.
   —to be creative and less inhibited by past practices.
3. "Remember the etc.," a simple, yet effective device.
4. Free ourselves from the insularity of an "all-wall."

The essence of this chapter is not the *avoidance* but the *awareness* of abstracting. Accordingly, it was asserted that decisiveness and viability *are* compatible.

DIFFERENTIATION FAILURES

1. Indiscrimination

Indiscrimination occurs when one fails to recognize differences among the similarities. The frequent result is that one reacts to blacks, police officers, politicians, business executives, Jews, and so forth, as if they were all identical—or at least enough alike to preclude any important differences. But people, situations, happenings, things, theories, and so forth, are unique. No two of anything are totally identical. And often there are differences that make a difference. The basic device for warding off dogmatic, unreasonable indiscriminations is the Which Index—$black_1$ is not the same as $black_2$, and so on.

2. Polarization

Polarization is the result of the confusion of *contraries* (situations involving graded variations, middle ground, alternatives) for *contradictories* (strict either-or, no-middle-ground affairs). It is the tendency to evaluate and communicate in black-and-white terms when shades of gray would be more appropriate.

An escalating conflict (the vicious pendulum effect) occurs when polarizers drive each other into extreme positions. This pattern of miscommunication is dangerous enough on the interpersonal level, but on the national and international levels, it can be catastrophic.

Polarization can be prevented, or at least diminished, if we learn to distinguish contraries from contradictories and to apply the How-Much Index.

To cope with the pendulum effect, it is helpful to regard differing perceptions as the consequence of differing conditioning and to concede that in complicated problems no one (including ourselves) has the one complete and incontestable solution.

3. The Frozen Evaluation

The frozen evaluation generally occurs when one assumes nonchange. It tends to occur when one unconsciously believes that the way it (a person, a process, a situation, an object, and so on) is now is the way it has always been—or always will be. This can be a troublesome and dangerous premise because literally nothing (especially human beings) remains the same. Perhaps the only constant aspect about the world in which we live is its inconstancy.

We can keep ourselves alert to the process nature of life by habitually When-Indexing (dating) out thoughts and statements. Man_1^{1973}, after all, is not the same as Man_1^{1986}.

INTENSIONAL ORIENTATION

1. A General Statement

The first chapter on intensional orientation did not deal with a specific pattern of miscommunication but rather with a general approach to reality. We are intensionally oriented when we go primarily, if not solely, by our maps (verbal and otherwise) of the territory rather than by the territory itself. An intensional mother, for example, might be guided by hazy memories of her own childhood, by the theories in Sunday supplement articles, and by various childrearing notions and nostrums of her generation to the virtual exclusion of her firsthand observations of the behavior of her child.

Intensional orientation invites trouble, confusion, and conflict (1) because often our maps (one's child-care theories and notions, for example) inadequately and fallaciously represent the territory (the flesh-and-blood child's feelings and behavior) and (2) because we may be unaware that we are dealing primarily with these maps and not with the respective territories that they represent. We may thus be led to react to the territory inappropriately, unintelligently, and even dangerously.

The basic remedy for diminishing the destructive effects of intensional orientation is to "get extensional." That is, develop a readiness to go out and examine the territory rather than be content to be deluded by one's often spurious maps. The byword of extensionality is to look first—then talk.

2. "Pointing" and "Associating"

Among the ways we use words are these: (1) simply to point to, or call attention to, what we are representing by the words and (2) to evoke associations (memories, feelings) for what we are referring to. "Jail," for example, may be used to point, figuratively, to the physical structure in which prisoners are housed. But it may also be used to elicit an emotional response, as when one is threatened with "jail."

When one is unaware that words may be used for these dual purposes, there is the possibility of a number of miscommunication patterns, including the "pointing-association" confusion (the tendency to respond to the associations evoked in one by words *as if* one were responding to what was being represented by the words); name-calling (the tendency for one's evaluation of a person to be influenced by the "associative" labels that have been applied to that person); and "associative" bypassing (the tendency for communicators to miss each other's "associative" meanings).

3. Blindering

My definition (i.e., my interpretation, size-up, perception, appraisal, and so on) of a problem greatly influences my attempts at solving the problem. But a definition is inevitably an abstraction, a leaving out of details. If, then, in defining a problem, I am unaware of leaving out details (especially if they are important or vital details), I am in danger of becoming blindered—of unconsciously permitting a narrowed perception to restrict my attack on the problem. The basic correctives are (1) to remember that definitions inevitably involve the exclusion of details (perhaps crucial ones) and (2) to recognize and remove your blinders.

UNDELAYED REACTIONS

Some undelayed reactions, such as reflex responses, are largely unavoidable, harmless, and even self-protective. Others, such as many reflexlike responses, may be highly useful when they have been properly conditioned and employed—the numerous actions of driving an automobile, for example. But some reflexlike responses—for instance, those manifested in fear and rage—are often destructive. It is the latter that should be controlled if we are to avoid contributing to the harm of ourselves and others.

In some respects, this is the key chapter of Part Three: Patterns of Miscommunication. Whereas the other chapters recommend various techniques, habits, and devices for avoiding and correcting the patterns of misevaluation and miscommunication, this chapter urged the basic setting for using them—the habit of delay-while-evaluating before action.

The basic corrective methods, then, have been to suggest techniques, first, for becoming (and remaining) aware of the insidious assumptions that influence our evaluation and communication and, second, to recommend the substitution of new, more adequate premises.

To implement these premises, I have suggested a number of evaluational habits as substitutes for, or modifications of, some existing habits. Let the reader be cautioned, however. The firm, enduring acquisition of these deceptively simple habits will not come easily. They will require practice and persistence. The experience will not be unlike that of a person who for years has typed with two fingers and is now learning the touch system of ten-finger typing. This individual may become discouraged, for efficiency may actually decrease at first. But eventually, the benefits—the ease and speed of touch typing—outweigh the temporary discomfort.

With cultivation, then, these evaluational habits (Which, When, and How-Much Indexing; remembering the etcetera; querying and paraphrasing; distinguishing inference from observation; and so forth) can become second-nature conditioned responses that will pay handsome rewards in terms of more intelligent, safe, productive, and mature communicative behavior.

BIBLIOGRAPHY

A Bibliography on Communication, Organizational Behavior, and Related Areas

COMMUNICATION, ORGANIZATIONAL BEHAVIOR

Adler, Mortimer. "Challenges of Philosophies in Communication," *Journalism Quarterly,* vol. 40, no. 3 (Summer 1963).

Adler, Ron. *Communicating at Work.* New York: Random House, 1983.

Adler, Ronald, and George Rodman. *Understanding Human Communication.* New York: Holt, Rinehart and Winston, 1982.

Allen, Richard K. *Organization Management through Communication.* New York: Harper & Row, 1977.

Applbaum, R. L., et al. *Fundamental Concepts in Human Communication.* San Francisco: Canfield Press, 1973.

Argyris, Chris. *Integrating the Individual and the Organization.* New York: John Wiley & Sons, 1964.

Arnold, Wm. E., and Robert O. Hirsch. *Communicating Through Behavior.* St. Paul, Minn.: West Publishing, 1977.

Balachandran, Sarojini. *Employee Communication.* Published by the American Business Communication Association, University of Illinois, 1976.

Bales, Robert F. *Personality and Interpersonal Behavior.* New York: Holt, Rinehart & Winston, 1970.

Bass, B. M. and Samuel D. Deep. *Studies in Organizational Psychology.* Boston: Allyn & Bacon, 1972.

Bateman, David N., and Jeffrey Miller. "Employee Communication: Messages for the 1980s." *The Journal of Business Communication,* vol. 18, no. 3, 1981, pp. 3–10.

Beer, Michael, et al. *Managing Human Assets: The Groundbreaking Harvard Business School Program.* New York: Free Press, 1985.

Bergen, G. L. and W. V. Haney. *Organizational Relations and Management Action.* New York: McGraw-Hill, 1966.

Berlo, David K. *The Process of Communication.* New York: Holt, Rinehart & Winston, 1960.

Blagdon, C. "Organization Communications." *American Business Communication Association Bulletin,* vol. 36, no. 3 (1973), pp. 12–27.

Blicq, Ron. *On the Move: Communication for Employees.* Englewood Cliffs, N.J.: Prentice-Hall, 1976.

Borden, George A. *An Introduction to Human Communication Theory.* Dubuque, Iowa: Wm. C. Brown, 1971.

Bowman, Joel P., and Bernadine P. Branchaw. *Understanding and Using Communication in Business.* New York: Canfield Press, 1977.

Brakel, Aat, ed. *People and Organizations Interacting.* New York: John Wiley & Sons, 1984.

Brennan, Lawrence D. *Organizational Behavior.* New York: McGraw-Hill, 1975.

Budd, Richard W., and Brent D. Ruben, eds.. *Approaches to Human Communication.* Rochelle Park, N.J.: Hayden Book Co., Inc., 1974.

Carter, Robert M., ed.. *Communication in Organizations.* Detroit: Gale Research Co., 1972.

Chase, Stuart. *Power of Words.* New York: Harcourt Brace Jovanovich, 1954.

_____. *Roads to Agreement.* New York: Harper & Row, 1951.

Cherry, Colin. *Pragmatic Aspects of Human Communication.* Boston: P. Reidel Publishing Co., 1974.

Cohen, Allan R., Stephen L. Fink, Herman Gadon, and Robin D. Willits. *Effective Behavior in Organizations.* 3d ed. Homewood, Ill.: Richard D. Irwin, 1984.

Coffin, Royce A. *The Communicator.* Scranton, Pa.: Barnes and Noble, 1976. *Communicating Effectively.* Reprint series. New York: American Management Association, Inc., 1975.

"Communication Climate," Atlanta Consulting Group, 1982.

Communicontents. Abstracts of communication books. Vol. 1. 1970—.

Conboy, William A. *Working Together: Communication in a Healthy Organization.* Columbus, Ohio: Charles E. Merrill Publishing, 1976.

Cronkhite, G. *Communication and Awareness.* Menlo Park, Calif.: Cummings Publishing Co., 1976.

Cummings, L. L., and Randall B. Dunham, *Introduction to Organizational Behavior.* Homewood, Ill.: Richard D. Irwin, 1980.

Cushman, Donald P., and Dudley D. Cahn, Jr. *Communication in Interpersonal Relationships.* Albany, N.Y.: State University of New York Press, 1984.

Cutlip, Scott M., et al. *Effective Public Relations.* 6th ed. Englewood Cliffs, N.J.: Prentice-Hall, 1985.

Darnell, Donald K. "Toward a Reconceptualization of Communication," *Journal of Communication,* vol. 21 (March 1971), pp. 5–16.

Davis, Keith, and J. Newstrom, *Human Behavior at Work.* 7th ed. New York: McGraw-Hill, 1985.

DiSalvo, Vincent; with Craig Monroe; and Benjamin Morse. *Business and Professional Communication: Basic Skills and Principles.* Columbus, Ohio: Charles E. Merrill Publishing, 1977.

Dittrich, John E., and Robert A. Zawacki. *People and Organizational Behavior,* 2d ed. Plano, Tex.: Business Publications, 1985.

Downs, Cal W.; Wil A. Linkugel; and David M. Berg. *The Organizational Communicator.* New York: Harper & Row, 1977.

Dunham, Randall B. *Organizational Behavior: People and Processes in Management.* Homewood, Ill.: Richard D. Irwin, 1984.

Eisenberg, Abne. *Communicating Effectively at Work.* Prospect Height, Ill.: Waveland Press, 1984.

Elbing, Alvar O. *Behavioral Decisions in Organizations.* Glenview, Ill.: Scott, Foresman, 1970.

Emmert, Philip, and William D. Brooks. *Methods of Research in Communication.* Boston: Houghton Mifflin, 1970.

Farace, Richard V.; Peter R. Monge; and Hemish M. Russell. *Communicating and Organizing.* Reading, Mass.: Addison-Wesley Publishing, 1977.

Flippo, Edwin B. *Management: A Behavioral Approach.* Boston: Allyn & Bacon, 1970.

Francis, Dave, and Mike Woodcock. *People at Work: A Practical Guide to Organizational Change.* La Jolla, Calif.: University Associates, Inc., 1975.

Froman, Robert. "How to Say What You Mean: Business Communication." *Nation's Business,* 45 (May 1957), pp. 76–78.

_____. "Make Words Fit the Job," *Nation's Business,* 47 (July 1959), pp. 76–79.

Fruehling, Rosemary T., and Roy W. Poe. *Business Communication: A Problem-Solving Approach.* New York: McGraw-Hill, 1984.

Gibson, James L., John M. Ivancevich, and James H. Donnelly, Jr. *Organizations: Behavior, Structure, Processes,* 4th ed. Plano, Tex.: Business Publications, 1985.

Gibson, James L., John M. Ivancevich, and James H. Donnelly, Jr. *Organizations Closeup: A Book of Readings,* 5th ed. Plano, Tex.: Business Publications, 1985.

Giffin, Kim, and Bobby R. Patton. *Basic Readings in Interpersonal Communication.* New York: Harper & Row, 1971.

_____, and _____. *Fundamentals of Interpersonal Communication.* New York: Harper & Row, 1971.

Glover, John Desmond, and Ralph M. Hower. *The Administrator: Cases on Human Relations in Business.* 5th ed. Homewood, Ill.: Richard D. Irwin, 1973.

Goldhaber, Gerald M. *Organizational Communication,* 3d ed. Dubuque, Iowa: Wm. C. Brown, 1983.

Goyer, Robert S. "Communication, Communicative Process, Meaning: Toward a Unified Theory," *Journal of Communication,* 20, no. 1 (March 1970), pp. 4–16.

Greenberg, Joseph H. *Language, Culture, and Communication.* Stanford, Calif.: Stanford University Press, 1971.

Greenwald, Howard H.; Susan A. Hellweg; Joseph W. Walter and Associates. *Organizational Communication: Abstracts, Analyses, and Overview,* 10. Beverly Hills, Calif.: Sage Publications, 1985. See also 5 (1980), 6 (1981), 7 (1982), 8 (1983), and 9 (1984).

Greenwood, James W., III, and James Greenwood, Jr. *Managing Executive Stress: A Systems Approach.* Tenafly, N.J.: Burrill-Ellsworth Assoc., 1984.

Hahn, Martin E., and Edward C Simmel. *Communication Behavior and Evolution.* Chicago: Academy Press, Ltd., 1976.

Hall, J. D. "Put Communication Theory into Practice," *American Business Communication Association Bulletin,* 36, no. 1 (1973), pp. 6–8.

Halpern, Jeanne W. "Differences Between Speaking and Writing and Their Implication for Teaching," *College Composition and Communication,* 35, October, 1984, pp. 345–57.

Haney, William V. "A Comparative Study of Unilateral and Bilateral Communication," *Academy of Management Journal,* 7, no. 2 (June 1964), pp. 128–36.

———. "Serial Communication of Information in Organization," in *Concepts and Issues in Administrative Behavior* Eds. Sidney Mailick and Edward H. Van Ness, pp. 150–65. Englewood Cliffs, N.J.: Prentice-Hall, 1962. Reprinted in *ETC: A Review of General Semantics,* 21, no. 1 (March 1964), pp. 13–29.

Hanneman, Gerhard J., and Wm. J. McEwen *Communication and Behavior.* Reading, Mass.: Addison-Wesley Publishing, 1975.

Hersey, Paul, and Blanchard, K. H. *Management of Organizational Behavior.* 7th ed. Englewood Cliffs, N.J.: Prentice-Hall, 1982.

Heyel, C. "How to Communicate Better with Employees," *American Business Communication Association Bulletin,* 37, no. 2 (1974), pp. 38–40.

Higgins, James M. *Organizational Behavior.* New York: Random House, 1985.

Himes, Gary K. "Communications: Your Most Valuable Skill: Parts I & II," *Supervision,* July and August, 1979.

Hodge, Billy J., and Herbert J. Johnson. *Management and Organizational Behavior.* New York: John Wiley & Sons, 1970.

Human Relations. Quarterly. 1 (1947–48).

Hunsicker, F. R. "Are We Educating Our Managers to Communicate?" *American Business Communication Association Bulletin,* 37, no. 4 (1974), pp. 10–16.

Huse, Edgar, and James Bowditch. *Behavior in Organizations,* 2d ed. Reading, Mass.: Addison-Wesley Publishing, 1977.

Huse, Edgar F., and Thomas Cummings. *Organization Development and Change,* 3d ed. St. Paul, Minn.: West Publishing, 1985.

Huseman, Richard C.; James M. Lahiff; and John D. Hatfield. *Interpersonal Communication in Organizations.* Boston: Holbrook Press, Inc., 1976.

———, Logue, Cal C., and Dwight L. Freshley. *Readings in Interpersonal and Organizational Communication,* 3d ed. Boston: Holbrook Press, Inc., 1977.

Jamieson, Harry. *Communication and Persuasion.* Dover, N.H.: Croom Helm, Ltd., 1985.

Johnson, Bonnie McDaniel. *Communication: The Process of Organizing.* Boston: Allyn and Bacon, 1977.

Johnson, Kenneth G. "Understanding the Communication Process," *Extension Insights.* Newsletter of the University of Wisconsin Extension Division, Madison, Wisconsin.

Johnson, Wendell. "The Fateful Process of Mr. A Talking to Mr. B." *Harvard Business Review,* 31 (January 1953), pp. 49–56.

Jones, John E., and Johanna J. Jones. *Dialog: A Program for Developing Work Relationships.* La Jolla, Calif.: University Associates, Inc., 1973.

Journal of Organizational Behavior Management. 1, (March 1977).

Kilpatrick, Donald L. *No-Nonsense Communication,* 3d ed. Elm Grove, WI: K & M Publishers, 1983.

Koehler, Jerry W.; Karl W. E. Anatol; and Ronald L. Applbaum. *Organizational Communication: Behavioral Perspectives,* 2d ed. New York: Holt, Rinehart & Winston, 1981.

Lawrence, Paul R.; John A. Seiler; Louis Barnes, and Jay W. Lorsch. *Organizational Behavior and Administration,* 3d ed. Homewood, Ill.: Richard D. Irwin, 1976.

Leavitt, Harold J. *Managerial Psychology,* 4th ed. Chicago: University of Chicago Press, 1978.

_____, and Pondy, Louis R. eds.. 3rd ed. *Readings in Managerial Psychology.* Chicago: University of Chicago Press, 1980.

Lee, Irving J. *Customs and Crises in Communication.* New York: Harper & Row, 1954.

_____. *How to Talk with People.* New York: Harper & Row, 1952.

_____. "Procedure for 'Coercing' Agreement," *Harvard Business Review,* 32, no. 1 (January 1954), pp. 39–45.

_____, and Laura L. Lee. *Handling Barriers in Communication.* New York: Harper & Row, 1957.

"Management's Dilemma—Theory 'X' v. Theory 'Y,'" *Chicago Purchaser,* August 1966, pp. 30–34.

Leitch, V. B. "Behavioral Objectives and Business Communications: Truth and Consequences," *American Business Communication Association Bulletin,* 38, no. 2 (1975), pp. 10–13.

Lesikar, Raymond V. *Basic Business Communication,* 3d ed. Homewood, Ill.: Richard D. Irwin, 1985.

_____. "The Meaning and Status of Organizational Communication." *The American Business Communication Association Bulletin.* September, 1981, pp. 2–4.

Lewis, Phillip V. *Organizational Communications: The Essence of Effective Management.* 2d ed. Columbus, Ohio: Grid, 1980.

Liggett, Sarah. "Speaking/Writing Relationships and Business Communication." *The Journal of Business Communication,* 22, no. 2, Spring, 1985, pp. 47–54.

Likert, Rensis. *The Human Organization: Its Management and Value.* New York: McGraw-Hill, 1967.

_____. *New Patterns in Management.* New York: McGraw-Hill, 1961.

Lippitt, Gordon L.; Leslie E. This; and Robert G. Bidwell. *Optimizing Human Resources.* Reading, Mass.: Addison-Wesley Publishing, 1971.

Longnecker, Justin G. *Principles of Management and Organizational Behavior,* 2d ed. Columbus, Ohio: Charles E. Merrill Publishing, 1969.

Luthans, F. *Organizational Behavior,* 4th ed. New York: McGraw-Hill, 1985.

McCroskey, James C.; Carl E. Larson; and Mark L. Knapp. *An Introduction to Interpersonal Communications.* Englewood Cliffs, N.J.: Prentice-Hall, 1971.

McGregor, Douglas. *The Human Side of Enterprise.* New York: McGraw-Hill, 1960.

McLuhan, Marshall. *Understanding Media.* New York: McGraw-Hill, 1964.

McQuail, Denis. *Communication.* New York: Longman, Inc., 1975.

Maidment, Robert, and William Bullock. *Meetings, Meetings, Meetings: Accomplishing More with Better and Fewer.* Reston, Va.: National Association of Secondary School Principals, 1984.

Maier, Norman R. F. *The Appraisal Interview.* La Jolla, Calif.: University Associates, Inc., 1976.

_____. *Superior-Subordinate Communication.* New York: American Management Association, Inc., 1961.

Mambert, W. A. *The Elements of Effective Communication.* Washington, D.C.: Acropolis Books, 1971.

Maslow, Abraham H. *Eupsychian Management.* Homewood, Ill.: Richard D. Irwin, and Dorsey Press, 1965.

_____. *Toward a Psychology of Being.* Princeton, N.J.: D. Van Nostrand Co., Inc., 1962.

Mescon, Michael, Michael Albert, and Franklin Khedouri. *Management: Individual and Organizational Effectiveness,* 2d ed. New York: Harper & Row, 1984.

Meyer, John W. and W. Richard Scott. *Organizational Environments.* Beverly Hills, Calif.: Sage Publications, 1983.

Micheli, Linda McJ., Frank V. Cespedes, Donald Byker, and Thomas J. C. Raymond. *Managerial Communication.* Glenview, Ill.: Scott, Foresman, 1984.

Miller, Sherod; Elam W. Nunnally; and Daniel B. Wackman. *Alive and Aware: Improving Communication in Relationships.* Minneapolis: Interpersonal Communication Programs, Inc., 1976.

Mortensen, C. Daniel ed. *Basic Readings in Communication Theory.* New York: Harper & Row, 1973.

Nelson, M. J. "Improving Interpersonal Business Relations through Effective Communication," *American Business Communication Association Bulletin,* 38, no. 1 (1975), pp. 18–20.

O'Connell, Sandra E. "Communication: Growth Field of the Seventies," *Journal of Business Communication* 15, no. 3 (Spring 1978), pp. 37–46.

O'Reilly, C. A., and K. H. Roberts. "Information Filtration in Organizations: Three Experiments," *Organizational Behavior and Human Performance,* 2, 1974, pp. 253–65.

_____, and _____. "Relationships among Components of Credibility and Communication in Work Units," *Journal of Applied Psychology,* 61 (1976), pp. 99–102.

Pace, R. Wayne. *Organizational Communication: Foundation for Human Resource Development.* Glenview, Ill.: Scott, Foresman, 1983.

Pearce, W. Barnett. "Trust in Interpersonal Communication." Unpublished manuscript delivered to the international Communication Association, Montreal, April 1973.

Penland, P. *Communication Science and Technology: An Introduction.* New York: Marcel Dekker, Inc., 1974.

Peterson, Brent D.; Gerald M. Goldhaber; and R. Wayne Pace. *Communication Probes.* Chicago: Science Research Associates, Inc., 1974.

Porter, L. W., and K. H. Roberts. *Communication in Organizations.* Harmondsworth Middlesex, England: Penguin Books, 1977.

———, and ———. "Organizational Communication." *Handbook of Industrial and Organizational Psychology.* Ed. M. D. Dunnette, pp. 1553–89. Chicago: Rand McNally, 1974.

Pugh, D. S., ed. *Organization Theory,* Rev. ed. New York: Penguin Books, 1984.

Putnam, Linda L., and Michael E. Pacanowsky. *Communication and Organizations.* Beverly Hills, Calif.: Sage Publications, 1983.

Redding, W. Charles. *Communication within the Organization.* New York: Industrial Communication Council, Inc., 1972.

Roberts, K. H. and C. A. O'Reilly. "Failures in Upward Communication in Organizations: Three Possible Culprits," *Academy of Management Journal,* 17 (1974), pp. 205–15.

———, and ———. "Measuring Organizational Communication," *Journal of Applied Psychology,* 59 (1974), pp. 321–26.

Rockey, Edward. *Communicating in Organizations.* Lanham, M.D.: University Press of America, 1985.

Roethlisberger, Fritz J.

———. "Barriers to Communication between Men," *Northwestern University Information,* 20, no. 25 (April 21, 1952).

———, and William J. Dickson. *Management and the Worker.* Cambridge, Mass.: Harvard Univ. Press, 1950.

Rogers, Donald P. "Organizational Communication Texts: A Selected Bibliography," *ABCA Bulletin,* 40, no. 2 (June 1977), pp. 31–33.

Sanford, Aubrey C.; Gary T. Hunt; and Hyler J. Bracey. *Communication Behavior in Organizations.* Columbus, Ohio: Charles E. Merrill Publishing, 1976.

Scanlon, Burt K. "Creating a Climate for Achievement," *Business Horizons,* March/April, 1981, pp. 5–9.

Schermerhorn, John R., Jr. *Managing Organizational Behavior,* 2d ed. New York: John Wiley & Sons, 1985.

Schramm, Wilbur. "How Communication Works," in *The Process and Effects of Mass Communication* (ed. W. Schramm). Urbana: University of Illinois Press, 1954.

———, and Donald F. Roberts. *The Process and Effects of Mass Communication,* rev. ed. Urbana: University of Illinois Press, 1971.

Scott, William E. and Larry L. Cummings. *Readings in Organizational Behavior and Human Performance, rev. ed. Homewood, Ill.: Richard D. Irwin, 1973.*

Scott, William G.

———, and Mitchell, Terrence R. *Organization Theory: A Structural and Behavioral Analysis,* rev. ed. Homewood, Ill.: Richard D. Irwin, 1972.

Sereno, Kenneth K., and C. David Morlensen. *Foundations of Communication.* New York: Harper & Row, 1970.

Sigband, Norman B. "Proaction, Not Reaction, for Effective Employee Communications," *Personnel,* March, 1982, pp. 190–2.

Sigband, Norman B. and David N. Bateman. *Communicating in Business,* 2d ed. Glenview, Ill.: Scott Foresman, 1984.

Sinetar, Larry R., and John L. Waltman. *Managerial Communication: A Strategic Approach.* New York: John Wiley & Sons, 1984.

Smith, Dennis L., and Keith Williamson. *Interpersonal Communication: Roles, Rules, Strategies and Games,* 3d ed. Dubuque, Iowa: Wm. C. Brown, 1985.

Solomon, Arthur. *Interpersonal Communication: A Cross-Disciplinary Approach.* Springfield, Ill.: Charles C Thomas, 1970.

Stewart, John. *Bridges Not Walls: A Book about Interpersonal Communication.* Reading, Mass.: Addison-Wesley Publishing, 1973.

Tannenbaum, Robert; Irving R. Wechsler; and Fred Massarik. *Leadership and Organization: A Behavioral Science Approach.* New York: McGraw-Hill, 1961.

Taylor, Anita, et al. *Communicating.* Englewood Cliffs, N.J.: Prentice-Hall, 1977.

Thayer, Lee O. *Communication and Communication Systems: In Organization, Management, and Interpersonal Relations.* Homewood, Ill.: Richard D. Irwin, 1970.

_____. *Organization-Communication: Emerging Perspectives.* Norwood, N.J.: Ablex Pub. Corp., 1985.

Tosi, Henry L., and W. Clay Hammer. *Organizational Behavior and Management,* 4th ed. Columbus, Ohio: Grid, 1985.

Vanderber, Rudolph F. *Communicate!.* Belmont, Calif.: Wadsworth, 1975.

Vardaman, George T. *Effective Communication of Ideas.* New York: Van Nostrand Reinhold, 1970.

_____; and Goerge T. Vardaman; Particia Black. *Communication in Modern Organizations.* New York: John Wiley & Sons, 1973.

Vroom, Victor H. "Industrial Social Psychology," in *Handbook of Social Psychology* (eds. G. Lindzey and E. Aronson), 2. 2d ed. Reading, Mass.: Addison-Wesley Publishing, 1968.

Weick, Karl E. *The Social Psychology of Organizing.* Reading, Mass.: Addison-Wesley Publishing, 1969.

Weissenberg, Peter. *Introduction to Organization Behavior.* Scranton, Pa.: Intext Educational Publishers, 1971.

Wenburg, John, and William Wilmot. *The Personal Communication Process.* New York: John Wiley & Sons, 1973.

Whyte, William F. *Men at Work.* Homewood, Ill.: Richard D. Irwin, 1961.

_____. *Organizational Behavior: Theory and Applications.* Homewood, Ill.: Richard D. Irwin, 1969.

Whyte, William H., and the Editors of *Fortune. Is Anybody Listening?* New York: Simon & Schuster, 1952.

Wiener, Norbert. *The Human Use of Human Beings.* Boston: Houghton Mifflin, 1950.

Wiksell, Wesley. *Do They Understand You?* New York: Macmillan, 1960.

Williams, John W. and Steven A. Eggland. *Communication in Action.* Cincinnati: South-Western Publishing, 1985.

Wilson, Gerald L., et al. *Interpersonal Growth Through Communication.* Dubuque, Iowa: Wm. C. Brown, 1984.

Winfield, Ian. *People in Business.* North Pomfret, VT: David and Charles, Inc., 1984.

Wofford, Jerry C.; Edwin A. Gerloff; and Robert C. Cumins. *Organizational Communication: The Keystone to Managerial Effectiveness.* New York: McGraw-Hill, 1977.

Wolf, Morris P., and Shirley Kuiper. *Effective Communication in Business,* 8th ed. Cincinnati: South-Western Publishing, 1984.

Wood, Roy V.; Joanne S. Yamauchi; and James J. Bradac. "The Communication of Meaning across Generations," *Journal of Communication.* vol. 21 (June 1971), pp. 160–69.

ORGANIZATION, MANAGEMENT

Adair, John. *Management Decision Making.* Brookfield, VT: Gower Pub. Co., 1985.

Adams, John D. ed. *New Technologies in Organizational Development: 2.* La Jolla, Calif.: University Associates, Inc., 1974.

Albers, Henry H. *Principles of Organization and Mangement,* 4th ed. New York: John Wiley & Sons, 1974.

Ashburn, Elizabeth A. *Motivation, Personality, and Work-Related Characteristics of Women in Male-Dominated Professions.* Washington, D.C.: National Association of Women Deans, 1977.

Austin, Larry M., and James R. Burns. *Management Science.* New York: Macmillan, 1985.

Baker, Kenneth R., and Dean H. Kropp. *Management Science: An Introduction to Decision Models.* New York: John Wiley & Sons, 1985.

Barnard, Chester, I. *TheFunctions of the Executive.* Cambridge, Mass.: Harvard Univ. Press, 1938.

Benge, Eugene J., and the editors of Alexander Hamilton Institute. *Elements of Modern Management.* New York: AMACOM, 1977.

Blake, Robert Rogers. *Corporate Excellence through Grid Organization Development.* Houston: Gulf Publishing, 1968.

Blanchard, Kenneth, Patricia Zigarmi and Drea Zigarmi. *Leadership and the One Minute Manager.* New York: Wm. Morrow, 1985.

Burke, W. Warner ed.. *New Technologies in Organizational Development: 1.* La Jolla, Calif.: University Associates, Inc., 1972.

Campbell, J., et al. *Managerial Behavior, Performance, and Effectiveness.* New York: McGraw-Hill, 1970.

Cox, Charles, and John Beck, eds. *Management Development: Advances in Practice and Theory.* New York: John Wiley & Sons, 1984.

Dessler, Gary. *Management Fundamentals,* 4th ed. Reston, Va.: Reston Publishing, 1985.

Diebold, John. *Managing Information: The Challenge and the Opportunity.* New York: AMACOM, 1985.

Donnelly, James H., Jr.; James L. Gibson; and John M. Ivancevich. *Fundamentals of Management: Functions, Behavior, Models.* 5th ed. Dallas: Business Publications, 1984.

_____; _____; and _____ eds. *Fundamentals of Management: Selected Readings,* 4th ed. Dallas: Business Publications, 1981.

Drucker, Peter F. *The Effective Executive.* New York: Harper & Row, 1967.

_____. *Management: Tasks, Responsibilities, Practices,* abridged and rev. ed. New York: Harper & Row, 1985.

_____. *Managing for Results.* New York: Harper & Row, 1964.

_____. *The Practice of Management.* New York: Harper & Row, 1954.

Erickson, Steve. *Management Tools for Everyone.* Princeton, N.J.: Petrocelli Books, 1985.

Etzioni, Amitai. *Modern Organizations.* Englewood Cliffs, N.J.: Prentice-Hall, 1964.

Farnsworth, Terry. *On the Way Up: The Executive's Guide to Company Politics.* New York: McGraw-Hill, 1976.

Flaherty;, John E. *Managing Change: Today's Challenge to Management.* New York: Irvington Pubs., 1984.

Flippo, Edwin B., and Gary M. Munsinger. *Management.* 5th ed. Boston: Allyn & Bacon, 1982.

French, Wendell L., and Cecil H. Bell, Jr. *Organization Development: Theory, Practice, and Research.* Dallas: Business Publications, 1978.

_____, and Don Hellriegel. *Personnel Management and Organization Development.* Boston: Houghton Mifflin, 1971.

Gabarro, John J., and John P. Kotter. "Managing Your Boss," *Harvard Business Review,* January/February, 1980, pp. 92–100.

Geneen, Harold S., and Alvin Moscow. *Managing.* New York: Doubleday Publishing, 1984.

Gibson, James L.; John M. Ivancevitch; and James H. Donnelly, Jr. *Organizations: Behavior, Structure, Processes,* 4th ed. Plano, Tex.: Business Publications, 1982.

Gordon, Thomas. *Leadership Effectiveness Training.* New York: Wyden Books, 1977.

Greene, Carles N., Everett E. Cedam, Jr., and Ronald J. Ebert. *Management for Effective Performance.* Englewood Cliffs, N.J.: Prentice-Hall, 1985.

Gregson, Shaun, and Frank Livesey. *Management and the Organization.* Pomfret, VT: David & Charles, Inc., 1984.

Greiner, L. "What Managers Think of Participative Leadership," *Harvard Business Review,* 5 (1973), pp. 111–17.

Hegarty, Edward J. *How to Succeed in Company Politics,* 2d ed. New York: McGraw-Hill, 1976.

Heirs, Ben, and Gordon Pehrson. *The Mind of the Organization.* New York: Harper & Row, 1977.

Helriegel, Don, and John W. Slocum, Jr. *Organizational Behavior: A Contingency View.* St. Paul, Minn.: West Publishing, 1976.

Hersey, Paul. *The Situational Leader.* New York: Warner Books, 1985.

Howard, Ann, and James A. Wilson. "Leadership in a Declining Work Ethic." *California Management Review,* vol. XXIV, no. 4, Summer, 1984, pp. 33–46.

Hunt, J. G., and L. L. Larson, eds. *Contingency Approaches to Leadership.* Carbondale: Southern Illinois University Press, 1974.

_____, and _____ eds. *Leadership Frontiers.* Kent State University Comparative Administrative Sciences, 1975.

Jucius, Michael I. *Personnel Management,* 9th ed. Homewood, Ill.: Richard D. Irwin, 1979.

Koontz, Harold, and O'Donnell, Cyril. *Essentials of Management,* 3d ed. New York: McGraw-Hill, 1982.

_____, *Management: A Book of Readings,* 4th ed. New York: McGraw-Hill, 1976.

Lassey, William R., and Richard R. Fernández eds. *Leadership and Social Change.* La Jolla, Calif.: University Associates. Inc., 1976.

Lawrence, Peter. *Management in Action.* Boston: Routledge & Kegan Paul, 1984.

Lee, Mary D., and Rabindra N. Kanugo. *Management of Work and Personal Life: Problems and Opportunities.* New York: Praeger Publishers, 1984.

Lee, Sang M. *Management Science,* 2d ed. Dubuque, Iowa: Wm. C. Brown, 1985.

Lippitt, Gordon L. *Organization Renewal: Achieving Viability in a Changing World.* New York: Appleton-Century-Crofts, 1969.

Llevada, E. Jerry. *Management of the Quality Function.* Reston, Va.: Reston Publishing, 1985.

London, Keith. *The People Side of Systems.* New York: McGraw-Hill, 1976.

Luthans, F., and R. Kreitner. *Organizational Behavior Modification.* Glenview, Ill.: Scott, Foresman, 1975.

McCoy, Charles S. *Management of Values: The Ethical Differences in Corporate Policy and Performance.* Marshfield, Mass.: Pitman Pub., Inc., 1985.

McFarland, Dalton E. *Management: Foundations and Practices,* 5th ed. New York: Macmillan, 1979.

McGregor, Douglas. *The Professional Manager.* New York: McGraw-Hill, 1967.

March, James G. *A Handbook of Organizations.* Skokie, Ill.: Rand McNally, 1965.

_____, and H. A. Simon, *Organizations.* New York: John Wiley & Sons, 1958.

Massie, Joseph L., and John Douglas, *Managing: A Contemporary Introduction,* 4th ed. Englewood Cliffs, N.J.: Prentice-Hall, 1985.

Mee, John F. *Management Thought in a Dynamic Society.* New York: New York University Press, 1963.

Myers, M. Scott. *Every Employee a Manager.* New York: McGraw-Hill, 1970.

Newman, Wm. H.; Summer, and E. Kirby Warren. *The Process of Management.* 5th ed. Englewood Cliffs, N.J.: Prentice-Hall, 1982.

Odiorne, George. *The Effective Executive's Guide to Managerial Excellence.* Westfield, Mass.: MBO, Inc., 1983.

Odiorne, George. *Personnel Administration by Objectives.* Homewood, Ill.: Richard D. Irwin, 1971.

Oncken, William, Jr. *Managing Management Time: Who's Got the Monkey?* Englewood Cliffs, N.J.: Prentice-Hall, 1984.

Organ, Dennis W., and Clay Hamner, *Organizational Behavior.* 2d ed. Dallas: Business Publications, 1982.

Parker, Frederick. *Management Techniques for The Effective. Company.* Pompano Beach, Fl.: Exposition Press of Florida Inc., 1984.

Peter, Lawrence. *The Peter Prescription.* New York: William Morrow and Co., 1972.

_____. *The Peter Principle.* New York: William Morrow and Co., 1969.

Peters, Thomas J., and Nancy K. Austin. *A Passion for Excellence.* New York: Random House, 1985.

Peters, Thomas J., and Robert H. Waterman, Jr. *In Search of Excellence: Lessons from America's Best-Run Companies.* New York: Harper & Row, 1982.

Pigors, Paul, and Charles A. Myers. *Personnel Administration.* 9th ed. New York: McGraw-Hill, 1981.

Raymond, H. Alan. *Management in the Third Wave.* Glenview, Ill.: Scott, Foresman, 1985.

Reddin, W. J. *Managerial Effectiveness.* New York: McGraw-Hill, 1970.

Reitz, H. Joseph. *Behavior in Organizations,* 2d ed. Homewood, Ill.: Richard D. Irwin, 1981.

Roger, R. E. *Organizational Theory.* Boston: Allyn & Bacon, 1975.

Schermerhorn, John R., Jr. *Management for Productivity.* New York: John Wiley & Sons, 1984.

Sears, Woodrow H., Jr. "Redefining HRD: Let's Cast Our Lot with Management." *Training,* May, 1984, p. 120.

Simon, H. A. *Administrative Behavior,* 3d ed. New York: Macmillan, 1976.

Steers, Richard M., Gerardo R. Ungson, and Richard T. Mowday. *Managing Effective Organizations: An Introduction.* Boston: Kent Pub. Co., 1985.

Tannenbaum, A. S., Bogdan Kavcic, Menachem Rosner, Mino Vianello, and Georg Wiesner. *Hierarchy in Organizations.* San Francisco: Jossey-Bass, Inc., Publishers, 1974.

Taylor, Bernard, and Gordon L. Lippitt. *Management Development and Training Handbook.* New York: McGraw-Hill, 1975.

Terry, George R., and S. G. Franklin. *Principles of Management,* 8th ed. Homewood, Ill.: Richard D. Irwin, 1982.

This, Leslie E. *A Guide to Effective Management: Practical Applications from Behavioral Science.* Reading, Mass.: Addison-Wesley Publishing, 1974.

Townsend, Robert. *Up the Organization.* New York: Alfred A. Knopf, 1970.

Wasmuth, William J., under the editorship of Joseph W. Porale. *Human Resources Administration: Problems of Growth and Change.* Boston: Houghton Mifflin, 1970.

Weick, Karl E. "Misconceptions About Managerial Productivity." *Business Horizons,* July/August, 1983, pp. 47–52.

PERCEPTION

Albano, Charles. *Transactional Analysis on the Job.* New York: AMACOM, American Management Association Inc., 1974.

Allport, F. H. *Theories of Perception and the Concept of Structure.* New York: John Wiley & Sons, 1955.

Blake, R. R. and G. V. Ramsey eds. *Perception: An Approach to Personality.* New York: Ronald Press Co., 1951.

Bower, Sharon Anthony, and Gordon H. Bower. *Asserting Yourself: A Practical Guide for Positive Change.* Reading, Mass.: Addison-Wesley Publishing, 1976.

Brouwer, Paul J. "The Power to See Ourselves." *Harvard Business Review,* vol. 42 (November 1964), pp. 156–62.

Brown, Harold L. *Perception, Theory and Commitment: The New Philosophy of Science.* Chicago: Precedent Press, 1977.

Bruner, Jerome S., and David Krech eds. *Perception and Personality.* New York: Greenwood Press, 1966.

Buros, Oscar K. ed. *Personality Tests and Review,* 2d ed. Highland Park, N.J.: Gryphon Press, 1975.

Combs, Arthur M. *Perceptual Psychology.* 3d ed. Evanston, Ill.: Harper & Row, 1976.

Cotler, Sherwin B., and Julio J. Guerra. *Assertion Training: A Humanistic-Behavioral Guide to Self-Dignity.* Champaign, Ill.: Research Press, 1976.

Dyer, Wayne W. *Your Erroneous Zones.* New York: Funk and Wagnalls, 1976.

Fensterheim, Herbert, and Jean Baer. *Don't Say Yes When You Want to Say No.* New York: David McKay, 1975.

Festinger, L. *a Theory of Cognitive Dissonance.* Evanston, Ill.: Row, Peterson, 1957.

Ford, George A., and Gordon L. Lippitt. *Planning Your Future: A Workbook for Personal Goal Setting.* La Jolla, Calif.: University Associates, Inc., 1976.

Forgus, Ronald H., and Lawrence E. Melamed. *Perception: A Cognitive-Stage Approach.* New York: McGraw-Hill, 1976.

Gibb, Jack R. "Defense Level and Influence Potential in Small Groups," in *Leadership and Interpersonal Behavior* (eds. L. Petrullo, and B. M. Bass), pp. 66–81. New York: Holt, Rinehart & Winston, 1961.

———. "Defensive Communication," *Journal of Communication,* vol. 11, no. 3 (September 1961), pp. 141–48.

Gumbert, Gary. "The Ambiguity of Perception," ETC., vol. 34, no. 2 (June 1977), pp. 192–203.

Hochberg, Julian. *Perception,* 2d ed. Englewood Cliffs, N.J.: Prentice-Hall, 1978.

Horney, Karen. *Neurosis and Human Growth: The Struggle toward Self-Realization.* New York: W. W. Norton, 1950.

Jackson, F. *Perception: A Representative Theory.* Cambridge: Cambridge University Press, 1977.

James, Muriel. *The O.K. Boss.* Reading, Mass.: Addison-Wesley Publishing, 1975.

Jones, F. N., et al. *Psychophysical Judgment and Measurement.* New York: Academic Press, 1974.

Jongeward, Dorothy, and Dru Scott. *Women as Winners: Transactional Analysis for Personal Growth.* Reading, Mass.: Addison-Wesley Publishing, 1976.

Kirn, Arthur, and Marie Kirn. *Lifework Planning.* La Jolla, Calif.: University Associates, Inc., 1974.

Liberman, Robert Paul, et al. *Personal Effectiveness: Guiding People to Assert Themselves and Improve Their Social Skills.* Champaign, Ill.: Research Press, 1975.

Livingston, J. Sterling. "Pygmalion in Management," *Harvard Business Review,* 47, no. 4 (July–August 1969), pp. 81–89.

McBurney, Donald H. and Collings, Virgina B. *Introduction to Sensation—Perception,* 2d ed. Englewood Cliffs, N.J.: Prentice-Hall, 1984.

Maddi, Salvatore R. *Personality Theories: A Comparative Analysis,* rev. ed. Homewood, Ill.: Dorsey Press, 1972.

Morrison, James H., and John J. O'Hearne. *Practical Transactional Analysis Management.* Reading, Mass.: Addison-Wesley Publishing, 1977.

Phelps, Stanley, and Nancy Austin. *The Assertive Woman.* San Luis Obispo, Calif.: Impact Press, 1975.

Richardson, Gisele. "A TA Approach to Diagnosing an Ailing Group," *Optimum,* vol. 8, no. 2 (1977). Bureau of Management Consulting, Government of Canada, Ottawa. Reprinted in *The Canadian Banker, & ICB Review,* 85, no. 1 (January–February 1978), pp. 44–48.

Rogers, C. R. *Client-Centered Therapy.* Boston: Houghton Mifflin Co., 1951.

_____. "Communication: Its Blocking and Its Facilitation," *Northwestern University Information,* 20, no. 25, pp. 9–15.

Simon, Sidney B. *Meeting Yourself Halfway: 31 Value Clarification Strategics for Daily Living.* Niles, Ill.: Argus Communications, 1974.

Smith, Manuel J. *When I Say No, I Feel Guilty: How to Cope—Using the Skills of Systematic Assertive Therapy.* New York: Dial Press, 1975.

Teutsch, Joel Marie, and Champion K. Teutsch.*From Here to Greater Happiness: Or How to Change Your Life for Good!* Los Angeles: Price/Stern/Sloan Publishing Co., Inc., 1975.

Thalberg, Irving. *Perception, Emotion, and Action: A Component Approach.* New Haven: Yale University Press, 1977.

Vroom, V. H. "The Effects of Attitudes on Perception of Organizational Goals," *Human Relations,* 13, no. 3 (1960), pp. 229–40.

Watzlavick, Paul, ed. *The Invented Reality: How Do We Know What We Believe We Know?* New York: W. W. Norton, 1984.

_____. *How Real is Real?: Confusion, Disinformation, Communication.* New York: Random House, 1977.

Webster, M., Jr., and B. I. Sobieszek. *Sources of Self-Evaluation: A Formal Theory of Significant Others and Social Influence.* New York: Wiley-Interscience, 1974.

Wright, H. B. *Executive Ease and Dis-Ease.* New York: John Wiley & Sons, 1975.

MOTIVATION, FRUSTRATION, COGNITIVE DISSONANCE

AtkInson, J. W., and J. O. Raynor. *Motivation and Achievement.* New York: Halsted Press, 1974.

Blake, Robert R., and Jane S. Mouton. *Managerial Grid III,* 3d ed. Houston: Gulf Publishing, 1984.

Dalton, Gene W., and Paul R. Lawrence. *Motivation and Control in Organizations.* Homewood, Ill.: Richard D. Irwin. 1971.

Ericson, Richard F. "Rationality and Executive Motivation," *Journal of the Academy of Management,* 5, no. 1 (April 1962), pp. 7–23.

Epstein, Eugene, and William C. Freund. *People and Productivity: The New York Stock Exchange Guide to Financial Incentives and the Quality of Work Life.* Homewood, Ill.: Dow Jones-Irwin, 1984.

Ferguson, E. D. *Motivation: An Experimental Approach.* New York: Holt, Rinehart & Winston, 1976.

Fershleiser, Russel. "Toward Wholistic Approach to Job Satisfaction," *MBA Society Journal,* III, no. 1, 1983, pp. 19–28.

Festinger, Leon A. "The Motivating Effect of Cognitive Dissonance," in *Assessment of Human Motives* (ed. G. Lindzey), pp. 65–86. New York: Holt, Rinehart & Winston, 1958.

_____. *A Theory of Cognitive Dissonance.* Stanford, Calif.: Stanford University Press, 1962.

Filley, A. C. *Interpersonal Conflict Resolution.* Glenview, Ill.: Scott, Foresman, 1975.

Gellerman, Saul W. *Management by Motivation.* New York: American Management Association, Inc., 1968.

_____. *Motivation and Productivity.* New York: American Management Association, Inc., 1963.

Goldberg, Joel A. *Manager's Guide to Productivity Improvement.* New York: Praeger Publishers, 1985.

Grant, Philip C. "Motivation, Myths and Misnomers," *Management World,* June, 1982.

Hall, D. T., and K. E. Nougaim. "An Examination of Maslow's Need Hierarchy in an Organizational Setting," *Organizational Behavior and Human Performance,* 5, no. 1 (February 1968), pp. 12–35.

Herzberg, Frederick. "One More Time: How Do You Motivate Employees?" *Harvard Business Review,* 46, no. 1 (January–February 1968) pp. 53–62.

_____. *Work and the Nature of Man.* Cleveland: World Publishing Co., 1966.

_____; B. Mausner; and B. Snyderman. *The Motivation to Work,* 2d ed. New York: John Wiley & Sons, 1962.

House, R. J., and L. A. Wigdor. "Herzberg's Dual-Factor Theory of Job Satisfaction and Motivation." *Personnel Psychology,* 20, no. 4 (Winter 1967), pp. 369–89.

Houston, John P. *Motivation.* New York: Macmillan, 1985.

Likert, Rensis, and Jane Gibson Likert. *New Ways of Managing Conflict.* New York: McGraw-Hill, 1976.

Losoncy, Lewis. *Motivating Leader.* Englewood Cliffs, N.J.: Prentice-Hall, 1985.

McClelland, David C. "Business Drive and National Achievement," in *Organization and Human Behavior (ed. G. D. Bell). Englewood Cliffs, N.J.: Prentice-Hall, 1967.*

McClelland, David C. *Motives, Personality and Society.* New York: Praeger Publishers, 1984.

Maslow, Abraham H. *Motivation and Personality,* 2d ed. New York: Harper & Row, 1970.

Myers, M. S. "Who Are Your Motivated Workers?" *Harvard Business Review* January–February 1966.

Organ, Dennis W. *The Applied Psychology of Work Behavior.* Dallas: Business Publications, 1978.

Quick, Thomas L. *Manager's Motivation Desk Book.* New York: John Wiley & Sons, 1985.

Shapero, Albert. *Managing Professional People: Understanding Creative Performance.* New York: Free Press, 1985.

Steers, Richard M., and Lyman W. Porter. *Motivation and Work Behavior.* New York: McGraw-Hill, 1975.

Thurow, Lester C., ed. *Management Challenge: The Japanese View.* Cambridge, Mass.: MIT Press, 1985.

Trowill, Jay A. *Motivation and Emotion.* St. Louis: C. V. Mosby Co., 1976.

Vroom, Victor H. *Work and Motivation.* New York: John Wiley & Sons, 1964.

Weihrich, H. *Management Excellence: Productivity Through MBO.* New York: McGraw-Hill, 1985.

Whyte, William F. *Money and Motivation.* New York: Harper & Row, 1955.

Yoder, Dale, and Herbert Heneman, Jr. eds. *Motivation and Commitment.* Washington, D.C.: Bureau of National Affairs, Inc., 1975.

COMMUNICATION PROCESSES

Speaking

Adams, Artie; Annette N. Shelby; and Jerry L. Tarver. *Speaking Up Successfully: Communication in Business and the Professions.* New York: Holt, Rinehart & Winston, 1984.

Anderson, Kenneth E. *Persuasion: Theory and Practice.* Boston: Allyn & Bacon, 1971.

Applbaum, Ronald, et al. *The Process of Group Communication,* 2d ed. Chicago: Science Research Associates, 1979.

Applbaum, Ronald L., and Karl W. Anatol. *Effective Oral Communications in Business and the Professions.* Chicago: Science Research Associates, 1982.

Applbaum, Ronald and Roderick Hart. *Business and Professional Speech.* Chicago: Science Research Associates, 1984.

Barker, Larry L. *Communication,* 3d ed. Englewood Cliffs, N.J.: Prentice-Hall, 1984.

Bell, Cary B. *Speaking in Business: A Basic Survival Guide.* Dubuque, Iowa: Kendall/Hunt Publishing, 1984.

Berdine, W. R. "Planning and Organizing a Business Speech," *American Business Communication Association Bulletin,* vol. 36, no. 4 (1973), pp. 28–32.

Brooks, William D. *Speech Communications,* 4th ed. Dubuque, Iowa: Wm. C. Brown, 1981.

Bryant, Donald C., and Karl R. Wallace. *Fundamentals of Public Speaking.* 5th ed. Englewood Cliffs, N.J.: Prentice-Hall, 1976.

_____, and _____. *Oral Communication,* 4th ed. New York: Appleton-Century-Crofts, 1976.

Capp, Glenn R. *Basic Oral Communication.* Englewood Cliffs, N.J.: Prentice-Hall, 1971.

Clevenger, Theodore, Jr., and Jack Matthews. *The Speech Communication Process.* Glenview, Ill.: Scott, Foresman, 1971.

Dance, Frank E. X., and Carl Larson. *The Function of Human Communication.* New York: Holt, Rinehart & Winston, 1976.

_____, and _____. *Speech Communication: Functions, Modes, and Roles.* New York: Holt, Rinehart & Winston, 1972.

Dickens, Milton. *Speech: Dynamic Communication,* 3d ed. New York: Harcourt, Brace & Jovanovich, 1974.

Gibson, James W. *Speech Organization—A Programmed Approach.* San Francisco: Rinehart Press, 1971.

Hance, Kenneth G.; David C. Ralph; and Milton J. Wiksell. *Principles of Speaking.* Belmont, Calif.: Wadsworth Publishing Co., Inc., 1962.

Howell, William S., and Ernest G. Bormann. *Presentational Speaking for Business and the Professions.* New York: Harper & Row, 1971.

Hugenberg, Lawrence W. and Donald D. Yoder. *Speaking in Modern Organizations: Skills and Strategies.* Glenview, Ill.: Scott, Foresman, 1984.

Jeffrey, Robert C., and Owen Peterson eds. *Speech: A Basic Text.* New York: Harper & Row, 1976.

_____, and _____. *Speech: A Text with Adapted Readings.* New York: Harper & Row, 1971.

Jensen, J. Vernon. *Perspectives on Oral Communication.* Boston: Holbrook Press, Inc., 1970.

Keltner, John W. *Interpersonal Speech Communication: Elements and Structures.* Belmont, Calif.: Wadsworth, 1970.

McBurney, James H., and Ernest J. Wrage. *The Art of Good Speech,* 4th ed. New York: Prentice-Hall, 1975.

Martin, Howard H., and Kenneth E. Anderson. *Speech Communication: Analyses and Readings.* Boston: Allyn & Bacon, 1971.

Minnick, Wayne C. *Public Speaking* 2d ed. Boston: Houghton Mifflin, 1983.

Monroe, Alan. *Principles and Types of Speech,* 8th ed. Glenview, Ill.: Scott, Foresman, 1978.

Neslon, M. J. "Speech Communication Methods and Concepts for Use in Organization Communication," *American Business Communication Association Bulletin,* 38, no. 1 (1975), pp. 17–18.

Newcombe, P. J., and K. F. Robinson. *Teaching Speech Communication: Methods and Materials.* New York: David McKay, 1975.

Nichols, Ralph G., and Thomas R. Lewis. *Listening and Speaking.* Dubuque, Iowa: Wm. C. Brown, 1954.

Pace, R. W.; R. Boren, and B. Peterson. *A Scientific Introduction to Speech Communication.* Belmont, Calif.: Wadsworth, 1974.

Phillips, Gerald M., Kathleen M. Cougl, and Lynne Kelly. *Speaking in Public and Private.* New York: Bobbs-Merrill, 1985.

Reinhart, Susan H. aa and Ira Fisher. *Speaking and Social Interaction.* Englewood Cliffs, N.J.: Prentice-Hall, 1985.

Ross, Raymond S. *Speech Communication: Fundamentals and Practice,* 4th ed. Englewood Cliffs, N.J.: Prentice-Hall, 1977.

Stedman, William. *A Guide to Public Speaking.* Englewood Cliffs, N.J.: Prentice-Hall, 1971.

Stewart, Charles J. ed. *On Speech Communication.* New York: Holt, Rinehart & Winston, 1972.

Tacey, William S. *Business and Professional Speaking.* Dubuque, Iowa: Wm. C. Brown, 1970.

Van Oosting, James. *The Business Speech: Speaker, Audience, and Text.* Englewood Cliffs, N.J.: Prentice-Hall, 1985.

Verderber, Rudolph. *The Challenge of Effective Speaking.* Belmont, Calif.: Wadsworth, 1970.

Weldon, Terry A., and Huber W. Ellingsworth. *Effective Speech Communication: Theory in Action.* Glenview, Ill.: Scott, Foresman, 1970.

Wiseman, Gordon, and Larry Barker. *Speech: Interpersonal Communication.* 2d ed. Scranton, Pa.: Chandler Publishing Co., 1974.

Zimmerman, Gordon I., et al. *Speech Communication: A Contemporary Introduction.* St. Paul, Minn.: West Publishing, 1977.

Writing

Adelstein, Michael. *Business of Better Writing Series.* Lexington, KY: KET, 1984.

Adelstein, Michael E. *Contemporary Business Writing.* New York: Random House, 1971.

Aurner, Robert R., and Paul S. Burtness. *Effective Communication in Business.* 6th ed. Cincinnati: South-Western Publishing, 1974.

Biddle, A. W. *Writer to Writer.* New York: McGraw-Hill, 1984.

Bonner, William H., and Jean Vogles. *Communicating in Business: Key to Success,* 3d ed. Houston: Dame Publications, 1983.

Bowman, Joel P., and Bernadine P. Branchow. *Business Repour Writing.* New York: Dryden Press, 1984.

Brown, Leland. *Communicating Facts and Ideas in Business.* 3d ed. Englewood Cliffs, N.J.: Prentice-Hall, 1982.

_____. *Effective Business Report Writing.* 4th ed. Englewood, Cliffs, N.J.: Prentice-Hall, 1985.

Brusau, Charles T., Gerald J. Alred, and Walter E. Olio. *Business Writer's Handbook.* New York: St. Martin's Press, 1977.

Burack, Sylvia, ed. *Writer's Handbook, 1985.* Boston: Writer, Inc., 1985.

Butenhoff, Carla. "Bad Writing Can Be Good Business," *ABCA Bulletin,* June 1977, pp. 31–33.

Colby, John, and Joseph A. Rice. *Writing to Express.* Minneapolis: Burgess Publishing Co., 1977.

Damerst, W., and A. B. Smith, Jr. "Techniques of Business Communication," *American Business Communication Association Bulletin,* vol. 36, no. 3 (1973), pp. 28–39.

Ewald, Helen Rothschild. "The Me in You-attitude: Business Communication as Transaction," *The Bulletin of the Association for Business Communication.* vol. XLVIII, no. 1, March, 1985, pp. 7–11.

Ewing, Jan. *Writing for Results in Business, Government, the Sciences, & the Professions,* 2d ed. New York: John Wiley & Sons, 1985.

Fear, David E. *Technical Communication.* Glenview, Ill.: Scott, Foresman, 1977.

Frew, Robert M., ed. *Writer's Workshop: A Self-Paced Program for Composition Mastery,* 3d ed. Sunnnyvale, Calif.: Peek Publications, 1984.

Gieselman, Robert D. *Readings in Business Communication,* 3d ed. Champaign, Ill.: Stipes Publishing Co., 1982.

Gieselman, Robert D. "Research in Business Communication: The State of the Art." *The Journal of Business Communication,* vol. 17, Summer, 1980, pp. 3–18.

Glathorn, Allan A. *Writing for Success.* Glenview, Ill: Scott, Foresman, 1985.

Halpern, Jeanne W., and Sarah Liggett. *Computers and Composing: How the New Techniques are Changing Writing.* Carbondale, Ill: Southern Illinois University Press, 1984.

Harrison, Nancy. *Writing English: A User's Manual.* Dover, N.H.: Croom Helm, Ltd., 1985.

Hatch, Richard. *Communicating in Business.* Chicago: Science Research Associates, Inc., 1976.

Henze, Geraldine. *From Murk to Masterpiece.* Homewood, Ill.: Richard D. Irwin, 1984.

Himstreet, W. D., and W. M. Baty. *Business Communications,* 7th ed. Belmont, Calif.: Wadsworth, 1983.

Huseman, Richard; James Lahiff; and John D. Hatfield. *Business Communication Strategies and Skills.* Hinsdale Ill: Dryden Press, 1981.

Iacone, Salvatore, J. *Modern Business Report Writing.* New York: Macmillan, 1985.

Janis, J. Harold. *Writing and Communicating in Business,* 3d ed. New York: Macmillan, 1978.

Jones, W. Paul, and Michael L. Keeue. *Writing Scientific Papers and Reports,* 8th ed. Dubuque, Iowa: Wm. C. Brown, 1981.

Journal of Technical Writing and Communication. 1971–

Journet, Debra, and Julie L. King. *Readings for Technical Writers.* Glenview, Ill.: Scott, Foresman, 1984.

Keithley, Erwin M., and Margaret H. Thompson. *English for Modern Business,* 4th ed. Homewood, Ill.: Richard D. Irwin, 1982.

Lahiff, J. M. "Effective Research—The Route to Good Reports." *American Business Communication Association Bulletin,* 37, no. 1 (1974), p. 25.

Lesikar, Raymond V. *Business Communication: Theory and Application,* 5th ed. Homewood, Ill.: Richard D. Irwin, 1984.

_____. *Report Writing for Business,* 6th ed. Homewood, Ill.: Richard D. Irwin, 1981.

Lindauer, J. S. *Writing in Business.* Riverside, N.J.: Macmillan, 1971.

Locker, Kitty O., and Francis Weeks. *Business Writing Cases and Problems.* Champaign, Ill: Stipes Publishing Co., 1984.

Manuel, Siegfried. *Writing for Science and Technology.* New York: Dell, 1970.

Mansfield, Carmella E., and Margaret Hilton Bahniuk. *Writing Business Letters and Reports.* Indianapolis, Ind.: Bobbs-Merrill, 1981.

Menning, J. H.; C. W. Wilkinson; and Peter B. Clarke. *Communicating through Letters and Reports,* 6th ed. Homewood, Ill.: Richard D. Irwin, 1976.

Meyers, Alan.*Writing with Confidence,* 2d ed. Glenview, Ill.: Scott, Foresman, 1984.

Murphy, Herta A., and Herbert W. Hildebrandt. *Effective Business Communication,* 4th ed. New York: McGraw-Hill, 1984.

Murray, Donald M. *Writer Teaches Writing.* Boston: Houghton Mifflin, 1984.

Oliu, Walter; Carles Brusaw; and Gerald Alred. *Writing that Works,* 2d ed. New York: St. Martin's Press, 1984.

Pearce, C. Glenn; Ross Figgins; and Steven P. Golen. *Principles of Business Communication: Theory, Application, and Technology.* New York: John Wiley & Sons, 1984.

Pearsall, Thomas E., and Donald G. Cunningham. *How to Write for the World of Work.* New York: Holt, Rinehart & Winston, 1978.

Perrin, Porter G., and Wilma R. Ebbitt. *Writer's Guide and Index to English.* 5th ed. Glenview, Ill.: Scott, Foresman, 1972.

Podis, Leonard A., and Joanne M. Podis. *Writing Invention, Form & Style.* Glenview, Ill.: Scott, Foresman, 1984.

Roundy, Nancy. "A Program for Revision in Business and Technical Writing." *The Journal of Business Communication,* vol. 20, 1983, pp. 55–66.

Schell, John, and John Stratton. *Writing on the Job.* New York and Scarborough, Ontario: New American Library, 1984.

Schley, Jim, ed. *Writing in a Nuclear Age.* Hanover, N.H.: University Press of New England, 1985.

Sigband, Norman B. *Communication for Management and Business.* 3d ed. Glenview, Ill.: Scott, Foresman, 1982.

Sigband, Norman B., and David N. Bateman. *Communicating in Business,*2d ed. Glenview, Ill.: Scott, Foresman, 1984.

Stott, Boll. *Write to the Point: And Feel Better About Your Writing.* New York: Doubleday Publishing, 1984.

Strunk, W., and E. B. White. *The Elements of Style.* 3d ed. New York: Macmillan, 1979.

Stultz, Russell A. *Writing & Publishing on Your Microcomputer.* Plano, Tex: WordWare Pub., Inc., 1984.

Tibbetts, Arn. "Ten Rules for Writing Readably." *The Journal of Business Communication,* 18, no. 4, 1981, pp. 53–62.

Walpole, Janey. *Writer's Grammar Guide.* New York: Simon & Schuster, 1984.

Walvoord, Barbara F. *Writing Strategies for All Disciplines.* Englewood Cliffs, N.J.: Prentice-Hall, 1985.

Weeks, Francis; Daphne Jameson; and Robert D. Gieselman. *Principles of Business Communication,* 3d ed. Champaign, Ill: Stipes Publishing Co., 1984.

Weiner, E. S. *Writing: A Diagnostic Approach.* Elmsford, N.Y.: Pergamon Press, 1984.

Wells, Walter. *Communication in Business,* 4th ed. Boston: Kent Publishing Co.,1985.

Wilcox, Roger. *Communication at Work: Writing and Speaking.* Boston: Houghton Mifflin, 1977.

Wilkenson, A. M. "Organizational Writing Vs. Business Writing." *American Business Communication Association Bulletin,* September, 1984, pp. 37–39.

Wilkenson, C. W.; Peter B. Clarke; and Dorothy C. Wilkenson. *Communicating Through Letters and Reports,* 8th ed. Homewood, Ill.: Richard D. Irwin, 1983.

Willingham, John R., and Donald F. Warders. *A Handbook for Student Writers.* New York: Harcourt Brace Jovanovich, 1978.

Woodman, Leonora, and Thomas P. Adler. *Writer's Choices.* Glenview, Ill.: Scott, Foresmen, 1984.

Listening

Barbara, Dominick A. *The Art of Listening.* Springfield, Ill.: Charles C Thomas, 1966.

_____. *How to Make People Listen to You.* Springfield, Ill.: Charles C Thomas, 1971.

Barker,Larry L. *Listening Behavior.* Englewood Cliffs, N.J.: Prentice-Hall, 1971.

Byrne, Donn P. *Listening.* New York: Longman, Inc., 1975.

Connelly, J. Campbell. *A Manager's Guide to Speaking and Listening.* New York: American Management Association, Inc., 1967.

Duker, Sam. *Listening Bibliography.* New York: Scarecrow Press, Inc., 1964.

_____. *Listening: Readings.* Metuchen, N.J.: Scarecrow Press, Inc., 1966.

_____, and C. R. Petrie, Jr. "What We Know about Listening: Continuation of a Controversy." *Journal of Communication,* 14, no. 4 (December 1964), pp. 245–52.

Floyd, James, J. *Listening: A Practical Approach.* Glenview, Ill.: Scott, Foreseman, 1984.

Glatthorn, Allan A., and Herbert R. Adams. *Listening Your Way to Management Success.* Glenview, Ill: Scott, Foresman, 1983.

Gunn, James E. *Listeners.* New York: Ballantine Books, 1985.

Hayakawa, S. I. "The Task of the Listener." *ETC.: A Review of General Semantics,* 7, no. 1 (Autumn 1949).

"Is Anybody Listening? Business Must Start Doing More Listening Itself." *Fortune,* 42 (September 1950), pp. 77–83.

Johnson, Wendell. "Do You Know How to Listen?" *ETC.: A Review of General Semantics,* 7, no. 1 (Autumn 1949).

Kerman, Joseph. *Listen,* 2d ed. New York: Worth Publishing Co., 1976.

Lewis, Carol R. *Listening to Children.* New York: Jason Aronson, Inc., 1985.

Mills, Ernest P. *Listening: Key to Communication.* New York: Petrocelli/Charter, Inc., 1974.

National Education Association and Sanford E. Taylor. *Listening.* West Haven, Conn.: National Education Association, 1977.

Nichols, Ralph G. "Listening Is a 10-Part Skill." *Nation's Business,* July 1957.

————, and Thomas R. Lewis. *Listening and Speaking.* Dubuque, Iowa: Wm. C. Brown, 1954.

————, and Leonard A. Stevens. *Are You Listening?* New York: McGraw-Hill, 1957.

Steil, Lyman K. *Listening: It Can Change Your Life.* New York: McGraw-Hill, 1985.

Wilhelm, Kate. *Listen, Listen.* New York: Berkley Pub. Corp., 1984.

Reading

Adams, W. Royce. *Reading Skills: A Guide for Better Reading.* New York: John Wiley & Sons, 1974.

Atkinson, Rhonda, and Debbie Longman. *Reading Enhancement and Development.* St. Paul, Minn.: West Publishing, 1985.

Drake, Duane D., and Margaret Rawson. *Reading, Perception, and Language.* Baltimore: York Press, Inc., 1975.

Duker, Sam. *Individualized Reading.* Springfield, Ill.: Charles C Thomas, 1971.

Herr, Selma E. *Read with Understanding.* Ontario, Calif.: Piequet Press, 1985.

McKeown, H. "Reading Critically and Summarizing Information." *American Business Communication Association Bulletin,* vol. 37, no. 1 (1974), pp. 26–29.

Ormerod, Jan. *Reading.* New York: Lothrop, Lee & Shepard Books, 1985.

Perfetti, Charles A. *Reading Ability.* New York: Oxford University Press, Inc., 1985.

Spache, G. D. *The Art of Efficient Reading,* 4th ed. New York: Macmillan, 1984.

Weiner, Harvey, and Charles Bazerman. *Reading Skills Handbook.* Boston: Houghton Mifflin, 1977.

Witty, Paul A. *How to Improve Your Reading.* Chicago: Science Research Associates, Inc., 1963.

Problem Solving, Decision Making, Creativity

Clark, Charles H. *Brainstorming.* Garden City, N.Y.: Doubleday Publishing, 1958.

Corson, J. J. "Innovation Challenges Conformity." *Harvard Business Review,* 40, no. 3 (1962), pp. 67–74.

Dunnette, M. D.; J. Campbell; and K. Jaastad. "The Effect of Group Participation on Brainstorming Effectiveness for Two Industrial Samples." *Journal of Applied Psychology,* 47 (1963), pp. 30–37.

Hoffman, L. R. "Conditions for Creative Problem-Solving." *Journal of Psychology,* 52 (1961), pp. 429–44.

Hyman, R. "Creativity and the Prepared Mind: The Role of Information and Induced Attitudes." *Widening Horizons in Creativity* (ed. C. Taylor). New York: John Wiley & Sons, 1964.

Kaufman, Roger. *Identifying and Solving Problems: A System Approach.* La Jolla, Calif.: University Associates, Inc., 1976.

Maier, N. R. F. *Problem-Solving Discussions and Conferences.* New York: McGraw-Hill, 1963.

Morgan, John S. *Improving Your Creativity on the Job.* New York: American Management Association, Inc., 1968.

Newall, A. N.; J. C. Shaw; and H. A. Simon. *Elements of a Theory of Human Problem-Solving.* Santa Monica, Calif.: Rand McNally, 1957.

Osborn, Alex F. *Applied Imagination: Principles and Procedures of Creative Thinking.* New York: Charles Scribner's Sons, 1953.

Parnes, S. J. "Effects of Extended Effort in Creative Problem Solving." *Journal of Educational Psychology,* 52 (June 1961), pp. 117–22.

Simon, H. A. *The New Science of Management Decision.* New York: Harper & Row, 1960.

Smith, E. E., and S. S. Kight. "Effects of Feedback on Insight and Problem-Solving Efficiency in Training Groups." *Journal of Applied Psychology,* 43 (1959), pp. 209–11.

Stein, Morris I., and Shirley J. Heinze. *Creativity and the Individual. New York: Free Press, 1960.*

GROUP PROCESSES: GROUP DYNAMICS, DISCUSSION, CONFERENCE

Bales, Robert F. *Interaction Process Analysis.* Reading, Mass.: Addison-Wesley Publishing, 1950.

Barnlund, Dean C., and Franklyn S. Haiman. *The Dynamics of Discussion.* Boston: Houghton Mifflin, 1960.

Blake, R. R., and J. S. Mouton. *Group Dynamics—Key to Decision-Making.* Houston: Gulf Publishing, 1961.

Bradford, Leland P. *Group Development.* La Jolla, Calif.: University Associates, Inc., 1974.

———. *Making Meetings Work: A Guide for Leaders and Group Members.* La Jolla, Calif.: University Associates, Inc., 1976.

Brillhart, John K. *Effective Group Discussion.* Dubuque, Iowa: Wm. C. Brown, 1967.

Cohen, Arthur M., and R. Douglas Smith. *The Critical Incident in Growth Groups: A Manual for Group Leaders.* La Jolla, Calif.: University Associates, Inc., 1976.

Fisher, B. Aubrey. "Communication Research and the Task-Oriented Group." *Journal of Communication,* 21 (June 1971), pp. 136–49.

Gergen, Kenneth J. *The Psychology of Behavior Exchange.* Reading, Mass.: Addison-Wesley Publishing, 1969.

Goldberg, Alvin, and Carl Larson. *Group Communication: Discussion Processes and Applications.* Englewood Cliffs, N.J.: Prentice-Hall, 1975.

Group Organization Studies: The International Journal for Group Facilitators. Quarterly. March 1976—. Published by University Associates, Inc., La Jolla, Calif.

Gulley, Halbert. *Discussion, Conference, and Group Process.* New York: Holt, Rinehart & Winston, 1960.

_____, and Dale G. Leathers. 3d ed. *Communication and Group Process.* New York: Holt, Rinehart & Winston, 1977.

Harnack, R. Victor. *Group Discussion: Theory and Technique,* 2d ed. Englewood Cliffs, N.J.: Prentice-Hall, 1977.

Hasling, Martin J. *Group Discussion and Decision Making.* New York: Thomas Y. Crowell Co., 1975.

Homans, George. *The Human Group.* New York: Harcourt Brace, Jovanovich, 1950.

_____. *Social Behavior: Its Elementary Forms.* New York: Harcourt Brace, Jovanovich, 1961.

Hunt, Gary T. *Group Communication Workbook.* Columbus, Ohio: Collegiate Publishing Co., 1973.

Jacobs, Alfred ed. *The Group as Agent of Change.* New York: Human Science Press, 1974.

Keltner, John. *Group Discussion Processes.* Westport, Conn.: Greenwood Press, Inc., 1974.

Lakin, Martin. *An Encounter with Sensitivity Training.* New York: McGraw-Hill, 1970.

_____. "Group Sensitivity Training: Uses and Abuses." *ETC.: A Review of General Semantics,* 28, no. 2 (June 1971), pp. 291–312.

Lee, Irving J. *How to Talk with People.* New York: Harper & Row, 1952.

McBurney, James H., and Kenneth G. Hance. *Discussion in Human Affairs.* New York: Harper & Row, 1950.

Maier, Norman R. F. *Problem Solving and Creativity in Individuals and Groups.* Belmont, Calif.: Brooks/Cole Publishing, 1970.

_____. *Problem-Solving Discussions and Conferences.* New York: McGraw-Hill, 1963.

Milman, D. S., and G. D. Goldman. eds. *Group Process Today: Evaluation and Perspective.* Springfield, Ill.: Charles C Thomas, 1974.

Phillips, Gerald M., and Eugene C. Erickson. *Interpersonal Dynamics in the Small Group.* New York: Random House, 1970.

Potter, David, and Martin P. Andersen. *Discussion: A Guide to Effective Practice.* 2d ed. Belmont, Calif.: Wadsworth, 1970.

Rogers, Carl. *Carl Rogers on Encounter Groups.* New York: Harper & Row, 1970.

Rosenfeld, H., and L. Rosenfeld. *Human Interaction in the Small Group Setting.* Columbus, Ohio: Charles E. Merrill Publishing, 1973.

Rowell, R. D. "Group Dynamics and Letter Writing." *American Business Communication Association Bulletin,* 38, no. 1 (1975), pp. 24–26.

Shaw, Marvin. *Group Dynamics: The Psychology of Small Group Behavior.* New York: McGraw-Hill, 1971.

Van de Ven, Andrew H. *Group Decision Making and Effectiveness.* Kent, Ohio: Kent State University Press, 1975.

RELATED STUDIES

General Semantics

Bauby, Cathrine. *Understanding Each Other.* San Francisco: International Society for General Semantics, 1976.

Beale, John. "A Short Critique of General Semantics." *ETC.: A Review of General Semantics,* 35, no. 1 (March 1978), pp. 58–60.

Berman, Sanford I. *Understanding and Being Understood.* San Diego: International Communication Institute, 1965.

Boardman, Phillip C. "Beware the Semantic Trap: Language and Propaganda." *ETC.: A Review of General Semantics,* 35, no. 1 (March 1977), pp. 78–85.

Bois, J. Samuel. *The Art of Awareness.* Dubuque, Iowa: Wm. C. Brown, 1966.

Bruner, R., and J. Pettet. "An Outline of General Semantics." *American Business Communication Association Bulletin,* 36, no. 3 (1973), pp. 2–11.

Chase, Stuart. *Danger! Men Talking.* New York: Parent's Magazine Press, 1969.

Condon, John C., Jr. "Bibliography of General Semantics." *ETC.: A Review of General Semantics,* part 1: 20 (May 1963), pp. 86–105; part 2: vol. 20 (September 1963), pp. 312–39; part 3: 21 (March 1964), pp. 73–100; part 4: 22 (March 1965), pp. 59–86.

_____. *Semantics and Communication.* New York: Macmillan, 1966.

Decker, John P. "A Human Engineering Approach to Conflict." *ETC.: A Review of General Semantics,* 28, no. 2 (June 1971), pp. 191–200.

ETC.: A Review of General Semantics. Quarterly. San Francisco: International Society for General Semantics, San Francisco State College.

Fleishman, Alfred. *Sense and Nonsense: A Study in Human Communication.* San Francisco: International Society for General Semantics, 1971.

Froman, Robert. "How to Say What You Mean; Business Communication." *Nation's Business,* 45 (May 1957), pp. 76–78.

_____. "Make Words Fit the Job." *Nation's Business,* 47 (July 1959), pp. 76–79.

_____. "Prevent Short Circuits when You Talk." *Nation's Business,* vol. 51 (January 1963), pp. 88–89.

_____. "Test Your Judgment." *Nation's Business,* 50 (January 1962), pp. 66–69.

_____. "Words Can Block Success." *Nation's Business,* 49 (September 1961), pp. 36 ff.

General Semantics Bulletin. A periodic publication of the Institute of General Semantics, Lakeville, Conn.

Haney, William V. "The Uncalculated Risk," (motion picture). Beverly Hills, Calif.. Round Table Films, Inc., 1971.

_____. "The Uncritical Inference Test: Research and Applications." *General Semantics Bulletin,* nos. 28 and 29, 1961.

Hayakawa, S. I. "How Words Change Our Lives." *Saturday Evening Post,* December 27, 1958, pp. 22–23.

_____. *Language in Thought and Action.* 2d ed. New York: Harcourt, Brace Jovanovich, 1964.

_____ ed. *Our Language and Our World.* New York: Harper & Row, 1959.

_____. *Symbol, Status, and Personality.* New York: Harcourt, Brace Jovanovich, 1963.

_____. *The Use and Misuse of Language.* New York: Fawcett World Library: Crest, Gold Medal & Premier Books, 1962.

Johnson, Wendell. *People in Quandaries.* New York: Harper & Row, 1946.

_____. *Your Most Enchanted Listener.* New York: Harper & Row, 1956.

Keyes, Kenneth S. *How to Develop Your Thinking Ability.* New York: McGraw-Hill, 1950.

Korzybski, Alfred. "General Semantics." *American People's Encyclopedia,* vol. 9. Chicago: Spencer International Press, 1948.

_____. *Manhood of Humanity* (1921). Lakeville, Conn.: Institute of General Semantics, 1950.

_____. "The Role of Language in the Perceptual Process." *Perception: An Approach to Personality* (eds. R. R. Blake and G. V. Ramsey). New York: Ronald Press Co., 1951.

_____. *Science and Sanity: An Introduction to Non-Aristotelian System and General Semantics* (1933). Lakeville, Conn.: Institute of General Semantics, 1948.

_____. *Time-Binding: The General Theory.* (Two Papers, 1924–26). Lakeville, Conn.: Institute of General Semantics, 1949.

_____, and M. Kendig. *Foreword: A Theory of Meaning Analyzed.* General Semantics Monographs, no. 3. Lakeville, Conn.: Institute of General Semantics, 1942.

Lee, Irving J. *How Do You Talk about People?* Freedom Pamphlet. New York: Anti-Defamation League of B'nai B'rith.

_____. *Language Habits in Human Affairs.* New York: Harper & Row, 1941.

_____, and Laura L. Lee. *Handling Barriers in Communication,* 2d ed. New York: Harper & Row, 1978.

Minteer, Catherine. *Understanding in a World of Words.* San Francisco: International Society for General Semantics, 1970.

Morain, Mary ed. *Bridging Worlds Through General Semantics.* San Francisco, Calif.: International Society for General Semantics, 1984.

_____. *Teaching General Semantics.* San Francisco: International Society for General Semantics, 1969.

O'Neill, William F., and George D. Demos. "The Semantics of Thought Reform." *ETC.: A Review of General Semantics,* 34, no. 4 (December 1977), pp. 413–30.

Rapoport, Anatol. *Fights, Games, and Debates.* New York: Harper & Row, 1960.

_____. "Letter to a Soviet Philosopher." *ETC.: A Review of General Semantics,* 19, no. 4 (February 1963).

Thayer, Lee O. ed. *Communication: General Semantics Perspectives.* New York: Spartan Books, 1970.

Wagner, Geoffrey. *On the Wisdom of Words.* Princeton, N.J.: D. Van Nostrand Co., Inc., 1968.

Weinberg, Harry L. *Levels of Knowing and Existence.* New York: Harper & Row, 1959.

Westcott, Malcolm R. "Creative Communication: Constructs, Associations, and Metaphors." *ETC.: A Review of General Semantics,* 34, no. 4 (December 1977), pp. 433–42.

Other Related Studies

Allport, Gordon W. *Pattern and Growth in Personality.* New York: Holt, Rinehart & Winston, 1961.

Beier, Ernst, and Daniel Sternberg. "Body Language." *Parade Magazine,* April 8, 1973.

Berelson, Bernard, and G. A. Steiner. *Human Behavior: An Inventory of Scientific Findings.* New York: Harcourt, Brace Jovanovich, 1964.

Birdwhistell, Ray L. *Kinesics and Context: Essays on Body Motion Communication.* Philadelphia: University of Pennsylvania Press, 1970.

Brown, Eric D. *Writing with a Word Processor: Communication in the Computer Age.* Reston, Va.: Reston Publishing, 1984.

Brown, Roger. *Social Psychology.* New York: Free Press, 1965.

Callahan, Joseph. *Communicating: How to Organize Meetings and Presentations.* Danbury, Conn.: Franklin Watts, Inc., 1984.

Chase, Stuart. *Guides to Straight Thinking.* New York: Harper & Row, 1956.

Clarke, P. ed. *New Models for Mass Communication Research.* Beverly Hills, Calif.: Sage Publications, 1973.

Collier, R. M. "The Word Processor and Revision Strategies." *College Composition and Communication,* 34, 1983, pp. 149–55.

Condon, John C., and Fathi S. Yousef. *An Introduction to Intercultural Communication.* New York: Bobbs-Merrill, 1975.

Dewey, John. *How We Think.* Boston: D. C. Heath, 1933.

Douglass, Merrill E., and Donna N. Douglass. *Manage Your Time, Manage Your Work, Manage Yourself.* New York: AMACOM, 1985.

Dutton, William H.; Janet Fulk; and Charles Steinfield. "Utilization of Video Conferencing." *Telecommunications Policy,* September, 1982, pp. 164–78.

Eisenberg, Abne M., and Ralph R. Smith, Jr. *Non-Verbal Communication.* Indianapolis, Ind.: Bobbs-Merrill, 1972.

Ekman, Paul. *Telling Lies.* New York: W. W. Norton, 1985.

Goodloe, Alfred. *Managing Yourself: How to Control Emotion, Stress, and Time.* Danbury, Conn.: Franklin Watts, 1985.

Greenberg, Joseph H. *Language, Culture, and Communication.* Stanford, Calif.: Stanford University Press, 1971.

Hall, Edward Twitchell. *The Silent Language.* Garden City, N.Y.: Doubleday Publishing, 1959.

Harris, Amy Bjork, and Thomas A. Harris. *Staying OK: How to Maximize Good Feelings and Minimize Bad Ones.* New York: Harper & Row, 1985.

Hinckley, Dan. *Writing with a Computer: Using Your Word Processor for a New Freedom and Creativity in Writing.* New York: Computer Books/Simon & Schuster.

Johnson, Alexander Bryan. *The Meaning of Words.* New York: Harper & Row, 1854. Now available in an edition published by John Winston Chamberlin, Milwaukee, Wis.

Knapp, Mark. *Nonverbal Communication in Human Interaction.* New York: Holt, Rinehart & Winston, 1972.

Kraemer, K. L., and J. L. King. "Telecommunications/Transportation Substitution and Energy Conservation," *Telecommunications Policy,* part 1: March, 1982, pp. 34–59; part 2: June, 1982, pp. 87–99.

Lee, Irving J. *The Language of Wisdom and Folly.* 3d ed. San Francisco: International Society for General Semantics, 1977.

Levinson, Harry. *Emotional Health in the World of Work.* New York: Harper & Row, 1964.

Liedlich, Raymond D. *Coming to Terms with Language.* New York: John Wiley & Sons, 1973.

McLuhan, Marshall. *Understanding Media: The Extensions of Man.* New York: McGraw-Hill, 1965.

Martinez, Benjamin, and Jacqueline Block, *Perception, Design, and Practice.* Englewood Cliffs, N.J.; Prentice-Hall, 1985.

Menninger, Karl A. *The Human Mind.* New York: Alfred A. Knopf, 1945.

Ogden, C. K., and I. A. Richards. *The Meaning of Meaning.* New York: Harcourt, Brace Jovanovich, 1952.

Penrose, John M. "Computer Software Review," *The American Business Communication Bulletin,* September, 1984, pp. 22–24.

Rokeach, Milton. *The Open and Closed Mind.* New York: Basic Books, Inc., 1960.

Rowan, T. G. *Managing With Computers.* North Pomfret, VT: David and Charles, Inc., 1984.

Russell, Bertrand. *Human Knowledge.* New York: Simon and Schuster, 1948.

Sekuler, Robert, and Randy Blake. *Perception.* New York: Alfred A. Knopf, 1985.

Sinclair, L. ed. *Ways of Mankind.* Boston: Beacon Press, 1954.

Smith, Alred G. ed. *Communication and Culture.* New York: Holt, Rinehart & Winston, 1966.

Stewart, Charles J., and William B. Cash, Jr. *Interviewing: Principles and Practices,* 4th ed. Dubuque, Iowa: Wm. C. Brown, 1984.

Toffler, Alvin. *Future Shock.* New York: Random House, 1970.

Ullman, Stephen. *Semantics: An Introduction to the Science of Meaning.* New York: Barnes & Noble, Inc., 1962.

Wiener, Norbert. *The Human Use of Human Beings.* Boston: Houghton Mifflin, 1950.

Zinsser, William. *Writing with a Word Processor.* New York: Harper & Row, 1983.

Index to Cases

Index

U

UAW, 12
Uncritical Inference Test, 213–14, 222
Undelayed reactions
 advance preparation, 529–30
 correctives, 527–30
 habit of delay, 528
 reflex-like responses, 524–27
  dangerous, 526–27
  useful, 525–26
 reflex responses, 524
 voluntary responses, 524
Understandability, 5
Unpopular Essays, 309

V–W

Vicious pendulum effect, 374–77
Videotaping, 137–40
Wallace, Amy, 260

Wallace, Irving, 260
Wallechinsky, David, 260
Waterman, Robert, Jr., 29n
Weaver, W., 199n
When Index, 420–23
Which Index, 354–55
Whitehead, Alfred North, 325
Whorf, Benjamin Lee, 495
Willits, Robin D., 127n
Wilson, James A., 12
Wolfe, Thomas, 200
Woman's Day, 501–03
Woodger, J. H., 209
Words and Women, 442
World Future Society, 413–14
Wouk, Herman, 371

Y–Z

Your Most Enchanted Listener, 318
Zaltman, Gerald, 166n, 168n

This book has been set Compugraphic in 10 and 9 point Century, leaded 2 points. Part numbers are 20 point Century Bold and chapter numbers are 42 point Century Semi-bold. Part and chapter titles are 18 point Century Bold. The size of the type page is 27 by 47 picas.

BEHIND THE WALLS

A Harper Jennings mystery

When Harper Jennings' staunchest rival at Cornell's archaeology department turns up on her doorstep, babbling about seeing a Pre-Columbian shape-shifter, Harper doesn't know what to think. But she can spot a great opportunity – Zina won a coveted post cataloguing a priceless collection of Pre-Columbian artifacts, and if Harper humours Zina, she'll be able to see them for herself. But then Zina is killed – and the more contact Harper has with the relics, the more her life starts going wrong. The artifacts can't really be cursed – can they?

BEHIND THE WALLS

A Harper Jennings Mystery

Merry Jones

Severn House Large Print
London & New York

This first large print edition published 2013
in Great Britain and the USA by
SEVERN HOUSE PUBLISHERS LTD of
19 Cedar Road, Sutton, Surrey, England, SM2 5DA.
First world regular print edition published 2012 by
Severn House Publishers Ltd., London and New York.

British Library Cataloguing in Publication Data

Jones, Merry Bloch. author.
  Behind the walls. -- Large print edition. -- (A Harper
  Jennings mystery ; 2)
  1. Jennings, Harper (Fictitious character)--Fiction.
  2. Women veterans--Fiction. 3. Iraq War, 2003-2011--
  Veterans--Fiction. 4. Post-traumatic stress disorder--
  Patients--Fiction. 5. Cornell University--Employees--
  Fiction. 6. Antiquities, Prehistoric--America--Catalogs--
  Fiction. 7. Blessing and cursing--Fiction. 8. Suspense
  fiction. 9. Large type books.
  I. Title II. Series
  813.6-dc23

  ISBN-13: 978-0-7278-9625-4

Severn House Publishers support the Forest Stewardship Council™
[FSC™], the leading international forest certification organisation. All
our titles that are printed on FSC certified paper carry the FSC logo.

Printed and bound in Great Britain by
T J International, Padstow, Cornwall.

To Robin, Baille and Neely

Acknowledgments

In writing *Behind the Walls*, I had support and encouragement from lots of people, too many to list. But special thanks to:

my agent, Rebecca Strauss at McIntosh and Otis;

my editor, Rachel Simpson Hutchens at Severn House Publishers;

my fellow Liars: Greg Frost, Jon McGoran, Jonathan Maberry, Don Lafferty, Kelly Simmons, Marie Lamba, Dennis Tafoya, Keith Strunk, Solomon Jones, Ed Pettit, Keith DeCandido;

my friends and family, especially Robin, Baille and Neely.

October, 1989

The crate was smaller than most, simply marked 'Utah'. No dates, like all the others. No specific dig sites either. Odd; Professor Langston was obsessive about labeling his collection. Maybe the labels were inside, taped to the lid? Or maybe they'd been lost.

Carla Prentiss sighed, glanced at her watch. Almost four. Without a list, there probably wouldn't be time to identify and catalogue the contents before sunset, and she didn't want to be caught there after dark. The professor's rambling old Victorian mansion was spooky enough in daylight. The place had been built in the early twentieth century by some hermetic silent movie star whose name she couldn't remember but who, in his paranoia, had designed the place with secret passages and hidden vaults, setting it deep in the woods outside Ithaca where, even now, it had no near neighbors. When he'd offered her the assistantship, Professor Langston had told her with some pride that his house was probably haunted.

'Haunted?' she'd parroted.

'Its inhabitants have led, shall we say ... uncommon lives,' He'd smiled, wheezing heavily as air forced its way through his dense nose

9

hairs. 'In the twenties, a young woman – a starlet named Chloe Manning – simply disappeared during a visit. Some say she's still in the house, wandering the passages in the walls.'

Carla had blinked at the walls of the study. Wondered if the bookshelves concealed secret doors. And bodies.

Under his white, unruly brows, Langston's eyes had twinkled, amused. He'd lowered his voice to a gravelly whisper. 'Some years later, a maid suddenly fell or jumped – or was pushed – over the balcony. Broke her neck. And then, in the fifties, well...' His eyes had narrowed, drifted across his study.

'What?' she'd pressed him. 'What happened in the fifties?'

He'd drawn a dramatic breath. 'Well, these things happen, even today.'

What things? She'd waited for him to explain.

'Sometimes men run amok. They snap and release pent-up aggressions on to their family members.'

'Professor, what happened?'

'Well.' He'd cleared his throat, reached for a pipe. 'The man of the house – Fredericks was his name. One night, he simply hacked his wife and three children to death. Damaged the walls a bit, too.'

Carla had felt a chill, held her breath.

'But it worked out well for me; I was able to acquire the place for a very reasonable price afterwards.' Professor Langston had smiled slyly. Pleased with himself.

Carla, of course, didn't believe in ghosts or

10

haunting. As an archeologist, she believed in history. In science. And so, despite the professor's grisly tales, she was thrilled at the opportunity to work with him, cataloguing the massive and disorganized collection of artifacts he'd accumulated in digs from Peru to Pennsylvania over the course of some five decades. Now in his seventies, Professor Langston had decided to write his will. And the Archeology Department, hoping that he'd leave a generous part of his conglomeration to the university, had offered to pay a graduate student to help him get it organized and itemized.

And that graduate student, Carla Prentiss, welcomed the income that came with the assistantship, not to mention the chance to see – to actually touch and examine – rare Pre-Columbian relics. So she overlooked the dusty cobwebs, eerie history and damp chill of the house. Not for the first time, she shook off the sense that she wasn't alone, and focused on the crate in front of her.

Utah.

An hour before dark. Maybe there would be time to do this one crate, depending on what was inside. Probably, it wouldn't take long. It wasn't heavy, might not have much in it. Glancing again at her watch, she reached for a lever to pry up the lid. As she wedged the tool in-between slats of wood, the light shifted. A shadow fell over her from behind.

'Professor?' She turned, expecting to see him. But, of course, he wasn't there – Professor Langston hobbled with a cane. Made thudding sounds

11

as he walked. Carla listened, heard no footsteps. Nothing. Just her own breathing and the silence of dust.

Uneasy, Carla surveyed the storage room. Saw nobody, just rows of metal shelves holding oddly shaped packages. Stacks of wooden crates and cardboard barrels lining the walls. The door slightly ajar. The row of cut-glass windows, revealing slivers of orange and red treetops, a gray cloud crossing above them.

The cloud – that was it. It must have blocked the sunlight for a moment, casting a shadow, darkening the room. That was all. She needed to relax.

Reinserting the lever into the crate, Carla pushed down on it to force up the lid. Her stomach growled with the exertion, complaining that she'd skipped lunch. Reminding her that it was her turn to cook dinner. Curried chicken with apricots. She could almost smell it.

Or no – wait. The smell wasn't her imagination. Nor was it curried chicken. What was it? She sniffed the crate where she'd loosened the lid, got a whiff of wood shavings and musty air. She straightened, sniffing, but couldn't figure out the source of the scent, so she continued her work. Inserting the lever on the other end of the crate. Pushing until the lid came up with a squeak of resistance. Or was the floor creaking? Carla looked around again. The smell was stronger. Musky and warm. Smoky. Sweet. Like incense? Or cheap cologne?

She thought of that starlet – Chloe somebody? The one who'd disappeared years ago, whose ghost might live in the walls. Oh God, was she smelling Chloe's stale perfume?

Ridiculous. Even so, the hairs on Carla's neck stood on alert, and she shivered at the idea. Probably, she reasoned, the odor was drifting up from downstairs. One of the professor's sons must be burning incense or scented candles. Or some exotic wood in the fireplace. That was all.

Calmer, Carla turned back to the crate just as another shadow fell over her. Not a cloud, this time. No, this shadow flickered from over head. And something darted above her – a bird? Lord, was there a bird trapped in the room? Cautiously, Carla looked up to see a tiny creature, flapping its wings, disappearing behind a beam high on the ceiling.

Damn. A bat? The house had bats? Cringing, she reached for the light switch and flipped it on. Examined the ceiling again. Saw no sign of the thing, couldn't see where it might have escaped. But, fine. Bats were harmless. They ate bugs, didn't they? Weren't they a sign of a healthy ecology? In an old house like the professor's, they probably weren't unusual, probably came out as the sun went down. No reason for alarm.

A little on edge, Carla continued her work. Carefully, she lifted the lid, set it on the table beside the crate. And looked inside.

When the first blow struck, she went down hard, her head banging the table. She tried to get up, but she was dizzy, blinded by pain. Carla huddled, protecting herself, trying to escape sharp swiping blows. Twisting, she had the impression of a large cat – a jaguar? Or no. A man?

13

She crawled, kicking, and, even as her flesh tore, she told herself that the attack was not possible. There was no such thing as a man who was also a cat. But this not-quite-man-not-quite-cat kept ripping at her. Digging at her chest.

Fading, Carla had three final thoughts. The first was that she never should have stayed to open the Utah crate.

The second was that she was having her final thoughts.

The third was that, damn, she wouldn't get to have that curried chicken.

October, 2011

At first, they didn't hear the banging. Maybe they mistook it for loose garbage cans clattering around in the driveway. Or maybe it got lost in the screaming howls of wind that gusted against the house, buzzing through cracks in the window frames, drowning out all other sounds.

Vicki Manning, clearing dinner plates, waited for the wind to subside before speaking. 'Wow. That was almost as loud as Trent's snoring.'

Harper Jennings laughed, nodding. She'd heard those snores; Vicki's husband could shake walls when he slept.

'Need. Putty. Fix.' Hank Jennings put down his wine glass. He'd cooked again, had become quite adept in the kitchen in the last year. 'In. Sulate. Before winter.'

'Put it on the to-do list.' Harper picked up a salad bowl, planted a kiss on his cheek on her way to the kitchen sink. She had become accustomed to Hank's speech; he had aphasia due to brain injuries from a fall from the roof. Most of the time, she understood his meaning perfectly, and she'd convinced herself that his speech was steadily improving.

Vicki took Hank's dish. 'The pasta was yummy, Hank. Thanks.' She'd been eating with

15

them on Tuesday nights while Trent taught an evening class. 'You should open a restaurant—'

Her voice was drowned out by rapping sounds and another anguished groan from the windows. Tree branches blew against the house, scraped against glass panes.

Hank shook his head. 'House com. Plaining. Old. Arth. Ritis.'

Indeed. The house was old, over a hundred years. And he and Harper had been renovating it, by themselves. To Harper, the process seemed endless, as if every job they completed led to ten more. But, with Hank's aphasia making him unable to teach, the endless work wasn't so bad; rehabbing gave Hank a focus. Something positive to work on.

Vicki poured herself the last of the wine as Harper washed pots and pans, gazing out the window into the darkness. Hedges, firs, branches of the oak tree bent to the wind. Night came early, felt stark and dangerous. But lights from the fraternity house next door spilled into the yard, defining shapes. Reminding her that she was safe, that the shadows held no snipers. That she was home in Ithaca not back in Iraq, surrounded by war and terror.

'Where's a towel? I'll dry.'

'There was one on the—' She stopped midsentence, interrupted by loud banging. It didn't sound like the wind. It came from the front door.

'Trent maybe?' Hank turned toward the sound. The dish towel was draped on his shoulder.

'Can't be,' Vicki glanced at the clock. 'He's still teaching.'

16

Harper grabbed the dish towel off of Hank, tossed it at Vicki as she headed for the door. The banging grew louder, more rapid. Urgent. Harper hurried, hearing shouts.

'Harper? Are you in there?'

She didn't recognize the voice.

Harper stopped beside the door, cautious. Old instincts, trained responses.

'Who?' Hank came up behind her, limping slightly.

Harper turned on the porch light, peered through the window. And saw Zina Salim. Zina Salim? Really? Why? But there she was, her hair flying in the wind, her dark eyes wide. Her fist raised to pound some more.

Harper swung the door open, and Zina rushed in, watching over her shoulder, repeating, 'Thank God. Thank God. Couldn't you hear me? I thought you'd never answer.'

Harper was speechless. But what was Zina Salim doing there? She and Zina weren't friends; they politely tolerated each other. Within the Archeology Department, they were staunch rivals, earning their PhDs under the same professors. Competing for assistantships, fellowships and teaching assignments, attention. And annoyingly, whatever Harper applied for, Zina Salim seemed to get. She was politically connected, the darling of the department – especially of Professor Wiggins, the graduate coordinator. There had been rumors, and more than once, Harper had wondered if a romance were involved.

'Thank God, Harper,' Zina breathed, rushing

17

into the house. 'Thank God you're home.'

'Come. In.' Hank welcomed her, scanning the front yard before shutting the door.

Zina was trembling as Harper led her into the living room, where Vicki stood staring, sipping her wine. 'Here, sit down. What happened, Zina? Are you OK?'

Panting, Zina sank on to the sofa, covered her face with her hands.

'Zina?' Harper watched her.

Zina hugged herself, silent and shivering. She seemed small, childlike. Harper pulled an afghan off the arm of the sofa, wrapped it around Zina's shoulders and sat beside her. Zina stared warily at Vicki.

'This is our friend, Vicki Manning,' Harper reassured her. 'Vicki, this is my colleague, Zina Salim.'

'Warm get. Now.' Hank threw some logs into the fireplace. Added some kindling. Zina watched him, transfixed, fingering an ornate bangle bracelet.

'What's wrong with her?' Vicki mouthed.

Harper shrugged, rolled her eyes. She thought Zina coy, manipulative. Affected, with her British accent and aristocratic attitudes. For everything she did, she seemed to have an ulterior motive. Harper didn't trust her, doubted she'd reveal her actual purpose for coming over. But clearly, she was frightened.

Hank's fire blazed, toasting the room. Zina watched the flames, became more collected. 'Better now?' he asked.

'Thank you,' Zina attempted a smile. She slip-

18

ped her bracelet on and off, nervously. 'This is so nice of you, opening your home to me.' She spoke in a sweet, controlled tone. 'I'm better now. Probably I was overreacting. I mean, obviously, I was. Just being silly. I hope I didn't interrupt your—'

'What happened, Zina?' Harper cut in.

Zina looked away, stared at the fire. Harper, Hank and Vicki stared at Zina. Moments passed. Finally, Zina turned to Harper.

'Harper,' her eyes were doubtful. 'Do you believe in the Nahual?'

'The Nahual,' Harper repeated.

Zina nodded, eyes shifting.

'In what?' Vicki asked.

'Shape-shifters.' Harper watched Zina, tried not to smirk.

'No – I know it sounds crazy. That's why I said I was overreacting. It was nothing—' She attempted a laugh, failed. Started to stand.

'Uh uh.' Harper grabbed her arm, pulled her back to the sofa. 'You're not leaving until you explain what the hell you're talking about.'

'Tell us.' Hank took a seat by the fire, waiting.

Vicki stepped closer. Zina's face reflected the fire. She looked from one to the other and finally caved, sinking back against the cushions.

'You'll think I'm making it up.'

'Just tell us.'

She drew a breath. Let it out. Drew another. And began. 'It was ... I was at work. At Langston's house.'

'Cataloguing?' Harper had applied for that assistantship, a plumb opportunity to document

19

the late professor's expansive Pre-Columbian collection. But Wiggins had selected Zina. Of course.

'Yes. Cataloguing.' Zina pushed hair off her face, still playing with her bracelet. 'But when the sun went down, the air – all of a sudden, it shifted. It actually moved. I felt someone there. Behind – or maybe in front – of me. I heard owls hooting. Dogs barking. And I smelled something – like incense. Smoky and musky ... And then wings were flapping—'

'Wings?'

'I swear. Like the wings of a bat.' Zina nodded, her face ghostlike, flickering orange. 'And boards – the floor was creaking. Someone was there. I looked but couldn't see anyone. And then, real low, I heard growling – soft and threatening, like a large cat about to pounce.' She stopped, checking their faces as if afraid they'd laugh at her.

Three faces watched her in firelight, not laughing.

'Then the lights flickered and suddenly – they went off. I stood, ready to run, but I smelled the thing in the dark. I couldn't see it, so I turned, feeling for it, and then something brushed my face – something furry. It was right up next to me – it growled right into my ear, so close that I felt its breath on my neck. I *smelled* it, like raw meat. I don't know what happened next. I ran – flew out of the room and down the steps, out of the house and into my car. Before I knew it, I was speeding back to town. On the way, I saw your lights were on...' She looked at Harper, then

20

Hank, then Vicki. Back at Harper. 'You all think I'm nuts, don't you?'

Everyone shook their heads, no. Politely. Even sympathetically.

'Of course we don't.' Harper knew all about panic, wasn't about to label it 'nuts'. She put a hand on Zina's shoulder. 'Whatever happened, real or imagined, you're safe. It's good you stopped here.'

'I did not imagine it.' She sat up straight, panting again.

'Breathe,' Harper ordered. 'Take deep slow breaths.'

Zina gazed around the room. Met their eyes directly, one pair at a time. And she took deep breaths. 'It was real,' she insisted. 'But they don't know the significance, do they?' She motioned at Vicki and Hank.

'Significance of what?' Vicki asked.

'Of the animals that were there. The bat is a sign of death. The owl represents the underworld; it's a messenger of the dead—'

'Oh, come on, Zina,' Harper interrupted. 'That's just mythology.'

'And the large cat – the jaguar – is the most revered and powerful of all animals. A symbol of power.'

'Since when? Sorry. That's just—' Vicki began.

'It's symbolism.' Zina insisted. 'Each of the animals has meaning. And I was surrounded by powerful symbols of death.'

For a moment, nobody spoke.

Finally, Hank stood. 'Get drinks. All of. Us.'

21

He headed for the kitchen.

'So? What do you think? It couldn't really have been a Nahual. There is no such thing, right?' Zina blinked at Harper.

'No. Of course there isn't,' Harper tried to answer as if the question were rational. Obviously, Zina had been frightened. But was she seriously asking if she'd encountered a Nahual?

'So how do you explain what happened? If not a Nahual, then what was it?'

'Here's what I think. You've been working alone in that spooky old mansion. The wind was howling, the boards were creaking, and the moon was full. You know about the house, what's happened there, so your imagination was predisposed to think scary thoughts. In the dark, it took off—'

'No, Harper. I swear to you. It was *not* my imagination.'

Harper tilted her head. 'Zina. Are you seriously saying that a bat or an owl changed into a jaguar and growled at you?'

'OK.' Zina's cheeks were ruddy from the warmth of the fire. 'OK, no. I mean, I know better. Even so, what I told you was real. It happened.'

'Zina.' Harper's voice was flat, definite. 'Whatever happened, it wasn't a Nahual. There is no such thing.'

Vicki lowered herself on to the cushioned chair beside Harper, leaned over. 'Will you please explain what you guys are talking about?'

Harper turned toward Vicki. 'Remember that research position I applied for – the one where

22

the professor died, and they needed someone to document his collection of artifacts?'

Vicki nodded. 'Of course I remember. You were pissed that they passed you over and gave it to the bitch you think is sleeping w—' She stopped short, her mouth forming an 'oh'.

Harper cleared her throat; Zina stared at the flames, handling her bracelet. She didn't seem to have been listening. 'Anyway, Zina got the position. She's been working on the collection for a few weeks, all alone in the professor's isolated old house.'

'So the floors might creak by themselves,' Vicki suggested. 'And with nobody living there, animals might have moved in—'

'How do you know there's no such thing?' Zina was still focused on Harper's comment. 'I mean, maybe there is. Because if it wasn't a Nahual, then what was it? How else can you explain it? Wings flapping, a big cat growling, fur and claws – and that smell...'

For a moment, Harper almost laughed; she thought Zina must be kidding. But no. Zina showed no signs of humor. 'Zina. Shape-shifters are mythological creatures. They're legends. Nothing more.'

Zina looked away, back into the fire.

'Shape-shifters?' Vicki asked. 'What?'

'They called them Nahuals. Pre-Columbians believed in shaman-like creatures that could take almost any form they wanted. They could change into men, large cats, dogs, deer, bats. Owls. Whatever shape they needed to protect their people or defend their territory—'

23

'Or their possessions.' Zina's voice was low. 'Their artifacts.'

'Seriously, Zina,' Harper began. 'Try to be—'

'Hot. Rum. Buttered.' Hank carried a tray of mugs and spice cookies.

The fire crackled; the drinks were warm and boozy. And Zina, warmer and relaxed by the rum, repeated her story to Hank.

'Ghost,' he concluded. 'Pro. Fessor. Haunting. House.' His eyes twinkled playfully.

Vicki grinned. 'Of course – he's probably changed his mind about donating his precious relics and wants to scare Zina away.'

'Cut it out.' Harper didn't see humor in Zina's fear. 'Nobody's haunting anybody. Nobody's shifting shapes. It's just – suggestion.' Harper put down her mug, thinking of the best way to explain. 'Look, Zina – it's like I said before. All those stories about the house, the history of the place – that's what's haunting you, nothing else.'

'Stories. What?' Hank asked.

Harper picked up a cookie and crossed her legs. She looked at Zina. 'You want to tell them?'

Zina emphatically shook her head, no.

So Harper began. 'In 1989, when Professor Langston first decided to will his collection to Cornell, he hired a young woman to catalogue it. One night, just before Halloween, the research assistant—' Harper stopped as the wind screeched through the windows, interrupting, as if to prevent her from going on.

'The research assistant got mauled to death,' Zina finished when the wind subsided. 'And the

24

killer cut her heart out.' She didn't look at Harper. She set her bangle bracelet down on the table, picked up her mug and gulped hot buttered rum.

'Well, we're not sure about her heart. But, yes, she was killed.'

'No. She was *mauled*. As if by a jaguar. Or a mountain lion. And her heart was dug out. Get your laptop,' Zina insisted. 'Let's Google it and I'll show you.'

In moments, the four were huddled around the screen, reading newspaper accounts of a mystery over two decades old.

Carla Prentiss had been found early Halloween morning, set out at the end of the professor's long, wooded driveway, positioned as if on display under a tree. Her wounds were extensive, and there was a lot of blood, so much that at first police didn't notice the hole in her chest where her heart should have been.

'See that?' Zina crossed her arms. 'They took her heart, the same way Pre-Columbians took human hearts—'

'But that's my point,' Harper interrupted. 'You got spooked by that horrible old crime. It's almost Halloween again – the anniversary of that murder. And you had that story in the back of your mind—'

'Read on,' Zina interrupted. '"Because of the missing heart, Professor Langston speculated that the murder was designed to resemble the work of a mythological shape-shifter who would sacrifice the hearts of enemies to the gods, or eat them to acquire their strength."'

25

'Yuck, they ate them?' Vicki winced.

'Read it for yourself.' Zina went on. 'Even Langston thought there was a Nahual—'

'Bull. Shit,' Hank interrupted. 'No such. Thing.'

Vicki was still reading. 'Hmm. It says that, for a while, police suspected the professor's Brazilian housekeeper. Oh, wow. He was having an affair with her, and she was jealous of the attention he paid to the dead girl. And there was another suspect – a kid who hung around with the professor's sons. His family pulled him out of school and sent him abroad.'

'OK, Vicki. We get it.' Harper was watching Zina, saw her biting her lip, holding her stomach.

'No.' Vicki wasn't finished. 'Wait, listen. That house – wow.' She looked up from the computer screen. 'Did you know about the family that lived there before the professor? The dad killed his wife and kids. With an axe. And he slit his own throat.'

Hank leaned over her shoulder, reading.

'And before that, a silent film actress disappeared there. Wait – oh, man – did you know the house has hidden passageways—'

'Vicki, enough. You're not helping.' Harper closed the lid of the laptop; the articles disappeared.

Hank scowled. 'Was reading.'

Zina cowered.

'OK,' Vicki sighed. 'I get why you're scared, Zina. That house has some bad karma.'

'Karma? Oh please, Vicki.' Harper was dismissive. 'It's just an old house, like this one, just

bigger. The professor raised his family there –
three sons, right? A couple of them still live
around here. Nothing out of the ordinary has
happened there in what? Twenty years? More?
Not since the murder.'

'Maybe that's because the professor locked the
collection up. No one's even looked at it since
that assistant got killed.' Zina curled herself into
a ball. 'Until now.'

The fire crackled. Harper began to argue, but
Zina cut her off. 'No – now I've gone and
messed with the relics again. So that shape-
shifter thing that killed the last researcher is
back. And, I swear, whether you believe me or
not – if I hadn't run out of that house tonight,
they'd have found my body tomorrow with my
heart cut out, just like hers.'

The fire crackled, but for a while nobody
spoke.

Then Vicki tried to help. 'But Zina. Think
about it – that murder was so long ago. The killer
would be an old man by now – if he's even still
alive.'

'A Nahual doesn't age—' Zina began, but the
wind moaned again, drowning out her voice.

When it stopped, Hank stood. 'Get. More
rum.' He collected their cups and went to refill
them.

'Actually, Vicki's right.' Harper chewed another cookie, 'Carla's murder might not have had
anything to do with the relics. Someone might
have just made it look that way.'

'Come on, Harper. Why would they do that?
Who would follow ancient rituals and cut out

someone's heart, just for fun? It has to be about the artifacts. They're cursed – lots of relics are. That's a known fact.'

'She's right,' Vicki agreed. 'Remember that story about Montezuma's gold? Trent and Hank told us about it. The gold was cursed, too.'

Harper scowled. 'Vicki, that's ridiculous. That's just a legend.'

But Vicki ignored her, turning to Zina. 'Back in 1910 or so, divers found a skeleton, deep in a lake. The thing was sitting up at the entrance to a cave, as if he were guarding it – I think it was somewhere in Mexico.'

'No, it was in Three Lakes Canyon,' Harper corrected. 'In Utah. And that story is bull, besides which it has absolutely nothing to do with the professor's collection.'

'Yes, it does. It's an example of how stuff can be cursed, Harper. People thought the skeleton was guarding gold, so they dug a tunnel to excavate it, but they all came down with a mysterious fever and died.'

'No, Vicki.' Harper closed her eyes, sighing. 'The only fever that those people got was *gold* fever. Nobody died.'

'Yes, they did.' Vicki sat up straight, eyes wide; her voice husky and low. The room was in shadows except for the fire, and its light flickered, dancing ghostlike on her skin. 'Then, divers went down to look but came up, terrified, refusing to go back. They said they'd been chased away by translucent figures without oxygen or diving gear. Spirits, protecting the gold. One diver swore that a figure had tried to

28

choke him, and when he took his gear off, they saw hand marks on his neck—'

'More rum!' Hank bellowed.

Harper jumped; Zina gasped. Vicki let out a shrill yelp. Startled, Hank juggled the tray, trying not to spill the drinks as the women dissolved into bouts of laughter.

'What?' He steadied himself. 'Scared crap. Out of me.'

'Sorry, Hank,' Vicki caught her breath. 'There's a lot of that going around.'

'Nonsense,' Harper insisted. 'Zina, pay no attention to Vicki's story. Gold is just a metal; relics are just old things. And whatever happened to you tonight, there's a logical explanation. No curse or spirit or Nahual was involved.' She grabbed another mug of rum and took a drink.

By the time Harper walked Zina to her car, the wind had died down. The night was quiet. Music no longer blared from the fraternity house next door.

'You're sure you want to go with me?' Zina asked. 'You don't really have to. The professor's sons usually come around in the daytime, and I'll be sure to leave before dark.'

'No. I'd love to come. I've been dying to see his collection.'

An awkward silence reflected that Zina had gotten the position that Harper had wanted.

'You know, you should have gotten the position. They only gave it to me because of my family. The business.'

'Business?'

'My family trades antiquities, so Professor Wiggins thought I'd have more experience handling relics. I mean, I've worked with them since I was a child.'

Oh really? 'Well, it doesn't matter. I'd just like to see it.'

'You realize that nothing is actually on display. All the pieces are packed up. I go box by box, identifying things, piece by piece. And half of the items aren't where they're supposed to be.'

'But Zina, maybe being there together, we'll be able to figure out what happened tonight.' Harper was sure that something tangible – maybe just the noise of the wind or a flicker of a shadow – had frightened Zina. That her imagination had taken over only after some real event had triggered it. 'Look, I've had a lot of experience with fear—'

'Oh, right. With Iraq and all.'

Harper nodded. Yes. With Iraq and all.

'But this is different. It's not a war – it was something unearthly. Unnatural.'

And war was earthly and natural? 'The point is that fear sets off reactions that aren't always appropriate or rational. If we explain what frightened you, you might not be afraid of it any more.' Lord, she sounded like Leslie, her shrink.

Zina looked away, into the night. Unconvinced. 'I know you don't believe me. But it was there. It was real.' She turned to get into her car, but Harper stopped her.

'Look, Zina. We don't know each other very well. But I've had my share of scare. And I can tell you that perceptions – what we think is happening – can be misleading.' Harper recalled a white flash, a blast, the feeling of flying through the air. Closed her eyes to shove the memory away. 'Just because something flies like a bat and has fur like a cat doesn't mean that it's a Nahual.'

Zina met her eyes, seemed defeated. 'Thanks for tonight, Harper. I know you mean well. And I'll be glad for your company tomorrow. But please don't try to convince me that I imagined everything. I was there. You weren't. I know what I know.'

With that, she opened the door of her electric-blue Smart Car, got in and drove away. Harper watched until the tail lights faded into the night. Then she went back to the house, finished clearing up. And noticed Zina's silver bangle bracelet on the coffee table.

Oh well. Harper popped it into her bag. She'd see Zina in the morning; she'd give it back to her then.

Vicki left after the dishes were done. And a while later, Harper finally crawled into bed, curling up against Hank.

'Think?' he asked.

Think? Harper considered the question.

'Zina,' Hank clarified.

Oh. 'I'm not sure. But clearly, something spooked her.'

'But bat. Cat. Man? Nuts.'

He was right. Zina's story sounded nuts. Then again, Harper, suffering from Post Traumatic Stress Disorder, had seen ambushes, explosions

31

and suicide bombers, had smelled gunfire and heard shots fired where there had been none, and her flashbacks had seemed real, as real as the bed she was lying in. As real as the silence of her reply. Hank's dismissal of Zina's perceptions felt personal, as if he were somehow dismissing hers, as well.

'What. Say. Your mind.'

'Just because you don't perceive something, Hank, doesn't mean it's not there.'

In the lamplight, she saw his eyebrow raise. 'Nahual? Hoppa. Really.' His eyes danced, laughing. Mocking?

'No. I don't mean a Nahual. But something.'

'Shadows.' Hank chuckled. 'Hallow. Ween. Ghosts. Nerves. Stories. Just.' He put his arm around her, kissed her forehead.

'It seemed real to her. She was terrified.'

'Nothing. Her mind. Weak. Zina.'

Wait, Zina was weak? Because she'd been frightened by her own mind?

'Sleep. Love.'

Harper leaned up, returned his goodnight kiss. And lay there, not sleeping, not moving. Cuddling against Hank, she tried to disregard both the weight of his judgments and the heaviness of his arm.

By morning, Zina was mortified. Goodness. Had she really gone running to, of all people, Harper Jennings, the person who probably disliked her more than anyone else in the entire Archeology Department, and told her – admitted to her out loud – that she'd been scared off the Langston

32

property? That she'd thought she'd encountered a Nahual? Really? Oh my. If that got back to her family, they'd kill her. And, if it got around the department, she'd never get over it. The gossip would ruin her career before she even started it. Rumors would fly. She'd be the brunt of countless pathetic not-even-funny jokes. She imagined them. 'What "shape" are you in today, Zina?' Or 'The Jaguar agency called; your Nahual's ready.' Stupid, stupid jokes.

OK. Never mind. She'd been in worse situations. She'd correct this one before it got out of control. Go to work and act as if nothing had happened. Actually, she'd go early and be there, fully composed and engrossed in her work, when Harper arrived. Goodness, how had she ever agreed to allow that woman soldier to come to work with her? As if she needed a combat officer to protect her and hold her hand. As if she couldn't manage on her own? Everyone knew Harper had wanted the Langston job, that she'd been jealous when Wiggins had given it to Zina. And now, Harper might use this incident to make it seem that Zina needed her help. Well, nothing doing. When Harper arrived, Zina would make light of the night before. Yes – she'd avoid being the brunt of jokes by laughing; she'd make fun of herself before anyone else could. And she'd be immersed in her work, too busy to do more than briefly show Harper around, pointing out the stacks of crates, letting her ogle a few relics. Then she'd send her on her way. Making it clear that she was in charge.

Zina showered, dressed, ate a stale donut, and

got into her little blue Smart Car, trying to recover some sense of dignity. There had to be logical explanations for everything that had happened. It had to have been the darkness. Creaking floors were normal in old homes. As were bats. And the lights? Well, the wind had probably blown down a wire. And the wind might even explain the feeling of fur – might have blown small pieces of fiberglass insulation into the room. Or, more likely, a cobweb or some packing paper had blown against her skin in the darkness. The wind, after all, had been terrible; tree branches had been blown down, now lay scattered on the road.

Her panic had simply been an overreaction. All she could do now was damage control. She'd explain it to Harper and hope the woman was decent enough to keep it to herself, not make her a laughing stock. But that wasn't likely; if the situation were reversed, she would certainly think the story was hysterical and share it with everyone. Oh dear.

The whole way to the Langston house, Zina considered what she'd say to Harper. How she'd convince her that she was fine, that her behavior the night before had been no big deal. That she'd been more amused than frightened – yes. That was it – she'd say that she'd stopped by Harper's house to share an odd but amusing anecdote. Like, would you believe it? Langston's house has its own Nahual. Haha. Isn't this a good spooky story for the week before Halloween?

She turned off Route 96 on to the long dirt road leading to the professor's driveway. About forty yards up, she stopped. A huge branch had toppled, blocking the way. Damn. She sat for a moment, considering her options. No way she could go around it; even her tiny car wouldn't fit between its top end and the trees. She could wait there for Harper; they could ride her motorcycle the rest of the way. Or she could park right there and walk the mile or so to the house.

Finally, Zina decided to get out and try to move the branch, to shove it just enough that she could drive around it. And if that didn't work, if it was too heavy, she'd park and walk.

Moving to the thinner end of the branch, she lifted her feet, stepped carefully through the tangle of twigs and lingering yellow leaves, took the central stem into her hands. She realized that moving without tripping on the foliage would be difficult; it might have been easier to grab the heavier, less dense end. Somewhere close, she heard the hooting of an owl. And, in the periphery of her vision, she saw something move. A man? No, something that looked like a big cat.

When her phone rang the next morning, Harper was straddling her Ninja, checking to make sure she had Zina's bracelet with her before leaving for Professor Langston's. She almost didn't answer it. But her new ringtone, the sound of a gong, kept chiming, and she realized the call might actually be from Zina. Maybe she needed to change the time. So, opening her storage compartment, she pulled out her big leather sack and felt around inside, finally locating the phone.

'Is this Harper?'

Not Zina. A man. Not a familiar voice.

'Who is this?'

'Is that you, Harper? Lieutenant Harper J. Reynolds of the United States Army?'

Harper tried to ignore a sudden rumble of gunfire. She took a breath. Looked around at her house, the gazebo in the yard. 'Who's calling?'

'Don't tell me you don't recognize my voice, Lieutenant. Honestly?'

She didn't. Or damn, no – maybe she did. It was smooth, liquid. Not quite deep enough. Sounded like – Burke Everett? But they hadn't talked in years, not since before the explosion had killed her patrol and sent her home, half dead. Why was he calling now? And how had he gotten her cell phone number? 'What's up, Everett?'

He laughed, triumphant. 'See that? I knew you wouldn't forget me.'

'It's not for lack of trying, trust me.'

'Same old Harper – still a ball-buster. How the hell are you?'

Harper looked at her watch. Almost nine. But the time made no sense; her mind whirled, trying to make sense of the voice in her ear. Images blurred. The air changed, felt dry and sandy, and she had the urge to check her bag for her gear – ammo, knife, goggles, sun block, water bottles, baby wipes...

'You survived that suicide attack – I knew that. But how are you now?'

How was she? Burke kept talking, not waiting for an answer. Harpcr tried to process what he was saying, but his words were too fast, made no

36

sense. She pictured him in uniform, heard him whining about the heat. Or the flies. Or the dust. Or the duty, whatever was bothering him at the moment. Burke Everett? After all this time?

'...because, I'll tell you what – I'll be in Ithaca Thursday. Day after tomorrow. It would be great to see you. You know, to catch up.'

What? No. No, it wouldn't. Harper swallowed. 'I don't know, Burke. I'm pretty busy—'

'Actually, thing is – it's kind of important. I need to talk to you about something. How's dinner Thursday night?'

Wait. Dinner? 'Burke, I'm married.' The words popped out of her mouth, unplanned. As if she'd assumed he'd wanted a date. Harper felt her face get hot.

Burke was laughing. An unpleasant, high-pitched sound. 'Well, congratulations. But I'm not asking for your hand. Just for dinner.'

'I didn't mean—'

'How about drinks then? A beer. Or lunch. Or coffee. Or frozen yogurt.'

'What do you want to talk to me about?'

He paused. 'It's not for the phone. Seriously. It's big. And I need to talk to you in person.'

A squirrel raced by, ran up a tree. Harper stared after it as it disappeared into dwindling orange leaves. In Iraq's stark sands, she'd missed the trees, the colors of summer and fall. She pictured it, that final patrol. Watching a car speed up to the checkpoint. Seeing a woman in a burqa crossing the street. And then, the sensation of flying through heat and fire. She remembered it clearly, even the smells of smoke and burnt flesh,

37

but her memories were just that: memories. Not flashbacks. Everett's unexpected voice had stirred up the past but hadn't entirely revived it. It wasn't engulfing her. At least, not yet.

'Harper? You there?'

'Yes.' Well, sort of.

'I'm just asking for half an hour – an hour at the most. You'll understand when we talk.'

She didn't answer. She tasted sand, felt it coating her sweaty skin. Heard Burke's voice only vaguely. Maybe she'd been too hasty deciding she wasn't having flashbacks.

'...wouldn't bother you after all this time ... wouldn't have come all the way from Milwaukee...'

'Fine.' Harper closed her eyes, bit her lip, concentrated on the pain of teeth puncturing skin to avoid falling into the past.

'Fine?'

'Yes. Fine. I'll meet you Thursday. Three o'clock. Ithaca Bakery.'

'Great, Harper. I'll be there—' Burke began. But Harper ended the call, tossed her phone into her bag and zoomed off on her Ninja before he finished his goodbye.

Harper roared downhill through the edge of town, heading out along Lake Cayuga, thinking about the phone call. Trying to figure out what Burke Everett wanted. In the war, he'd been a wimp. A tall, lanky guy, always keeping his head down, bucking tough details. Complaining even about the easy ones. Not someone she'd want protecting her back. Not someone she'd spent

38

much time with.

So why was he calling her now? It had been – what? Seven? Eight years since she'd seen him? What could he want?

Harper didn't want to think about Iraq. Didn't want to remember. She'd spent years trying to recover from her injuries, still had a bad leg. Not to mention the flashbacks. She'd been better lately, not having as many. Leslie, her shrink, had helped, had shown her how to diminish their intensity, employing scents, sensations or sharp flavors to keep focused on the present. She wondered if Burke Everett had flashbacks. No, probably not. Burke hadn't risked much, usually had soft duty, chauffeuring visiting brass through the Green Zone or base camps. He'd never been wounded. Had never seen his buddies blown up by IEDs or suicide bombers. Again, Harper saw the woman crossing the street, approaching the detail of soldiers at the checkpoint. White heat flashed, and Harper felt herself fly.

But this time, she was flying past the lake, not through the air. And the noise was the engine of her Ninja, not bursts of explosives. She needed to stay grounded. In the moment. To focus on colored leaves. Traffic. The cloudless sky and crisp air. Anything except Iraq.

Her mind, however, remained on precisely that. The past. And the unexpected reappearance of someone she'd almost forgotten. Someone she'd chosen not to stay in contact with. Why had Burke Everett called? What could he possibly want? Harper was so intent on those questions that it wasn't until she turned on to the

39

unpaved road leading to the professor's long rocky driveway that she gave a thought to Zina and the relics, the reason she was there, racing along a darkly overgrown path in the middle of nowhere.

She hoped that Zina would be waiting outside, that she wouldn't have gone into the house alone after her panic the night before. On the other hand, maybe Zina felt better, wasn't as shaken now that it was daylight. Looking up the curved narrow road through the trees, Harper tried to spot the house up ahead, wondering about its history. The missing actress, the murdered family. The dead research assistant. Zina's fear.

Engrossed in her thoughts, Harper sped ahead. She almost didn't notice a mass of electric blue just off the narrow road, half hidden by trees. Almost didn't bother to glance back to see what it was, a color that didn't belong. Almost didn't turn and go back to investigate.

But when she did, she barely recognized the heap of mangled metal as the little blue Smart Car that had been Zina's, smashed against a thick old oak.

Harper jumped off the bike and raced to the wreck, shouting, calling Zina's name. She tore through trees, around shrubs and over undergrowth. Twigs snapped underfoot like sniper fire, but Harper ignored them, kept moving until she could peer through tangles of foliage, broken glass and twisted metal. Only when she saw what was left of Zina, her blood-drenched body slumped beside the car, her eyes fixed on nothing

... only then did she stop and stay still.

The air smelled of oil and blood. Harper stared; sweat poured down her torso. And somewhere, guns began firing. Men cried out. No, she insisted. Not now. But, even as she told herself that the fighting around her wasn't real, that it was a flashback, she ducked low to the ground, dodging bullets, feeling them whizz past her ears. Guns popped. Smoke clouded her vision. Someone screamed. She reached for her weapon, couldn't find it. Realized that, damn, it must be back with her gear. So half crawling, half scooting, she made it back to her Ninja, pulled out her leather bag, reached inside for a pistol, found a phone. Dug some more. And pulled out a lemon.

A lemon? She blinked at it, forcing herself to remember what it was doing in her gear. A voice deep in her head commanded: *Bite it*. Bite it? The lemon? But wait – a woman was crossing the street, her hand reaching inside her burqa, and a green car was speeding toward the checkpoint. She knew the explosion was coming, needed to warn the patrol ... *Bite it!*

Harper jammed the lemon into her mouth and chomped; sour acidic juice spilled on to her tongue, startling her. Overpowering her mind. Making her focus on taste. On the moment. And suddenly, the checkpoint, the car, the woman suicide bomber – the war faded away, leaving Harper alone on the wooded path to Professor Langston's, a phone in her hand, a lemon in her mouth. And, a few feet away, Zina, dead, huddled beside her car.

* * *

Lights and sirens. Sirens and lights. Harper sat on a large rock, watching as police and firemen and medical technicians scurried around. The coroner's van pulled up. A tow truck. A television crew. She didn't know what to do, where to be, so she stayed off to the side, huddling. Trying to understand what had happened. Zina had to have been speeding, must have lost control of her car and hit the tree. Must have crawled out, injured, and died. But why had she been speeding? What was her hurry? Was she being chased, maybe? Here? On this unpaved back road? Something nagged at her about Zina's body. She was almost sitting up. And there was so much blood. Not much, if any, inside the car. None visible on the seat. What had caused her to bleed so much?

A man wandered over, balding, maybe in his forties. Tall, lanky. Prominent cheekbones. Wearing jeans, a tweed blazer. He nodded in her direction, stood watching the commotion. Hands in his pockets.

'Hell of a thing.' He didn't look at Harper, kept his eyes on the wreck.

Harper didn't answer. But he was right; it was a hell of a thing.

Finally, the man turned to her. 'Angus Langston.'

Langston. One of the professor's sons? Angus held out his right hand. As if introducing himself at a social function.

Harper shook the hand. It was large and lean, smooth-skinned. 'Harper Jennings.'

Police and EMTs huddled around Zina's body.

'So, Ms Harper Jennings, they tell me you're the one who found this? You called it in?'

Harper nodded.

He nodded, silently watching the scene. After a while, he looked at her. 'Well, if you don't mind my asking, Ms Jennings, what exactly brought you here to this spot this morning?'

Harper opened her mouth to reply, but Angus continued. 'Being as this is private property. A private road. Which would make you a trespasser.'

Wow. Harper's mouth was still open. She closed it, stunned. Zina was dead, her body still crumpled beside battered blue metal, and this guy was bothering her about her presence on his property? Slowly, deliberately, she stood to her full five foot three-and-almost-a-half inches, assumed an officer's stance.

'You live here, Mr Langston?' She used her most authoritative military voice. Had to arch her neck to meet his eyes. 'In the professor's house?'

Her tone surprised him; he took an instinctive step back. 'No, I stay in the cottage. But where I sleep isn't your concern. The house and property belong to me and my brothers.' He shifted his weight, eyed her. Lost some bluster. Looked away.

'Look, I'm aware that this is private property,' Harper continued. 'But I am not trespassing. I was invited here.'

His eyebrows rose. 'Really. Because I sure don't remember inviting you. And I doubt my brother invited you—'

43

'Actually, I was invited by the woman over there.'

Angus crossed his arms. 'Well, that's interesting. Because the fact is, that woman didn't have the right to invite anyone here. It's bad enough she was here, wandering around. Which by the way, she didn't have the right to do. Now she's brought you. Next, everyone and his uncle Fred will be here.'

'Hey, Mrs Jennings? Harper?'

Harper turned. Saw a face from the past. Detective Charlene Rivers. She shut her eyes, opened them again. Still saw the detective approaching, walking across the road. Not a flashback. Rivers was actually there. Oh God. Memories swirled: a student jumping out of a window. Another, dead on her front porch...

'I saw your Ninja over there.' Rivers smirked. 'I thought I was done dealing with you.'

Harper nodded. 'Good to see you, too, Detective.' She rubbed her eyes, pushing away bloody memories. She hadn't had contact with the Rivers since that debacle with stolen drugs over a year ago.

'Who's your friend?' Rivers eyed Angus Langston who introduced himself just as another news van pulled up the road.

'Aw, hell,' he scowled. 'Who the fuck let them on the grounds? Doesn't anyone understand the words "private property"? What's next? Rock bands? Concession stands? What is this, goddam Woodstock?' He stomped off toward the television van.

'Friendly guy.' Rivers watched him, turned to

44

Harper. 'So tell me. What are you doing here? You know the victim?'

Wait, the 'victim'? Harper drew a breath. Looked across the road to the empty coroner's gurney awaiting Zina's body. And, as she began to answer, remembered that Detective Rivers was in homicide.

What was a homicide detective doing at the scene of a car accident?

Rivers and Harper walked along the road, heads down, voices low, as Harper summarized the events of the night before. Gravel crunched underfoot; the air smelled of dry leaves. 'So basically, you're saying that your friend was afraid for her life?'

'I guess. But she wasn't entirely rational, at least not at first. She thought a Nahual was after her. But Nahuals aren't real.'

'So you think it's just a coincidence that the very next morning she's dead?'

Harper shrugged, shook her head. She had no idea. 'Detective, what are you saying? That Zina was murdered?'

Rivers stopped walking, looked back at the crash site. 'Truth is, I don't know what I'm saying. I have to wait for the coroner's report before I draw any conclusions. All I know is I heard the dispatch that there was a fatality out at Langston's, so I came out to see what went down.' She looked at Harper. 'You know about this place? The history?'

'Some.'

'Then you know what I'm talking about. This

45

dead woman was a researcher for the university. Just like the last dead woman way back in – I think it was eighty-nine? That's the kind of thing that sends alarms bells off in my head. I don't believe much in coincidence.'

Somewhere nearby, an owl hooted. Odd. An owl, in daytime? Weren't they nocturnal? Owls were supposedly one of the Nahual's favorite shapes. Ridiculous. But maybe not to Zina. In fact, maybe Zina had seen an owl – or even a deer or a fox. Or a large cat. Maybe she'd thought the animal was the shape-shifter again, coming after her, and she'd panicked, smashed her car into a tree. It was possible.

Damn. Harper should have arranged to drive with her, not to meet her at the house. If she had, Zina would still be alive. Far away, guns fired; Harper felt snipers watching her from the shadows. She scanned the ground for IEDs. The detective was still talking.

'...press will go bonkers, especially now at Halloween time with all the ghosts this house supposedly has. So I wanted to see for myself. Find out what really happened. And, frankly, after talking to you, I'm not happy.'

Oh dear. 'Why?'

The detective shifted her weight, sighing. 'Harper. People do not normally freak out and claim that someone's trying to kill them. And, even when they do, they don't normally die within hours. Unless someone was really trying to kill them.'

Oh. That was why.

'No. My gut tells me this car accident is wrong.

46

This woman didn't just floor her gas pedal and drive into a tree. And, superficially? Her heavy bleeding from the chest, those wounds seem wrong for a car accident.' Rivers sighed, shook her head. Looked at her feet, then back at the car. 'No. I can't prove it, at least not yet, but this woman, Zina Salim? I'd put money on it: she was murdered.'

Rivers had been right about the press. Instantly, the news media focused on Zina's death, presenting it not as a tragic accident, but as just the most recent of a long list of bizarre occurrences at the old house. By the six o'clock news, tales of the missing actress, the fallen maid, and the murderous father gone amok were resurrected along with that of the mutilated former research assistant. Anchors indicated that the huge house was haunted or cursed, noting that none of the current owners actually lived in it, speculating that they didn't dare reside under its roof.

Hank was not pleased. He turned off the television, glowering. 'Dead. Fault. My.' His eyebrows furrowed.

Trent had stopped by for Happy Hour. He poured Scotch. 'I'm not sure I follow. You're saying it's your fault that the woman drove into a tree?'

'Came here. Help. Asked.'

'Stop it, Hank.' Harper felt bad enough without Hank's help. 'This isn't on us. What were we supposed to do? I was going with her to the house. I was on my way—'

47

'Not. You, Hoppa. I. Man. Can't.' He swallowed his Scotch and stood. Eyes fierce. 'Can't.
Man. Do.' His fist tightened. 'No use.'

'That's not true—'

'What's he saying?' Trent broke in. 'That he's
useless? Come on, Hank – you're strong as an
ox—'

'There was no way either one of us could have
foreseen or prevented what happened.'

'—you've come a hell of a long way since last
year.'

Harper and Trent spoke together, reassuring
Hank, but he wasn't listening. He turned and
stomped away, wobbling slightly.

Harper was on her feet, following, calling.
'Hank – wait.' She caught up to him, took his
arm.

'No, Hoppa.' He resisted, pulled himself away.
'Me. My. Self. Lone.'

Harper let him go, and hugged herself, stunned. Hank had never before pushed her away.
Her chest hurt when she took a breath. Trent
walked over to her, concerned, smelling of
Scotch, asking if she was all right. And as she
lied, nodding, and saying, 'Of course,' they
heard the front door slam.

Trent poured himself another Scotch. 'What's
going on? He's not himself.'

Harper wasn't sure what was going on. But she
didn't want to discuss the possibilities, not even
with Hank's best friend. She sat on the sofa,
picked up her glass.

'Are you two all right?'

What? 'Of course – yes.' The question sur-

48

prised her. Did Trent think there were problems? Did he know something she didn't? 'Everything's fine.'

'Well, it's got to be tough.' Trent stared into his glass.

Tough?

'Hank and all. Now. You didn't sign up for this life.'

Really? What was he saying? Trent had been there when Hank had fallen off the roof. Before that, he'd been Hank's colleague in Cornell's Geology Department. They'd been inseparable, had taught, consulted, conducted research, published articles, even climbed mountains together. But now, Hank could barely speak and had trouble moving on his right side while Trent had become a tenured professor, secure in the lifestyle to which Hank had aspired. And Trent thought that was 'tough'?

Harper's jaw tightened. 'He gets frustrated.' So did she. Frustrated, sad and tired. The day already seemed endless, and it wasn't even dinner time.

Trent drank. 'But he seemed to be doing so well.'

'He *is* doing well, Trent.' Her tone was sharp. 'He's doing incredibly well.'

Silence.

'I didn't mean that he wasn't doing well.' Trent tried again. 'I just meant I've never seen him resentful about his condition before. Not that I blame him – he has every right to—'

'He's adapted amazingly well.' Harper wasn't going to discuss Hank behind his back. 'He's

49

entitled to take a moment.' She tried to convince herself. Remembered the shock of his bear-like body shoving her away.

'Of course. We all need that sometimes.'

The moment strained; Trent had come for a drink with Hank, not awkward and self-conscious exchanges with Harper.

'Well...' they both said it at the same time. Both stood.

'I ought to get home.'

'Vicki must be waiting.'

A quick hug, and Trent took off. Harper sat on the sofa, drinking Scotch, until half an hour later, when Hank reappeared.

'Eat.' He went into the kitchen, took out some eggs.

Harper followed, started chopping onions and tomatoes. Neither of them mentioned Zina or the part they had or hadn't played in her death. Neither referred to Hank's stomping out of the house. They cooked an omelet, ate it quietly and washed up. But they had no real conversation, and Harper, unwilling to be pushed away, didn't even try to touch him for the rest of the night.

Emails and text messages regarding Zina's death flooded the Archeology Department, whose faculty and graduate students assembled in Goldwyn-Smith Hall on Wednesday morning to share their shock and sadness, and to discuss the prospect of a memorial service. They met in a lecture hall, about twenty people huddling in a couple of rows surrounded by a hundred empty seats. Professor Wiggins, Zina's advisor, began by extolling Zina's spirit. Phillip Conrad, a PhD candidate, said he'd arrange to have the service held in the Annabel Taylor chapel. Professor Schmerling, temporary department chair, offered to provide an organist and a tenor. Marge Thomas, one of the secretaries, volunteered punch and cookies.

Harper's attention drifted; she hadn't slept well, tormented by images of Zina's mangled body and disturbed by Hank, who'd tossed and kicked all night. She didn't volunteer for any of the committees, didn't offer to read or to select readings, or to order floral arrangements, or to help print a program with Zina's photo and biographical material. She felt distant from the others, unable to participate. And when the meeting finally broke up, she was the first one out the door, dropping a twenty into the memorial fund; it seemed a trivial amount, but it was all she had in her bag.

'Harper – hold up a minute, would you?' Professor Schmerling called to her from the front of the lecture hall.

She stopped, felt caught. Like a kid trying to skip class. 'Of course.' She turned and smiled, watching him approach. Wondering what he wanted.

'Do you have a couple of minutes?' He looked troubled. Weather and life had carved lines deep into his face, and his half-lenses rode tentatively on the middle of his nose.

Actually, she'd promised Hank she'd take him shopping for work boots. 'Of course...'

'Because – here. Let's sit.' He led her to a back

51

corner of the hall, away from the others.

They sat. He looked at her closely. His eyes were dark, probing.

Harper tried not to squirm.

'So, how are you doing? I understand you were there, at the, uh, scene. You found her; correct?'

Oh Lord. He wanted details? That's why he'd stopped her? Harper nodded. 'Yes. But I'm all right. Thank you for asking.' She started to get up.

'Wait! Sorry, that's not actually what I want to discuss – although, believe me, I do care about how you're doing; don't misunderstand. I imagine it must have been quite terrible to find a colleague that way. Or anyone, really. It would have had to be...' He fumbled with words, reddened, looked away. Folded his hands. 'Nonetheless. Well. As they say: life goes on.'

Harper had no idea what Schmerling was trying to say. 'Yes. It does.' She didn't know how else to respond.

He looked at her again, smiling sadly. 'Good. I'm glad you agree. Because, under the circumstances, what I'm about to say might otherwise seem, well, indelicate.' He paused, cleared his throat. 'Harper. I'd like to know if you're still interested in the Langston research assistantship.'

The Langston research assistantship? Harper's mouth opened. Speechless.

'I'm aware that you'd applied for it last summer, but that it was assigned to Ms Salim. But now that she's unfortunately – that is to say, tragically – unable to complete it, I'm ... The

52

department and the university are hoping you'll be willing to take over.'

Harper's head tilted; her mouth dropped. 'Professor, Zina just died yesterday. She hasn't even been buried.'

'I'm aware.' He stiffened. 'Do you not think I'm aware of that, Harper? I told you it would seem indelicate, didn't I? Nevertheless. The fact remains that Professor Emeritus Langston has left the university his entire priceless collection of Pre-Columbian artifacts, gathered over a distinguished fifty-year career, and, regardless of your or my own personal grief and sympathies, that collection still requires the careful and meticulous attention of a knowledgeable, qualified person so that it can be documented accurately for probate, insurance and tax purposes.' He stopped for a breath.

Harper didn't move. She watched him for a moment. 'With all respect, Professor, what's the hurry?'

Schmerling cleared his throat again. Crossed his legs. Looked over at his colleagues and students lingering across the lecture hall. Finally, he faced Harper. 'I'll be completely candid, but our conversation is confidential, agreed?'

She agreed.

'There has been some ... reluctance among the Langston family to adhere to the terms of the professor's will.' He paused. 'Speaking plainly, the sons are planning to challenge it. They're claiming that Langston was ill, physically and mentally impaired when he drew up the will, that he left his collection to the university while

53

suffering paranoid delusions, and so on. Naturally, their claims are completely without merit, but the university would like to be aware of exactly what is included in the collection, given that the sons have access to it until we actually take possession of it, which we want to do as soon as we can, but might not be able to do if the sons contest the will. In fact, any day now, they might even prevent us from examining the collection because it's on premises willed to them.'

Harper thought of Angus Langston, his indignation that she was on his property.

'So, as insensitive as it seems to press onward, the sooner the cataloguing can be completed, the better. As you know, the terms of the assistantship are generous – your tuition and fees would be covered completely for the term. Professors Hayes and Wiggins would advise you. Frankly, Harper, you're the best-qualified candidate for this. The university needs your help. All else aside, it's a golden opportunity for you, and I'd consider it a personal favor if you'd accept.'

He watched her, waiting. Did he expect her to answer here? Right now?

'Have I overwhelmed you?' He smiled. The lines on his face deepened, became crevices.

'Just a little.' Harper tried to absorb what she'd just heard. She wanted the assistantship, but so soon? Wouldn't grabbing it so quickly be like profiting from Zina's death? 'It's a lot to take in.'

'Not really. All you need to think about is the work itself. Documenting the collection. Any

54

chance you're still interested?'

God help her and Zina forgive her, yes, she was interested. Extremely, avidly, passionately interested. Pre-Columbian symbolism was a focus of her dissertation – the only part of her PhD still to be completed. Of course, definitely yes, she wanted the position, was thrilled at the chance to accept it, to see and examine and touch precious rare artifacts. She couldn't imagine them, couldn't wait to begin. And couldn't say so, not there at the meeting to plan Zina's memorial. Harper sat perfectly still. She opened her mouth, but words wouldn't come out.

Professor Schmerling waited. Cleared his throat. 'Well, I understand that you'll want to think about it. Especially under the circumstances...'

Harper nodded, relieved.

'Why don't you sleep on it? Let me know tomorrow? Or as soon as you can?'

She nodded again. What now? Was she supposed to thank him? It didn't seem appropriate, since the offer had resulted from Zina's death. And he'd labeled it a 'personal favor'; she shouldn't thank someone for asking her a favor. Still silent, unable to figure out what to say, she stood when he did and grabbed her bag.

'I'll call you tomorrow, Professor,' she managed. And hurried for the door.

Harper had walked to campus that morning, feeling restless. In the morning, sunlight had sparkled on red and orange leaves; the breeze had been gentle and warm. But the walk home,

55

just an hour later, was different. The sky had darkened with heavy gray clouds, and the air chilled her. Not only that; the long walk had stressed her left leg. Her war injuries tingled and ached, her leg threatening to cave under her weight.

Slowly, carefully, she made her way to the Suspension Bridge, heading home, replaying her conversation with Professor Schmerling. Absorbed in her thoughts, Harper paid little attention to the Big Red band, practicing for the weekend's Homecoming, marching toward her across the Quad. Students gathered along their path, listening, singing. Sometimes cheering. Harper took a breath, not in the mood for marching bands or team spirit or fun. Even so, as she walked away, she found herself moving in time to a fight song. Drumbeats marking her steps, urging her on.

Crossing the bridge, she didn't make her customary stop to take in the view of the gorge. Didn't pause for even a glance at the rocky walls or gurgling stream below. She simply wanted to get home and talk to Hank about the offer. To think about it someplace quiet and calm.

Approaching her house, though, she realized that it would be neither. Rock music blared, electric and grating, from the fraternity house next door. Members were outside, decorating for Halloween, hanging skeletons from trees, building a fake cemetery in the yard. Planting plastic hands beside Styrofoam headstones, making it look like the dead were clawing out of their graves. Frat boys tottered around, imitating Zombies.

Partying. Starting the Homecoming/Halloween weekend on Wednesday morning.

'Beer?' One called to her in greeting.

Harper smiled, waved. 'Too early for me.'

'Early? I thought it was late – we're still going from last night.' He grinned, turned away.

She limped to the mailbox, took out a pile of mostly junk mail and headed to the house, wondering if Hank was ready to go boot shopping. Noticed an envelope hand-addressed to her.

Postmarked Atlanta. Who did she know in Atlanta? She stopped for a moment, staring at the envelope as if it would explain itself. Not recognizing the handwriting. Then, stuffing the rest of the mail into her big leather bag, she opened it.

Inside was a newspaper clipping. Harper unfolded it, saw an obituary column. With one notice circled: Peter Murray. His picture was there, looking handsome and young. In uniform.

Harper froze, staring at the photo, reading and rereading, trying to understand. Peter Murray. He'd died on October fifth, 'suddenly'. Suddenly? What the hell did suddenly mean? A car crash like Zina? An overdose? A heart attack? A gun to the head? What? She pictured him, back in Iraq, hanging out with Burke Everett. Pete was polite, a gentleman. Almost an anachronism. Opening doors for women, offering his jacket in the cold. Never sitting until women sat. Never cursing or telling a dirty joke in mixed company. Blushing when she did both. Pete Murray was dead?

Harper stood in the front yard, oblivious now to the music blaring next door, not noticing the

57

raucous frat boys rough-housing not twenty feet away. She was absorbed, reading and rereading a death notice. Remembering Burke's call. His insistence on seeing her. Obviously, the call and the death were connected. In fact, Burke had probably mailed her the obituary. Probably wanted to talk about Pete, his death. But that made no sense; he could talk to her about that on the phone. Why did he need to come all the way to Ithaca? Burke was from Milwaukee. How could he have mailed the envelope from Atlanta?

Nothing made sense. Not the letter, not the call, not the offer from Schmerling, not Zina's death. Harper was puzzled, troubled. Her leg throbbed; she needed to sit. To collect her thoughts. Heading into the house, she held on to the obituary as she set the mail and her leather sack on the foyer table.

'Hank – I'm back.' She passed the living room, limped down the hall. Passed the kitchen, looked in. Didn't see him. Heard nothing. 'Hank? You ready to go?' she called again, approaching the study. No Hank. Where was he? Oh God – had something happened?

Her heart skipped, and she saw him again, lying in the hedges, his head cracked and bleeding ... But she kept moving, out of the study, up the stairs, past the nursery, the spare room, going into the bedroom.

'Hank?' she stopped at the door, staring at the bed.

Hank didn't answer. He just lay there, his face blank, watching her.

'What are you doing in bed? It's noon. We're

58

supposed to go get you new boots?' She went to the bed, sat beside him. Rubbed her nagging leg. 'Are you OK?'

Hank stared ahead at nothing. 'Fine.'

Obviously, he wasn't. His eyes were dull, not twinkling.

'What's wrong? You never stay in bed all day. Come on.' She stopped rubbing her leg, tugged at his arm.

He didn't resist. Didn't react at all. When she stopped tugging and let it go, his arm dropped like a stone.

'Hank? Stop. You're scaring me. Get up.'

He blinked, not moving. 'Get. Up.' He finally repeated. 'Why?'

'Why?' Harper sputtered, searching for a reply. But she couldn't find one. Because, other than to follow a conventional routine, there really was no reason for Hank to get up.

She sat on the edge of the bed, silent. Seeing his point of view. Why, after all, should he bother? What was there for him to do? He didn't drive any more. Had trouble walking long distances. Didn't work. Couldn't even do chores, given his weakened right side. Maybe he was sick of going with her to the grocery store or the farmer's market. Of tinkering alone on the house, laying tiles in the bathroom and painting walls, remodeling the house. Of being disabled. Of not being able to speak and live his life the way he wanted to. And, if he were sick of all that, no one could blame him.

She pictured him, the old Hank. The way he'd been before the accident. A hiker, a swimmer, a runner. An athlete in top physical condition. She looked at him now, lying slack against his pillows, felt a familiar pain ripple through her. God, she missed him.

And if she missed the old Hank, Hank certainly must miss him more. The man had every right to mope. When he'd fallen, he'd lost everything: his career as a professor, his ability to speak, his agility, his goals ... hell, his sense of self.

Harper moved closer, lay down beside him. Listened to his breathing.

'We're lucky.' She lifted his hand, kissed it.

He turned his head, scowling doubtfully. 'Not. So. Much. Useless. Should have. Died.'

His answer stung. He wished he'd died? Really? No matter what he'd lost, they still had each other. Wasn't that worth living for? Harper remembered her fear at almost losing him. Watching him fall from the roof. Seeing him unconscious. Waiting through the days of his coma, the weeks of intensive care. The months of intense therapies – physical, speech, occupational, psychological, experimental. And suddenly she felt not just gratitude, but almost painfully intense joy that he was still there, warm and alive, alert enough to be depressed by his condition. Well enough to mourn his lost self.

'But we are lucky.' She propped herself up on an elbow. Touched his stubbly cheek with her free hand. Turned his head and planted a kiss on his lips. 'We have each other. And I love you,' she whispered, kissing him again. 'Even more since I almost lost you.' And again. 'Even more since I see how strong you are, every day.' And she kept it up, kissing his mouth, his cheek, his neck, his chest. Moving down his body and not stopping until he wrapped his arms around her and lifted her to meet her mouth with his. Even then, she didn't let go. She hung on to him with all her strength, as if her love could pull him out of his grief and sadness and make him want to live.

It seemed to work, too, even though it didn't get him out of bed. They lay there together, tangled in each other's arms, legs entwined, Harper's clothes lost in the sheets. Bodies relaxed, eyes closed.

'Mad.' Hank finally sighed. 'I. Can't man. Be.'

'If you were any more of a man, you'd kill me.' Harper grinned at him.

He didn't smile. 'Man. Keeps. Safe. Prot. Tects.'

Of course. This mood was about Zina. That he hadn't been able to help her.

'Friend. Your. Asked help. From.' He paused, licked his lips. Struggling with words. 'I was no help. Now dead.'

Harper kissed his shoulder. 'It wasn't your fault, Hank. Nobody could have predicted what happened.'

'No. Not able.' His body tensed as he repeated. 'Not able. Me. Not. Self. Gone.' His tone was factual, flat. Not maudlin. Not emotional. He kissed her forehead.

Harper wanted to console or encourage him. But what could she say? That he was wrong? That he hadn't changed, that he was still lit and strong and could do whatever he wanted? Enter

61

triathlons? Compete in Iron-man? No. The truth was that his life had changed. A lot. Resting her head on his shoulder, she sighed, feeling helpless. Searching for words. Finding none. Harper lay silent, wondering if either of them would ever get out of bed.

But they did get up. Soon, Hank made an announcement: 'Food.'

In a flash, he was on his feet and in the shower. Then downstairs, cooking. It wasn't until Harper was halfway through a stack of pecan and banana pancakes that she thought about the events of the morning. The envelope containing Peter Murray's obituary. And the offer of the assistantship from Professor Schmerling.

She wanted to talk with Hank about both. But, given his earlier mood, she didn't expect that Hank would welcome either topic. At the moment, mentioning Pete, yet another dead acquaintance, didn't seem like a good idea. But maybe Hank would see the assistantship as a good opportunity, despite the reasons it was available. Maybe she just had to present it positively.

'Pancakes are incredible.' She chewed, assessing his mood. He seemed less bothered. But his eyes seemed altered, as if looking inward. Lacking their usual laughter.

'Secret.' He swallowed. 'Batter.'

Really? She tasted it now, a trace of liquor. 'Cognac? You're a genius.'

'No.' He shook his head. 'Magi. Shun.'

Good. Hank was feeling better. So why was

she hesitant about talking to him? Usually, they were completely open with each other. She should just go ahead and tell him about the offer; Professor Schmerling wanted a quick reply. Harper took a breath, swallowed. Opened her mouth to speak.

'Boots.' Hank began at the same time.

'Hank, there's something I—'

'Go buy? After we. Eat.'

Harper paused. 'Sure. As soon as we're done.'

'Hoppa. What? You were saying?'

Harper put her fork down. Looked at her plate. She might as well just tell him. 'Professor Schmerling took me aside after the meeting this morning.'

Hank chewed, listening.

'He wanted to talk about Professor Langston's collection. He said Langston's family is contesting the professor's will – something like that. So the university wants the collection documented before the lawyers put a halt to it. Which means as quickly as possible.'

'And?' Hank's eyes darkened. He stopped chewing.

'He asked me to take over Zina's job.'

Hank's eyes were cold, stone-like. He didn't move. Didn't say anything.

'He apologized for offering it so soon after Zina's death. But the work needs to be done, and he needs an answer.'

Hank remained silent.

'Look, it would pay my tuition for the whole semester. And I'd probably be able to apply some of the work to my dissertation research.'

Still nothing from Hank.

Harper kept talking. 'The thing is, someone has to do it. And I'm the most qualified of the available grad students, and it's an unbelievable opportunity to work with those actual artifacts, even though, obviously, it's terrible what happened.'

'Know. You.' Or maybe, 'No. You'?

'What?'

'Do. What you. Want. Will.'

Harper crossed her arms. 'What's that supposed to mean? I'm talking to you about it because I want to know what you think before I do anything—'

'No. You. Know. Already made mind. Up.'

'Not true. That's not fair.'

'OK.' Hank pushed his plate away. 'Hoppa. You want my oh. Pinion?'

'Of course I do.'

He scowled, crossed his arms. 'Job. Not good. Bad. Karma. Juju. Vibes.'

'Seriously? Karma? Juju? Vibes? How about shape-shifters? Nahuals? You didn't mention *them*.'

'See. You did know. Do what. You want. Told you. Thoughts. My.' He stood, picked up plates.

'Hank, am I supposed to turn down a great opportunity because you think its bad luck? Because of superstitions? You know we can really use the money.' Especially now that he wasn't working, but she stopped short, didn't say that. Didn't have to.

'Not money only. About.' He turned to face her, dishes in each hand. 'Choice. Yours. Not

64

mine. I'm hus. Band. Not your boss.'

He was right. If he told her not to take the job, she'd resent him for trying to control her. She needed to decide on her own. And, actually, she had. Talking about the artifacts had reminded her how badly she wanted to work with them and convinced her to accept the assistantship.

Harper followed Hank, carrying cups to the sink. Then, as he washed the griddle, she put her arms around him and squeezed. He allowed it, but didn't stop washing. Didn't return the hug. Harper moved away, wondering if she'd been wrong to tell him about the offer. If he was getting depressed again. If her new opportunity was reminding him of his own lost ones. Still, she had a right, even a responsibility to accomplish as much as she could. In fact, she ought to call Schmerling and make it official. Find out when she would start.

She started into the hall to get her phone. But Hank turned off the water, dried his hands and came with her.

'Boots.' He announced. 'Go and buy. Now?'

And they did. Heavy-duty Timberland's. They joked about the frat boys next door. Discussed the music, costumes, Halloween candy, the weather, what they'd have for dinner. But Harper didn't tell Hank about Pete Murray's obituary, and for the rest of the day, made no mention of Zina or the assistantship.

Vicki's hair was darker. She'd rinsed it again, a bluish shade of maroon. 'Are you fucking nuts?' Coffee splashed out of her cup as she set it down, gaping at Harper.

Harper bit off the tip of a bacon slice.

'You're crazy. There is *no* way you should take that job.' Apparently Vicki agreed with Hank.

'Too late. I already called him to accept.'

'So? You can call him back.'

'Why? Vicki, it's a great position. I get to work with actual relics and—'

'And the last two people who did that are dead, Harper. How is it that you do not get that?' Vicki shook her head, looked out the window of State Street Diner where they'd met for breakfast.

'No one's going to hurt me.' Harper shoveled a wad of French toast into her mouth. Chewed. 'Look, you yourself said that whoever killed that researcher twenty some years ago is either old or dead now. And—'

'I said that to calm Zina, who is now dead. Dead, Harper. I saw how scared she was about working there. And now she's dead.'

Vicki sounded like Detective Rivers. 'In a freak car accident. It had nothing to do with the research assistantship.' Besides, Harper was a trained combat officer; she could take care of herself.

Vicki sputtered. 'You asked my opinion. I gave it.'

'The university needs the documentation.'

'If the university is so hell-bent on document-ing that collection, they can move it to university property and post security guards.'

'They can't take it anywhere until the will is settled.'

'Fine. Then let them wait until it's settled.'

66

'But the brothers might mess with it unless it's catalogued. Besides, settling the will could take years; who knows where I'll be then.' Clearly, Vicki, a dentist, had no idea how rare an opportunity Harper had been offered. Not a clue how thrilling it would be to work with rare, Pre-Columbian treasures.

'What did Hank say?' Vicki stuck her chin out, a non-verbal challenge.

Harper hesitated.

'I knew it. Hank doesn't want you to do it either.'

'I didn't say that.'

'Then tell me. What did he say?'

Harper mumbled her answer. 'Basically, he said it was up to me.' Well, not really. Really, he'd indicated that she wouldn't listen to his opinion. That she would do what she wanted to do regardless. That, once again, he felt powerless.

Vicki shook her head again, leaning on her elbows, watching Harper. 'No one who loves you wants you to do this.'

Harper hid behind her coffee cup. They were silent for a while. Finally, a gong rang inside Harper's bag. Harper reached in, dug around for her phone.

'That's your new ringtone?' Vicki frowned.

The gong continued while Harper rifled through keys, flashlight, water bottle, Zina's bangle bracelet, wallet, baby wipes, pens, tampons, chapstick, sunblock ... Damn, where was her phone? Maybe it was Professor Schmerling's office, calling about paperwork. Or maybe

67

Burke Everett was canceling their coffee date.

But when she finally found her phone, caller ID announced Ithaca Police Dept. And by the time she answered, the caller had hung up. She tried to return the call; it went to the switchboard. No way to find out who'd called.

'The cops are calling you?' Vicki wiped her mouth, dropped her napkin on the table. 'Why? Something about Zina?'

'Vicki.' Harper was losing patience. 'How can I possibly know why they're calling? No one was on the line.' She stared at the phone, trying to dismiss her ominous feelings. Telling herself that the caller hadn't been Detective Rivers. That Rivers' instincts hadn't been right; the Coroner's report hadn't indicated that Zina had been murdered. That the police didn't need to talk to her again.

But neither her feelings nor Vicki's chatter would let up. 'Something's wrong, Harper. You know what? I'm thinking maybe Zina's accident wasn't just an accident.' She paused. Then added, 'I'm thinking the police don't want you to take that position either.'

Harper was early for her appointment with Leslie. She'd been seeing her less often – every other week. Now that her flashbacks seemed under control and Hank's health had stabilized, she didn't feel an intense need for a therapist. Until today. Today, she couldn't wait for Leslie to open the door to her cozy, candle-scented, plant-filled inner sanctum with its green leather sofa and steaming sweet teas.

Waiting, she sat, breathed evenly, tried to clear her mind. To think of nothing. Not sure how to do that, not able to picture 'nothing'. So she envisioned an empty room, but Zina appeared inside it, her chest blood-soaked – no. She took another breath, started over. Closed her eyes. Counted, focusing on the numbers. One. She saw it, '1', straight as a spear, strong as an impaling rod. Great. She'd counted all the way to one.

Harper stood, began pacing around the tiny waiting room. Heard Detective Rivers saying that people didn't usually spend the night fearing for their lives and coincidentally end up dead the next morning. Heard Vicki telling her not to take the assistantship, Hank withholding his support. Hank. She worried about him. He was changing. Harper walked in circles, literally spinning. When would Leslie open up? What time was it, anyway?

Finally, the door swung wide, and warm green eyes and a cup of hot spicy chai greeted her. Harper took her place on the sofa beside Leslie and spewed words. About Zina's death. About the assistantship. About Hank.

'He was just lying in bed. Hadn't showered or shaved. He said he didn't see any reason to get up.' Unexpected tears welled in Harper's eyes. 'Which sounded like he didn't see any reason to live. He said he wasn't a man any more. That he couldn't help Zina, couldn't protect her or any-one else.'

Leslie tilted her head, nodded slowly.

When Harper blinked, a tear rolled down her cheek. She swatted at it, despised crying. 'I reminded him that it wasn't his fault, what happened to Zina. And that we're lucky that he survived. And that we still have each other. '

Leslie said nothing.

'And he seemed all right again, for a while. But when I told him about the assistantship, he got distant again. He said that the position was bad luck, but that it didn't matter what he thought because I'd do what I wanted to do anyway. As if his opinion was irrelevant. And the truth? The truth is he was right; I took the position even knowing he didn't want me to.'

Harper stopped. Realized that she was whining. These weren't survival issues. They were trivial, in the scope of life's calamities. What the hell? Why was she sniveling about her husband's moods, her job opportunity? She was tougher than that, Army strong. Not a self-pitying sniveler. And yet, here she was, sniveling the hell out of her hour with Leslie: oh, poor me. Look at what a bad time I'm having.

She began to back off, change the subject.

'No, Harper. Don't try to gloss over this. It's important.'

It was?

'Fact is I've been waiting for something like this to come up.'

Really?

'Sadly, the catalyst was the death of your friend, which we also need to talk about. But one thing at a time. First, let's focus on you and Hank.'

Oh dear. 'OK.'

'Frankly, I think it's a good thing that he's

70

expressing his feelings. Given all that's he's been through, don't you think his attitude has been a little too positive this last year?'

Maybe. Yes, actually.

'Look, Harper. After his accident, the two of you went through incredible stress and anxiety. Both your lives changed dramatically, but – face it, Hank's changed far more than yours. He suffered physical losses like his speech, and professional ones like his professorship. Beyond that, he's inevitably coping with psychological and emotional issues. He's a strong guy, but he's still only human. How has his injury affected his sense of self? His identity? The fact is that Hank needs to rediscover himself and find out a new way to be Hank.'

Harper nodded. She'd known all that. She thought Hank had been working it out, that he'd find his new path with time. 'He's been dealing with all that. It's been over a year, and so far, he's been fine.'

Leslie paused, pursed her lips. 'Hank's had a lot of physical healing to do. That took his energy for quite a while. And you've said he's pretty macho, right? So I imagine he'd fight his emotions. He wouldn't let himself admit how powerless he feels, or how depressed. I mean, would he?'

No. Definitely not. Harper should have known, should have anticipated Hank's emotional reactions to his accident. After all, she'd been terribly depressed after her injuries in Iraq; she was still suffering Post Traumatic Stress Disorder. Why should she expect Hank to be any

71

less vulnerable?

Obviously, because she'd wanted him to be. She'd wanted to believe he was basically unchanged. Still the old Hank.

Leslie went on. 'The fact is that to fully recover, Hank needs to go through this phase. He needs to see himself as he is, to mourn what he isn't any more, to accept what he's lost. He can't really heal or integrate what happened without allowing these feelings to emerge, however sad or angry or frustrated they may be. So in a way, it's a healthy sign that he's not pretending any more that everything's just dandy. He's admitting his emotions, and that's a big step toward coming to terms with what's happened.'

So Hank's depression was a good thing? Harper thought of his losses. Remembered him preparing a lecture, hiking up a mountain trail, setting up a tent in the woods. Whooshing past her downhill on skis ... No. She couldn't go there. That Hank was gone.

The hour was almost up. Harper's chai sat untouched on the coffee table.

'Next time, we'll need to talk about your friend's death and that assistantship. But about Hank – given his tough exterior, I'd bet that he's struggling a lot more than he's letting on. I'd keep a close eye on him.'

She would?

'Make sure he knows that help is available. It's good that you remind him how important he is to you, but he's dealing fundamentally with himself, not your relationship. You can't fix it for him, Harper.'

Leslie's voice was soft but firm. She waited for her comment to sink in. Then added, 'I can refer him to someone. If he's willing. If he'd go.'

Oh God. Did Leslie think Hank was seriously in a crisis? That he needed professional help? 'What are you saying?'

Leslie paused, her eyes steady on Harper's. 'What I'm saying is this: you love this man. You helped him survive. Now, he's got to want to.'

On her Ninja, Harper roared down the hill, letting the chill air slap her. Thinking about Hank. How insensitive she'd been. How oblivious to his feelings. She'd been wrapped up in their life, getting it back, having him home. Continuing her PhD program as if he'd never been hurt. Pretending he was fine. How selfish of her. How superficial. How lonely he must feel.

Well, she'd make it up to him. She'd encourage him to explore new options. Maybe suggest he see a therapist? She pictured it. 'Hank, Leslie has a referral for you. A colleague who can help you.'

He'd resent it. He'd glare. Maybe snarl. 'You think. Need. I. Damned. Shrink?' And stomp out of the room. Slamming the door.

No. Better to be supportive. Wait and see.

Harper stopped for a red light. Looked around the intersection. Pedestrians crossing. Cars waiting. Leaves scattering the street, golden and red. The sky pillowed with purple clouds, foreshadowing winter. She closed her eyes, collecting herself. Focusing on the moment.

Almost time to meet Burke Everett. Damn, she

hadn't even mentioned him to Leslie. Or Peter Murray's obituary. Who had sent it? And why?

The light changed. Harper rode, taking a long route to the Ithaca Bakery, concentrating on motion, the wind on her face, the chill of the air. Trying to think of nothing.

Burke had lost his swagger. He dashed into the Ithaca Bakery, looking over his shoulders, glancing out windows. Drawing attention to himself by trying not to. Spotting Harper at a table near the door, sliding into the seat opposite her.

'We should move.'

Not, hi. Not, good to see you. Not, you look great.

'Move?'

'To the corner.'

He was on his feet, leading the way. Harper followed. Burke positioned himself where he'd have the greatest view of the area: against the wall, facing the room, windows nearby. He looked around, satisfying himself that no one was watching him. Not the table of students across the room, not the elderly man reading the paper, not the guys behind the counter, not the construction workers buying coffee.

Finally, Burke's eyes stopped wandering, settled on Harper. 'You look good.'

'What's going on?' She pictured him back in Iraq. Complaining about the rations. Or the ninety-second showers. Or the heaviness of his gear. Complaining. Always. 'Why are you so jumpy?'

He snickered. 'So much for foreplay.'

'You didn't come all the way from Milwaukee for foreplay.'

'No.' He looked around again. Shifted in his seat. 'Thanks for meeting me.'

Harper riveted her gaze on him. He was practically quivering. 'You hear about Murray?'

Burke's eyes looked away, darted side to side. He hunched forward. Lowered his voice. 'You got the obituary? I sent it while I was there, down in Atlanta. For the funeral.'

Why was he whispering? The funeral was no secret. Burke seemed downright paranoid. Was he having a breakdown? Some vets had trouble adjusting to civilian life, lost their grip. He looked thin, gaunt. Maybe he should eat something. Aromas of fresh bread, sugar, chocolate and cinnamon surrounded them, closing in.

'Why don't we get some food?'

'No – don't get up. Just let's stay here a while.' More looking around. At the door. Out the windows.

'So you drove here all the way from Atlanta?'

He nodded. 'Couldn't risk buying a ticket. Look, I can't stay long. Gotta keep moving.'

'Burke.' Harper leaned back. 'I've got to say it: you seem – nuts.'

He let out a harsh, cough-like laugh, made a nervous, twitchy nod. And looked around again. 'Don't hold back, Harper. Tell me what you really think.'

'Why do you keep looking around? Are you paranoid? You think someone's following you?'

'Shh – not so loud.'

'Burke. No one's listening.' She picked up the sugar dispenser, looked underneath, pointed to the bottom of the glass. 'See? No wires. No bugs. No one's here but you and me.'

She wondered if he was dangerous. Delusional people could get violent. She readied herself, sat alert just in case.

'It's not a joke, Harper. Not after Pete. But you're right; I can see where you're coming from. I'm on edge.' His leg bounced, vibrating the table. 'But I'm not crazy. I swear.'

Harper said nothing, doubtful. Wondered what her responsibilities were, what she should – or even could do for him.

'You got to believe me, Harper; you're one of the good ones. I mean I think about the people I've known. There aren't many I can trust. No matter what, though, even in the worst times, I always knew – right from the beginning back in Iraq, at that camp outside of Mosul – I could count on you. I knew that the first time I saw you.'

He did? Harper tried to recall meeting Burke. Pictured him sweating in his T-shirt, filling a Humvee's gas tank, swatting at flies.

'That's why I came to you. I swear this thing is out of control. People are fucking killing each other.'

Harper watched him. 'Burke. I'm thinking you need to sign yourself into a VA clinic. Get some meds.'

'Fuck I do.' Another quick look around. 'OK. Let me explain. James Henry Baxter. Remember him? Our detail?'

Their detail? The walls of the bakery faded; Harper recalled sweat and sand coating her skin, the grumble of a Humvee's engine, a hot white rocky road stretching out ahead. An ambush. Yes, she remembered. She'd been in charge of the special detail, driving the colonel around Iraq. 'Sure. What about it?'

Burke smirked. 'We thought we lucked out, getting assigned to light duty escorting Baxter. A real plum. You, me, Maurice Shaw, Pete Murray and Rick Owens.'

The detail had lasted just one week. They'd taken Colonel Baxter around so he could attend meetings, befriend local leaders, boost troop morale, inspect projects and sites. Except for one minor skirmish, it had been nothing memorable.

'Turned out the duty wasn't so light – with that ambush. We saved the Colonel's life.'

OK. So what? They'd saved the Colonel from a ragtag bunch of insurgents who'd tossed explosives at their caravan. It hadn't been all that difficult or memorable.

'Shaw never came home, you know. IED.'

Harper hadn't heard. 'Shit. I didn't know.' A flashback rumbled; she saw a burst of white, felt herself flying on to the top of a burnt-out car. Lifting pieces of her sergeant off of her belly. She bit her lip hard, grounding herself with pain. Focused on the smells of cinnamon and baking bread. Burke was still talking.

'...and now, Murray's bought it.'

Murray? Oh, right. The obituary. 'What happened? The obituary didn't say.'

'Because they think he fucking killed himself.'

77

What? Pete Murray? He'd been in her unit. Handsome, in a gingery freckled way. And good-natured, a gentleman even in war. Saying please and thank you even when asking for rounds of ammo. Promising to have people over for sand-free Sunday pot roast when they got home. Never ever cursing, careful to say 'gosh' instead of 'God'...

'His mom found him on the end of a rope in her garage.'

Pete Murray had hung himself? Wow. But then, lots of war veterans had invisible emotional and psychological wounds. Maybe Pete had PTSD. Lord knew that could be deadly. If she hadn't found support – if she hadn't met Hank and found help from Leslie – who knew what would have happened? Maybe she'd have hanged herself, too. Post Traumatic Stress Disorder could rip your mind apart. Could be lethal.

'At least, that's what they say. But you and I know better.'

What? 'Wait. You're saying he didn't hang himself?'

'You knew Pete. He wouldn't impose on his family that way. No, he would never off himself. Listen, Harper – you were Baxter's temporary assistant. Think back. There were five of us in that detail. Two are already dead. And one is the Colonel's personal secretary.'

Interesting. Nice gig. 'Rick Owens? Owens works for the Colonel?'

'He's his fucking personal butt kisser. Which leaves just the two of us loose.'

Loose? What the hell was he talking about?

78

'I'm getting some coffee. You want anything?' She started to stand.

'Wait.' Burke grabbed her arm, stopping her. 'Remember when he – when Baxter left? How we loaded the helicopter?'

Vaguely.

'Remember he had us transfer a bunch of crates?'

She thought back, felt the heat, the dust. Heard the Humvees' motors. The deafening whirr of the helicopter's blades. And she saw the men: Owens, Everett, Murray and Shaw loading it with supplies. Knapsacks. And stacks of boxes.

'I remember. So?'

'So great. Would you testify to that?'

Testify? What? 'Burke.' She tried to sound non-judgmental. 'I don't have a clue what's going on with you, but – honestly. You need help.'

'Listen to me, Harper. Put it together,' Burke sputtered. He still held her arm, tightened his grip. 'Jesus Christ. What do you think was in those boxes?'

She shrugged. 'Supplies?'

His eyes were too bright. 'Guess again.'

Not supplies? What was Burke thinking? That the crates held drugs? Or – oh God – stolen artifacts? She'd heard about priceless ancient relics being looted from Iraq ... But no, that was ridiculous. The Colonel's crates had been legit supplies. 'Burke, this is bullshit. Get help.' She removed his hand from her arm.

His whisper was raw. 'You know that Baxter started his own foundation. It sponsors some serious organizations. Militias and such. Survivalist stuff.'

Really? Harper doubted it; Burke was unbalanced. If he was right, Baxter's activities were surprising. Maybe even disturbing. But it was his right to sponsor organizations, wasn't it? This was a free country.

'Not just your usual survivalist groups, either. I'm talking dangerous people. People infiltrating high places. People who make all those skinhead militia extremist freaks look like your grandma's Canasta club.'

Actually, Burke sounded kind of like a dangerous extremist freak himself. What had happened to him? And why was he so fixated on Colonel Baxter?

His eyes gleamed. 'And now, guess what? Baxter is running for the United States Senate. State of Tennessee.'

So what? Again, even if it was even true, what difference did it make? What did he expect her to do about it? 'Burke. Seriously. What point are you trying to make?'

'Harper – he's funding the campaign with his own cash. Don't you get it? He's spent a few million so far.'

And? Wasn't that his right? 'So?'

Burke's eyes darted from the window to the door to Harper. 'Baxter didn't get rich on a military salary. And he didn't inherit any big money either. His dad was a high school history teacher. And he didn't marry money.'

'How do you know all that?'

'The Internet – you can find shit out about

anybody.'

Harper sighed. She wanted to get Burke help but didn't think he'd allow it. 'So you're saying what? That Baxter got his money from Iraq? That he stole something?'

Burke smiled. 'Bingo.'

'What did he steal?'

He tilted his head, scowling. 'Money. Harper – the US sent billions over there to be used at the discretion of the military.'

She knew about it. Everyone did. The Commander's Emergency Response Program was set up to provide cash for local programs and projects. Funds were supposed to turn enemies into friends, sponsor local initiatives, counter the root causes of instability and marginalize extremist groups.

'Literally, billions are missing. Tons of crates filled with hundred dollar bills.'

'So you think Baxter dipped into CERP and he's using that money to fund his campaign?'

'And his lifestyle. And his foundation. Believe me, our Colonel is one ambitious and dangerous dude.' He looked around again.

Harper frowned. It was no secret that CERP funds had been badly managed. But Burke had no evidence. He was irrational, pooling together unrelated events, jumping to conclusions. 'I don't know—'

'You think I'm nuts.' His leg wouldn't stop twitching. 'Believe me – I thought it was fucking nuts, too, when Pete called to talk about it. But a couple weeks later, boom – Pete shows up on the fucking end of a rope. This is for real, Harper. A

81

lot is at stake. You and I are in danger.'

'No, Burke. I don't—'

'We're the only ones left who knew about the theft!'

'Except that I didn't know about it. In fact, I still don't—'

'That doesn't matter, don't you get it, Harper? He *thinks* you know. Or that you *might* know. And he can't afford to have anyone knowing or even *maybe* knowing. That's why he hired Rick. He bought him off.'

Burke's eyes popped, pupils dilated. There was no point trying to reason with him. Harper let him go on ranting. When he finished, she simply asked, 'Bottom line, Burke. What do you want from me?'

He let out a long sigh. His eyes drilled into hers. 'I need to know that you'll back me up.'

Back him up? 'Back you up how?'

'I'm going to expose him. So if and when the time comes, I need to know you'll confirm what happened with the boxes. Testify that we loaded all that cargo at the Colonel's orders.'

'Burke, I'm sorry. I'm not agreeing to do anything until I'm sure what's going on. Because, frankly, I see not one real piece of evidence to back up your accusations. In fact, the only evidence I see here indicates that you need help and some serious meds.'

'I swear, I'll get you evidence.'

'Aren't you married, Burke?' She interrupted, redirected his attention. 'How's your wife?'

Burke's eyes narrowed. 'How'd you know about that?'

82

'About what?'

'Who told you?'

'Nobody told me anything. I'm just asking—'

'She threw me out. Said it was the war.'

Harper nodded, unsurprised. 'Sorry. Maybe she was right. You should get help.'

'I'm not fucking nuts, Harper.' His gaze pierced her.

A man in a tan suede jacket walked into the bakery, looked around. Talked on his cell phone. Went to buy a Danish.

Burke stiffened, eyeing the man. 'Gotta go. It's not safe. Look – I get that you won't believe me until you see proof. But at least be cautious, will you? Oh – and don't tell anyone you saw me. Don't even mention my name.'

'Burke, that's—'

'Harper, you and I are the only witnesses left. We're liabilities. I'm not fucking with you – Rick's his lackey. And Pete's dead. That's evidence enough, isn't it? That should show you how big this is.' He stood, whispered in her ear. 'I'll explain more next time we meet.'

'What makes you think –' Harper began, but Burke darted away before she could finish her sentence – 'that there'll be a next time?'

The Ninja sped back up the hill, found its way to Stewart Avenue, then up to College Town. Seeing Burke Everett had rattled her. Brought back images Harper didn't want to see. She fought with her memory, focusing on shops windows filled with Halloween decorations: jack-o'-lanterns, skeletons, witches, ghosts. Reminding

83

herself that pedestrians, not checkpoint patrols, stood at intersections; that students toting backpacks, not soldiers lugging heavy gear, occupied the sidewalks. Snipers weren't aiming at her; IEDs weren't buried in the road. Harper raced ahead, trying not to think of Burke Everett or their time in Iraq. But as she crossed the bridge toward campus, she distinctly saw the woman in a burqa standing beside the street. And, oh God. She recognized her. Had seen her before. Knew what she was planning. And this time – even if it killed her – this time, she would stop her...

Harper swerved, made a U-turn, got off her bike. Set out on foot, chasing after the woman, and, locating her, Harper raised a weapon, confronted her. Ordered the woman to put her hands on her head and get on the ground. But the woman stood there, defiant, unmoving. Harper repeated her orders. Asked if the woman understood English. Gradually became aware of voices behind her. People crowding around...

'She has a bomb,' Harper warned. 'It's hidden in her burqa. Stay away – she'll detonate it!'

Nobody responded. Nobody ran to help. Nobody seemed concerned. They stood still, watching her. Tittering. And laughing.

Harper blinked, looked around. Slowly, the sand of Iraq faded, became the concrete of Ithaca. The soldiers became students. Oh God – her gun turned into a flashlight. And the woman – the suicide bomber? Her burqa was flowing, long and black. She stood outside a hookah shop, an inanimate mannequin dressed like a Halloween witch. Complete with broom.

Oh God. Harper felt her face burn. She hadn't had so severe a flashback in more than a year. Faces surrounded her, leering, questioning, mocking.

'Look out – the mannequin has a bomb.' Someone snickered.

'What is she on?'

'Whatever it is, I want some!'

'Cut it out – she's mentally ill.'

'Right. Listen to the Psych major.'

'Seriously.' Someone touched her arm. 'Are you OK?'

Harper took a step back. Looked at the faces. Oh God. 'Fine.' Another step back. 'I was just – I'm fine.' She fled to her bike, set it right, jumped on and sped away, feeling eyes on her all the way across campus until, ignoring the grave-yard, pumpkins and skeletons in the yard next door, she finally made it home.

Hank looked up from a soup pot. His eyes were twinkling like usual, and something smelled wonderful. 'Chili.' He told her. 'Veggie.'

'Yum.' Harper tried to smile. Tried to stop trembling and act normal. She kissed him, asked how he was.

'Mood. Better.' He stirred in some cumin. 'Busy. Helps.'

He was talking about his feelings. A good sign. 'You?'

Harper looked away. He wanted to know how she was. What should she say? That she'd just had a humiliating flashback? Or endured a crazy visit with paranoid Burke Everett? Or accepted

85

Zina's assistantship, about which he'd had serious reservations? No. She couldn't risk talking about any of those things, at least not yet. Hank was feeling better but his mood was probably still fragile. She didn't want to upset him and send him into another bout of depression. 'I'm fine. I had a busy day, too.'

He nodded. 'Good. Stuff done?'

He assumed she'd been in the library, gathering research for her dissertation. It was where she should have been. 'Not a whole lot. I wasted time.'

He shrugged, tasted his chili. 'Some days. Happens.'

'Need any help?' Harper took out her phone, texted Leslie: *Can U C me? Bad flashback.*

'Salad. Make.'

Harper took out a bag of pre-washed lettuce, a bag of walnuts. Maybe it wasn't really a relapse. Maybe her PTSD wasn't getting worse; she'd just been reacting to seeing Burke again, and the flashback had been like an allergic response. A case of emotional hives; embarrassing, but not really a big deal. Her face reddened at the thought of the witch in College Town. The crowd staring at her...

'Today. Nahual here.'

What? Harper looked up, saw Hank's playful smile. She crumbled blue cheese into the salad bowl. Why would he ask that? 'A Nahual. You saw one?'

'Yes. True.'

'Not funny.' What was he doing? Why would he make light of Zina's fears? Was he mocking a

86

dead woman? No, Hank wouldn't do that. So what was he doing? Harper began slicing an onion.

'Want. To meet. Him?'

Really? 'You're asking if I want to meet a Nahual?' He was going to introduce her to a shape-shifter? Harper looked at him, confused.

Hank turned off the stove, stepped over to her, took the knife from her hands and set it on the counter. When she turned, he engulfed her in his arms and kissed her.

'Hoppa. I am. Nahual.' His breath tickled her ear. 'Shift. My shape.'

Oh my, Harper thought as Hank pressed against her, and, feeling what he meant, she laughed out loud. It was funny. Hank was joking, must really be feeling better. And so, despite her troubling day and unsettled thoughts, she accompanied him upstairs, hoping that Hank's depression was easing and that his big warm body would comfort her. Or at least for a while, empty her mind.

Afterwards, eating dinner, Harper intended to tell Hank about her day. But every time she began, she stopped herself, heard Leslie warn, 'He's probably struggling more than he lets on.' Was he struggling? She watched him eating, spooning up his chili with gusto.

'Something?' Hank felt her watching him.

'No.' She smiled. 'Not really.' A lie. Why not just blurt out the truth, that, after taking the assistantship despite his objections, she'd had a disturbing visit from a paranoid guy she'd served with, followed by her worst flashback in a year?

'Know you. Tell me. What?'

Damn. Hank was no fool; he knew something was bothering her. But she heard Leslie warn that Hank was vulnerable: 'I'd keep a close eye on him if I were you.' Harper wasn't sure how stable Hank was, didn't want to send him spiraling back into feelings of powerlessness and depression. He was watching her, waiting for an answer.

'It's been a long day, that's all.' Not a lie. That was true. Harper took a sip of wine. Avoided eye contact.

'Talk. Me.' He ripped off a chunk of fresh bread. 'Want?' He held the chunk out.

'Thanks.' Harper took it, stalling by spreading butter on it. Maybe she should just tell him part of what had happened. Maybe about the assistantship. But that might start a whole chain of anguished conversation about Zina's death and bad karma and danger, would no doubt depress him again. Better if she began with Burke Everett's visit and his insane claims about the Colonel; after that, she could tell him about her flashback.

'OK? Chili?' Hank watched her. No doubt wondering why she was so quiet.

'Delicious.' It was, too. Rich and spicy. But why was she making small talk? She needed to be open and talk to Hank even if it might affect his mood. She took a long sip of wine. Drew a breath. Opened her mouth, ready to begin. Chickened out. 'Where'd you get the recipe?' What was wrong with her?

'Book. But changed. Improvised.'

Wow. He'd just said, 'improvised'? That might have been the biggest word he'd managed since his accident. 'You're an amazing man, Hank.'

He winked. 'Not bad. Nahual. Too.'

She met his eyes, returned his grin. Oh God. What was she doing? Playing happy housewife after publicly attacking a mannequin?

Harper took another gulp of wine. Blurted, 'I had a visit today. From a guy I served with.'

Hank broke off a piece of bread. 'Wow. The blue. Out of?'

'Pretty much. He looked me up because another guy we knew there – Pete Murray – died. Hanged himself.'

Hank frowned, stopped buttering and looked at her. But his eyes sparkled, alert. Not depressed.

She swallowed more wine, measuring Hank's mood, deciding that he was fine. It was all right to continue. She was about to tell him about Burke's conspiracy theory that Colonel Baxter had stolen millions from Iraq's CERP funds to start his own extreme political movement, that he'd killed Peter Murray for figuring it out. That he might kill Burke for the same reason. And might come after her.

'The guy – his name is Burke. He's got lots of issues. Seems paranoid.'

Hank frowned. 'How?'

Harper was about to explain all about Colonel Baxter and Burke's theories. And she would have, too, but just then, the doorbell rang.

The fraternity next door was celebrating in

89

anticipation of the weekend: the rare and spectacular simultaneity of Homecoming and Halloween. The smell of beer and marijuana permeated its yard, drifted through the neighborhood. Detective Rivers had beeped her siren and flashed her lights, just to give them a scare, had watched the brothers scurry for cover, disappearing into bushes, turning lights out inside the house. When Harper opened the door, she was still shaking her head.

'Year after year,' she sighed. 'It never changes. The government ought to give up already and make all that stuff legal. Make it a lot easier on us cops.'

Harper wasn't sure exactly what Rivers was talking about. 'Come in,' she held the door open.

Rivers looked haggard. 'I called you earlier, Mrs Jennings, but you didn't pick up. So I thought I'd stop by.'

Harper swallowed. 'We're just eating. Join us? Want some chili?' Her heart rate sped up a notch. Why had Rivers come over?

'I shouldn't—'

'How are. You?' Hank stood at the kitchen door, remembered the detective from the drug incident a year earlier. 'Come in. Eat.'

'Good to see you looking so well, Mr Jennings.'

'Hank. Call me.' He led her into the kitchen.

Harper filled another bowl with chili. 'Something to drink, Detective?'

'Water, thanks.'

The three of them sat at the table. Rivers marveled at the chili. 'Delicious. Who's the cook?'

'Hank.'

Hank beamed. 'Chef. I'm good.'

'You sure are. This is perfect.'

Harper refilled her wine glass. Drank. What the hell was Rivers doing at their dinner table? Why were they sitting around chatting like old friends?

Rivers swallowed. 'So.' She turned to Harper. 'I hear you've taken that Langston assistantship.'

Damn – Harper hadn't formally told Hank yet. She glanced at him, caught his frown. Did he think she was hiding her acceptance? 'That's right. I accepted it just this morning. How did you find out so fast?'

Rivers smirked. 'Mrs Jennings, I'm an investigator.' She lifted her spoon to her mouth, chewed. 'Frankly, between you and me, I'm not thrilled with your decision, given that the last two research assistants were murdered.'

'Murdered?' Harper echoed as Hank said:

'What?'

Hank dropped his hunk of bread on to the table. Stopped eating.

'Oh damn. You didn't know?'

Harper saw Zina, sitting in the woods, blood-drenched and lifeless.

'I tried to call and give you a heads up, but by now, I assumed you'd heard.' Rivers looked from one stunned face to the other. 'I guess you haven't seen the news.'

No. Not since the morning paper.

'Well, it's been reported all day. It'll be on the eleven o'clock news and tomorrow's headlines.'

What would?

91

'Zina Salim's death was no accident. Definitely a homicide.'

Harper swallowed. Stiffened. 'But I thought the crash...?'

'No. The crash didn't kill her.' Rivers paused, put down her spoon. Cleared her throat. 'We don't know why the car hit the tree. Maybe she was driving fast, being pursued by someone. Or dodging something, so she lost control of her car. But when Ms Salim got out of the car, she wasn't bleeding much, if at all.'

'So? Then?' Hank's voice was hushed.

'So then someone killed her. And they posed her body upright, in a sitting position.'

Harper swallowed wine, remembering the last research assistant, the one from twenty-odd years ago. Hadn't her body been propped up, seated like a sentry?

Even so, she couldn't accept it. 'Maybe the crash caused Zina's injuries. Maybe she fell or crawled out of the car and tried to get up but couldn't and died in a sitting position.'

Again, the detective paused, dabbed her mouth with her napkin and looked directly at Hank, then at Harper. 'Well, I suppose that would have been a possibility. Except for one thing.'

'What?' Harper looked at Hank; his face was blank. Puzzled.

Rivers pursed her lips. 'The fatal injuries weren't caused by the car crash. This murder is exactly like the one from 1989.' She met Harper's eyes. 'Zina Salim's body was mutilated. The killer took her heart.'

* * *

They washed the dishes in silence. They both knew the implications. Had discussed them at length with Rivers. Harper rolled the conversation around in her mind.

'What do you think it means?' Rivers had addressed them both.

Hank had been silent, waiting for Harper to answer. Knowing what she'd say.

'I have no idea.' Harper had condensed her comments. 'But in many Pre-Columbian cultures, taking hearts was an accepted practice. Victors cut them out of vanquished enemies. Priests would sacrifice the hearts of conquered warriors to the gods.' She'd stopped, leaving it at that.

'Go. On.' Hank had pressed. 'Tell eating them.'

Oh Lord, really? Why was that relevant?

Rivers looked puzzled. 'Eating?'

Harper sighed. 'Well, it's not proven. But, yes. Some scholars theorize that Pre-Columbians believed that a person's strength was located in the heart. So, to acquire someone's strength, they took the heart out and ... ate it.'

She'd cleared her throat, tried not to think about the fate of Zina's heart.

Rivers had folded her hands on the table. 'So this heart-taking is Pre-Columbian in origin.'

Harper had shrugged. 'It may be. But we can't be sure—'

'Pre-Columbian, just like Langston's relics. The ones that both victims just happened to be working on when they were killed.'

Harper had nodded.

'Is it common knowledge about the hearts? Would lots of people know about this practice?'

'Not. Lots.' Hank shook his head.

'But it's no secret,' Harper added. 'Anyone who's read about Pre-Columbian history would know. Or traveled and visited ruins. Or studied—'

'OK. I get it,' Rivers cut her off. 'So there's a select group who'd see the connection. But they don't have to be experts or scholars like yourself.'

Like herself? What? Had Rivers been implying that she'd had something to do with Zina's death? Harper had bristled, straightened her posture. Prepared to defend herself.

But Rivers had simply sighed and asked Harper and Hank to let her know if they had further thoughts concerning the murder. Then, thanking them for the chili, she'd taken off, advising Harper to be careful working with the relics. 'Remember, two women have already died at that place.'

Silently, Harper and Hank finished in the kitchen. It wasn't until they were in bed that she finally spoke. 'Just so you know, I was going to tell you I'd taken the assistantship. I just didn't—'

'You can. Still. Quit.'

She took his hand. 'I know.'

'Will you?'

She probably should. Under the circumstances, no one would blame her. 'I promised Schmerling I'd do it. They're counting on me.'

'Schmer. Ling would. Understand.'

'But I can't just quit – I haven't even started yet.'

'Can turn down. Murderer. Loose.' He lay on his side, facing her, his eyebrows furrowed. 'Zina. Saw Nahual. Sensed danger.'

'Her imagination ran away with her.'

'She's dead, Hoppa. Not imagined. Killed. Real. Job bad. Karma. Evil.'

There he was with his bad Karma Juju Hoodoo Vibes again. 'Hank, don't even pretend to believe in superstitious mumbo—'

'Places. Things. Can. Be bad.' He didn't smile. Seemed serious. But how could he be? Hank was a geologist, had a PhD. Had traveled all over the world. How could he believe that locations could possess 'good' or 'bad' vibes?

Obviously, he must not mean it literally. He must just be worried about her. 'It's OK, Hank. I can take care of myself. I'm not like Zina – I'm Army. A trained combat officer. I mean it – bring it on. Let her killer try to mess with me – I'll take him down in a heartbeat.' Oops. Wrong expression.

'Damn Hoppa.' Hank wasn't impressed. He sighed. 'OK. But. With. I'm going.'

Really? He'd go with her? And do what? Hold her hand? Hang around bored all day? 'How about this: I'll go and assess the situation. If it seems even the least bit dangerous, you can come along—'

'No, this how about? Come. Me. Along. Assess. With. You.' He sounded adamant.

'It's not necessary.' She leaned over and kissed him. 'But thank you.'

95

'Hoppa.' He wasn't backing down. 'Dead. Serious.'

He was right. It was serious. Harper saw Zina's slumped, blood-soaked body. Why was she making light of the danger, ignoring Hank's concerns? Maybe he was right that she should turn down the assistantship, forget about working with the relics. She pictured herself at Langston's – personally examining rare, never-displayed ancient artifacts, documenting them, holding them in her hands. Making tangible contact with a culture lost centuries ago – how could she explain to Hank the thrill she felt even thinking about it? No, she didn't want to give up this opportunity, wouldn't be so easily scared off.

'Killer. There.' Hank persisted. 'Zina. Nahual saw.'

'What are you implying? That an actual Nahual was protecting the artifacts, that he killed Zina and took her heart? Because that is utterly beyond ridiculous.'

Hank didn't reply. He lay back, folding his hands on his chest, staring at the ceiling, leaving Harper to think about her attitude. Was she being foolish? Was there, as Detective Rivers suspected, a connection between Zina's terrors of a Nahual and her murder the very next morning? Had someone been stalking her, someone she'd mistaken for a shape-shifter? And, if so, what was his motive? Did it have to do with the collection? Was everyone who worked with it going to be targeted?

Maybe. Even probably.

Damn. Hank was right. She should at least let the murder investigation proceed before recklessly putting herself in danger.

'OK. You win. I'll talk to Schmerling.' She sighed. 'I'll tell him I don't want to work there unless he can guarantee it's safe.'

'Hoppa. For real.' Hank raised an eyebrow, doubtful. 'Promise.'

Harper bit her nail, and her voice was husky with resentment. 'Promise.'

She lay back against her pillows, but she tossed, picturing crates filled with carved vessels and masks, figurines of marble, silver and gold. And when she finally drifted off, she dreamed of an immense ebony warrior, poisonous serpents emerging from his mouth, his helmet and the twist of his belt.

The memorial service was well attended. The chapel in Annabel Taylor Hall was full. The press was there, as was the entire Archeology Department, along with members of the press, a number of university bigwigs, including the Provost, the Chancellor, the Dean, and a slew of people who hadn't even known Zina, who were simply curious about the murder.

Harper sat with other graduate students, between Philip Conrad and Stacey Cohen. As a small choir sang 'Amazing Grace', Philip leaned over, whispering, 'Sad about her family, isn't it?'

It was? 'Why?'

'Well.' He looked around. 'She has four brothers and family living in New York. Not one of them came.' He shook his head, disapproving.

97

Covered his mouth with his hand as he whispered. 'They wouldn't have any part of this. Flatly refused. They said it was a matter of honor.'

Honor? Why? Getting murdered was dishonorable?

'I don't get it. It's about women in their culture or their religion.' He stopped abruptly as the singing ended and the chapel hushed.

A pastor led the twenty-third psalm, then invited people to speak. One of Zina's housemates read a poem. 'I Did Not Die,' she recited. 'By Mary E. Faye. Do not stand at my grave and forever weep. I am not there. I do not sleep...'

Another housemate talked about how ambitious and smart Zina was, how she'd overcome the constraints of her family and fought to establish her own identity on her own terms. The third one broke down and couldn't read, so someone volunteered to read her notes, in which she promised never to forget Zina, her strength, and her spicy couscous dishes.

Harper listened, moved by the statements, wondering why she'd never seen in Zina the qualities extolled by her friends. Maybe she'd been foolish to resent her, competing against her instead of getting to know her.

Professor Wiggins stood and talked about Zina's commitment to Archeology. He confessed to being awed by her uniquely powerful and determined spirit. His affect seemed wrong, almost joyous, and his comments were followed by awkward silence until Phil got up and talked.

Phil described first meeting Zina, being intimidated by her dark, enchanting beauty, and trying to impress her with his knowledge of Indian culture, only to find out later that her family was from Syria, and that he must have sounded idiotic.

Finally, Professor Schmerling gave a eulogy, praising Zina's initiative, persistence and talent. He closed by inviting everyone to mingle and honor Zina by informally sharing their memories. One of Zina's friends played the Beatles' 'Blackbird' on the guitar as people filed out to the lobby where Marge, the department secretary, was serving cookies and punch.

'That was nice.' Tears swelled in Stacey's eyes, threatening her mascara. 'You did a great job, Phil. You lightened it up.'

'Someone had to. Especially without her family here.'

'Yeah. That's terrible.'

Phil picked up a piece of shortbread. 'You have to give her credit, though. Standing up to them.'

'Standing up to them?' Harper had no idea what they were talking about.

'Yeah,' Stacey sniffed. 'Her housemate Sonja, the one who read the poem—'

'I talked to her while I was arranging this,' Phil interrupted. 'I wanted to include Zina's family, but Sonja told me that was out of the question. That they'd told her she was dead to them.'

'What? Why?'

Phil sighed. 'Long story.'

'They arranged a marriage for her—' Stacey began.

Again, Phil cut her off. 'She said they did it for business. They're into international importing

99

and exporting. Art, antiques, high-end collectibles – that kind of stuff. Apparently, to promote their interests, they promised Zina to a wealthy client back in Syria. She'd never even met him.'

'Never mind he was thirty years older than she was and had two other wives. Can you believe it? Zina was accomplished and independent, getting a PhD from an Ivy League university.' Stacey was incensed. 'And her family was forcing her into an arranged polygamous marriage? Positively medieval.'

Harper agreed.

'Zina refused, of course,' Phil added. 'She wouldn't go back to Syria, wouldn't meet with her brothers in New York, wouldn't agree to the marriage. She flat out defied her family, which evidently infuriated them. I assume that's why they wouldn't attend the service.'

Harper didn't know what to say. Zina had been stronger, far more complicated than Harper had imagined.

'And that's the least of it.' Stacey swallowed a bite of sugar cookie. 'Sonja said that by refusing the wedding, Zina had dishonored her family. And she was worried there would be consequences.'

Consequences? Like what? They'd ground her? 'What consequences? They couldn't force her to get married.' Could they?

Stacey looked at Phil. Phil looked away, shrugged. 'Harper,' he said, 'in some cultures, women represent the honor of the family. Being dishonored isn't taken lightly.'

Harper blinked, as if snapping back to consciousness. Of course – she ought to have realized, having dealt with some of those cultures during the war. She knew what he was about to say even before the words left his mouth.

'At the time, Sonja assumed "dead" was just a figure of speech. But Zina told her otherwise. Because she'd dishonored her family, she was literally dead to them. And, if they ever saw her again, or if she ever tried to go home, they'd kill her.'

An honor killing? Harper pictured Zina, her confident, assertive attitude. Her ambition. And her lifeless, bloodied body. Was it possible that her own relatives had murdered her for defying them? For shaming them?

Harper had first heard of such things while in Iraq. Incidents where family members – brothers, husbands, fathers or even mothers – killed their sisters, wives or daughters for shaming them. For not being virgins. For falling in love with the wrong man. For trying to get a divorce. For going out alone in public, dressing and behaving too 'westernized'. She'd heard about these killings and maimings of women, but, in Iraq, she'd never personally encountered any.

But now there was Zina. Was it possible that Zina had been killed by her own family? Harper couldn't imagine it. And yet, it was possible. Maybe even likely.

'Do the police know about this?' she began.

Phil nodded. 'I told them myself – and I know Sonja did.'

'I mentioned it to that woman detective who came to the Archeology office.'

101

So Rivers knew about the honor killing possibility. Why hadn't she mentioned it?

'So is it true you're taking over Zina's assistantship?' Phil asked. 'There's a rumor—'

'Lovely memorial, wasn't it?' Professor Schultz, a member of Phil's dissertation committee joined their cluster, and Phil began chatting him up. Stacey went to refill her punch.

'Harper.' Dean Van Arsdale suddenly approached, Professor Schmerling at his side. 'Thank you for stepping up on the Langston project.' He put a hand on her shoulder and squeezed. 'Especially in these circumstances – we all appreciate it. Myself especially. Good luck with it.' He flashed some teeth and kept moving, releasing her shoulder in order to extend his hand to someone else.

Oh dear. How awkward – she'd promised Hank she'd turn the position down. But Professor Schmerling was still standing there, handing her an envelope. 'Contract, detailed instructions and the keys to Langston's,' he said. 'Return all four signed contract copies to my office any time next week. And again, thank you.' He nodded, started to walk off.

'Wait – Professor? I need to talk about this.' She held out the envelope, trying to return it.

Schmerling kept nodding, walking away. 'Call me with any questions. The instructions are quite clear.' The Dean joined him, pulled him away.

Harper stood in the middle of the crowded lobby, holding the envelope, surrounded by the buzz of conversation, thinking of the assistantship and how embarrassing it was going to be to turn it down. But how could she complain? Embarrassment was nothing compared to what Zina had endured. She thought of Zina's last minutes. The horror of knowing that her own flesh and blood were taking her life – if, in fact, they had. But it made sense, didn't it? The family wouldn't even come to her memorial service; maybe that was because they were responsible for her death.

It was too much, too awful. Hoping for quiet, Harper stepped outside but was immediately assaulted by blaring brass and pounding drums. The Big Red Band paraded down College Avenue, promoting the next day's Homecoming game. Life and football went on as usual, not even pausing for a woman's murder.

Harper closed her eyes, leaned against Annabel Taylor's wall, absorbing the vibrations of the band, holding the envelope with the contract and the Langston keys. Damn. She'd promised Hank she'd turn it down, but according to Phil, everyone in the department had already heard she'd taken it. And Dean Van Arsdale and Professor Schmerling – the whole university was counting on her to get started. She pictured rooms filled with relics. Mysteries of time preserved in boxes. She opened the envelope, took out the keys. Looked at them.

She could just go over and glance at the collection. Just take the briefest peek. What would be the harm in that?

No – what was she thinking? She'd promised Hank she wouldn't go until she was sure it was safe.

But that was before she'd known about Zina's family. Now, it seemed that Zina's death had been an honor killing, that she'd been killed by her own relatives. In that case, there was no danger to anyone else. What would be the harm in just stopping by?

She could just go look at it. Not actually begin work – merely peek at a few pieces. See how Zina had left things. What the place looked like. How it was set up. She'd spend just two or three minutes – at most five.

She'd call Hank and let him know that it was safe, that he didn't need to worry – maybe just send a text message to avoid a discussion. Harper dug around her bag, pushed aside the flashlight, her wallet and Zina's bracelet, located her phone. Saw that she'd missed some calls. Good God, three voicemails from Burke Everett. The lunatic was stalking her. She played back his first voice message.

'Harper – I'm being followed. You might be, too. Keep your eyes open and be careful. I'll be in touch.'

The next: 'Harper, they know I'm here. Watch your back. They've figured out I came here to see you. So they know you know what I know – sorry I put you in danger.'

The last: 'I have to ditch my cell. They're tracking me on it. I'll call you when it's safe.'

Burke had completely lost it. Wherever he was, he needed help. Lord. She hoped he wouldn't harm anyone. Hoped he'd call again so she could get him to a hospital.

The last message was from Leslie, her soothing

104

voice agreeing to could see Harper at four o'clock.

Good. Four o'clock.

It was hours away. She had plenty of time.

Before she went to her Ninja, Harper sent Hank a text. *No need 2 quit! Will explain. Making a stop. C U 2ish.*

Then, dropping the keys and phone into her bag, she headed to her motorcycle and roared away. She had gone all the way to the Langston's long private driveway before the question came to mind.

If her family had killed Zina, why had they taken her heart?

She didn't have an answer. She'd never heard of it being part of any honor killing before. But then, she was no expert on the subject. Maybe it was symbolic in some cultures. Harper was still considering the missing heart as she confronted the yellow police tape still draped across the drive, blocking the road to the Langston house. Police and the press had been gone for some time; evidence had been gathered and removed. But the tape remained, wrapped around the area where Zina's body and car had been found. Harper didn't want to mess with the police, so she got off her bike and walked it through the trees around the taped off area, parking it near the house.

Up close, the place was much larger than she'd imagined. Like some once grand and elegant hotel. Rambling and endless, hollow and forlorn. Haunted, even. Odd that Zina hadn't mentioned that paint crumbled on the porch pillars, that wood rotted on the frames of windows and double doors. A riser was missing on the front steps. The roof sagged. Parts of the house literally seemed to be crumbling. Well, never mind. Harper was well acquainted with worn-out floorboards and loose shingles; she and Hank had been renovating their own old house for years. And in Iraq, sometimes, living conditions made this place look like five star luxury. So, undaunted, Harper left her Ninja and plowed through ankle deep fallen leaves toward the house.

Climbing the front steps, she reached into her bag for the house key, found her cell phone instead, thought briefly of calling Hank, decided that there was no reason to; she'd be on her way home in a few minutes. Finding the key, she unlocked the elaborately carved double door, stepped inside. And sneezed.

Dust was everywhere. Clouds of it. Specks as large as snowflakes. She saw it floating around her, illuminated by light beaming from the windows. Harper looked around the foyer, saw a high, rounded dome with a heavy crystal chandelier, a spiral staircase, marble floor, ragged Oriental rug.

Harper noted the worn carpet leading to the second floor. The faded wallpaper, curling at the corners. To her right, walnut panels and closed doors. Corridors leading to various wings of the house. To her left, another corridor, and the entrance to a cluttered living room, the surfaces of sofas and chairs buried beneath journals and publications. A large marble fireplace gaped from the opposite wall, filled with burned wood and ashes, surrounded by stacks of firewood.

Harper was tempted to explore the publications – the professor probably had a treasure trove of archeology literature. But that was his personal property; besides, she couldn't wait to get a look at the collection, which her instructions said was on the third floor, at the east end of the building. In seconds, she'd gone up the spiral staircase to the landing, then up another flight of steps to the floor above. Then down a long hallway, passing door after door until she came to an arch that divided the east wing from the core of the house. On the other side of the arch, she confronted the collection.

No one had prepared her for what she saw. Not Professor Schmerling, not Zina. No one. When she entered the east wing, Harper stopped, gaping at the dozens of pine crates stacked in the hall. She stepped around them, looked into the first room she passed. Saw a few worktables, a computer. Shelves of small cases, notebooks and more boxes.

The next two rooms were loaded wall to wall with various-sized containers and boxes. Harper gaped, overwhelmed. The collection was huge – far larger than she'd imagined. She stepped into the last room, squeezing between rows of mid-sized cartons, noticing that each had a note taped to it. She stooped to read one:

Early/Middle Mohica, Loma Negra, 300 BC–300 AD. 6 ¾ inches high. Copper warrior mask, slight damage. Est. $5000–$7000.

Really? She had to see it. Box cutters were all

over the place. Harper took one and slit the seal of the package. Opened it. Began removing the packing material wadded up inside—

'Excuse me!'

Harper jumped, sent the box cutter clattering to the floor.

'You want to tell me what you're doing in there?'

A man stood in the doorway, glaring. At first she thought it was Angus. His hairline was receding like Angus's, and he was thin and tall. Same prominent cheekbones. But this man had a ponytail. Wasn't Angus. Another of the professor's sons?

Harper's heart was still somersaulting. She took a breath. 'Sorry if I startled you.' Actually, she was the one who'd been startled. 'I'm here from the university.'

'The what? You're fucking kidding me.' He shook his head. 'Those sons of bitches don't waste any time, do they? That last one isn't even buried yet.'

Actually, Zina was going to be cremated. But Harper didn't explain that; she got his point.

'Well, go ahead. Knock yourself out – make all the lists and labels you want. But you're wasting your time.' He watched her for a moment, must have realized he'd been acting belligerently. Backed down a notch, nodded at her. 'I'm Jake Langston.'

Harper breathed. 'Harper Jennings.'

'So you're a grad student like the last one – like Zina?'

'Yes. Same department.'

Jake reached into his vest, pulled out a pack of Camels, offered her one with tobacco-stained fingers. Lit up when she declined. 'I'll share something with you, Harper Jennings. It doesn't matter how many lists you make or pictures you take. The university isn't getting any of this collection. Not one single arrowhead. Everything here belongs to my family.'

Oh great. Jake was going to argue with her about the professor's will? Get into details of the lawsuit? Harper didn't want to hear about it, had no part in the dispute. She just wanted to take a look at the mask in the box she'd opened. 'Look, I'm just here to document—'

'Even so. You ought to know what you're getting into. The will that leaves the collection to the university is, excuse the expression, a piece of shit. My father didn't have a clue what he was doing when he wrote it. For the last few years, his mind was gone. He was senile.'

'But I thought he made the donation decades ago.' Back in the eighties, before the first research assistant had been killed.

Jake exhaled a smoke ring, shook his head. 'No.'

'But wasn't there a research assistant—?'

'Yes, Carla. Pretty Carla.' He picked a shred of tobacco off his tongue. 'I was in my first year of college, fantasizing about asking her out. I was too shy, of course. Still, all of us tried to catch her eye. Angus, Caleb—'

Caleb?

'He's the oldest. Married, lives in Oregon.' Jake smiled, shook his head. 'But Carla stole my heart.' He stopped, cleared his throat. 'Sorry. Poor choice of expression. But all of us were smitten. Even Angus's friend, Digger. And Digger wasn't easily impressed.'

Why was Jake telling her all this?

'You know, they never found out who did it. And now, Zina's dead, too.' He looked at Harper too steadily. For too long. As if testing her reaction.

Harper met his eyes. Stared back. Wondered how well he'd known Zina. Obviously, well enough to call her by her first name.

Finally, Jake looked away. 'My father was still teaching back then; Carla was one of his research assistants, and he assigned her to inventory everything. For insurance purposes, I guess. But his will? No. He wrote that a few months before he died, when he had dementia. Otherwise, he'd never have given everything away.'

Harper chewed her lip, not sure what to say. She eyed the open box, trying to glimpse a bit of copper. Wished he would leave.

But Jake didn't leave. He stood there, tall, gangly. Middle-aged skin loose under his jaw. Spewing smoke into dust-filled air. 'It's obvious how confused he was – you can see for yourself. Father was always meticulous. He kept neat, careful records, labeled everything.' Jake let out a harsh, ragged cough. 'But the last few years, as his mind went, he took relics out, repacked them someplace else but didn't write down or remember where. Then he'd search for them. I'd come by to check on him and find an artifact worth fifty thousand in the laundry basket – or worse, in the washing machine. Some never turned up. You'll see how it is. Clutter and chaos. The collection – hell, the whole house – is a portrait of Dad's confusion.'

Oh dear. How sad for Professor Langston. Harper imagined him digging through the myriad of packages, searching for a priceless artifact he'd placed beside his frozen peas. 'Poor guy.' She meant it.

'We took care of him, my brothers and I. We kept him from harm. Then he died, and guess what? He left us nothing. Just this pathetic old house that needs more repair than it's worth. But the collection worth millions – the relics he spent his life gathering? That, he left to the university. To strangers.' Jake shook his head. He took a final long deep puff of his cigarette, crushed it against a wooden crate, leaving an ash mark. Stuck the stub into his pocket. 'Father wasn't in his right mind. He got manipulated, plain and simple.'

Maybe it was true. Harper had no idea. Either way, it wasn't her issue. The open box beside her gaped, teasing, inviting her to look inside. But she felt awkward with Jake standing over her, claiming the contents rightfully belonged to him. She cleared her throat, leaned against a stack of crates, crossed her arms. Smiled. Hoped he'd move along.

Jake didn't budge, didn't say anything. Seemed comfortable right where he was, took out another Camel, lit up in silence.

Damn.

Harper fidgeted, ran her fingers through her

hair.

Jake blew smoke rings.

'You live here?' she finally gave in, broke the silence.

'Seriously? Here?' he scoffed. 'No, no. I have a place down the road. My brother Angus lives on the property, though. In the guest house.'

'I've met him. He accused me of trespassing.'

Jake grinned. 'That's Angus. He's our guard dog. Protects our domicile. He and Digger – they love these relics. When they were young, my father took them along on digs. In fact, that's how Digger got his nickname. His love for all things archeological. But no. Nobody should live in this old thing. The plumbing's shot. Wiring's fried. Roof leaks. Stairs are loose, and there are rotting boards all over the place. Walls about to collapse in on the passageways.'

Passageways? 'It's true about those?' Harper remembered the story about the film star – that actress who'd disappeared in them.

'Quite true.' Jake grinned. 'This house has false walls, hidden doors, secret passages. Vaults. Trapdoors. Tunnels.' His grin didn't fade as he winked. 'Be careful where you step and what you touch.'

Harper told herself she should leave, come back another time when Jake wasn't around. But no. She had a legitimate job to do, shouldn't let him interfere with it. She needed to check out the work Zina had done, see her notes and how she'd left things. Besides, she wasn't willing to leave without seeing even one single relic.

'Well, I'd better get started here. Get some

stuff done,' she reached for the box.

'Like I said, knock yourself out.' Jake remained where he was, leaning against the doorframe, watching her.

Harper felt his stare as she turned away and reached for a handful of packing material. 'I won't stay long. I just need to get myself oriented.'

He was quiet.

She set the material on the top of a crate, took out another handful. Looked into the box, still didn't see the mask.

'Well, remember what I said: be careful. Watch your step.' Jake's voice sounded different, kind of thin.

'Thanks,' Harper turned to say goodbye, but Jake wasn't there. She went to the door, into the hall, over to the stairway. Didn't see him anywhere. Gooseflesh rose on her arms. She hadn't seen him leave; Jake was simply gone.

Probably she'd been so engrossed in finding the mask that she hadn't heard him go. But finally, he was gone and she could explore the collection. She went back to the box, dug in with her hands, feeling for a mask.

Finding nothing.

She pulled out clumps of packing material, let it drop to the floor, until the box was empty.

Nothing.

Oh God. Jake must have been right. The professor must have tampered with his collection, moving pieces around, relocating them, misplacing them. The mask could be in the micro-

113

wave. In a shoebox. Under a cushion. Who knew? What a nightmare. Not only was the collection larger than she'd imagined; it was also completely disorganized. She gazed around at the boxes and crates, realizing how much had to be done. It could take months or even years to sort things out.

Sighing, Harper headed down the hall, back to the room with the computer. Maybe Zina had left useful notes. Booting up, she looked around. The room was pristine, dust-free. The shelves held cleaning chemicals, disposable smocks and gloves. And a row of notebooks. Harper took one at random, opened it. Saw the name on the inside of the cover: Carla Prentiss.

Oh dear. The handwriting, the book belonged to the first research assistant. She turned the pages, scanning lists of crate numbers and itemizations of content. Harper couldn't believe the relics listed – objects thousands of years old, representing the craftsmanship and symbols of Pre-Columbian cultures, most in perfect and near-perfect condition. Vessels. Bowls. Masks. Figurines. Oddly, several pages of the logbook indicated that a few items were missing. Maybe the professor hadn't been as competent and organized as Jake thought. Maybe he'd been misplacing relics even back in the eighties.

Harper replaced the notebook, sat at the computer. Found Zina's records. They were scant; she'd only been working a short time. Probably had spent most of her energy getting organized, setting up the computer file, arranging the crates. Like Carla, Zina had approached the artifacts box by box, labeling each with a code number. Like Carla, she'd itemized their contents as she'd proceeded, comparing actual content to that listed on the lids or sides of the boxes. And, like Carla, she'd found disparities.

Relics listed on the boxes were not always found inside. Missing from Crate A-1 was a ten-inch high Mayan gold figure of a turtle with the Maize god, AD 900–1200, valued at $70,000. From Crate A-3, a Honduran vessel, mosaic marble, eight and a half inches tall, a thousand to fifteen hundred years old, value $55,000. Harper read on. Saw that out of seven crates and twenty-four items Zina had catalogued, four items were missing.

Strange. But probably not a big deal, Harper decided. Over the years, the professor had probably removed some of the items – might have put some on display, sold some or donated them to museums. Her job was to make a record of what was there, not to explain what had been done with what wasn't. She'd simply follow Zina's technique, code each crate, open one at a time, record the contents. Indicate any discrepancies.

Saving the file, she shut down the computer and turned to the stacks of boxes, noting the labels: A-1, A-2, A-3. Zina had made it to A-7. For a moment, Harper felt her presence, imagined her working there alone at dusk. Saw a bat flap out from the rafters, heard the wind scream through the walls, watched the lights flicker and go out. She could understand how Zina's imagination had taken off, how she'd panicked. Even now, in daylight, the massive house was eerily quiet. Stacks of boxes cast ominous shadows and concealed dark corners, and the air seemed bathed in a haze. Harper shook her head, refusing to acknowledge the chilly draft on her shoulders. Reminding herself that she ought to get going. She had to get home. Had only a few minutes to peek at relics.

But where should she begin? Actually, she'd already opened a box. The one without the mask. Maybe she'd just go back there and look through that stack. Or she could just stay here and continue with the crates Zina hadn't looked at yet. That made more sense.

Harper took a lever and jimmied it under the lid of an unlabeled large pine crate. She pushed down, loosening the lid a bit. Moved the lever along, shoving it into the gap, pushing on it, repeating the process until one side of the lid had lifted up. Then she started on the opposite side, inserting, pushing, reinserting, pushing, until, finally, the lid came off.

Underneath, on the inside of the lid, was a list of contents. Harper didn't bother to read it; her hands were already sifting through shredded fabric and papers, feeling for smaller packages. Closing around a carved Styrofoam container. Lifting it, carefully. Unwrapping the tape. Removing the Styrofoam. Gasping.

Staring.

She was just over a foot long. Clay with a dark patina. Probably Proto-Classic. Harper cradled her in her hands, admiring her. Picturing the artist as he formed her, never imagining his work would endure, connecting him to people over two thousand years later. Harper checked the list inside the lid of the crate; yes, the piece was Proto-Classic, created between 100 BC and 450 AD. And its estimated worth was – oh dear – $70,000.

Harper's hands trembled as she laid the figurine on the black fabric, photographing it from different angles. Then, replacing it in its Styrofoam bed, she wrapped fresh tape around it and set it back into the crate. She really should go. Soon. After she looked at just one more piece.

Again, she reached into the packing, retrieved an item. Unraveled the tape, opened the Styrofoam casement. This time, she found a late-Classic jaguar – a guardian effigy, made between 550 and 950 AD. In perfect condition, multicolored, two feet high. It had a thick collar, claws, bared fangs. And stood on its rear haunches, its front legs flexed. The lid listed its value at $65,000.

Harper's hand fished in the crate, pulled out another package. Unwrapped it. Discovered a Chimu silver beaker, shaped like a human figure in a loincloth and headband. Made between 1100 and 1400 AD. Worth $8,000.

She couldn't stop. Photographed and logged them and moved on to the next crate. Used the lever to open it. Pulled out a golden Teotihuacán mask, made around 450 AD, worth around $85,000. A Mayan polychrome vessel, decorated with detailed images of humans and animals, made around 600 AD. Valued at $70,000.

Harper was agog. Completely absorbed. She stopped replacing the relics, arranged them instead on the worktable, surrounding herself

117

with the artistry of lost cultures. Lost times. She examined one then another, then returned to the first, admiring the craftsmanship, the combination of utility and symbolism in each piece. The pristine quality of the pieces, their thousands of years of undamaged existence. Rapt, she pictured the people who'd owned them. Their belief in the power of animals – jaguars, turtles, owls, deer, bats. And men mystical enough to take those forms. She picked up the jaguar, felt the inspired awe of the artist worked into the sculpture's smooth sinews.

It wasn't until the room darkened that she realized she'd lost track of time. Harper stood and looked out a window, saw the sun disappearing behind the tree line. What? How could the sun be setting already? What time was it? Disoriented, she looked for a clock. Saw none. Where was her bag with her phone? Damn. She'd left it in the other room when she'd been talking to Jake, needed to go get it and leave. But no – she couldn't just leave, not with all those relics lying exposed on the table; she had to put them away. Where was the light switch? She scanned the walls, found one. Flipped it, but no light came on. She looked up, saw a blackened blown-out bulb hanging from the ceiling between the rafters. Damn. Carefully, Harper worked in fading light to pack up the array of precious masks, vessels and figurines. She squinted through increasing dimness to fit them into their snug individual packing, and set them into their proper crates. How had she gotten so engrossed in the collection that she'd forgotten the time? Lord – Hank must be worried. Must wonder where she was.

Finally, the last artifact was safely in its crate. Harper hurried down the hall to get her bag, noticed again how quiet the house was. Palpably, deathly quiet. She moved alone through shadows, aware of Zina, picturing her there in the dark, imagining creatures closing in on her. Bats. Cougars. Harper kept moving, rejecting the sense that someone was watching her. That time had slowed. That it was taking forever to move a few yards down the hall to get her bag. She picked up her pace, nearly tripped as a floorboard sagged under her weight and the ankle of her war-ravaged left leg twisted. Damn. Pain shot through her. She shifted her weight, stopped. Winced. Saw a shadow shift behind some crates. No, ridiculous – it was she who'd wobbled, not the shadow. Even so, her heart rate picked up. Harper looked around, tense and alert as she half hopped, half ran down the cluttered hall to the storage room, grabbed her bag, and flew through the arch, down the hallway to the stairs through deepening darkness. Looking over her shoulder, braced for the unknown, she scolded herself. She wasn't afraid of the dark; she'd survived places far more frightening than a creaky old house.

Still, as she left the Langston place, Harper thought she heard the distant hoot of an owl, was sure she saw someone rustling among the trees. She told herself it was Angus or Jake. Even called their names.

No one answered.

Harper hurried to the Ninja. Heart pounding, trying to reign in her imagination, she told herself she was not smelling incense, was not seeing a bat fluttering above her. But her hands shook as she tossed her bag into the storage compartment, pulled on her helmet, jumped on to her bike and roared away, tearing right through the police tape, determined to be off the property and home before dusk became night.

When she got to Ithaca, stopped at a red light, she finally pulled her phone out and looked to see what time it was. Almost five thirty. What? Lord, she'd been at Langston's for four and a half hours? Appalling. And confusing. OK, she'd stayed longer than she'd planned, had gotten involved with the relics, but – four and a half hours?

Damn. She'd also missed a bunch of calls, hadn't heard her phone ringing down the hall. She played back the first voicemail.

'Where. Hoppa? OK?' Oh boy. Hank hardly ever called, didn't feel comfortable on the phone. Must really be worried.

The next call began. 'Harper, it's four fifteen.'

Oh God. Leslie. Harper had forgotten all about their four o'clock appointment. Had missed it entirely.

'Are you coming? Give me a call.'

Harper's face got hot, mortified. Leslie had done her a favor, squeezing her into a busy schedule as an emergency, and she'd simply *forgotten* to go? She thought about the flashback, remembered standing on the sidewalk, trying to arrest a mannequin. No question, she needed to see Leslie. Needed to call and apologize. Reschedule. Oh man.

The light changed, but Harper stayed near the curb, listening to the rest of the messages. Hank had called again. 'OK you? Hoppa? Call me.'

Oh dear. How could she explain herself? She'd apologize. Admit that she'd been selfish...

But a man's voice whispered from the phone. Hoarse. Raspy.

'Be careful, Harper. They almost got me today.' Burke Everett. He was panting. Possibly hurt? 'They might come after you, too, so watch your back. I'm trying to lose them, but they're everywhere and—'

Harper sighed, pushed the 'end' button. She had enough on her mind without Burke's paranoid ranting. She'd screwed up, needed to get home and make amends, first to Hank, then to Leslie. She sped through dark streets, planning what she'd say, how she'd explain. Not noticing the rented black sedan closing in on her until it almost ran into the Ninja. At the last second, Harper realized the car wasn't going to slow, and she swerved right, nearly smashing a parked car, flying past it up on to the sidewalk, avoiding a startled pedestrian walking his corgi. Barely righting her bike and stopping as the sedan sped away.

'Did you see that?' she sputtered.

'What's the matter with you? You could kill somebody,' the man scolded. 'Keep that thing off the walkway.' Scowling under the streetlight, he turned and walked away.

Harper stared at him, then the street. She took several slow deep breaths, muttered some curse words, and walked the Ninja through parked cars, on to the asphalt, climbed on and rode home. Finally, prepared to gush apologies on to her husband, she pulled into her driveway and noticed that, though the fraternity next door was decorated and blazing with light, the windows of her house were completely dark.

Harper parked her bike and stood for a moment, chewing her lip, watching the house. Picturing Hank sitting inside, alone in darkness, deep in another bout of depression. Maybe drinking? And it was her fault – she'd known his moods were fragile; Leslie had warned that he was struggling emotionally.

And then, she'd disappeared on him. She'd said she was coming home, but hadn't, reminding him, once again, of how dependent he was, how powerless he felt. He couldn't reach her by phone. Hadn't driven since his accident, so couldn't go looking for her. Couldn't figure out where she'd gone, why she hadn't returned. Could only sit and wait, helplessly.

Oh God. She'd really messed up.

But, hell, she'd only been gone a few hours. Was that a crime? Was Hank so fragile that he'd panic if she spent one single afternoon somewhere without telling him? And if he was indeed that fragile, how long could he – how long could either of them – stand it?

Music blared from the fraternity. *The Monster Mash*. A Halloween oldie. Oh Lord. It was going to be a long party weekend. Homecoming Saturday. Halloween Sunday. Hank's depression every day...

But she was getting ahead of herself, making assumptions – she needed to go inside and talk to Hank. Turn on some lights. Apologize. Taking in a deep breath, Harper straightened, took her bag out of the Ninja's storage box and started along the row of Hemlocks toward the house. The music had changed. The trees, the ground, and Harper's nerves vibrated to *Bad Moon Rising*.

Harper let herself into the house, turned on the light in the entranceway. Called out Hank's name. Heard no answer. Tossed her bag on to the hall table and saw light spilling from his office near the back of the house. She hurried toward it, eager to see him. Passing the kitchen, she realized she'd underestimated him. She'd been wrong to think he'd so easily fall apart and mope, sitting alone in the dark. Hank was strong, resilient. He was in his office, no doubt, reading some obscure geology journal article on his computer. Everything was fine; she'd apologize for being late, for losing track of the time. And he'd understand.

'Hank?' She approached his office door. Again, Hank didn't answer. Didn't come out to meet her. Harper stopped, listening to his silence, remembering his accident, his fall from the roof. She closed her eyes; saw him sliding over the shingles, falling. Hitting his head against concrete. Oddly, in the same moment, she saw a black sedan close in on her Ninja, nearly hitting it ... Felt the surge of the motorcycle as she

123

swerved away just in time...

'Hank!' Still she didn't move. She stood at the door, calling his name louder this time, again picturing the car coming out of the darkness, straight at her. Deliberately. Accelerating. Aiming? Was it possible that Burke was right? Were people actually coming after her? Had they already been there – was Hank all right?

'Hank?' This time, her voice was edgy and ragged. She thrust herself into the office, scanning the desk chair, the big leather easy chair, the carpet, the corners ... 'Hank,' she called as she spun around, looking again. 'Hank,' she repeated over and over. First as a question, later as a wail. But Hank didn't appear. Nor did he answer.

Oh God.

Harper went through the house, quietly now, turning on every light as she went. Hank wasn't in the kitchen. Not in the powder room, dining room, living room. Harper's chest tightened; breathing was an effort. She kept seeing his accident, watched him fall, over and over. No, she wouldn't go there, wouldn't relive it. Needed to stay in the moment. To find Hank. Climbing the stairs, to the dark second story, she felt a sharp pang in her stomach. Clutched it. And heard Leslie's voice: 'He's struggling more than he lets on ... I'd keep a close eye on him if I were you.'

Harper stopped, suddenly chilled. Shivering. Again picturing Hank alone in the house, depressed. Unable to reach her. Feeling abandoned and hopeless...

No. Ridiculous. Unthinkable. Hank would

124

never hurt himself. Never. Not ever. No.

Still, Harper remained on the steps, unable to move. Unable to shake her icy paralysing fear of what she might find at the top of the staircase.

'Hank?' Her voice this time was thin. Broken.

He probably just dozed off, she told herself. Probably was asleep.

Unconvinced, her feet refused to move, and she had to force them up the final few steps. Had to push herself on to the landing, down the hall into the bedroom.

Where she found Hank.

He was standing by the window, staring out at the fraternity. His back to her.

'Hank?'

He didn't answer. Turned slowly to face her.

'Didn't you hear me?' Harper was annoyed. 'I've been calling your name – why didn't you answer?'

His voice was low. 'Why didn't *you*? Answer? Phone.'

Harper switched on the light. Hank was still in his robe. Unshaven. Hadn't gotten dressed all day.

'Called you.' Hank glowered.

'I know – I'm sorry. I didn't hear the phone.' He hadn't gotten dressed again. Had he stayed in the bedroom all day? 'Look, I'm sorry. I messed up. I got involved with the Langston project – it turns out Zina was most likely killed by her own family. Some kind of horrible honor killing. But, if that's the case, there's no danger to anyone else, and I might as well take it. So I went over just to take a look for a few minutes, and I lost

125

track of—'

'Friend came. Here.' Hank's eyes sizzled. He wasn't even listening. 'Burke. Iraq from.'

What? 'Burke? Came here?'

'Told me. You saw him.'

Damn. What had Burke done? Had he shown up at the house and told Hank the whole cockamamie story about Colonel? That his militia was out to assassinate them both? No wonder Hank had been upset when he couldn't reach her.

'I told you about him, remember? Burke's got some serious mental issues. I guess the war messed him—'

'Not told me. Burke's story. About. Not told me. Zina's job. Took. Lots. Hoppa.' Hank didn't move. He stood at the window, broad shoulders stiff. Jaw tight. 'Why? Don't trust. Me?'

'That's ridiculous.' Harper wanted to go to him, touch him. She took a step forward, but stopped, held back by his glare. 'Of course I trust you.'

'Then tell me. Now.'

Oh God. Where to start? 'OK. Burke came into town. We met for coffee, and he started making wild accusations about some guys we knew in Iraq. He's paranoid.'

'And?'

And?

'Burke. And. What else?'

What else? 'Oh. You mean the assistantship?'

He stared, didn't reply.

'OK.' She swallowed. Took a breath. 'I know I told you I'd turn it down. But that was because of the murder, right? But this morning, I found

126

out about Zina's family – they thought she'd disgraced them by refusing an arranged marriage and probably killed her.'

'And? Also?'

'Also what?'

Hank stepped forward, a towering, lumbering infuriated bear. His mouth twisted into a grimace. 'Also. About. Us.'

Us?

'Not tell me. Not talk to me. Not trust. Not good. Not. Us.'

Oh God. 'Hank – how can you say that? We're good. I do trust you...'

He moved past her, toward the door.

'OK. Lately, I've held things back. But the only reason I've done that is that you've been depressed. I haven't wanted to upset you—'

'Depressed. Me?' He spun around more quickly than she'd thought he could. 'Think. So?'

'Yes, but I get it – you have a right to be.' She stepped toward him. Again felt the invisible wall. 'I understand you have to work through your feelings after everything—'

'Think I can't. Manage? Need my. Wife. Protecting. Me?'

'Of course not, don't even—'

'Think. I'm not. Strong. Man?'

'—suggest that!'

'Maybe. Hoppa.' He turned, walked out of the bedroom. 'Maybe. Right.'

Harper followed him down the hall, talking to him. Telling him to stop. To sit down and talk. But Hank ignored her. Pulling off his bathrobe,

127

he pulled on jeans, a jacket, stepped into his new boots, stopped at the door to point to the hall table.

'Burke. Phone. Number,' he said. Then he left.

Harper started after him, opened the front door, but stopped. What was she going to do – wrestle him to the ground? Force him back into the house? She bit her lip, refused tears. Hank was going through a phase, wavering between sadness and anger, just as she'd done after her war injuries. His moods were natural, inevitable. And he needed to work through them on his own. She hadn't helped by going AWOL that afternoon, but he'd forgive her in time. They'd talk. He'd be all right. They'd be all right.

Wouldn't they?

She stood in the hall, facing the door, hoping he'd come back inside. After all, Hank wouldn't go far. Would he? She watched the door.

Damn. Harper couldn't help it. She hurried after him on to the front porch; *Season of the Witch* blasted from next door. But where was Hank? She looked around. Scolded herself for upsetting him. She was supposed to be there for him, helping him through this crisis. Instead, she'd gone off on her own without even telling him, just to look at some relics – well, some incredible relics. But she hadn't even considered how he'd feel...

Nearby, through the music, she thought she heard the revving of a car's engine. And suddenly, Hank's Jeep, parked for months in the garage beside the house, zoomed in reverse down the driveway into the street, jerked into drive and sped away.

Harper stood in the middle of the front yard, chilled and ankle-deep in leaves, her mouth hanging open. Hank hadn't driven in over a year, not since his accident. His right side was weaker than the left. Would he be able to steer? To control the gas and brake? Damn it. What was he doing?

Cursing and worried, she ran to the street, saw tail lights disappear around the corner. Stood there, staring. Considered taking off after him on the Ninja, pictured catching up with him, how he'd react. Not difficult to figure out: he'd be furious. Would feel emasculated, as if she didn't think he could manage on his own.

Amplifiers screamed, 'Must be ... must be ... the season of the witch!'

Harper trudged back to the house and slammed the door, refusing, absolutely refusing to cry. She paced. Took out the Scotch. Walked away from it. Paced some more, feeling helpless and furious about being helpless. Worrying about Hank. Pouring a drink. Staring into the glass as she drank. Seeing Hank fall from the roof, hit his head ... No. Refusing to relive that. Closing her eyes, thinking of Leslie ... Oh God. She needed to call her. That was, if Leslie would even speak to her after her missed appointment.

Quickly, unsteadily, Harper dug her phone out of her bag, made the call. Got Leslie's voicemail, of course. Left a message apologizing, saying she'd gotten caught up earlier but really needed to talk, asking her to call back. Hearing herself sound needy.

Damn. Harper stood in the front hall, phone in hand. Where had Hank gone? She pictured him driving, taking a turn too fast, losing control of the car. Thank goodness it was a Jeep, sturdy. Not likely to get totaled if he crashed. Unless it rolled into the gorge. Or the lake. Harper clutched her phone, walked in circles, waited for Leslie to call. Get a grip, she told herself. Hank is fine. He's just proving himself. Testing himself. He'll come back, having shown that he can still drive. He'll be in a better mood. She needed to calm down, be patient.

But she couldn't. Tossing her phone on to the table beside her bag, she noticed a piece of paper there. A number was scrawled on it. Burke's number. Lord. She'd almost forgotten about him, how he'd shown up at her house, gotten Hank all riled up. Furious, she made the call, waited for him to pick up so she could yell at him. But he didn't pick up. A computerized voice told her to leave a message at the tone. So she did.

'What the hell's wrong with you, Burke?' The words flew out, unplanned. 'What did you say to my husband? Did you share your genius theory about Colonel Baxter? Did you say that he's trying to kill us? Have you completely lost it? Did you not happen to notice that my husband has his own problems? Could you not realize that maybe you should leave him out of your damned paranoid bullshit?' She paused to catch her breath, composed herself. Lowered her voice. 'Here's the deal, Burke. Don't ... do not bother me or my husband again. Ever. Don't come over, don't call. Don't send obituaries in the mail. Just take your frickin' conspiracy theories and sign yourself into a VA hospital. Get help. But go away.'

Harper felt a pang. Pictured Burke, how jumpy and pathetic he'd been, almost twitching with fear. The guy was sick; he hadn't deliberately caused harm. She was being too harsh, didn't want to be cruel.

'Sorry, Burke,' she softened. 'It's just too much right now. I've got my own stuff, can't help you with yours.'

And then she hung up.

Waiting wasn't easy. Harper waited on the front porch, on the living room sofa, at the kitchen table. She poured another finger of Scotch, blinked at it, gulped it down, poured another. Left the glass on the table. Walked up and down the hall, looked out windows, sat down, stood up, went to her phone, picked it up, thought of calling someone – but couldn't decide who. Leslie again? Vicki? Detective Rivers? What would she say? That she was frantic, almost hysterical because Hank had left their property?

Even she could hear how irrational that sounded. Clearly, she was overreacting. Didn't need to be frightened. Hank was fine. Would be fine. But she kept seeing him fall off the roof. Kept imagining him crashing the car. She put the phone down, tried to ignore the rumble of gunfire closing in on her. Too late ... Suddenly, to her left, something exploded; burning air scalded her face, and she smelled burning flesh, heard screams of pain. Started to run for cover – no.

131

Damn it. She fought back. Closed her eyes. Wouldn't, couldn't allow a flashback. But the bullets still flew. Whizzed past, barely missing her head. Ducking, hunkering low to the ground, Harper dashed back to the base – or maybe the kitchen? She grabbed a grenade from the cold drawer in the arsenal, and bit off the pin. Dug her teeth in. Instantly, the grenade's sharp sour taste jolted her, banishing the battleground. Returning her to the moment where she stood by the refrigerator, holding a half-eaten lemon.

Even so, her skin still burned. Her lungs felt raw, and she tasted copper. Danger reared up and roared, but no matter how much she wanted to, she didn't know how to confront it. Not this time.

This time, the battle wasn't hers. It was Hank's.

So Harper stood and sat and stood again in her kitchen, downed another glass of Scotch, poured another. And waited.

At ten before two in the morning, Hank pulled into the driveway, parked the Jeep in the garage. He came in, looking frazzled. Relieved, Harper didn't say a word. She just ran to him.

'Sorry.' Hank seemed straighter. Taller.

'No. I am.'

'Both. Should. Be.'

He was right. They broke apart, stood awkwardly near the front door.

'Want a drink?' By then, she'd had more than a few.

'No. Late.'

'We should talk.' She needed to apologize, explain. Tell him about Burke, the assistantship – about her selfishness.

'Not now, Hoppa. Sleep.'

He headed to the stairs. Acted like nothing had happened. Harper was drained and exhausted. Unable to let go.

'I was worried about you.' She followed him.

'Why?'

Why? Really? 'Because you were upset. And you haven't driven since—'

'Fine. I'm. Fine.'

They went upstairs, got ready for bed. Harper stayed close to him, needing to connect. Uneasy about his silence. But Hank simply got into bed, rolled over and turned out the light. Harper snuggled against him.

'No kiss?'

He turned and kissed her. A dutiful peck on the forehead.

'Uh uh.' She pulled his face to hers, kissed his mouth.

But even though he lay facing her, their arms and legs entwined, Harper felt his distance. In seconds, his breathing became deep and even. Harper tried to but couldn't relax.

'Hank?'

'Huh.'

'Where did you go?'

Hank didn't answer. Softly, he began to snore.

Harper had just fallen asleep when the doorbell rang. She opened her eyes, looked around. The sun blazed through slats of the bedroom blinds.

Clock said nine thirty. Hank's side of the bed was empty.

Oh God. Harper jumped out of bed, raced to the window, looked outside for the Jeep. Saw it there, right where Hank had parked it, inside the open garage – thank God.

But where was Hank?

'Harper?' Vicki's cheery voice floated up the staircase. 'Get your lazy butt down here!'

Damn. It was Saturday morning. She and Vicki usually had coffee during the week. But this was Homecoming; Trent was attending a brunch, glad-handing alumni to stimulate contributions. Vicki didn't want to go, so she'd offered to come by with scones.

'What, were you out partying all night? Get up!' Vicki called.

Harper groaned. She ached all over, didn't feel like getting her butt anywhere but back to bed. Her left leg ached as she dragged herself to the bathroom; the rest of her complained as she splashed water on to her face and moved her toothbrush around her mouth. The face in the mirror was blotchy; her hair clumped into tangled blonde stumps. Harper stuck her tongue out at the reflection, ran her fingers through the tangles, and plodded down the stairs, looking for Hank.

Finding Vicki. She'd dyed her hair again. This time, too dark. Almost black.

'Where's Hank?' Harper looked down the hall, toward the kitchen.

'Wow. Hello to you, too.'

'Have you seen him?'

Vicki nodded at the front door. Harper went to the window, looked out.

Hank was in the front yard, raking leaves. What? She stood, frozen, watching. He was off balance, his movements short. But they were steady. Persistent.

'Are you sick?' Vicki came up behind her, frowning. 'You look terrible.'

Really? 'Hank took the Jeep out last night.'

Vicki's mouth dropped. 'What?'

Harper kept watching him, amazed. 'He drove. He was gone for hours, alone. In the middle of the night. I have no idea where he went. He wouldn't tell me. And now, look.' She pointed at the window. 'He's...'

'He's raking. He had half the yard done when I got here.' Vicki stood beside Harper, watching Hank. She shrugged. 'So. This is all good, right?'

It was?

Harper turned to Vicki, about to tell her about Hank's moods, but her voice choked and her eyes had filled. Why? What was wrong with her? Hank was fine, working outside on a brisk October morning. Recovering, testing his capabilities. Getting a renewed sense of self. She should be glad.

'Oh, Harper.' Vicki hugged her. 'You've been a soldier through this whole ordeal. Thanks to you, Hank's come back from hell. Look how strong he is. He's out there, pushing himself. Not giving up. You guys are going to be fine – both of you.'

Harper gazed out the window. Watched Hank work the rake, pulling leaves into speckled heaps of red, yellow, orange.

Vicki seemed convinced that there was no problem. That Hank's exertion was unremarkable, a positive sign of progress. She led Harper to the kitchen. Freshly baked scones – a variety of cinnamon nut, chocolate chip and cranberry orange – were set out on a plate near butter and honey and jam.

'So.' Vicki poured coffee. 'Hank's driving again. Doing lawn work. He's full of surprises. What do you think he'll do next?'

Vicki meant well, but Harper tensed. Grabbed a scone, forced a smile. 'I can't even guess.'

Leslie hadn't called back yet. And Harper needed to talk. Vicki knew Hank well; she'd probably have insights as to his moods and behavior. Would have ideas about how Harper should respond.

'What do you think?' Vicki primped her chin-length hair. 'You like it?'

Harper thought it looked witchy, appropriate for Halloween. 'It's different.' She shrugged. 'Something new.' Two days ago, it had been auburn. Vicki was constantly changing her look.

'Different good? Or different bad? Maybe I should cut it real short—'

'No, it's good. It's a change – it's fun.' Kind of. 'Look, Vicki. Can I talk to you? About something...'

'Of course you can talk to me. What a question. What's up?' She bit into a chocolate chip scone. Crumbs tumbled on to the table.

Harper took a breath. Didn't know where to start. Maybe she should back up to yesterday, her visit to Professor Langston's house. As soon as she began, Vicki stopped her.

'Wait. You took that assistantship? Are you crazy? After Zina was killed there? I thought—'

'No. It's OK. Turns out, her family probably did it.' Harper explained that Zina had refused an arranged marriage. That it was likely she'd been the victim of an honor killing.

Vicki's eyes widened. 'Wait. You're saying her own brothers killed her?'

'Maybe. Or an uncle. Or her father – even her mother.' Harper began to move on. 'Anyway, when I got there, the collection—'

'Hold on.' Vick shook her head. Bit her lip. 'Her own *parents* might have killed her?'

'I know. It's horrible.' She pictured Zina's slumped, mutilated body. Blinked the image away. Picked up her coffee. 'But the thing is that, if they did it, then Zina's death wasn't a random murder. Which means there isn't some crazed killer out there.'

Vicki shook her head. 'Imagine.'

'And if there's no crazed killer out there, there's no reason I shouldn't take the assistantship. So I decided to accept it, and I went there to get—'

'No wait.' Vicki frowned. 'Remember the night before she died, when Zina came here, terrified of that newel—'

'Nahual.'

'Whatever. Do you think ... maybe she had real reasons to be afraid. Maybe somebody was actually there – one of her brothers or her father might have been stalking her, and she thought it was a nowl.'

'Nahual.' Harper didn't want to dwell on the murder. She wanted advice about Hank and had mentioned the honor killing theory only to explain why, instead of turning down the assistantship, she'd gone to Langston's where she'd lost track of time and not come home, infuriating Hank, setting him off on a rampage of unpredictable activity. 'Anyway, I'm sure the police are—'

'Did Zina ever mention the arranged marriage? Did she talk about problems with her family?'

'No.' Harper sighed. 'Not to me. But we were not close. Vicki, can we please talk about—'

'What about her roommates? Did she tell them? Did she say she was afraid of her family?' Vicki swallowed coffee. 'Because, I mean, if it were me, I'd carry a gun and mace and pepper spray. I'd be petrified – wouldn't you?'

Harper chewed her lip, impatient. 'Yes. I'd carry a damned arsenal. But can we come back to this? I want to tell you what hap—'

'Hold on a second, OK? We'll talk about whatever you want, but this is important.'

'And what? I'm not?' God, had she just said that? It sounded whiny and petulant. Like a jealous kid. She bit into a scone.

'Don't be stupid.'

'I'm not being stupid.' Her mouth was full. 'I just want to talk to you. A lot's been going on.'

'Fine. A lot's been going on with me, too. I haven't told you about the drama in my office now that Pam's leaving.' Vicki was a dentist and Pam was her office manager. 'Or about Trent's

138

promise to stop drinking and join AA. But Trent and I and Hank and you can wait until we talk about Zina.'

Harper put the scone down, wiped her hands. 'We aren't going to accomplish anything by—'

'I didn't say we were. But honestly, Harper. We were with her the night before she died. So I want to talk about it, OK? Can't you put your devastating, earth-shattering problems on hold for just five minutes?'

Her devastating, earth-shattering problems? Vicki was mocking her? Really? Harper's jaw tightened. She was tempted to say or do something regrettable, maybe hurl the rest of the scones at Vicki's perky little nose. But she refrained. Zina's death wasn't a topic to be glossed over; it deserved respect and attention. So, calming herself, Harper picked up her cup. Sipped. Sat silent, stiff. Drummed her fingers on the table.

'So here's my thinking.' Vicki leaned forward, elbows on the table. 'From what I've heard, Zina wasn't carrying any weapons. Was she?'

'No.'

'Not even scissors or a steak knife. Not one thing to protect herself?'

'No.' Harper bit off a chunk of scone, unsettled. Wondering what mood Hank was in. Why he hadn't even said 'good morning' before going outside.

'So?' Vicki seemed to think her point was obvious. 'So, I think that means that Zina wasn't afraid of her family. She didn't believe she was in danger.'

'Well, I guess she was wrong.' Harper drew a breath. Maybe she was being selfish to want her issues to take precedence over Zina's. Maybe Vicki was right that discussing the murder was more important. Even so, Harper drifted away, thinking about Hank, how she should approach him. What she should say. She looked out the kitchen window. Didn't see him. Wanted to go outside. To talk to him.

Vicki went on. 'But, obviously, she knew her family and their beliefs. She had to know—'

'Maybe she didn't take the beliefs seriously, Vicki.' Harper finished her coffee. 'No one had any reason to think her family would commit an honor killing until after the murder.'

'Well, that's just weird.' Vicki held her cup, sat straight. 'Imagine you come from a family – from a culture – that dictates the death penalty for certain acts. And you knowingly commit one of those acts. Can you imagine not considering that? Not taking precautions to protect yourself?'

'No, I can't.' Neither could she imagine Zina's mindset, her background and its conflicting values. 'But we're Westerners. We really can't know what Zina was thinking. We can't comprehend being part of a culture where women get killed for having relationships with men. Or wearing make-up. Or going out alone, or—'

'But Zina wasn't a fool. She was a bright woman. Worldly. Educated. And yet she seems to have been oblivious to the dangers of going against her culture.' Vicki broke off a piece of scone, toyed with it.

'What are you saying?'

'I guess I just don't want to believe her family would, you know ... do that.'

'You'd prefer it if a random stranger had killed her?' Harper didn't want to consider that possibility.

'You know what?' Vicki chewed slowly. 'I would. Yes.'

Harper felt a chill, pictured the moment Zina realized that her own flesh and blood was taking her life. She imagined meeting the killer's familiar eyes, searching them for compassion, feeling cold steel pushed through her body...

Harper stood, went to rinse out her coffee mug, realizing that, yes, she no longer wanted to talk about Hank. Compared to Zina's death – the betrayal by her family – she and Hank had no problems at all. She looked out the window, saw Hank pushing a wheelbarrow filled with leaves. A year ago, he'd struggled even to walk. Now, he was doing yard work. And driving the car.

Vicki had stopped talking, was waiting for a response. 'Harper?'

'Sorry.' She had no idea what Vicki had been saying. But, suddenly, watching Hank, she thought she knew why Zina hadn't been afraid. She'd known the culture and its rules, but had been too close to her family to see them objectively. Zina had underestimated the people closest to her, hadn't grasped the extent of their passion or the depth of their resolve.

Zina made a fatal, though not uncommon mistake.

'I have to go out,' Harper ran to the closet and pulled on a fleece jacket.

141

'What? Harper?' Vicki stood up, gaping. 'I thought you wanted to talk!'

'Not now. Don't have time.' Harper hurried to the door. 'Sorry to run off. Just leave everything, OK? I'll clean up later...' And she was out the front door, rushing over to Hank.

He looked up as she approached, didn't say anything. Nodded, as he balanced carefully and pulled the rake, gathering leaves. Harper went to a pile a few yards away, ordered her left leg to bend, and, despite its complaints, began picking up arm-loads, dropping them into the wheelbarrow. When it was full, she rolled it to the back of the house, tossed them over the fence on to the floor of the woods. Then she returned to the front yard, repeated the process. Again and again. And again.

At some point, Vicki came out, looking confused. 'So. I guess I'll go.'

Harper picked up some leaves, wiped her brow. 'OK. Yeah. I have to do this. Thanks for the scones.'

'Trent. Say. Hi.' Hank called.

Vicki wandered off. 'Dinner Tuesday?' she shouted.

Harper nodded, waved back. 'Bring dessert!'

At some point, Harper noticed that her left leg was seriously throbbing. But she didn't give in, wouldn't stop until Hank did. And Hank wouldn't stop.

It took a few hours to clear the front lawn. Finally, they returned the wheelbarrow and the rake to the garage.

Hank was sweating, flushed with exertion. But

his eyes twinkled with energy. And as he put an arm around her, he was smiling. 'Talk. Now.'

Harper's phone was ringing when they went inside, but Harper let it go, interested only in talking to Hank. He led her into the kitchen, poured coffee. Two mugs. Sat at the table. Waited until she sat. Met her eyes. The twinkle had faded.

'I was mad.'

'I know.'

'I was. Wrong.'

'No. You had a right to be mad. I was wrong. I should have called and—'

He put a hand up. 'Me first. Talk.'

OK. Harper lifted her coffee, took a sip.

'I've been. Thinking. Hoppa.'

She waited.

'Whole year now. I've. Not had a. Life. Too much on. On you. Leaned on you. Burden.'

'No, you've never been—'

He covered her lips with his finger, hushing her. Harper wanted to assure him that he had never been, never could be a burden, but he wouldn't let her speak.

'Me first. Talk first.'

OK.

'Hoppa. You.' He stopped, took a breath, rearranging his lips and tongue. 'You need your life.' He swished coffee in his mouth, moistening it. Swallowed coffee. 'To do. Your thing. Go where you want. Not worry. Poor. Hank.'

What? Harper's chest fluttered a warning. 'But I don't—'

143

'No. Listen.' Again, he stopped her. 'Change. We need. We. Both need change.'

Harper's throat tightened. Her hand rose to her mouth. What kind of changes? What was he saying?

'I can't be. Any more. Pris–prisoner.'

A prisoner? 'You haven't—'

'Not your fault. Not about. You. About. Me.'

Her stomach flipped, heart raced. Was Hank giving her the old 'it's not you it's me' line? Dumping her? No, of course not. He couldn't be.

'I need to. Go. Work. Do. Man be.'

Harper couldn't move, couldn't breathe. She sat riveted. Frozen.

'You do.' He strained to form the syllables. 'What you want. Where. And when. You want.'

Was this really happening? Was Hank telling her to just go wherever she wanted? Tears filled her eyes, blurred her vision.

'I need also. Need to go. Drive. Do. What I want.' He paused, watching her. Not looking quite like himself. Altered in some way. Hank, but not Hank. He inhaled. 'Indy. Pendent.' Exhaled.

Harper's eyes swam. Do not cry, she ordered herself. You are stronger than that. You love this man, and if he's dumping you to prove he can be independent, that sucks. But at least sit up straight and show some spine. Harper sat up, but blinking, she sent a single fat teardrop spilling on to her cheek. She slapped it away.

'Crying? Don't.' Hank reached out, touched her face. 'Not bad. Change. Good. Both. For us.'

Really? Harper's chest hurt when she breathed.

She crossed her arms, bracing herself. She wondered what she could say. Whether she'd even be able to speak, with her throat so choked.

'The truth. I'm saying. Not. Pretend.' Hank who wasn't quite Hank paused to lick his lips. Moved them around as if limbering them up. This was more than he'd said at one time since his accident. 'You need, Hoppa. To tell truth, too.'

Hold on. Was he saying she hadn't been honest with him? 'What are you talking about?' Instantly, hurt became anger, and Harper's finger rose, jabbing the air. 'I have never lied to you, not ever. About anything.'

'No.' His eyes were steady, his voice grave. 'But truth not said. Same as lies.'

Harper felt as if he'd slapped her, covered her cheek. 'Hank, I have not hidden the truth!'

'Burke.' One syllable. It struck like a thunderclap. 'And took Zina's. Job.' His voice was a low rumble. Or no – was that gunfire?

Harper heard shots, felt the ground explode as she scanned the area for something – anything to fend off the flashback. She saw napkins, jam. Leftover scones. A butter knife. Picked up the knife, pressed it deep into the palm of her hand until sharp pain pushed the encroaching battle away, grounding her. She closed her eyes, wincing, and made a fist.

'Told me. You weren't taking. Job. But took. It.'

Harper listened, heard no guns. Looked around for snipers, saw only her kitchen walls. Focused. 'We've already been over this, Hank. I was

145

going to tell you about all of that, but I didn't get a chance. Let me explain everything now—'

'Missing point.' Hank cut her off.

What point? 'No. You said I'm not truthful. But that's not fair; I haven't tried to hide anything from you.'

'Me either.'

'You? You mean you're hiding things from me?'

'No. Just do. Now. My thing. Own. Like you.'

Harper pictured him backing out of the driveway in the night. Staying out for hours. Raking the leaves. Doing things without her for the first time in over a year.

'Two lives. Do own things. Each. Apart.'

'Apart?' Her voice wobbled.

His eyes hardened, held on to hers. 'Each. Hoppa. I love. You.' He paused. 'But we can't. Like before. Be. Need change. Big.'

Harper drew a breath. She understood Hank was going through dramatic changes. But did that mean he wanted to separate? Was he breaking up their marriage in order to prove he could be independent? And who put him in charge of dictating what was to change? Was he saying that things had to be his way or no way, putting her on some kind of ultimatum, a wife probation? Well, no thank you. That wasn't going to fly. She stood, pushed her chair away from the table.

'Listen, Hank. It's my turn to speak now. Maybe I've screwed up. Maybe I've done something – or a bunch of things – that really pissed you off. But I have never ever deliberately hurt

146

you or stood in your way. I have been your staunchest ally since I married you. I love you. If that's not good enough, then fine. Be as independent and apart as you want. Do your thing. You want change? You got it.'

She spun around, accidentally knocking the coffee mug off the table. Heard it shatter on the floor. Heard Hank call, 'Hoppa, wait – look. Hand. Bleeding,' as she sped from the room.

He stood, yelling, 'Hoppa, stop. Come back – please!' But Harper didn't hear him; she'd already left the kitchen and was halfway to the door.

Burke Everett hadn't shaved in a couple of days. Kept the hood of his sweatshirt up, concealing his face. Moved around College Town, never staying in one place long, crashing overnight in some apartment with a bunch of stoners, half in Halloween costumes where nobody knew who anybody was. Spending the day trying to blend in with scruffy potheads who hung out around there. Keeping his eyes open.

So far this morning, he'd seen three of the Colonel's people. Three that he was sure of: two in a black sedan. Christ, they might as well have carried a sign announcing themselves. One was subtler, hanging out near a pizza shop. His shoes had given him away, all laced up with their military shine. With tattered jeans? Really? Did they think he was stupid? At least they hadn't spotted him – so far, he'd seen them first and disappeared.

Meantime, he'd tried to reach Harper, even had

gone to her house to warn her. But she'd been out, and her husband, well. No point telling him anything. There was something seriously wrong with that dude. Big guy, good-looking, but he moved like a wounded gorilla. Couldn't even talk. Maybe he was one of those brain injury guys. Burke had heard that a lot of guys got head wounds from IEDs, got all kinds of weird afterwards. Harper had called afterwards, left a pissed-off message, telling him not to come to the house. Probably she was embarrassed about the guy, trying to shield him from people. Burke understood. Harper was one of the good ones, all about being strong. Being loyal.

Which was probably why she hesitated to take a stand against the Colonel – he was her superior officer. She probably couldn't believe a man of his stature could be so corrupt. Well, she was wrong. And, by the way, speaking of loyalty, Burke was Army, too, wasn't he? Where was her loyalty to him?

Someone bumped smack into him, walking fast. Fuck – he hadn't seen the guy coming. If that had been one of them, he'd be dead. Just like Pete. Time to move on. Burke kept his head down as he walked. Time to get out of town. Leave them here, crawling all over Ithaca look-ing for him. His car was parked off Stewart Avenue, and he headed that way. Watching over his shoulder. Feeling eyes on him. What was that guy doing across the street, just standing there as if smoking a cigarette? Why was the guy looking at him? Burke quickened his step. The guy didn't follow. Didn't make a call. False alarm.

At the corner, he turned sharply, suddenly, watching to see if anyone was on his tail. Some chick, yakking on her cell. He stood against the wall, watching until she passed. Then backtracked. She didn't follow. Didn't even glance his way.

But those guys were good. Might have tag teams. The chick might right that second be telling her contact on the phone where he was headed. Burke slipped a hand into the pocket of his sweatshirt, clutched his 9 mm. Felt better. Life was better with a Beretta. He chuckled; not a bad slogan. He should send it to the company. Maybe they'd buy it from him. But first, he had to get out of town. Kept his head down. Kept walking.

Harper's hand was bleeding. Her palm was wet and sticky, a small incision right smack in the center. Who knew a butter knife could break skin? And who cared? It was only fitting that she'd bleed after what she'd just heard. Harper sped to the door, aware that Hank was coming after her, calling her name. But she didn't stop, couldn't. She grabbed her bag from the front table and kept moving, not stopping for Hank, the sharp pain in her left leg, her bloody palm, the frat guys' raucous Homecoming party revving up in the yard next door, her phone chiming its gong sound. Smearing tears off her face, Harper popped her helmet on, hopped on to her Ninja and rode away, aware of Hank on the front porch, yelling words her engine drowned out.

Harper sped down the hill to the lake, barely aware of traffic or surroundings, immune to the chilling wind in her face, aware only of pain. How could Hank accuse *her* of not being honest with him when he was the reason she didn't tell him things. He was the one whose moods kept shifting, who was often too depressed or frustrated to have a conversation. And how could he accuse her of 'doing her own thing'? As if she hadn't put her PhD program, her friendships – her entire *life* – on hold when he'd been hurt. As if she hadn't devoted herself completely to his recovery, rejoicing about each triumph no matter how small. Coaxing him through his therapies. Cheering his progress.

Harper stopped at a red light. Looked around, saw no one coming. No cops. Went through it. Besides, who said she had to tell Hank about every single decision she made or every conversation she had? She was his wife, not his possession. She had a perfect right to go where she wanted and say and do what she wanted.

But wait. Wasn't that pretty much what Hank had said? She replayed his voice: 'You do. What you want. Where you want.' Had he been complaining about that? Or just stating a fact?

Oh God. Was it possible that she had seriously overreacted?

Harper slowed down. Replayed Hank's words again. And again. Had he been saying he wanted them to go their separate ways? Or just that he needed to be more independent, like she was? Near the railroad station, Harper pulled to the side of the road, stopped the bike. Thought.

Her phone chimed. Hank? She reached around for her bag, dug it out of the storage unit and retrieved her phone. By then, she'd missed the call. Damn. She checked missed calls, hoping to see Hank's number, but no. It hadn't been Hank. She didn't recognize the number, not even the area code. And she saw that she'd missed a bunch of other calls, too. She took out a tissue, wiped drying blood off her hand. Blew her nose. Thought about going home, what she should do. Wondered why Hank hadn't called. What he really wanted. Rubbed her eyes. Glanced at the list of missed calls.

Good God – Burke Everett had left three voicemails. Vicki had called, too, and Harper's mother, just back from a cruise. And Leslie. Thank goodness – maybe Leslie could see her today even though it was the weekend – maybe she was even free now...

But Leslie's message said that she was away for the weekend. At a wedding. She could see Harper Monday at noon.

Harper bit her lip, looked at her cut hand, then off into the hills. She closed her eyes and drew a breath. Monday was a long, long time away.

Burke stopped cold, looked over his shoulder. Gazed quickly across the street. Seeing no one, he turned back to his car and stared.

The thread was gone. The thread he'd hung on the door handle had fallen to the ground. Which meant someone had tried to get into his car.

They'd found it. The Colonel's people had probably booby-trapped it, attached an explosive

151

device to it. He didn't dare stop to look for it. They had to be nearby, watching for him. If he lingered or poked around, they'd see him. No. No way he was even going to touch that car. No one was going to blow him to hell.

Burke kept walking, deciding what to do. Finally figuring out that he'd been wrong: there was no bomb. An explosion at a major university would draw too much attention. What they'd probably done was much less obvious, though just as dangerous to him; they'd put a tracking device in the car. That way, they could keep tabs on him. Follow his every move. Get to him later, with less fanfare.

But Burke wasn't going to let that happen. He walked on, not clear where he was headed. Used his phone to find a rental car office. But before they even picked up, he realized what an idiot he was: to rent a car, he'd have to use his credit card. They'd be watching for his card number, would track him that way.

In fact, now that he thought about it, he shouldn't use his credit card at all – even to go to a damned ATM for some cash. Did they think he was an idiot? That he couldn't figure out how they worked? Fuck them. His feet slammed the sidewalk. Pissed. What the fuck was he supposed to do now? He couldn't even get a fucking bus ticket without them finding about it. He felt trapped, cornered. Looked around. Lowered his head.

OK. OK. They couldn't stick around Ithaca forever, could they? He'd just have to outsmart them, stay out of sight. He needed to talk to

Harper; he'd already called a thousand times, would keep calling until he reached her. She didn't want to be part of this. But she was smart, would figure out that she had no choice; she was part of it, like it or not. Just like he was. She'd give him some cash and some food. Maybe even put him up for a while. He pulled out his phone, called her again. Got her voicemail again. Damn, couldn't she just pick up her damned phone? Just once? Why did he keep getting her voicemail? It made no sense...

Unless the Colonel had already gotten to her.

Christ. Burke stopped walking. Put his hands over his eyes. Pictured Harper dead somewhere, murdered like Pete.

Burke had to know. Had to find out if Harper was still alive, if he was the only one left. Taking side streets, watching pedestrians, he made his way back to her house.

Harper rode around Ithaca, uphill, down again. Rode around to the stadium, heard percussion bursting from the Big Red Band, roars from the Homecoming crowd. Kept riding. Across campus, past the Quad. Through College Town. Back downhill, across town to the lake. Barely aware of traffic or her location, Harper headed to nowhere in particular, riding her way through time. Unsure what she should do. Alone.

The Ninja cut through crisp air; the wind slapped her face raw, but she kept moving, determined to go faster than her heart. Eventually, though, like a homing pigeon, she found herself approaching the turn-off to the long dirt road

153

through the woods, the sign that said, PRIVATE PROPERTY: KEEP OUT. And without hesitation, as if that had been her destination all along, she took the turn on to Langston's place.

Slowing down too quickly, Harper felt the bike skid on pebbles and leaves. The engine was too loud, disturbed the stillness of the place, so she parked it. Decided to walk the rest of the way to the house. She pictured the crates, the hundreds of relics waiting for her, and picked up her pace. Work would help, she decided. She'd spend some time on the collection, think about something besides Hank for a while. Maybe she'd get a fresh perspective. Or at least escape the present one.

Leaves crunched under her feet. Around her, the woods were silent. Nothing moved. She wondered if Angus was around, if he'd pop out from behind a tree, challenging her right to be there. Or if Jake would appear again inside. Never mind. She had every right to be there, would simply insist that they allow her to work. She thought back to the relics she'd already seen: vessels, masks, bowls, figurines. Imagined the thrill of unpacking them, examining them.

Something rustled among the trees. Harper kept walking. Probably a squirrel. Maybe a fox. She looked around, though. Saw just foliage. Light filtering through branches. Dense clusters of trees. And one, along the road, that was missing a chunk of bark – oh God. Zina's tree.

Harper didn't stop to look. She picked up her pace, kept it up until she got inside the house. And even then, she kept moving, not letting the

shadows or stillness bother her. She went directly to the third floor, along the long hall to the east
wing, focusing only on her task. Determined to
ignore the nagging memory of Hank's declaration of independence. His voice, repeating, 'Two
lives. Do own things. Apart.'

No. She wouldn't let herself dissolve. She was
strong. Would survive somehow. Fine. He wanted her to do her own thing? She would. Starting
now. Tears kept filling her eyes, but she resolved
to get a grip. She'd concentrate on other times,
lost peoples. Escape into the past until she figured out how to bear the present.

Wiping her eyes, Harper booted up the computer, logged on to the documentation page.
Picked up a crate, set it on the worktable.
Methodically, efficiently, she removed the lid
and checked the items listed on the crate's content sheet. Took out the packing materials. Lifted
a Styrofoam packing case from the box, carefully removed the tape. Took an excited deep
breath. Opened it.

And froze, staring.

The case was empty.

A space had been carved, precisely shaped to
hold a vessel. But the vessel wasn't there. It was
gone. Harper rechecked the content sheet, scanned the list of items for a vessel. Saw: Mayan
polychrome vessel, 550–950 AD, five and a
quarter inches high. Estimated value $75,000.

Oh God. Harper couldn't breathe. A piece
worth that much money was missing? She looked around the room as if it might suddenly
appear. Damn. But how could it be missing? The

crate had been sealed. Obviously, someone must have opened it, taken the bowl and then resealed the crate. But who could have done that? The professor? Was this one of the pieces he'd moved to the laundry room?

And even if it was, how could she prove it? Would she be suspected of stealing it? Would Zina? No, that was ridiculous – anyone could have taken it. There was no security at all, no one guarding the collection. The only lock was a hundred years old, on the front door. Other than that, the place was abandoned, unprotected. They might as well put a sign up, advertising the place to thieves.

Lord. For all she knew, all the crates were empty. She scanned the stacks of boxes in the room. And suddenly thought of Jake – maybe Jake had found the vessel. Maybe he'd know where it was. Or at least, he'd vouch for the fact that the professor had moved pieces around and forgotten about them.

Harper let out a breath. Of course. The vessel hadn't been stolen, would turn up in a soup pot or under a pillow, if it hadn't already.

Still, Harper made a note of the missing piece before taking out another packing case. She was uneasy as she unwrapped and opened it, afraid it would be empty. Let out a sigh of relief when she saw that the case still held its relic: a figure of a priest with beadwork around his belt and on his headdress. Fourteen inches high. Made between 500 BC and 500 AD, estimated value of $20,000. Harper photographed and logged it. Took out the next box, opened it to find a

Teotihuacán mask, eight and a quarter inches high, made about 500 AD. It was nicked slightly at the top, but still estimated to be worth about $75,000.

Harper's phone rang a few times, but she let it go. If Hank was calling, she wasn't ready to talk to him yet, and if it was someone else, she'd rather work than take the call. Harper proceeded, unpacking the crate, item by item. Logging and photographing each relic. Finding bowls and gold pieces. Another copper mask, early to middle Mohica, Loma Negra, from around 300 BC, six and a half inches high, valued at $4,000. Even damaged, its expression was mesmerizing, powerful. Merciless.

Finally, she replaced everything in the crate, marked it as logged, and made notes of the discrepancies between the original content sheet and her itemized log. In addition to the vessel, two small sculptures valued at $40,000, were unaccounted for. Might be in the professor's sock drawer.

Harper logged off the computer, noticing that three hours had passed since she'd begun working. And that she hadn't dwelt on Hank in all that time. Had been completely absorbed. In fact, she felt stronger now, and refreshed. Stable. Ready to go home and face him, for better or worse.

Walking back to the Ninja, Harper braced herself for the latter. Hank's voice had begun again, telling her that their lives were going to change. Repeating, 'Need change. Dig.' And, 'Do own thing. Apart.' She refused to cry again, but her stomach churned, and she realized she hadn't eaten since early morning. Not that she had an appetite. Still, she was thinking about eating as she approached the tree hit by Zina's car. And the spot where she'd found Zina' body.

Up ahead, Harper saw the bald trunk, the dented part missing bark. She shuddered, picturing it. Had Zina's family ambushed her there? Had one of them run in front of the car, causing her to steer into a tree? She imagined them yanking Zina out of the smashed vehicle as she begged them to let her live. Harper stopped herself, didn't want to envision the killing, made herself focus on the leaves, the sound of her footsteps.

She moved through the woods, furious at the brutality of Zina's death. Closing her eyes, she reminded herself that, by comparison, her own family problems were trivial. At least she and Hank could be civil. They could solve their problems without shedding blood.

Passing the damaged tree, Harper steeled herself and glanced into the woods where she'd found Zina's body. She blinked, at first assuming she was having a flashback, seeing Zina lying there again. But the image wouldn't go away. There really was another body there. Only, this one was a man.

A big party was going on next door to Harper's house. Fraternity brothers, dates, alumni, wives. Lots of beer. A big banner, saying, 'Welcome Alumni'. A fancy buffet set up under an open tent in the side yard. A band blasted music from the balcony. Half the people were in costumes – one guy was dressed as a pirate, another as a zombie. Several were in drag. There was a chick in a way-short skirt, her top so low she might as well not have worn it, but somehow it had a badge pinned to it, and she had a cop hat on. An electric witch cackled whenever someone came too close, which was always. Skeletons and zombies swung in the breeze, hanging from trees. Fake tombstones were everywhere. A lot of noise, a rowdy half-in-the-bag crowd.

A good place, Burke figured, to fade into the background. He wandered, trying to be invisible. Pretending that his clothes were a thug costume. People stood in small clusters around the yard, yelling over the music, laughing, drinking, eating. He managed to grab a roast beef sandwich from the tent, wolf it down with a beer, smile and nod when someone said, 'Some game today, huh? Did we whoop Brown, or what?' Everything was going all right until a guy in Gucci walked up with an extended hand and suspicious eyes, introducing himself.

'Jeff Wasserman.' He moved his lips to show teeth. 'Class of oh-six.'

Jeff Wasserman asked what class Burke had been in. Burke shook Jeff's purposely too firm hand, returned the smile. Fumbled for an answer. The guy looked about his age, obviously could tell that he didn't belong there, that he'd never been at Cornell, let alone in the fraternity. Burke was dressed way wrong, didn't have a preppy blazer or an actual costume. Didn't fit. Shouldn't have taken the sandwich. The guy had probably

159

seen him take it, pegged him as a homeless guy stealing food. Well, hell – he had to eat. And he couldn't exactly go into a restaurant or food market.

Burke decided he'd come up with some bullshit about how he'd never graduated. Had flunked out and gone to Iraq. Which would explain his clothes, right? Vets could dress in old jeans and hoodies or whatever they wanted – even at parties. Even on Halloween.

'Mike. Mike Burke,' he began. But he didn't have to go on.

'Hey, Wassy!' a guy in a chicken suit called from the porch. 'We need a legal opinion.'

And so Jeff Wasserman and his Gucci blazer excused himself and took off, leaving Burke to grab another sandwich, refill his beer and wander to the back of the house where no one would notice him. Where he could watch Harper's house and look for her or anyone else who approached it. Where the trees would shield him from anyone tailing him.

But after almost an hour, no one had stirred at Harper's house. Damn. Where the hell was she? He wondered if she'd gotten the letter he'd sent, outlining everything just in case something happened to him. Every detail was there, implicating the Colonel. He'd wanted to give it to her personally, to make sure it didn't get intercepted, but ended up mailing it. And now, Harper was AWOL. Was it because she'd read the letter? Because they knew she knew?

Burke thought of calling again. What was the point? He'd called her dozens of times, gotten no response. And he had to ditch the phone soon – his third in as many days, afraid they'd trace his calls to Harper and find him from the signal. But he couldn't buy another phone without using his credit card, so he couldn't toss this one quite yet, just turned it off. Felt his sweatshirt pocket for the Beretta as he looked around. He could feel them around him, closing in. He'd seen them that morning, a black sedan following him along Seneca, so he'd ducked between buildings, stayed away from traffic after that. Moved as he'd been trained: efficiently, invisibly. Holding them off.

But they weren't far. He sensed them, the searing beams of their eyes. Smelled the tension, the adrenalin. They might even be here, mingling with the frat boys, disguised in costumes. He checked out a guy dressed like a hula dancer. Was he packing under his leis? And the dude in the chicken suit – he could have a whole arsenal under all those feathers. Burke shifted positions, scanned the perimeter. Saw nothing definite. But he wasn't fooled. They were watching him even now. Closing in.

Harper froze, staring at the body. Dark hair, dark skin. Lying exactly where Zina had been. Looking very much like she had looked. Perfectly still.

Damn. How was it possible that there was another body there? Right there, in that exact spot. Not a week after Zina had died there.

Harper listened, looked behind her. Heard nothing, saw no one. The body was on top of a pile of leaves, as if resting against them. She edged closer, peering through the trees. Looked for a wound, for blood. Saw neither. So how had he died? Strangling? Poison? Was there a knife in his back? Oh God. Who was this man? And who'd killed him? She thought of Angus, the way he disliked having people on the property. Had he completely lost it and killed a trespasser?

Or could it have been Jake? She remembered being alone in the house with him. His anger about his father's will, about losing the collection. Maybe this guy was a lawyer and Jake had taken his revenge? Ridiculous. Jake had made her uneasy, but that was no reason to assume he was a killer. Was it?

Besides, she shouldn't be standing there, staring at a dead body. She should leave it alone, shouldn't mess up the scene. Should simply take her phone out and call the police. Except maybe he was still alive ... Before she did anything else, she should at least find out if he had a pulse. Maybe she could help him. Maybe he was still alive and needed first aid. CPR.

Cautiously, quickly, Harper moved toward the man. Kneeling beside him, she reached for his throat, hesitating for a moment to touch him, to invade the privacy of his death. Dreading the absence of a heartbeat, the sensation of cool, lifeless flesh. But she stiffened, took a breath, and put her hand directly over his carotid artery, as she'd been trained. And, just before he sat up, yelling, swinging and grabbing at her, she saw the half-gallon of Cutty Sark near his feet, almost a quarter gone.

For a couple of hours, Burke managed to dig in and hold his position behind the fraternity. He drank beer, tried to blend in. Kept watch on the woods and Harper's house. Saw nothing. But he wasn't fooled. He sensed their presence. Where the hell were they? What were they planning? They weren't simply going to leave him alone and go away; they were up to something. His face itched from nerves. A tic had begun in one eyelid. It was like Iraq, being on alert, not knowing what was coming.

Around dusk, the party began to wrap up. Burke thought he'd grab a final sandwich when he heard rustling in the trees. Instinctively, he dropped, stayed close to the ground. Peered into the growth. The music pounded, shook the ground. And suddenly, something large shook the foliage, darted away – damn. A deer. A fucking deer. Burke released a breath and stood up again, relieved.

Remembering the sandwich, he stepped around to the side of the house. People were drifting away. Probably, he should ignore Harper's order to leave her alone. Probably, he should go back to her house and simply knock on the door. If she was out, he could wait for her there. What else, really, was there for him to do? He had no other options – she'd have to let him stay there until it was safe. Maybe she'd even have an idea for their next move.

Unless – fuck! Again, the unacceptable possibility hit him: it might already be too late. Harper might not be home because the Colonel had already gotten to her. In which case ... Well, in which case, he wouldn't let them take him, too. His hand closed around the Beretta. No way would he let the Colonel have that satisfaction.

The chip bowl was empty, and the potato salad was gone. Oh well. Burke grabbed his sandwich and headed out of the tent. He was taking a bite, thinking about ringing Harper's bell when he saw the guy in the chicken costume walking toward him. A cat burglar had moved in, blocking his path to the woods. OK. Time to take off. Still chewing, Burke pivoted, hurrying toward Harper's.

The guy took her by surprise, but Harper instantly shifted into combat mode, pinning him effortlessly. He didn't have much bulk, and she'd been trained. Had dropped men twice his size. She'd rolled him over, had a knee in his spine, held his arms behind him.

'What do you want?' he panted. He wriggled, still trying to free himself. 'Who are you? Let go of me.'

Harper smelled the booze in his breath. She tightened her grip. 'Hold still.'

'You want my wallet? Take it.'

'Who are you?' Actually, it was none of her business who he was. Or what he was doing there. He was trespassing, but that wasn't her concern; the property wasn't hers.

'Get off of me.' He twisted his neck, trying to look at her.

'Answer me.'

'No, I won't answer you. I won't tell you

164

anything until you get off of me.' He bucked.

'Hold still.'

'I will not hold still.' The guy was stubborn; even flattened on the ground, his face buried in dead leaves, he argued. Refused to give in.

Harper stayed put, but her left leg complained, didn't like bending for long periods. Soon it would throb. 'Look. I can stay here all day,' she lied. 'Tell me what you're doing here.'

'Tell me why you've assaulted me.'

Really? 'Dude. You're the one who did the assaulting. I saw you lying here not moving, and I came to help you. I was afraid you might be dead—'

'Well, now you know. I'm not dead. And I don't need your help. So just—'

'But you started swinging at me.'

'Well, of course. Naturally, I did. I was sleeping here, and suddenly you came at me out of nowhere!' He sputtered, but she felt his body relax. 'You put your hands on my neck – what would anyone in that situation do?'

Good point. In that situation, she'd have probably decked somebody. Then again, she wouldn't have been sleeping out here in the woods on the Langston's private property. Her left leg was tired of bending, beginning to throb. And she really needed to get home. 'OK. If I let you up, will you promise not to try to hit me?'

'If you leave me alone, I'll leave you alone.'

More conditions. Why wouldn't the guy just give in? Probably, she'd wounded his pride. Never mind. They both knew she'd flattened him and that he didn't dare mess with her again. She slid off his back, watched as he rolled over and sat up. He gazed at the trees. Then at her.

'So.' Harper crossed her arms. 'Who are you? And what are you doing here?'

'I might ask you the same.' He spoke formally, looked up at her with steady dark eyes. Familiar eyes.

'I'm Harper Jennings. I have a research position here.'

He nodded, then reached for his bottle of Cutty Sark. 'Nice to meet you, Harper Jennings who has a research position here.' He took off the cap. 'Would you like a drink?'

Burke didn't get far. Looking over his shoulder, he stumbled over a tombstone and hit the ground. Lost the roast beef sandwich. Regaining his balance, he reached for the 9 mm that had fallen from his pocket. Looked around to make sure no one had noticed him dropping it.

Saw a guy in a blazer approaching from his right. Recognized him.

'That him?' The chicken pointed a wing at him.

'You all right there, Burke?' The guy smiled at him. Held out an arm to help him to his feet.

Burke hesitated, feigning pain and surprise. 'Rick? What the hell are you doing here?'

Shit shit shit. They'd found him. Rick Owens, the Colonel's right hand man, was an arm's length away. Reaching for him.

Burke moaned, pretended to be unable to get up. Then, as Rick and the chicken stepped forward, he scrambled. Grabbing the ground for balance, he fumbled the gun, had to let it go.

166

Took off in a full out run. Made it past Rick, faked a move to the left, made it past the chicken and into the woods. Heard Rick calling, 'Everett! Hey. Wait – stop!' As if they were buddies and he wanted to catch a beer.

Burke zigzagged through the trees, uphill. Slipped on leaves, nearly tripping over stuff hidden beneath them – twigs or undergrowth. His breath was ragged, his lungs scraped raw, but he kept going. Felt Rick right behind him, didn't dare slow down to look. Heard his shoes crushing leaves. Heard his panting. Ahead, Burke faced a steep incline. Damn, maybe four feet straight up. No choice, no time – he bent his knees and jumped, legs out. Grabbed a tree trunk and held on. Steadying himself, he saw the fence.

It was ten feet tall. Extended at least fifty feet in each direction. And it stood just a few yards in front of him, blocking his way.

Instinctively, Burke whirled, kicking. His heel landed in Rick's gut, and the guy folded, sounded like a dying cat. Burke spun left, didn't see anyone else. Rick was recovering, climbing to his feet, pissed.

'What the fuck's wrong with you?' He wheezed, coughed, held his stomach. 'Are you nuts?'

Burke didn't want to get trapped following the fence, needed to get back down the hill, past Rick.

'I just want to fuckin' talk to you. Have a conversation.' Rick brushed dirt off his slacks, catching his breath. Reaching into his pocket.

Burke wasn't going to wait for the gun to

167

appear. Before Rick could say another word, he lunged straight at him, knocking him aside, and charged back down the ledge, through the trees, past the fraternity with its Halloween zombies and graveyard markers, its gaggle of costumed pot-smokers on the porch.

Burke didn't stop to look around. Was sure that Rick hadn't come for him alone, that others were nearby, lurking, about to pounce. He raced along Wyckoff, Thurston. Headed towards a bridge. Saw a gang of them coming towards him, some of them in disguises. One dressed as a clown. Really? A clown? But there were too many to take on. And Rick was behind him; he couldn't slow down, couldn't wait for Harper, couldn't rest, didn't dare. Rick was fast – Burke could hear him panting, closing in, just a few steps behind. He ran even after he'd lost his breath, even when his muscles burned. He sprinted on to the bridge, kept going even when he knew they had him. He was trapped, Rick behind him, the others ahead. Out of options, Burke looked around, grit his teeth. And did the only thing he could.

The man took a swig of Cutty. Held the bottle out for Harper.

Harper shook her head, no thanks. It was getting dark. And she had to get home.

'I have no diseases.'

Well, what was the harm? The encounter had left her jittery, and one sip wouldn't hurt, might even settle her nerves. Lord knew they'd had a rough day. Harper took the bottle, raised it to her mouth. Swallowed. Felt the heat of booze slide down her throat, warming her. She handed the bottle back.

'I am Salih.' Salih drank again. 'Salih Salim.'

Salih *Salim*? As in Zina Salim? Harper drew a breath, felt cold again.

'And, I admit it.' He stopped to hiccup. 'I am trespassing.' He blinked at her. 'Do you want to call the police, Harper Jennings? Do you think I should be arrested?'

'No. I'm sorry – I didn't realize. Are you related to Zina?' She didn't know what to say.

He tilted his head, looking at her. 'You knew my sister?'

Harper nodded. 'I ... yes. Actually, I found her. Here.' Why had she said that?

'You?'

Harper nodded.

They were silent for a moment.

'And when I saw you lying in the same spot, I thought ... Well, I thought there was another body.'

Salih nodded, 'Of course.' He gestured to a fallen trunk beside him. 'Have a seat.' Another hiccup. 'I'm afraid I'm not dead. I've simply been drinking for a while. I must have dozed off.'

Harper sat, assessing Salih. His body was beefy and long. His features fuller than Zina's, his eyes round and fiery. If Zina's death had been an honor killing, had he known about it? Had he actually committed it? Harper imagined it: Salih holding his sister while their father wielded a knife. Or the other way around. Oh God. This

169

man, Salih – was he Zina's murderer?

Harper stiffened and glanced at the path, ready to bolt. Salih blinked, his back sagging against a tree trunk. He'd had too much to drink to be a threat. Besides, she'd already taken him down once, could do it again. And she wanted to find out more about Zina's family.

'My little sister was a rebel.' He shook his head. 'Even more than me. I – well, as you can see – I take a drink. My family doesn't approve.'

Harper said nothing.

'But Zina defied our parents. Always, from the time she was a little child. She had to do things her way. So stubborn.' He chuckled. 'There are seven of us – oops. Were seven of us. Now we are six.'

Harper nodded. 'I'm sorry.' Salih couldn't have participated in Zina's murder. Her loss clearly pained him.

'We grew up in Britain. Our parents and three brothers are still there. But our business expanded to the United States, so some of us moved here. Zina was the youngest. She came over for school, and, right away, she was American. Watching *Friends*. Or *90210*. Or whatever. Getting ideas about men, about dating. Dressing in tight jeans, showing her body. She became a different person.'

He lifted the bottle, offered it to Harper. She accepted, took a polite sip. Passed it back.

'Zina came to my house the night before she was killed.' Harper thought he might want to know. 'She was frightened.'

Salih's eyebrows lifted. Interested.

'She was working here, at the house. And she thought she was being followed.'

'So she knew she was in danger?'

'Well...' How was she to explain that Zina thought she was being followed by a mythological creature? 'I think working here stimulated her imagination. She thought she was being followed by a shape-shifter.'

'A shape-shifter.'

'Yes. A Nahual.' Harper explained the Pre-Columbian belief in men who could change forms to guard their land and people.

When she finished, Salih blinked at her. 'My sister believed such a thing was real? A – what did you call it? A Nahual? That this Nahual was chasing her?'

'Zina was shaken. She thought something was chasing her. I don't know why.'

'A premonition.'

Harper didn't comment.

'Do you think that's what it was? A premonition of her death?'

Harper hadn't considered that possibility. Didn't know how to answer. 'I don't know.'

'They say these things happen. That people sometimes have a sign that the end is coming.'

Harper doubted it. 'All I know is that she was frightened. Not herself. Up until then, Zina had seemed very ... calm and realistic.' She'd wanted to say very competitive and aloof. 'Your sister was very strong willed. Very ambitious.'

'Too strong willed. Too ambitious. Forget the Nahual or whatever you call it. Her stubbornness and ambitions are what got her killed.'

171

Her stubbornness and ambitions? Why would he say that? Was Salih acknowledging that there had been an honor killing? Admitting that Zina had been killed because she was too Westernized? 'I don't understand...'

'If she hadn't been here –' Salih gazed into the trees – 'if she hadn't been working on that research position and insisting on that doctorate degree, if she'd just gone along as part of the family, helped with the business and gotten married like our parents wanted, she'd still be alive.' His voice broke; he looked away.

'You were close?' Stupid question. Obviously, they'd been close. The man was here, where Zina's body had been found, getting drunk and fighting tears.

His shoulders sagged. 'She was my little sister.'

But Harper was confused. 'There was a memorial for her at the university. You weren't there – nobody from the family came.'

'We have our own ways of mourning.'

Harper pictured family members laundering blood from their clothes after the honor killing. 'Still. It might have helped to see how many people cared about her. You said you were close.'

'I said *I* was close with Zina. I didn't say my family was. My family is ... We come from a different culture. I don't expect you to understand. But my sister parted ways with it. It's a long and bitter story. She defied our parents constantly. Whatever the line was, she crossed it. Many times. She embarrassed them publicly. She refused to participate in the family's business enterprises. She even refused to marry the man to whom our father promised her.'

'Well, of course she did, Salih. Nobody's parents arrange marriages for them in America—'

'My family is not American.' Salih cut her off. 'We were raised here and in Britain, but we are Syrian. Traditional and proud. Zina was part of our family. She knew our ways, but she resisted. When she turned her back on the family interests, my parents declared her dead. So there it is: why would they come to a memorial service for her when, to them, she'd already been dead for some time?'

Harper sat straight. 'What do you mean they declared her "dead"?' Had they issued her death sentence?

'I mean "dead". They cut off all ties. Including funds, even for education. I'm the only one who even talked to her. I kept urging her to make amends. To perform symbolic acts of humility and penance. I did it secretly, but I suspect my mother knows – knew.'

Again, he took a drink, passed the bottle to Harper.

'Who do you think killed her?' Harper took a sip, watching his eyes.

'That's a question, isn't it?' Salih shifted positions. 'Trust me, I think about it every minute. About who killed her...' He lifted the bottle, gulped booze. 'I know several who might have done it. Including close members of my family.'

Oh God. He suspected an honor killing, too? 'Are you talking about an honor killing?' Had

173

she just said that out loud?

Salih didn't answer, didn't seem surprised or offended by the question. He took another long drink, looked at Harper with a resigned smile. 'Honestly, you want to hear the truth? Whoever did it, my sister understood why. And whoever did it, no one else will ever know.'

By the time Harper returned to her Ninja, Salih had put away much of what was left in the Cutty Sark bottle. And among other things, he had confided that he believed his family was behind Zina's murder, that despite living in the West, they still held to the old ways of their heritage. His aunt had wanted a divorce and had been stabbed to death years before – no doubt at his uncle's hand. Before Harper had thought about the time, the sun had dipped to the horizon.

Salih promised he was perfectly fine and able to drive, but Harper insisted that he leave his car parked on the main road where it was. She was sober, having swallowed only a few sips of liquor, but Salih was slurring his words and teetering, in no shape to get behind the wheel. Harper insisted on taking him to his hotel. She dropped him at the Embassy Inn on Dryden Road, and, as darkness fell, watched him wobble inside. Then, she headed home.

Oh dear. Hank. What was she supposed to say to him? Maybe she should call and let him know she was all right. Then again, if he was ready to break up their marriage, he ought to get used to not knowing how she was. A hot pang ripped through her belly, into her chest. Was Hank

174

really doing this? Why? 'Why' didn't matter, she scolded herself. It wasn't about reasons or arguments; it was about feelings. Needs. And she couldn't make Hank need her or feel for her. Maybe Leslie was right that his healing required him to rediscover himself. Maybe his fall had damaged not just his bones and brain, but his ego. Before she'd met him, Hank had been quite a player. Maybe he needed to prove that he could still be one. That he was still hot, could still score with the ladies – well, if so, if that was what he needed, they were over for sure. Done. No way she'd stick around for that.

Cut it out, she told herself. She had no reason to think that Hank wanted other women. She was imagining things, needed to stop.

Harper revved the engine, sped down Dryden to Hoy, along Hoy to Campus Road, Campus to East. East to Thurston. Along the way, she passed Homecoming events, parties in transition from happy hour to Halloween Eve bashes. Something was going on at the Alumni House. Music pounded out of fraternities, sororities. Dorms. Harper kept moving, zipping past. Going home.

Finally, she pulled into the driveway. Saw the house dark. The Jeep gone.

Damn.

Harper got off her bike and stood, arms folded, feeling the chill of the night, dreading going into the empty house.

'Hey, Mrs Jennings!'

She turned, saw a kid from the frat next door. Dressed as a chicken. 'We still got some beer –

come on over!'

Harper waved. Thanked him and backed off. Turned away and headed toward the house. The last thing she wanted was to hang out with drunk college kids in Halloween costumes.

Or no. Maybe not the last thing.

Inside, she turned on the hall light, took out her phone and checked her messages. Nothing more from Burke, thank God. But Hank had called. Once. An hour ago.

Harper hesitated, afraid to hear the message. What was wrong with her? Why was she scared of a damned telephone message? Squaring her shoulders, she braced herself and played it back.

'Damn. Hoppa. Answer.' That was all. Not, 'Come home. I'm worried.' Not, 'I'm sorry. I love you.' Just a curse word and a command.

She played it again. His voice sounded strained. Hank was upset.

She pushed the 'send' button, returning his call. Waited, breathing unevenly for him to pick up. Heard his phone ringing in the kitchen.

Lord. Hank hadn't taken his phone? Where had he gone without it? And when was he coming back?

Or more to the point: *was* he coming back?

Harper closed her eyes, imagining their bedroom. His half of the closet empty. His razor missing from the bathroom sink. No. He wouldn't have moved out. Not so suddenly. It hadn't – couldn't have – come to that yet.

Even so, she didn't want to go upstairs. Damn Where had he gone? She thought of calling Vicki and Trent to see if Hank was there. But if he

176

weren't, she'd have to explain why she didn't know where he was. And she wasn't ready to do that.

Cursing, Harper flung her phone into her bag, stomped into the kitchen. Her stomach felt hollow; she'd been drinking but not eating. She opened the refrigerator, took out an apple, bit into it. Gagged. Her stomach was empty and rumbling but her body rejected food, refused to eat. Fine. She opened a cabinet, found the Halloween candy. Ripped open a mini-bag of M&Ms, poured them into her mouth. No gagging. Her body didn't object, accepted chocolate. Grabbing a second bagful, she didn't know what to do with herself, where to be. She couldn't stay in the kitchen. Couldn't stay anywhere. Walked in circles until she finally went back outside, on to the front porch.

She watched the street for a while, saw cars drive by, none of them Hank's.

The music from next store had quieted; it was dark now, and their post-game party was over. Alumni and their wives had gone; pledges were filling trash bags and folding tables, cleaning up. A few couples in Halloween costumes lingered in the yard, drinking and smoking dope among the plastic tombstones and hanging skeletons. A guy in a hoodie darted across the lawn, activating a mechanical witch who cackled and danced.

Harper wandered off the porch, down to the sidewalk, not ready to go back into her empty house. The night air was brisk. Harper shivered as a gust of wind picked up leaves, swirling them around. Maybe she should reconsider calling

Vicki and Trent. She could call just to say 'hi', not even mention Hank. If he were there, they'd tell her, wouldn't they?

Harper stopped mid-thought. Something was out there in the trees – running. An animal? No – a man. He wore a blazer and khakis, and, though he didn't seem to notice her, he was running right towards her.

Harper froze, gaping as he sped past. It had to be the darkness. She had to be mistaken. She turned, walking after him, staring into the night long after he was out of sight.

He'd been moving fast, she reminded herself. And it was dark; she hadn't gotten a good look. Even so, she could almost swear she'd recognized him. She was almost positive it was the guy Burke had said was following him: Rick Owens, from their detail in Iraq.

But that made no sense. Obviously, it hadn't been Rick. Why would Rick Owens be high-tailing it out of the woods behind her house in the middle of the night? In Ithaca? Burke had colored her thinking; she was taking on his paranoia.

The wind was picking up. Harper went back to the house, hearing sirens nearby, wondered what college pranks had gone too far this time. Inside, she changed into flannel PJs and listened for Hank's car. She went downstairs to make a sandwich. Found a can of tuna, a half-empty jar of mayo. A lone bagel, not too stale to toast. Mindlessly, she went through the motions of preparing food, on alert for the sounds of tires on the driveway.

178

Waiting, she chewed tuna. Swallowed beer. Thought of Salih and Zina. Her family alienated enough to declare her dead. Even to kill her. Thought of the relics to get her mind off of that.

Finally, headlights flared through the windows. Harper heard a car in the driveway and couldn't help it. She ran to the door, expecting to see Hank climbing out of his Jeep.

But the car wasn't Hank's. It had red and blue lights on top, and letters on the side, spelling POLICE.

And the person walking along the path to the house wasn't her husband. It was the homicide detective, Charlene Rivers.

Hank? Oh God. Something had happened to Hank – Rivers was in homicide. Had Hank been – oh God...

Harper couldn't move, couldn't speak. She watched Rivers' approach in slow motion, through a haze. This wasn't real. The detective wasn't actually there. Neither was Harper. Her mind was tricking her. Snipers fired; she felt the whizz of bullets flying past her cheek. Heard men scream. Smelled smoke as Rivers took a step, then another, wading through thickened air. And then, ever so slowly, Rivers smiled.

Wait. She smiled? How could Rivers smile at a woman whose husband had just been killed?

'Good evening, Mrs Jennings.' The words were dim, distant. The smile disappeared. Rivers kept coming. Spoke again, asking a question.

Harper's heart raged against her ribs, threatened to burst through.

179

Rivers stood facing her, watching her. Making words.

Harper strained to hear her over the roaring sounds of her blood.

'Mrs Jennings? You all right?'

She moved her head up and down, yes. Hugged herself, shaking.

'Well? Can I come in?'

Oh God, oh God. Rivers wanted to come in? Bad sign. Obviously, she didn't want to deliver bad news on the doorstep. Harper wanted to refuse her. To say, no, you can't come in. Because, somehow, if nobody told her that Hank was dead, he wouldn't be. Officially, anyway. As far as she knew, he'd still be alive. Wouldn't he?

Rivers took a step forward.

Harper's head moved again, up and down. She opened the door. Rivers went in. Harper hesitated, gripping the doorframe. Making herself breathe. Finally, she followed the detective into the house.

'Can we sit?'

Harper had to read Rivers' lips; blood rushed through her head like a waterfall, drowning out all other sounds. She was shivering violently, couldn't get warm so she pulled Hank's parka from the closet, put it on. Hunkered into it. Smelled Hank. Oh God.

Rivers was touching her arm, asking questions. Moving her lips: 'What's wrong? Are you sick?'

Harper wrapped the jacket around her. 'Chilled,' she managed.

They sat at the kitchen table, Rivers across from her. Studying her.

Harper waited, aware that time had slowed. That each moment was stretching and distorting. She heard her pulse, her lungs. She felt like screaming. Dammit, why couldn't Rivers just get it over with and tell her what happened to Hank?

Ask her, she told herself. Just go ahead and ask.

But she didn't have to. As soon as she opened her mouth to speak, Rivers reached into her pocket and took out an envelope. 'Mrs Jennings,' she began. 'I'm afraid I have some unpleasant news. There was a suicide tonight.'

Suicide?

'A man jumped off the Thurston Avenue Bridge.'

A man? Harper waited for Rivers to utter Hank's name. Why was she being so oblique? Shouldn't she be more empathetic? Shouldn't she prepare the widow for her loss, offer condolences?

'A bunch of students saw him. A man was there, trying to talk him down. The kids tried to help.'

Harper strained to listen to Rivers' details. Apparently, as the students approached, the man had tried to help him, offered him a job. But the jumper had refused, cursing and shouting that he'd never take a deal with 'that fucker'. Promising that 'your boss is going down'. Then he'd jumped.

The kids had called 911; in a matter of minutes, the body had been retrieved from the gorge.

Harper's pulse slowed. Rivers still hadn't said

181

Hank's name. Hadn't even hinted at it. And the story – well, the guy didn't sound like Hank. For one thing, Hank wouldn't have made such coherent statements. His words would have come out differently, in short spurts. So this dead man wasn't, couldn't be Hank.

Relief washed over her, made her giddy. Hank was alive. Although, if he didn't come home soon, he might not be that way long; she might kill him herself. Where the hell was he? She pictured him out at a bar. With another woman. His head too close to hers. Damn, she needed to stop imagining—

'Mrs Jennings?'

Lord. She hadn't heard a word the detective had been saying.

'I gotta tell you, you don't seem like yourself. You might be coming down with something.'

'Sorry. I'm ... fine.'

'As I was saying, his cell phone shows that he's called you several times today.'

What? Harper felt blood drain from her head.

'And there's another reason we think you know him. He had this in his pocket when he died.'

Rivers held up a piece of scrap paper. Handwritten letters spelled: HARPER REYNOLDS. Reynolds was crossed out, replaced with JENNINGS. And her address and phone number.

The realization hit Harper hard: it was Burke. He was dead. Burke Everett had jumped off a bridge.

Harper couldn't get warm. She wrapped Hank's

parka around herself and heated up some coffee, but kept shivering anyway.

Burke was dead? Oh God.

If she'd taken his phone calls, agreed to help him, would he still be alive? Was his death her fault?

She pictured him flying off the bridge. Lying limp and lifeless in the gorge.

A detail about his death resonated in her mind. She tried to figure out what. But Rivers kept interrupting, asking questions. Wanting to know who Burke was, how Harper knew him. Why he'd been calling her.

Harper told the detectives about serving with Burke in Iraq. About his recent visit and urgent need to talk with her.

Damn you, Harper. Don't tell them another word. She heard Burke's voice as clearly as if he'd been sitting beside her. *They won't believe you anyway. They'll tell the Colonel anything you say – you're digging your grave.*

Rivers frowned. 'After all these years, Mrs Jennings? Isn't it strange that Mr Everett suddenly came all this way for a visit?'

'Not really. Another guy we served with just died. Burke came here after the funeral.' And suddenly, Harper knew what had been bothering her: Peter Murray. He hadn't simply died; he had hanged himself.

First Pete, now Burke. Both dead. Both suicides. Harper shivered.

Rivers nodded. 'I see.'

'Actually, our friend committed suicide.'

Burke hissed: *Shut the fuck up, Harper – you*

183

can't trust her. Baxter has the cops—

'Suicide?'

Harper swallowed hot coffee. Felt it cool as it made contact with her icy gut. 'His name was Peter Murray. He hanged himself.'

Rivers met Harper's eyes.

'Also a suicide,' Rivers repeated.

Harper nodded. Hugged herself inside the parka.

'And when was this funeral?'

'Recently. A week or two ago.'

Rivers jotted down notes. Raised an eyebrow, waited for Harper to go on.

'Burke was torn up about Pete's death. In fact, he ... he sounded paranoid. Truthfully, I think he'd lost it.'

Stop, Harper. I mean it – button your trap.

'What do you mean "lost it"?'

Harper slid deeper into the parka. 'He had a theory about why Pete died. He was positive everyone who'd served on a special detail was in danger from a retired Colonel who was having us followed.'

Shut the fuck up, Harper!

'He said that, with Pete dead, he and I were the only ones left who could bring this Colonel down – he was irrational.'

Rivers watched her for a moment, then sighed. 'Some of these military guys, they come home changed. They can't readjust. My cousin's kid is like that. Can't hold a job, doesn't want to do anything. We worry about him.'

Harper wrapped her hands around her coffee mug, trying to warm them. 'Burke said his mar-

184

riage broke up.'

'See? That might have been what sent him off. What about work? Do you know if he had a job?'

Harper didn't. But she knew something else: that Burke's death was her fault. 'I told him to get lost. He was calling constantly, warning me about the danger we were in. He even showed up here at the house and got Hank upset – the guy was out of control.' She paused. 'But instead of getting him some help, I told him to buzz off. I just ... abandoned him.'

Rivers crossed her arms. 'So you're blaming yourself for this man's death?'

Maybe. A little. Yes. 'He needed help. I didn't look out for him. I left him on his own.'

They sat in silence for a few moments, drinking coffee.

'It wasn't your job to take care of this guy.' Rivers finally spoke. 'You're not in Iraq any more; he's not your responsibility.'

But he was. He'd been one of her guys; he'd come to her and she'd let him down.

'You couldn't have known what would happen and probably couldn't have stopped it anyway.'

Harper wasn't sure about that. She nodded anyway, so the detective would stop talking.

More silence. Harper stared at her coffee mug. Saw Burke diving off the bridge, the laces of his sneakers flying.

'Well. Anything else you can share on this guy?' Rivers pushed her chair away from the table. 'Because, first glance, seems pretty open and shut.'

It did?

'Guy was having a breakdown. He was depressed, losing control. Becoming delusional. Finally committed suicide.'

Suicide. Something icy ricocheted inside Harper's chest. She pictured Burke waiting for her to call back. Not daring to come to her home because she'd forbidden it. And, while she'd been out drinking with Salih, he'd given up. Lost all hope. Gone to the bridge and jumped. She heard the thud of his landing. Shuddered. Closed her eyes.

Detective Rivers stood. 'Where's your husband?'

Her husband? The question startled her. All evening, she'd been listening for Hank's car to pull into the driveway, but Detective Rivers didn't know that – why was she asking about him? What did she know?

'You're not in great shape, Mrs Jennings. I don't want to leave you here alone.'

Harper released a breath. 'I'm fine. Hank'll be back soon.' She hoped.

She glanced at the clock. Twenty after nine. Where was Hank?

As if in answer, a car door slammed outside. Hank was back. Unless it was more cops. No. She recognized the footsteps coming up the back stairs. Hank's gait. Harper froze, couldn't move. Rivers took their cups to the sink. Getting ready to go.

The kitchen door opened and Hank burst in wild-eyed. 'Hoppa?' He looked around the kitchen. 'Happened? Police.'

Rivers sat again, reviewing what had happened

for Hank. Asking what he knew about Burke. What Burke had said the day he'd come to the house.

'Jumpy. Wanted to see. Hoppa.' Hank didn't look at her. 'Wouldn't tell. Said urgent. Danger. Not. Why.'

'He was jumpy?'

Hank nodded. His eyes glowered. 'Looking. Behind him.'

Rivers sighed. 'Well, that fits.'

'Fits what?'

'What we know so far.' Rivers' eyes travelled from Hank to Harper, back to Hank. 'Mr Everett was extremely troubled. Possibly troubled enough to take his own life.'

'Self killed?'

'He jumped off a bridge.'

'Damn. But kill. Why?'

'Because of me.' Harper finally spoke. 'Burke asked me to help him. And I didn't.' Harper wanted Hank to hold her, warm her in his big muscled arms. But he didn't. Might not ever. She huddled into his parka across the kitchen from those arms, speaking to him for the first time since she'd left the house that morning. 'He must have come here looking for help again, and I wasn't here.'

'But kill self? He wait could. Or come back.'

'Mr Jennings, the guy wasn't thinking straight.' Rivers folded her arms. 'His buddy just killed himself. His marriage fell apart. He never readjusted to civilian life. He came to his old army pal but even she couldn't help him.'

The words felt like a blow to the gut; Harper let

187

out a soft involuntary grunt.

'Not to say it's your fault. You didn't do anything wrong. Mrs Jennings, look, statistically, each year there are twice as many suicides as murders – and that number is even higher among war vets. Given all the factors I just rattled off, it looks like a cut and dry suicide.'

Harper sat silent, only half listening to the detective, her thoughts spinning. It wasn't her fault that Burke had died – was it? She didn't dare look at Hank. Wished he would do something to reassure her – move his chair closer. Take her hand. Something. And, oh God – the detective would leave soon. What would happen then? Would Hank want to talk? Later, would they sleep in the same bed? She bit her lip, looked at her hands, began her spiral again. Oh God, Burke was dead. But it wasn't her fault, was it?

Harper watched Rivers, not listening any more. But Rivers was looking at her, so she tuned in, heard: '...second dead body connected to your wife in as many weeks...'

Harper sat straight. Cleared her throat. Tuned in.

'...don't seem connected to each other, but they're both connected to her ... understandable if she's shaken up.' Rivers eyed her but talked to Hank. '...keep an eye on her if I were you.'

Two bodies. Harper saw Zina again, her slumped body bathed in blood. And she imagined Burke, battered on the floor of the gorge. She recalled the indifferent stillness of Zina's flesh.

'Any news? Zina case?'

'Nothing I can discuss yet.' Rivers watched Harper. 'Mrs Jennings, are you OK?'

She wasn't. Zina had come to her for help and died. The same thing had happened to Burke. No question. Somehow, everything was her fault. She was toxic. No wonder Hank was done with her. Her stomach wrenched and she tasted bile. Harper stood and dashed to the powder room, about to be sick.

'Hoppa?' Hank waited outside in the hall.

Harper rinsed her face, patted it dry. 'I'm OK.' She stepped out of the powder room, drained.

Hank didn't say anything, just followed as she walked back to the kitchen.

'Are you all right?' Rivers stared at her. She was standing, as if about to go.

Harper's face got hot. 'I'm fine. Just upset – I haven't eaten much, and I guess I had too much to drink this afternoon.'

Silence. Two pairs of eyes watched her.

'I ... I was working at Langston's. And I ran into Zina's brother. He was there, at the exact spot where I found her—'

'Excuse me?' Rivers interrupted. 'You ran into who?'

Harper felt Hank's glare. 'He was drinking, visiting the place where she died.'

The detective's mouth dropped. 'Which brother?'

'Salih. Salih Salim – musical, isn't it?'

'You discussed the murder with him?'

Well, sort of. 'A little. I mean, I said I'd found her.'

189

Rivers sighed, crossed her arms. 'Mrs Jennings, tell me exactly what was said.'

'He ... actually, he thinks their family killed Zina. He suspects an honor killing because Zina defied their parents.'

'Where is Salih?'

Harper told her where she'd dropped him off, and the detective headed for the door. 'Mrs Jennings,' Rivers stopped as she was leaving. 'If Salih Salim contacts you again, let me know immediately.'

'But why? He's not the one who—'

'We've been trying to contact Zina's family since her murder. So far, we haven't been able to locate a soul. Every single one of them seems to have left the country.'

Harper waited, but Hank didn't say anything. After Detective Rivers left, he turned to the refrigerator, got out some sliced turkey and cheddar cheese. Started to make a sandwich.

A sandwich? He was hungry? Ignoring her?

Finally, she couldn't take it any more. 'Are you going to offer me one?'

He didn't turn around. 'Want?'

Her stomach still hurt, but it was empty; she'd lost her tuna sandwich. 'No cheese on mine.' Was he giving her the silent treatment? Acting as if nothing had happened? Didn't he care about Burke's death?

Harper took two beers from the refrigerator.

'Not enough. Drink. With Salih?' Hank's voice was flat.

He was mad that she'd been drinking? 'I didn't

really drink that much—'

'Wrong with. You?' Hank spun around, facing her, the mayonnaise jar in his hand. 'Killer. Zina. Might be this man!'

'Salih didn't kill her.'

'You know? How?'

How did she know? Well, because he'd told her. 'He wasn't dangerous. We just talked.'

Hank replaced the mayonnaise in the refrigerator, brought two plates, two sandwiches to the table. Didn't say a word. Began eating.

'Why are you so mad?'

'Mad?' His mouth was full. 'Why? Really?'

'It's not because I had some drinks with Zina's brother. You've been mad all day, right?'

Hank fumed, chewed. 'Just walked out. You. Today.'

Well, what had he expected her to do? 'I was upset. You said we needed to be apart. So I *let* you be apart!'

'Not talked. Not said. Just left.'

'What was there to say? You want to be on your own!'

Hank slammed a fist on the table; the plates bounced. 'Damn. Hoppa.'

She blinked, stunned. Hank, with all the frustration he'd had in his recovery, had never pounded a table. Never lost control. Tears rushed to Harper's eyes. She started to get up, but Hank put his sandwich down and grabbed her wrist.

'Sit.'

She sat. Felt his hand gripping her without tenderness.

'I've had a hell of a day, Hank.'

191

'Too.' Or two. 'Wife walked mad out. Killed could be, like Zina.'

'Really, Hank. I was in no danger.'

'No calls. No idea. Where you—'

'I didn't know where you were either. I got home and you weren't here. I tried to call, but you left your phone in the house—'

'Got dark. Went looking.'

'—so I was waiting for you, and meantime, they found Burke—'

'Drove all over. Trent's. Ruth's. Leslie's. No Hoppa. Not anywhere.'

'—and had no idea where you were or how to find you. So how do you like it so far, us being apart?'

They both stopped, stared at each other. Hank's eyes were flames, searing her. Harper's nostrils flared. Suddenly, Hank leaned over, grabbed her head and pressed his mouth against hers, hard, expressing his fury and frustration without the need for words.

When he released her, Harper was breathless, couldn't speak. Hank glared.

'Apart. Means. Not me leaning. Always on you. Doesn't mean. Not talking.'

What? Had she mistaken his meaning that morning? Overreacted to the word 'apart'?

'OK,' she began. 'I get that you're stronger and don't have to lean on me any more. But I don't see why you're so damned mad.'

Hank glowered. 'Why? Told you. You hide. Secrets.'

'I do not have secrets.'

'Bullshit. Burke. Didn't tell—'

'There was nothing *to* tell!'

'Man was crazy. Could you have. Hurt. Killed.'

No, Burke wouldn't have hurt her – but Hank kept talking. Repeating his list of Things She Hadn't Told Him. 'You took job Zina's. Didn't tell.' Hank paused, puckered and stretched his lips, limbering them to speak. 'Found maybe out family killed. Her. Didn't tell. Now today. Left. Drank with maybe man killed Zina. Wrong.' He stopped, reworked his lips again. 'What's wrong with. You. Hoppa? Want danger? Why?'

He went on for a while, scolding, listing things she'd done that were wrong or reckless. Or inconsiderate, secretive, selfish. Harper had never seen him so exasperated, wanted to calm him down. She didn't defend herself or try to explain; that would only fuel his temper. Besides, she didn't have the energy. Instead, she nibbled at her sandwich, strangely at peace. Because despite everything – her husband's complaints, the shock of Burke's death, the horror of Zina's murder – one fact was clear: Hank didn't want to split up. No matter what else was happening or how furious he was, he still loved her. She knew that from his kiss.

Harper awoke Halloween morning, not sure if Hank had come to bed or not. She'd fallen asleep as soon as her head had hit the pillow, too exhausted to dream. And the sheets beside her were empty.

It was after ten. She'd slept for eleven hours? Lord. Harper hurried downstairs, smelling coffee.

'Hank?'

He didn't answer. He'd left a note in the kitchen. He hadn't wanted to wake her, was out running errands. Would be home about three.

Harper held the note, sank into a kitchen chair. Listened to the silence of the house. Told herself to get it together, not to be so easily hurt. This was just a phase. Hank was proving that he could be independent. Once he'd shown that he could do things solo, he wouldn't need to any more. Would include her again. Meantime, she would not waste time and energy feeling sorry for herself.

She poured a cup of coffee, gazed out at the wooded spot behind the house. In the daylight, almost bare of leaves, the trees seemed sparse. She thought of Burke. How could he have killed himself? Had he been entirely without hope? Felt trapped by his delusions? Had he imagined he was being chased by the cluster of students and that man who'd been trying to help him?

Harper wasn't sure. But she couldn't stop thinking about Burke, his calls, his death. Setting down her coffee, she went for her phone, brought it back to the kitchen. Sat and played his last messages again.

'They found my car.' His voice was ragged, whispering. 'I don't dare use it, so I'm on foot. I know you don't want me to come over. Can you meet me somewhere? Harper, it's serious. They're all over the place, watching for me. I can't use my credit cards or they'll find me. Can you get me some cash? Call me back. We're not safe.'

His next call was breathless. More urgent. 'I gotta keep moving, can't carry the evidence. So check your mailbox. They're closing in and they'll do anything to shut me up. I'm on my way to your place. It's fuckin' showdown time.'

And the last: 'Damn, Harper. Where are you? Did they get to you already? At least call me the fuck back and let me know you're still breathing.'

No question. Burke had reached out to her for help, and she'd let him down. Harper sat at the table, drinking coffee. Thought about her mailbox. Maybe he'd left something for her? She ran outside to the street, checked the box. Found it empty. Burke hadn't left anything there. He'd just been rambling.

Back in the house, she popped a piece of rye bread into the toaster oven, looked for the butter. Damn – there was no butter. No jam either. She hadn't shopped all week. Maybe Hank would go to the grocery store on his 'errands'.

Reaching for a jar of peanut butter, she glanced out the window again. Heard Burke's desperate whisper, 'It's fuckin' showdown time.'

Showdown time. Burke believed that Colonel Baxter had people looking for him. That his car had been tampered with, his credit cards tagged. But he was getting ready to take his enemies on, face to face. Was that the attitude of a man about to take his own life?

Harper didn't think so.

Then again, Burke was unbalanced. Who knew what an unbalanced man's attitudes would be?

She heard him explaining Colonel Baxter's

195

theft. Telling her about the detail in Iraq. The cargo of stolen cash they'd loaded on to the helicopter.

It seemed preposterous. Probably, Burke had concocted it all as a way to blame his problems on somebody else, as his marriage, job and mental health were falling apart.

But Peter Murray was dead – Burke hadn't concocted that. And now Burke was dead, too. She thought of the other member of their team, Rick Owens. Had she seen him near her house?

The ding of the toaster oven jangled her; Harper spun around, grabbing her knife. Wow. Maybe paranoia was contagious. Harper took out her toast, used the knife to slap on some extra chunky. Took a bite. And thought about the only other living member of their detail. She ought to tell him about Burke.

Unless, of course, he already knew.

Thank the Lord for Google. In seconds, she'd grabbed her laptop and located hundreds of Rick Owenses. In a few more seconds, she'd found her particular Rick Owens and his business contact information in Washington DC. Rick, it seemed, was a political consultant. And if there was any truth to Burke's story, one of his major clients was Colonel Baxter, candidate for Senator.

Chewing her toast, she punched Rick's number into her cell. On the third ring, Rick's voicemail picked up. The recording was smooth, professional, positive, slick.

She pictured Rick in fatigues, covered with sweat and dust, swatting flies. Tried to put the voice with the image. Couldn't.

At the sound of the tone, she wasn't ready, hadn't planned what to say. It wasn't right to give bad news by voicemail; she shouldn't mention that Burke was dead. Still, she had to speak – her silence was being recorded. Finally, she spurted. 'Rick? Hi Rick, it's Harper – Lieutenant Reynolds. From Iraq. Give me a call when you get a chance? Thanks.'

She ended the call, after leaving her number, feeling clumsy. Had she really said that? 'It's Harper. Lieutenant Reynolds. From Iraq?' Like he wouldn't know who Harper was? They'd served together, for God's sake. And how many Harpers did he know? Well, it didn't matter what she'd said. The important thing was that he'd get the call, return it, and answer some questions about Burke and the Colonel.

Meantime, Harper had a blank day ahead of her. She should go to the grocery store. Maybe work at Langston's for a while. She rinsed her coffee mug and put the peanut butter away, headed up to shower. She was drying off, wrapped in a towel when her cell phone gonged.

She reached for it, hoping it was Hank. Saw the incoming call number, didn't recognize it. The area code was 202. Washington DC.

Rick was calling back. Harper grabbed the phone, answered the call. 'Hey, there, soldier. How are you?' she began.

'Just fine, Lieutenant. I hope you are, as well.'

The voice wasn't Rick's. Harper's hand tightened on the phone and her chest tightened as she recognized the gravely voice of Colonel Baxter.

Why was the Colonel calling? Did he know that, minutes ago, she'd called Rick Owens? Was he responding to that call?

She heard Burke's voice, whispering a warning: *They're closing in. They're watching.* But that was ridiculous. Rick worked for the Colonel; they were probably together. Rick must have seen the message and shown it to the Colonel, who just wanted to say hello.

'Heard you got hitched.'

He had?

'Sounds like he's a good guy. Sorry about his accident.'

What? How did he know about that? 'How did you know—'

'Oh, make no mistake: I keep tabs on my people, Lieutenant.'

What did I tell you? They're watching you. A chill rattled Harper's bones; she pulled Hank's robe off the hook, put it on.

'The older I get, the more I realize how few people I can truly rely on. And I never forget a person who's helped me out – let alone saved my life.'

Or who can expose his crimes, Burke interrupted.

'Back in Iraq, you proved to be one of those people. So I've kept tabs on you from afar to make sure you're doing OK.' He wheezed as he chuckled. 'Think of me like your crazy old uncle.'

Her uncle? How creepy. Harper gathered the robe around her, covering up. That detail in Iraq had lasted only what – five days? And based on

198

that, all these years later, he was her 'uncle'? Harper bristled.

I told you, Harper. He kept tabs on all of us because we can ruin him.

'Truthfully, sir, that's not called for—'

'Oh, trust me. It's not simply for your sake. It's for my own, as well. If a man has ambition in life, which, God help me, I do, he needs to surround himself with good people. When you find them, you're a fool not to keep them close, or at least to keep track of them in case you'll need to bring them close later. That little cadre of yours, that detail back in Iraq – you got us out of that ambush. If you hadn't, I wouldn't be here today. You proved yourselves to be people I could trust and rely upon. So I've kept track of each and every one of you, just in case.'

'Really?' Harper looked around, half expecting to see cameras in the woodwork. 'Well, then you know there aren't many of us left.'

A loud sigh. 'I know. Tragic about Peter Murray.'

Only Peter Murray? Didn't he know about Burke? 'And Burke Everett.'

A pause. 'Everett?'

'Yesterday. He went off a bridge.'

'Holy Mother of God.' The Colonel growled. He sounded genuinely stunned, dismayed. 'What in God's good earth is wrong with people? First Murray. Now Everett? Two suicides in – what? Two weeks? God almighty.'

Suicides? Harper scowled; she hadn't said it was suicide. But she guessed it was a safe assumption; probably, death by bridge was rarely anything else. 'And Shaw never made it home. So that leaves Owens and me; we're the only ones left.'

Harper heard paper shuffling in the background. People moving around. An unintelligible whisper. Then, 'Yes, Harper. Sadly, you're correct. The numbers are dwindling. Which brings me to the point of my phone call. You've heard about my Senate run?'

'Yes, Sir.'

'Harper, my opponent is formidable and it's a tough race. But I'm confident that I'll come out on top. And when I do, I'm going to need dedicated, trustworthy staffers. Rick Owens is already on board.'

Burke's voice interrupted: *Here it comes, Harper. He's going to try to sign you on. It's a pay off.*

'Frankly, my staff is off-balance. I need a strong woman's point of view. Someone who's a leader, who's smart, gutsy, innovative, articulate. And savvy. In other words: you.'

What did I tell you?

It took Harper a moment to speak. 'Colonel, I'm enrolled in graduate school. I'm about to write my dissertation.'

'I know all about it, Harper. Look. Archeology isn't going to go away if you put it off for a while. And, since your husband isn't employed, even with his disability payments, I know that you can use some income—'

What?

'—especially since graduate school doesn't come cheap at an Ivy League school like

200

Cornell.'

'Colonel.' Harper clutched the phone. 'This conversation – you're making me very uncomfortable.'

'I understand. You've thought you were all alone and on your own. It's an adjustment to realize that you're neither. Given your circumstances, Harper, I'm prepared to go even farther. I'll offer your husband a job, too – there's plenty of non-verbal work to be done...'

Harper stood with her mouth open, appalled. Colonel Baxter knew all about Hank, the nature of his injuries, their finances. He'd not just been watching from afar; he'd been downright spying on them, just like Burke had said. What the hell?

'...believe me, I take care of my people. Come on board; you won't have to worry about another bill. I'll talk to Professor Schmerling. Dean Van Arsdale, too. They'll give you an extension on your—'

He even knew her professor? 'How do you know Schmerling and Van Arsdale?'

Another sigh. 'Harper. Like I said: it's my business to be connected. I've kept my eye on you. You're one of the people I've wanted to keep close.'

In her mind, she heard Burke: *Be careful, Harper. He's not just trying to buy you off; he's also warning that he knows everything about you, including how to hurt you. It sounds like an offer, but it's really a threat.*

'I'm a little overwhelmed here.' She felt bullied and spied upon. Tried to hide the indignation in her voice.

'Understandably. No need to answer me today. Just consider what I've said.'

'But I assure you, my husband and I don't need—'

'Harper,' he interrupted, 'let me ask you this: out of all the places in the world, why do you think Burke Everett killed himself right in the town where you live?'

'I didn't say he—'

'I think I know why. Everett came to you because he trusted you, because of the bond formed between you when you served in that detail. Owens and I saw him at Murray's funeral, and he was almost irrational. He had wild notions about the past. Tell me, did Everett share those notions with you?'

'No.' It came out of her mouth too fast. Sounded untrue.

'Really? Didn't you see him?'

'No.' Damn – the lies just kept coming. Why was she denying it? If the Colonel had been 'keeping tabs' on her, he already knew she'd seen Burke.

'You're saying you never saw him?' His voice sharpened; he knew.

'No, wait – I forgot.' She scrambled to change her story. 'When he first came to town, we had coffee. That's how I found out you were running for Senate – he told me. After that, he called a few times, but we didn't connect.'

'And? Did he seem stable? Say anything unusual?'

Don't tell him anything. He's fishing.

'Well, he was depressed about Pete. He took

202

the loss real hard.'

'Murray's death. That's all he talked about?'

'Yes, pretty much. Why?' Harper sat stiffly on the edge of her bed, biting her lip.

The Colonel sighed. 'I understand you don't want to betray a comrade, Harper. But I can't help but think that Burke came to you for a reason. Probably to confide something he considered important. And I have to think that it's no coincidence his death took place in your neighborhood. In fact, I'm betting it was a symbolic message to you, reinforcing whatever he confided. Am I completely off base here?'

Sonofabitch. He's threatening you. Saying that my death was a symbolic warning. A message telling you how close his people are, how much they can get away with.

Harper heard whispering on the Colonel's end of the line. A chair creaking and background shuffling. Then his blustery voice again. 'Sorry – I keep getting interrupted. But that's my thinking. Terrible news about Everett. A real waste. Makes me even more determined to reach out and gather my people close. Think about what I've said, Harper. I can take care of you and your husband, and you can be of service. We both win. Sound good?'

'Thank you, sir,' Harper's jaws were clenched. Something told her not to stand up to him. Not even to turn him down flat. 'I'll think about what you've said.'

When she got off the phone, Harper stayed on the bed, replaying the conversation. Feeling invaded. Exposed. The Colonel knew way too

203

much about her life. Was way too pushy. How odd that a man running for Senate from a state she'd never been to, a man she hadn't seen or heard from in years and had served with for only a few days – how odd that such a man would spy on her for years and call right after Burke's death to offer jobs for her and her husband.

It made no sense at all.

Unless, as Burke said, the Colonel was trying to buy her silence about what happened back in Iraq.

Harper thought back to the detail, loading cargo on to the Colonel's helicopter. Had those crates been loaded not with supplies, but with millions in stolen hundred-dollar bills? Was that why the Colonel had kept an eye on everyone who'd worked that detail? Was it possible that, for all his seemingly irrational paranoia, Burke had been right? Why else would the Colonel take time out of his busy campaign, just a few days before the election, to suddenly call her and out of the blue offer her a job?

Because he thinks you know the truth and he wants to scare you silent.

'Shut up, Burke.' She said that out loud. Good God, what was wrong with her, hearing Burke's voice in her head? Answering it? Enough. She needed to get away, out of the house. Harper pulled on jeans and a heavy sweatshirt, grabbed her phone and bag. Hesitated for a moment, long enough to text Hank: *See you later*. No need to give details; he hadn't given her any.

She was in the driveway, about to climb on to her

Ninja when Detective Rivers pulled up. Oh God. What now?

'Your friend wasn't at the hotel when we got there, Mrs Jennings,' she called as she got out of the car.

Her friend? Oh, Salih.

'No one by that name was even registered.'

'But I dropped him there...'

'Might have used a false identity. Fake name on the credit card.'

Really? 'I don't know why he'd do that.' She felt as if she knew him. As if they were friends.

Rivers looked off into the woods behind the house. 'Well, it's probably not all that complicated. In my experience, people use false IDs when they're up to no good.'

'Detective, Salih didn't kill his sister.'

Now Rivers looked at Harper. 'You know that for sure?'

Of course not. 'He was terribly upset about her murder. He didn't seem capable of—'

'I looked into the honor killing theory, Mrs Jennings. Lots of times, people kill their relatives even though they love them. They see the murder as a sacrifice necessary for the good of the entire family. A man might feel obligated to kill, let's say, his sister. It would be his duty. That's not to say he wouldn't then deeply mourn her loss.'

Harper tried to imagine Salih cutting Zina. She couldn't. Salih hadn't done it. Had he?

'These are people from a different culture. Different rules. If the brother did it, he thought he was doing the right thing. And his family will respect him for it. But I doubt we'll get the chance to find out for sure. Salih wasn't at the hotel, and the family's cleared out of their place in New York.'

A breeze scattered leaves around their feet.

'I don't suppose he told you where he was going from here?'

Harper shook her head. 'Sorry.'

'Damn. Looks like this one's going cold.' Rivers frowned. Didn't leave. Just stared past the garage at the trees behind the house.

Harper wanted to get going, sensed that she wouldn't want to hear whatever Rivers was going to say next.

'You or your husband own a Beretta, Mrs Jennings?'

A Beretta? 'No.'

'We asked the frat boys next door. Odd. None of them claimed it either.'

'I'm sorry – I'm not following you.'

Rivers shook her head. 'Of course you don't; I haven't explained. The fraternity boys were cleaning up after their party, and one of them found a gun by a ledge uphill back there – unregistered. So we're asking if it belongs to anyone in the area.'

Harper nodded. 'Well, it's not ours.'

'I didn't expect it would be. The only prints on it belonged to the suicide victim.'

Burke? Why would Burke's gun be in the trees behind her house?

'And that leaves us with a conundrum, Mrs Jennings.' Rivers' brown eyes narrowed, and she crossed her arms. 'How would you rather die, by jumping off a bridge or taking a bullet in the head?'

Seriously?

'Because, between you and me? I can't see why a man who had a loaded gun in his possession would go to all the trouble of climbing on to the wall and jumping off a bridge.' She paused. 'Of course, his gun was all the way back here. Maybe he dropped it. Couldn't find it. Still. Something about this one doesn't seem right.'

Burke had had a gun? Not a surprise, given his state of mind. But, as experienced in combat as he was, Harper knew that he wouldn't have accidentally dropped it. He would never have lost his weapon; someone must have taken it. Must have ambushed him. There must have been a struggle, and he must have dropped the gun as they fought. Harper envisioned it; saw Burke running for his life, heading in the dark on to the Thurston Avenue Bridge. Feeling trapped there. Climbing on to the ledge.

But that was ridiculous. Students had seen him jump. They'd tried to stop him.

And they'd said someone else had tried, too. A man had been there, talking to Burke.

And Harper had seen a man run past her – a man who'd looked a lot like Rick.

Stop, she told herself. You're imagining things. Buying into Burke's delusions.

But what if Rick had been there, had struggled with Burke back in the trees. What if Burke had dropped his gun and run off, and Rick had followed, running right past her? What if they'd confronted each other on the bridge, and Rick had not been talking Burke down, but had been threatening him?

No question: rather than surrender, Burke would have jumped.

After Rivers drove off, Harper rode around town, replaying snippets of conversations with the Colonel, Hank, Salih, Burke. And, finally, with Rivers. Memories fragmented and bumped each other. She was finding Hank's abrupt note, then hearing about Burke. Then finding Zina's body. Or drinking with Salih. Or listening to the Colonel.

She thought of Rivers' reaction to Burke's fears of Colonel Baxter.

Rivers had scoffed. 'Let me get this straight. The man is running for Senate from the state of Tennessee?'

Yes.

'And supposedly, he stole millions of dollars from Iraq, yet he's never been accused or even suspected of this theft.'

Again, yes. Harper had explained that she was just repeating what Burke had told her.

'And this guy, Baxter – he's suddenly having everyone who served on your detail killed in order to prevent potential accusations that, even if they were made, nobody could prove?'

Harper had agreed that it sounded crazy; she hadn't believed it either. But then, Burke had died. Peter Murray had died. And the Colonel had suddenly offered her a job.

'He what?'

Harper had told Rivers about the phone call. The Colonel's too intimate knowledge of her life.

Rivers had shaken her head. 'Mrs Jennings. This is all – well, no question, it's odd. Nevertheless, other than an unexpected job offer and your buddy's unsubstantiated claims, there's no evidence that Colonel Baxter has broken any laws. Am I right?'

She had been. Unless Burke actually had possessed the proof as he'd claimed. But even if he had, who knew where it was? Harper rode her Ninja, airing her mind out, trying to think of other things. Like where Hank was. Or no, not that. And not about Zina and Salih, either...

She refused to think about them even as she pulled on to the turn-off that led to the only place where she could find stillness and peace, where she could escape. She parked the Ninja not far from the spot where she'd found Zina's body. When she heard the gong of her phone, she grabbed inside her bag, hoping it was Hank. Fumbling, she grabbed her flashlight instead of her phone. Then her wallet. When she finally pulled the phone out, she saw that it wasn't Hank at all. She recognized the number on the screen, though. It was Richard Owens.

He knew that the Colonel had called her. 'I'm following up.' He sounded smooth, cheerful. Like a political consultant, not a hitman.

'There's nothing to follow up on, Rick. He made an offer, but I'm not interested.'

'Hell, Harper. You called earlier – I got your message.'

Right – why was she snapping at him? He was just returning her call. 'I wanted to tell you about

Burke.'

'Yeah, Baxter told me. It sucks, doesn't it.'

It did.

'But the very fact that you called me, that proves you still feel connected.'

Connected?

'That's what Baxter and I want to point out to you: we three share history. We're linked, like family. Look, I know the Colonel pretty damn well. He's a good guy. He comes across a little too strong. But he's for real, I swear.'

For real? As real as Burke's 'suicide'? Harper wasn't sure about Burke's death, but she didn't want anything to do with Rick. She started toward the Langston house. No way she was letting the Colonel or his people anywhere close to her. Even a punk like Rick.

'Listen, Harper, I'm actually not far from you.'

Harper stopped walking. He wasn't far? So that man she'd seen running – had it really been him?

'I had to visit a big backer in Rochester, and before I head back south, tell you what – I'd love to sit down with you.'

Oh no. Harper tensed. Heard Burke warn: *Don't let him.*

'I can come by, catch up, and we can iron out the specifics of your offer.'

What? 'You mean today?' Harper looked around, as if Rick would walk out of the woods.

'Sure. How's this afternoon?'

'Sorry. Can't today, Rick. I'm ... busy.'

'Busy? It's Sunday. And Halloween. What arc you doing, trick or treating?'

'I'm working.' None of your business.

'Working? On what?'

Seriously? 'It's archeology stuff. Nothing—'

'You're on a dig?'

'No. I'm documenting a collection of—'

'OK. So you're on campus? I can come by.'

'No, I work at a professor's house. Off campus.'

'So, I've got a car – how far away will you be?'

Man, he was pushy. Why was he pressing so hard? 'Rick. It's not going to work. Besides, like I said, I'm not interested in working for the Colonel.'

'At least hear me out before you make up your mind. No harm in listening, right? Are you at work now?'

Good God. 'Yes. I am. And I've got to get back to it. So—'

'OK. I get it. I know when I'm shot down. Hey. Good to talk to you, Harper. Catch you later.'

Harper stood on the gravel road, baffled. Irritated. What was Rick's problem? Why had he been so persistent? Was he the Colonel's duty officer? Had Rick sent people to quiet Burke? And Murray? Would he come after her next? She looked around, saw nobody among the trees. Of course she didn't. Colonel Baxter was ambitious, overbearing. Possibly dishonest. But a killer? Doubtful. Even if he'd stolen the money, he wouldn't assassinate every potential witness. He was a renowned public figure with a distinguished military record. The idea of him putting hits on people – well, it was absurd.

211

Enough. She wasn't going to think about them now. In fact, she wasn't going to think about anything that was newer than Pre-Columbian. Tossing her phone back into her bag, she closed her eyes. Took slow deep breaths. Relaxed her shoulders. Felt the stillness of the air and the trees. Opened her eyes again.

The gray sky sent soft light through the branches; yellow and copper leaves speckled the ground. The air smelled of crispness, of autumn. Harper walked on, her shoes crunching pebbles, crushing leaves. One step. Another. Gradually, though, she noticed another sound – soft and muted. Echoing her steps. She stopped, listening. Looking around. Bracing herself to fight – was someone following her? One of the Colonel's people?

Silence. Then a breeze skittering through the trees. Damn. Now, she was the paranoid one; Burke's fear had infiltrated her psyche. *You shouldn't be alone*, she heard him warn. *They're all around, watching. Closing in.*

'Shut up,' she muttered, walking on, feeling an ache in her left leg, hearing the sound again. Deciding that it wasn't actually a sound; it was more like imperfect timing, as if her footsteps were slightly out of sync with the noise they made.

Harper kept going, reaching into her bag, searching for her pocket knife, finding her flashlight and phone, her water bottle. Pretending not to notice the sound, she tried to identify its direction. And when she did, even without a weapon, she spun around to face it, adopting a

212

combat stance.

A young buck stood among the trees. Bambi? That's who'd shaken her up? She exhaled, shook her head. Noticed the odd coincidence: deer were the Pre-Columbian symbol of the Seventh Day. And it was Sunday – the seventh day of the week. Chills skittered up Harper's spine even as she dismissed the fact as meaningless. Big deal. So she'd seen a deer on a Sunday – Pre-Columbian beliefs were fascinating but had no basis in reality. After all, they were nothing but myths. Deer symbolized many things: they stood for the hunt; they were the rescuer of the moon goddess. And they were a favored shape taken by Nahuals.

The deer lifted its head and met Harper's eyes, stared right at her, directly, as if challenging her. But of course, it wasn't doing anything of the kind. Deer were meek; deer didn't challenge. The creature was probably terrified, frozen in fear. Harper stood motionless, watching it, recalling Zina raving about a Nahual. Swearing she'd encountered a cat-man-bat-owl ... Deer?

No. Absurd. Still, for a long moment, neither of them moved. The deer watched Harper; Harper watched the deer. A stand-off. Harper assured herself that the deer would not change forms and turn into a hunter. Wouldn't come after her heart. A Nahual hadn't killed Zina; there was no such thing as a Nahual, and Zina's family had killed her.

Still, the animal was large. Muscular. And its eyes were steady, holding her gaze. Harper told herself to get moving, asked herself why she was in a staring contest with a four-legged furry opponent. Decided that she would end it. Breaking her stare, she took a deliberate step forward and looked at the path ahead.

A few steps later, Harper turned to look back. She didn't see the deer, but she heard an odd sound for daytime: the mournful hoot of an owl.

Inside the house, Harper went straight upstairs, through the main house to the east wing. She needed to work, to focus on concrete items and tasks. So she hurried to the workroom with the logbooks, cameras and computer.

And saw that the boxes had been moved.

She'd left the crates that she'd already itemized and labeled neatly arranged in stacks. But they weren't stacked any more; they stood side by side at odd angles, sloppy and disorganized. Harper stood at the door, surveying the room, her senses on alert. The intruder might still be around, hiding behind stacked boxes. Silently, she reached into her bag, feeling for cylindrical shapes, sifting through granola bars, water bottle, pens, pocket knife, tampons – until, finally, she retrieved her flashlight and slowly stepped into the room, aiming the light into dark corners behind the hodgepodge of boxes. Finding no one, she moved out, down the hall, searching each shadowed room. Nobody was there.

Could she be mistaken? Had she been so upset that she hadn't actually left the boxes as neatly arranged as she'd thought? No. Absolutely, no. She clearly remembered separating the boxes

214

she'd examined from the others, leaving them in order, clearly coded. Stacked neatly one on top of the other.

One of the brothers must have been there. Angus or Jake – both resented her presence. One of them must have come in to see what she'd done, messed around with the boxes, probably to annoy her. Well, they'd succeeded. Now that the boxes had been tampered with, she'd have to reopen them and confirm that the contents were still there as she'd logged them, undisturbed. Damn.

Harper shoved her flashlight into her belt, went back to the workroom. Put on the protective gloves and got to work, rechecking the crates one after another, confirming their contents, redoing what she'd already done. Finally, when she'd made sure everything was intact, she re-stacked the boxes neatly in the corner and lifted a new crate on to the worktable. It had a mark on the side: Utah. She reached for the lever to pry the top up. Opened it. And stared.

Nothing was in the box. Not even packing material. OK. There could be a lot of reasons it was empty. The professor might have removed everything. Or the contents could have been loaned out to a museum. Or broken during shipping, or sold. She read the list fastened to the inside of the lid. Three vessels and a gold mask were supposed to have been in the container. The note said nothing about lending or selling the relics.

Harper did the only thing she could; she added the items to her growing list of missing relics.

215

Then she resealed the empty box, placed it in the corner with the others she'd examined, and opened another crate. Lifting the lid, she hesitated, worried that this box might be empty, too. But it wasn't. Wads of packing material cushioned individual casings. She pulled each out carefully, and opened them, one by one.

There were seven Narino ornamental gold pieces from around 750 AD. Each with dramatic projecting human faces, valued at $15,000.

A detailed avian sculpture from 2200 BC, thirteen and a quarter inches high, decorated with a double row of onyx knobs, valued at $10,000.

Two early classic Veracruz warrior sculptures from about 300 AD, with black skin, elaborate ornamental clothing, even detailed helmets. Valued at $15,000 apiece.

The final object on the contents' list was missing. A Honduran marble vessel from the Ulua Valley, early post-classic period, about 1000 AD. Eight and one eighth inches deep, with geometric patterns and a projecting feline face with open mouth and jaguar fangs, handles in jaguar forms. Valued at $55,000.

Damn. The most valuable and intriguing piece in the crate was missing. Harper looked inside again, found only packing materials. The vessel wasn't there. Why were so many pieces missing? Even if the professor had been absent minded, could he have removed all these missing pieces? Could he really have stashed unique $55,000 treasures in his soup pots?

Harper stared at the empty crate, frustrated. Too many important pieces were simply not accounted for. Someone would probably have to search the house, look under cushions, behind books. Even inside those legendary hidden passageways, if they existed.

Under the work light, the gold ornaments glowed. The warriors stood strong. Photographing them, Harper calculated that, according to the listed insurance estimates, even without the vessel, this one box contained about $130,000 worth of artifacts. She glanced around the room. Counted fourteen crates. The hallway and other rooms held dozens more. She did some rough math, estimated that the collection was worth several million. Possibly tens of millions.

Lord. She'd known that it was valuable. But now, adding up the estimates on the itemized lists, she couldn't quite grasp the numbers. Or the incredible fact that she had the opportunity to actually put her eyes and hands – well, her gloves – on such rare and high-priced relics.

Carefully, Harper made a note of the missing vessel; recorded and verified the presence of the other objects. Then, before repacking them, she studied each piece. Felt their textures and weights, studied their detail and aesthetics. She held them, sensing the presence of their creators, as if the hands that had crafted the pieces could reach across centuries, touching her through their work. Who had formed these gold ornaments? Or clothed the figurines? Had the bird sculpture signified the soul of a dead warrior? She was examining its wings when, suddenly, her concentration broke. Harper sat up, alert. Hearing – no, *feeling* – someone coming up the

217

stairs.

No one's there, she told herself. But her instincts knew better. She'd had this sense many times in Iraq; it wasn't a sound or a visual. In fact, it wasn't anything with a name – just a certainty that someone was approaching. Maybe it came from a stirring of the air or the beating of a heart. But it was a certainty that she'd learned not to question, that had saved her life more than once.

Silently, Harper slid off her stool. Grabbing the lever, she stepped toward the door. And didn't even breathe.

Rick Owens walked past the 'No Trespassing' sign, proud of himself. He'd played Harper like a fiddle, got her to tell him everything he needed to know without her suspecting a thing. In fact, she probably thought she'd brushed him off. No way she had a clue that he was right here in Ithaca. Let alone, not far behind her on the road, following her Ninja.

He stopped to admire her bike. Not a bad choice for a female. Nice chrome—

Rick spun around, hearing a rustle in the bushes. Saw a squirrel scampering up a trunk. Rolled his eyes at his own jumpiness. He continued along the gravel path, his sneakers almost silent. Not that anyone would hear him; the place was deserted. Well, except for Harper. She was here. The Ninja said so, and so had her cell phone. Nice to have connections who could trace calls.

But he wouldn't have any more fuck ups. Not

to brag, but despite what had happened with Burke, he was good. Efficient. Persuasive. He'd get the job done, according to plan. He'd show her how urgent things were, how the country was at war – not just war like the public ones in Iraq or Afghanistan or the rest of the hot spots. No it was fighting another, almost invisible war; one much more destructive and insidious than those others. One being fought right here at home, quietly, untalked about. A war that was eating the country from its gut, taking it down. The only hope was strong leadership by someone who could get people off their asses, inspire the military, mobilize the general public, close the borders. Make America strong again. A country not to be messed with.

First, this infernal, internal cancerous war had to be won. And Harper could be – no, she *needed* to be part of it. She had to choose a side. Step up. Not like Murray and Burke. Rick pursed his lips, felt the soreness of their loss, the betrayal.

For a few minutes, he hung back in the darkness of the trees, scouting out the front of the monstrous old house. The place was like a damned hotel, seemed wide as football field. But no problem; he'd find her. He could move like a shadow, disappear into dust. And he'd done his homework on Harper, on this place. Had studied the unsolved murder that had occurred here on this very site a week ago. The way the woman had died. The location, the position in which Harper had found her.

It was almost as if someone had set that murder up to make his worst-case scenario easy for him.

Not that he'd have to take Harper out; his mission was to persuade, not necessarily eliminate her. Even so, combat images he'd tried to erase kept reviving themselves, popping into his head. Like the open eyes of a dead Iraqi boy, their look of disappointment. Rick blinked, trying to shake the boy from his mind, but he heard familiar screams and rifle fire; saw a leg in the middle of the road, smelled burning rubber and flesh. He rubbed his eyes. Felt the ground shake. Sweat rolled down his back, and his arms tingled from the vibration of his machine gun. Finally, he slid into a crouch beside a tree trunk, grounding himself against its rough bark.

When the images faded, he sat for a moment, recovering. Then, making sure he was safe, he checked his watch. He'd lost half an hour. Damn. Recovering, he looked over his shoulder, made sure no one was around, and darted to French doors at the side of the house. Jimmied the lock. Swung the door and snuck in. All of this in less than fifteen seconds.

Rick checked the pistol in his pocket. He wouldn't need it, of course, but kept it at hand always, even when he slept. Just in case. He moved silently across the house, along a long hall to the foyer. He wandered through the first floor, looking for Harper. There were way too many rooms. A library or study. A formal living room, a dining room that could seat dozens. A big room with a high ceiling, completely empty. A huge kitchen, divided into three large rooms. A laundry room and servants' quarters. Rick turned and went back to the stairs. Harper wasn't on this floor; he was wasting time.

He started up the staircase, his hand on his pistol, prepared. He took the steps quickly, invisibly, without a sound. Wandered through the second-floor bedrooms. One after another, like a damned dormitory. There had to be a dozen, some empty, some cluttered with random junk, a few full of heavy, old bedroom furniture.

And lots of dust. As he exited the first bedroom, Rick barely stifled a sneeze. Shit. The fucking dust was up his nose; he'd caught the sneeze this time, but the damn thing would come back. He stepped into a corner, rubbed his nose against his sleeve, pressed his nostrils with two fingers, waiting for the tickle to subside. Damn dust anyhow. He hated the stuff, had fought in it, slept in it, eaten it ... In Iraq, it had coated every inch of him – even the crack of his ass. That dust had been hell, but it was sand dust. Clean. Not like this dust that smelled of old age and decay. And death. Like that saying: dust to dust.

When he was sure he wasn't going to sneeze, Rick continued, easing from room to room, checking each even though he was sure Harper wasn't in any of them. He'd developed a clear image of where Harper was, sensed her presence the way he used to sense an unseen silent insurgent. Rick took his time, relishing the hunt, using old skills. Verifying his instinct that Harper was upstairs.

Finally, he moved to the stairway, glided up the steps. Followed his instinct to go east. Crept along the long hallway to the arch, saw wooden boxes stacked in the hall. Headed for the room with a light on. His heart rate picked up, his breathing shortened; he smelled Harper's scent above his own sweat. Rick felt his weapon in his jacket pocket where he could get to it, but reminded himself this wasn't going to be a battle. It was going to be a conversation between friends. And, even if it went wrong, compared to combat, this was nothing. This would be a piece of cake.

Slowly, Harper moved away from the worktable, gripping the lever. Who was there? Probably, just Jake or Angus. Nobody to worry about. Still, she was careful to be silent as she stood at the door, peering into the hall. A man was coming up the stairs. Wearing a camouflage jacket.

Her glimpse was quick, but she saw he wasn't Jake or Angus. He was shorter. Beefier. Familiar.

Harper moved into the hall. 'Rick?' She glared at him in disbelief. 'How – what are you doing here?'

Rick froze, mouth open, eyes darting. Instinctively, his hand went to his pocket, quickly relaxed and moved away. Harper recognized the reflex; Rick was carrying a gun.

'Harper. Surprise!' He forced a grin, took the final two stairs and headed towards her, his arms wide for a hug. 'You look terrific. Great to see you.'

Harper didn't return the smile, didn't allow the hug. Her scowl stopped Rick mid-step, yards away.

Rick sighed, looked at the lever. 'Wow. What were you going to do with that?'

'Knock your brains out.'

'I guess I shouldn't have surprised you.'

'I told you on the phone I couldn't see you. Did you miss that? Go away, Rick.' She turned to go back to the workroom, dismissing him.

'Seriously? After all this time, that's all you have to say? "Go away"?'

Harper didn't answer.

'OK. You're right. I'm too pushy.' He followed her, stepping around stacks of crates to get in the door. 'But it's important that we talk. Critically important.'

Harper moved through the aisle between stacks, returning to her spot behind the work-table, sat on her stool. Put the lever down. Folded her hands like an angry schoolmarm. 'Fine. You have two minutes. What do you want?'

Rick smiled, opened his mouth to answer. But she cut him off. 'No – no, wait. First, I want to know how you even knew where I was. What did you do, follow me here?'

He lost the smile. 'I had to do what I had to do.'

'And how did you get in?'

Rick met her eyes.

'Really. You broke in. What did you do, break a window?'

He grinned. 'No. I'm better than that.'

'What the hell do you want?'

'I had to see you. To convince you to join us.'

She tilted her head. 'This is about Baxter. His job offer?'

'He needs to know you're with him, Harper. He wants you on his team – our team. Look, you and I are the only ones left from our detail. He trusts us. He feels indebted because we risked our lives to save his.'

'That was war. It was our duty.'

'He's personally committed to us. And he wants to bring us together again as a team. He's authorized me to increase his offer – name it, Harper. What would it take to bring you on board?'

Burke's voice echoed, warning her. *He's trying to buy you off. Tell him to fuck off.*

Harper shook her head. 'You know what, Rick? I'll tell you what I told him: I'm not interested in working for him. So you're finished here. Bye, now. Have a safe trip home.'

Harper picked up one of the gold ornaments, began repackaging it.

'Harper, let me tell you about Baxter's plans for the country. Will you at least listen? All he wants to do is bring you on board. Think of him as a rich uncle, who wants to make your life easier.'

'Why would he want to do that?'

'Because he takes care of the people who've helped him get to where he is.'

'Lovely.' Harper heard Burke cursing. 'Please give the Colonel my best.'

She carefully sealed the package, wrapped it in tape, set it back into the layer of foam in the crate. When she looked up again, Rick was gone.

She listened for the sounds of his steps on the stairs, heard nothing. Rick was stealthy and he was wearing sneakers, but still, she should have heard a creak in the floor, a brush of fabric

224

against wood. But she heard nothing. Harper sensed his presence, knew that Rick was close. Probably just outside the door, in the hall. With a gun in his pocket – or in his hand. Why wouldn't he leave?

'Rick?' she called to him. 'I know you're out there.'

He didn't answer.

Cursing, she grabbed the lever, waiting. Certain that Rick would reappear. And in a matter of seconds, he did.

'I can't leave.' He stood in the doorway. 'I made a commitment to recruit you. I can't accept a "no".'

Harper stood. Rick came closer, his hand near his pocket. Harper anticipated his movements, bracing herself. What did he intend to do, shoot her? Or convince her to jump off a bridge?

Harper waited, silent, not moving. Rick came closer, a smile slithering across his face. 'All he wants is your loyalty.'

'Rick,' she decided to be frank. 'I didn't have a clue about our detail's real purpose or the money Baxter stole until Burke explained it to me.'

Rick scrunched his face, scratched his ear. 'What are you talking about?'

'Even now, I don't know for sure what happened. But no way I'm risking that it might be true. I'm not taking a pay-off "job" from a thief who betrayed his own country. Baxter may have bought you, but he can't buy me.'

Rick sighed, leaned against the wall. Dropped pretense. 'How can you be so fucking naïve, Harper? Baxter did what he did *for* his country.

So he'd be in a position to get it back on track.'

'Spare me, Rick. Just go before I call the cops.'

'The cops? What, because I broke in? Seriously?'

Harper looked him in the eye. 'Tell me you didn't force Burke to jump. Tell me you had nothing to do with Pet—'

Rick cleared his throat, bent his knees and suddenly leapt up on to the worktable, crouched among the priceless relics, pointing his gun at her head.

Before Harper had a chance to react, he frowned. 'Harper, I really can't accept another "no". Are you sure you won't reconsider?'

Harper froze.

'Put that down.' Rick meant the lever.

Harper let go of the lever and eyed the muzzle, mind racing. He could easily have killed her. Could kill her even now. He had the advantage, had taken her by surprise. So why he wasn't he shooting her?

Probably, he didn't intend to shoot her. So what did he want? For her to accept a pay-off from Colonel Baxter? Was it really that simple? Or was it more – maybe the relics? Was Rick there to steal them? Had he already stolen the missing pieces? For the Colonel? After all, the Colonel had stolen all that money in Iraq – maybe he was also stealing relics?

'Come on, let's go. Let's talk.' He faced her from the tabletop. 'I don't want to hurt you, Harper.'

'What the hell, Rick?'

'I'll do whatever it takes to convince you to

accept Baxter's excellent offer. Can't I persuade you to rearrange your schedule and find some time?'

She eyed the gun, thought of Burke diving off the bridge. Had Rick held a gun on him, too? Had he forced Burke to jump? Did he plan to stage her suicide, as well? Good God, stop thinking, she scolded herself. Just take the asshole down. Get the damned gun.

Finally, her training resurfaced. Harper took a breath, centered herself, leaned back, and crashed her forehead directly against Rick's, sending him flying backwards on to the floor. Relics rolled and rattled, even fell. Were they broken? Harper couldn't stop to look. She dashed around the table and crates, pouncing on Rick as he scurried to his feet.

Something hard – probably his gun – smacked the side of her head. Pain stunned her; darkness and white light flashed in her skull, but she wasn't down. Harper grabbed his ankles as he tried to run, pulled at his shoes. A sneaker came off in her hand; she tossed it aside, pulled his foot with both hands. He hit the floor with a sharp slap. Half crawling, Harper came at him, but he rolled, bent his knee and slammed his leg full into her chest, launching her backwards. Harper flew. And flying, she suddenly smelled smoke, heard an explosion, waited to land on top of a burned out car. To see pieces of the guys in her patrol scattered in the street, on her stomach – no. She couldn't get sucked into a flashback. Even as she sailed through air, she struggled to anchor herself in the moment.

The impact of smacking into the wall accomplished that, jolting her into the present. Proving that she was not in Iraq, but at Langston's house. Landing not on a car but against a wall. And bouncing off of it without a weapon, facing a former comrade who, though wobbly, still held a gun. Half dazed, breathing heard, she readied herself for his approach.

'Fuck.' Rick grunted as he stepped closer, pointing the gun at her. 'Settle down. I just came to talk. Just listen to what I have to say.'

Harper waited, hunched, feigning injury. As soon as he came within reach, she swung her strong leg, trying to kick the gun away. She missed, felt the momentum of her foot crunching ribs, heard the simultaneous roar of pain and blast of pistol.

In a final surge, Rick charged forward, falling against her, knocking her against a wall panel. Which gave way under her weight. Harper tumbled through it, falling into darkness. The fall probably lasted just a second, maybe two. But in that time, Harper had several distinct thoughts. First, she wondered if she'd been shot or even killed, and if she was falling into hell. Next, she recalled Hank falling off the roof, wondered if his fall had seemed this endless. Finally, she felt a pang of unbearable sorrow, picturing Hank and realizing that, if she were dead, she'd never ever see him again.

Rick stumbled to his feet. Bitch had knocked the air out of him, broken his fucking ribs. Dazed, he realized his left calf stung. And it was bleeding.

228

Fuck. Fuck. Fuck. She'd fucking made him shoot himself in the leg?

Where was she? Where the fuck was she? Forget about the Colonel's plans – he'd blow her cute fucking little head off.

But she wasn't there. Rick turned in circles, rotated, swinging the gun up and down, back and forth. Looking behind the boxes, even though she hadn't been anywhere near them.

It was like she'd disappeared. Like she'd gone right through the wall.

Maybe he'd passed out and she'd run off? Damn, had he let her get away? No. He was sure. The gun went off and he'd hit the ground, but he'd gotten right up again. No lost moments. He would know if he'd been unconscious; wasn't new to battle or wounds. Still, where the hell was she?

Rick stumbled around, gun still dangling from his hand, trying to think. One thing was sure: he needed to stop bleeding or he'd fall down and die right there. Needed to make a tourniquet. Turned in circles, confused. Fumbled around, wincing, groaning. Reaching hurt; moving any part of him hurt. Even breathing. She must have smashed six ribs. Might have sent one into his lungs.

Damn. Blood was pooling in his sneaker, the one he still had on. He leaned against the wall, dragging his wounded leg because it buckled when he put weight on it. Finally lowered himself to the floor and managed to steady his torso while his arms unbuttoned his jacket and pulled his T-shirt over his head. He slapped himself in the face. 'Do not pass out,' he said aloud as he bit a hole in the shirt. Blinking, shaking his head, refusing the darkness that tried to wash through his head, he ripped the shirt into strips, rolled his pant leg up, exposing the wound. The bullet had gone at an angle, passing through the muscle, going in the back of his calf and out the front. Bleeding like a motherfucker. Damn T-shirt strips kept stretching. He had to keep tightening them, yanking, annoying the wound, and the damn thing killed. Well, he was no pussy, could take the pain. Still, this shit was messed up, shouldn't have happened. As soon as he got the bleeding under control, he'd go find Harper and settle this. Miss PhD. Miss I-don't-want-a-job-in-Washington, even for Baxter. Miss I'm-better-than-you-are, too-good-even-to-hear-you-out.

Rick tightened the tourniquet, took off his remaining sneaker. Leaned against the wall just for a second, to regain his wind. No matter what it took, he'd show her, once and for all, how wrong she was.

The impact of landing reverberated through her body. Each bone, each nerve had its own collision and reaction. Harper couldn't move; pain jolted her limbs, her back, her skull. Worst of all, she couldn't see. Oh God – was she blind?

'Help.' She screamed, but her voice was a croak. 'Somebody!' She tried again but began to cough. Her ribs raged with each cough, and she tasted blood and dust. Finally, her body quieted, and she lay still, her breath ragged, hearing nothing else. Seeing nothing but blackness.

After a moment, she yelled again. 'Hey, Rick!'

Her voice was stronger now. 'Rick! Can you hear me?'

No answer. Maybe he was dead? Had been shot in the struggle? Damn. Why couldn't she see? Panic surged in her belly. Maybe the blindness was temporary. From the blow to her head when she hit the ground. Maybe it would pass. Meantime, she couldn't just lie there; she needed to get up, told her legs to bend, her head to lift. But her parts didn't care what she said, refused to obey. Harper lay back, staring into the dark, felt it creeping into her head, wandering through her veins, seeping over her thoughts, and finally carrying her away.

Sitting there, his leg on fire, Rick realized the mess he was in. Even if he found Harper, he probably wouldn't be able to get through to her and get her to sign on. But now, if he dispatched her, it wasn't going to look like a suicide with his damned blood all over the hallway. And he wasn't strong enough to clean it up. Let alone to set the scene. He was in shit. Deep in shit.

Grimacing, he reached for his phone. The Colonel would send someone to pick him up, help him out. Karl, the guy who'd helped him tail Everett – he must still be in town. Should have come along on this job, too. They'd underestimated its difficulty.

His hands were bloody, left marks all over his Blackberry as he made the call.

But before anyone could pick up, he pressed 'end'. Closed his eyes, put his head back, cursed. What the hell was he thinking? Was he really going to call the Colonel and tell him that he'd fucked up yet again, even let the target get away? Oh, and by the way, that he'd shot himself?

From the beginning, the Colonel had made it clear; there was no room for failure. Too much was at stake. People were with him or they weren't. No middle ground. His Senate seat was a critical phase of a history-making plan. No one – certainly not Rick – would be considered valuable enough to jeopardize it with scandal or worse. If Rick admitted to screwing up, the Colonel would no doubt send Karl, but not to rescue him.

Rick struggled to his feet, grunting, deciding to do what it would take to survive. His wound wasn't all that bad; he'd seen plenty worse. He had to keep focused, on task. Had to find Harper and get his job done. If they found her outside, maybe hanging from a tree, they might not come inside for a while. Might not see the blood right away. He'd have a chance to come back and bleach the place later.

Limping, he stuck the gun back into his belt, pocketed his phone. Where the hell had she gone? He checked behind the crates again, searched every room on the floor, gazed down the stairs. But before going down them, he had an idea. Rick went back to the wall where he'd last seen Harper and began tapping, listening for hollow sounds.

When Harper opened her eyes again, she saw nothing. Her sight had not returned. Oh God. She stopped breathing, felt her chest tighten. Do not panic, she commanded herself. Do not panic? Really? She couldn't see. Wasn't sure where she was or how badly she was hurt. Or how long she'd been there. Or if anyone would ever find her. She listened, called out.

'Hello?'

Hollow, empty silence.

'Anybody?' Darkness swallowed her voice.

OK. Enough. Time to get up and find a way out of there. Except that she couldn't quite get up. Could barely lift her head. She was dizzy, shivering. Her thoughts broke apart incoherent, fragmented before she could grasp them. She closed her eyes again, smelled old wood, dirt. Mildew. Mold. And thought of Leslie, how she'd helped her to remember things through hypnosis. Relax, she heard Leslie's voice in her head. Let the tension out of your feet, your legs, your thighs. Breathe slowly, from your diaphragm. Gradually, Harper replayed what had happened. She saw herself upstairs, working with the collection. Upset that so many pieces were missing. She'd been about to pack up and go when – out of nowhere – Rick had shown up with a gun in his pocket.

She remembered his claim that he just wanted to 'talk'. But his weapon had spoken for itself. She remembered headbutting him, but everything after that was a blur of blows and kicks until she'd slammed a hallway wall, and – what? Gone right through it? Had she fallen through a wall?

Harper replayed the fight, not sure her memory was right. After injuries, people often had memory gaps or distortions. But she was certain. She'd hit the wall and *passed right through it*.

How was that possible? Besides, if she'd broken through a wall, wouldn't she have just landed in the next room? Or in a closet? How had she fallen down a whole story or two – into nothing?

Something tickled her memory but wouldn't show itself. Her mind was swollen and foggy, and she closed her eyes, trying to control her shallow breathing and quell her jagged pulse. And, all at once, a memory surfaced, and Harper knew exactly where she was.

The tales about secret passageways in the Langston house weren't just lore; they were true. The wall she'd hit must have been a false panel that led into a passageway, and it had given way, sending her into a hidden corridor. She thought of the stories about the passageways. The one about an actress who'd never been found. Harper shivered.

Never mind. That was just a story. She pushed herself up on to her elbows. Damn. Her head and back pulsed with pain. Something warm and wet – had to be blood – oozed down her face; she touched her head, found the source. A gash on her temple. Vaguely, she remembered getting hit there. Asshole Rick had slugged her with his gun. Harper put her hands on the ground, pushed, managed to sit up. Checking her body, part by part, she found no breaks, no bullet wounds or other cuts. Slowly, she bent her legs and climbed to her feet. She stood unsteadily, unbalanced in the dark. Suddenly dizzy, she crouched again, steadying herself. Her thoughts were tedious and muddled, the darkness disorienting.

Relax; she replayed Leslie's voice. *Breathe.*

Harper inhaled. Concentrated on breathing. Thought about Burke and Murray. The Colonel offering her a bribe. Rick coming at her with a gun. After a moment, she straightened her back, winced in pain. And cursed as she stood again.

Blind or not, she was going to find her way out of there. And when she did, she'd settle things with Rick Owens. And Colonel Baxter, too.

Damn. The whole wall sounded hollow. As if there were a room or empty space behind it. Harper must have known, must have escaped through a hidden door. Rick looked up and down, felt the panels, trying to open the thing. He pressed against it. Pushed on the top, the bottom, the middle, trying to find a latch or a hinge. He backed away, examining the wall from a different vantage point, trying to see if the molding looked uneven. He moved up close, pressing his cheek against the plaster, trying to find tiny inconsistencies in the texture.

Nothing.

Shit. He had to find her. He stood still, staring at the wall. Picturing what was on the other side. Of course – probably, it was a secret room, and she was in there hiding. Maybe huddling in fear? Breathing heavily? He leaned against the wall again, holding his breath, listening. Hearing nothing. Fuck.

But who was in there. She had to be. People

didn't just disappear, and there was no place else she could be. Rick leaned against the wall and called, 'Harper. I know you're in there. It's no use.'

Listened again. Heard no movement. Damn. The woman was smart, well trained. She could probably stay there for hours. Maybe a couple of days. The only way to get her out would be to go in and get her. Fine, no problem. Surely, he could break through a flimsy old wall.

Again, Rick tapped the plaster, this time listening not for what was behind it, but for what was in it. Deciding it was neither too sturdy nor too thick, he stepped back, leaned away and pounded the thing with his fist. And recoiled, howling, having overestimated his strength. Whimpering, he saw flashing lights, felt pain shooting through his hand and arm, along his bones. He cradled his hand, cursing the thin swatches of plaster that had splintered and fallen to the floor.

OK. He needed something heavier. A tool. There were tools in the room where he'd found Harper. His leg throbbed, resenting the walk, but he limped back there. Found a hammer on the shelf – exactly what he needed. Encouraged, Rick felt more optimistic. Actually had a glimmer of hope as he made his way back to the wall.

Harper knelt, feeling her way around. There was a boarded wall a few feet away on either side of her; the floor felt like wood, only grainy. Was it dust? She patted her way ahead, but – damn.

236

Something sliced her fingertip. What the hell? A knife? She pulled her hand away, sucked blood from the cut. Cautiously, she put her hand back, felt the thing. Something smooth with a jagged edge, like a broken dish. A shard of – oh God. A shard of pottery? A broken relic?

For the first time since she'd seen Rick, Harper thought of the relics. She'd left them unpacked on the worktable, out in the open. Exposed. And when she'd fought with Rick, some had been knocked over, might have been broken. Oh God. Had a piece of one gotten caught in her clothing? Fallen with her? Gently, she felt the piece, avoiding its sharp edge, trying to identify its shape and texture. But the fragment wasn't definite enough. She couldn't be sure. Damn – was it part of the bird? Or one of those exquisite warriors?

Harper set the piece down, gaped into darkness, seeing nothing. She turned the opposite way, say the same nothing. Nothing. Do not panic, she ordered herself. Think. Make a plan. But wait, was something slithering around her ankle? Oh God. She kicked air, slapping her ankle, shaking off whatever it was. If it was anything other than her imagination. But, damn, it felt like a snake. She kicked again and stomped the ground, smashing whatever it was. If it was. Were there snakes in there? Spiders? Rats? Who knew what creatures were creeping around in the darkness? Harper told herself to take charge. Make a plan. But how? What could she do? She was trapped behind a wall – inside a hidden, secret, possibly unknown passageway. Not only that. It was completely pitch dark. She had no

237

idea which way to turn, how to get out. And if she found her way out, Rick and the Colonel's other lackeys would be waiting for her.

Harper's muscles tensed. Her stomach lurched. She smelled blood and burning rubber, heard gunfire. Men shouting. Flies buzzing around her eyes ... Damn. She bit her tongue sharply, grounding herself in the moment. She couldn't afford a flashback; the situation was already bad enough. She needed to focus and find her way out. Because, except for Rick Owens who no doubt wanted to assist her in a fake suicide, nobody – not a single soul – knew where she was. She was on her own.

Fine. If she couldn't see, she'd feel her way out. Hands on each wall, she took baby steps in a randomly selected direction, exploring the ground ahead with her toes, slowly testing the solidity of the ground before shifting her weight. After a few steps, her shoe bumped something; she stooped to feel what it was. Found something straight and long. Not her lever. Something shorter, smoother. With a knob at the end.

Her flashlight! She actually squealed with joy as she grabbed it. She'd forgotten about it; it must have fallen from her pocket. But here it was. Oh God. A miracle. Her flashlight.

The walls seemed liquid, as if they were swaying. Rick knew better. He'd been hurt before, knew the signs. Damn Harper had knocked him flat and he'd hit his head. Plus he'd lost blood. It wasn't the walls that were swaying; it was him. Not to worry, though. He'd been hurt worse.

Even now, he could hear the explosions ringing in his ears. Could see Humvees burning, smell charred flesh. No, this was nothing. No ambushes. No IEDs. No snipers waiting to pop him. Even half conscious, this was still a piece of cake.

The hammer seemed awfully heavy. He was losing strength. Even so, he swung at the wall, hit the spot where he'd cracked the plaster. Sent more chunks flying. Swung again. Again and again until, finally, a small blotch of darkness appeared. He'd broken through to the other side.

Encouraged, he kept the hammer going, slamming the wall, breaking off pieces of plaster and lath, widening the gap. When the hole was baseball sized, he leaned forward to peer through it. And lost his balance and nearly fell when the entire panel gave way, swinging open. Rick pulled back, stumbling. The panel snapped shut.

Apparently, he'd accidentally pressed the spot that opened the door. He blinked, trying to identify it. Pressed the panel. Nothing happened. Pressed it again, a little to the left. Then to the right. Then higher, lower. Frustrated, he punched the wall. The door swung open. Before it could snap shut, Rick put his shoulder there, holding it open. He looked inside, expecting to see Harper somewhere in the room. But Harper wasn't there. Neither was the room. Rick gazed into the space behind the wall and saw a well of black, nothing else.

He looked down, saw a rotted staircase, collapsed on to itself. Couldn't see how deep the hole was. 'Harper?' he yelled. His voice disappeared into darkness. He coughed. 'Harper – are you OK?'

Of course she didn't answer. Was too stubborn. Would die before she surrendered an inch. Well, fine. He'd do it her way. But he couldn't stand there, wedged in the doorway. And, if he moved away, the wall would close again. He had to get down there, but what if he couldn't get the fucking wall to open again?

For a few seconds, he stood, considering his options. Looking for something to stick into the doorway to stop it from shutting. Seeing the crates. Contemplating ways to shove one into place without letting the door close. He leaned his torso toward the stack of crates, pressed his fingers around the closest one. Tugged. It inched forward. His leg screamed with the exertion, the shifting of weight. But he kept it up, leaning, pulling until the crate toppled off the stack, close enough for him to slide it against his leg. He held the door open with his back, moved the crate against the molding, careful not to drop it into the gaping darkness. And he stepped away.

The wall snapped against the crate, knocking it back into the hallway.

Fuck. Fuck fuck fuck. This was taking way too much time. Frustrated, Rick grabbed the hammer and smacked the wall again and again, widening the hole. He smeared sweat out of his eyes with bloodstained hands, but kept at it until the gash was big enough for him to lean inside. He fished his penlight out of his belt and cast a thin, powerful beam through the gash in the wall, aiming straight down.

Saw the rotted staircase. Scattered broken boards on the floor below. He moved the light, trying to see where Harper had landed, how far she'd fallen. How badly she'd been hurt. If maybe she was dead. He squinted, straining to see.

'Harper?' he yelled.

No answer. No body. Where was she? Had she somehow gotten away? God, if she talked to the press, his ass was grass. Rick listened, heard nothing. Couldn't be sure. Again, the darkness prevailed, engulfing his call and inking out his feeble ray of light.

Her flashlight wasn't strong, and its beam was narrow. But it reassured Harper that she wasn't blind; when she turned it on, her panic subsided. She could actually see a few yards ahead. Visibility wasn't great, but she was able to orient herself enough to know that she was in a tunnel. The floor was of panels and planks coated with thick patches of what seemed to be sawdust and littered with broken boards and debris. At her feet were shards – probably one of them had cut her finger. In the dim thread of light, she saw what looked like a shattered relic – something with a mosaic pattern? And she remembered the missing vessel. Mosaic pattern, with a jaguar head.

Harper stooped, began collecting various chips and pieces, trying to reassemble them, but stopped herself. What was she doing? Was she crazy? She needed to find her way out of there. The relic – if it even was a relic – could wait.

Gently, Harper moved the pieces to the side of the path and stood again, moving the skinny beam of light, scanning her surroundings. Beside her, against the wall, was a decayed stairway, a rotted platform at its top. There must be a hidden entrance up there; she must have passed right through it. Which meant that, even though it had seemed like more, she'd fallen just one story. And that she must now be on the second level of the house.

A narrow, hollowed-out passageway extended ahead of and behind her. Nothing moved in either direction. No visible snakes. Maybe spiders? Oh Lord, she hoped not. She flashed the light along the floor, then upward. She saw no spiders. But she stood gasping, swallowing air, staring at bats. Dozens of them. Hanging upside down from every exposed rafter like leaves from an oak tree.

OK, she told herself. They're just bats. Harmless. Good for the environment. They ate bugs, probably spiders, too. Besides, they were sleeping. And blind. If she left them alone, they wouldn't even notice her.

Harper moved the light, trying not to disturb them. Deciding not to look at them, to pretend they weren't there. Realizing that the bats were good news: if they'd been able to get inside the passageway, there must be an opening. Which meant a way out. She needed to stop gawking at the fauna, move her butt and find it.

She walked on, hearing a harsh sudden bang. Then another. Pieces of plaster loosened from the overhead wall, fell to the ground behind her.

242

For a heartbeat, she thought of calling out; maybe someone had come to rescue her. But no – more likely, the person up there was Rick, incensed that she'd eluded him. He was coming after her, rabid enough to demolish the wall. Harper moved forward, picking up her pace, aiming the light on the floor ahead as her eyes grew accustomed to dimness, discerning more detail.

A dozen yards ahead, the passageway split into two. She stopped, considering: right or left? Which way should she go? She closed her eyes, trying to sense the exit, picturing the layout of the house. Probably, she was between walls of the bedrooms on the second floor. Which meant she had no idea which direction would be better. She pointed her finger, whispered, Eeny meeny miny mo. From the darkness behind her, she heard Rick calling her name. His voice sounded close, tore at her like a claw.

Harper veered right, hurrying. Several steps later, she thought, damn. Maybe I should have gone left.

Rick pressed his shoulders against the wall and stuck his head through the hole, the penlight in his mouth. The light was weak, but he could see the floor. She simply wasn't down there.

But how could that be? How could she have survived that fall? He turned his head, moving the light, thinking that maybe she'd crawled a few feet away before collapsing. But she wasn't there.

Fuck. What was he supposed to do now?

Obviously, he couldn't admit that he'd let her get away. Obviously, he had to find her.

But how? She was somewhere inside the fucking *walls*. He stuck his head back in the hole, this time examining the space. Beyond the decrepit stairway, there appeared to be a passageway, a tunnel. And the walls beyond the stairs were fairly smooth. OK.

Rick smiled, relieved. He'd go down there after her. Even with his damned leg, it wasn't that far. All he had to do was attach a rope up here and rappel off the wall. Except that, damn. He didn't have a rope.

Think, he told himself. But his thinking was blurry, messed up. He couldn't keep his mind on one topic for very long. Probably, he needed water, orange juice. Something to offset his blood loss. Whiskey. Rye. Bourbon. Anything. He looked around the hallway, hoping to find a Coke, saw crates. What the hell was in all these crates?

And then it occurred to him: he could use them to climb down into the hole. He could drop them down, one at a time, until they piled up into a mound, like a mini-mountain. He could ease on to them and climb down to the tunnel floor. Genius. Absolute genius.

First, he had to make the hole wide enough and high enough. It took many more slams of the hammer, but he pulled away large wads of the wall. Then he went for a crate. It was lighter than he'd expected, light enough to heft it up to the opening, shove it through, hear it fall. He got his penlight, flashed it down. The crate had come apart, revealing piles of shredded foam. Damn. Well, it was a start – he'd probably need to toss in a couple dozen to make a high enough mound to climb onto. He'd better hurry. Harper had a head start, and his leg was slowing him down.

Rick limped to the crates, picked up another, brought it to the hole, shoved it through, let it go. Listened for the crash. Went for the third, repeated the process. Felt dizzy, but kept going. Army Strong, he told himself, and he moved back and forth, lifting and dropping boxes, losing count of the number. Driven by the knowledge that he couldn't let Harper get away. At some point, he peered through the hole and saw a mess of wood and packing stuff all over the floor. Not high enough. Nowhere near high enough. So he kept on tossing boxes until, finally, he realized he had no choice: he had to rest. Just for a minute.

Rick leaned against the wall beside the remaining crates, leaned on one to ease down to the floor. His leg was still oozing through the tourniquet. The pain had moved beyond the wound, occupied his head, his back. He'd be OK, though, in a minute. He needed just a minute to rest, and he'd be OK.

Harper faced a wall. A blank, flat plaster wall. She flashed the light up and down, refusing to accept that, after wandering through twists and turns, thirsty and sore, she had come to this: a dead end.

But it couldn't be a dead end. Why would someone go to all the trouble of building a secret passageway only to have it lead nowhere? They wouldn't, would they? And yet, here it was. A tunnel leading to nothing.

But wait. A blank wall was the way she'd gotten in there. Maybe this was the same thing, a fake obstruction. A secret door. She felt it gently, pressed on the corners, the middle. Nothing gave way. She pushed harder, leaned her back against it and shoved with her whole body, rammed it with her shoulder. Nothing happened. The wall was just a wall.

Harper leaned against it, sinking to the floor, flashing her light back along the path she'd just taken. Wondering how long she'd been walking. How long her flashlight batteries would last.

Oh God. What if they died? She'd be blind again, engulfed by thick black air. Buried in it. She turned off the light. Sat in the dark. Closed her eyes, frustrated, spilling tears. Her left leg throbbed; her head pulsed pain. She'd lost track of time. Lost her sense of direction. What if she'd been wandering in circles? Or tangled in false passages leading to dead ends? She might never find her way out.

She thought of Hank. Of never seeing him again. Of dying here, unseen, inside walls. Harper's body tensed. She ran her arm across her blood-smeared face, refusing to let herself cry. She needed to get a grip. After all, she was resourceful. Trained to overcome the harshest conditions and survive the most hostile environments. She could certainly survive in a decaying old mansion.

Besides, she probably wouldn't have to find

her way out. Any minute, someone would come and find her. When he'd seen that she hadn't come home, Hank would have gotten help. Would have sent for the police. Detective Rivers was probably right that moment talking to Angus and Jake, who would know all about the tunnels and how to get around in them. Any minute, one of them would climb in and get her out.

Unless Rick found her first.

She listened for him. Earlier, she'd heard violent smashing. But not for a while. Now, sitting still in the pitch darkness, she heard nothing. Or wait. Something? Were those footsteps? Grunts? Dragging? Was someone there? Was it Rick?

She stopped breathing, strained to pick up the faintest hint of sound. And then, suddenly, a burst of music. Not just music. Meatloaf. That song, 'Paradise by the Dashboard Light'. The girl was singing that she had to know if he'd love her forever, that he had to tell her right now.

Harper got to her feet, trying to locate its source. Was it coming from behind her? Back in the tunnels? Through the wall ahead? Why couldn't she be sure? She turned in circles, listening, unable to determine a direction. Each way she turned seemed wrong.

'Let me sleep on it,' Meatloaf sang.

Maybe it wasn't real. Maybe that was why she couldn't locate it. Maybe the music was in her head. After all, she hadn't seen anything but a dim swatch of light, hadn't heard much except her almost silent footsteps in God knew how long ... Minutes? Hours? She had no idea. And

247

sensory deprivation could cause hallucinations; she'd learned that back in psych class. So maybe she was hallucinating now. Creating Meatloaf in her mind because her mind needed to hear something.

Then again, maybe she wasn't.

Which would mean that someone was actually within hearing distance. If she could hear them, then they could hear her. She yelled, 'Hel—' and stopped halfway through the word. What if it was Rick blasting the music, luring her to him with a friendly sound so he could ambush her?

Well, fine, she decided. If it was Rick, she'd deal with him.

'Hello?' she bellowed. Her voice swam into empty air, drowned by the music. 'Can anyone hear me?'

The girl answered, repeating that she had to know right now.

The music sounded real. But Harper had endured countless flashbacks that had seemed real; she was well aware that the mind could play incredible tricks. Even so, she couldn't stay there, at a dead end. Had to move, to keep searching for a way out. She turned the flashlight back on and started down the tunnel, away from the wall. She stopped, though, when she saw a bent nail on the ground, and she knelt slowly, wincing in pain to pick it up. It wasn't as sharp as her pocketknife would have been, but the nail was pointed enough to carve an 'X' on the wall.

From now on, at least she'd know if she was backtracking. From now on, she'd leave a trail.

* * *

Rick pushed himself to his feet. If he fell asleep, he was a goner. He might die right there. No, he had to find Harper, complete his job. His sweat chilled him, and he shivered. His leg was on fire. Vaguely, he noticed his phone on the floor. It must have fallen from his pocket; he'd get it in a minute. But first, he went back to his task, shoving boxes through the secret door until, finally, the pile was close enough to stand on. He secured his gun in his tool belt, took the hammer for good measure, grabbed his penlight, and lowered himself into the hole.

The stack was unstable, composed of broken and off balanced crates, and it gave way under his weight, sending him sliding to the ground. A howl escaped his throat; a jolt tore through his leg. He landed on his ass, legs akimbo, and lay panting until his body stopped reverberating. Thinking, even as he shook with pain, about his phone. That it was still out there on the floor. That he'd forgotten to pick it up. Fuck.

Gradually, his nerves stopped screaming, and he rolled to his side. Light from the open door was dim; he turned on his penlight, looked around. Saw a tunnel extending ahead and behind him. Saw some broken pottery a few steps away. Harper had been there, had gathered the pieces.

Leaning on a broken crate, Rick climbed to his feet. His leg wound was bleeding again, so he played with the tourniquet, tightening it, grimacing. His hands wet and slipping, he rested for a moment, allowing the pain. Snapped a yard-long board off a broken crate to use as a walking stick.

Then, gripping his stick in one hand, his gun in the other, his penlight in his mouth, he set out after Harper.

Almost instantly, music began to blare; he couldn't tell from where. Really? Music? Fucking Meatloaf? Shit. He stopped for a second, absorbing this new development. What the hell did it mean? Was someone else in the house? Were they having a damned party? Wonderful, all he needed were more complications. Witnesses. As if this job hadn't gone to hell already. Now, he'd have collateral damage, too? He'd have to take care of extraneous people? This day just got suckier and suckier. Fuck fuck fuck.

Rick limped ahead, moving in the direction of the broken pottery. Furious about the music. How was he supposed to listen for Harper when someone was blasting fucking Meatloaf?

On the other hand, when he found her, the music would cover screams and gunshots.

Every few steps, he had to stop to steady himself, fight the dizziness. Overcome the gnashing pain. But relentlessly, he kept on. Until, goddammit, the tunnel split.

Of course it did. Everything else was fucked up, why wouldn't the tunnel be, too? Rick felt like shooting the walls, blowing the whole damned place up. He needed to get it together; he was better, smarter than to lose it. He needed to psyche out his prey, that was all. OK. Which way would she have gone, right or left? He closed his eyes, pictured Harper standing there, choosing. She would go right; he was sure of that. She was right-handed. And she'd been

250

wounded on her left side. To her, left was vulnerable, so reflex would make her go right.

But she was smart, too. Wouldn't choose her first impulse. Would know he'd psyche her out.

Rick clutched his gun, leaned on his board, flashed the penlight ahead. And went left.

Harper's mouth was dry, parched. Beyond thirsty. But she kept on going, stopping every few yards to scratch the walls with an 'X.' Taking a route different from the one she'd taken earlier. Listening to identify the direction of the music, to move towards it. But the tunnel moved in its own complicated directions, twisting, turning, moving up and down ramps, taking her through stretches where the ceiling lowered and the walls narrowed. Once, she had to move sideways, couldn't fit through any other way. What if the ceiling collapsed? What if she were buried alive there? But she kept on. Had no choice. Behind her was a dead end.

At some point, as abruptly as it had started, the music stopped. Harper called out, hoping whoever was there would hear her. 'Hello? Can you hear me? Is somebody there?'

She kept calling, listening. Heard no reply. Fought tears. Kept walking, marking the wall. Her body became numb, her steps automatic, zombie-like. She stopped thinking, stopped being afraid. Motion, motion and breathing were the only constants. For a while, she counted steps, then lost track. Couldn't remember whether she was on one hundred twelve or twenty. Vaguely, it occurred to her that all the exits might be hidden like the one she'd fallen through. That she might have passed a dozen of them without knowing it. How could she find a door if it looked like the rest of the passageway? She couldn't. She'd wander forever, trapped in the walls. She wiped away more tears, this time of exhaustion. Told herself that the exits must have some marker. That they would have to. Harper walked on slowly, shining her light on ceilings and walls, looking for irregularities. Symbols.

The passageway veered around a corner. She flashed the light above her head, to her left and right. Finally, she aimed it straight ahead. And then the hallucination began.

It had to be a hallucination. Couldn't be real.

But there she was: a woman in a fur coat. Curled up on the floor, her head lolling forward, as if asleep.

It's sensory deprivation, Harper warned herself. She's not there. She's like an oasis in the desert; your mind is creating her. Harper closed her eyes, held them shut. Opened them again. The woman was still there.

Oh God. Someone was actually there. A person, maybe trapped like she was. Maybe hurt. Harper rushed to her. 'Miss – miss? Are you all right?'

Harper knelt, touched the woman's shoulder. Aiming the light on to her head.

Slowly, as if deflating, the woman caved in. Before Harper realized that her coat was empty, the woman's head rolled off of her shoulders, her hair falling free, her skull tumbling to the floor.

* * *

His leg raging, Rick wondered if people could go insane from pain. Decided that, of course, yes, they could. Briefly, he wondered if he was going insane right then, breaking down a wall, hobbling down some hidden corridor, hunting a woman down so he could kill her. It definitely sounded insane. But it wasn't; it was war. And when fighting a war, a little insanity never hurt.

Besides, he could take the pain. Pain was nothing, just a physical reaction. Nerves sending impulses to the brain. He was trained. He could overpower them. But it was tough; he could imagine those impulses getting stronger, taking over his mind. Pissing him off. Sending him on a rampage where he'd kill anything that breathed. Maybe even himself.

He walked on, angry at his pain, leaning on his cane, blinking rapidly to steady himself. His gun got too heavy for his hand, and his lips were tired, aching from holding the penlight. He put the gun back into his belt, used the gun hand to hold the penlight. There. That was better. Oops. His balance was off. He stumbled, would have fallen if not for the walking stick.

The corridor again veered sharply to the left, sloped down gradually. The air became chilly and damp. The walls became more clay than plaster; the planks of the floor covered rocks and earth. Obviously, the path had led him underground. The further he walked, the louder the music seemed. Damn. What if he didn't find Harper, but walked right into a damned Halloween party?

253

He stopped, considering what he should do. Wondering if Harper had already found the party, if they'd called the police. Damn.

He looked behind him, considered going back, climbing out the hole he'd made, finding Harper another time. Maybe waiting for her at home. She'd have to go home sometime; he could wait for her, and bang bang, do the job in two seconds.

That was probably the smart thing to do. Rick didn't relish the trek back up the passageway, but he turned, started back. Went about ten yards when, bam, the music stopped. And from somewhere – he couldn't tell where – a woman called, 'Hello? Can you hear me? Is somebody there?'

Harper was close. He stood alert, waiting for her to yell again. But when she did, he still couldn't identify her direction. Except he was sure she wasn't behind him; he'd have seen her. Unless, back at the fork, he'd taken the wrong turn. Maybe he should have gone the other way. Damn. His leg pulsed, distracting him. OK, he'd keep going forward for a while. If he didn't find her in like ten minutes, he'd go back to the fork and start over.

Rick smelled something smoky, musky. Maybe a fire? Oh God, was the house burning down? No, the scent was too mild. Almost like incense. Odd. He crept forward, sniffing, his skin itching, nerves prickling. His instincts on red alert, warning of danger up ahead, probably Harper. He stayed close to the wall, edging forward. Coming to a dead end – no, not a dead end. Too late, he noticed the sudden drop, the ladder leading straight down. Rick fell, landing hard on his leg, letting out a shattering yowl.

Instantly, someone pounced on him, pressing an arm against his throat. Rick swung and punched, couldn't breathe. Fuck. He tried to reach for his gun, but his arms were pinned, couldn't move. Damn. The fucker was choking him. Who the hell was it? Rick thrashed and twisted.

Even with his desperation and pain, his mind raced, able to get his bearings. A cave-like room. A ramp that led up to daylight. A table covered with small packages. And finally, as darkness overtook him, a creature above him unlike any he'd seen before; it had fought like a man, but had feathers like a bird. And the head of a wild cat.

Harper jumped, howling, and ran backwards around the corner. Heart pounding, swallowing air, she stood for a moment, hugging herself. The woman wasn't, couldn't have been real. The body had to be a creation of Harper's own terrified, sensory-deprived mind.

Finally, her breathing quieted, her heart rate slowed. Prepared to see an empty hallway ahead, she rounded the corner, flashed the light. And saw the skull, patched with blackened leathery skin, lying on the path. A champagne bottle on its end beside her, along with a crystal glass. The fur coat draping a decomposed skeleton against the wall.

Oh my God. Harper stared, remembering the stories about the house. Trying to recall a name

– Carole? Camille? No – Chloe. Chloe Manning. The glamorous silent movie actress who'd disappeared during a party in the Twenties or Thirties, whose body had never been found. Until now. Harper stood, staring at the remains, doubting her own perceptions. After all, people had supposedly searched the passages for the actress and never found her. How could Harper have chanced upon her?

Unless she, too, was hopelessly lost.

Harper imagined the woman stumbling in the dark without a candle or flashlight. How long had she wandered around? Had she been drugged? Too drunk to know what was happening? Had she screamed, pounded the walls in despair and panic? Passed out? Never mind. It was too late to worry about her; she'd been dead for almost a century. And now, Harper was as lost as Chloe Manning had been. Very irretrievably lost. Was the body an omen? Would she share Chloe Manning's fate? Would she die there, alone?

She thought of Hank. Wondered how long he'd search for her. When he'd give up. If he'd have her declared dead so he could marry again. A hot stab of jealousy surged through her, resenting his new wife. Oh God, would she really never see him again? Damn. Was this really how she'd die? Sniper fire whizzed past her head, a bomb exploded nearby. Harper smelled smoke, heard screams of the wounded. And something else: from faraway, she heard Hank's voice. Calling her. 'Hoppa!'

How sad. How pathetic. She was so desperate, so without hope of ever seeing him again that she

was manufacturing him. Hallucinating. She heard it again: 'Hoppa!'

'Hank? I'm here!' she called, knowing that he wasn't really there. That she was calling to her own imagination. Even so, she stared into the tunnel and pictured him coming for her, emerging from the darkness with his powerful, uneven gait, bearing a flaming bright torch, his eyes reflecting the fire.

'Hoppa!'

'Stop it,' she scolded her mind, aching for Hank. Sorry she'd ever argued with him.

Stop it. She pinched herself, concentrated on the sharpness of the pinch, then on the ache in her leg, aborting the hallucination with pain. Pleased that she could feel it. Pain, after all, meant there was still hope: unlike Chloe Manning, she wasn't dead. Yet.

Don't look at her, Harper told herself. Just mark the wall and keep going. She kept going, but couldn't help looking back, aiming her light one more time on the remains of Chloe Manning, her skull staring from the shadows, watching Harper leave.

Her throat was parched. Don't think about it, she told herself. Don't think about Rick or the Colonel or Hank or anything. Just walk.

She walked. She marked the wall. And walked and marked the wall. Maybe it wasn't really for a long time. Maybe it was only a few minutes. Half an hour that felt like days? She had no idea. Time could be misleading. Like darkness. She felt like collapsing, or at least like sitting for a while. Didn't do either. The passageway kept

257

changing. Now it turned at right angles, zigzagging. Somehow she'd gotten off her original path, which had been relatively straight. Now, there were right angles, as if she were moving around the perimeters of rooms. As if she were in between them. She tapped on the wall, wondered if she could kick through. Decided to try. Stopped, put her weight on to her weak left leg and slammed the wall with her right. The impact sent her flying to the ground, cursing. White pain reverberating through her right leg.

But she kept going. After a while, the ground sloped down, probably leading to the first floor. Harper sped up; there had to be an exit down there. Had to be. The slant made moving easier, quicker. And suddenly, the passage became damp, cooler. She smelled earth. Must be underground? Yes. The walls had become rock and clay. Damn. And after a while, she smelled something sweet. Mold? No, muskier. Spicier. More like incense? A few steps later, she heard voices and almost screamed with joy.

Except she didn't. She crouched against the wall, listening. Making sure that Rick hadn't sent for reinforcements. That she wasn't walking right into his arms.

'I'll go back later,' a man said. 'Maybe there's something else even better.'

'Asshole.' This voice was gruffer, deeper.

'It wasn't my fault. She was right there.'

'Stop making excuses for yourself, will you? You fucked up.'

'I know that. Don't you think I know that?' The first man again, whining.

Silence. The scent of smoky incense was stronger.

'I paid you a week ago. Our customers expect delivery tonight. Trust me, we don't want to piss them off.'

More silence.

Harper crept forward, leaned around a corner, expecting to see them. Saw a blank wall several feet ahead. What? Where were the men? She inched closer to the wall, trying to hear the voices, and stepped forward, setting her foot down on empty air. She swam, arms flailing and grabbing at the wall as she shifted her weight, hopped backwards, lost her balance and landed on her butt. She sat for a moment, catching her breath. Shit. She'd almost fallen into a gaping hole at the end of the passageway. Soft golden light rose from the opening. Harper shut off her flashlight and rolled on to her belly. She lay flat, crawled to the edge, peeked down. Saw a cave-like room, dimly lit with lanterns. A man, pacing. And, directly under her, limbs sprawled, lying not far from a rope ladder, she saw Rick.

Rick was looking right at her, but didn't move, didn't let on. Had he seen her? Harper waved her hand, watched for a reaction. Saw none. Rick's eyes remained fixed, and he lay perfectly still. Oh God. Was he dead? Maybe not. Maybe he was just hurt. Dazed or unconscious. But who were those men? Couldn't they see him lying there? Why weren't they helping him?

She strained to hear their conversation.

'...figure out who he is and how in God's name he got here.'

'There are dozens of openings.'

'You know that. But how did he? How did he even know that there are passageways?'

Silence.

'You have no idea? Either one of you? Because other than the three of us, who could possibly know?'

'We don't know any more than you do, Joe.'

'Great. Just great,' Joe growled. 'So some random burglar just *happens* to break into this house? Just *happens* to find a passageway? Just *happens* to drop in on us today, right when we're about to make a serious delivery?'

'So what are you saying, Joe? That this guy's a spy? Someone's been spying on us?'

'It sure looks that way. But he couldn't be in it alone. Somebody sent him. Somebody who wants part of the take.'

'No, wait.' The guy who wasn't Joe argued. 'Except for us, who could that be?'

Silence.

Harper inched forward, trying to get a better view of the room, to see who was in there. Missed a comment or two.

Then heard Not Joe say, 'You serious?'

'I am.'

'Really? The blonde from the university?'

She froze, not daring to breathe.

'Not all alone,' Joe reasoned. 'But obviously she knows the dollars these pieces can bring in, so she might have made her own deal. Or it might be the other way – this guy might have come to her with a deal.'

'And they spied on us to find out about the

260

tunnel. It makes sense. Except what happened to his leg?'

'Who knows. Perhaps she double-crossed him?'

'Well, we'll never know, thanks to Chief Cat-feathers over there. That guy sure isn't going to tell us.'

Harper looked down at Rick. His eyes hadn't moved. For sure, he was dead.

'For your information, I hardly touched him. Guy was half dead to begin with – look at all the blood on him.'

'You went at him like a rabid hyena. We should have talked to him.'

Harper looked down at Rick. A blood-drenched rag formed a feeble tourniquet around his leg. His eyes gazed her way, not blinking.

'Well, since we're speaking of mistakes, genius, let's get back to yours.'

'I already told you, Joe. It wasn't my fault.'

'So whose fault was it? Mine? His?' Work boots paced into Harper's view. Then out. 'Shit. All right, it doesn't matter now. We've got a situation here. What am I supposed to tell them? That my idiot supplier fell down a shaft and broke a one-of-a-kind priceless pot for which they've prepaid fifty-five thousand?'

Fifty-five thousand? Harper strained her neck, leaning over the hole to see more of the room. Saw a table stacked with Styrofoam packing cases like the ones up in the crates. Were they relics? She tried to count them, got to nine.

'We can refund their money,' the guy who wasn't Joe suggested.

These guys had stolen relics and were selling them. Of course. That was why so many were missing from the collection. The professor hadn't misplaced them as Jake had said. The missing pieces removed by these guys. Was Angus one of them? Was Jake? Were they stealing what they believed should have been their legacy?

Suddenly, right below her, Rick began to slide across the floor.

'Oh no,' the man who wasn't Joe groaned.

'What's he doing? Hey, what the hell are you doing?' Joe barked.

Rick's arms splayed over his head as someone dragged him by the feet, moving him out of Harper's line of sight.

'Shit. Does he have to do that again?' Joe asked. 'What the hell's the matter with him?'

'Let's not bother him.' First guy sounded edgy. 'Just let him do his thing. You don't want to start something with him.'

'He's fucked up,' Joe said. 'Seriously. He needs help.' His voice sounded familiar. Slightly accented.

'You think I can't hear you?' A third voice. Kind of throaty. Also familiar?

'You're talking about me as if I'm not here. I can hear everything you're saying.'

'Good. I'll say it to your face. You fucking need to go someplace and get locked up. You're ill. It's sick, what you're doing.'

'I appreciate your opinion. But you have no inkling what you're talking about. I'd advise you not to speak to me.'

'Really, Digger? You're telling me what I can do?'

Digger? Wait. Jake had talked about Digger – had said he was Angus's friend. Was this the same 'Digger'?

'Move away. You're interfering with the rite.'

'Rite? Are you serious? You look like a fucking chicken.'

'You're speaking out of ignorance. And as a priest, I can't be bothered with your opinions. This rite is essential for our continued success. It strengthens us.'

'It does, does it?' Joe was unconvinced.

'It does.'

'It's not his fault.' The first guy spoke up. 'The old guy got him started.'

'Neither of you can possibly understand.' Digger sounded winded. Probably from dragging Rick.

'He's being doing this since the eighties.'

'Since the eighties?' Joe's voice again. 'Shit. How old were you then? Like ten?'

'Fifteen. Digger was sixteen.'

'No, I started younger. By sixteen, I'd performed a dozen rituals.'

'Bullshit! We'd have heard if—'

'I began with a dog.'

'You did what? Fuck you, Digger – that was you? You fucking killed our dog?'

That had to be Angus.

'Not his spirit. That still lives within me. The professor didn't realize what I was doing until my fourteenth – which was Carla.'

Carla? Harper drew a breath. Carla Prentiss.

263

Langston's murdered researcher. Angus's friend killed her?

'What is he talking about?' Joe scoffed.

'The old guy used to take us on digs. Digger was fascinated by the old rituals, how they were done.'

'Shit. You're saying you killed that girl?' Joe sounded stunned.

'Not killed; sacrificed,' Digger corrected. 'She was a virgin. A pure offering.'

'And the professor knew?'

'Well, he figured it out. Quietly arranged for his protégé here to be sent on a long vacation to the Happy Home.'

'It was a private academy. My parents thought it best that I study abroad.'

'Whatever. I can't believe you killed my fuckin' dog.'

Harper thought she must have misheard. Because she could swear that the third guy, Digger, had just admitted that he had killed Carla Prentiss. And Angus was down there, explaining the past to Joe. She pictured him at the site where she'd found Zina. Had he acted as if he'd killed her? Or maybe Jake had done it. Maybe it hadn't been an honor killing at all. She shivered, recalling being alone with him in the house. The way he'd lingered. But the men were still talking.

'...and the professor chose me as his assistant. He taught me the mystical secrets and rites of the ancients.'

Harper edged sideways, craning her neck, stretching to see them. Saw two pairs of legs in

264

jeans and work boots. No faces. Nobody else.

'So now you're what? The high priest of fuck-upness?' Joe mocked. 'I'll tell you what, Father Fuckup: stop what you're doing. I warned you the last time, and I'm warning you again. Stop it. Now. Hey – I'm talking to you, you sick—'

Harper heard a clank. A scuffle. Pushing? Stumbling? The first guy yelling: 'Settle down, both of you. Jesus. You'll break everything. Get it together, would you? Anybody remember why we're here? Joe's got a delivery to make.'

A pause. 'Don't you ever fucking touch me again, you hear me?' Joe was breathless, his voice wind and thunder.

'Actually, I'd prefer not to have any contact with you whatsoever. But I promise you this: if you attack me again, my physical touch will be the least of your problems. I'll gather all the powers and—'

'I swear to you, I'm going to rip your fucking powers right out of—'

'Enough!' The first guy intervened.

Silence. Harper smelled tension and incense.

Joe broke it. 'So what do you think? She still up there?'

She? Oh God. Harper ducked away from the opening. Had they seen her? Were they looking up at her? Wait, of course not. They had no idea she was there. Besides, if she couldn't see them, they couldn't see her. Even so, Joe was talking about her. Who the hell was he?

'She must be. Isn't her bike still out there?'

'Yeah. Was when I got here, anyway.'

Lord. They'd seen her Ninja, were definitely

265

talking about her. And she was convinced, almost sure that two of them were Angus and Jake.

'What's she doing, sleeping up there?' A pause. 'Oh shit.'

'If she was mad enough to shoot *him*—'

'She might be dead up there.'

'—what do you think he did to *her*?'

Silence.

'Should we go see? If she's alive, we could talk to her about this guy.'

'No, not now.' Joe grunted. 'Focus, would you? First, we've got to make this delivery. Even if she's dead up there, we don't have time to go looking for a suitable replacement piece right now. So here's what we'll do. I'll tell them their vessel got damaged in transit. I'll offer to make it good with another piece of equal or greater value. Which you will supply.'

'That ought to work.'

'But, I'll tell you this, Butterfingers,' Joe went on. 'If they don't go for it, it comes out of your pocket.'

'The hell it does.' The first guy raised his voice. 'I'm not paying for—'

'Really? Well. Then you better hope they'll go for it.' Joe's voice rumbled, dangerous.

A pause. Then the first guy mumbled, 'Whatever.'

'So, are we done here, ladies? Let's load up.' Joe's voice called from farther away. 'That means all three of us, Your High Priest of Poultry Feathers.'

The first guy lowered his voice, urging, 'Come

266

on, leave that for now. We got to move this stuff. Besides, aren't you supposed to do that in daylight?'

'It's almost daylight.' The third guy bristled. 'But he has no respect. He's an ignorant nonbeliever who doesn't understand even the most basic aspects of the spirit world. And yet, he continually challenges me.'

'Gentlemen,' Joe called. 'We got a date. Move it!'

There were grumbling replies, but the voices faded, too difficult to understand. In a few moments, Harper heard doors slam, a car drive off, and then no sound at all.

Harper waited. Still heard nothing. And decided to move.

Cautiously, she got to her feet, lowered herself down the rope ladder to the open space below. Light flowed in across the room. She squinted, covered her eyes. Looked again. Saw a dirt ramp leading up out of the room. A dark sky, black trees above the open exit.

A dark sky? Harper blinked, disoriented; she'd arrived in the middle of the day. How long had she been there? Wait – one of the men had said it would be daylight soon. So she'd been inside all night?

Oh God. Hank must be frantic. But where was he? Why wasn't he here, looking for her? Never mind; it wasn't the time to think about Hank. Harper ran for it, not even looking to see if any of the men were still there. Passing the table, she noticed that the packages were gone, loaded up

267

for delivery. She dashed toward the ramp, aware of each breath, of the effort of each step. Of her exposure and vulnerability. She ran, oblivious of her wimpy leg, ignoring her exhaustion and pain, made it to the bottom of the ramp where she lowered her body, hugged the wall, peered up, actually inhaling fresh air again.

Seeing no one, she started up the ramp, but stopped and turned, headed back inside. No matter what he'd done, she couldn't leave Rick there without checking; she needed to be sure that he was definitely dead. Squinting in the dimness, she turned, scanned the room.

Rick was lying against the wall on a pyramid of rocks that resembled an altar. A pile of colored feathers lay on the floor beside him, and all around him, scented oil burned in small pots. Primitive painted images covered the wall: a deer. A dog. A bird. An owl. A jaguar. A man with a jaguar head. Harper stepped closer.

'Oh God.' She stopped breathing and stared.

Rick's shirt was ripped open. And his chest sliced in an X, the skin pulled back above the heart.

Harper ran in a haze, cool dew misting her face, leaves crunching underfoot. She glimpsed trees as she sped past them, vaguely aware that she'd emerged far from the house. That the ramp had led her to a familiar spot – exactly where she'd found Zina's body. But then she was on her bike, roaring away, hoping the cops would stop her for speeding and take her away.

But they didn't. She raced along the highway,

through Ithaca and up the hill, around campus and, turning on to Hanshaw Street, she saw the police cars in her driveway. All the lights on in her house.

She spun on to the property, dropping the Ninja on its side as she slid off. She ran, calling Hank's name.

The front door was open; she flew inside, shouting, 'Hank?'

In the living room, she scanned faces, searching for his and found it in a cluster. Hank was on his feet, coming to her, reaching for her. 'Hoppa!'

Harper jumped into his arms, relieved. And she stayed there, pressed against him until, gradually, she became aware of other voices, other people. Vicki. Trent. Detective Rivers. Uniformed police. Everyone was asking questions. 'Harper, where have you been?'

'Are you all right, Mrs Jennings?'

'Good God, she's covered with blood!'

'We've been so worried...'

Hank raised a hand, stopping them. 'Hoppa. Sit.' He started for the sofa, but Harper pulled him back.

'No – no, we have to go back. To Langston's. Rick's dead, and these other guys ... One of them killed Carla. And they're selling the relics!'

'Mrs Jennings.' Detective Rivers stepped forward, put an arm around her shoulders. 'Breathe.'

Everyone stood around her, a circle of staring faces. Harper looked from one to another. Vicki's eyes were swollen and red; she'd been crying.

Trent's were liquid and boozy. Hank's – Hank's were steady and dark, making her want to stay there, lingering in their heat. But Detective Rivers led her to the sofa, made her sit.

'Slowly now. In complete sentences. What are you trying to say?'

Vicki dabbed the cut on her head with a damp washcloth. Trent offered her a Scotch. She took it, her hands trembling. Took a gulp with a parched throat, coughed at the burn. Remembered how thirsty she was. Vicki brought water and more damp towels, dabbed at Harper's face even as she drank. Harper repeated herself, insisting that Rivers go with her back to Langston's. Explaining that a man had been killed there. That she'd encountered a group who were trafficking illegal antiquities.

Rivers wanted more details. She asked questions. Who had been killed? Harper was impatient. Why did she need to explain now? Couldn't they talk on the way? But Rivers wasn't moving, so Harper told her that the dead man was someone she'd known in the army, that he'd been stalking her. That he'd been sent to kill her. That he'd probably killed Burke Everett and Pete Murray, another guy they'd served with.

Rivers was frowning.

Harper hurried on, explaining that men at the house were stealing the relics. That one of them was called Joe and another might have been Angus. Or maybe Jake. But either way, one was Angus's friend Digger, and Digger had admitted killing Carla Prentiss, and he might have killed Zina, too. Oh, and she'd found Chloe Manning,

270

the actress—

Harper stopped, bothered by the look in Rivers' eyes. It was soft, like sympathy. Sympathy? It reminded her of the way she herself had looked at Burke when she'd thought he was nuts. Damn, didn't Rivers believe her? Did she think she was just ranting? Why wasn't Rivers calling for backup, taking off for Langston's with lights and sirens? Five, maybe ten whole minutes must have passed since she'd walked in, and every moment counted.

Sighing, Rivers got to her feet. 'Do you feel up to going back there, Mrs Jennings? So you can show me exactly where the body is?'

It wasn't until she peeled herself off the sofa that Harper realized exactly how drained she was. 'Of course.' She teetered as she started for the door.

'Going with.' Hank's beefy hand closed around hers. And suddenly, she wasn't quite as exhausted any more.

A patrol car followed them. Rivers didn't turn on the sirens; there was almost no traffic at this early hour. Harper sat in the back seat with Hank, leaning against his shoulder.

'Got dark out. Waited. Thought you mad still with me. Stayed out.'

Harper shook her head, no. She hadn't been mad.

'Got mad, too. Thought OK. Games. Let her play. Late got though. Finally, called you. Not answer.'

'But I wouldn't do that. I don't play games,

Hank.'

'Midnight after. Worried. Tried to find house. Lang. Ston's. Didn't know. Where. Had to find. Came there. Looked for you.'

Wait. Hank had gone to Langston's? He'd been there?

'Drove there.' Hank's eyebrows furrowed. 'Window broken found. Looked whole house. Your bike. Your. Bag. Phone. Broken rel. Licks. Blood. Lots. And hole big in wall. No you.'

Harper's eyes filled. Hank had gone to look for her. She wondered – in the tunnel, had she really heard his voice? 'Did you call my name?'

He went on. 'Looked in wall. Yelled "Hoppa". Tried to go through hole. Arm. Leg. Caught, stuck. Couldn't get in. Help.'

'Your husband was quite alarmed, Mrs Jennings. He called us, and we went out about one in the morning, looking for you. When we saw the blood, we got concerned. Took samples. Made the third floor east wing into a crime scene. We sent an officer into that hole with a rope, so he wouldn't get lost. He got to the end of his rope, literally, and came back. Frankly, we were all pretty concerned. We were about to get a dog to follow your scent.'

Wait, the police had been to Langston's? Why hadn't they seen the thieves? And why hadn't the thieves seen them?

'Meantime, I took your husband back home and kept him company until your friends got here. He's had a hell of a night, and I didn't want him to be alone. When you suddenly showed up, you can imagine how relieved we were.'

Hank leaned over, planted a tender kiss on her forehead. Harper leaned up; her lips met his. She stayed tightly secured in his arms until Rivers pulled on to the road leading to the Langston house.

Then, Harper sat up, gazing out the window as they approached the spot where she'd found Zina. 'I came out of the tunnel somewhere in there.'

Rivers stopped; the patrol car parked behind them. Everyone got out.

Harper tensed, preparing herself to go back.

'OK?' Hank whispered.

She met his eyes, took a breath, and led the way into the thicket of trees and bushes, past the clearing where she'd had drinks with Zina's brother, looking for the opening in the ground. Damn. Why hadn't she paid closer attention? Why hadn't she marked the spot?

She walked in circles. The opening wasn't small, had been large enough for large men carrying packages to walk through. But then she saw a subtle path, crushed foliage leading to the road, and she followed it around a fallen tree trunk.

From the outside, hidden in the thicket, the ramp seemed small and harmless. Kind of like a large animal had burrowed there.

'He's down here,' Harper started into the tunnel.

Detective Rivers grabbed her arm. 'Mrs Jennings. Wait here.' She motioned the officers to go first, handing each a flashlight. 'Give us the all clear.'

273

One at a time, preceded by thin, white beams, the two men lowered themselves through the opening on to the ramp, guns drawn.

'We're clear, Detective.' The call came almost immediately. Too soon.

Rivers went in, Harper right behind her, leaving Hank to lumber behind.

'Do you see him?' Harper asked as Rivers entered the hollowed out room. 'He's in the back—' She stopped at the bottom of the ramp, and stared.

The room, except for a few broken crates and a couple of black and white bird feathers, was empty. Rick was gone, along with the altar that had held him. There were no lanterns, no pots of burning oil. All that remained of what she'd seen were primitive paintings on the wall: a deer, a dog, an owl, a jaguar, and a man with a jaguar head.

Harper was furious. If Rivers hadn't stalled, wasting precious minutes back at home, they'd have caught the men. But now, there was no proof of anything, not even of Rick's murder.

Harper showed them the opening to the tunnel. 'This leads back to the house. And all through the house. Chloe Manning's in there. I can show you.'

Hank's arm was around her. 'Tired too.'

Harper twisted, freeing herself. 'No. I'm not too tired. I should show you before these guys have time to make more evidence disappear.'

Rivers bristled. 'Look, Mrs Jennings. If you're implying that I—'

'We should have come right back here, like I said.'

Rivers stood tall, looked down a few inches at Harper's face. 'Listen, ma'am. When you came into your house, you were in no condition to go anywhere. You had a head wound and you were rambling. Before I moved, I needed to understand what you were saying, as well as to assess the accuracy – actually, the credibility – of your claims. I acted as quickly as I thought reasonable. Within a matter of minutes.'

'But we missed them.'

Rivers crossed her arms, met Harper's eyes. 'Mrs Jennings, if what you say is true—'

'*If?*'

'—then I'm pretty sure your relic traffickers had removed the body by the time you got home.'

The two women stared at each other for a moment, Harper steaming.

'I understand you're frustrated and exhausted, but I need to conduct an investigation, and I'd appreciate your calm cooperation. How about you show us exactly what happened back in the house?'

Hank had stepped close, silently took Harper's hand. Then, as a group, they went back to the cars and drove up to the house where they found two very agitated men, standing at the door.

Angus spoke first. 'What the hell's been going on here?'

'We were just about to call the police. We thought someone murdered you.' Jake glared at Harper.

275

She said nothing, was listening to their voices, wondering which of them was the relic thief.

'So you called the cops? What the hell went on up there!'

'I told you, Jake,' Angus grumbled. 'It's the damned university and all their publicity. Someone fucking broke in and robbed us. The collection's been in the news so much, we might as well have had an open house for burglars.'

'Gentlemen,' Rivers interrupted, 'can we take a look inside?'

On the way upstairs, Angus went on, 'Man, I wish I'd come by earlier. I'd have caught those sons of bitches.'

'Why did you come by, Mr Langston?'

'I come by every day. To check on the place.'

'What time was did you get here?'

'Dunno. Before six.'

'Awfully early, isn't it?'

'Not for me. I'm up at sunrise.'

By the time they'd arrived on the third floor, Angus had explained that he'd seen the missing windowpane and called Jake. Together, they'd gone into the house and found mayhem upstairs. A smashed wall. Broken artifacts. And blood.

'We thought it was your blood,' Jake moved closer to Harper.

Hank took a step forward, stood between them.

But Harper wasn't paying attention. She was concerned; the crates that had been stacked in the hallway were missing. Where were they? On an impulse, she peeked through the gash in the wall and in the dim light below saw a heap of mangled wood and packing boxes.

A sound – kind of a groan – escaped her belly as, oblivious to the others, she rushed to check the workroom. Thank God, the crates there remained unharmed. But there was damage there, too. Despite the stiffness of her leg, Harper knelt and carefully picked up the pieces, cradling a broken ancient bird.

It was a catastrophe.

Harper grabbed her stomach, felt the loss as physical pain. 'Oh my God. Oh God,' seemed to be all she could say. She stood, gently replacing the broken artifacts on the worktable and rushed back to hall where Angus and Jake were shouting, cursing, pacing in distraught concentric circles.

Hank had looked at the breakage. As had Rivers and the two officers. Harper shoved her head back through the hole, gawking at the devastation, baffled about what could have happened. Replaying the night before, her encounter with Rick.

She'd fallen through the wall and escaped into the tunnel. But she hadn't broken the wall, had she? No, it had merely given way.

So Rick must have tried bashing the wall in. And then found out how to open the door before throwing the crates down into the passageway? Why?

Rick had had no idea what the crates held. To him, they'd merely been big wooden boxes. So he'd dropped priceless, irreplaceable objects so he could climb down the boxes that held them.

'She was up here. She must know what happened.' Angus came at Harper from the left,

Hank half a step behind him. 'Did you have anything do to with this?' Angus raised his hand to grab her arm; Hank's went up to intercept it. Angus wheeled around, swinging, his fist thudding into Hank's jaw. Harper leapt at his back, jabbing his ribs, but the officers pounced on her, one from each side while Rivers separated Angus and Hank, cautioning Jake against moving a muscle.

'Mother of God,' she breathed. 'What is wrong with you people?' She shook her head. 'No, don't answer that. Don't say a single word, anybody. Unless I ask you to.'

Harper went to Hank. His gum was bleeding. She glared at Angus, who glared back.

When the room was silent, Rivers looked at them, one after another. Then she said, 'So. Who wants to tell me what you all are fighting about?'

They all began talking at once. But Rivers made them take turns, and finally came to understand the significance of the smashed crates, that the treasures they held were part of Professor Langston's renowned, disputed, and controversial collection.

'It was Rick. The dead guy who wasn't there just now – the one who attacked me—'

'Hold on – a dead guy who wasn't there attacked you?' Jake rolled his eyes.

Rivers scowled, held up her hand. It made sense to her.

'Rick had no idea about the relics,' Harper went on. 'He came here for me. And when I fell through the wall, hc must have smashed his way through and piled up the crates so he could come

278

down after me.'

'After you?' Angus looked at Jake. 'She was in the passageway?'

'How'd you get in there? Actually, how did you even know about it?' Jake's head didn't move, but he glanced at his brother.

Again, Rivers quieted them. 'You guys interrupt again, I swear, I'll arrest you.'

'What the hell? We can talk if we want. We own this damned house and—' Angus began. Harper thought she recognized his whiny tone.

Rivers' gaze seared him, made him stop mid-sentence.

'So this guy broke in downstairs,' Rivers summarized. 'But he didn't know about the relics. So what did he want?'

Hank squeezed Harper's hand a little too tightly. Letting her know he had questions, too.

'Me.' She couldn't stop thinking about the broken relics. The incalculable loss Rick had caused. She heard him urging her to cooperate with Colonel Baxter, to work with them. But he'd known she wouldn't agree, had brought a gun. 'He came here to offer me a job.'

'A job.' Rivers looked skeptical.

'Job?' Hank echoed.

'The same "job" he'd offered Burke. Right before Burke jumped off the bridge.'

'Hoppa? What. Saying—' Hank began.

'Rick tried to bribe everyone from our special detail.' Harper tried to explain, had trouble knowing where to start. 'He wanted to keep us quiet about what happened in Iraq. See, turns out, Burke's conspiracy theories weren't totally

279

delusional. I think he was correct that our detail unknowingly aided a superior officer in a heist – a theft of millions of dollars in cash.'

Rivers frowned. 'That superior officer was—'

'Yes,' Harper interrupted. 'Colonel James Henry Baxter. The Senate candidate.'

The frown deepened.

Harper continued. 'Pete Murray figured it out – maybe he knew from the start. Anyhow, I think Murray threatened to expose him. Maybe even tried to blackmail him. After that, the Colonel must have assumed that everyone in the detail knew; we were all liabilities. He couldn't afford a scandal – let alone prison – so he hired Rick ... Rick was on the detail, too. And Rick's job was to pay the rest of us off. To convince us to keep silent. Suddenly, soon afterwards, Pete "committed suicide". Then Burke. Who knows? If I hadn't fallen into the tunnel, I might have "killed myself" too.'

For a moment, nobody spoke. Hank's nostrils flared and his breath was heavy, but he said nothing, containing himself. Angus cleared his throat, looking at his feet.

Finally, Rivers sighed, shook her head. 'OK. Clearly, this is going to take a longer, more private interview. Right now, I don't know what we've got here. The blood indicates that there might indeed have been a homicide. And we have a burglary, an assault with intent to kill by a person unknown. Destruction of property. For now, this whole house is a crime scene. Nobody comes in; after we leave, nobody goes out.'

'But we need to find—' Harper began.

'Don't worry, Mrs Jennings. If your buddy is anywhere in the house, we'll find him.'

Her buddy? Rick? Harper nodded and walked with Hank back to the car, not bothering to correct the detective. She hadn't been talking about finding Rick; she'd been talking about the relics. Hoping to find some that had survived the fall.

On the way home, Rivers said nothing, just drove. Harper leaned against Hank, struggling to stay awake. Wondering how many artifacts had been destroyed. Where Rick's body was. What the brothers knew about the stolen relics – if they had been the men with Joe. Her eyes flittered closed, and she saw the passageways again, the endless corridors of darkness, twists and angles. She saw Chloe Manning's skull fall from her fur coat. And Rick's dead eyes, his open chest.

Damn. She couldn't let herself sleep. Had to stay awake and tell Rivers about the men who'd been stealing the relics. About Digger, who'd killed Carla. About her certainty that Angus or Jake was involved. And about Joe, who seemed to be the leader. And she had to talk about the Colonel – who needed to be stopped.

But the steady rhythm of the car relaxed her, and a day and a half without sleep took over. When Harper woke up, she was in her bed, and the sky out the window was black. Night time again.

She bolted up, sank back, dizzy. Sat again, more slowly. 'Hank?' Her throat was dry. She got out of bed, started for the stairs.

Hank called from the kitchen. 'Awake?'

The aroma of roasted chicken wafted upwards. Lord, she was hungry. When had she eaten last? What time was it? How long had she slept?

Harper held the banister, descending slowly. Still off balance.

'Slept thirteen hours.' Hank answered her unasked questions. 'Now. Eight o'clock. Made dinner.' He reached for her hand, helped her down. 'First, something. Else.'

What? Hank led her down the hall to the bathroom. A bubble bath was steaming there, ready for her.

A bubble bath?

Since the war, Harper had taken only combat showers. Ninety seconds long, exactly. Divided into precise divisions for soaping and rinsing. But Hank had prepared this. How had he known when she'd wake up?

'Third one I made. You. Kept sleeping.'

Oh. He hadn't known. Had refreshed the bath again and again. How dear. Harper's eyes misted.

'Need wash, Hoppa.'

She glanced in the mirror, saw a clotted cut on her temple, lumps and bloody smudges, clumps of sooty hair.

Hank was undressing her, helping her into the water. Harper sank back, raw skin stinging, then soothed by the heat. She listened to bubbles popping. Felt warm water sway with her breath. Ninety seconds passed; she knew the duration. But she hadn't even begun to wash yet. Hank sat on the edge of the tub, reached into the water and retrieved one of her feet. He began to scrub her, tenderly, part by part.

When she stepped out of the tub twenty minutes later, Harper was shiny clean and refreshed. Not tired, but ready to go back to bed.

They didn't make it upstairs, only to Hank's office across the hall. Their love-making was spontaneous, wordless. Both desperate and tender. Full of apologies, of promises conveyed through touching.

Afterwards, Hank set out comfort food – roast chicken, mashed potatoes, green beans, apple crisp. He spoke little, made no allusions to their conflicts, the Langston relics or the deaths. Harper was relieved. She was ravenously hungry, didn't want to do anything but eat. She was almost through her second helping of apple crisp when the doorbell rang.

'Rivers.' Hank glanced at the clock, started for the door.

Rivers?

'Coming now. Tell.'

What? Had she made an appointment? Why hadn't Hank warned her? Harper wiped her mouth, started to get up. But Hank was already back, leading Detective Rivers into the kitchen.

'Coffee?' he offered. 'Crisp?'

'Coffee would be great. I seem to be eating here a lot these days.' Rivers took a seat across from Harper. 'You look better.'

Harper smirked. She was cleaner, but hadn't as much as combed her hair. 'I slept.'

'That's the best medicine.' Rivers thanked

283

Hank as he handed her a steaming mug. 'I've had guys going through that passageway. Mrs Jennings, I got to tell you, that thing snakes all over. Hither and yon and back again.'

Harper nodded. She'd seen that for herself.

'I'd heard about the secret passages. Everybody's heard about them. That house has a hundred stories about it. But I never imagined anything this complex. It seems like every single room has a passageway wrapped around it. Separating it from the next room and the hall, sometimes from the room above. I see how you'd have gotten lost. You might have been looping around the same circuit, zigzagging, retracing your steps for hours.'

Harper's hand stiffened around her coffee mug. She recalled the darkness, the never-ending angles, divides, dead ends and turns.

'You're lucky you didn't get seriously hurt. Sections of the floors are rotted; you could have fallen right through.'

Actually, she had.

'But other sections are in good repair. In fact, they seem to have been maintained carefully. New floors, even ramps leading to the lower levels. Which indicates that they've been in recent use.'

Of course they had. The traffickers had snuck through them to pilfer relics, probably even while the professor was still alive.

Detective Rivers poured two per cent into her coffee. 'So. If you have a few minutes, I have some more questions for you about—'

'No, wait. Tell me, did you find Rick?'

284

Rivers swallowed coffee. 'No sign of him. Other than the blood.'

Harper nodded. Where had they put Rick? And why had they moved him?

'Apple. Crisp.' Hank put a dish in front of Detective Rivers, handed her a fork.

'Looks delicious.'

'I'm good. Cook.'

'What about Chloe Manning?'

Rivers hesitated, chewing. She glanced at Hank, then back at Harper. 'They followed your X marks and found some remains. Yes. Initially, they seem consistent with Chloe Manning – the fur coat has her initials in the lining.'

Harper played with her spoon. Saw a skull rolling, hair falling free.

Rivers was ready for Harper's statement, and Harper began, repeating much of what she'd already told them. In one non-stop burst, she repeated Burke's assertions about the theft in Iraq that had funded the Colonel's rise to power. She described how the Colonel had tried to buy off everyone who could threaten him. How he'd sent Rick to deal with her and Burke. Harper skipped over her time in the tunnel, didn't mention her terror or doubts about ever getting out. But she talked about finding the missing actress. And Rick's body. And hearing the men with the stolen relics, their discussion of the long-ago murder of Carla Prentiss.

Finally, she stopped, certain there was more to tell, not sure what it was. Rivers was making notes. Hank frowned and took her hand. 'Now?'

Now? What did he mean, 'now'? Now. Harper

285

fudged. 'I don't know. I guess there will be consternation about the collection. And the police will try to find Rick's body.'

'No. You. Now. Danger still.'

What?

Rivers looked at Hank. Swallowed the last of her apple crisp.

'Colonel. Still.'

Oh. The Colonel.

'The allegations against this man need to be substantiated, Mr Jennings. Remember, he's a prominent figure, a leading candidate for the Senate, and the election is just a day away.'

Hank took a breath. 'Rick didn't. On his own. Come. See Hoppa.'

He was right. And if the Colonel thought she posed a threat, he'd send someone else to deal with her.

'What are you suggesting, Mr Jennings?'

'Wife my. Not safe.' He moved close, took her arm. 'Famous man. Crap. Stop him. Need to.'

Rivers responded with warnings about making premature conclusions and false accusations. She talked about suspicion versus proof, the importance of procedure and evidence. Harper wasn't listening. She didn't know how or exactly when it had happened. But the problems she and Hank had been having seemed unimportant, insignificant. At least for now, they'd disappeared. She and Hank were solid again.

Rivers didn't seem to think that Harper was in imminent danger. She packed up her notebook, getting ready to leave.

286

'A few more things before I go.' She folded her hands. 'I took statements from the Langston brothers today.'

Harper pursed her lips, wondered if she should mention her suspicions. But she had no proof that Angus and Jake were stealing the relics. No evidence at all.

'Those guys are pretty upset about their inheritance. They insist that the collection should be theirs. In fact, Jake's so opposed to the will that he said he'd rather see the pieces stolen by traffickers than taken by the university.'

Especially if he was one of the traffickers, Harper thought.

'He also said that, as boys, he and Angus used to play in the passageways. That they know how to get around in them, how to avoid the dead ends like the one where Ms Manning got lost. But he said, as far as he knows, he and Angus are the only ones who know how to get in and out of the passageways. So he doesn't buy the idea that traffickers have been using them.'

Harper met Rivers' eyes. Didn't the detective see what she was saying?

Hank finally said it. 'So. Maybe traff. Ickers. Are brothers.'

Rivers smirked. 'Again, Mr Jennings. That's an interesting theory. But we need evidence. We have none.'

'Find.' Hank suggested.

Rivers looked at him directly, then at Harper. 'And there's this.' She reached into her satchel, pulled out a plastic evidence bag containing a cell phone. 'We found this in the hall near your

287

workroom. Recognize it?'

'No.' Was it Rick's? She reached for it, took a closer look.

'Seems several calls were made on it to your phone. And several more to a private number in Tennessee. Which happens to be the private line of your old friend, Colonel Baxter.'

Harper sat up straight. This was it: evidence to support her story. 'See? The calls prove that Rick worked—'

'All it indicates is that the owner of the phone had contact with both you and Baxter. You said Rick worked for him; it makes sense they'd talk. But working and talking don't mean—'

'Not by themselves. But Rick knocked the wall down to come after me.'

'Possibly to try to save you after you fell through. There are lots of interpretations possible, here, Mrs Jennings. I admit that your story is compelling, but like I've said, it needs to be substantiated. Right before an election, I can't go making wild accusations against a candidate.'

'What about after the election?'

Rivers started again, repeating her speech about the need for evidence, and Harper nodded as if paying attention while she lowered the phone to her lap, pushed a button through the plastic, turning it on. Pressed the send button. Saw numbers come up, recognized hers, memorized another. Shut the phone off and gave it back, repeating a phone number in her mind.

Vicki still liked newspapers, but Trent did his reading online. Both sat with Hank and Harper at their kitchen table, summarizing what the media were reporting as they munched bagels and breakfast scones. Tales of the Langston house were sweeping not just through Ithaca, but through the country.

'Says here that Chloe Manning was nude beneath her fur coat.' Trent seemed amused. 'Must have been quite a party.'

'Apparently, one to die for.' Vicki took a bite of cinnamon walnut.

'And you, my dear Harper, are the celebrity *du jour*.'

Harper's phone gonged again. It sat on the counter, had been ringing non-stop; Harper had stopped answering. Mostly the calls were from reporters wanting sound bites.

'Turn off?' Hank offered.

Harper shrugged. She didn't care. Hank stood, heading for the phone. The gong stopped.

Trent went on. 'Your ordeal in the passage-ways fascinates the public. Coupled with the discovery of the long lost starlet. Goodness, I'm amazed there was anything left to find. It's been, what, almost a century since she wandered off?'

'It must have been cool and dry in there.' Vicki offered. 'She'd be, like, mummified. Was she, Harper?'

Harper spread butter on to her scone, thinking again about Rick.

'Was she?' Vicki repeated.

'Hoppa. Tired.' Hank chided Vicki. 'Too much.'

'Oh, of course. Sorry. Trent, we are so insensitive. Are you feeling OK, Harper?'

289

Everyone looked at her, assessing her wellness. She put down the butter knife. 'Fine. I'm fine.' She glanced at the newspaper. 'What else does it say?'

'You're sure you want to hear?' Vicki looked at Hank.

'Hoppa. Not. Need. Now.'

'No, I'm fine. Tell me.'

'Well,' Trent drawled, 'the media seem to delight in the fact that as one corpse is found, another has vanished.'

Rick. Where was Rick?

'They make it sound like Langston's house has grabbed fresh meat, relinquishing Chloe Manning only after it swallowed your assailant, whom they say you've identified, but they don't give his name.'

Harper saw his open eyes, open chest. Had she mentioned his chest to Rivers? She couldn't remember, doubted that she had. Needed to remember.

'And Dean Van Arsdale is quoted, addressing the university's dismay at the damage to the collection. They quote him as being appalled and pained at the loss. He says that these traffickers have looted perhaps the most unique and enlightening collection of Pre-Columbian artifacts in the world. And on and on.'

'What did he say about the broken artifacts?'

'Broken artifacts?' Trent scanned his computer screen.

'It just refers to "damage".' Vicki rechecked the article. 'What got broken?'

Harper shrugged. 'Don't know yet.'

'More coffee?' Hank changed the subject.

Harper stared at her scone. None of the news items, directly or indirectly, had mentioned Colonel Baxter. Of course they hadn't. Rivers wouldn't have revealed anything, had insisted there wasn't any hard evidence against him. Baxter had led to the destruction of relics, the deaths of Pete, Burke and Rick. But nothing would happen to him? He'd be elected to the Senate. Then what? Amass more power, run for president? Burke had said the Colonel had bigger plans than she could imagine.

Harper tried to figure out how to stop him, but her thoughts disconnected, interrupted by questions. Who were the traffickers? Who was Joe? Or Digger, the 'priest' who'd killed Carla Prentiss? Where was Rick's body?

She tried to shove these thought aside; the election was less than twenty-four hours away. There was limited time to get to the Colonel. She needed to think, to be away from the chatter. Harper pushed her chair away from the table. 'I'll be right back.'

Apparently, she'd interrupted Trent in the middle of a sentence; he frowned, offended.

'OK? Hoppa? You?'

'Yes. Fine.' She pecked Hank's cheek, squeezed his shoulder as she passed.

'Want company?' Vicki started to get up.

Harper's, 'No,' was too emphatic. She added, 'Thanks, Vicki. I just need a second or two.'

Not certain what she was going to do, Harper headed for the hall. On the way, she grabbed her phone.

When he picked up the call, he said, 'Harper?' He didn't sound surprised to hear from her. In fact he sounded glad. 'I'm glad you called.'

'Rick's dead.' She closed the door, leaned against the bathroom wall.

Silence. Then, 'What?' His voice was thin.

'He's dead. They haven't found his body yet, but I saw him.'

'What the hell happened?'

'What do you think?' she snapped, had no patience for bullshit.

He hesitated. 'I have no idea.'

'You sent him after me and Burke, didn't you?'

'What?' A pause. 'Harper, are you telling me that you killed him?'

'Me?' Why would he say that? 'No. But I would have if I hadn't fallen.'

'Look, I don't understand what you're saying. I asked Rick to bring you guys on board. I owe you – all of you. And I'm finally in a position to pay you back. Harper – I thought I explained all this last time we talked. Rick was supposed to convince you, Everett and Murray to accept my offers, that's all.'

The man was buttery smooth, sounded sincere, caring. No wonder voters loved him. Harper sat on the toilet lid. 'Well, Rick's idea of "convincing" us was rather forceful. It involved a gun.'

A slight pause. 'That's not – no, that's just Rick. He's carried since the war. It's legal; he has a permit – the gun has nothing to do with what he's doing for me.'

'Really? Because Rick stalked me, broke into

my workplace, snuck up on me with his weapon. Tried to force me at gunpoint to accept your offer.'

The Colonel swore under his breath. 'Harper, I swear I have no idea what you're talking about. What you're describing is unbelievable. It's way beyond what we'd ... I'd never have imagined...'

Really? 'Well, you better imagine it, sir. Because while he was attacking me last night, somebody killed him.'

Baxter didn't reply for a moment. Harper heard background voices. Papers shuffling. Machines whirring. The sounds of a political campaign in its final hours.

Finally, 'It's chaos here today, sorry for the interruptions. Now, tell me. How? Who?'

'How is still uncertain. But it was some guys who traffic stolen antiquities. He ran into them while coming after me.'

'Antiquities? What? Look – damn. Hold a sec.' His voice muffled as he covered the phone and spoke to someone. When he came back, he sounded shaken. 'Harper, this is terrible news. Terrible. Rick was like a kid brother. He was my go-to guy. I trusted him with my life.'

And with the truth about the money you stole? Harper couldn't help it; she had to ask. 'Sir, back in Iraq—'

'I'll never forget how the four of you saved my life.'

'Yes, sir – but—'

'I've told you, I'll never forget your courage. I'm deeply indebted.'

'It was our job to protect you. But, sir, that

293

cargo we loaded. What was it?'

Oh God. Had she really just said that?

'The cargo? I don't remember. Supplies. Standard stuff. Why?' He didn't sound elusive. Not even a little shady.

Was he that good a liar?

'It wasn't money?'

'Money?' He let out a low whistle. 'What gave you that idea?'

Harper fudged. 'Just a rumor.'

'Great, wonderful. That's all I need. Another rumor. Ever since I started running for office, there's been one after another. Now, what are they saying? That I did what, stole a helicopter full of money? What's next? That I started the war? Who thinks this stuff up, anyhow?' He sounded indignant. Wounded. Honest.

Could Burke have been wrong? Had he or Pete invented the cargo story?

'Wait.' The Colonel changed focus. 'Didn't you say they haven't found Rick? So are you sure? How do you know he's actually dead?'

God. Did he think she didn't know dead when she saw it? 'Because, like I said, I saw him.'

More background sounds. Another interruption.

Then: 'Thanks for letting me know.' Colonel Baxter lowered his voice. 'The election's tomorrow, Harper.'

'Don't worry, nothing about Rick will hit the news before then. It won't interfere.'

'What? Oh. No. I didn't mean that, Harper. I meant I'm tied up completely today and tomorrow. After that, let's talk some more. You'll fill

294

me in on what happened, what you said about Rick's odd behavior – his breaking in and so on; you'll explain the details, OK? So we can figure this out? Remember, I can put in a good word for you with Van Arsdale. Or fix your husband up with a new position. Maybe you'll reconsider my offer. I'd appreciate having you around, especially now that you're the only one left.'

When she got off the phone, Harper stayed in the bathroom, holding her head in her hands, trying to make sense of the conversation. Colonel Baxter was blustery and pushy, but he'd almost convinced her that he was a stand-up guy. That the story of the theft had been invented by Pete or Burke. That the violence and deaths to members of their detail had been the work of Rick alone.

When she came back into the kitchen, the conversation stopped and three heads turned toward her.

'OK?' Hank folded the newspaper, slid it into the recycling bin.

'We've decided you need a diversion, Harper.' Vicki stood. 'How about a girls' day? A facial? Or a massage?'

'What?' Harper sat.

'I called my favorite spa. They have openings in an hour. A facial or a massage – aromatherapy, deep tissue. You choose, whatever you want. It's on Trent and me.'

'Go,' Hank urged. 'Relax you.'

'Consider it a sign of our love.' Trent refilled his coffee mug.

Really? Harper thought about it. A massage? Zina and Burke were dead. Rick, too. Relics had been ruined – what good was a massage?

Then again, it would only last an hour. Might help her release some tension. Besides, she had most of the day free. She had an appointment with Leslie later, but that was all she had planned. Still, what was the point? Harper stood, carrying plates to the sink.

'No, don't.' Trent put up a hand.

'Clean up. We'll.' Hank took the plates from her.

Harper went for her bag.

'Leave it. You won't need it.' Vicki grabbed her arm, led her out the door. 'I'll drive.'

'No, it's OK.' She headed for the Ninja. 'I'll take the bike. You won't have to drive me home.'

'I don't mind. The whole point is that you can relax.'

But Harper climbed on to her motorcycle, rolled it down the driveway to Vicki's car, following her into town.

The first day of November was brisk, the air refreshing. The sky bulging with blue-gray clouds. Harper sped along, trying to be in the moment, but kept seeing herself wandering an endless dark tunnel that led to Chloe Manning's skeleton. Zina's lifeless body. Rick's dead eyes. Or a mound of broken crates and smashed artifacts.

Her mind mimicked the passageways, tangled with thoughts that led nowhere, or into and around themselves in an endless loop.

A massage, she decided. She would have a

massage and let go, stop thinking for an hour. A whole hour.

Ahead of her, Vicki turned right. The spa was just a few blocks away, on Audubon. Harper followed, was halfway through her turn when she noticed some pedestrians standing at the corner. One of them was Salih Salim.

Harper was surprised to see him; Rivers had said that she couldn't find him or his family. That they had disappeared. But there he was, right out on the street.

Harper pulled over to the curb. 'Salih?' She pulled off her helmet.

He turned, startled. 'Harper?' He seemed surprised to see her, but grinned, stepped over to embrace her. 'Good to see you again!'

'Where have you been, Salih? The police wanted to talk to you about your sister and—'

'No, no. I've been away.' His smile vanished; he looked away. 'With the family. It's been a difficult time for us.'

Harper nodded. Of course it had. Zina had been murdered.

'Our business is shaky at best.'

What? He was upset about business? Not Zina? 'And your sister...?'

'Well, of course.' His eyes didn't rest, kept moving. 'My sister. Despite my family's claims to the contrary, they all feel Zina's loss. In fact, that's where we've been. I convinced my ... my father decided to provide for her funeral. We all went back home to bury her.' He paused, took a breath. 'I got back just yesterday. A quick trip.'

Harper nodded, didn't know what to say.

'So there's nothing to do for her any more. She's at peace. And now, I have to hurry and salvage our business or it will die, too.' His mouth formed a sad twisted smile. 'Good to see you again, my friend.'

They hugged, separated, waving goodbye. Then Harper remembered Zina's bracelet. It was back home, still in her bag. 'Oh – Salih? I have something to give you.'

'To give me?' he called as he walked away. 'What is it?'

'Something of Zina's.'

He stopped, turned. Met her eyes. Looked away, at traffic. Hurried.

'I can bring it to you.'

'Good, if you don't mind – I'm at the same hotel as before. Oh – I don't use my own name. I'm registered as Smith. Come by, say, around three?' He waved, turned, and, as the light was green, headed across the street.

Naked under a sheet, listening to music that sounded like water, Harper smelled scented oils that reminded her of the oil burning around Rick's body. She thought of seeing Salih, of how hurried he'd seemed. Of taking Zina's bracelet to him. But her thoughts wandered and waned, and gradually faded altogether as she paid attention only to the hands of Kara, the masseuse.

The hands worked steadily, slippery and lubricated, building friction, causing waves of heat to roll through her muscles, one by one. Soreness Harper hadn't known about rose up and fought, only to be vanquished, banished by Kara's hands. Aches she'd tolerated as permanent were soothed. Her left leg almost wept with sweet release. For an hour, the hands of a stranger pulled the tension from her tissues, and Harper was immersed in sensations, indifferent to time.

Afterwards, wrapped in a terry robe, she sat with Vicki, sipping water with lemon slices. Vicki's face was bright red, glowing.

'Was yours good?'

Harper nodded, closed her eyes, almost too relaxed to speak. 'Yours?'

'Mmmm.'

They sat, speechless. Sipping. Finally, forced themselves to shower and dress. Harper thanked Vicki. Hugged her. Reminded her of their Tuesday night dinner. And got back on the Ninja, almost too relaxed to drive.

But she did drive, floating on her Ninja all the way home. Hank was outside, working a leaf blower. He shut it down, beaming. 'Bought today this.'

Half the front yard was already clear, the rest a speckled sea of leaves, even though they'd raked just days ago.

Harper forced a smile, aware that, until recently, Hank would have discussed the purchase with her before making it. And would have wanted her to go with him to the mall. But never mind. Hank was his own man again, and that was good. She walked over, gave him a hug. He smelled like the outdoors, hard work.

She looked at the leaf blower. 'So you have a new toy.'

'More. Snow blower. Bought. On sale. And

mower. Drill set. Saw, too. All.'

Really? He'd bought all that? Without even mentioning it? Harper felt stung, as if disenfranchised in decision-making. The tools would allow Hank to work around the property, but where would they get the money to pay for them? Hank's disability didn't provide much. And she had tuition debts to pay off. Harper bit her lip, didn't comment. Didn't want another argument.

'Massage? Good?'

'Yes. Very.' But tension was already building up in her shoulders, tightness in the small of her back. She pecked his cheek. 'I have to go – an appointment with Leslie.' Then, because she was practicing openness, she added. 'I ran into Zina's brother before. He's back in town.'

'From where back?'

'He said the whole family went home to bury Zina. Maybe he meant England? Or Syria? Anyhow, I'm going to stop by and drop off Zina's bracelet.'

'Bracelet?'

'Remember? She left it here that night—'

'Rivers no?' Or Rivers know?

Know? Oh right; she'd wanted to talk to Salih. 'I'll let her know he's back.'

Hank yanked the electric cord of the leaf blower, began winding it around his arm. 'With you go.'

'No, Hank. Stay here. Do what you're doing.' Her stubbornness rose, resisting him. Insisting that, if he could do things alone, she could, too. 'I'm seeing Leslie in an hour. I'll just stop by the

Embassy Inn on the way.' She started for the house.

'Hoppa. Letter for you. Sad. Burke. Came,' Hank called.

'A letter?' Sad? Burke?

Hank had started the leaf blower again, couldn't hear her. So Harper went inside, where she saw it in the foyer. She picked it up, looked at the envelope, sighed. The name on the return address was Burke Everett. It had been sent Friday, right before Burke died.

She tore it open. Looked for a note, an explanation. Found none. Only a list of serial numbers, crate numbers, shipment numbers. Receipts dated the final day of their assignment with Colonel Baxter, all with his signature. Itemized accountings of parcels, crates and containers – the shipment her detail had nearly died to protect, the one that they had loaded on to a helicopter in Iraq.

The one Baxter had insisted was full of supplies.

And that Burke had insisted was full of cash.

Harper stared at the papers, picturing Burke in his last hours, desperate, unable to reach her, increasingly certain that he wouldn't survive. Managing to mail these papers to her, hoping that she'd act on them, since neither he nor Pete could. She recalled his jittery hands, his darting eyes. Burke had been unbalanced, paranoid. Might have invented the theft in his mind. Might have sent her a list of serial numbers of standard supplies. Did she really believe that this envelope contained proof of a major multimillion-

301

dollar heist? And, even if she did, did she really want to create a scandal, embarrassing the Colonel – potentially ruining his political career by asking the army to confirm the contents of his shipment?

Harper rubbed her forehead, fighting a headache. The relaxation of her massage had evaporated; her legs felt heavy and her shoulders ached. She stared at the papers, uncertain about what to do. The possibility was undeniable that they might incriminate the Colonel in a huge theft, might even implicate him and Rick in Burke's and Peter's deaths.

Then again, they might not.

She walked in a circle, gazed out the window at Hank, pushed her fingers through her hair, looked again at the papers, the signatures. Finally, she came to a realization: she wasn't in charge of investigating either theft or homicide. And it wasn't her place to approach the army, not her job to launch an inquiry that could ruin a man's life.

Harper folded the paper, replaced it in its envelope, set the envelope back on the foyer table. She'd give it to Detective Rivers and let her follow up. Rivers could contact the army as part of her official investigation into Burke's death. The army would confirm the contents of the shipments, would determine whether a theft had actually occurred.

Relieved, Harper took her phone out of her bag and made the call, left a voicemail for Rivers. Told her that she'd received mail from Burke, asked her to call. Added that Salih was back, registered as 'Smith' at the Embassy Inn on Dryden Road.

Then at three o'clock, Harper grabbed her bag, went outside and climbed back on to her Ninja. When she shouted goodbye to Hank, the leaf blower was making a lot of noise. He didn't hear her, but he looked up and waved as she drove off.

The Embassy Inn was on the other side of campus. Harper got there about three fifteen, plenty of time to see Salih and make her appointment with Leslie. She asked at the desk for Mr Smith; the clerk made a call. In moments, Salih came into the lobby, still dressed in his pinstriped business suit, his red tie. He greeted Harper with a grin, a warm hug.

'Thank you for coming all this way.'

'No problem.' She reached into her bag, feeling for the bracelet. 'Let me give you—'

'No, no. Not so fast. First, you have to join me for a drink. I have a selection set up in my suite.'

Was he asking her to his room? 'Really – I have to get to an appointment.'

'So you don't have to stay long. And I promise not to make a pass.' He winked playfully, took her hand, tugged on it. 'Come, my drinking buddy. Just one drink. We'll catch up.'

Harper shook her head. 'I can't.'

Salih kept it up. 'When's your appointment? I'll have you on your way in plenty of time.'

Fine. What was the harm in one drink?

His suite contained a sitting room stocked with liquor. Stoli, Johnny Walker Black, Chablis. The fridge was full of beer. Salih had set up his

303

own bar.

He poured her a Scotch, himself a vodka. Raised his glass in a toast. 'To friendship.'

They clinked glasses, sipped. Sat. She on an easy chair, he on the love seat. Cartons wrapped in brown paper were stacked along the far wall, as if ready for shipping.

'Tell me, Harper,' he eyed the cut on her forehead. 'What happened to you? Were you in an accident?'

'No, it's nothing serious.' She took a sip of Scotch. 'I fell at the Langston house.' It wasn't a lie.

'And how is it, working there?'

Really? He was asking how she liked his dead sister's job? 'Well, I don't like how I got the position.'

'Of course not. I didn't mean to imply that. I meant only what I asked. How is the work going?'

Harper thought of the missing pieces, the traffickers. Rick's body, the crates he'd dropped into the passageway. 'It's been complicated.'

Salih raised his eyebrows, tilted his head. 'Complicated?'

She didn't want to talk about it, couldn't bear to. So she changed the subject. 'How did your business meeting go?'

He crossed his legs. The cuffs of his slacks revealed unmatched socks. Both black, but of different fabric. Odd, for a man so meticulous. 'It's a difficult time. Did I mention it last time? What we do? We deal in fine art, sculpture and some antiques. But our passion is artifacts.

That's how Zina first came to archeology. As a child, she tagged along with our father to auctions and such. But the problem today is that many countries are determined to repossess their relics. Even decades or centuries after they've been traded. Just recently, the Chinese filed a suit against us to prevent us from auctioning several exquisite pieces.' He uncrossed his legs, took a drink. 'But you don't want to hear about my troubles. Let's talk about you. The Pre-Columbian collection.'

'What do you want to know?' Harper swallowed Scotch. Checked her watch. She had to leave in a few minutes. But the Scotch had warmed her and it wasn't often that someone was really interested in talking about artifacts.

'Tell me about the collection itself.'

Harper shook her head. 'It's beyond description. It's vast. The collection includes pieces from South America through the south-west US. Some pieces are more than three thousand years old – and many are pristine.' Well, maybe not the ones smashed to smithereens. 'The other day, I held a three-thousand-year-old jaguar—'

She stopped at the sound of a key turning. 'Hey, Joe? I found that replacement.' The door swung open and Angus Langston walked in, carrying a small package. His mouth opened when he saw Harper, then he turned to Salih. 'Shit, Joe. How was I supposed to know you had company?'

Joe? Why was Angus calling Salih 'Joe'?

How did Angus even know Salih?

And why were they both staring at her?

Instantly, Harper flashed back to the tunnel, the traffickers, their voices. The argument about a relic worth $55,000; Joe scolding someone for breaking it. Threatening to make him pay for it out of his own pocket. Oh God. No question: Joe was Salih – and Angus was one of the traffickers.

'No need to look so confused, Harper.' Salih forced a smile. 'I go by "Joe Smith" when doing business. I've found it easier to get along in this country if I use an American-sounding name.'

Harper nodded, feigning indifference. Told herself to be cool. After all, neither Salih nor Angus were aware that she'd heard them from the passageway. Or that she knew they were stealing relics. Or that they'd been involved in Rick's death.

'Hello, Angus.' She smiled, put her glass down and stood, trying to sound casual. Forgot about returning Zina's bracelet, the reason she'd come. 'Well, I'll leave you to your business.'

'What are you up to, Joe?' Angus snapped. 'What's she doing here?' He squinted, suspicious. 'Is she trying to undercut us? Are you two making a separate deal?'

'Good God, Angus. We're having a drink.' Salih finished his and set the empty glass beside Harper's. 'Not that it's your business.' The men glared at each other.

Harper cleared her throat, excused herself. 'Well. Thanks for the drink, Salih.' She started for the door.

Angus stood in her way, wouldn't step aside.

'Excuse me, Angus.' Harper looked up at him. He was a foot taller than she was, maybe ninety pounds heavier. She counted her options, ways to take him down as she stepped sideways, trying to get around him.

'This bitch is the reason half our stuff is broken.' He blocked her, moving with her to the side. A pas de deux. 'She cost us a fortune!'

'Wait just a moment, please, Harper.' Salih put up a hand. He addressed Angus. 'What are you talking about? Broken? What's broken?'

'You've been gone, Joe. Out of touch. You don't even know what happened. This broad and the guy Digger offed? Somehow, they dumped about twenty crates of relics into the—'

'I had nothing to do with—' Harper stopped. Replaying. *That guy Digger offed.*

Angus went on, telling Salih about the damaged and destroyed treasures they'd found in the passageway. But Harper wasn't listening. She was putting pieces together. Unbelievably, Salih must be – *had* to be – Joe. That he'd been there when someone named Digger killed Rick. That he was the leader of the traffickers.

Salih sighed, rubbed his eyes, reacting to the bad news. When he looked up, his gaze moved from Angus to Harper, back to Angus. 'This is disturbing.'

'Yeah, that's what I'm trying to tell you. She's even worse than your sister. This bitch cost us a fortune.'

Salih blinked at him. 'You really are an ass, Angus.' He turned back to Harper. 'My apologies, my friend. Professor Langston was a long-time client of my family. Until his death, we dealt with him with some regularity. But now, we seem to have inherited his sons.'

'What kind of bullshit is that?' Angus interrupted. '*You* came to *us*!'

'Look,' Harper feigned indifference, frowned as if confused. 'I'm going to be late. I'll go and leave you two to discuss whatever it is you—'

'Don't think so, darling.' Angus stepped forward. 'You're what they call a liability.'

Salih sat back against the love-seat cushions, sighing. 'Angus. You aren't just an ass. You're a complete moron.'

'Well, what do you suggest we do, Joe? Let her walk out of here? She's competition!'

'She has no role in this business whatsoever.'

'Yeah? Then ask her what she and that dead guy were doing in the passageway.'

Salih's eyes darkened and he turned to Harper. 'Actually, it's a good question. However, at this point, after all that's been said, the answer is irrelevant.'

Harper assessed the situation, eyeing Angus. She'd do a one-two move, knocking the wind out of him by slamming his solar plexus, then, as he sank, she'd chop his neck. And dash for the door. She drew a breath, ready, set—

And Salih called her name in a menacing tone.

Harper looked over her shoulder, saw the gun in Salih's hand. Damn. Would he really shoot her? She doubted it. She met Salih's eyes, debating whether or not he would. Whether she should test him and take Angus down. Suddenly, though, her debate ended unresolved as she went blank, dropping to the floor even before she could feel the blow.

The smell was sickening. Musky and sweet, moldy and smoky. She could actually taste it. Harper grimaced and turned her head, initiating a sudden sharp pain in her neck. She groaned, waiting for the pain to subside. Tried to sit up, couldn't move. Couldn't move an arm or a leg. Nothing. Oh God.

Slowly, warily, she opened an eye. Saw a small flame inches from her face. A candle? Then she inhaled the noxious scent. Recognized it, though it was stronger now; she was closer to it. Some kind of incense was burning. Or scented oils.

OK, she was stuck in a dream, a nightmare. One of those where she thought she was paralysed but it was just a phase of sleep. So she started over. Closed her eyes, tried again to sit. Couldn't move. And she felt restraints around her wrists, her ankles.

It wasn't a dream. Damn – where was she?

Harper lay still, squinting to focus and see beyond the flame. Gradually, in the dim light, she looked to her left. Saw a wall of stone and clay, like a cave. And pictures painted on it. A deer. An owl. A dog ... Oh God. She was at Langston's. In that room at the end of the passageway, the one where she'd seen Rick—

Images surfaced. The hotel room. Salih. And Angus. Salih holding a gun. Lord. What had happened? Had Salih shot her? Harper closed her eyes again, carefully took an inventory of her body, searching for the pain of a bullet wound. The scent of fresh blood. Found none. So she hadn't been shot, but somehow, they'd knocked her out. She'd been unconscious. But for how long? Never mind – that was irrelevant. She needed to figure out how to untie herself. How to escape.

Something moved near her – softly, like footsteps, coming closer. Harper kept her eyes closed, playing possum. The steps stopped. She felt subtle swirls of air, and a man's voice chanting syllables she didn't understand.

Carefully, she opened her right eye a crack. Just enough to reveal a sliver of vision. At first, she saw shadows darting directly above her. Then something glimmering, reflecting the flame. She closed her eye, listening, trying to calm herself. But she sensed someone close to her, peeked again. And saw a man leaning over her. He was talking to himself, and suddenly, he pressed something – a rag? – over her mouth and nose. Harper smelled chemicals, wriggled and resisted, struggling to breathe. Fading, she realized that, no – it wasn't a man. It had a man's body, but it was covered with feathers like an owl. And it had a jaguar's head.

The Nahual was hungry. Not the kind of hunger known to men. This was the hunger of the jaguar, the hunger of mountains and of the moon. It was the hunger, also, of the hunt. And of the dead.

He'd finished with the man, taking his power in, engulfing his spirit. Had offered the remains, as was his calling, to the wolves, the ravens, the foxes and dogs. He could feel his strength even now, raging in his blood like the screams of a warrior. The man was completely unlike the

310

trader's sister. She'd been meek; despite her superior intellect. Her spirit had been marred, defeated by the betrayal of her dying.

Having fasted and cleansed himself, he slipped into his owl form, becoming himself an omen of death. Again, he observed the woman on his altar. She was small but muscular, almost as firm as the man. She wore a wedding ring, and so was clearly not a virgin, but never mind. He'd incorporated purity decades ago. Now, his goal was to enhance his spirit, increase his potency. At times during rituals, soaring above earth, he felt godlike.

He took the form of the jaguar, preparing himself. Stepped beside her, beginning his incantations. Presenting her with the sedating drug, releasing her limbs to free her spirit.

Yes, this one would make an excellent addition. For one thing, she was still alive. If he acted quickly, when he began to take it in, her heart would still be beating.

That now familiar, sickening scent of pungent and sweet smoke was her first sensation. And second was nausea, not quite bad enough to make her retch. But bad. Harper didn't want to open her eyes. She was afraid to see that creature again. It must have been a dream. But how had it been a dream? It had been so vivid – she could have sworn that she'd actually seen a creature of many shapes. Maybe a Nahual. So she kept her eyes closed, not looking yet. She reached out for Hank, felt empty air. Where was he? What time was it? What was that smell? Her back ached, and she was chilly. She reached for the blanket. Found none. No Hank. No blanket. Oh God. Harper opened her eyes. Saw the vessels of burning oil. The paintings of animals on the wall. Remembered Salih and Angus. And waking up here with that creature...

Harper sat up, was overtaken by nausea. And pain in the back of her skull. She stayed still, waiting for the waves to pass. Damn. What had they done to her? She touched the back of her head, felt a mushy, golf-ball-sized lump. Her last memory was back in Salih's room. Trying to leave. One of them ... Angus must have knocked her out. Maybe she'd been delirious from the blow to her head, imagining that strange bird-cat-man. Maybe she'd never even been tied up. Never mind. It didn't matter. She needed to get out of there, and her arms and legs were unbound now. She could move.

Slowly, she turned her head, looking around the dim cave-like room, seeing no one. She was alone. Fabric tickled her belly. Harper glanced down, saw that her shirt had been ripped open, her bra removed. Her chest exposed. Reflexively, without thinking, she gathered the torn fabric, covering herself. Pictured Rick lying dead in that same room, his exposed chest sliced open. She took a breath, recalled the creature she'd seen before she'd passed out, something – a knife? – glittering in his hand.

Oh God. She thought of the conversation she'd heard when she was lost in the passageway. A man claiming he'd learned the rites and rituals of the ancients. Bragging that he'd sacrificed Carla

Prentiss. And the other guy mocking him, calling him The High Priest of Owl Feathers? Telling him he looked like a feather duster.

Harper closed her eyes, saw the feather-covered creature with a man's shape and a jaguar head. It hadn't been a dream, was not a trauma-induced hallucination. It had been a guy dressed in ritual costume. Wearing the head of a jaguar, the most revered of all beasts, the embodiment of power. And the feathers of owls, the messengers between the living and the dead.

Even before she'd processed these thoughts, Harper had hopped off the table and begun to run. But she'd stood too fast. Dizziness overcame her, and she buckled with nausea and pain. Bent over, she kept moving toward the door to the woods. Told herself she was almost there. Counted her steps to take her mind off her dizziness. When she got to seven, she stopped. Listening.

Men were talking. Just outside, on the ramp to the woods.

Damn. Harper hugged the wall, listening.

'You have to dispose of her anyway.'

'Thanks to this idiot, yes. We have no options.'

Salih? Was that his voice? Salih was agreeing to kill her?

'Me? How is it my fault you decided to—'

'Let's not waste more time going through it again.'

'Exactly. I need to continue the rite before she wakes up.'

'You're not going to lay a hand on her.' Salih insisted. 'It's enough you mutilated my sister. I

313

won't let you—'

'I am not the one who killed your sister. You should thank me; I resurrected her strength.'

'Thank you? I should kill you!'

'Meantime, what did you do with the guy?' That voice was Angus's.

'The guy?'

'Where is he? Are the cops going to descend on us like last time?'

'No, it isn't like before. His remains are where no one but wolves and spirits will find them.'

'Except for the heart, right?' Salih's voice was a growl. 'What do you do with the hearts, you sick bastard – what did you do with my sister's?'

'What the hell difference does it make, Joe?' Angus tried to appease him. 'Let him get on with it. It's all the same to us. And to her – I mean when you're dead, you're dead.'

'How can I say this in a way you two morons will understand?' Salih spoke slowly and clearly. 'There are such things as human dignity, loyalty and honor. That woman has done nothing to defile herself or anyone else. She may need to be eliminated for practical reasons, but she deserves—'

'No.' The third man interrupted. 'The woman has exquisite power. It emanates from her visibly, like a corona. And I intend to acquire it through the practices of my predecessors. End of discussion.'

'If you as much as touch her, consider our relationship and business dealings finished. I mean this.'

'Cut it out, Joe. You aren't going to end anything,' Angus whined. 'We depend on each other.'

'Get out of the way, Angus. If he wants to cut her, he'll have to get past me.'

There was scuffling outside. The sounds of punches landing. Of grunting and cursing. Then, of someone coming.

Harper dashed back into the cave. Maybe she could get to the rope ladder, climb up into the passageway. But, no – not enough time. They'd grab her and yank her back down. She had to stay there. Take them on face to face? Or better – she could lie back on the table, feigning unconsciousness and, when the guy approached her, take him by surprise. Grab his weapon and turn it against him. Harper took her position, wounded, dizzy. Wondering if she'd be able to overpower him. If she were strong enough.

In the end, it didn't matter; it was the only plan she had.

The Nahual shoved the man aside, pummeling his face, slamming him to the ground. How dare he challenge him? This day would mark the end of their collaboration. The man had mere materialistic goals, had no concept of the real significance of their work. The acquisition of spiritual enlightenment and power were far more valuable than any tangible wealth. But Joe Smith would never understand. He wasn't even worth sacrificing; his spirit was tainted and slimy. Incorporating Joe's heart might actually harm him, might stunt his growth.

But the woman was different. She glowed with

315

life energy, moved catlike with power and purpose. She was a fighter, too, and of a fertile age. She lay along the wall under the images of death, of the souls of warriors, of the hunt, of the mountains. Her lungs would be filled with the mystical scented oils, the fires of priests. He'd never taken in a living organ, but, in moments, that would change. Her heart would be beating in his hands, in his mouth. Her life would enter his body, become his, uniting with his soul, joining the others – the dog, owl, bat, deer, butterfly, turtle, rabbit, toad. The young woman of his youth. The man from the tunnel. He remembered each of them, the surge of awareness each had brought. The struggle with the turtle's shell. The mottled skin of the toad. The bloody ribs of the virgin.

Slowly, he resumed the chanting that the others had interrupted. He readied his blade to open her chest, prepared for the soaking volcano of blood that would spew. He closed his eyes, repeating syllables he'd memorized decades ago at the professor's side. Words that praised the bravery, strength, spirit, beauty of the creature about to die. He touched her face, covered her eyes with his hand, spread his wings to cast a shadow over her body. Then, taking one last look at her, he held his weapon above her chest, silently taking aim.

The guy was standing beside her, mumbling syllables in a language she'd never heard. Careful not to lift her eyelids too far, Harper peeked at him. Saw the head of a wild cat on top of his, askew like a lopsided headdress or crown. And a

316

jacket of feathers, speckled in red. Damn. Was this the Nahual that had scared Zina? Some guy dressed in feathers and stuffed animal parts? 'You look like a damn feather duster,' Joe – or, rather Salih – had said.

Harper watched through her sliver of vision as he waved his arms like wings and rotated in circles, swooping, whirling, spinning and chanting. Reaching up, bowing low. Spinning again.

She thought of jumping on him while his back was turned, but he moved quickly, unpredictably. She might miss him and land on the ground. So she watched, waiting for the right moment, legs tensed, ready to push off the wooden slab. Finally, he stopped dancing around and stood silent and unmoving, looking down at her, both hands poised above her chest, holding a long thin blade.

Harper roared, startling him as she flew off the altar, springing at him with all her hundred and twenty pounds. He was clumsy, off balance with two heads, unprepared for an assault, and he keeled over with Harper attached to him by all fours. The spines of feathers pricked her skin as she pounced on him, scratched her as he hit the ground and twisted to get free. Harper held on, looking for the knife, not finding it, feeling his empty fists instead as they pounded her sides. Still, she didn't let go, stayed on top despite his squirming body and dizzying blows. She hung on with her thighs as if riding a bull, punched his face, jabbed his ribs. Scanned the floor again for the knife. Saw it a few yards away. Too far to reach. Harper took a breath, shifted her weight and thrust her strong knee into his belly, winding him so she could crawl off of him to get it. But he grabbed her leg, yanked it, pulling her back as he rolled to his side, then up on to his knees. He clamped one, then both hands around her throat as he stood, lifting her by her neck. Holding her face in front of his, meeting her eyes.

Harper's feet left the ground. She couldn't breathe. She kicked, aiming for his gut. She punched like a machine, reflexively repeating her combat training. She poked at his eyes. But her clarity was failing, her vision spotty. Her mind was disconnecting from her body, not obeying its commands. Flailing, Harper glared, trying to focus, and just as she began to black out, oh God, she recognized his face.

Professor Wiggins? She blinked, saw him again. Staring at her with glowing, hot eyes. Watching her die. Harper's mind fought, kept thinking. Was Professor Wiggins the Nahual? Was he really killing her? Was his face the last thing she'd ever see? Their eyes locked. Harper scratched, pulled skin off his face, but he didn't even wince. He kept the pressure on her neck, and she felt the blood pulsing behind her eyes, pooling inside her head. The strength was draining from her limbs. For a moment, she thought of Hank. And then, the Nahual's eyes widened, his mouth opened as if to scream. Slowly, he released her neck and they both, in unison, dropped to the floor.

Harper rolled, coughing, gasping, struggling to breathe. Unable to get up. Unsure what had happened. Sensing that she was still in danger, she tried to get to her feet, to run. Someone else was there with her – maybe Hank? Had he come for her? A man knelt beside her. She strained her neck to turn her head and look. Saw not Hank, but Salih.

'Harper,' he spoke softly, touched her shoulder. 'Are you all right? I'm very sorry about this.'

His face was a mess. An eye was swollen half-closed, his lip and nose bleeding. Harper skitter-ed away from him, still coughing.

'You don't have to be afraid. I'm a business-man, Harper, nothing more.' He smiled, reveal-ing bloody teeth.

From the doorway to the ramp, Angus shouted. 'Jeezus H, Joe. What the fuck happened now?'

Still coughing, Harper followed Angus' gaze. Professor Wiggins lay on the ground, his ritual knife protruding from his back. Salih had stab-bed him, had rescued her. She tried to speak, but provoked more grating coughs. Salih looked concerned.

'I wish I had something – water, maybe – to help you. But I don't. Angus? Do we have water in the van?'

Angus stood at the ramp, scratching his head. 'What did you do, fucking kill Digger? What in hell's the matter with you?'

'Go see if there's water.'

'What the fuck for? This is so fucked up. Let's just get this over with and clean up, OK?' Angus stepped closer to the body, gaping at Wiggins.

Salih sighed, shook his head. 'I'm sorry you got involved in this mess, Harper. I truly like you.' He got to his feet, rubbed his hands.

319

Harper eyed him, unable to talk.

'But sometimes, unfortunately, our own survival requires us to deal with unsavory people and to perform unsavory tasks.' Another sigh. 'And, once again, I'm charged with the wellbeing – indeed, the survival – of my family. Protecting both its honor and its business interests. Despite my personal feelings and attachments, I cannot let this mess be revealed. You understand?'

Harper shook her head, no.

Salih chuckled grimly. 'Just like Zina. Stubborn to the end.'

Zina?

'My sister also claimed she had no idea why she had to die. This, despite her own deliberate defiance and dishonorable actions. Her refusal to marry the man my father had chosen for her. Her refusal to participate in the family business – even after we managed to obtain that research position for her.'

Harper blinked, wheezing.

'All she had to do was compromise. If she had procured even a few items for us, I could have convinced my father to overlook the marriage issue and spare her.' Salih shook his head. 'But she was so incredibly stubborn. Zina threatened to expose her own family, to publicly shame us. What was I to do? It was my responsibility. But when she realized what was coming, she pretended to be surprised. She must have thought she was immune, that her actions would never provoke consequences.' He paused, misty-eyed. 'I loved my sister.'

Harper blinked, trying to clear her head and

320

understand what Salih was saying. He had killed Zina? She was pretty sure he'd just admitted that he had.

'She knew her responsibilities from the start. We partnered with Wiggins to get her the position for the very purpose of obtaining artifacts.'

Of course. Professor Wiggins had openly favored Zina, had lobbied hard for her to get the assistantship. Now Harper knew why. She glanced at his body. Had his leg been extended before? Had he moved?

'Little Zina. She was my favorite sister.' Salih looked into the distance. 'It was painful. Still is. But I did what was necessary.' He turned to her. 'I hope you understand. If I would kill my own sister whom I dearly loved for the sake of the family, I must certainly not hesitate to kill you.'

'Digger's still breathing.' Angus stood beside Wiggins. 'What do you want to do?'

Salih rubbed his swelling jaw. 'He's an abomination. Leave him.'

'Leave him? What, here?'

Salih stepped over to Wiggins. Looked down at him. 'No, you're right. We should dispose of him. Go get a cart.'

Angus hesitated, frowning.

'Well, unless you want to carry him.'

'This is messed up, Joe.' Angus headed to the ramp. 'I don't like it one bit.'

'And now, Harper. I guess it's you and me.'

Salih reached into his jacket, took out a pocket knife. It wasn't big, wasn't fancy. But it was more knife than she had. Her neck throbbed and ached from Wiggins' choking grasp, but she

321

braced herself for yet another assault. Salih stepped closer confidently, as if he thought she was too weak to fight, too defeated. But Harper had been trained for battle and, as soon as he was within reach, she drew a deep breath, centered herself and swung, landing her fist hard in his eye, the one that was already swollen closed; then, as he reeled, she aimed and slammed her right foot up hard between his legs.

The Nahual listened, waiting silently, gathering his fury and strength. Assessing the severity of his wound. Testing each limb, refusing the pain. He never should have gotten involved with these philistines. Never should have trusted that their lust for monetary gain could interface with his for spiritual growth. No, it had been a mistake, but he would correct it here, today.

He was bleeding, though. Leaking strength. He'd need to act soon, before the moron Angus returned with his cart. He wasn't sure, given a choice, with whom Angus would side. Angus had known him decades longer; they'd grown up together. And he'd been the protégé of Angus's father. But Joe had all the money. And Angus, being a fool, might go either way. Given his condition, he didn't want to risk facing two opponents.

Not to mention the woman.

He'd injured her throat, had felt her windpipe collapsing under his grip. But she was already recovering; he heard her ragged coughing. Heard Joe rambling, apologizing that he had to kill her. Talking about honor, about family. As if his family had such a thing as honor. As if anyone did in this era where the earth itself was spat upon and defiled, where revered beasts were slaughtered, starved or caged. Joe's family, indeed. How did this insignificant creature have the audacity to think that he and those who'd spawned him had the capacity to possess such a thing as 'honor'? Honor belonged to the ageless spirits, the creatures of death and sky and rivers and mountains and wind. It didn't belong to petty criminals and thieves. No, he should never have gotten involved. But Joe had offered – no, had *promised* – him access to the relics, that he could select among them for his studies.

The Nahual played dead, lying still as Joe finished simpering about murdering his sister. He watched as the woman bludgeoned him and ran for the rope ladder, as Joe moaned and stumbled, chasing after her. Recognizing his moment, the Nahual chanted softly, calling upon the spirit of Joe's sister, and he felt it stir within him, raging, seeking revenge. He called up the spirit of the dead male from the tunnel, too, and summoned all the creatures he'd ever embodied, and then he drew a breath, drawing fury from his own pain. Finally, he pulled the power of all those spirits together and leapt to his feet, hurling himself at Joe with a warrior's cry, landing a crushing blow to the base of his skull. Knocking him down. Standing over him with a triumphant bellow. Dragging him to the altar where he would take his life, his heart. And his spirit.

She was weak, sore all over, her neck felt sprained, and air scraped like dull razors in her raw throat, but Harper made it to the rope ladder and, by the time Salih had chased her to the bottom, she'd pulled herself up into the passageway. Spent and wheezing, she stopped to glance back. Damn – Salih was already halfway up the ladder. She turned, ready to run. But before she'd taken a step, she heard a shout, a thud, a groan. Harper stepped back, looked down the ladder once more. Salih lay flat on his back on the ground, staring up at her exactly as Rick had. And exactly as Rick had, Salih began sliding away. Someone was dragging him.

Harper couldn't see who it was. Angus? Had he gone after Salih and slugged him? She lowered herself on to the floor of the passageway, stuck her head out the opening. And saw the Nahual – Professor Wiggins – the knife still in his back, holding Salih by his armpits and pulling him across the cave.

Salih seemed conscious. His eyes were alert, open, fixed on her as Wiggins moved him. And when Wiggins stopped to rest, Salih rolled over and jumped to his feet, fists flying. Wiggins fought back with amazing vigor. Punching and grunting, they moved out of her view. Leaning further down, careful of her neck as she lowered her head, Harper saw them again; the Nahual costume now ripped, the jaguar head dangling loose, Wiggins stumbled toward the ramp with Salih close behind. Salih reached, took hold of the hilt of the blade and twisted it before pulling it out. A gut-twisting scream resounded through the cave as the Nahual fell to his knees, both of his heads bent, the back of his feathered jacket blood-soaked, his arms raised to the sky. Salih stood behind him, raised the blade high with both hands and unceremoniously shoved it down into the Nahual's back, piercing his heart.

Salih remained there, breathless and bloodied beside the pile of feathers until Angus came in with a wheelbarrow.

'Hey, how'd he get all the way over there? Shit, Joe. Your face looks like—'

Harper couldn't hear Salih's response. But she saw him pointing toward the house, gesturing emphatically, showing Angus where to go. Damn. He was sending him to the other end of the passageway, to Rick's broken wall. The only way Harper knew to get out.

'Shit. This just gets worse and worse, man. Jake's gonna find out and then we'll all be dead.'

Salih said something, gesturing again, and Angus rushed up the ramp, cursing and whining.

Slowly, Salih lifted his gaze to the top of the rope ladder, meeting Harper's eyes.

Faster, she told herself as she yanked at the ladder. Hurry. She tugged on the thick, heavy ropes, taking them up rung by rung, expecting at any moment that Salih would pull down from the other end. But he didn't. The ladder was difficult to maneuver and weighed more than she'd expected, but, sweating and wheezing, she managed to pull it all up and gather it into a pile. Favoring her neck, she lay flat beside the rope and peered down into the cave for Salih. Saw the wheelbarrow, the dead Nahual. The vessels of burning oil. The altar ... And finally,

325

Salih, apparently returning to the cave after stepping out for supplies. He was lumbering across the cave with his arms full, carrying an extension ladder and a flashlight. On his shoulder, she saw a holster.

OK, time to go. Harper got to her feet and turned, gazed into the passageway. Saw a well of total darkness. Damn. This time, she had no flashlight, would be completely blind. But Salih had a gun. She had no choice.

Harper plunged into blackness, her hands on the walls, feeling for the trail of X's she'd carved with a nail. Hearing the clunk of the ladder against the opening, Salih's heavy footsteps on the rungs. His panting as he climbed into the passageway. His voice calling, 'Harper?'

She kept moving blindly, cautiously, testing the floor with her feet, following the wall with her fingers. Was that an X? Or just a random scratch? She traced the line, touched the intersection in the middle – yes, it was an X! She wouldn't get lost if she stuck to the trail.

'Harper, stop. You'll get lost. Look, I'm a businessman; we can negotiate.'

Harper hurried away from the voice, deeper into the passageways, trying to remember the turns, the dead ends. Remembering with dismay that the Xs didn't lead to an exit; they led to the spot where she'd found Chloe Manning. Following them was useless. Oh God, what if she got lost again, this time in the dark? Familiar panic bubbled in her belly. What a joke. After escaping against all odds, she'd come back to die here after all?

Shut up, she told herself. Stop whimpering and just go. Salih was not far behind; she could hear his steps. Imagined his bloody breath on her neck, his gun at her ribs. She hurried on, suddenly felt the air shift. Just ahead, her fingers felt empty air. A gap in the wall. Was this a turn in the passageway? She didn't remember one so close to the rope ladder, but she'd been exhausted, half-delusional and dehydrated, might not have noticed. And the wall definitely had a gap. So the tunnel turned. Except, no – she felt gaps on both sides. So the tunnel divided left and right. She stepped forward, arms outstretched. Found no wall ahead either. She was at a crossroads, could go straight, left or right. She couldn't take time to think; Salih was too close. Needed to choose and move. Oh God. Harper had no idea where she was. Taking a breath, she chose without a reason and turned right. Her hand skimmed the surface of the wall, feeling her way. Counting her steps in case she had to retrace them.

At the ninth step, Salih called again, his voice not as close. 'Harper – there's no point wandering. There's no way out for you. Come back. We'll have a bottle of wine and talk things out.'

A bottle of wine? Really? Harper kept moving. Counting steps, she turned and zigzagged blindly, feeling oddly calm. Gradually, Salih's voice became more distant. After a while, she didn't hear it at all.

She'd lost count of her steps somewhere after two hundred thirty. And she'd forgotten the

327

sequence of her turns, even though she'd tried to make a marching song out of them: right, right, left, right, left. But she couldn't remember them, wouldn't be able to find her way back if she had to. Harper wandered lost, listening for Salih, not hearing him. But soon, she heard other voices.

'Mrs Jennings?' A man.

'Hoppa!' Hank?

And the barking of a dog.

A dog?

Harper stopped walking and shouted to them, but her voice was thin and hoarse. And using it, she began to cough again. Could they hear her? She waited until they called again, tried to identify their direction, to go towards them. Running, stumbling on the uneven floor, turning corners she wasn't sure would take her closer, she called out as loudly and often as her throat would allow until, finally, she saw a glow of light ahead. Squinting, shading her eyes from the brightness of flashlights, Harper stopped walking and let herself sink to the tunnel floor.

A golden Lab pulled on his leash, dragging the officer behind him; when he reached Harper, he sat beside her. Panting. And Harper sat panting in unison.

'Mrs Jennings?' The officer aimed his flashlight at her face, blinding her. 'It's OK, Mrs Jennings. We've got you.'

'Hoppa? Hoppa – OK?'

She couldn't see him, but Hank's winded voice came to her from somewhere behind the policeman. And then, as the officer talked into a radio, Hank was moving in front of him. And around

328

the dog. And as he reached for her, Harper half jumped, half fell into his arms.

Hank handed her up through the hole in the wall to the EMTs who'd been waiting. He stood on Rick's pile of broken crates and smashed relics. They'd set up lights down there, illuminating a whole section of the passageway, but Harper couldn't bear to look. Didn't want to see the wreckage of relics on the ground.

The EMTs placed her on a stretcher. Began checking her out. Frowned at her face, her torso. Her throat. Conferred with each other then asked if someone had choked her. She started to nod, but the older one stopped her. 'No, no – don't move your head. Stay still.'

Harper kept still, but moved her eyes, searching for Hank. 'How'd you know where—' she started but her voice again broke, instigating a fit of coughing and alarming the EMTs.

'Leslie,' Hank said.

Leslie?

'Called. Said you. Shown up. Not.'

What? Shown up where? Harper tried but couldn't remember anything about Leslie. Couldn't even recall how she'd gotten to Langston's.

'Thank goodness you're all right, Mrs Jennings.' Detective Rivers climbed out of the hole in the wall, talking as she strained to lift a German shepherd out and helped an officer climb after her. 'We've been scared sick about you. Especially after we got to Mr Salim's hotel and saw what was in his room,'

His room? Harper pictured it, the suite, its

well-stocked bar. Wait. Her memories were resurfacing – she'd gone to Salih's hotel to give him Zina's bracelet, and he'd offered her a drink. 'Just one,' because she didn't want to be late. Wait – late? Oh – late for Leslie! Yes, she'd had an appointment with Leslie, but hadn't shown up.

Even so, why had Leslie called Hank? If Leslie had a concern, she should have called Harper. Except that maybe she had. Harper wouldn't have answered her phone, didn't even know where it was. And, given Harper's role in the headlines of the last week, Leslie would have worried when Harper hadn't shown up and wasn't answering her phone. Which would explain why she'd called Hank.

Harper's head hurt, resisted thinking. Something pierced her arm. She looked down, saw one of the EMTs – the younger one – inserting a butterfly needle into her arm. Damn. They were giving her an IV.

'I don't need that!' She started to sit up, tried to push him away. Didn't want to go to the hospital.

'Lie back, ma'am. It's just in case.' He connected a saline bag to her arm while his partner strapped cold packs to her torso.

Detective Rivers was still talking.

'...your motorcycle outside and your leather bag in his room. But that wasn't all.' She folded her arms. 'We found over a dozen relics in there, packaged and ready to go. Do you know anything about those?'

Harper tried to shake her head but couldn't. They'd put something around her head and neck, immobilizing her. When had they done that? How, without her noticing? Cold fluids streamed into Harper's arm. Breathing hurt. The detective talked on.

'...my untrained eye, Mrs Jennings, those relics look to be Pre-Columbian, and I suspect they might belong to the Langston collection. Given that Mr Salim's sister used to work with the collection, and that her body was found at the Langston house, and that these relics might have been stolen from there, I thought I should stop over there and see what was going on.'

Harper was still confused. How had they known to search the passageway? Why would they think she was in there?

'When we arrived, we saw a van parked outside that cave you showed us. We went inside, and, Mrs Jennings, there was a lot of blood in that cave.'

Blood? Wait. Not Wiggins' body? The EMT was checking her blood pressure, distracting her.

'Frankly, with so much blood, I feared the worst, but your husband – he's a keen observer – he noticed something odd: the rope ladder to the passageway had been pulled up. So we thought – we hoped – you'd skedaddled up and taken it up with you.'

'Enough.' Hank put a hand up, scolding. 'Hoppa. Hurt. Talk later not more now.'

The older EMT nodded agreement. 'We're ready to roll.' He rechecked the stabilizing equipment around her neck.

'One minute.' Rivers stopped them. She eyed Harper. 'Mrs Jennings, please. If you know, tell

331

me: where is Salih Salim?'

Harper pointed to the passageway, mouthed, 'In there.'

'In the passageway? He was with you?'

Harper tried, but couldn't shake her head, managed to croak, 'Following me.' And then something else occurred to her. 'Where's Angus?'

Harper woke up, full of painkillers, staring at an IV pole and bag of fluids. In the hospital. Again, she saw the explosion at the checkpoint, her patrol blowing up. Felt the thud of landing on a burn-out car, her leg ... She reached down, felt her leg. No bandages. What? She tried to turn her head to look around, but couldn't move it. Wait – how come—?

'You up, Hoppa.' Hank stood above her, taking her hand. 'Feel how?' He leaned over, kissed her.

Harper closed her eyes, her memory spotty. 'I'm in the hospital.'

He explained that, yes, she was. And had been for two days under heavy doses of pain medicine. She'd been X-rayed, MRI'd, examined all over. Tests had shown that her neck was sprained, her larynx bruised, a couple of vertebrae dislocated. Her ribs were bruised, her hands raw from rope burn. From head to toe, she was banged up and scraped. While she'd been running from Salih, adrenalin had probably masked the pain of these injuries, but once she was safe, it had erupted hot and fierce. The pain medications had made her groggy, and, when she'd been awake, she'd had flashbacks of being injured in Iraq, of the explosion that had killed most of her patrol and nearly taken her left leg. She'd cried out, she'd fought. And then she'd slept again.

Hank held her hand. 'Hungry?'

Harper couldn't see the tray, but she smelled something sweet. Trying to sit, she reached for the control, couldn't find it. Hank pushed the button and raised the bed for her; sitting up, she regarded the tray in front of her. Hospital pancakes. A scrambled egg. Some kind of pink meat. Apple juice. Jello. Jello?

Hank pulled the tray over, cut the pancakes for her. Harper couldn't remember when she'd last eaten. Wasn't sure if she wanted food. But Hank held a syrupy blob to her mouth, and she ate.

'Good,' Hank beamed as if she'd finished a marathon. 'Good eating, Hoppa.'

She chewed in a haze. Felt grimy, wanted a shower.

'Mother your called.' Hank shoveled more pancake.

Oh God.

'Wants come out here.'

Harper almost choked. Her mother? 'Uh uh.' Her mouth was full, and her voice unaccustomed to talking. '*No.*' Harper's mother meant well, but required too much attention. Harper always took care of her, not the other way.

'Told her. Visit later. Better.'

Harper let out a breath, swallowed. On her own, she lifted the juice, pulled the top off with shaky hands. Lord, she was weak.

'Help you?'

'I got it.' Almost. She pulled, finally lifted the foil top from the plastic cup, took a drink. All

333

without moving her head and neck, which were still stabilized in the brace. 'Can they take this thing off?'

'Soon.' Hank took the empty cup. Cut another slab of pancake.

Harper was still chewing when Detective Rivers came in. And that's when breakfast stopped.

'She better today? Think she's coherent?' Rivers addressed Hank.

'Eating.' Hank stood bear-like, blocking the detective. Protective.

'Good. So she can keep on eating. I won't stay long.'

'Not strong.'

Harper sat chewing, listening to them discuss her as if she weren't there.

'I'm not going to give her a workout, Mr Jennings. I'm just going to talk.'

'It's OK, Hank. Good morning, Detective.' She had a few questions for Rivers, was eager for the chance to ask them.

Rivers came around the bed, took a seat opposite Hank, beside the window. 'You look better.'

Harper hadn't considered how she looked. Knew it couldn't be good.

'You up for talking a bit?'

Harper swallowed. 'Sure.'

'Because you might have some insights about what's happened. After we sent you off in the ambulance, we found another body.'

Harper couldn't turn her head. Her eyes moved from side to side, Rivers to Hank. Hank to

Rivers. Waiting. Whose body? Rick's? Salih's?

'Turns out he was a professor of Archeology. Frederick Charles Wiggins. He had deep scratches on his arms and face, bruises on his sides as if he'd been beaten up. And two knife wounds – one that pierced the heart.'

Made sense; Harper had fought him pretty hard.

'And he was posed, just like Zina. Leaning against a tree outside, right where she was.'

Against a tree? How had he gotten there? Maybe Angus moved him? He must have. He was the only one—

'He was dressed in some kind of costume. Feathers...'

'He wanted to be a shape-shifter. Recreating Pre-Columbian rituals.' Harper's voice was weak, still hoarse.

Rivers tilted her head. 'Mrs Jennings, did those rituals involve taking out people's hearts?'

Harper stiffened.

'If they did, he wasn't the only one recreating them. Because someone took his.'

Someone took Wiggins' heart? But who? And why? Wiggins was the guy trying to become a Nahual. He'd been the only one with even a remote reason to take hearts.

'I don't get it – Wiggins was the one taking the hearts.'

Rivers squinted. 'How do you know that?'

'Because I heard them talking about what he'd done to Zina.' She hesitated. 'And because he tried to take mine.'

Hank's mouth opened. 'Hoppa.' He took her

335

hand, turned to Rivers. 'Upset now. Enough.'

'Just a few more things.' Rivers leaned forward so Harper could see her more easily. 'It's interesting what you've just said, Mrs Jennings. Because it's consistent with our findings. Wiggins's heart was removed, but not the way Zina's was. Zina's body had minimal damage. The cuts were neat and skilful. The breastbone opened with almost surgical precision.'

Or with the care of a Nahual.

'This one was ripped open, mangled. Looked like it got hacked with an axe. Clearly, not the work of the same guy.' She paused. 'So do you have any idea who could have done it?'

Maybe. 'Angus Langston was the only other person there.' But she couldn't figure out why Angus would mess with Wiggins' body, let alone take his heart.

'Interesting. Because Angus took off. He tried to split.'

Tried?

'We picked him up for a DUI yesterday. He was speeding out of town.'

Had Angus taken the time to cut out Wiggins' heart before he ran? Harper couldn't picture it. Didn't want to.

'That it?' Hank asked.

'It'll do for now. It's good to see you getting better, Mrs Jennings.' Rivers stood, started for the door. 'I'll be in touch.'

As she was leaving, Harper remembered what she'd wanted to ask. 'Detective – wait. Have you found Rick Owens? And what about Salih?'

* * *

Neither had been found.

The police had looked for Salih in the passageway, had watched the house and the ramp exit to make sure he couldn't leave. They'd scoured the tunnels with dogs. But the dogs ran into dead ends or seemed to lose the scent. Two days after he'd entered them, Salih hadn't emerged from the passageways. Harper wasn't surprised. Chloe Manning's body had gone undiscovered for almost a hundred years. The secret corridors were too twisted and gnarled to be untangled so quickly by a few men and dogs.

Harper came home the next day with a cervical collar and pain pills that made her mind foggy. She disliked dozing off, disliked more the shuddering pain that radiated through her body without them. Despite her loopiness, Harper played hostess to a stream of visitors. Detective Rivers and her sometime partner, Detective Boschi, checked in, reporting that Angus had confessed to stealing relics, but vehemently denied having anything to do with killing Wiggins, whom he called Digger, or anyone else. He admitted that he had information about other crimes, but, hoping to make a deal, he refused to give details until he could negotiate.

Vicki and Trent came with flowers, balloons, bonbons and Scotch. The Archeology Department sent a fruit basket. Professor Schmerling and Dean Van Arsdale came by with chocolates, awkwardly apologizing for Professor Wiggins, muttering that they'd known he'd been eccentric but had never dreamed he'd been so disturbed. Phil and Stacey arrived with questions and a

337

huge tin of candy corn. The press called often; Harper's mom called even more often, still wanting to fly out, refusing to believe that Harper was 'fine' as she claimed. Hank stayed steadfastly by Harper's side, answering the phone, limiting the number and length of visits. He seemed to relish his role of caretaker, making decisions, taking control.

Harper's throat began to heal, but she still didn't speak much. Found herself listening more, thinking that most of what people – even her friends and professors – said was blither. She wondered if Hank, unable to converse well, felt the same distance as she did from others. She thought of them as 'talkers'. Of herself and Hank as 'watchers' and 'listeners'.

The first few days home passed in a haze of medication. Harper saw the news reports about the murder at Langston's, heard reporters' references to the election held earlier in the week. Even with the references, she didn't think of Colonel Baxter right away, and she didn't remember Burke's letter. She didn't think of the letter even when she watched a feature about the landslide victory of an Iraqi war veteran, a former army colonel elected to Senate from the state of Tennessee. That news upset Harper, but it wasn't until Friday, walking past the front door, that she actually saw Burke's envelope under a paperweight on the foyer table. That was when she remembered the list of shipment dates and serial numbers. And it was when, with Hank hovering and telling her not to lift her heavy leather bag by herself, she went to get her phone.

338

'You said you needed evidence of theft,' she said. 'These shipment numbers will prove that Baxter stole millions.'

'Mrs Jennings,' Detective Rivers sounded tired. 'The man is now a United States senator. He just won by an overwhelming majority. And, frankly, this alleged theft occurred years ago, while I have more than a couple of open homicides to investigate.'

'I hope those include Burke Everett's. Because I think these papers will show motive for his murder, evidence that it wasn't suicide. And they'll show why Rick Owens was coming after me.'

'Mrs Jennings, maybe you should—'

'Baxter sent Rick.' Harper's voice was hoarse and strained. 'To silence Burke and me. About Iraq. Ask Angus – he was there when Wiggins killed him.'

'Hoppa. Calm down.' Hank stroked her back. Hovering.

'Detective, Rick killed Burke – I'm sure of it!'

'Hoppa – stop.'

Harper scowled, pushed Hank's hand away. 'And Wiggins killed Rick after he chased me through the passageway, and—'

'Whoa. Settle down, Mrs Jennings – your husband will have my hide.' She paused, sighed loudly. 'All right. You win. I'll stop by and check out the letter.'

Relieved, Harper ended the call and set the envelope back on the foyer table under the paperweight. And noticed Hank glowering.

'What's wrong?'

339

He simmered. 'You. Don't listen. Need rest.'

'I'm fine, Hank. You don't need to stand over me every second.'

As soon as she said it, she was sorry. Lord, how ungrateful was she?

'I didn't mean that...'

But it was too late. Wounded, Hank turned away, started for the door. 'Super. Market. Going. Now. OK?'

Harper went after him, called to him, but he didn't stop. Who could blame him? All week, he'd helped her eat and bathe and dress and move. And now, she'd snapped at him? What was wrong with her?

When he came back, she'd apologize. Meantime, it would be good for Hank to take off for a little while. It would be fine.

Harper dozed on the den sofa, felt someone standing beside her, assumed it was Hank. She opened her eyes and saw not Hank, but Angus, staring at her. Smiling. Harper froze – when had Angus been released? Slowly, cautiously, she sat up. Looked around for Hank, remembered he was gone...

'Sorry. Didn't mean to startle you – the door was open.'

It was? Harper didn't remember it being open. But she felt relieved. And foolish. It wasn't Angus who'd come to see her; it was Jake. She greeted him, moved to the end of the couch. 'Come sit down.'

'So. You doing OK?' he sat, studying the cervical collar, her bruises.

'Better.'

'Look. I want you to know. I had no idea what my brother was doing. He knew better than to tell me.'

Harper still couldn't turn her head much, so she twisted her body to face him.

'Angus.' Jake shook his head. 'He probably started selling relics after he found out about the will. Probably thought that by ripping off the collection, he was taking what was rightly his. But the killing? Zina?'

'Angus didn't kill her. That was Zina's brother,' said Harper.

'What about Digger? You must have seen him. You were there, right? The guy in the feather jacket with a stuffed cat on his head. Wiggins.'

Oh. Wiggins, Digger, the Nahual. All the same person. 'Salih Salim killed him. Not Angus.' But it struck her that the detectives hadn't mentioned Wiggins' cathead. Maybe they'd thought it unnecessary, too much gruesome detail.

Jake paused, took a breath. 'You know, Angus and I – we've known Wiggins for just about always. Digger. His dad was our dentist. And his mom was a drunk, so he hung around our house until he became part of the family. Went on digs with us – that's how he got the name. Growing up, he was like a brother.'

Really? Wiggins?

'After a while, my father spent more time with Digger than he did with us.'

Harper didn't know what to say. 'Maybe it just seemed that way.'

'No. He did. Digger became father's protégé.

341

They were always in the study, talked about research, spiritualism, symbolism. God knows what all. My father brought him to conferences. To South America. Utah. All over. Until that girl died. Carla.' Jake looked into the air. 'After that, Digger went away for a while.' He looked at Harper, smiled oddly.

'All this time, you knew?'

'Yep. She wasn't his first, either.'

Jake's grin was crooked. 'We had a dog. Aubrey. I found him behind the house. His chest was ripped open.'

Harper recoiled.

'There were also birds. A cat. Even a deer. Over the years, all over the property, animal corpses would show up, *sans* hearts. The owls were the messiest. He plucked out their feathers.'

'You're saying Wiggins—?'

'Oh, for sure. I told my father about it. Know what he did? He laughed. He shook his head, but he laughed. He told me not to worry, that long ago, spiritual men sacrificed the hearts of creatures for their religions. Probably someone was doing that again. He said he'd talk to the person.'

Harper sat silent.

'But my father didn't do anything. Not even when Digger killed Aubrey. So when Digger went on to Carla, it was my father's fault.' Jake's eyes became steely. 'I was mad – I liked Carla.'

'What did you do?'

Jake's jaw rippled. 'Told my father what I knew. This time he didn't laugh. But he didn't go

342

to the police. He arranged with Digger's family to send him abroad. Supposedly to get help. But I don't know about that. Because some years later, all educated and grown up, Wiggins came back with his PhD. I think he expected to be welcomed home like a prodigal son. My father got him a position at the university, helped him get a start. But he would have nothing to do with him. Wouldn't let him near the relics. Hell, he wouldn't let him in the house.'

Harper listened, chilled. And wondered why Jake was telling the story to her, not the police.

'Thing is. Once he was back, dead animals started showing up again, without their hearts. This time, I was a grown man. I went to him, told him what I knew. He denied it. He said it wasn't him, that it had been Angus all along. That Angus had killed the girl. He'd just taken the fall.'

'Jake. This is—'

'Unbelievable? Is that what you were going to say?'

She'd been about to say: '—something you should tell the police.'

'Well, it is. Meantime, the cops have Angus in custody. But Angus is no killer. He's spineless. And a sneak. My own brother, and he was ripping me off. With Wiggins. I can't figure out when it started. But they got together and decided to steal pieces from the collection. Which meant from me – because that will won't stand up. Wiggins took my dog, my father, and now he's taken my brother and my inheritance from me.' He closed his mouth, clenched his jaw, and slid closer to Harper on the sofa.

'You know why I'm telling you this?'

She didn't. But she didn't like the look in his eyes. Or the nearness of his body.

'Fact is, nobody but you can testify against Angus in any of this. Not the thefts. Not the killings.' He met her eyes. 'Angus is a pussy, but he's all I've got left.'

For a moment, neither spoke.

Harper stood, her eyes still on his. Jake stood smoothly, like a jaguar about to spring. She spun around, headed for the foyer, the door.

Jake followed, unhurried. 'Wait, I'm not finished – don't you want to hear what he did with them?'

She broke into a run, made it into the foyer, to the table by the door. Saw Burke's letter, the paperweight.

Jake grabbed Harper's shoulder, spun her around. Leaned close and spoke softly. 'Wiggins thought that a creature's heart contained its power and spirit. So that each heart he ate made him more powerful.'

Harper felt his breath on her face, tried to turn away, but couldn't move her neck. Inched her arm toward the table.

'I finally got him, though.' Jake smiled. 'My dog. And all those "spirits" he spent years gathering – all his so-called powers. Who's got them now?' He licked his lips, tightening his grip on her. 'Guess who's the Nahual now?'

Harper swung the paperweight.

When Hank came in with his arms full of

grocery bags, he found Jake hog-tied with duct tape in the foyer, Harper calmly watching, reading in the living room, waiting for Detective Rivers to arrive.

The search for Salih continued. His family offered rewards, but he remained missing, apparently lost in the twisted bowels of the Langston house. Angus traded information about the murders of Carla Prentiss, Zina Salim, and Rick Owens to reduce the multiple charges against him. Rick's bones were found in the woods, his flesh devoured by scavengers. Jake was charged with abusing Wiggins' corpse and assaulting Harper with intent to kill, even though he'd never actually laid a hand on her.

The Tuesday before Thanksgiving, Rivers stopped by. She turned down the offer of coffee, said she couldn't stay. 'I heard back about those serial numbers you gave me. The FBI and the Army – all the powers that be – say that the shipment list isn't enough to launch an investigation. They don't even want to bother checking the numbers, because merely loading cargo on to a helicopter – well, that wouldn't prove that there was a crime or even misconduct. And there's no other evidence to indicate wrongdoing. Not even any witnesses.'

No. Except for her, all the witnesses were dead.

'Anyhow, it's a good thing you didn't try to sabotage Baxter's election over this, Mrs Jennings. There'd have been hell to pay. They say he's a rising star – there's already talk about him running for president.'

She handed Harper a file folder. Inside was a

345

copy of Burke's letter and a pile of correspondence going up the chain of command from Rivers to her boss to the FBI, the Army and the Justice Department.

After Rivers left, Harper put the file aside, didn't want to think about Burke, Rick, Pete, the Colonel, his election or a theft that might or might not have happened back in Iraq.

The next day was gray and wet, but she walked to the bridge where Burke had died, spent some time just standing in the rain, remembering.

'How was Thanksgiving?' Leslie's office smelled of cinnamon. She sipped tea, curled on to the green leather sofa beside Harper.

'My mother came out.'

Leslie nodded. 'Got it. How bad?'

'Pretty bad. But she means well. She's just high maintenance.'

Silence. Harper didn't know what to say, where to begin. Avoided the Big Stuff. 'I'm back working on my dissertation. It's going well.'

'Good.' Leslie's voice was like silk. Or maybe cotton balls.

Harper nodded. More silence. Tell her, she thought. But she didn't. Instead, she said, 'The department asked if I wanted to be part of the relic assessment. To identify all the damage. I declined.'

'I'm sure they understood.'

Harper nodded. 'Professor Schmerling said they did. It's kind of funny – I mean, in a terrible way: after everything that's happened so they could acquire that collection, the university isn't even keeping it.'

'Seriously?' Leslie put her mug down. 'Why not?'

'Most of the pieces are going back to the countries of origin. After all the attention in the press, countries requested their return. I guess the university wants to avoid more trouble.'

Silence again. Tell her, Harper thought. But she didn't.

'You're all better. Physically?'

'Pretty much.' Harper demonstrated, turning her head just a little.

'And how are things with Hank?'

Harper sipped tea, stalling. The truth was that she and Hank were still cautious. Dancing around each other, not sure how tightly to hold on, how much to let go. 'Better.' Maybe.

'Is he more comfortable with independence?'

With his independence? Or with hers? 'He doesn't like me to be out of his sight. He worries about me. It's the opposite of how things were – I used to be the one worrying, taking care of him. Now, he's helicopter husband, always hovering.'

Leslie smiled. 'Have you told him how you feel about that?'

No. She hadn't. She would, but not until she was sure she wanted him to stop. Harper still had nightmares about endless corridors, men with bloody grins. Or feathered creatures feasting on beating hearts. In the night, she often climbed on to Hank, clinging to him in her sleep.

Or waking him up to make love.

Often without birth control.

Tell her, she thought. But she didn't, wasn't

ready to talk about that. Not even to Leslie.

Not even to Hank.

Leslie was talking, assuring Harper that she and Hank were solid, just finding their way. Going through a new phase.

Harper toyed with the bangle bracelet on her wrist, thinking about new phases. About the name Zina. About what to buy Hank for Christmas. About the nursery. About her dissertation. About the changes the New Year would bring.